D1329356

THE URBAN POLICEMAN IN TRANSITION

A Psychological and Sociological Review

THE URBAN
POLICEMAN
IN TRANSITION

A PSYCHOLOGICAL AND SOCIOLOGICAL REVIEW

By

JOHN R. SNIBBE, Ph.D.
Los Angeles County
University of Southern California Medical Center
Instructor in Psychiatry
University of Southern California
School of Medicine

HOMA M. SNIBBE, Ph.D.
Physiological Fitness Research Project
Department of Personnel
County of Los Angeles
Los Angeles County Sheriff's Department

CHARLES C THOMAS · PUBLISHER
Springfield · Illinois · U.S.A.

Published and Distributed Throughout the World by
CHARLES C THOMAS • PUBLISHER
BANNERSTONE HOUSE
301-327 East Lawrence Avenue, Springfield, Illinois, U.S.A.

© *1973, by* CHARLES C THOMAS • PUBLISHER
ISBN 0-398-02661-0
Library of Congress Catalog Card Number: 72-88473

With THOMAS BOOKS *careful attention is given to all details of manufacturing and design. It is the Publisher's desire to present books that are satisfactory as to their physical qualities and artistic possibilities and appropriate for their particular use.* THOMAS BOOKS *will be true to those laws of quality that assure a good name and good will.*

Printed in the United States of America
N-1

TO OUR PARENTS

Dr. Jalil Mahmoudi
Mrs. Badri Mahmoudi

Mr. Richard W. Snibbe
Mrs. Miriam B. Snibbe

CONTRIBUTORS

STANLEY P. AZEN, PH.D., *Schools of Electrical Engineering and Medicine University of Southern California.*

MELANEY E. BAEHR, PH.D., *Chicago Police Department, Industrial Relations Center Project, University of Chicago.*

MORTON BARD, PH.D., *Department of Psychology, City University of New York.*

ALLAN BERMAN, PH.D., *Department of Psychology, University of Rhode Island.*

VYAUTAS J. BIELIANSKAS, PH.D., *Department of Psychology, Xavier (Ohio) University.*

ARTHUR M. BODIN, PH.D., *Mental Research Institute,*

COLETTE C. JACKSON, M.A., *Research Analysis Corporation, McLean, Virginia.*

WILLIAM CRAVEN, M.S.W., *Department of Public Social Services, County of Los Angeles.*

STEVEN J. DANISH, PH.D., *College of Human Development, Penn State University.*

TERRY EISENBERG, PH.D., *Professional Standards Division, International Association of Chiefs of Police.*

NANCY FERGUSON, M.A., *Counseling and Testing Center, Southern Illinois University.*

ERNEST C. FROEMEL, M.A., *Chicago Police Department, Industrial Relations Center Project, University of Chicago.*

JOHN E. FURCON, M.A., *Chicago Police Department, Industrial Relations Center Project, University of Chicago.*

DAVID T. HELLKAMP, PH.D., *Department of Psychology, Xavier (Ohio) University.*

DORIS JACOBSON, PH.D., *School of Social Welfare, University of California at Los Angeles.*

vii

RITA M. KELLY, PH.D., *American Institutes for Research, Kensington, Maryland.*

SUSAN KUSHNER, M.S.W., *Psychiatric Social Work Department, County of Los Angeles, University of Southern California Medical Center.*

JOEL LEFKOWITZ, PH.D., *Department of Psychology, Baruch College, City University of New York.*

BJORN D. LEIREN, B.A., *Psychology Department, California State College at Los Angeles.*

RUTH J. LEVY, PH.D., *Institute for Local Self Government.*

DONALD A. LIEBMAN, PH.D., *San Francisco Police Department.*

STEWART H. MARSH, M.S.P.A., *Department of Personnel, County of Los Angeles.*

SHIRLEY D. MCCUNE, PH.D., *National Education Association.*

DAVIS B. MCENTIRE (DECEASED), *American Council on Race Relations.*

HUGH R. MONTGOMERY, PH.D., *Department of Personnel—Sheriff's Department, County of Los Angeles.*

ARMANDO MORALES, M.S.W., *School of Social and Community Psychiatry, University of California at Los Angeles.*

BRUCE T. OLSON, PH.D., *Department of Sociology, University of Tulsa.*

ROBERT B. POWERS (DECEASED), *California Department of Justice.*
DAVID R. SAUNDERS, PH.D., *Department of Psychology, University of Colorado.*

JEFFREY A. SCHWARTZ, PH.D., *Richmond Police Department.*

MELVIN P. SIKES, PH.D., *Department of Educational Psychology University of Texas.*

DAVID H. SMITH, M.A., *Department of Psychology, University of Washington.*

HOMA M. SNIBBE, PH.D., *Department of Personnel—Sheriff's Department, County of Los Angeles.*

JOHN R. SNIBBE, PH.D., *Psychology Department, County of Los Angeles, University of Southern California Medical Center.*

ROBERT J. SOKOL, M.D., *Department of Psychology, Los Angeles Police Department.*

LAWRENCE SOLOMON, PH.D., *Psychology Department, United States International University.*

Kathleen B. Stoddard, M.A., *Department of Educational Psychology, University of Utah.*

Ezra Stotland, Ph.D., Psychology Department, University of Washington.

Hans Toch, Ph.D., *School of Criminal Justice, State University of New York at Albany.*

Robert C. Trojanowicz, Ph.D., *School of Criminal Justice, Michigan State University.*

Kenneth Visser, M.A., *Psychology Department, United States International University.*

Irving A. Wallach, Ph.D., *Research Analysis Corporation, McLean, Virginia.*

Regis H. Walther, Ph.D., *Manpower Research Projects, George Washington University.*

Gorman West Jr., M.A., *American Institutes for Research.*

PREFACE

THE *Urban Policeman in Transition* is a presentation, representing various contemporary directions police departments are taking with the help of behavioral scientists.

There is little doubt that the police have in the past few years, been subjected to massive psychological and sociological review. Active interventions in various departments have also increased until it is the rare urban police department that does not have a psychologist on staff or an active research program to improve such areas as selection, training or community relations.

The reasons behind this renewed interest are complex. The police and police methods have come under increasing criticism and concern in the face of radical changes in our culture. The individual officer and the department's ability to meet the challenge of changing times has ceased to be an area of minor speculation. Hard data, evaluative studies and consultations are now essential for the survival and smooth functioning of police departments. Innovations in training and selection are now critical and cannot be a matter for next year's budget meeting.

Police departments, like all institutions in our society, must meet the needs of changing times. The police are by no means unique in this pressing demand. Government, the military, educational institutions, hospitals and industry are all reevaluating past policies, practices and roles.

This volume strives to put forward positive solutions and research data which both attempt to solve problems and illuminate areas of concern. It represents a cross section of opinions and disciplines. It is by no means complete, however; the number of research programs now being conducted in the United States is staggering. It will undoubtedly take years for the data to be implemented into positive change. The authors hope that this inevitable "time lag" will be reduced with this volume.

ACKNOWLEDGMENTS

THE AUTHORS wish to express deep appreciation to Mrs. Lynn Lee and Jeanne Bryant for their help in the preparation of this volume, and to Mrs. Edith Richardson for typing part of the manuscript. To Sergeant Ken Olson and Deputy Dorine Owens of the Los Angeles Sheriff's Department, we give our special thanks for their administrative and editorial assistance.

CONTENTS

THE URBAN POLICEMAN IN TRANSITION

A Psychological and Sociological Review

SECTION I

SELECTION AND PREDICTION

INTRODUCTION

SELECTION AND PREDICTION

THIS CHAPTER REPRESENTS SEVERAL SIGNIFICANT ATTEMPTS TO DEVELOP SELECTION CRITERIA FOR POLICE OFFICERS. RECENTLY MANY RESEARCHERS HAVE BECOME INTERESTED IN HOW TO SELECT AND KEEP COMPETENT OFFICERS. ALTHOUGH FRAUGHT WITH METHODOLOGICAL COMPLEXITIES, THE REALITIES OF CONTEMPORARY POLICE WORK REQUIRE THOUGHTFUL, EMPIRICAL, AND STANDARDIZED PROCEDURES FOR THE EMPLOYMENT OF LAW OFFICERS.

THE SMITH AND STOTLAND ARTICLE REPRESENTS A REVIEW OF THE LITERATURE ON RESEARCH ON SELECTION AND AN EXAMINATION OF SOME MODELS FOR TRAINING AND ASSESSMENT.

RUTH LEVY'S ARTICLE ON IDENTIFICATION OF HIGH-RISK APPLICANTS GENERATES SEVERAL USEFUL VARIABLES THAT ARE EFFECTIVE IN DECREASING PREDICTIVE ERRORS.

THE TWO ARTICLES BY FURCON, FROEMEL, BAEHR AND SAUNDERS REPRESENT PIONEERING WORK IN THE DEVELOPMENT OF PREDICTION FOR PERFORMANCE OF POLICE OFFICERS. THESE STUDIES HAVE DONE MUCH TO PROVIDE MORE REALISTIC AND EQUITABLE SELECTION AND PERFORMANCE CRITERIA.

BJORN LEIRENS' ARTICLE ON SELECTION OF DEPUTY MARSHALS OFFERS MASSIVE EMPIRICAL EVIDENCE USING A WIDE VARIETY OF PREDICTORS. IN MANY WAYS IT REPRESENTS THE NEW DIRECTION OF RESEARCH AND A SOUND CONDEMNATION OF PAST PRACTICES. IT IS INDICATIVE OF THE PAINSTAKING AND COMPLEX PROCESS NECESSARY FOR COMPETENT DATA AND SELECTION.

THE SNIBBE, AZEN, MONTGOMERY AND MARSH STUDY IS A CLASSIC, SIMPLY BECAUSE THERE ARE SO FEW MEANINGFUL LONGITUDINAL STUDIES ON POLICE OFFICERS. IT DELINEATES SEVERAL VALUABLE VARIABLES THAT SEEM TO PREDICT TENURE AND PERFORMANCE AND USES A SOPHISTICATED STATISTICAL PROCEDURE (I.E. STEPWISE DISCRIMINANT ANALYSIS) THAT MAY WELL BECOME ONE OF OUR MOST USEFUL TOOLS IN PREDICTIVE AND SELECTION RESEARCH.

4

Chapter 1

A NEW LOOK AT
POLICE OFFICER SELECTION

DAVID H. SMITH AND EZRA STOTLAND

IN RECENT YEARS, the public has increasingly demanded better police service both in controlling crime and maintaining civil peace. These demands have not been adequately met, partly because of a shortage of police officers. The President's Commission on Law Enforcement and the Administration of Justice (1967A) has pointed out that 10 percent of the nation's police forces are understrength. In a single year, as many as 50,000 new officers may be needed. The difficulty in finding new officers does not stem from a sufficient number of applicants, since only 22 percent of the applicants become police officers (O'Conner, 1962). Accordingly, the problem in meeting the public's demand for better police service is in part a matter of selecting the best potential officers from among the candidates. The issue then is finding a valid basis for predicting which candidates will become successful officers.

The usual procedures for selecting police are background checks, medical examinations, tests of physical agility and prowess, oral examinations and written civil service tests. One weakness of these procedures is that the civil service tests are not only unstandardized, but their ability to predict who will be a successful officer has not been widely demonstrated. On the other hand, the use of psychiatric screening and psychological testing has greatly increased in the past twenty years (Oglesby, 1958; International Association of Chiefs of Police, 1961). Furthermore, there is pressure to use these tests on an even larger scale. The U.S. President's Commission on Law Enforcement and Administrations of Justice states that, "psychological tests, such as the MMPI, and interviews to determine emotional stability should be conducted in all de-

5

partments." As Reiser states (1970), "Today the emphasis in police departments and in most industrial organizations is still on the mechanical-technical approach to problem solving. Comparably less thought and consideration seem to be given to the human side, although it is human beings involved in social systems we are concerned with. Police Departments will be increasingly utilizing psychological and other behavioral science professionals in various areas of police functions as routine procedures."

Since 1950, approximately two dozen articles by psychologists have appeared which directly report research on methods of research selecting police officers. In addition, a number of articles have reviewed the research reports and other publications related to police selection. Still other publications report on surveys of the extent of use of tests. In the present paper, we will first critically review all of these types of publications. Next, we will suggest a new approach to police selection.

SURVEYS OF USAGE OF PSYCHOLOGICAL AND PSYCHIATRIC METHODS

Since 1950, four surveys have been conducted relevant to the use of psychological and psychiatric methods in police selection. Frost (1955) sent questionnaires to 33 centers of population over 150,000 of which 25 responded. He found that most departments used a variety of screening devices, including age, residency requirements, veterans preferences, and character checks by means of oral board examinations and background checks. No tests of a psychological nature were reported used by the 25 cities—neither personality, intelligence or tests standardized or validated on police populations.

Oglesby (1958) sent questionnaires to 111 centers of population over 100,000, of which 90 replied. He discovered that only 14 centers, or 16 percent, had formalized programs of psychiatric or psychological testing of applicants. Of the 14, 10 employed a psychiatrist, 2 a psychologist, and one employed both a psychiatrist and a psychologist. Oglesby recommends that the evaluation of emotional stability of police applicants should consist of three parts: (1) projective psychological testing (2) psychiatric interview and (3) retesting after a period of employment to detect personality changes and to provide more data for developing criteria for predicting success on the job.

In 1956 and again in 1961, the International Association of Chiefs of Police sent out questionnaires to all districts of population of over 25,000 (O'Conner, 1962). Sixty-nine of the cities answered the 1956 questionnaires. Of the cities, 8 percent or 30 cities, indicated that they routinely screened candidates for emotional fitness. In seven additional cities, psychiatric evaluations were given to those candidates who were diagnosed by the examining physician as exhibiting nervous or emotional disorders. The cities which responded to the original survey were resurveyed in 1961. Of these, 16 percent or 49 cities now used psychiatric screening on a routine basis, and an additional two cities on a selected case basis. The screening devices ranged from paper and pencil mental health inventories to extensive projective testing and interviewing by psychiatrists. However, psychiatric screening was the least commonly used device. Thirty psychiatrists, thirteen clinical psychologists, and a scattering of physicians and other personnel were employed. (It is interesting to note that, although all cities had some form of formalized screening, 15 percent indicated that they had no training for police prior to employment.)

Narrol and Levitt (1963) in the most recent nationwide survey sent questionnaires to 61 cities with population greater than 150,000. Of the 55 who responded, all used some kind of instrument that could broadly be called a psychological test (intelligence, personality, etc.). The bulk of these were self- or mass-administered intelligence or aptitude tests. In only three cities were the tests administered by a psychologist face to face with an individual applicant. Only 22 percent use personality tests, and only one reports any original research. Only six cities employed a psychologist in their recruitment programs.

From the surveys, it is clear that the use of personality screening techniques is not widespread, but is increasing. One of the major problems is that many cities are using tests that have not been validated on police populations. Further, many departments use test data without any clear criteria on occupational success.

Several departments place heavy emphasis on the use of intelligence tests, accepting the assumption that intelligence, as measured by I.Q. tests, is positively correlated with success as a police officer. This appears to be a rather uncritical use of these instruments.

TRAIT STUDIES

Since 1950, 22 reported studies have involved the administration of psychological tests to policemen, although not always in connection with selection procedures. The tests and test batteries used have varied widely, as follows: Strong Vocational Interest Blank (Kates, 1950; Zaice, 1962; Matarazzo, 1964); the Kuder Personal Preference Record (Sterne, 1960; Marsh, 1962; Colrarelli and Siegel, 1964; Matarazzo, 1964; Nowici, 1966); the Rorschach, either group or individually administered (Kates, 1950; Rankin, 1957; Matarazzo, 1964; Rhead *et al*, 1968; Peterson, 1970); Edwards Personal Preference Schedule (Zaice, 1962; Colarelli and Siegel, 1964; Matarazzo, 1964); the California F Scale (Adorno, *et al*, 1950) or modification of it (Matarazzo, 1964; Smith, Locke and Walker, 1967; Carlson, Thayer and Germann, 1970); the Dogmatism Scale (Rokeach, 1960; Smith, Locke and Walker, 1968; Smith, Locke and Fenster, 1970); and sundry other standardized tests. Generally, these studies have involved comparisons between policemen and civilians and determine differences between the groups. Unfortunately, seldom is there any effort to repeat the studies to determine how reliable the differences are.

The most comprehensive student of policemen's performance on personality tests, has been Baehr (1968). She administered five standard tests and twelve tests especially developed at the University of Chicago to a large group of Chicago policemen with the purpose of examining their ability to predict police performance.

In addition, she attempted "to identify 'patrolmen types' which would exhibit distinctive performance styles in the field and would not be adequately described by the concept of average patrolmen." To determine the relationship between these tests and police performance, eight criterion variables were used as follows: a paired-comparison procedure in which supervisors rated each of the men they knew in comparison with each of the others; supervisor's regular semi-annual field performance ratings; tenure in the department; departmental awards; complaints registered in the Internal Investigation Division; departmental disciplinary action; attendance; and the number of arrests made.

On the basis of her results, Baehr concluded, "there was an acceptably high and statistically significant relationship between the test battery scores and independent measures of performance." This was especially true of the paired-comparison rating, the regular supervisor rating, and tenure. The tests predicted especially well for the black policemen.

Baehr also identified the group profile of successful patrolmen. Successful patrolmen were characterized by "stability in parental and personal family situations, stability stemming from personal self-confidence and the control of emotional impulses; stability in the maintenance of cooperative rather than hostile or competitive attitudes, and stability deriving from resistance to stress and a realistic rather than a subjective orientation toward life." Baehr's study should be extended by examining the ability of her test battery to predict the future performance of recruits, rather than the correlation between tests and performance of functioning policemen. In addition, the study needs to be repeated on non-volunteers instead of the volunteers used by Baehr, and the study should be repeated in other police departments and on police groups other than patrolmen. Overall, the Chicago study is an important step toward developing valid prediction of police performance.

LONGITUDINAL STUDIES

Very little longitudinal research has been done, i.e. attempts to use tests to predict the performance of police over long periods of time. Colrarelli and Seigel (1964) (C.F. Rush, 1963) tested Kansas Highway patrolmen. They then correlated the test scores with indices of performance on the job. Finally, they planned to give the tests on new recruits to determine whether the tests could predict their future performance. No results have yet been published of the last phase of the project.

Marsh (1962) and Snibbe, *et al* (1971) have undertaken perhaps the most ambitious longitudinal study to date. From 1947 to 1950, 100 of the 619 recruits to the Los Angeles Sheriff's Department were given a series of tests: civil service written tests; Guilford-Martin Temperament Inventory; the Kuder Preference Record; and the MMPI. In 1958, each of the men was rated by his supervisor in terms of overall performance. In addition, the researchers recorded the discharge rate, accident rate, and tenure of the recruits. The most statistically significant finding was that those who had scored in the upper 3 percent on the civil service written test were more successful than the others. Other predictions that correlated significantly with performance were the Hy Scale of the MMPI, C Scale of the GMTS, height and scores in recruit school. Those who had done promotional work, such as insurance and real estate sales, before recruitment also fared better as police officers. Snibbe, *et al,* conducted a further follow-up study on these 100 officers to "assess the efficiency of the predictions for the time period 1950 to 1970." They correlated the same previously used prediction variables with the following indices of performance by 1970: position held, annual ratings by supervisors, workmen's compensation claims, and present rank.

RETROSPECTIVE STUDIES

Retrospective studies based on police personnel files have not been highly successful. Cross and Hammond (1951) compared the personnel records of discharged and retained Colorado Highway Patrolmen. They found that successful patrolmen were likely to be single or married without children and had previously been employed in agriculture, in skilled work, or in private protective agencies.

Levy (1967) examined 4,287 personnel files of former and current policemen from 14 agencies in California from 1952 to 1962. She found, "Officers who are terminated for cause by their departments tend to be younger at the time of appointment, to have a greater number of years of education, a greater number of marriages, shorter work histories, more citations for vehicle code and other violations, and, in general, to present a pattern of greater mobility and uncontrolled impulsivity than do the officers who are retained (Levy, 1967) ."

Subsequently, Levy, (1971) continued the project by testing new recruits to California Police agencies, and using these tests to predict who would be discharged for cause. After 100 cases were recorded, Education/Research, Incorporated of Berkeley tested the accuracy of the predictions. This organization found that the tests were only slightly better than chance in predicting who should be retained. These researchers also pointed out that the original results gave only a "rough estimate of their true worth and cannot be confidently applied to a set of individuals different from the base group." They also argued that the use of the tests in predicting police tenure would involve many false negatives; "How many good men can you afford to turn away in your attempt to avoid the hiring of a bad one?" Finally, they maintained that it has not been "determined if a police force primarily made up of individuals from groups classified as 'currents' would be desirable."

PERFORMANCE CRITERIA

In the course of describing research in the area of selection of policemen, we have referred to a number of criteria of police performance, e.g. number of arrests, tenure on the job, or supervisor's ratings. Despite their wide usage, a number of questions can be raised about the value of such criteria. First, different criteria may be needed for different police jobs. Some officers may concentrate on traffic, so that felony arrests may be of little importance. Different districts may require different types of police work. Some officers may stay in one district, while others are rotated. Thus, the tests for the validity of the predictions should be made with appropriate statistical controls for these differences. Furthermore, several different types of officers may be needed to fill the various types of needs. Secondly, ratings and evaluations by supervisors are often made on the basis of such difficult to define global characteristics as "wholesomeness" or "opinionated" (Blum, *et al*, 1961, 1962). Thirdly, there is little agreement on what does in fact constitute good police work. Is a good police officer one who arrests frequently or one who settles minor problems on the street? Is a good police officer one who maintains the peace or one who "disturbs the peace" to enforce the law? Using objective or available criteria only avoids facing this issue.

JOB ANALYSIS

Now that we have seen that most of the personality testing to select police officers has been found wanting, we need to go back to fundamentals. We need to look directly and clearly at the role for which we are selecting men and then work back from our analysis of this role to ascertain the most important characteristics to seek out in police recruits. It is not sufficient just to look for such broadly defined personality characteristics like "emotional maturity," or "ego strength." Standard personality tests do not tap sufficiently those particular aspects of emotional maturity or ego strength which are most pertinent to the role of police officers. We need to be more specific. We need to take a stab at systematic job analysis despite the reluctance of police departments to do so (Lefkowitz, 1971).

Furthermore, it is not sufficient simply to weed out applicants who have some gross pathology. We need to do more than select by rejection. Meeting the demands for the general up-grading of police work in America requires that the quality of the average police officer be raised, that higher general standards be attained. We need to select positively rather than only negatively.

CONFLICTS IN POLICE WORK

An examination of the role of the police officer indicates that the central problem he faces is the management of conflict, both intra and interpersonal (Neiderhoffer, 1967; U.S. President's Commission on Law Enforcement and the Administration of Justice, 1967A). Let us spell out what these conflicts are, turning first to the interpersonal.

Many, if not most of the contacts an officer has with the public involves a conflict between himself and one or more civilians: stopping a car for a traffic violation; removing a drunk from the streets; catching a robber in the act or shortly thereafter; confronting a group which assaults him verbally, sometimes in order to provoke him; etc. The prevalence of this type of conflict is obvious.

In fact, one of the most dreaded and potentially fatal types of contact for a policeman is the family fight. But police also have to intervene in street fights, barroom brawls, and so forth. Furthermore, police may become involved in confrontations between groups in society: labor and management; union jurisdictional disputes; black demonstrators and white bystanders; students vs. administrators; prison inmates vs. guards; black families newly moved into white neighborhoods and their new neighbors; etc., etc.

Frequently a conflict between two groups of civilians can turn into a conflict between the police officer and one or both of the groups. In family fights, the policeman's efforts to protect a wife from her assaultive husband may provoke her into an attack on her protector. Police officers attempting to keep one group from assaulting another may become the enemy of the former group. Thus dual conflicts become three-sided conflicts.

Despite the pervasiveness of interpersonal conflicts, the most difficult and probably most important conflicts for police officers are intrapersonal. The conflicts of values and groups supporting these values are legion. Let us explicate but a few of these types of conflict.

One conflict a new officer quickly encounters is between the value of enforcing the laws and the fact that he simply does not have the capability of enforcing all of the laws. He must be selective with respect to which laws to enforce. He cannot stop every car which goes one mile over the speed limit; he cannot enforce every blue law on the books; he cannot cite every jaywalker he sees (U.S. President's Commission on Law Enforcement and Administration of Justice, 1967).

Furthermore, the officer may be in a conflict about differential enforcement of laws. In some jurisdictions a middle-class drunk is often handled quite differently from the skid roader. Violence between blacks is considered less serious than violence between whites. As Wilson (1968) has pointed out that the violation of laws may sometimes be accepted because enforcing them would "disturb the peace." If social gambling is discrete and hidden, the officer may choose not to disturb it. A little juvenile misbehavior may be sometimes disregarded as being "just what kids will do." Some dope addicts or even pushers may be let off because they are good informers.

A similar conflict may arise from the fact that some activities are lawful under certain circumstances and not lawful under others. Gambling is legal at a race track but not off. Streetwalking is illegal, but call girls are seldom ever arrested by the police. Homicide in war is legal but not in many other circumstances. Laws may be changed making the illegal legal and vice versa. Drinking was once illegal and now is not. Smoking marijuana is illegal, but the moral and practical bases of keeping it illegal are being questioned. And the penalties for various drug offenses vary tremendously from location to location, and *sometimes* from judge to judge. Homosexuality is illegal, but there is much pressure to make it legal.

Even when an officer makes an arrest which he "knows" is a good one, the punishment may be discrepant with what he believes to be just. He may be in conflict about making an arrest when it might only lead to "plea bargaining," or freeing of the prisoner for what appears to be a legal technicality (Skolnick, 1966).

In his relationships with his fellow officers there are many potential sources of conflict of values. The new officer may be in conflict about what he learned in the police academy and what he learns from the old-timers. An officer may be in conflict about his knowledge of corruption or other misconduct by a fellow officer and code of secrecy among police officers. He may be in conflict between the need to share information with other officers in his department and with other police departments to make arrests on the one hand and the credit the other agencies may receive for making the arrests on the other. He may be in conflict between the new professionalism on the one hand and the old-timers common sense and seniority on the other. He may be in conflict over his recognition of the values of education and his respect for experience.

Conflicts may arise out of his relationships with the community. He is expected to protect a community which sometimes holds him in low regard. Conflicting demands may be placed on him for more police protection and less police work on the streets. He may be required to solve crimes committed against people who appear to invite the transgressor, e.g. cars left with keys in the ignition, girls raped by their boyfriends in their own apartments, and burglaries committed in homes left unlocked. He may be expected to remain professionally cool in the face of verbal attacks. Even "positive" actions by the community may place him in conflict: a grateful businessman offers him a cup of coffee on the job. Because of his peculiar hours he may be isolated from the very community he protects.

REACTION TO CONFLICTS

There is no need to extend this catalogue of conflicts. But there is a need to point out that not only does the role of policeman involve conflicts which are at least comparable to those in other professions, but the conflicts are more difficult to resolve in an orderly, reasoned, systematic way. The officer sometimes has to make almost instantaneous decisions about how to act, even when he has only partial information regarding the conflict. He may never be able to find out "who provoked whom" in a family fight. He may only be able to guess whether the fleeing suspect is armed. Furthermore, there is often little in his training, and less in official police policy, about how to resolve these conflicts (President's Commission, 1967A). He is told to use his "common sense," but what "common sense" means is seldom explained. Furthermore, officers are rarely motivated to resolve conflicts in as orderly, systematic and time consuming a way as is used by such other professions as law, science, accounting. They are rarely trained to use such methods. Officers themselves tend to place high value on action, on controlling situations, on appearing effective rather than on waiting or seeking alternatives. The pressure to engage in immediately effective public action stems partly from the value systems of police officers, partly from their need to maintain their public image of being authoritative. In addition, officers receive few rewards from their peers or superiors for taking time to examine alternative courses of action. All of these pressures toward immediate and effective action thus force the officer to resolve conflicts often with little compelling justification for choosing one particular line of action in preference to another.

Another important aspect of the police officer's attempts to resolve conflicts is that the conflicts often have long-range consequences both for civilians, his fellow officers, and himself. The decisions he often makes are not trivial and sometimes involve human life.

DISSONANCE REDUCTION

Situations in which people make decisions of consequence in the face of conflicting ideas or information have been shown to lead to states of what has been termed cognitive dissonance (Festinger, 1957; Festinger, 1964; Abelson, et al., 1968). Individuals react negatively to such states, i.e. to the knowledge that they have made choices to act in a given way, with significant consequences, even when those choices were based on inadequate or conflicting information. As we have seen, a policeman often finds himself in such situations. Thus, especially when he is a "rookie," he will frequently be in situations in which he is likely to attempt to reduce this state of cognitive dissonance. One of the most common ways to reduce dissonance is to come to think that there was in fact less conflict and more justification for having made a given choice than originally believed—that is, a person can engage in garden-variety rationalization. Specifically, he can come to believe that, after all, gambling can not be so bad since it is widely practiced and even condoned in some situations. He can come to believe that the man he arrested on slight suspicion is really guilty. He can come to believe that his partner's acceptance of a free meal is not wrong since policemen are underpaid by the community anyway.

Suppose an officer reacts in a given way to reduce dissonance and this way is effective in doing so. The next time he confronts a dissonance-arousing situation he is likely to react in the same way because it has been effective for him in the past. Thus after repeatedly encountering such situations, the officer will no doubt develop a set of beliefs which permit him to function without ever really experiencing very much dissonance. He may develop a high level of suspiciousness about mankind in general so that he believes arrests on suspicion are really based on factual grounds. He may develop a high level of cynicism about the significance of certain values and moral precepts. Many people have noted the generally dour view of human existence common to police officers (Niederhoffer, 1967) ; in part this view may be a result of repeated attempts to reduce dissonance—attempts that culminate in a set of beliefs which avoid dissonance. For example, a policeman who believes that all people have committed some criminal acts for which they have not been punished will find little dissonance in arresting someone on flimsy grounds. These beliefs not only are often developed by the individual policeman, they are shared by other police officers who support one another in these beliefs. They have in some instances become part of a police ideology. This sharing results from the officers communicating about their common experiences and their ways of reducing dissonance in these situations.

In one sense the development of such shared ways of avoiding dissonance are highly functional because they permit the police officers to continue to function with less stress. Further, the ideology is not necessarily wrong—double, triple, quadruple standards for human conduct abound everywhere and injustice is widespread in human society. And the police officer is in a position in which he encounters a disproportionate amount of duplicity and injustice.

Nonetheless, a heavy price is paid both by police officers and by society at large because of the very strength of these dissonance-avoiding beliefs. Because of the strong motivational basis of these beliefs and because of the norms supporting them, police officers may be less willing to recognize exceptions, to perceive changes in situations, to react to situations flexibly and openly. The officer may condemn young black males as criminally inclined, may see public officials as corrupt, may see gambling as acceptable, may think all suspects are guilty, etc. In a fast changing and complex society such as America, such inflexible thinking can lead to harm because of the discrepancy inherent between such thinking and reality.

TOLERANCE OF DISSONANCE

The question then arises of how to minimize or even avoid the development of such inflexible beliefs among police officers. One way of doing so stems from the proposition that not all people are equally motivated to reduce dissonance. Some people can live more comfortably with the fact that they have had to make decisions in conflict situations with often ambiguous and incomplete justification. Some people may be less likely to have to find very strong justifications for the difficult choices they have had to make. Police officers who have a high tolerance for dissonance thus would no doubt in the long run be better officers. They would be more open to change, to perceiving exceptions, to seeing the value of alternative courses of action which they have not chosen. They would be more likely to try out new, flexible ways of functioning as police officers in a changing society.

Unfortunately, no well-established valid measure of individual differences in tolerance for dissonance has yet been developed. Nevertheless, we would like to propose a way of measuring such differences. This way is simply to place potential recruits in situations of conflict similar to those of police work and observe how they react, that is, to place candidates for police work in role-playing situations in which they would be confronted with some conflict typical of police work.* Not only would their behavior during the actual role playing be evaluated, but immediately after the role playing session their perceptions and evaluations of their own behavior could be obtained to determine how *flexibly* they were thinking about what had happened.

---

*Chenoweth (1962) has already suggested the use of role playing in police selection. A beginning in use of role playing as a selection device for police officers has been made by Mills, McDevitt, and Tonkin (1968). However, the situations they used were not selected to measure reactions to conflict.

Role Playing

An example would be to have the candidate enact the role of a police officer responding to a complaint late at night from a ghetto housewife that a group of young black men were making so much noise in the street that the neighborhood was kept awake. The candidate would then be faced with the problem of deciding how much noise is too much, of reacting to the probable verbal hostility from the young men which may tend to provoke him to anger and thereby to violate the dictum to be professional, etc. The role of the young men could be enacted by actors who are instructed to "give the officer a hard time." After the candidate has enacted the role to the point at which he has committed himself to a line of action and has followed it through for a reasonable time, the role playing might be stopped and the candidate given some questions, either orally or in writing, to determine how well he tolerated dissonance without reducing it. This tolerance would be reflected in his continued perception and relatively high evaluation of courses of action which he did not take. The tolerance would also be reflected in his admission of a lack of certainty about his perception of the motivation of the young man and in the candidate's willingness to admit that there were ambiguities in the situation.

Not only might such a procedure provide information about the ability of the candidate to deal with the situation without having to engage in an excessive amount of dissonance reduction, but the candidate's enactment of the role might also provide information about other of his characteristics which might be relevant to police work: his ability to maintain his "cool", his ability to communicate with others, his imagination in devising ways of coping with the situation, etc. Furthermore, these situations could be selected to tap the candidate's ability to handle the first type of conflict mentioned above—between himself and the community and between or among members of the community. The candidate could be observed by several raters either directly or by means of videotape. A series of such role-playing episodes might be devised, each representing a difficult type of conflict which police officers often encounter.

One advantage to this procedure is that it minimizes the problem of using completely paper and pencil measures with a group of people who are more oriented to action than to writing. Another is that it can also be used as a training procedure so that there would be a continuity between selection and training. The progress of a recruit from his selection role playing through to his training would be apparent both to him and to the trainer.*

The intended result of such a selection technique would be to select those recruits who are flexible and therefore could handle and tolerate the inherent ambiguities of a policeman's job and select out those individuals who are unable to tolerate the cognitive dissonance and stress resulting from ambiguity and uncertainty. Inclusion of a tolerance for dissonance procedure individually administered to recruits in addition to other relevant selection methods would be much more realistic and fundamental than many of the current psychological measuring devices currently in use.

Training by Means of Role Playing

In addition to using role playing as a technique of selecting officers, it might also be used to train them. Recruits who watched actors play scenes involving psychological stress might become better equipped to deal with such situations on the street. Some departments have begun to use TV or filmed role playing for this purpose (Fakler, 1970; Danish, 1970). Recruits might be placed in a series of stress situations for training purposes (Office of Strategic Services, 1948; Chenoweth, 1961; Mille, McDevitt and Tonkin, 1966; Mille, 1969).

A LOOK TOWARDS THE FUTURE

Although methodological and theoretical difficulties abound in personality assessment and prediction of future job performance with police populations, future research in this area is very much needed. There is a very real need for sample informational research. Very little is known about a great many things with regard

---

*The use of role playing as a gauge of improvement in performance by the recruit was suggested by a recruit in the Seattle Police Academy.

to policemen. A study of the reasons why men want to become policemen would be a good starting place. An inquiry into why policemen leave their jobs or why certain policemen "go bad" is also in order. It has been estimated that it takes about $10,000 (IACP, 1962) to train and equip a policeman today and an additional $25,000 to sustain him for the rest of his working life. In addition, policemen often make decisions involving continuation or discontinuance of life itself. We cannot afford to be less than rigorous in our attempts to place the best men in positions of such responsibility.

Beyond informational research, assessment studies which have been the bulk of published data, are still very much required. Methodologically-sound studies need to be developed and standardized on the kinds of populations we identify as successful patrolmen. This may not be a unitary construct as the Baehr study would suggest. We may well find that there are many successful personality "types" in police work.

REFERENCES

Abelson, R.P., Aronson, E. ,McGuire, W.J., Newcomb, T.M., Rosenberg, M.J., and Tannenbaum, P.H. (Eds.) : *Theories of Cognitive Dissonance: A Sourcebook*. Rand McNally, 1968.

Adorno, T.W. et al.: *The Authoritarian Personality*. Harper, 1950.

Baehr, M. et al.: *Psychological Assessment of Patrolman Qualifications in Relation to field Performance*. Law Enforcement Assistance Administration, U.S. Department of Justice, 1968.

Blum, Richard H.: "Police Selection in Europe," *Police*, 1960, Part I,5, No. 4, pp. 39-43, Part II,5, pp. 32-35, Part III,5, No. 6, pp. 72-74.

Blum, Richard H.: *Police Selection*. Thomas, 1964.

Blum, Richard H. et al.: "A Study of Deputy Sheriff Selection Procedures," *Police, 6,2,* 59-63, 1961.

Blum, Richard H.: "A Further Study of Deputy Sheriff Selection Procedures." *Police, 6,4,* 77-79, 1962.

Brereton, George H.: "The Importance of Training and Education in the Professionalization of Law Enforcement." *Journal of Criminal Law, Criminology, and Police Science, 51,* 11-121, 1960.

Carlson, Helena, R.E. Thayer, and A.C. Germann.: "Social Attitudes and Personality Differences Among Members of Two Kinds of Police Departments (Innovative vs. Traditional) and Students." Presented at the Western Psychological Association Convention, Los Angeles, April, 1970.

Chenoweth, James H.: "Situational Tests—A new Attempt at Assessing Police Candidates." *Journal of Criminal Law, Criminology, and Police Science, 52,* 232-38, 1962.

Colarelli, Nick J. and N.J. Siegel.: "A Method of Police Personnel Selection." *Journal of Criminal Law, Criminology, and Police Science, 58,* 287-89, 1964.

Cross, Arthur C. and K.R. Hammond.: "Social Differences Between "Successful" and "Unsuccessful" State Highway Patrolmen." *Public Personnel Review, 12,* 159-61, 1951.

Danish, Steven J.: "Training of Policemen in Emotional Control and Awareness." *American Psychologist, 25,4,* 368-9, April, 1970.

Fakler, John: "T.V. Role-playing for Training." *Law and Order,* February, 1970.

Festinger, Leon: *A Theory Cognitive Dissonance.* Stanford, 1957.

Festinger, Leon: *Conflict, Decision, and Dissonance.* Stanford, 1964.

Frost, Thomas M.: "Selection Methods for Police Recruits." *Journal of Criminal Law, Criminology, and Police Science, 46,1,* 135-45, 1955.

Gallati, Robert: "Police Personnel Testing Experience of New York City Police Department." *Police,* May-June, 1960 and July-August, 1960.

Kagan, Norman et al.: "Studies in Human Intersection: Interpersonal Process Recall Stimulated by Videotape." Educational Publications Services, College of Education, Michigan State University, December, 1967.

Kates, Solis L.: "Rorschach Responses, Strong Blank Scales, and Job Satisfaction Among Policemen." *Journal of Applied Psychology, 34,* 249-54, 1950.

Kimble, Joseph P.: "Police Training Today and the Challenge for Tomorrow." *Police,* September-October, 1964.

Lefkowitz, Joel.: *Job Attitudes of Police.* Pilot Project, National Institutes of Law Enforcement and Criminal Justice, Law Enforcement Assistance Administration, 1971.

Levy, Ruth J.: "Predicting Police Failures." *Journal of Criminal Law, Criminology, and Police Science, 58,2,*265-276, 1967.

Marsh, Stewart H.: "Validating the Selection of Deputy Sheriffs." *Public Personnel Review, 23,*1,41-44, January, 1962.

Matarazzo, Joseph D. et al.: "Characteristics of Successful Policemen and Firemen Applicants." *Journal of Applied Psychology, 48,2,* 123-33, 1964.

McAllister, John A.: "A Study of the Prediction and Measurement of Police Performance." *Police,* March-April, 1970.

Mills, Robert B., R.J. McDevitt, and S. Tonkin: "Situational Tests in Metropolitan Police Recruit Selection." *Journal of Criminal Law, Criminology and Police Science, 57,*1, 99-106, 1966.

Mills, Robert B.: "Use of Diagnostic Small Groups in Police Recruit Selection and Training." *Journal of Criminal Law, Criminology, and Police Science, 60,2,* 238-41, 1969.

Mullineaux, Jewel E.: "An Evaluation of the Predictors Used to Select Patrolmen," *Public Personnel Review, 16,2,* April, 1955.

Narrol, Harvey G. and E.E. Levitt: "Formal Assessment Procedures in Police Selection." *Psychological Reports, 12,* 691-693, 1963.

Neiderhoffer, Arthur: *Behind the Shield; The Police in Urban Society.* Doubleday, 1967.

Nowicki, Stephen Jr.: "A Study of the Personality Characteristics of Successful Policemen." *Police, 10,3* January-February, 1966.

O'Conner, George W.: *Survey of Selection Methods,* International Association of Chiefs of Police, Washington D.C., 1962.

Oglesby, Thomas W.: "The Use of Emotional Screening in the Selection of Police Applicants." *Police,* January-February, 1958.

Office of Strategic Services: *Assessment of Men,* Rinehart & Co., Inc. 1948.

Peterson, Margaret H. and F.D. Strider: "Psychiatric Screening of Policemen." Presented at the Midwest Divisional Meeting, American Psychiatric Association, November, 1968.

President's Commission on Law Enforcement and the Administration of Justice, 1967A: *Task Force Report: The Police.*

President's Commission on Law Enforcement and the Administration of Justice, 1967B: *The Challenge of Crime in a Free Society.*

Rankin, James H.: "Preventive Psychiatry in the Los Angeles Police Department." *Police,* July-August, 1957.

Rhead, Clifton et al.: "The Psychological Assessment of Police Candidates." *American Journal of Psychiatry, 124,*11, May, 1968.

Rokeach, M.: *The Open and Closed Mind.* New York, Basic Books, 1960.

Reiser, Martin: "Psychological Research in an Urban Police Department." Presented at the American Psychological Association Convention, Miami Beach, Florida, September, 1970.

Reiser, Martin: "The Police Psychologist as Consultant." Presented at the Western Psychological Association Convention, Los Angeles, California April, 1970.

Reiser, Martin: "A Psychologist's View of the Badge." *Police Chief,* September, 1970.

Rush, Allen C.: "Better Police Personnel Selection." *Police Chief,* September, 1963.

Shev, Edward D.: "Psychiatric Techniques in the Selection and Training of a Police Officer." *Police Chief,* April, 1968.

Skolnick, J. H.: *Justice Without Trial.* John Wiley, 1966.

Smith, A. B., Locke, B. and Walker, W. F.: "Authoritarianism in College and Non-college Oriented Police." *Journal of Criminal Law, Criminology, and Police Science, 58,*1, 128-32, 1967.

Smith, A.B., B. Locke and W.F. Walker: "Authoritarianism in Police College Students and Non-police College Students." *Journal of Criminal Law, Criminology, and Police Science, 59,*3, 440-443, 1968.

Smith, A.B., B. Locke and A. Fenster: "Authoritarianism in Policemen who are College Graduates and Non-college Police." *Journal of Criminal Law, Criminology, and Police Science, 61,2,* 313-315, 1970.

Snibbe, Homa, J. Grenick, H. Montgomery, and L. Maruyama: "They Wore a Badge for Twenty Years: A longitudinal Predictive Study of Law Enforcement Officers." Presented at the Western Psychological Association, 1970.

Sterne, David M.: "Use of the Kuder Preference Record, Personal, with Police Officers. *"Journal of Applied Psychology, 44,5,* 323-24, 1960.

Wilson, James Q.: *Varieties of Police Behavior.* Harvard University Press, 1968.

Wolfe, Jerry B.: "Some Psychological Characteristics of American Policemen: A critical "Review of the Literature." Proceedings of the Annual Convention of the American Psychological Association, 1970.

Chapter 2

A METHOD FOR IDENTIFICATION OF
THE HIGH-RISK POLICE APPLICANT

Ruth J. Levy

INTRODUCTION

For over a decade law enforcement has been working assiduously at improving and refining its selection techniques by research, by improvisation, by borrowing from business and management techniques, by collaboration with behavioral scientists, and finally, by trial and error. Tremendous strides have been made, but there still remains a long hard row to hoe before the goal of professionalization is reached. It is hoped that the investigation described herein will contribute to shortening the row and facilitating the burdens encountered.

The proliferation of articles, journals, and books flowing from the pens of law enforcement officers in recent years would seem to reflect a change in self-image among men who were formerly so ink shy, and this must bring in its wake a salutary change in their public image. Selection is complicated by the fact that we keep adding new functions to the law enforcement officer's job. A Los Angeles police sergeant, in discussing the multifaceted situations encountered in police work, talks of, "an endless number of problems that a policeman is not qualified to solve, but must make an attempt to solve."[1] In the United States police functions are sometimes sloppily conceived, often poorly delineated, and continuously misunderstood, both within and without law enforcement. Supreme Court decisions intended to insure justice and civil liberty[2] are frequently considered by law enforcement officers as making their job more difficult. Does the problem lie in our concept of justice? Our definition of law enforcement? The charac-

This research was supported by a Ford Foundation Grant.

25

teristics of our police officers? Most of us agree that some revamping of our system for administration of justice is overdue, but while we await this more global task we cannot neglect the task of upgrading and improving police selection.

The President's Crime Commission of 1967 and the President's Riot Commission of 1968, while addressing themselves to the overall search for root causes of violence, simultaneously recommend "improved screening of police candidates to eliminate those with undesirable characteristics."[3] The former United States Attorney General, declared that, "The police mission these next several years may be the most important in public service,"[4] and maintains that, "The basic shortcoming of police service today is in its quality, not its quantity."[5]

In 1967 we completed a study which examined minutely the histories of 4,000 officers employed in California by ten municipal police departments, three sheriffs' offices and the California Highway Patrol. Of these, 613 had been terminated for cause over a ten-year period.[6] When we compared their pre-employment histories with those of officers who had not been found occupationally wanting, it was found that they possessed certain combinations of demographic factors which significantly differentiated them from men not terminated for cause. This discovery has a predictive usefulness not heretofore exploited.

Up to the present time there have been two major methods used in screening. One involves services of psychiatrists and/or clinical psychologists to identify emotional pathology. Obviously a man with such gross pathology as to be out of contact with reality cannot function as a police officer. However, among the finer nuances of personality and character constellations, it avails us little to attach nosologic labels for purposes of police selection. Too often it is taken for granted that anxiety, compulsivity, or immaturity should bar a candidate from police employment. We used to take for granted that height under 5'9" should bar a candidate from police employment. Now that height requirements have been reduced by an inch or more, we find that the shorter recruits are no less able than their taller colleagues. Obviously, then, former height requirements were either arbitrary or at least in need of modification.

Are some of our requirements in the area of emotional factors equally arbitrary? The standards we must raise are not arbitrary ones, but job-related standards. Mere addition of pre-employment tests and examinations is valueless unless they help identify capacities of an applicant to perform certain tasks. "It cannot be said that any of the conventional personality measures have demonstrated really general usefulness as selection tools in employment practice."[7] Ghiselli and Barthol warn that such tests have proved ineffective for numerous "occupations in which these factors could reasonably be expected to be of paramount importance."[8] Interesting and relevant is a study evaluating the Edwards Personal Preference Schedule as a predictor of success in naval flight training. It shows failure to discriminate in any way among aviators who successfully completed their training, those who left the program voluntarily, and those who were failed by the Navy.[9] There are even those who believe that "certain traits ordinarily considered to be 'pathological' are essential ingredients of the personality structure of the 'normal' police officer."[10] Unless and until we know which emotional components militate against satisfactory police work, it is a waste of time, energy, and money to seek the candidates with greatest amount of "emotional stability." It is emotional *suitability,* not "emotional stability" which we should be seeking.

The second screening method has scientific merit. Through in-depth investigations in individual police departments[11] it attempts to create and/or select pre-employment tests validated on the basis of correlation between predictor variables and criterion variables. This is an excellent approach. Unfortunately, we have over 40,000 law enforcement agencies in the United States and the applicability of this method is confined to a police department on whose data the program is based.

It was because neither of these methods seemed optimum, and because we already had empirically derived variables which discriminated between officers terminated for cause and other officers across the board in fourteen police jurisdictions that we proceeded with the present study.

BACKGROUND

In order to understand the present investigation it is necessary to mention briefly the retrospective study referred to above since the former is based on the results of the latter. In the earlier study we determined that the fourteen participating jurisdictions had a total of 613 failure terminations during the decade 1952-1962. They had an almost identical number of non-failure terminations, i.e. men who left their jobs voluntarily and remained eligible for rehire. An occupational failure was defined as any separated officer "whose services were no longer considered by his department to be of value to that Department because of inefficiency on the job (caused by reasons other than physical disability) or because of non-job-connected behavior intolerable to the Department."[12] This definition lumped together men fired when criminal charges were brought against them for alleged mistreatment of arrestees, men fired for excessive use of alcohol during off-duty hours, and men unable to meet departmental expectations for a variety of other reasons. Such lumping makes little sense except that all such behaviors are intolerable to law enforcement. We collected the personnel files of all of these failures and non-failures, and after recording the year of hire for each, pulled the personnel files of all still-employed officers who had been hired during the same calendar years as had been the ex-officers. The total number of subjects was 4,000.

From the 4,000 personnel files we abstracted and coded the various demographic and life-historical data which law enforcement agencies collect from each applicant. Cross comparisons proved that certain demographic factors discriminated among the failures, non-failures, and those still in service at a statistical level not accountable for by chance. Thus, for example, the non-failures had completed more years of education before appointment than either of the other two groups. Of men who had taken police science courses before hire 52 percent were still in service, 32 percent had terminated as non-failures, and 16 percent had been terminated by their departments and were ineligible for rehire. Length of residence in city of application correlated significantly with later occupational status, those still in service having lived there longest, and non-failure terminations having lived there the shortest length of time. The still-employed reported the lowest number of residences, while the non-failure terminations reported the highest number. Of the applicants about whom it was known at the time of appointment that they had been married at least twice, 32 percent became occupational failures, 12 percent became non-failure terminations, and 11 percent were still employed.

The rationale in attempting to validate a method for identifying the high-risk applicant rather than the potentially successful officer, is that we have been able to identify a cluster of characteristics and life experiences which many police failures have in common. The converse is not true. The so-called "successful" officer possesses traits which vary from city to city, from chief to chief, from year to year, from one set of social pressures to another. Longevity of employment alone must not be mistaken for "success." Therefore, characteristics of the long-time employee are not necessarily the ones we should be seeking in recruits if we have any standards of selection in mind other than, "Will this candidate remain on the force?" It may be that the backgrounds, behavior patterns, and performance of the non-failures comes closer to the ideal being sought by many communities. If this be true, then it behooves the employer to work at changing the intramural structure so that the potential non-failure will not leave law enforcement to seek more challenging and more rewarding employment elsewhere.

PRESENT STUDY

All 14 departments from which the empirical data had been derived, and which had been selected for heterogenity of size, location, and function agreed to cooperate again for the purpose of validating a demographic model to predict for each applicant the probability of his remaining in law enforcement, terminating as a nonfailure, or becoming an occupational failure.*

To the 14 original participants was added one sheriff's office

---

*This two-year project was supported by a financial grant from the Ford Foundation to the Institute for Local Self-Government.

which had not been included in the earlier investigation. The participating jurisdictions hired a total of 1,765 officers during the period November 1, 1968 through October 31, 1969. The complete personnel files of all 1,765 recruits were reproduced and 62 variables were abstracted from each file. These included personal history, applicant's ordinal position in family, physical examination results, assessments and recommendations by references, prior employment history, residence history, military experience, marital status, and selected social history factors. Of these variables, the following, which had been shown empirically to have discriminated among the failures, the non-failures, and the still-employed in the original 4,000 subjects entered into a predictive model which was applied to the data on each of the 1,765 recruits:

1. Number of marriages
2. Had police science courses prior to application
3. Majored in police science prior to application
4. Applicant had been married, but marriage ended in divorce, separation or annulment
5. Discharged from previous job (s)
6. Number of years education
7. Was sworn peace officer prior to application
8. Was employed as law enforcer, but not sworn peace officer (e.g. guard, corrections officer, etc.)
9. Was Military Policeman (or equivalent such as Shore Patrolman)
10. Number of jobs held
11. Served in some branch of the military forces
12. Served as active member of U.S. Navy
13. Total number of residences listed by applicant
14. Total number of years residence in California after age 16
15. Applicant born in city where he resided at time of application
16. Number of adult arrests for penal code violations
17. Number of juvenile arrests for penal code violations

First attempts to establish a predictive model were mildly successful. Use of a three-way discriminant equation, as well as an assortment of two-way approaches, was discarded because necessary flexibility was lacking. These methods precluded identification of predictive occupational status for any man whose pre-employment background was atypical of men who became failures of non-failures or remained in law enforcement and application of an effective procedure for establishing a confidence level for each prediction. Accordingly, to obviate these deficiencies we developed three separate submodels for independently classifying each recruit within each occupational status (failure, non-failure, continuous employment). This approach permits identification of any given recruit as having pre-employment factors found in all three occupational status groups, in two of them, in one of them, or in none of them. Each man was ranked along each of three continua, representing occupational status, and level of confidence was calculated for each prediction.

To derive the appropriate equations, the following steps were applied to the data from the cases in the original study:

1. Application of program BMDO7M[13] to obtain recorded pre-employment factors in each department which discriminated still-employed from failures and non-failures; failures from non-failures and still-employed; and non-failures from failures and still-employed at the 20 percent level of confidence.

2. Grouping together of departments into four groups, in each of which discriminations were based on similar pre-employment factors. (This grouping was done in order to insure a sufficient number of cases in each computation and to avoid inclusion of spurious variables.)

3. Re-application of program BMDO7M to the department groups (2. above) to identify pre-employment factors which discriminated at 5 percent level of confidence, or better.

4. Application of discriminant program BMDO4M[13] to derive discriminant equations based on these empirically derived pre-employment factors (3. above) and a rank ordering of the cases. From these rankings the numbers of misclassified cases were calculated and levels of confidence determined. (For example, in a run of 100 cases, if our equation made incorrect occupational calssifications in two of the ten top-ranking cases, then the a posteriori percent of correct classifications for those ten top-ranking cases would have been 80 percent.)

5. In conjunction with these equations (4, above) we devised intuitive or logical discriminative equations which attempted to accomplish the following:

a. Modify pre-employment factors in the empirically derived equations so as to correspond to the profile of pre-employment factors abstracted from the 1,765 cases in the present investigation. (For example, at time of hire of the 4,000 officers in the earlier study residence history was generally requested and reported for only ten years preceding the time of application, whereas at present many departments ask applicants to give residence history since birth.)

b. Modify weightings when pre-employment factors in the empirically derived equations showed changes between the earlier study and this one. (For example, in the original study 12 percent of the applicants had taken police science courses prior to police employment, whereas of the 1,765 subjects in this investigation 33 percent had accumulated credits in police science courses prior to their application.)

c. Add to the predictive model theoretically "good" life historical factors which had not been examined in the earlier study due to absence of information.

THEORETICAL CONSIDERATIONS

Regardless of the specific reasons leading to the termination in the 613 occupational failures previously studied, scrutiny of their records revealed that they had been unable to make a satisfactory adjustment to the "chain of command" expectations in the law enforcement milieu and that they had been unable to act in authoritative (as distinguished from authoritarian) manner in both crisis and routine situations.

We know that certain personality components tend to be associated with inabilities. For example, denigration of self-worth, often accompanied by denigration of worth of others, militates against acceptance of a subordinate role and is more likely to produce tension-producing authoritarianism than an authoritative stance. Nomenclature alone will not characterize the high-risk police applicant, but the men most likely to fail as law enforcement officers seem to closely resemble the passive-aggressive personality, aggressive type, whose deep dependency needs have been met but erratically and who continues to deny these needs overtly (e.g. through open hostility) or covertly (e.g. through alcoholism), or the sociopathic personality who does not profit from experience.

One of the best indices of self-realization can be found in an individual's past affiliations. Therefore, if we can elicit and measure these past affiliations we should be able to predict at a better level of confidence than heretofore, which police applicants constitute the high risk population. Rigidity in selection practice serves no purpose. The important consideration is to match individual capacities with job-duties rather than to expect conformity to an inflexible and often arbitrary standard.[14] A United States Congressman from New York contends that, "If the selection of policemen is characterized by lack of appropriate high standards on the one hand, it can also be criticized for an overabundance of poorly conceived and irrelevant limitations on the other. Police departments often impose a number of requirements that are simply not as important or relevant as they once were—if indeed they were ever important or relevant at all. These must be reviewed in the light of the duties the modern policeman is required to perform and the character traits and physical capability he must apply to that performance."[15]

If the above premises are applicable, the searching questions we must ask concern past affiliations which warn that the police applicant will probably be unable to make the necessary adjustments at the opposite ends of the authority pole which characterize the functions of the law enforcement officer. In quite another context, Dr. Christopher Leggo, former Medical Examiner for the California State Personnel Board, stated very directly and simply, "In our culture, the father is the first central figure of authority, and the attitude toward the paternal parent is likely to be the attitude with which all subsequent authority is viewed."[16] Although this may be an oversimplification, nevertheless it is interesting to note that in the fourteen jurisdictions which participated in this study, heterogeneous as to size, location, wealth, level of sophistication, age, and function, not a single one has explored the candidate's relations with his father. In most of the fourteen, pre-employment information does not include data on father's whereabouts, whether or not he remained married to applicant's mother, or the simplest kind of vital statistics. Some of the departments fail to inquire whether the applicant's father is alive or dead, and in those departments whose background investigators do make such inquiry, we have never seen this information incorporated into an evaluation of the applicant's own authority stance. In those departments which use psychiatric interview as part of the selection armamentarium, psychiatric reports have not included discussion of father-son relationships as a significant datum in assessing the applicant's suitability. In the departments which use polygraph testing as part of the selection process, considerable attention is paid to an applicant's past sexual behavior, drug use, as well as falsifications in self-reporting, but we have never seen reference to inquiries into applicant-father relationships.

Chief Al Nelder of the San Francisco Police Department, discussing police recruitment, is quoted as saying of the officers on his department: "We want them to treat and regard everybody as whole human beings."[17] An infant's first regarded human being is usually his mother. His self-image is tailored by his earliest relations with her and by his later relations with father and siblings. Information on relations with mother and siblings is as conspicuous by its absence from recruit investigations, as reported in police personnel files, as is information on father-son relations. In an effort to obtain some vital statistics not contained in police personnel files (the parameters of this study did not permit anything more) we administered a one-page questionnaire to each of the 1,765 recruits on the day of appointment. From the replies we were able to calculate ordinal position in parental family for each officer.

The not inconsiderable research on effects of ordinal position suggests use of this variable in a predictive model with the following considerations:

1. First-borns tend to identify most particularly with authority, discipline, and parental prohibitions and moral values.[18]
2. First-borns, in relation to second-borns, exercise dominance and use more physical power and this relationship within the dyad is not affected by differences in family size.[19]
3. Only children and first-borns have a greater tendency to conform under group pressure and under conditions of stress than do later-born children.[19]
4. Later-born siblings who have been "seriously overpowered" may feel the need to repeat the treatment they received to those less powerful than themselves.[20]

On the basis of the above considerations, we gave status of first-born a negative value for police failure in our predictive model, i.e. the assumption is made that a first-born applicant will be less likely to fail than a later-born if all other variables are identical.

Continuing the investigation of past experiences and affiliations as tools for assessing self-attitude and attitude toward others, we explored another variable not heretofore studied in this connection, namely what might be called name-style. If there is merit in the idea that the first-born is less likely to fail than a later born if all other variables are identical, what effects is imprinted on a man's character and behavior if given his father's name? (John Doe, Jr.). A man's name is felt to be an integral part of himself. It has been suggested by Robert Holt[21] in a well-documented treatment of the subject, that most people feel their names to be as much parts of themselves as are their arms and legs. When a son is given his father's name he becomes, symbolically, an extension of his father. It is possible that a man named for his father, clothed at birth with the father's symbol, will experience less overt conflict with the father's authority than will his other-named brother. He may concomitantly, vis-a-vis others than his father, feel the weight of authority emanating from him through the strength of a reinforced ego. On the basis of these considerations, we gave the variable "Jr." after surname a negative value for police failure in our predictive model; i.e. the assumption is made that an applicant with "Jr." after his surname will be less likely to fail than another if all other variables are identical.

The next variable we treated is not completely unique as a selection tool and is included in police selection in at least one eastern city. Until now, however, there has been no validation of its predictive usefulness. This variable is the presence of tattooing. Information on this variable was spotty in our original 4,000 police personnel files. It is still spotty in the present 1,765 cases, in which we were able to positively identify presence of tattooing in 32 applicants. If one views tattooing as a type of self-disfigurement, often motivated by a desire to project a strong masculine image,[22] one must evaluate the tattooed man as an individual who, at least at one time, was dissatisfied with himself to the point of inducing an almost irreversible change in persona. Does the history of such nonacceptance of self augur poorly in predicting acceptance of others, specifically in law enforcement, acceptance of superiors as well as acceptance of service recipients? Hypothesizing an affirmative answer, we gave the variable tattooing a positive value for police failure in our predictive model.

As a result of the foregoing and other considerations, the following variables entered our predictive model in addition to the empirically derived factors:

1. Applicant's ordinal position (birth order)
2. Applicant is last-born (in family of 2 or more)
3. Applicant is first-born (in family of 2 or more)
4. Applicant is "Jr."
5. Applicant has tattoo(s)
6. Applicant received "dishonors" in military (e.g. court martial) or in school (e.g. academic probation, suspension, expulsion)
7. Poorly-executed application (failure to follow directions or falsifications)
8. Father is (was) police officer
9. Any negative reference
10. Negative reference from employer
11. Negative reference from character reference
12. Negative reference from school
13. Negative reference from neighbor, landlord or wife
14. Negative recommendation from background investigator
15. Negative recommendation from interviewer
16. Negative recommendation by examining physician, psychiatrist, or psychologist
17. Age
18. G.E.D. or other high-school equivalent in lieu of high-school diploma

The above logically-derived variables had to be utilized in a fashion which would not detract from the value of the empirically derived variables, since the latter had already shown power to discriminate significantly between police terminations and non-terminations. Therefore, we created a second predictive model consisting of the empirically derived variables *plus* the logically derived variables. In addition, since the background information on the 1,765 men hired between November 1, 1968 and November 1, 1969 was in some areas different from the information elicited from the earlier 4,000 personnel files, it was necessary to adjust accordingly the weightings of the empirically-derived variables.

This study concerns itself with the qualifications an applicant brings to his job, but we dare not forget that the job environment and non-job-connected events are constantly influencing his progress. In addition to the recruit's personality as an omen of success or failure as a law enforcement officer, there is the personality of his employer and his department, which help determine an officer's occupational future. The man with a "drinking problem" who is employed by a department with rigid strictures against drinking steers a more difficult occupational course than he would if he were employed by a department which sees his problem as one for which the department should give counsel, guidance, and possibly even treatment. We need to devise methods of measuring the job environment in a way which will add new dimension to predictions. Non-job-connected events and circumstances add their contribution to determining occupational future. Wives of some officers are sympathetic and supportive while others are demanding and destructive. No instrument will predict these events and circumstances. However, greater knowledge of an applicant's past affiliations can contribute some information regarding the likelihood of a recruit's marrying a supportive versus a destructive partner.

RESULTS

All pre-employment information available to the fourteen participating jurisdictions was obtained at the time of hire for each of the 1,765 subjects of this investigation. The number of new hires during the data collection period of November 1, 1968 to November 1, 1969 ranged from 6 in one department to 851 in another. The extent of information requested of and obtained from each recruit varied from department to department. One hundred and sixty-six cases were found to lack some crucial information and were eliminated from computations. In all of the remaining 1,599 cases there was a completed law enforcement application questionnaire containing information on residence history, education, marital status, military experience, job history, illnesses, surgical interventions, arrest record, and vehicle code violations. In some cases there were letters from primary references; in some school transcripts; in some, military documents; in some, photocopies of birth certificates and marriage certificates; in two jurisdictions there were copies of psychological test reports and psychiatric evaluations; from all departments but one we received copies of completed Civil Service application questionnaires and the scores obtained by applicants on Civil Service written and oral tests. Each recruit completed a one-page questionnaire (See Figure 2-1), containing information on reason for

FIG. 2-1

QUESTIONS TO BE ADDED TO P.D. QUESTIONNAIRE

NAME_____DATE_____

1. The MAIN reason I want to be a peace officer is because (check the statement which comes *closest*, even if not exact):
    a) Desire to work with people
    b) Influence of relatives or friends who are or were peace officers
    c) Interest and/or experience
    d) Service to mankind
2. Total number of times I have been married is (circle one):
    0   1   2   3   4   more than 4
3. IF married (now or previously), age at time of first marriage was (circle one):
    Less than 18   18   19   20   21   22   more than 22
4. Age when first child (if any) was born was (circle one):
    Less than 18   18   19   20   21   22   more than 22
5. If ever divorced, plantiff in dirovce was (check one):
    a) Myself
    b) Ex-wife
6. Total number of older brothers (circle one):
    0   1   2   3   4   5   more than 5
7. Total number of older sisters (circle one):
    0   1   2   3   4   5   more than 5
8. Total number of younger brothers (circle one):
    0   1   2   3   4   5   more than 5
9. Total number of younger sisters (circle one):
    0   1   2   3   4   5   more than 5

wanting to enter law enforcement, marital status, age at time of first marriage, age at time of birth of applicant's first child, and applicant's ordinal position in his parental family.

The reason most frequently given by recruits on their applications regarding desire to join a police force is referable to the many benefits attached to police employment; viz. salary (in San Francisco beginning salary for patrolmen in 1970 was $10,000 per annum, with educational requirement of high school graduation) and "fringe benefits" (health insurance, retirement pensions, disability awards, etc.) . Since these "security" reasons constitute the overwhelming majority and did not discriminate among subjects in our earlier study, we eliminated them from our one-page questionnaire (Fig. 2-1) , forcing each recruit in the present study to choose from among the four next most frequently given reasons for wanting to become a police officer.

Inclusion of questions regarding age at time of first marriage and age at birth of first child was the result of two considerations: (A) Their absence from the data collected from some of the participating departments; and (B) A series of cases in our earlier study wherein this particular behavioral expression of responsibility-assumption hinted at correlation with later occupational status, with a positive correlation between failure termination and extreme youth at time of first marriage and birth of applicant's first child. (This finding differs from that found among Chicago patrolmen.[23]) .

Information on each of the 62 variables was abstracted from each of the 1,599 cases. The cases from the sheriff's office which had not been part of the original study were temporarily set aside for separate treatment.

Table 2-I shows the empirically derived pre-employment factors which occurred most frequently; in the discriminant epuations. With two exceptions, all empirically derived pre-employment factors consistently discriminated in the same direction for any given occupational status (failure, non-failure, continued employment) . "Number of previous full-time jobs" and "served in Navy" entered the predictive equations in one direction in some departments, and in the opposite direction in other departments.

(The predictive significance of Navy service may be related to whether or not the city of application is a coastal city.) Table 2-II gives the logically derived pre-employment factors which were used in weighted combinations with the discriminant

TABLE 2-I

EMPIRICALLY DERIVED VARIABLES USED IN PREDICTIVE MODEL

Failure	Non-Failure	Continued Employment
Few years residence in California	Few years in California	Many years in California
Number of jobs	Greater than average education	Less education than average
Tattooed	Served in navy	Served in navy
Was sworn peace officer previously	Older than average	Never before a sworn peace officer
Discharged from previous job(s)		Never divorced

Example of a discriminant equation based on empirically derived variables: Score for predicting continued employment (i.e. no termination within the first seven years after hire)— 2 (number years residence in California) plus 5 if applicant had served in navy minus 4(number years education).

TABLE 2-II

LOGICALLY-DERIVED VARIABLES USED IN PREDICTIVE MODEL

Failure	Non-Failure	Continued employment
Last-born	First-born	Born in city of application
Negative recommendations	No negative recommendations	No negative recommendations
Poor application	Arrested as juvenile	Application not poor
Parental home broken	No adult arrests	Parental home intact
Low military rank in relation to years served	"Jr."	Military rank not low in relation to number of years served
Age 21 or 22	Greater than average number of residences	Fewer than average number of residences
Earned high school certificate thru G.E.D. or equivalent	Father is sworn peace officer	Does not give "service to mankind" as reason for joining
Gives "Service to Mankind" as reason for application		Never failed entrance exam to any other police department
Failure to pass entrance exam for another police department		
Parent deceased		
"Dishonors"		
First child born to applicant when very young		

Example of a second discriminant equation including logically derived variables: Score for predicting continued employment of at least seven years —
Score from empirical equation (Table I)
plus 9 if born in city of application minus 12
if application were poorly executed or contained
falsifications.

equation resulting from the empirically derived factors. These data formed the basis of the second set of discriminant equations in the predictive model.

Of the 1,599 recruits on whom predictions were made, 1,056 were hired by departments studied in the first investigation. We applied to the pre-employment information on each recruit the equations derived on the basis of the empirical variables and the logical variables appropriate to the hiring department. From the discriminant scores, all recruits were ranked within their departments. An a posteriori percent for each occupational status was then assigned, as illustrated in the sample below:

Computation for Officer "X" Using Empirical Equation

	Score	Rank	a posteriori %
Failure	40	5	70%
Non-Failure	30	20	70%
Continued employment	50	100	10%

Computation for Officer "X" Using Logical Equation

	Score	Rank	a posteriori %
Failure	40	30	30%
Non-Failure	50	3	70%
Continued employment	45	90	10%

The a posteriori percentages become the print-outs most meaningful in communicating to the employer the degree to which Officer "X" resembles, in terms of his pre-employment history, other officers in the employing department. Using the comparisons rendered by applying empirical equation alone, it is readily seen that Officer "X" has very little resemblance to other officers who have remained on the employing department for seven years or longer. On the other hand, demographic factors in his file moderately resemble men who have voluntarily resigned or been fired from this department, without however distinguishing between the two types of termination. Now using the predictive equations into which the logically derived variables have entered, the picture changes. Again the a-posteriori percentage indicates a background very dissimilar from the background of most officers

Fig. 2-2
Distribution of Predicted Terminations
Made by Logically Derived Equations

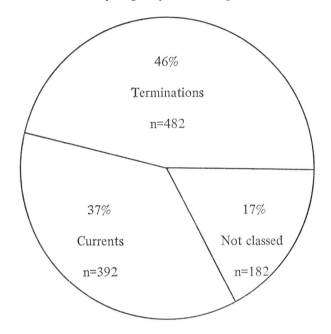

Total n = 1056

Fig. 2-3
Distribution of Predicted Classifications
Made by Logically Derived Equations

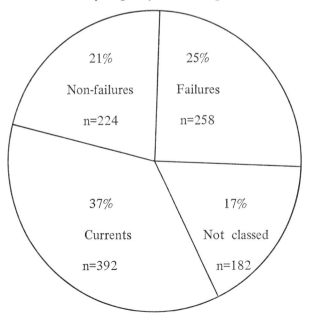

Total n = 1056

Fig. 2-4

Distribution of Predictions Made by Logical Equations
On the Actual Terminations as of 2/70

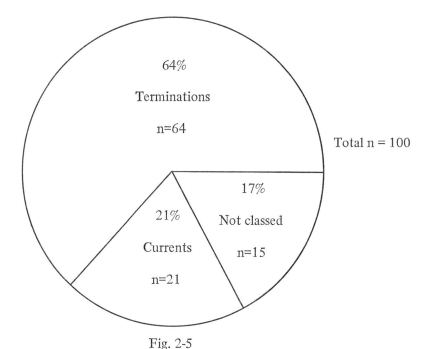

Total n = 100

Fig. 2-5

Distribution of Predictions Made by Logical Equations
On the Actual Failures as of 2/70

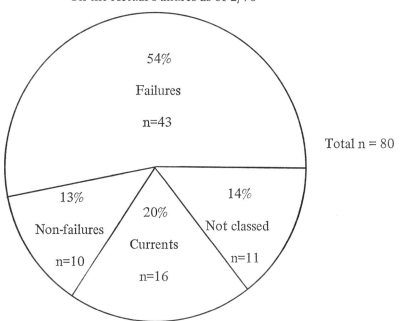

Total n = 80

who have remained on this department. Again the a-posteriori percentage shows moderate similarity to non-failures in this jurisdiction. But the addition of the logically derived variables to the predictive equation has changed the comparison to former failures, now showing much less similarity to such failures.

In January, 1970, fourteen months after the first subject had been hired and two months after the last subject had been hired, we computed a preliminary validation of our predictive approach. By that time 100 of the 1,056 recruits had either voluntarily resigned or had been asked by their employers to leave. Of these 100, 80 were considered by their employers to have failed and were ineligible for rehire; 13 were considered by their employers to have been non-failure terminations, eligible for rehire should they so request; and 7 terminations could not be classified due to insufficient information. Analysis of the effectiveness of the predictive model when using the equation with empirically-derived variables shows only mild significance. But use of the model when using the equation with the added logical variables is significant beyond mere chance factors. Figures 2-2 and 2-3 give predicted occupational status, Figure 2-2 grouping all terminations together, Figure 2-3 breaking the termination predictions down into failures and non-failures. Figure 2-4 examines the extent to which we were able to predict correctly terminations for the 100 officers who actually had terminated or been terminated as of January, 1970. Figure 2-5 illustrates our predictions for the 80 men who had become failures as of that time. Table 2-III shows the probability scores for effectiveness of the predictive model.

TABLE 2-III

P-VALUES FROM TESTS ON THE EFFECTIVENESS OF THE PREDICTIVE MODEL

| | Discriminant Equations Used | |
	Empirical	Logical
Distribution of Predicted Terminations vs. Distribution of Actual Terminations	$p = .14$	$p < .001$
Distribution of Predicted Classification vs. Distribution of Actual Failures	$p = .05$	$p < .000001$

DISCUSSION

On the basis of our results to date it appears as though our selection approach has demonstrated its usefulness in identifying, before hire, the high-risk police applicant. The approach, very simply stated, is to identify the demographic factors which distinguish occupational failures from others, and to examine each new applicant for the presence or absence of these factors. Certain basic correlations applied to all fourteen jurisdictions we studied. For example, we found a significant positive correlation between amount of education and non-failure termination, i.e. the greater the recruit's amount of education, the greater the likelihood that he would leave law enforcement voluntarily within seven years of his appointment. A single predictive equation with identical factors, identically weighted, is not universally applicable. One starts with an equation containing the universally applicable factors and then adjusts and modifies the basic formula so as to meet the unique needs and experiences of a given community.

Germaine to the central issue of developing a method for identification of the high-risk police officer are several important milieu factors briefly alluded to below which require investigation and exploration simultaneously with research involving the backgrounds and life histories of the recruits themselves.

Civil Service

A police applicant is twice screened before he ever presents himself to a law enforcement agency. First comes the self-selection process which occurs. The distribution of some demographic factors (e.g. branch of armed services in which applicant met his military obligations) is different from that of an unselected U.S. male population in the age bracket under consideration. Next comes a process of Civil Service elimination from this self-selected group. An applicant who fails to meet Civil Service ordained prerequisites in the city, county, or state where he seeks employment is eliminated without further consideration. If he passes this barrier he is generally required to take a Civil Service composed written test, often unstandardized, frequently resembling a test of general information. A large percentage of applicants is eliminated at this point. If he gets over the written test hurdle he is asked to appear before an oral review board, consisting of representatives from Civil Service, law enforcement, and the outside community. The reviewers change, their predilections and interviewing skills vary, and the results of these oral reviews seem dictated at times by happenstance or even in opposition to the needs of law enforcement. There is generally an applicant attrition of approximately 90 percent from the time of original application with a Civil Service department to the time of appointment. We cannot help but speculate on the number of "false negatives" which occur among that 90 percent. How many men who could upgrade a police department are eliminated without justification? The "common failure of examining boards to select well-qualified men for appointment"[24] is not being rectified fast enough.

On the other side of this coin, whereby law enforcement may be arbitrarily deprived of good potential, is the system of supplying a police agency with a list of "eligible" candidates who have passed all Civil Service obstacles and from whom the chief or sheriff or commissioner must choose in an order similar to that in which they won the obstacle race. Thus if a Civil Service Commission presents a law enforcement administrator with a list of ten "eligibles" and there exists only one job opening on the police department, it would be difficult, if not impossible, to appoint applicant number ten (i.e. the man with the lowest Civil Service rating) even though police agency considered him to be the best qualified among the ten to fill the vacancy, and even though no correlation has been demonstrated between Civil Service ranking and later occupational status.

None of us wishes to regress to a spoils system nor to remove some of the necessary checks and balances, but our present system denies to the police administrator freedom of choice in selection. Better communication is needed between our law enforcement agencies and the respective governmental bodies under which they function.

Administrative Bias

In view of the departmental differences in policies of recruitment, selection, retention, and promotion, we tried to isolate some of the administrative philosophies and prejudices affecting occupational status. Accordingly, it was requested of each participating administrator that he rank fifteen demographic variables, some of which significantly discriminated among men in the three occupational status groups (failure, non-failure, and continued employment) in the order in which he believed they contributed to an officer's failing, an officer's voluntary termination, or an officer's retention. The results of this cursory survey demonstrate a complete lack of concensus among the fourteen departments. Again we reaffirm the view that reduction of occupational failures depends not only on an improved selection process but on the "police system itself."[25]

Job Satisfaction

Law enforcement is justifiably concerned about the many non-failure terminations, i.e. the voluntary resignations of men who give good service but eventually leave the profession because it fails to adequately recognize, compensate, or reward this service. The potential long-term employee or potential non-failure may, in the absence of job satisfactions become a failure. When success and satisfaction are not available through legitimate routes, "illegitimate means may be used."[26] It is up to administrative and supervisory personnel to recognize the man with potential for good service and to use whatever innovative means are possible to insure against his disillusionment. Identification of a recruit as a potential non-failure alerts his department to his similarity with others who have given good service in the past but left when they became disenchanted. Thus alerted, administration is in a better position to examine and meet the recruit's needs.

Two-Level Entry

The report of the National Commission of the Causes and Prevention of Violence states, "Effective police administration is hard to find. The great majority of police agencies are headed by chiefs who started as patrolmen and whose training in modern management techniques, finance, personnel, communications and community relations is limited." The report continues with reference to the difficulties attendant on changing the present system because of "antiquated civil service concepts." We are familiar with the rationale of some police chiefs who have faith in the system which requires upward movement through the ranks and who warn that lateral entry will have a "demoralizing" effect. Nevertheless, the two-level entry system, long in practice on the European continent, seems to have many advantages. Under it, a man applies either for the job of patrolman, a service occupation in which he can rise to the highest non-administrative post, or for the job of police administrator, whose emphasis is on managerial skills. The prerequisites for entrance differ, the functions differ, and there is greater likelihood of promotion for any given man within his category of employment. The educational requirements for the two categories differ both horizontally and vertically. Some police chiefs in the United States argue that police administrators cannot do an effective job unless they have had experience "on the street." Even if this is true, it should be possible to give a prospective administrator the needed "street" experience over a briefer period of time rather than demanding that he spend the most productive years of his life working his way to the top.

Background Investigation

Law enforcement agencies have not yet agreed on the type of information to elicit in assessing a candidate's potential, nor in the methods most appropriate to elicit it. Uniformity has little value as an end in itself, but departments can give no cogent reasons why some, for example, ask applicants to give residence histories going back in time for three years preceding date of application, while others require applicants to give residence histories going back to the time of birth. All departments want to know the extent of an applicant's education and his marital status, and yet these two areas are often explored via ambiguous questions. If an applicant gives school grade completion as "12," this response still leaves unanswered whether he attended school for 12 years or achieved the equivalency of high school completion through other means. Since number of years of school attendance is correlated with occupational status, it is important for the employer to obtain this information. Or, an applicant is asked to give his marital status. Since number of marriages at the time of application is correlated with later occupational status, this datum should be known to the employer but is not always elicited.

Over and beyond the need to modify avenues of investigation so as to enrich meaningful knowledge about applicants, there are whole areas of personal history and past affiliations which law enforcement fails to explore. For example, in one department where information is available on the stability of an applicant's parental home, 15 percent of recruits in a single calendar year came from broken homes, i.e. homes in which the parents were divorced or separated, but 33 percent of the occupational failures came from broken homes.

The improvement in personal history forms and application questionnaires has been so great during the past decade, that law enforcement is obviously aware of their contribution to eliciting background data with predictive significance and will assuredly lose no opportunity to continue their refinement in keeping with new insights as the latter emerge and are reported.

CONCLUSIONS

Law enforcement must improve its techniques for recognizing as high-risks, before hiring the sheriff's deputy who lost control over his impulses to the point where he used his service revolver to kill the shopkeeper who moved too slowly in response to the deputy's order; the two police sergeants who celebrated a colleague's promotion by engaging in a "shooting spree"; the patrolman who, while under the influence of alcohol, shot at howling cats in his backyard, and two months later, after suspension and reinstatement, was arrested for hit-run driving; the three off-duty policemen who decided, after consuming quantities of beer, to bait a group of hippies by pelting them with eggs at three o'clock in the morning and then exchanged gunfire with their victims;

the police officer convicted of bad check charges; the uniformed patrolman arrested while molesting two teen-age girls; the policeman who pleaded guilty to felony charges of grand theft; or the thirty-two narcotics agents who peddled some of the drugs they seized as contraband. These men might have served admirably in other professions. No man has a constitutional right to be a policeman.[27] These men are not typical police officers but they besmirch the law enforcement profession, demean the police image, and complicate recruitment. The approach we have used will better identify these men as high risks before they are hired.

In his address to the 1969 annual conference of the International Association of Chiefs of Police, Charles H. Rogovin, Administrator of the Law Enforcement Assistance Administration, U.S. Department of Justice, chided that, "Police have robbed themselves by being slow to change, to innovate, to take a candid look at themselves, to fully utilize what resources have been made available." We have been encouraged to find that quite to the contrary, at least in the case of the fourteen participants in this research, requests for assistance have been aggressive and changes have been made whenever resources were provided. We tend to agree with Mr. Quinn Tamm, Executive Director of the International Association of Chiefs of Police who said, at the same meeting as that addressed by Mr. Rogovin, "The next decade may be the most productive in the history of law enforcement."

REFERENCES

1. Wambaugh, Joseph: *The New Centurions.* Little, Brown, and Co., 1970, pp. 215-216.
2. Miranda v Arizona, 384 US 436, 86 SCT, 1602 L 2nd ed., 694 and Escobedo v Illinois, 378 US 478, 84 SCT, 1758 12 L 2nd ed., 977.
3. See also Doig, James W.: "Police Problems, Proposals and Strategies for Change." In Symposium on the Police in a Democratic Society. *Public Administration Review,* Sept.-Oct., 1968, pp. 393-407.
4. Clark, Ramsay: *Crime in America.* Simon and Shuster, N.Y., 1970, p. 137.
5. Ibid, p. 148.
6. Levy, Ruth J.: "Predicting Police Failures." *J. of Crim. Law, Criminology and Police Science, Vol. 58,* No. 2, 1967.
7. Guion, R.M. and Gottier, R.F.: "Validity of Personality Measures in Personnel Selection." *Personnel Psychology, Vol. 18,* No. 2, 1965, p. 140.

8. The Validity of Personality Inventories in the Selection of Employees. *J. of Applied Psychology, Vol. 37,* No. 1, Feb., 1953, pp. 18-20.

9. Peterson, F.E., Lane, N.E., and Kennedy, R.S.: "The Relationship of the Edwards Personal Preference Schedule to Success in Naval Flight. Training." *Bureau of Medicine and Surgery, Project MFO 22.01.02-5001, Subtask 1, Report No. 46,* U.S. Naval Aerospace Medical Institute, U.S. Naval Aviation Center, Pensacola, Fla., Oct. 8, 1965.

10. Rhead, C., Abrams, A., Trosman, H., and Margolis, P., "The Psychological Assessment of Police Candidates." *Amer. J. of Psychiatry, Vol. 124,* No. 11, May, 1968, p. 135.

11. Baer, M.E., Furcon, J.E., and Froemel, E.C.: "Psychological Assessment of Patrolman Qualifications in Relation to Field Performance." *LEAA Project Grant No. 046;* also Peterson, M.H. and Strider, F.D.: "Psychiatric Screening of Policemen." *Proceedings of the Meeting, Amer. Psychiatric Assn., Midwest Division,* November, 1968.

12. Levy, Ruth J.: "Retrospective Study of Peace Officer Personnel Files." San Jose City Health Dept., 1966, unpublished.

13. Dixon, W.J. (Ed.): *Biomedical Computer Programs,* Health Sciences Computing Facility, Dept. of Preventive Medicine and Public Health, School of Medicine, U.C.L.A., 1967.

14. Leggo, Christopher: "Standards for the Employment of Former Mental Hospital Patients." *J. of Occupational Med., Vol. 8,* No. 3, March, 1966, p. 135.

15. Scheuer, James H.: *To Walk the Streets Safely.* Doubleday & Co., Inc., Garden City, N.Y., 1969, p. 127.

16. "Resentment—An Obstacle to Recovery." *Industrial Medicine and Surgery, Vol. 22,* No. 6, June, 1953, p. 242.

17. *San Jose News:* April 2, 1968.

18. Palmer, Robert D.: "Birth Order and Identification." *J. of Consulting Psychology, Vol. 130,* No. 2, 1966, pp. 129-135.

19. Conners, C.K.: "Birth Order and Needs for Affiliation." *J. of Personality, Vol. 31,* No. 2, Sept., 1963, pp. 408-416.

20. Sutton-Smith, B. and Rosenberg, B.G.: "Sibling Concensus on Power Tactics." *J. of Genetic Psychology, Vol. 112,* No. 1, March, 1968, pp. 63-72.

21. "Studies in the psychology of names." Princeton U., 1939, unpublished thesis.

22. Yamamoto, J., Seeman, W., and Lester, B.K.: "The Tattooed Man." *Medical World News, April 24,* 1964, p. 22.

23. Baehr, M.E., Saunders, D.R., Froemel, E.C., and Furcon, J.E., "The Prediction of Performance for Black and for White Patrolmen." *Professional Psychology, Vol. 2,* No. 1, Winter, 1971, pp. 46-57.

24. Hopkins, E.J.: *Our Lawless Police.* Viking Press, N.Y., 1931.

25. Niederhoffer, A.: *Behind the Shield.* Doubleday & Co., Inc., 1967, p. 40 and Chevigny, P.G.: *Police Power.* Pantheon Books, N.Y., 1969.

26. Chwast, J., "Value Conflicts in Law Enforcement." *Crime and Delinquency, Vol. 11,* No. 2, April, 1965, pp. 151-162.

27. Statement attributed to former Los Angeles Chief of Police, Tom Reddin, as quoted in *Life,* July 30, 1965.

Chapter 3

PSYCHOLOGICAL PREDICTORS AND PATTERNS OF PATROLMAN FIELD PERFORMANCE

JOHN E. FURCON, ERNEST C. FROEMEL AND MELANEY E. BAEHR

IN VIEW of the importance of the law enforcement function in our society and the great authority and responsibility vested in the individual police officer, it seems strange that the contribution of behavioral scientists to the task of identifying, selecting, training, and placing the men best fitted to do the job has generally not equalled the effort expended on improving police technology and weaponry. Of course, the value of psychological testing in patrolman selection has been long recognized. However, there has been an unfortunate preoccupation with tests of intellectual ability,[1] and little or no awareness on the part of police organizations of the need to validate the tests used, i.e. to establish evidence of a relationship between scores and actual on-the-job performance. Blum,[2] for example, makes the following comment about police selection:

> If we restrict the scope of our survey of research to studies which have been made by trained social scientists using acceptable scientific methods for observation and treatment of data, we find that there has been very little such work directed to the evaluation of the usefulness of psychological tests for the selection of policemen.

Recent guidelines issued by the federal government[3,4] suggest that selection test validation can no longer be considered a research "luxury." It is a legal necessity if such tests are to be used at all.

In the light of this necessity and with the cooperation of the Office of Law Enforcement Assistance, U.S. Department of Justice,

Reprinted with the permission of Illinois Institute for Technology Research Institute, Chicago, Illinois and the Authors.

and the Chicago Police Department, a research study[5] was implemented which focused upon: (1) the identification of psychological tests with potential for contributing information in police officer selection; (2) the validation of these tests by demonstrating a statistical relationship between test results and on-the-job performance; (3) the investigation of problems of using selection tests in a racially-mixed group; and (4) the identification of "patrolman types" which would exhibit distinctive performance styles in the field and which would not be adequately described by the concept of the "average patrolman." This paper provides an overview of the methods and principal findings of the study.

IMPLEMENTATION

The first step in the study was an occupational analysis aimed at identifying specific personal qualifications necessary for successful performance of the patrolman's job. A review of formal job descriptions and case reports provided an important *entree* into the police organization, but extensive field observation in many police districts in the city was the most important part of the occupational analysis. Directly observing police officers in their day-to-day activities by riding in patrol and command cars and responding to calls provided real insight into the behavioral requirements of the patrolman's job. The product of this experience was a list of twenty essential requirements, emphasizing behavioral rather than formal or "official" aspects of the job.

The information and experience gained in the occupational analysis was used as the basis for selecting psychological tests for use in the study. These tests were classified into three general categories: (1) motivational measures (e.g. biographical data, work interests) ; (2) measures of intellectual ability (e.g. reasoning ability, perceptual skills, special aptitudes) ; and (3) behavioral measures (e.g. temperament, stress tolerance) . Various criteria were used in making the actual selections. Preference was given to standardized, paper-and-pencil tests which could be group administered and which did not require elaborate apparatus. Objective rather than subjective scoring was emphasized. In fact, all the tests finally chosen could be administered and scored by suitably trained clerical personnel, although the interpretation and use of results were, of course, matters for properly qualified professionals.

SELECTION OF PATROLMAN PERFORMANCE MEASURES

Once the battery of psychological tests had been chosen, the next step was the identification of meaningful indices of patrolman performance against which to gauge the relative value of the tests. Obtaining an accurate index of employee performance is one of the more difficult tasks facing any organization, and this difficulty increases in the case of police officers because of the complexity and independence of their job.

Fortunately, the Chicago Police Department (CPD) routinely compiles information in a number of significant areas of patrolman performance. The semiannual departmental performance rating, tenure, departmental awards, Internal Investigation Division record, disciplinary actions, arrest performance, and attendance were selected for inclusion in the study. In addition to this selected information already on file, the results of a rating technique developed by the Industrial Relations Center (IRC) for use in industry were also employed as one performance index. This method, the paired-comparison appraisal technique, uses a man-to-man comparison to provide a composite performance index based upon the combined ratings of supervisors who are familiar with an individual's performance. Furthermore, it provides several checks on the meaningfulness and accuracy of the ratings, including measures of the internal consistency of each rater and his agreement with others rating the same men. Two supervisory (subjective) ratings (the paired-comparison and the semiannual departmental rating) and six objective performance indicators were thus used to assess on-the-job performance. These performance measures, described in Table 3-I served as the criterion variables in the validation study, and were thought to provide a comprehensive picture of the many facets of patrolman performance.

TABLE 3-I
PATROLMAN PERFORMANCE CRITERION MEASURES

MEASURE	DESCRIPTION
1. Paired-Comparison Rating	From the performance appraisal conducted by the IRC staff
2. 1966 CPD Performance Rating	The average of the two half year totals from the CPD
3. CPD Tenure	Years of service on the CPD
4. CPD Total Awards	Honorable mentions + commendations + higher awards averaged for 1961 through 1966
5. CPD I I D Complaints	Ratio of I I D complaints over I I D sustained complaints
6. Disciplinary Actions	Disciplinary actions averaged for 1961 through 1966 + I I D sustained complaints
7. Number of Arrests, 1966	Total arrest record for 1966
8. Times Absent	Total incidence of absence for 1966

SELECTION OF PATROLMAN TESTING SAMPLE

In twelve police districts reflecting the wide spectrum of large city police work, a total of 253 sergeants and lieutenants used the paired-comparison technique to rate the field performance of 2,327 patrolmen assigned to patrol duty (approximately 85 percent of the uniformed officers in these districts). On the average, each man was rated by three supervisors, and each supervisor rated the performance of 30 men. The results of these ratings were used to select officers for testing. Approximately 60 percent of the men in the twelve districts volunteered to participate as subjects to complete the four-hour battery of tests. From these volunteers 490 officers were chosen, all of whom had been (1) rated by at least two supervisors; (2) rated with acceptable individual rater consistency and combined rater agreement; and (3) rated clearly in either the top third or bottom third in level of field performance. These men received a $15 stipend for their assistance during off-duty hours.

VALIDATION RESULTS

The 490 men were tested in two separate groups, about five months apart. In Table 3-II, these groups are called the "primary validation sample" (consisting of 242 men, and referred to during the study as Wave I) and the "cross-validation sample" (consisting of 240 men, and referred to as Wave II). The size of the two groups in the table is less than the total number tested, since some cases were dropped because of missing performance data or test results. The final analysis was confined to cases with complete data records.

TABLE 3-II
MULTIPLE CORRELATIONS OF TEST BATTERIES WITH PERFORMANCE
CRITERION MEASURES

								Number	
TEST BATTERIES							*Disci-*	*of*	
Racial		*PC*	*1966 CPD*	*CPD*	*CPD*	*IID*	*plinary*	*Arrests*	*Times*
Groups	*N*	*Rating*	*Rating*	*Tenure*	*Awards*	*Complaints*	*Actions*	*1966*	*Absent*
PRIMARY VALIDATION SAMPLE									
Primary Validation Tests									
Total	175	.60	.67	.72	.57	.53	.47	.53	.55
White	128	.62	.66	.74	.59	.64	.51	.63	.67
Negro	47	.92	.90	.92	.85	.91	.89	.84	.96
CROSS-VALIDATION SAMPLE									
Cross-Validation Tests									
Total	192	.67	.63	.81	.57	.54	.66	.61	.60
White	126	.77	.69	.84	.60	.55	.77	.65	.74
Negro	66	.98	.88	.97	.88	.88	.88	.95	.95

The column header spanning the criterion measures reads *CRITERION MEASURES*.

Preliminary analysis of results for the primary validation sample (Wave I) led to the removal of the least promising tests and their replacement with more promising ones for the Wave II test administration. The findings for the Wave II sample justified these substitutions in that there were increases in the predictive efficiency of the test battery. Table 3-II gives the specific concurrent validity coefficients obtained in Waves I and II for the eight criterion measures. The figures in this table are multiple correlations which show the relationship between selected weighted variables (scores) from the test battery and on-the-job patrolman performance.

The first conclusion to be drawn from these results was that, for the total group of patrolmen, there was a statistically significant and meaningful relationship between the test battery scores and independent measures of police officer performance. This was especially true of the three major performance criteria—the paired-comparison rating, the departmental rating, and tenure—but also held for all other performance measures used in the study. These results provide strong evidence for the relevance and validity of these tests for the selection of patrolmen. As already noted, the substitutions made in the Wave II test administration resulted in some small increases in predictive efficiency, but the results for Wave II essentially replicate those of Wave I.

The second result was less expected. While significant relationships between test battery scores and performance could be demonstrated for the total group of patrolmen, the degree of this relationship increased when the subsample of white patrolmen was treated separately and increased even more spectacularly and significantly when the sub-sample of black patrolmen was treated separately. These findings were checked with a cross-validation procedure. In this procedure, the weights for specific test scores established on one sample of patrolmen were applied to another sample in an attempt to gauge the effectiveness of the weighting procedures for predicting performance in the new sample.

The results of the cross-validation analysis indicated that the best prediction of performance was obtained when weights based on a specific racial group were applied to members of that group. In contrast, poorest predictions (sometimes a zero or even negative relationship between test scores and performance) were obtained when weights based on one racial group were applied to another. Applying weights based on the total racially-mixed group to the separate racial groups produced inconsistent results, sometimes yielding reasonably acceptable predictions and at other times predictions at no more than the level of pure chance. These results suggest that separate validations will result in selection procedures which are equitable to candidates from both racial groups without lowering the effectiveness of the organization, since the same on-the-job *performance* (rather than test) standards will be applied to all candidates.

The results of the validation analyses identified the specific psychological test areas which assessed characteristics likely to be most predictive of patrolman success. In the area of personal background, early assumption of family responsibility by establishing a family and home and evidence of family and occupational stability are important. A history of better than average general health is also helpful. Apart from at least an average level of general intellectual ability and good visual perceptual skills, some of the most important attributes for success in the intellectual area are the levels of aptitude exhibited in dealing with problematical interpersonal situations. The desirable response for a patrolman was found to be one of cooperation and active endeavor to solve the problem rather than withdrawal, undue competitiveness, or an expression of hostility. In the area of personality and behavior, the desirable attributes were found to be a realistic control of impulses and emotions, and a "work" rather than "social" orientation. Other important characteristics were personal self-confidence, capacity to tolerate stress, and a "common sense" rather than a subjective and feeling-oriented approach to life.

Perhaps the best way to summarize these findings is to say that the critical attributes for patrolman success are related to stability —stability in the parental, personal family, and occupational situations, stability in the maintenance of cooperative rather than competitive or hostile problem-solving modes, stability stemming from personal self-confidence and control of emotional impulses, and stability deriving from a capacity to tolerate stress and from a realistic rather than a subjective orientation to life. This summary is much more than a literary description of an ideal patrolman. The desirable attributes mentioned above can all be measured by psychological tests. Further, patrolmen who scored in the desirable direction in these test areas were those who were independently given higher ratings for performance by police supervisors, and who exhibited higher levels of performance on the more objective measures of police officer performance.

PATTERNS OF PATROLMAN PERFORMANCE

As the complexity of an occupation increases, its demands become more diverse, and there is increasing latitude for individuality of style in meeting these demands. Under these circumstances, the occupational group will no longer be composed exclusively of members approximating a single behavioral prototype, all performing with varying degrees of success along a unified dimension or criterion. Instead, occupational subgroups will begin to emerge, internally homogeneous but differing among themselves in style of performance.

Defining performance in terms of the subjective (supervisory) and objective measures described in Table 3-I, it was possible to identify eight subgroups of patrolman performance, each of which was clearly distinct from the others and also from the "basic" or average performance pattern. As indicated in Table 3-III, five subgroups were regarded as showing desirable or acceptable per-

TABLE 3-III
PATROLMAN PERFORMANCE PATTERN SUBGROUPS
EIGHT PERFORMANCE PATTERN SUBGROUPS

SUCCESSFUL PERFORMANCE	LESS-THAN-SUCCESSFUL PERFORMANCE
NEWCOMERS TO THE DEPARTMENT	
SUBGROUP 1 Low Tenure—Excellent Performance	
SUBGROUP 2 Low Tenure—Good Performance	
	SUBGROUP 3 Low Tenure—Poor Performance
ESTABLISHED PATROLMEN	
SUBGROUP 4 Average Tenure—Excellent Performance	
	SUBGROUP 5 Average Tenure—Poor Performance with Disciplinary Actions
	SUBGROUP 6 Average Tenure—Conflicting Ratings & General Disciplinary Problems
OLD - TIMERS	
SUBGROUP 7 Long Tenure—Excellent Performance	
SUBGROUP 8 Long Tenure—Good Performance	

formance patterns, while the remaining three were characterized by generally poor performance. Successful and less-successful performance occurs at most stages of police tenure. There are three low-tenure or relatively newcomer subgroups. Their performance exhibits a complete range from excellent through poor. There are also three subgroups of established, average-tenure patrolmen, one of which exhibited excellent performance, and the remaining two the poorest performance patterns identified. The two remaining subgroups are composed of long-tenured old-timers, showing excellent or good performance.

The objective in studying the performance subgroups was to identify the behavioral attributes characterizing the members of each as measured by the psychological test battery. This information would make it possible to compare the psychological attributes of candidates with those of the various subgroups. Similarities to good or poor subgroup membership could then be used in selection and placement decisions. For example, Figure 3-1 contrasts the performance records of Subgroup 1 and Subgroup 6. Although much lower in tenure, Subgroup 1 is clearly superior in performance as measured by supervisory ratings and objective measures of performance. The paired-comparison ratings of Subgroup 6 patrolmen were characterized by low agreement between raters, and the subgroup's performance in the areas of complaints, disciplinary actions, and absences is much poorer than the average.

Analysis of the test results of the members of these two subgroups, in contrast with the "basic" or average patrolman group, evidenced some important differences, as presented in Table 3-IV. The results of Subgroups 1 and 6 may be summarized by saying that the first (Low Tenure—Excellent Performance) is similar to the basic group but often scores higher on critical dimensions or else adds high scores on attributes which logically would seem to contribute to superior performance. On the other hand, the second (Average Tenure—Conflicting Ratings) scores below the basic group on a number of important dimensions. In some cases, their profile is actually the reverse of that of the basic group. These results provide additional evidence for the validity of the psychological areas measured by the tests and are encouraging in

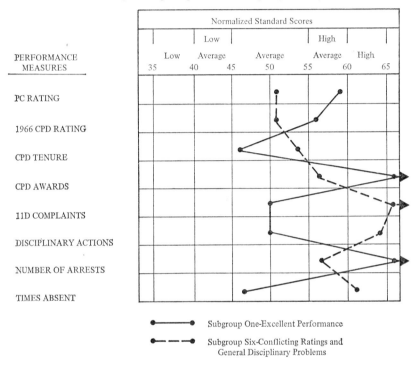

Figure 3-1
Performance Patterns
of Subgroups One (Excellent Performance)
and Six (Conflicting Ratings and General Disciplinary Problems)

that they point the way to the possibility of identifying—at the time of application to a police department—those who are likely to show good or poor patterns of patrolman performance.

IMPLICATIONS FOR POLICE MANAGEMENT AND RESEARCH

In this age of unprecedented technological advances, the *human* resources of an organization remain the most crucial input in the attainment of organizational goals. This is particularly true of the law enforcement organization, where the individual police officer serves as a direct representative in providing service to the public. The results of this study bear directly upon the procedures

TABLE 3-IV
CONTRAST OF ATTRIBUTES OF SUBGROUP ONE AND SUBGROUP SIX
PATROLMEN WITH THE BASIC PATROLMAN GROUP

SUBGROUP I EXCELLENT PERFORMANCE	SUBGROUP 6 CONFLICTING RATINGS AND GENERAL DISCIPLINARY PROBLEMS
BACKGROUND AND EXPERIENCE	
Higher drive, higher vocational satisfaction than basic group	Lack of assumption of family responsibility
MENTAL ABILITIES	
Strong perceptual skills and fast reaction time	Below average perceptual skills and slow reaction time
APTITUDES	
High cooperation and low withdrawal	High withdrawal
BEHAVIOR	
High energy level and high spontaneity	Low self-reliance and conflicting impulse control—low on realistic control

for setting meaningful standards for the identification, selection, and placement of candidates in police organizations.

Two advances are thought to be particularly significant in the area of psychological testing in law enforcement organizations. The results of the occupational analysis suggested that tests of aptitude, personality, and motivation were relevant to the selection of police officers. Thus a type of testing which extended beyond the scope of intelligence testing was brought to bear in this study. Of even more significance is the fact that a test battery composed of tests of motivation, intellectual ability, and behavior showed a meaningful relationship to measures of on-the-job performance in police work. The results of the study are an advance over earlier attempts (e.g. DuBois and Watson[6]) in which relationships were established between test scores and training academy performance but not between scores and actual on-the-job or field performance.

The fact that the Chicago Police Department has a multi-racial force with a patrolman composition of about one-quarter black and three-quarters white provided the opportunity to make a worthwhile contribution to the general body of knowledge in the field of minority group testing. The importance of these findings to police officer selection procedures and policies will increase for all law enforcement organizations as their racial compositions move to correspond more closely with the racial composition of the jurisdiction being served.

The subgroup analysis helped to verify the basic findings of the project and is promising as pointing the way to better procedures for placement and assignment of police officers. In addition, these results are thought to add to our general insight into the psychological functioning of police officers on the job. The application of a new (to law enforcement) form of performance appraisal, the paired-comparison method, and the opportunity to contrast it with other subjective and objective performance indices added to our knowledge of performance evaluation techniques.

The study has two broad implications for selection testing in police organizations. The first is the need to broaden the scope of testing procedures to include measures of personality, motivation, and aptitude in addition to measures of intelligence. The second is the critical need to validate the use of these procedures if law enforcement organizations desire to use tests responsibly. The implications for training are less apparent, since many of the psychological areas covered in the study are relatively fixed in the individual, such as reaction speed and general temperament pattern. It is significant that one of the areas found to be most predictive of success, that dealing with interpersonal skills and social aptitude, was one in which virtually no differences were found between the racial groups and one relatively more open to modification via training or experience.

The basic contribution of the study has been the identification and validation of psychological tests for use in police organizations. The specific implementation of the test battery itself is probably of foremost interest to the police manager.

This discussion has attempted to show the necessity for, and logic behind, a test validation study. If these results are to be utilized elsewhere, it is essential that a technically sound validation study precede or at least be conducted concurrently with the use of any of the tests. Although it is quite likely that the tests have relevance to police officer selection in the large cities of our country, the specific findings should be generalized quite cautiously. A definite standard appropriate in Chicago may be inappropriate in other departments. Until more replicating studies have been reported, a local validation in any jurisdiction desiring to utilize these procedures properly remains a most stringent necessity.

The means for conducting such validation studies are probably as close as the nearest college or university. The planning and implementation of the present project can serve as a case study of a successful relationship between a law enforcement organization, an educational institution, and the federal government. In particular, the study could not have been conducted without the existence of a law enforcement organization at a stage of development which would permit scientific access and freedom of inquiry while at the same time providing complete support and commitment to the project.

REFERENCES

1. Narrol, H.G. and Levitt, E.E.: "Formal Assessment Procedures in Police Selection." *Psychological Reports, 12,* 691-694, 1963.
2. Blum, R.H. (Ed.) : *Police Selection.* Springfield, Ill., Charles C Thomas, Publisher, 1964.
3. Equal Employment Opportunity Commission: *Guidelines on Employment Testing Procedures.* Washington, D.C., EEOC, August 24, 1966.
4. Wirtz, W.W.: "Order on Validation of Employment Tests (September 9, 1968). *"Labor Policy and Practice, Fair Employment Practices, No. 95,* 401:225 Washington, D.C., Bureau of National Affairs.
5. Baehr, M.E., Furcon, J.E., and Froemel, E.C.: *Psychological Assessment of Patrolman Qualifications in Relation to Field Performance.* Washington, D.C., U.S. Government Printing Office, 1969.
6. DuBois, P.H. and Watson, R.J.: "The Selection of Patrolmen." *Journal of Applied Psychology, 34,* 90-95, 1950.

Chapter 4

THE PREDICTION OF PERFORMANCE
FOR BLACK AND FOR WHITE
POLICE PATROLMEN[1]

MELANY BAEHR,* DAVID R. SAUNDERS,
ERNEST C. FROEMEL AND JOHN E. FURCON

THIS PAPER derives from a study done in the Chicago Police Department (CPD) with support from the U. S. Department of Justice (Baehr, Furcon, and Froemel, 1968). A primary aim of the study was to establish general standards and effective procedures for the selection of patrolmen. Basic in this endeavor was the design and validation of a psychological test battery which would ultimately be used to differentiate potential good performers from potential poor performers.

The predictor variables for the validation came from a test battery designed to cover four broad areas of measurement—motivation, mental ability, aptitude, and behavior. In the areas of motivation, measures of background and experience and of work interests were used. Mental ability was assessed with tests of reasoning, language facility, and perception. The aptitude section of the battery covered creative potential and social insight. The behavior dimension tapped various aspects of temperament and personality, including pressure tolerance. The tests which were most useful, and which will most probably be used in a forthcoming predictive study, are listed in the References by author(s) and title (Baehr, Burns, and McMurry, 1965; Baehr

Reprinted from *Professional Psychology, 2,* 46-58, 1971.

[1]This research was supported in part by the U.S. Department of Justice through Grant No. 046, Office of Law Enforcement Assistance, and Grant No. 0010, National Institute of Law Enforcement and Criminal Justice.

*The Authors wish to thank Frances M. Burns for her editorial assistance in the preparation of this paper.

and Corsini, 1965; Baehr and Pranis, 1961; Baehr, Renck, and Burns, 1959; Cassel, 1959; Corsini, 1966; Dombrose and Slobin, 1957; Thurstone, L. L. and Jeffrey, 1956 [three tests]; Thurstone, T. G., 1956; and Thurstone, T. G. and Mellinger, 1957).

Two somewhat different versions of this battery, one containing 14 tests and one 11, were administered to two samples of patrolmen, referred to as Wave I and Wave II. In selecting these samples, we made every effort to ensure that they were representative of the patrolman population, not only as to demographic and racial characteristics but also as to the varying kinds of police performance and behavior called for in different districts. In all, 540 patrolmen were tested. Using a further principle of selection, we drew this total sample in about equal parts from the upper-rated third and the lower-rated third of the uniformed patrolmen in the Patrol Division of the department. The ratings in question came from one of the criterion variables chosen for the study—the results of a special performance appraisal done by supervisors, using a form of the paired-comparisons technique. The other criterion variables used were as follows:

1966 CPD rating—the average of the two regular semiannual CPD performance ratings for 1966

CPD tenure—years of service on the CPD

CPD total awards—honorable mentions plus commendations plus higher awards averaged for 1961 through 1966

CPD IID complaints—ratio of Internal Investigation Division complaints over IID sustained complaints

Disciplinary actions—disciplinary actions averaged for 1961 through 1966 plus IID sustained complaints

Number of arrests—total arrest record for 1966

Times absent—total absences for 1966

From the start, it was clear that the validation based on the predictor and criterion variables summarized above was going to present points of interest and challenge, since the population involved was multi-racial, being 75 percent white and 25 percent black. This fact was significant because the Civil Rights Act of

1964 forbids any use of tests which can result in "discrimination" against any racial group. For the Chicago Police Department, this ruling dictated a validation procedure which would make the interpretation of results from the final battery fair and nondiscriminatory for both groups involved. Actually, the problems posed by such a validation are neither new nor unique. The theoretical avenues of approach are relatively well known. However, the opportunity to employ these approaches in a real situation, without shortcuts, has not often been available until recently.

Logically, preparing to validate a selection test battery for a multiracial population involves at least three and sometimes four successive steps.

1. Determining whether or not the racial groups show different results on any of the predictor (test) variables.

2. Determining whether or not the racial groups show different results on any of the criterion (job-performance) variables.

3. Determining whether or not any differences which exist could lead to discrimination against either of the groups. If a given test score always corresponds with a given level of performance, then that test cannot be held to discriminate, even if one racial group scores and performs consistently higher than does the other. However, if a given test score corresponds with different levels of performance for the different racial groups, then the test can be held to discriminate, and the fourth step is needed.

4. Determining what statistical technique will provide the most accurate and equitable representation of the relationships between the predictor and criterion variables for each racial group in the sample.

Our results in following these four steps for our specific sample of white and black patrolmen are discussed and illustrated in the remainder of this paper.

RACIAL GROUP DIFFERENCES ON THE PREDICTOR VARIABLES

Analysis of test results for the two racial groups indicated that the groups were more often similar on the predictor variables than they were different. In addition, the distributions of the groups overlapped considerably on all variables. However, in spite of these facts, our inescapable finding was that there were "significant" differences between the group means in virtually all areas of the test battery.

It is now generally accepted that black groups will score lower than white groups on a wide variety of ability and aptitude tests, as indicated by such fairly recent studies as those of Ash (1966), Dugan (1966), Krug (1966), Lopez (1966), Lucas (1953), and others. It is also widely accepted that the lower scores of black groups are the result of educational, social, and cultural deprivation rather than of innate or genetic influences. However, the patrolmen in our samples had been prescreened by the Civil Service Commission for general intelligence, by the Chicago Police Department for personal background, and by psychiatric examination for emotional health. We were thus somewhat surprised at the pervasiveness of the differences we found between the white and black groups. The general nature of these differences is summarized in Table 4-I.

TABLE 4-1

GENERAL WHITE AND BLACK GROUP DIFFERENCES IN SCORES ON THE TEST BATTERY

AREA OF MEASUREMENT	
MOTIVATION	
Background & Experience	White group significantly higher on a third of the dimensions
MENTAL ABILITY	White group higher on all dimensions & significantly higher on half of them
SPECIAL APTITUDES	
Social Insight	Virtually no differences
BEHAVIOR	
Pressure Tolerance	White group significantly higher
Personality	Occasional variable differences

On the measure of background and experience, the white group scored higher on the dimensions indicating drive to achievement, financial responsibility, early assumption of personal family responsibilities, and adjustment to the parental family environment. The hypothesis that the black group scores generally lower on these background dimensions because of social, educational, and vocational deprivation seems a tenable one. This hypothesis would also explain the single instance in which the black group scored significantly higher—on the dimension called School Achievement. If educational standards are usually lower in predominantly black schools, the black patrolman applicants would need to have reached a higher school grade level to pass the Civil Service screening procedure than would their white counterparts. In this study, we were probably dealing with a relatively highly-selected black group.

Results in the area of mental ability revealed a rather interesting relationship between the time limits set for a test and the significance of the difference between the racial group scores on that test. Table 4-II summarizes the fairly well-defined inverse relationship between the time limit of the test and the magnitude of "t." Since only the Wave I sample took all five of the tests cited, these results reflect the performance of only a part of our total population.

Discovery of this relationship prompted us next to examine results on the test of pressure tolerance (The Press Test), which

TABLE 4-II

DIFFERENCES IN FAVOR OF THE WHITE GROUP COMPARED WITH TIME LIMIT OF THE MENTAL ABILITY TESTS FOR THE WAVE I SAMPLE

Test	White Group			Black Group			Time Limits	t	p
	N	Mean	S.D.	N	Mean	S.D.			
Non-Verbal Reasoning	170	31.89	5.23	62	30.63	4.83	Untimed (25 mins.)	1.71	.085
Understanding Communication	170	29.75	5.01	62	28.00	5.66	15 mins.	2.14	.032*(W)
Closure Flexibility	170	54.15	26.72	62	48.37	22.25	10 mins	1.64	.098
Perceptual Speed	160	51.68	13.83	61	47.11	12.27	5 mins.	2.37	.018*(W)
Closure Speed	170	12.65	5.13	62	10.26	4.13	3 mins.	3.63	.001***(W)

*p < .05
***p < .001
(W) = White group mean higher

is specifically designed to gauge reaction time under pressure. The test is in three parts, measuring, first, speed of reaction to verbal stimuli, second, speed of reaction to color stimuli, and, third, speed of reaction to color in the presence of distracting verbal material. Each part is timed for 90 seconds. Differences between the racial groups were significant on all parts, generally beyond the .001 level. These results are shown in Table 4-III. While these results are not definitive, they are certainly suggestive, and we hope to have the opportunity to investigate them further in our continuation of the study.

TABLE 4-III

DIFFERENCES FOR THE TOTAL SAMPLE IN FAVOR OF THE WHITE GROUP ON A TEST OF PRESSURE TOLERANCE.

The Press Test	White Group			Black Group			Time Limits	t	p
	N	Mean	S.D.	N	Mean	S.D.			
Part I Verbal Stimuli	353	75.75	15.85	154	70.55	17.04	90 secs.	3.22	.002**(W)
Part II Color Stimuli	353	72.97	14.92	154	65.01	15.56	90 secs.	5.35	.000***(W)
Part III Color with Stress	352	59.23	14.48	153	54.22	13.73	90 secs.	3.70	.000***(W)

p<.01
***p<.001
(W) = White group mean higher

In contrast to the findings described above, there were no consistent racial differences in social aptitude on the Test of Social Insight, developed by Russell N. Cassel. This test measures the individual's relative preference for five possible modes of response to difficult or problem social situations. These modes are characterized as Withdrawal, Passivity, Cooperativeness, Competitiveness, and Aggressiveness.

RACIAL GROUP DIFFERENCES ON THE CRITERION VARIABLES

The next step in planning the validation procedure to be used was to determine whether the white and black groups differed on the job-performance or criterion variables. Our findings are presented in Table 4-IV. The data here are by no means as clear-cut as those obtained from the predictor variables. Only four of the

TABLE 4-IV
WHITE AND BLACK GROUP DIFFERENCES ON THE JOB-PERFORMANCE OR
CRITERION VARIABLES.

| | WAVE I SAMPLE | | | | | | | |
| | White Group | | | Black Group | | | | |
Criterion Variable	N	Mean	S.D.	N	Mean	S.D.	t	p
Paired-Comparisons Rating	170	51.02	11.86	62	50.03	11.82	0.56	.580
1966 CPD Rating	170	85.72	3.34	61	84.67	3.98	1.83	.065
CPD Tenure	167	9.32	7.46	60	9.37	3.99	0.06	.954
CPD Total Awards	170	1.05	1.38	62	0.64	0.75	2.90	.004**(W)
CPD IID Complaints	170	1.68	2.57	62	2.98	2.84	3.16	.002**(B)
Disciplinary Actions	170	.85	1.20	62	2.57	2.42	5.33	.000***(B)
Number of Arrests	170	40.42	28.74	62	80.66	60.54	4.99	.000***(B)
Times Absent	170	3.25	3.58	62	2.94	2.65	0.73	.525

| | WAVE II SAMPLE | | | | | | | |
| | White Group | | | Black Group | | | | |
Criterion Variable	N	Mean	S.D.	N	Mean	S.D.	t	p
Paired-Comparisons Rating	144	52.10	11.21	84	48.25	11.38	2.47	.014*(W)
1966 CPD Rating	184	86.39	3.91	90	83.58	4.11	5.37	.000***(W)
CPD Tenure	188	6.62	5.17	92	7.43	5.18	1.23	.218
CPD Total Awards	188	0.84	0.94	91	0.73	0.74	1.03	.305
CPD IID Complaints	188	1.54	2.72	92	2.16	2.97	1.68	.091
Disciplinary Actions	188	3.46	4.28	91	7.27	6.98	4.76	.000***(B)
Number of Arrests	188	48.18	39.77	90	68.14	51.76	3.22	.002**(B)
Times Absent	187	2.48	2.47	89	3.20	3.33	1.81	.068

*p<.05
**p<.01
***p<.001
(W) = White group mean higher
(B) = Black group mean higher

criterion variables yield consistent results across the Wave I and
Wave II samples. These results show that the white and black
groups do not differ significantly in tenure on the force or in
absenteeism. However, the black patrolmen made significantly
more arrests and had significantly more disciplinary actions taken
against them. A ready explanation for these latter findings is the
existence of different conditions in different districts of assignment. Black officers are very often assigned to predominantly
black districts, which, in many instances, are high-crime areas.
One would expect that patrolmen in such districts would need to

make more arrests than those assigned to low-crime areas. Also, they might well have more disciplinary actions against them because they are constantly "in the thick of it" and under pressure to respond to difficult and "touchy" situations. Furthermore. it is not uncommon for an arrested person to file a complaint against an officer with the intention of "bargaining" for a lesser charge.

On the subjective performance appraisals—the paired-comparisons rating and the 1966 CPD rating—only the Wave II sample produced significant differences between the racial groups. We therefore have no clear evidence that members of one group are regarded by their supervisors as better performers than members of the other. Clarification of this point will be an important objective of the continuation study, in which we plan to analyze both sets of subjective ratings for more than 2,000 patrolmen. These ratings will be weighed against conditions of performance, the race of the rater, and the race of the individual rated.

Reverting to the present study, with the first two steps of preparing for the validation completed, we were faced with clear-cut racial group differences on the predictor variables and ambiguous differences on the criterion variables. Plainly, no assumptions could be made as to any precise correspondence between predictor results for the two races on the one hand and their results on the criterion variables on the other. We therefore proceeded to the next step—the selection of an appropriate statistical technique to implement a validation for a racially-mixed sample.

CROSS-VALIDATION FOR A RACIALLY-MIXED GROUP

Under the circumstances described above, traditional multiple regression analyses based on the total sample are clearly inapplicable, even when members of the different racial groups are equally represented in that sample. Instead, current best thinking and practice favor the use of a "moderator" variable in implementing the multiple regressions. Examples in which the contribution of such a moderator is significant have been presented by Kirkpatrick, et al. (1967) and others.

The moderator approach, originally suggested by Saunders (1956), has the not inconsiderable advantage that the total sample can be used as a single sample for determining the best weights. The difficulties of its use center around the selection and development of the actual moderator variable to be used. However, when this moderator variable is simply membership or nonmembership in a subgroup, e.g. a racial group, the method should obtain results which are numerically indistinguishable from those that would be obtained by analyzing the subgroups separately.

In the present study, the Wave I and Wave II samples were treated individually because of the modifications introduced into the Wave II test battery. Within each Wave, a design of discrete validations was employed for the total group and for its component black and white patrolman groups. The multiple correlations obtained for these groups across the eight criterion measures used in the study show the same pattern (Baehr, et al., 1969, p. 146). That is, the coefficient for the white patrolmen increases slightly over the estimate for the total sample and that for the black patrolmen more strikingly. T-tests of the significance of the differences between the correlation coefficients—corrected for bias (Guilford, 1956, p. 399)—obtained by the black and white patrolman groups were generally significant beyond the .01 level of confidence for the three major criteria. The only exception occurred in the Wave II sample, where the significance of the difference between correlation coefficients was beyond the .05 level of confidence for the tenure criterion.

In order to create "hold-out samples" for calculating both cross- and primary validity coefficients, the white group, the black group, and the total sample within each Wave were each divided randomly into two parts. Regression weights established for each of the resulting six within-Wave subgroups were then used to predict scores for every other subgroup in the Wave sample. A summary of these results if given below for the three major criterion variables—the paired-comparisons rating, the 1966 CPD rating, and tenure.

In Figure 4-1, the multiple correlations between the parts of each group on the paired-comparisons rating are shown in the blocks with solid lines. The primary validation coefficients are the diagonal, the cross-validation coefficients the off-diagonal, en-

Fig. 4-1

ANALYSIS OF WITHIN-WAVE MULTIPLE CORRELATIONS
FOR PAIRED-COMPARISONS PERFORMANCE CRITERION

WAVE I SAMPLE

	TOTAL GROUP(T)		*WHITE GROUP(W)*		*BLACK GROUP(B)*	
	PART 1	*PART 2*	*PART 1*	*PART 2*	*PART 1*	*PART 2*
SUBGROUP						
N	80	101	58	73	22	28
M	5	4	7	8	7	6
SUBGROUP						
T_1	.38	.23	.36	.21	.22	.19
T_2	.27	.41	.24	.47	.26	.29
W_1	.37	.17	.59	.21	.05	.12
W_2	.33	.42	.21	.53	.19	.19
B_1	.41	.44	-.02	.25	.73	.36
B_2	.14	.40	.29	.37	.46	.66

WAVE II SAMPLE

	TOTAL GROUP(T)		*WHITE GROUP(W)*		*BLACK GROUP(B)*	
SUBGROUP						
N	97	95	61	65	36	30
M	6	5	9	7	7	7
SUBGROUP						
T_1	.49	.25	.35	.05	.46	.32
T_2	.24	.46	.19	.40	.01	.12
W_1	.36	.33	.59	.12	.25	.22
W_2	.11	.48	.24	.61	-.14	-.17
B_1	.57	.15	-.05	-.11	.66	.51
B_2	.49	.46	.04	.08	.34	.75

tries. "N" indicates the number of cases in each part and "m" the number of variables used for the prediction.

Trends for the two Wave samples are generally similar. In Wave I, the primary validation results for the racially-mixed subgroups (.38, .41) are lower than those for either racial subgroup treated separately (white .59, .53; black .73, .66). In Wave II, coefficients for the mixed subgroups are again moderate (.49, .46), increase for the white subgroups (.59, .61), and increase still further for the black subgroups (.66, .75). For the crossvalidations (the off-diagonal entries), the best coefficients were obtained on the black subgroups in both samples, although there is some shrinkage from the primary coefficients. In contrast, figures for the white subgroups are no better than those for the subgroups of the total sample.

However, the generally poorest validity coefficients, as shown in the blocks with broken lines, were obtained when predicting the performance of blacks from weights established on white samples and vice versa. All of these coefficients are low, and some sink to zero or even become negative.

White and black subgroup coefficients based on weights obtained from the racially-mixed groups are inconsistent. For example, we find .33 for one part of the white group in Wave II as compared with .11 for the other part.

Figure 4-2 shows results for the CPD rating performance criterion. These are not so clear-cut as those for the paired-comparisons criterion, but the trends are the same.

Results for the tenure performance criterion are given in Figure 4-3. Unlike those in the two previous tables, all coefficients, both for the primary validation and for the cross-validation, are at relatively high levels. However, the trend for higher cross-validity coefficients within racial groups and especially within the black group is repeated.

In the final design which was forced upon our study, the samples are small and the results necessarily unstable. However, the trends for the three major criterion variables seem to be clear. The best cross-validation coefficients were obtained when weights based on a given racial group were used to predict scores for

Fig. 4-2

ANALYSIS OF WITHIN-WAVE MULTIPLE CORRELATIONS FOR CPD-RATING PERFORMANCE CRITERION

WAVE I SAMPLE

	TOTAL GROUP(T)		*WHITE GROUP(W)*		*BLACK GROUP(B)*	
	PART 1	*PART 2*	*PART 1*	*PART 2*	*PART 1*	*PART 2*
SUBGROUP						
N	80	101	58	73	22	28
M	11	4	9	6	5	7
SUBGROUP						
T$_1$	.63	.20	.52	.24	.45	.07
T$_2$	.19	.53	.18	.39	.02	.37
W$_1$	.54	.10	.61	.21	.24	.01
W$_2$	.25	.53	.28	.54	-.01	.23
B$_1$	.67	.25	.38	.19	.65	.35
B$_2$	-.03	.52	-.10	-.03	.11	.71

WAVE II SAMPLE

SUBGROUP						
N	97	95	61	65	36	30
M	6	5	10	5	11	6
SUBGROUP						
T$_1$	.54	.25	.39	-.07	.35	.24
T$_2$	.23	.44	.24	.25	.10	.29
W$_1$	.44	.33	.62	.15	.06	.08
W$_2$	.12	.38	.25	.39	.03	.10
B$_1$	.57	.17	.20	-.46	.80	.34
B$_2$	.37	.63	.20	-.05	.37	.74

The Urban Policeman in Transition

Fig. 4-3

ANALYSIS OF WITHIN-WAVE MULTIPLE CORRELATIONS
FOR TENURE PERFORMANCE CRITERION

WAVE I SAMPLE

	TOTAL GROUP(T)		*WHITE GROUP(W)*		*BLACK GROUP(B)*	
	PART 1	*PART 2*	*PART 1*	*PART 2*	*PART 1*	*PART 2*
SUBGROUP						
N	80	101	58	73	22	28
M	11	12	7	14	6	8
SUBGROUP						
T_1	.69	.52	.67	.47	.53	.50
T_2	.57	.68	.51	.66	.57	.65
W_1	.72	.52	.70	.47	.51	.49
W_2	.50	.62	.45	.66	.49	.57
B_1	.70	.62	.62	.48	.80	.70
B_2	.77	.89	.69	.62	.83	.94

WAVE II SAMPLE

	TOTAL GROUP(T)		*WHITE GROUP(W)*		*BLACK GROUP(B)*	
	PART 1	*PART 2*	*PART 1*	*PART 2*	*PART 1*	*PART 2*
SUBGROUP						
N	97	95	61	65	36	30
M	22	17	19	12	8	9
SUBGROUP						
T_1	.85	.75	.80	.75	.77	.66
T_2	.69	.77	.66	.74	.68	.57
W_1	.88	.77	.89	.79	.73	.63
W_2	.69	.80	.67	.87	.67	.44
B_1	.81	.71	.63	.68	.86	.71
B_2	.71	.70	.69	.59	.71	.81

members of that same group. Conversely, the poorest cross-validation coefficients (some zero or negative) were obtained when predicting across racial groups. When the groups were treated separately, better prediction resulted for the black group. Evidence of the stability of this result can be inferred from the fact that it was obtained first for the total Wave samples and replicated through six sub-sectionings of these samples.

At this point in our research, we can do little more than speculate about the possible reasons for the better prediction for black patrolmen. One hypothesis that seems tenable to the writers is that results on ability tests for advantaged groups may be disguised by the effects of remedial training, special tutoring, or even of a generally favorable developmental environment. Such effects would serve to curtail the range of ability test scores by compressing them at the upper end of the scale. The disadvantaged groups would not ordinarily have been influenced by these effects, and would thus present a wider range of ability test scores, leading to larger correlations and subsequent larger multiple correlations. An alternate hypothesis concerns the effects of differential sample sizes. Although the appropriate technical precautions were taken (as in the correction of the multiple correlation coefficients), it is possible that the multiple correlations for the black sample may be somewhat exaggerated because of its relatively higher ratio of number of predictor variables to number of cases.

In any event, it is important to stress that separate validations defining racially-distinct prediction equations (with distinct yet overlapping sets of predictor variables) hold the most promise for accurate and equitable predictions for members of both racial groups. Such procedures would lead to the setting of appropriate test standards for each group to reflect identical standards of job performance. Since a given performance level is generally associated with a lower test score for the black group as compared to the white, it should follow that a greater number of black applicants can be hired with some assurance that this will not result in a loss of efficiency in the organization.

ATTRIBUTES RELATED TO SUCCESSFUL PERFORMANCE

Once the multiple regressions had been completed, our next step was to analyze the beta-weights of the predictor variables which had appeared in them. This analysis enabled us to identify those tests and variables most likely to be effective in the ensuing predictive validation study. Furthermore, on the basis of these tests and variables we were able to pinpoint some of the attributes which were common to the more successful of the currently employed white and black patrolmen which distinguished them from unsuccessful patrolmen. These attributes are summarized in Table 4-V.

TABLE 4-V
ESSENTIAL ATTRIBUTES FOR SUCCESS PATROLMAN PERFORMANCE.

BACKGROUND & EXPERIENCE
Early Family Responsibility
Parental Family Adjustment
Good General Health

MENTAL ABILITY
Acceptable Level of General Mental Functioning
Visual Perceptual Skills

SPECIAL APTITUDES
Social Insight—Cooperation vs. Withdrawal or Aggression

BEHAVIOR
Controlled vs. Impulsive Behavioral Response
Personal Self-Reliance vs. Dependence
"Work" vs. "Social" Orientation
"Realistic" vs. "Subjective-Emotional" Approach to Life

The successful patrolman of either race has usually assumed family responsibility early by marrying and establishing a home. He has evidenced stability in both his childhood and his occupational environment. A history of generally better than average health is also characteristic.

Not unexpectedly, in view of the screening procedures applied, the successful patrolman possesses at least an average level of functioning intelligence. Over and above this, he has better visual-perceptual skills. He indicates a stronger capacity to provide meaningful organization to an ambiguous visual field and to discriminate differences in his perceptual field rapidly and accurately.

In the area of special aptitudes and skills, the most important attribute is the characteristic mode of dealing with interpersonal and social problem situations. The desirable response to such situations is cooperation and an active endeavor to solve the problem rather than physical retreat from it or expressions of competiveness or aggression toward the other individuals involved.

As to behavior, success as a patrolman entails the ability to resist stress and to control any purely impulsive or emotional responses. A lack of adequate impulse control is predictive of poor performance. So too is unrealistic overcontrol. Balanced and realistic handling of impulses is a positive indication of patrolman success. Another important characteristic is personal self-reliance. Phrased another way, the successful patrolman is not dependent on the badge or the pistol for ego support and personal confidence. Other characteristics in this area are a "work" rather than a "social" orientation and a realistic rather than a subjective approach to life.

The attributes described above may all be seen as reflecting stability—stability in the parental and personal family situations, stability in the maintenance of cooperative rather than competitive or hostile social attitudes, stability stemming from self-confidence, resistance to stress, and ability to control emotional impulses, and, finally, stability deriving from a realistic orientation to life.

REFERENCES

Ash, Philip: Race, employment test, and equal opportunity. *Industrial Management, 8,* March, 8-12, 1966.

Baehr, Melany E., Burns, Robert K., and McMurry, Robert N.: *Personal history index.* (Research ed.) Chicago: Industrial Relations Center, University of Chicago, 1965.

Baehr, Melany E. and Corsini, Raymond J.: *The Press Test.* Chicago, Industrial Relations Center, University of Chicago, 1965.

Baehr, Melany E., Furcon, John E., and Froemel, Ernest C.: *Psychological assessment of patrolman qualifications in relation to field performance.* Washington, D. C., U. S. Government Printing Office, 1969.

Baehr, Melany E. and Pranis, R. W.: *The temperament comparator.* Chicago: Industrial Relations Center, University of Chicago, 1961.

Baehr, Melany E., Renck, Richard, and Burns, Robert K.: *Work interest index.* Chicago: Industrial Relations Center, University of Chicago, 1959.

Cassel, R. N.: *Test of social insight.* (Adult ed.) New Rochelle, N. Y.: Martin M. Bruce, 1969.

Corsini, Raymond J.: *Non-verbal reasoning test.* Chicago: Industrial Relations Center, University of Chicago, 1966.

Dombrose, Lawrence A. and Slobin, Morton S.: *Arrow-dot test.* (Modification by Industrial Relations Center) Missoula, Montana: Psychological Test Specialists, 1957 (IRC modifications, 1966).

Dugan, Robert D.: Current problems in test performance of job applicants: II. *Personnel Psychology, 19,* Spring, 18-24, 1966.

Guilford, J. P.: *Psychometric Methods,* (2nd ed.). New York: McGraw-Hill Book Company, Inc., 1954.

Kirkpatrick, James J. et al.: *Differential selection among applicants from different sociometric or ethnic background.* Final Report to The Ford Foundation, May, 1967 (Unpublished).

Krug, Robert E.: Some suggested approaches for test development and measurement. *Personnel Psychology, 19,* Spring, 24-35, 1966.

Lopez, Felix M., Jr.: Current problems in test performance of job applicants: I. *Personnel Psychology, 19,* Spring, 10-18, 1966.

Lucas, C. M.: Survey of the literature relating to the effects of cultural background on aptitude scores. *Research Bulletin, 15-13.* Princeton, N. J.: Educational Testing Service, 1953 (multilithed report).

Saunders, David R.: Moderator variables in prediction. *Educational and Psychological Measurement, 16,* 209-222, 1956.

Thurstone, L. L. and Jeffrey, T. E.: *Closure flexibility (Concealed figures)* (Form A). Chicago: Industrial Relations Center, University of Chicago, 1956.

Thurstone, L. L. and Jeffrey, T. E.: *Closure speed (Gestalt completion).* Chicago: Industrial Relations Center, University of Chicago, 1956.

Thurstone, L. L. and Jeffrey, T. E.: *Perceptual speed (Identical forms).* Chicago: Education-Industry Service, 1225 E. 60th Street, 1956.

Thurstone, Thelma G.: *Understanding communication.* Chicago: Industrial Relations Center, University of Chicago, 1956.

Thurstone, Thelma G. and Mellinger, John: *Cree questionnaire.* Chicago: Industrial Relations Center, University of Chicago, 1957.

Chapter 5

VALIDATING THE SELECTION
OF DEPUTY MARSHALS

Bjorn D. Leiren

THE President's Crime Commission of 1967 and the President's Riot Commission of 1968, while looking for preventative measures to cope with urban ills, recommended that local agencies improve screening of police candidates to eliminate those with undesirable characteristics.

Just exactly what form that improvement should take was not stated, but an arm of the Federal government, the Equal Employment Opportunities Commission (EEOC), has laid down guidelines for the selection of employees by all Federal contractors (Federal Register, 1970). These guidelines require "evidence of a test's validity (based on) experimental data demonstrating that the test is predictive of or significantly correlated with important elements of work behavior . . . for which candidates are being evaluated."

Concern with valid selection of candidates for police-type work did not, however, begin with these commissions. Terman, in 1917, described the use of "mental and pedagogical tests" in the selection of policemen for the city of San Jose, California.

Terman's efforts were among the first in this area and others have followed. The work of DuBois and Watson (1950) is characteristic of the types of research done on the police selection problem. They used a series of achievement tests (e.g. Army General Classification Test) and personality measures (e.g. Rosenzweig Picture Frustration Test) to predict police academy and in-service rating scores. They reported multiple R's of .60 (p<.01) for academy grades and .29 (p<.05) for service ratings.

The author wishes to express thanks to Vernon L. Kiker and Joseph G. Phelan, California State University at Los Angeles.

Marsh[1] (1962) reports a study on Los Angeles County Deputy Sheriffs. The procedure used by Marsh was very similar to that of DuBois and Watson. However, Marsh also concerned himself with tenure and auto accidents as additional criteria. He found that some general abilities tests were predictive of tenure, and that the Hypomanic and Depression Scales of the MMPI were predictive of auto accidents.

We see, then, that researchers on this problem have long been of the opinion that personality is an important variable to consider when selecting police candidates. Bass et al. (1954) directed themselves to this problem specifically. Their investigation of 37 Baton Rouge city policemen indicated that sometimes biographical and personality factors were better than aptitude measures for predicting police "success."

These three studies are representative of most of the work done in this field from Terman in 1917 to the middle sixties. Then it seems that the growing concern about the role of the policemen in the American society created an atmosphere which was highly conducive to research on police positions. Matarazzo, Allen, Saslow and Wiens (1964) replicated Terman's 1917 work. Johnson (1965) made a critical appraisal of the changes in the selection of police candidates from Terman's time to that of Matarazzo et al. Robinson (1970) investigated the value of self reports by policemen as predictors of effectiveness on the job. Spencer and Nichols (1971) did an exhaustive study with the Chicago Police Department which covered several years. Cunningham[2] conducted a second study of the deputy sheriffs in Los Angeles augmenting Marsh's earlier work.

All the recent work, however, has been with departments involved with criminal law enforcement. The purpose of this study was to examine the selection procedures of a civil law enforcement

---

[1]Marsh's deputy sheriffs and the deputy marshals of this study are both members of separate departments in Los Angeles County. Both are policing agencies in the Los Angeles area, but the sheriffs are concerned with the enforcement of criminal law while the deputy marshals are concerned with the enforcement of civil law.

[2]This is an unpublished study which can be obtained from the County of Los Angeles Personnel Department Library, Rm. 546, 222 North Grand Avenue, Los Angeles, California.

agency to determine the validity of those procedures and how that validity might be increased. The study was a cooperative project involving the resources of both the Department of the Marshal and the Department of Personnel of Los Angeles County.

The study was intended to demonstrate that certain tests are predictive of both training and field performance of deputy marshals. This was to be done by correlating biographical data, achievement test scores and personality trait scores with measures of training and field success.

METHOD

General Approach: Data was collected on various measures of job success, and some potentially useful predictors of that success.

To cut down on the number of variables used, the different types of variables were subjected to factor analysis. The groupings for these analyses were as follows: (a) criteria, (b) biographical data, (c) personality data. Aptitude tests were used without subjection to factor analysis for reasons which will be discussed later. This procedure was necessary to limit the number of variables involved since the increased capitalization on chance relationships by the inclusion of all the data, with the sample sizes involved, would greatly reduce the significance of any relationship that would come out.

The factor analyses were carried out by the use of a FORTRAN IV program for minimum residual factor analysis. The program was designed to carry out a complete factor analysis including extraction of factors by the minimum residual method (Comrey, 1962; Comrey & Ahumada, 1964) and rotation by the normal varimax method (Kaiser, 1958).

The factors obtained by this method were treated in two ways. In the cases of the criteria and personality measures, factor scores were formed by combining (unweighted) the variables which loaded in the same factor with a loading of .4 or above. Variables that did not load in a major factor were dropped or, in the cases of the criteria, were retained as individual criteria. In the case of the biographical data the variable with the highest loading in a factor was retained as representative of the factor while the others were dropped. Regardless of which method was employed, the resulting predictor variables were then scrutinized to determine which should be included on the basis of a potential logical criterion-predictor relationship. Those variables which could not be supported on the basis that such a relationship might logically exist, and be useful, were discarded.

Once the variables to be used had been decided on, the next step was a series of multiple regression analyses. Separate analyses were run for each criterion.

First, the sample was divided into two random halves. Then for each kind of predictor, separate stepwise regressions were performed for each half of the sample. There was a separate analysis for the aptitude tests, the personality tests, and the biographical items. For this purpose the BMDO2R (Biomedical Computer Programs, 1968) program was used with an F-to-enter of 3.0, an F-to-delete of 2.0, and a tolerance of .10-these terms being defined in the program and refering to the significance of the contribution, at any given step, of each predictor variable to the prediction of a particular criterion.

Second, the reduced sets of each kind of variable were combined and this combined set of predictors was again entered into the BMDO2R in the same way as before, except that now an F-to-enter of 4.0 was used. The predictors selected in either subsample in the initial run through were applied to both subsamples at this stage.

Third, the combination of predictors which come out in each subsample for each criterion was then cross-validated in the other. This was done by (a) weighting the appropriate predictors in the second subsample by the beta weights developed in the first, (b) combining these weighted scores into composite scores, and (c) correlating the composite scores in the second subsample with the criterion scores for that subsample.

Fourth, if the zero order cross-validation correlation coefficients in either or both subsamples was statistically significant, the subsamples were recombined and BMDO2R was applied a final time. The predictors which were included in a significant cross-validation equation were allowed to enter or delete, using the same standards as were applied in the second step, to obtain the beta weights for the combined sample and the estimate of the multiple correlation in the population.

A comment should also be made here concerning the interpretation of the multiple correlation coefficients computed in this study. The significance levels which are reported are based on the actual number of variables in the multiple regression equations. There is a school of thought that contends that the significance levels should be based on the total number of variables which might possibly have entered the equation. Such an attitude, for this type of study, seemed overly conservative. However, it was felt that some consideration should be given to the fact that more advantage might be taken of chance than the significance tables for the multiple R (Guilford, 1965) were intended to control for. For that reason multiple correlation coefficients are reported only for those combinations of variables that resulted, also, in a significant cross-validation, zero order r. The reasoning behind this approach is that it is most unlikely that the beta weights which resulted in a significant multiple R, when that significance was due to an artifact of the data, would also result in a significant correlation when those beta weights are applied to an independent sample.

Subjects: The subjects used in this study were 121 male deputy marshals (ages 23 to 35) who had been selected at random from the 390 deputy marshals in Los Angeles County. All the deputies had been a member of the Marshal's Department for at least one year but not more than three years. Also, they had all completed the marshal's training academy consisting of ten weeks of police officer's standard training and five weeks of civil law enforcement training. These two training programs will be referred to as "post" and "civil" respectively.

Of the total number of deputies tested, 9 percent had had some type of prior police experience. On the average they had 1 to 2 years of college. Seventy-nine percent were married, and 28 percent designated themselves as belonging to an ethnic minority.

Nineteen of the subjects either did not indicate their ethnic background, or complete data were not available for them; these subjects were not used in the cross-validations.

Criteria: The nature of the criteria used was threefold. First, there were personal history data on each individual for the time he had been with the department including the number of absences over an 18-month period, the number of letters of commendation the individual had received over the same period, and the number of automobile accidents he had been involved in since joining the department.

Secondly, supervisory ratings were obtained for three catagories: emotional stability—how well he handles the "pressures" of the job; appearance—does he look the way a deputy marshal "ought to" look; and overall—the supervisor's sum-total feeling about the individual. For 21 of the deputies it was possible to obtain these ratings from a previous as well as his present supervisor. The correlation between these two sets of ratings was .664 (N = 21, p<.01). This tends to indicate that the ratings are to some extent stable over time.

Third, standardized scores for both the post and civil portions of the training academy were obtained.

As was mentioned earlier, this is a study of both field and training performance. The first two criterion areas listed above constitute the field criteria; the third represents the training criterion.

The three criterion areas, consisting of eight sub-criteria, were intercorrelated and the resulting matrix was subjected to a factor analysis, yielding four factors. Table 5-I represents the varimax factor loadings and communalities.

The number of auto accidents had loadings of .4 on two of the factors. These loadings were not reasonable on an a priori basis; also the increase in loadings on a fourth factor extracted to a higher level than those for Factor III was indicative of spurious factor. Therefore, it was decided to retain auto accidents only as a separate, single criterion. The final criteria used in the study were as follows: (a) absenteeism; (b) overall supervisory rating; (c)

TABLE 5-I
LOADINGS AND COMMUNALITIES OF CRITERION FACTORS

Criterion	Factors				h^2 [a]
	I	*II*	*III*	*IV*	
Absenteeism	—.127	.018	*.399*	—.125	.192
E. S. Rating	*.676*	.118	—.014	—.120	.486
App Rating	*.496*	.155	—.243	.121	.344
O. A. Rating	*.923*	.115	—.101	.059	.880
Commends	—.096	—.007	—.084	*.520*	.287
Auto Accs.	.021	—*.409*	.219	*.418*	.390
Post	.177	*.511*	.016	—.038	.294
Civil	.025	*.513*	.103	.041	.276

[a]h^2 = Communality

letters of commendation from the community; (d) number of auto accidents; and (e) composite academy scores.

Predictors: Following the guidelines set down by the DuBois and Watson, Cunningham, and Marsh studies, three types of predictors were selected. These consisted of eight aptitude tests, two personality tests, and a biographical questionnaire consisting of 53 items.

The aptitude tests were not factor analyzed. Seven of the tests had been developed to be relatively independent of each other. This development was completed on populations much larger than those used in this study, so it was decided to accept these tests as measures of separate and distinct aptitudes.

The aptitude test predictors were as follows:

a. Five speeded tests distributed by Psychological Services, Inc., Los Angeles (Ruch and Ruch, 1963)
   i. Vocabulary (RH1)
   ii. Basic math (RH2)
   iii. Spacial visualization (RH3)
   iv. Numerical reasoning (RH6)
   v. Verbal reasoning (RH7)
b. Two tests developed by J. P. Guilford[3]

---

[3]These tests were developed under U.S. Government Contract Nonr-228(20) by J. P. Guilford and were used with his permission.

    i. Best trend name (G1)

    ii. Letter triangle (G2)

  c. The General Abilities employment test (4-1) currently used by Los Angeles county for selection of deputy marshals. None of the subjects in this study was selected on the basis of this particular test, however.

Factor analysis of the biographical items indicated that the bulk of the common variance in the questionnaire could be accounted for by 13 of the items. These were as follows:

  a. Prior police experience

  b. Time on last job

  c. Minority group status

  d. Amount of school completed

  e. Type of grades received in school

  f. Amount of mother's education

  g. Marital status

  h. Height

  i. Selling experience

  j. How long unemployed before hire

  k. Number of police science units

  l. Firearm experience

  m. Number of siblings

These items were then scrutinized to see if some of them could be eliminated and the number of variables to be considered further reduced. "Marital status" (g) was eliminated because the question was poorly phrased. There was no indication if the deputy married before or after hire, so even if this variable did correlate with any of the criteria it could not be used for selection purposes. "Time on last job" (b) and "How long unemployed" (j) were eliminated since they refer to tenure, which was not a criterion. "Firearm experience" (l) may or may not have been answered from the standpoint of academy training, so this item was eliminated. "Amount of school" (d), "Type of grades" (e), and "Number of Police Science Units" (k) were shown in Cunningham's study on deputy sheriffs to be highly correlated with written test scores. Since test scores are generally more reliable than biographical information, especially self-report items, these were dropped. "Amount of mother's education" (f) and "Height" (h) were not logically related to any of the criteria, and were dropped. "Selling experience" (i) is a consideration in the interview, and since the interview is of considerably more interest, this item was also dropped.

The result was that three of the biographical items were retained as potential predictors. They were: (a) Prior police experience; (c) Minority group status; and (m) Number of younger siblings. "Prior police experience" was retained because of its obvious relevance to law enforcement. "Minority group status" was retained because of its relevance to recent court decisions, the EEOC Guidelines, and Los Angeles County's concern with Affirmative Action. "Number of younger siblings" was retained because it was the item with the highest loading on what might be termed a *Financial—Marital Stability* factor, and a similar factor was found in Cunningham's study to be very useful as a predictor.

Factor analysis of the personality tests resulted in three personality measures being retained as predictors. They were as follows:

a. Rotter—Internal vs. External Control of Reinforcement, as measured by the Rotter I-E scale (Rotter, 1966).

b. FI—Aggressive Self-Assurance vs. Lack of Decisiveness, as measured by a composite of the Autonomy, Heterosexuality, Intraception, and Agression scales of the Edwards Personal Preference Schedule (EPPS).

c. FII—People Orientation vs. Production Orientation, as measured by a composite of the Order, Affiliation, Succorance, Endurance and Nurturance scales of the EPPS (Edwards, 1959).

Table 5-II represents the factor loadings and communalities for the factor analysis performed on the scales of the Edwards Personal Preference Schedule. Six of the EPPS scales (Exhibitionism, Achievement, Dominance, Abasement, Change, Deference) were dropped as variables because they did not fall into one of the two main factors, and were not regarded as being of enough interest to retain as individual predictors.

When compared to Edwards' normative group for the EPPS,

the Ss varied considerably above and below the normative means depending on the scales. However, perhaps more meaningful than the scores on the individual scales, in this case, is the results from the factor analysis on those scores. As was mentioned earlier, two main factors came out.

The first was a combination of the (a) Autonomy, (b) Heterosexuality, (c) Aggression, and (d) Intraception scales. The loading on intraception was opposite in sign (i.e. negative) to the other three. This factor was named "Aggressive Self Assurance vs. Lack of Decisiveness."

What this combination of four scales seems to be picking up is the "all man" self-image of these officers. They see themselves as loners (Autonomy), virile (their average Heterosexuality score was as at the 80th percentile), go-getters (Aggression), and less concerned with people's reasons than their actions (negative loading on intraception).

The second major factor was "Production Orientation vs. People Orientation," a combination of the (a) Order, (b) Endurance, (c) Affiliation, (d) Succorance and (e) Nurturance scales. The latter three scales had negative loadings. This seems to be picking up the rigid and structured attitude commonly attributed to law enforcement officers.

They feel it's a job that must be done; one must do it in a proper, specified manner (Order). One must be persistant, for the people that are dealt with will avoid contact if possible (Endurance). And, one cannot allow his personal feelings to affect his work (negative loadings on Affiliation, Succorance, and Nurturance). In general then, it appears that the deputies have a definite opinion of how to approach their work. They feel that they themselves are extremely capable of performing their job, and that if they are forced to choose between duty and people, duty will come first.

These attributes seem to be confirmed by discussions with many of the individual deputies. They do seem to have a need to feel thay are serving a higher good, namely society. How else could they evict a tenant and his family for back rent, or repossess the furniture of a senior citizen for non-payment of a doctor bill.

TABLE 5-II
LOADINGS AND COMMUNALITIES OF THE EDWARDS PERSONAL
PREFERENCE SCHEDULE

	Factors		
Scale	I	II	h^2 [a]
Sch	—.029	.296	.089
Def	.096	.344	.128
Ord	—.060	.489	.242
Exh	—.366	—.047	.136
Aut	—.561	—.075	.320
Aff	.391	—.557	.463
Int	.530	.101	.292
Suc	—.081	—.455	.213
Dom	0.33	.120	.016
Aba	.337	—.080	.120
Nur	.487	—.640	.646
Chg	—.220	.042	.050
End	.320	.519	.371
Het	—.500	—.063	.255
Agg	—.497	—.078	.253

[a] h^2 = Communality

In general, the deputies scored above average on the achievement tests. For example, on the verbal comprehension, basic math, numerical reasoning, and verbal reasoning tests their average score was consistently above the 80th percentile, relative to the male population used in the standardization process. On the visual pursuit test, their average score was at the 50th percentile. Their standard deviations on these five measures were $\frac{1}{2}$ to 1 times the size of the population sigmas.

On the Rotter Internal—External Scale, their average score ($\overline{X}$ = 8.77) and standard deviation (S = 3.89) were extremely close to the mean (M = 8.15) and standard deviation (sigma = 3.88) reported by Rotter for his standardization population of 575 males.

The interview score received by the deputy at the time of his initial application was also introduced as a predictor; the composite training score was used as a predictor of field performance.

In all a total of 14 predictors were correlated with training success, and 15 with field success.

Procedure: Testing of the deputies was done in three group sessions. The actual testing time was three and one-half hours, with a one-half hour break after the first two hours. The sessions were held during regular working hours and the deputies were compensated in that manner for their time. The order of the tests was randomized for each administration.

RESULTS

Intercorrelations of the predictors and the criteria: Significant relationships were found between the predictor battery and each of the criteria. Table 5-III illustrates each criterion and the particular predictors found to be significantly related to them. Since observations and scores for every subject on every variable were not obtained, the correlations and significance levels reported are those computed using only those subjects for whom scores were available.

Absenteeism was negatively correlated with one of the bio-

TABLE 5-III
CORRELATION MATRIX FOR PREDICTORS AND CRITERIA
(TOTAL GROUP)

Predictors		Abs.	Rate.	Criteria Coms.	Accs.	Train.
Sibs	(102)	—.223*	—.043	—.103	—.058	.031
PPD	(102)	—.053	.242*	.075	.138	—.053
Min	(102)	—.045	—.112	.204*	.018	—.115
RH1	(103)	.099	.003	—.066	—.206*	.317**
RH2	(104)	—.125	.098	—.103	—.096	.227*
RH3	(105)	—.030	.016	.014	—.064	.328**
RH6	(105)	—.059	.201*	—.052	—.160	.329**
RH7	(102)	—.041	.201*	.198*	—.282**	.294**
4-1	(101)	—.117	.182	—.110	—.190	.355**
Rott	(106)	—.058	—.041	.100	.246*	—.222*
F I	(101)	—.077	.265**	—.018	—.054	.017
F II	(101)	—.056	—.112	—.075	—.120	.046
Int	(110)	—.014	.132	—.035	.039	.187
Train	(101)	.012	.146	—.028	—.186	1.000

Note—The number of Ss on which the correlations were performed is indicated in parentheses after the predictor, except for the correlations involving training as a variable for which there were 101 Ss in every case.

*p<.05
**p<.01

graphical items, "number of younger siblings." It was hypothesized that perhaps persons with a larger number of younger siblings would be more responsible and hence tend to be absent less.

Supervisory ratings were found to be related to scores on the numerical reasoning and the verbal reasoning aptitude tests, and the FI scale of the EPPS. This tends to indicate that the supervisors preferred persons who demonstrate reasoning ability and are aggressively self-assured.

Letters of commendation from the community was positively correlated a high score on the verbal reasoning achievement test and whether or not the person is a member of an ethnic minority.

The number of automobile accidents a deputy had been involved in was negatively correlated with scores on the vocabulary and verbal reasoning tests of the achievement test. This tends to indicate that the less "intelligent" have more auto accidents. It is interesting to note here the policy of many automobile insurance companies to charge lower premiums to students who maintain a high scholastic average.

Also correlated with the number of auto accidents was the scores on the Internal-External Reinforcement Scale. This indicated that those deputies who were externally "controlled," more fatalistic in their attitude, had a higher number of auto accidents.

The composite academy training score proved to be the most predictable of all the criteria. Here, six of the achievement tests, including the one being used at present by the county of Los Angeles for selection of Deputy Marshals, were significantly correlated with success. In addition, two of the personality measures proved to be related. This may be explained by the nature of the training situation. It is a combination of classroom work, for which one would expect academic type tests to be predictive, and physical strain with mental harassment, for which it is reasonable that some type of personality variable would be associated.

Cross-validation: For the purpose of cross-validation, several multiple regression analyses were performed. The procedure used was the one described earlier in the Methods Section under *General Approach.*

The results obtained with the predictors for training success are illustrated in Table 5-IV.

TABLE 5-IV
CORRELATIONS FOR TRAINING SUCCESS

Group	Predictor	Initial	N	Correlation Coefficients Cross-validation	N
I	RH7 + Rot	R = .50**	51	r = .27*	50
II	RH3 + RH1 + 4-1	R = .57**	50	r = .28*	51

*p<.05
**p<.01

In this case, since both cross-validation r's were significant, the subsamples were recombined and the final beta weights for prediction of the composite training scores obtained.

The predictors included in the final regression equation were (a) the test presently used for selection of deputies (beta = .220), (b) the visual pursuit test (beta = .253), (c) the vocabulary test (beta = .207), and (d) the Rotter I-E Scale (beta = −.187). This resulted in a multiple correlation of .518 (p<.01). This correlation was then corrected for bias and the shrunken R ($\bar{R}$) of .504 (p<.01) was obtained.

The beta weights developed from each subsample for prediction of the four field criteria failed to produce statistically significant correlations when applied to the cross-validation sample.

This indicates that, for the total group, the relationships existing between scores on the predictors and the measures of job success were strong enough to be useful when considering training success, but not when considering field success.

DISCUSSION

The results showed that both the personality-biography and aptitude tests used here are useful predictors of success as a deputy marshal. Both showed strong relationships to the training criterion and the field criteria.

Similar to the DuBois and Watson study, both types of predictors resulted in significant multiple R's for all the groups considered. However, some of predictor combinations did not hold up under cross-validation. As in the Marsh study, a personality measure (Rotter I-E) displayed a strong relation to auto accidents. As in the Cunningham work, aptitude measures seemed to hold up best for prediction of training success. Also, the selection devices used here meet the EEOC requirements for proper selection of candidates.

There is no indication in the data that success in training is a useful indicator of potential field success. Even considering the range restriction that has occurred due to preselection of this sample on the basis of academy success, the results strongly point out a need for a reevaluation by the marshal's department of the relevancy of the training given new deputies to actual job (field) performance.

Given, however, that the criteria of success now being used are not changed, three conclusions are suggested by these results:

1. Personality, biographical, and aptitude measures are significantly correlated with measures of deputy marshal success.
2. Success in training has not been shown to be a good predictor of field performance.
3. Further study is needed to determine predictors which might be useful for prediction of field success.

Finally, there are some limiting considerations regarding these results that should be noted. The present study was conducted within a concurrent validity design. As such there is always the danger that, when the results are applied to an applicant population, any or all of the predictive relationships will not hold up.

What this points up is the need to consider this study not as a terminal point in the establishment of selection procedures for deputy marshal, but as the first in a continuing series of studies. To continue investigation along this line would allow for: (a) a check on the results reported here; (b) changes in the selection procedures to accommodate needed revamping of the criteria of success; (c) the establishment of valid procedures to predict those criteria that could not be predicted successfully in this study; and (d) a needed predictive study of deputy marshal selection.

COMMENTS

There are several points alluded to in this study that I feel should be commented on and specifically elaborated.

The first is the problem of differential selection. The data, as it is reported here, concerns itself with prediction of success of *all* the deputies, regardless of their particular ethnic or cultural background. There is considerable evidence to suggest that this may not be the most practical or desirable approach to the analysis of the data.[4]

The EEOC Guidelines *(Federal Register, 1970)* requires that, where technically feasible, "data must be generated and results separately reported for minority and non-minority groups." Preliminary work on the present data indicates that criteria which were not predictable from total group scores, do show predictor-criterion relationships when the information is analyzed separately for caucasian and minority subgroups. Further work, however, is required to establish the strength of these relationships.

What this points out is the need to consider ethnic background when trying to predict job success. These factors, it seems reasonable, are especially important in police-type work, both from the standpoint of community reactions and supervisory ratings.

The second point which deserves further investigation is that of the policeman's personality. Even though the deputy marshals are not policemen in the usual sense, their scores on the EPPS indicates that the persons who gravitate to the field do exhibit many of the personality characteristics which have come to be associated with the profession, in the minds of the general populace. These characteristics include the virile, "he-man" self image, and a (per-

---

[4]Four papers presented in a symposium at the 1971 American Psychological Association Convention in Washington D.C. dealt with the problem of differential prediction specifically. Three out of the four found the differential selection approach to selection to yield more useful results. The symposium was entitled "Prediction of Performance and Personnel Selection from Racially Mixed Groups" (Division 14).

haps over-zealous) concern for the common good, coupled with a relative disregard for individual problems and situations.

Finally, question is raised as to the propriety of a quasi-military approach to the training of police officers. This is the approach which has traditionally been used to train new officers (at least in California), but this study has not shown any meaningful relationship to exist between that training and actual job performance.

It seems worse than ludicrous for taxpayers to subsidize training programs for policemen that do not prepare the officers to do their job.[5] My intent with this statement is not to instigate a movement against police training. Rather, I am attempting to point out the need for further investigation of police training programs with the idea in mind that, if study shows that present training is irrelevant, the programs and emphases should be changed to actually meet the needs for which the training programs were designed.

And, further, that these changes may necessitate a reevaluation on the parts of police departments as to the desirability of a quasi-military approach to law enforcement.

REFERENCES

Bass, B. M., Karstendiek, B., McCullough, G., and Pruitt, R. C.: Validity information exchange, No. 7-024. *Personnel Psychology, 7,* 159-160, 1954.

Comrey, A. L.: The minimum residual method of factor analysis. *Psychological Reports, 11,* 15-18, 1962.

Comrey, A. L., and Ahumada, A.: An improved procedure and program for minimum residual factor analysis. *Psychological Reports, 15,* 91-96, 1964.

Dixon, W. J. (Ed.) : *Biomedical Computer Programs.* Los Angeles, University of California Press, 1968.

Du Bois, P. H., and Watson, R. I.: The selection of patrolmen. *Journal of Applied Psychology, 32(2),* 90-95, 1950.

Edwards, A. L.: *Edwards Personal Preference Schedule.* New York, Psychological Corp., 1959.

Federal Register Doc. 70-9967. Washington, D. C.: U. S. Government Printing Office, 1970, 35 (149) .

Guilford, J. P.: *Fundamental Statistics in Psychology and Education,* 4th ed. New York, McGraw-Hill, 1965.

---

[5]The deputy marshal training program lasts 5 months and cadets receive full pay ($842/mo.) and benefits during training.

Johnson, R. W.: Successful policemen and firemen applicants: then and now. *Journal of Applied Psychology, 49(4)*, 299-301, 1965.

Kaiser, H. F.: The varimax criterion for analytic rotation in factor analysis. *Psychometrika, 23*, 187-200, 1958.

Marsh, S. H.: Validating the selection of deputy sheriffs. *Public Personnel Review, 23*, 41-44, 1962.

Matarazzo, J. D., Allen, B. V., Saslow, G., and Wiens, A. N.: Characteristics of successful policemen and firemen applicants. *Journal of Applied Psychology, 48*, 123-133, 1964.

Robinson, D. D.: Predicting police effectiveness from self reports of relative time spent in task performance. *Personnel Psychology, 23*, 327-345, 1970.

Rotter, J. B.: Generalized expectancies for internal versus external control of reinforcement. *Psychological Monographs, 80* (1, Whole N .609), 1966.

Ruch, F. L. and Ruch, W. W.: *Employee Aptitude Survey Technical Report.* Los Angeles, Psychological Services, 1963.

Spencer, G. and Nichols, R.: A study of Chicago police recruits. *The Police Chief, 38(6)*, 50-55, 1971.

Terman, L. M.: A trail of mental and pedagogical tests in a Civil Service examination for policemen and firemen. *Journal of Applied Psychology, 1*, 17-29, 1917.

Chapter 6

PREDICTING JOB PERFORMANCE OF LAW ENFORCEMENT OFFICERS: A TEN- AND TWENTY-YEAR STUDY*

HOMA M. SNIBBE, STANLEY P. AZEN,[2]
HUGH R. MONTGOMERY AND STEWART H. MARSH

IN THIS CHAPTER we present the results of two longitudinal studies which attempted to delineate variables contributing to and predicting successful police performance. Subjects for both studies were law enforcement officers appointed to the Los Angeles County Sheriff's Department during the years 1947-1950. The first study, a ten-year predictive efficiency study, was undertaken by one of the authors, Stewart Marsh of the Los Angeles County Department of Personnel, in 1958 (Marsh, 1962). His findings identified certain psychological, aptitudinal, and biographical variables which showed promise in differentiating between successful and unsuccessful officers. The second study, a twenty-year follow-up study, was undertaken by the authors in 1970 (Azen et al., 1972). The purposes of this study were to validate Marsh's findings and to evaluate Marsh's significant variables as twenty-year predictors of success and performance of the same law enforcement officers. The latter study also derived classification decision rules which may be used for future selection of officers.

*Work on this study was supported by LEAA Grant No. 72-DF-09-0005, administered under the auspices of the Los Angeles County Sheriff's Department and The Department of Personnel. The Physiological Fitness Standards Research Project staff psychologists are: Drs. J. Grencik, H. Snibbe, and H. Montgomery. The authors would like to express deep appreciation to Mrs. Lynn Lee whose energy has contributed greatly to these efforts.

[2]Departments of Electrical Engineering and Medicine, University of Southern California, Los Angeles.

101

THE MARSH TEN-YEAR STUDY

The subjects for this study were 619 male law enforcement officers appointed as deputy sheriffs in Los Angeles County between the years 1947 and 1950. Data on two sets of variables were collected and analyzed. The first set, called the *subject variables,* consisted of Civil Service test scores, personal and biographical information, and the grade received in the Sheriff's Academy. These data were collected at the time of appointment. The subject variables also included a battery of personality and interest test scores for 95 of the 619 officers. Psychological tests were administered at the time of appointment by the Counselling Center of the University of Southern California. Detailed description of the subject variables is given as follows:

Subject Variables

Civil Service Test Scores

1. Written test scores on the Civil Service entrance examination. These are standard scores based on general ability, practical judgment and memory.
2. Interview score on the Civil Service entrance examination.
3. Weighted average of the total written test scores (weighted 60%) and the interview score (weighted 40%).

Personal and Biographical Data

4. Age (years) at time of entry in the Department.
5. Height (inches).
6. Percentile rating at the Sheriff's Recruit Training Center (the Sheriff's Academy) prior to appointment.
7. Years of school completed after high school.
8. Occupational status before recruitment as an officer.

Personality Tests

9. Guilford-Martin Temperament Inventory; C-scores based on a general male population (Guilford and Martin, 1934).
10. Kuder Preference Record, Vocational, Form C; T scores based on a general male population (Kuder, 1951).
11. Minnesota Multiphasic Personality Inventory (MMPI);

T scores based on a general male population (Hathaway and McKinley, 1943).

The second set of variables for which data were collected and analyzed is called the *criterion variables*. These variables measured the success and field performance of the officer during his period of employment up to 1958 or just prior to his termination date. The description of these variables is given below:

Criterion Variables

1. Tenure—whether the officer was still employed by the department as of April, 1958.
2. Accident record—the number of job-related preventable automobile accidents prior to 1958.
3. Job performance—the average of a special five-category rating developed by Marsh. This average rating will be denoted by MSPR throughout this chapter.

A few comments are in order about the Marsh special job performance rating. Much effort went into securing the MSPR in a usable form which would minimize the effects of weaknesses inherent in such evaluations. Each supervisor was given a group of cards, each of which contained the name of one of his officers. He was then asked to sort the cards into five approximately equal subgroups according to the officers' work performance as deputy sheriffs. The subgroups were ordered from 1 to 5. Since each officer had more than one supervisor, his average rating was calculated. This average is the MSPR score. From this information it was decided that officers with extreme average ratings would be compared in the study. Thus, officers with mean rating between 4.0 and 5.0 (High) and those with mean rating between 1.0 and 2.0 (Low) were used in the analysis. Furthermore, an even more extreme comparison was made between officers with a High MSPR and those who had been discharged or had resigned in lieu of discharge.

The objective of the study was to determine whether there were any significant relationships between the subject and criterion variables. For this purpose, 2 × 2 contingency tables were analyzed using the chi-square test for homogeneity (Afifi and Azen, 1972, Section 2.5) . Thus, for each subject variable the following four contingency tables were studied:

Criterion Variables

	Tenure		*Accident Record*		*Job Performance*		*Job Performance*	
	Yes	No	None	1 or More	High MSPR	Low MSPR	High MSPR	Discharge
High								
Low								

Subject Variable (vertical label at left)

Figure 6-1.

The cut-off between "High" and "Low" for each subject variable was determined by Marsh to be that value of the variable yielding the largest chi-square value for the test of homogeneity. The significant subject variables are designated as *predictor variables* throughout this chapter.

The significant subject variables, i.e. predictors, of job performance are presented in Table 6-I. Note the distinction between High MSPR vs. Low MSPR and High MSPR vs. Discharge given in the column labeled *Criterion groups*. Further, note that some of the results are given only for officers on patrol assignment. Finally, observe that the cut-off between "High" and "Low", the proportions in each criterion group at or above, and below this cut-off, the number of cases analyzed, and the calculated chi-square value are given for each predictor.

Thus, when comparing officers with High MSPR with those who had been discharged, five subject variables are shown to be significant predictors. Viewing each predictor separately, a high ($\geqslant$ 97th percentile) civil service written test total score, high ($\geqslant$ 84th percentile) sentence-completion score, and high ($\geqslant$ 73rd percentile) weighted average were indicative of a High MSPR. Further, being tall ($\geqslant$ 72 inches) , or having a high ($\geqslant$ 80%) Academy rating was also predictive of High MSPR. When comparing officers with High MSPR and those with Low MSPR, low scores on three personality test scales—the General Activity scale on the Guilford-Martin, scales 9 (Hypomania) and 1 (Hypochondriasis) on the MMPI—were shown to be significant predictors of High MSPR. Further, tall officers, patrolmen with a high number-series-completion score, or patrolmen with a "promotional" (e.g. public relations, insurance, real estate) background were potentially high performers.

Table 6-II presents predictors of automobile accidents and tenure. For accidents, two scales on the MMPI—scales 9 (Hypomania) and 2 (Depression) and two scales on the Kuder Preference Record—Mechanical and Social Service—were isolated. Examining each predictor individually, officers with a high scale 9 or a low scale 2 on the MMPI, a low Mechanical or a high Social Service score on the Kuder, were shown to be potential accident risks. Finally, high scores on either the civil service written test total, interview, or weighted average were indicative of shorter job tenure.

This study is interesting and valuable since it identifies certain biographical, aptitudinal and personality variables as predictors of success and job performance. However, the chi-square technique used for this study is not the most effective method for analyzing the subject variables since it neither takes into account the dependence of the subject variables, nor does it yield an ordering of the resulting predictors. In the next section we present the results of a twenty-year follow-up study in which most of the predictors from the Marsh study are analyzed as to their continued significance as twenty-year predictors. That study also determines the "best" predictor (s) among the significant predictors and derives decision rules for classifying an officer as potential success or failure.

TWENTY-YEAR STUDY

The subjects for this study were 95 of the 619 male law enforcement officers for whom the psychological test data were available. The subject variables chosen for this study were most of the predictors found significant by Marsh. Basic differences be-

TABLE 6-1
PREDICTORS OF JOB PERFORMANCE

Predictor	Criterion Groups	Cut-off Found Significant	Effect of Cut-off On Ratio Between Criterion Groups		Chi Square[1]	No. of Cases
			At & Above Cut-off	Below Cut-off		
Civil Service Test Scores						
Total written test	High vs. discharged	97th percentile[4]	12.5 to 1	2.5 to 1	3.87	165
Sentence completion items	High vs. discharged	84th percentile	5 to 1	2 to 1	5.38	165
Number series completion items	High vs. low (patrol assignment)	73rd percentile	3 to 2	2 to 5	7.79	121
Weighted average of written test and interview[5]	High vs. discharged	73rd percentile	5 to 1	1.2 to 1	12.03	165
	High vs. low	73rd percentile	3 to 2	2 to 3	6.88	226
Personality Tests						
Guilford-Martin General Activity Scale	High vs. low	C-score of 6	1 to 7	1.5 to 1	4.28	51
	High vs. low (patrol assignment)	C-score of 6	1 to 6	2 to 1	4.15	36
MMPI Hypomania Scale[6]	High vs. low	T-score of 55	1 to 1.3	3.5 to 1	4.65	53
	High vs. low (patrol assignment)	T-score of 55	1 to 2	6.5 to 1	8.03	36
MMPI Hypochondriasis Scale	High vs. low	T-score of 55	1 to 3	2 to 1	5.34	53
Personal & Biographical Data						
Height	High vs. discharged	72 inches	6 to 1	2 to 1	7.46	164
	High vs. low	72 inches	1.7 to 1	1 to 1	5.17	225

Previous occupation	High vs. low (patrol assignment)	Subjects listing "promotional" work[7] vs. all others	Promotional: 2 to 1	All others: 1 to 1	4.30	254
	High vs. low (patrol assignment)	Subjects listing "police and fire"[8] vs. all others	Police & Fire: 1 to 2	All others: 1 to 1	4.45	254
Grade in Sheriff's Recruit School	High vs. discharged	Grade of 80%	17 to 1	1.5 to 1	12.48	81

[3]For data in this report, a χ^2 of 3.84 is significant at the 5% level; a χ^2 of 6.64 is significant at the 1% level. Yates' correction was applied whenever one of the expected cell frequencies was smaller than 25.

[4]Percentiles are based upon the original distribution of unselected-candidates scores.

[5]A near-significant (positive) relationship was found for the interview at the 58th percentile ($\chi^2 = 3.75$; $n = 226$).

[6]A similar finding was that this scale correlates —.23 with overall effectiveness as an Air Force officer. (Mackinnon, Donald W., *An Assessment Study of Air Force Officers*, Part V *Summary and Applications*. Lackland Air Force Base, Tex.: Personnel Laboratory, Wright Air Development Center, Dec., 1958. (*Technical Report* WADC-TR-58-91 (V), ASTIA Document No. AD 210 220) p. 26.

[7]Included such jobs as public relations, insurance and real estate sales, and advertising.

[8]Included patrolman, detectives, baliffs, firemen, health inspectors.

TABLE 6-II
PREDICTORS OF ACCIDENT RECORD AND TENURE

Predictors of Accident Record

Predictor[9]	Cut-off Found Significant	Effect of Cut-off on Ratio Between Control and Accident Groups		Chi Square	No. of Cases
		At and above Cut-off	Below Cut-off		
MMPI					
Hypomania Scale	T-score of 55	1 to 1.2	4 to 1	6.44	66
Depression Scale	T-score of 50	2.5 to 1	1 to 1.5	5.04	66
Kuder Preference Record					
Mechanical Scale	T-score of 30	2 to 1	1 to 2	4.23	67
Social Service Scale	T-score of 50	1 to 1	4 to 1	4.00	67

Predictors of Tenure

Predictor[10]	Cut-off Found Significant	Proportion Still Employed		Chi Square ($n = 591$)
		Below Cut-off	At or Above Cut-off	
Score on total written test	95th percentile	62%	49%	7.02
Interview score	Scores falling between 73rd and 82nd percentile	68%	56%	9.57
Weighted average	84th percentile	68%	55%	10.11
	65th percentile	73%	57%	10.17

[9] A near-significant finding was that subjects 71 inches or more in height tended to have fewer accidents ($\chi^2 = 3.65$; $n = 337$).
[10] Relationships were computed only for the three predictors listed.

tween the subject variables of the twenty-year study and the predictors of the ten-year study are due to changes in the techniques of analysis. For example, only the civil service written test total score was considered for the twenty-year study; the breakdown into "sentence-completion items" and "number-series completion items," as well as the interview and weighted average were not studied. In addition, the occupational status before recruitment was deleted from this study since it is a nominal variable and hence, not suitable for either analysis of variance or discriminant analysis techniques. Also, since Academy ratings were available for only 45 out of 95 officers, the significance of this variable as a predictor was analyzed independently of the other subject variables. In addition, the actual percentile Academy rating has been transformed into an ordinal variable measured on a seven point scale. Finally, age was included as a subject variable although it was not found to be significant in the ten-year study. In summary, the subject variables for the twenty-year study are given as follows:

Subject Variables

Civil Service Test Score

1. Written test total score on the Civil Service examination.

Personal and Biographical Data

2. Age (years) at time of entry in the department.
3. Height (inches).
4. Rating at the Sheriff's Recruit Training Center prior to appointment. (1 = outstanding, 2 = good, 3 = better than average, 4 = acceptable, 5 = doubtful, 6 = weak, and 7 = not satisfactory.)

Personality Test Scales

5. General Activity scale on the Guilford-Martin Temperament Inventory.
6. Mechanical scale on the Kuder Preference Record.
7. Social Service scale on the Kuder Preference Record.
8. Scale 1 (Hypochondriasis) on the MMPI.
9. Scale 2 (Depression) on the MMPI.
10. Scale 9 (Hypomania) on the MMPI.

Data on a set of criterion variables, differing somewhat from those of the ten-year study, were collected for each subject up to 1970 or just prior to his termination date. For each criterion variable, the officers were divided into two distinct criterion groups, characterized by specific values of the criterion variable. The description of these variables and the corresponding groups is as follows:

Criterion Variables

1. *Employment status as of 1970.*
   Criterion Group 1: in service as of 1970 $(n_1 = 45)$.
   Criterion Group 2: not in service, i.e. resigned, retired, or dismissed $(n_2 = 48)$.
   Deceased officers were eliminated from this analysis $(n = 2)$.

2. *Rank status as of 1970.*
   Criterion Group 1: deputy sheriff or senior deputy sheriff $(n_1 = 14)$.
   Criterion Group 2: sergeant, lieutenant, captain, inspector, chief $(n_2 = 31)$.
   Officers who were not in service as of 1970 were removed from this analysis $(n = 50)$.

3. *Job type as of 1970 or termination date.*
   Criterion Group 1: patrol $(n_1 = 38)$.
   Criterion Group 2: non-patrol $(n_2 = 56)$.
   One unidentified officer was removed from this analysis.

4. *Average supervisors' rating.* This is the average of all ratings prior to 1970 or to the last year of employment.
   Criterion Group 1: low rating $(n_1 = 11)$.
   Criterion Group 2: high rating $(n_2 = 22)$.
   Three officers with unknown rating and 59 officers with average rating were removed from this sample.

5. *Number of job-related auto accidents prior to 1958.*
   Criterion Group 1: no accidents $(n_1 = 70)$.
   Criterion Group 2: at least one accident $(n_2 = 25)$.

6. *Number of job-related auto accidents prior to 1970.*
   Criterion Group 1: no accidents $(n_1 = 65)$.
   Criterion Group 2: at least one accident $(n_2 = 30)$.

7. *Number of Workmen's Compensation claims prior to 1970.*
   Criterion Group 1: no claims $(n_1 = 30)$.
   Criterion Group 2: at least one claim $(n_2 = 65)$.

8. *Type of on-job injury prior to 1970.*
   Criterion Group 1: no injury, external non-police related body injury, back injury, police related injury, or other injury $(n_1 = 80)$.
   Criterion Group 2: cardiovascular disease or gastrointestinal ulceration, stress-strain injury $(n_2 = 15)$.

Note from this list that the criterion "tenure" from the ten-year study is now defined as "employment status." This criterion also includes those officers dismissed from the Department. Also observe the two additional job performance criteria—rank status and job type. The criterion "supervisors' rating," not the same as MSPR in the Marsh study, is the average of all supervisors' routine semiannual ratings from time of appointment to termination or 1970. Both automobile accident criteria (1958 and 1970) were studied to test for the sensitivity of the resulting predictors. The number of Workmen's Compensation claims was studied because of its bearing on job performance as well as the economic implications of injury and illness. Finally, "on-job injury" was investigated since statistics compiled by the U. S. Department of Health, Education, and Welfare in 1967 indicate that persons engaged in police work suffer from a higher prevalence and incidence of heart attacks than do those in other careers.

As stated above, one objective of this study was to evaluate the ten-year predictors as to their continued significance as twenty-year predictors. For this purpose, one-way analysis of variance (Afifi and Azen, 1972, Chap. 4) was performed on all subject variables for each criterion. The resulting significant subject variables are designated as *predictors*. The second objective was to determine the "best" predictor(s) for each criterion. For each criterion, the *single best predictor* is that predictor which is most significant (i.e. smallest p) among the predictors of that criterion. To derive a classification decision rule for a single best predictor, and to identify a potential *second "best" predictor* given the single best predictor, we used the technique of *stepwise discriminant analysis* (Afifi and Azen, 1972, Chap. 5).

TABLE 6-III
SIGNIFICANT PREDICTORS FOR THE TWENTY-YEAR STUDY

Criterion	Predictor	F	p <
Job Performance			
Rank Status	Written Test Total	6.71	.025
	Mechanical	6.44	.025
	Scale 1 (MMPI)	4.05	.025
Job Type	Age	5.62	.025
	Mechanical	2.89	.10
Supervisors' Ratings	Mechanical	5.57	.025
Accident Record			
1958	Scale 9 (MMPI)	4.61	.05
	Scale 2 (MMPI)	2.76	.10
	Height	2.75	.10
1970	Scale 9 (MMPI)	9.10	.005
	Scale 2 (MMPI)	3.69	.10
Tenure			
Employment Status	General Activity	5.11	.025
Other			
Workmen's Compensation	None	—	—
On-Job Injury	None	—	—

Table 6-III presents the results of the analysis of variance for each criterion. Note that seven of Marsh's predictors (excluding "age") have continued significance after twenty years. Also, observe that there are no significant predictors of "Workmen's Compensation claims" and "on-job injury."

Table 6-IV presents the results of the stepwise discriminant analysis. In this table, each criterion has at most two "best" predictors. The measure of the significance of each "best" predictor is given by the *p* value in the footnote of the table. Thus, the single best predictor for *rank status* is the civil service written test total score; for *job type,* age; for *average supervisors' rating,* the Mechanical score on the Kuder Preference Record; for *automobile accidents 1958 and 1970,* scale 9 of the MMPI; and for *employment status,* the General Activity scale on the Guilford-Martin Inventory. Given the single best predictors, the second best pre-

TABLE 6-IV
SINGLE AND SECOND BEST PREDICTORS FOR THE TWENTY-YEAR STUDY

Criterion	Predictor	Classification Decision Rule for Predicting Criterion Group	Criterion Group	Reliability
Job Performance				
Rank Status	Written Test Total[c]	Test Total > 67.9	Promoted in 20 yrs.	66%
	Mechanical[c]	Test Total −.31 (Mech.) > 50.1	Promoted in 20 yrs.	72%
Job Type	Age[c]	Age $\leq$ 25.1	Patrol Duty for 20 yrs.	60%
	Mechanical[a]	Age + .07 (Mech.) $\leq$ 29.3	Patrol Duty for 20 yrs.	63%
Supervisors' Ratings	Mechanical[c]	(Mech.) > 44.9	High Average Rating	67%
Accident Record				
Auto — 1958	Scale 9 (MMPI)[b]	Scale 9 $\leq$ 59.3	No accidents in 10 yrs.	60%
	Height[a]	Scale 9 −3.6 Height $\geq$ —201	No accidents in 10 yrs.	63%
Auto — 1970	Scale 9 (MMPI)[d]	Scale 9 > 59.4	No accidents in 20 yrs.	64%
Tenure				
Employment Status	General Activity[b]	Gen. Act. $\leq$ 3.9	In service after 20 yrs.	59%

(a) $p < .10$,   (b) $p < .05$,   (c) $p < .025$,   (d) $p < .005$

dictor for *rank status* and *job type* is the Mechanical score on the Kuder Preference Record, and finally, the second best predictor for *automobile accidents,* 1958, is height.

For each single best predictor (or for each pair of single and second best predictors), a classification decision rule is also given in this table. The decision rule can be used to predict the criterion group with a given probability of correct classification. This probability is the "reliability" given in the last column of the table.

Two examples will illustrate the use of the decision rules. Suppose we wish to predict the twenty-year rank status of a new recruit based on the civil service written test total score. If his score is larger than 67.9 (see column 3) then we predict with 66 percent reliability (column 5) that he will be promoted within twenty years (column 4). If his total score is less than or equal to 67.9, we predict with the same reliability that the converse is true, i.e. that he will not be promoted in 20 years. Using both the test total and the Kuder Mechanical score of the new recruit, we predict twenty-year rank status as follows. If the quantity (test total − .31 × Mechanical score) is greater than 50.1, we predict with 72 percent reliability (an increase of 6 percentage points) that he will be promoted. If this quantity is less than or equal to 50.1, we predict with 72 percent reliability that he will not be promoted. Similar conclusions can be drawn from the other classification decision rules.

DISCUSSION

The results of the ten-year study indicate that certain biographical and aptitudinal variables (e.g., height, previous occupational status, civil service test scores and the grade in the Sheriff's Academy) as well as some psychological test variables (e.g. scales 1, 2 and 9 of the MMPI, Mechanical and Social Service scales on the Kuder, and the General Activity scale on the Guilford-Martin) are significant predictors of tenure, automobile accident risk and job performance. It is not surprising that the civil service test results are directly related to High MSPR. On the other hand, the inverse relationship of these tests with tenure may appear to be contradictory but possibly can be explained by the fact that officers with high test scores are likely to change careers within the civil service system. Interesting findings of the ten-year study include the identification of five psychological test predictors of police performance, since in fact, there has been a dearth of studies successfully using psychological tests to predict field performance (see bibliography compiled by Becker and Felkenes, 1968).

The twenty-year study indicated that seven of the predictors found significant at 10 years were significantly related to one or more criteria at 20 years. Variations in the results of both studies can be attributed to differences in the criterion variables, criterion groups, and the statistical techniques used. Outstanding predictors, recommending themselves for inclusion in a selection battery, include the Mechanical score on the Kuder Preference Record, scale 9 of the MMPI, and the General Activity scale on the Guilford-Martin. The importance of the Mechanical score is anticipated in the work of Cattell, Eber and Tatsuoka (1970), who found that mechanics and police officers have similar personality characteristics and interests. Clinical implications of a high scale 9 on the MMPI include impulsiveness and rash actions—both consistent with low MSPR (ten-year study) and increased accident rate (both studies). Finally, an elevated General Activity score is prognostic of Low MSPR (ten-year study) and short employment history (twenty-year study). Both results are consistent with the fact that high General Activity scale characterizes individuals with strong emotional reactions, mood fluctuations and personal instability.

The fact that Academy rating was a significant predictor in the Marsh study but was not significant for any criterion in the twenty-year study is probably due to the decreased sample size and to the fact that this variable was made discrete (from 1 to 7) in the twenty-year study.

CONCLUSIONS

The conclusions drawn from the ten and twenty-year longitudinal studies of police performance are threefold. First, it has been shown that various aspects of the success and performance of a law enforcement officer may be predicted by certain biographical, psychological, and aptitudinal variables. In fact, scale 9 (Hypomania) on the MMPI and the Mechanical scale on the Kuder Vocational Preference Record are two valuable psychological predictors. Secondly, the twenty-year study has reinforced some previous positive findings (e.g. Marsh, 1962, Cattell *et al.*, 1970). Thirdly, the stepwise discriminant technique was shown to be effective in determining "best" predictor variables and yielding classification procedures.

One problem with our results is a generic problem with longitudinal studies: some of the tests have undergone revision and the forms demonstrated to have validity at that time may not be generally available. This includes both the Guilford-Martin and the civil service test. Finally, since the role of the officer is changing (Silver, 1967), there is increasing need for research into the selection of qualified personnel, including new definitions of successful job performance.

REFERENCES

Afifi, A. A. and Azen, S. P.: *Statistical Analysis: A Computer Oriented Approach.* Academic Press, New York, 1972.

Azen, S. P., Snibbe, H. M., and Montgomery, H. R.: "A longitudinal predictive study of success and performance of law enforcement officers." *Journal of Applied Psychology* (in press).

Becker, H. K. and Felkenes, G. T.: *Law Enforcement: A Selected Bibliography.* Scarecrow press, Metuchen, New Jersey, 1968.

Cattell, R. B., Eber, H. W., and Tatsuoka, M. M.: *Handbook for the Sixteen Personality Factor Questionnaire.* Institute for Personality and Ability Testing, Champagne, Illinois, 1970.

Guilford, J. P. and Martin, H. G.: *Guilford-Martin Temperament Profile Charts.* Sheridan Supply Company, Chicago, 1934.

Hathaway, J. C. and McKinley, J. C.: *The Minnesota Multiphasic Personality Inventory.* Psychological Corporation, Minneapolis, 1943.

Kuder, G. G.: *Kuder Preference Record, Vocational, Form C.* Science Research Associates, Chicago, 1951.

Marsh, S. H.: "Validating the selection of Deputy Sheriffs." *Public Personnel Review, 23,* 41-44, 1962.

Silver, A.: The demand for order in civil society: A review of some themes in the history of urban crime, police, and riot. In Bordua, D. J. (Ed.): *The Police.* John Wiley and Sons, New York, 1-24, 1967.

SECTION **II**

POLICE AND
THE COMMUNITY

INTRODUCTION

THIS CHAPTER DELINEATES A CONTROVERSIAL DIRECTION MANY URBAN POLICE DEPARTMENTS HAVE TAKEN IN THE PAST FEW YEARS. THE COMMUNITY-RELATIONS MODEL REPRESENTS AN ATTEMPT ON THE PART OF VARIOUS DEPARTMENTS TO RE-OPEN LINES OF COMMUNICATION BETWEEN POLICE AND THE COMMUNITY. THE TASK, OF COURSE, IS AS COMPLEX AS IT IS INNOVATIVE. POLICE COMMUNITY-RELATIONS ALSO HAS BECOME A NEW SPECIALIZED ROLE FOR POLICE OFFICERS. THIS NEW DIRECTION HAS PROMPTED INNOVATIVE RESEARCH PROGRAMS, NEW COMMUNITY-RELATIONS MODELS AND INSTITUTES. THIS CHAPTER REPORTS ON SIGNIFICANT STUDIES IN THIS AREA.

THE TROJANOWICZ ARTICLE IS A DISCUSSION OF PROBLEMS AND FALSE ASSUMPTIONS THAT HAVE PLAGUED COMMUNITY-RELATION PROGRAMS IN THE PAST. SUGGESTIONS FOR CHANGE AND REDIRECTION, HOWEVER, REPRESENT A SUBSTANTIAL CONTRIBUTION TO THE FIELD.

EISENBERG'S REPORT IN PROJECT PACE IS THOUGHTFUL, CREATIVE AND TIMELY. HE ALSO SUGGESTS DIRECTIONS FOR REEMPHASIS IN POLICE COMMUNITY-RELATION PROGRAMS.

THE FINAL TWO CHAPTERS IN THIS SECTION REPRESENT EVALUATION OF SEPARATE BUT SIMILAR PROGRAMS DEVELOPED TO MEET THE NEEDS OF BOTH COMMUNITY AND POLICE. EACH IS UNIQUE BUT ADDRESSES ITSELF TO PROBLEMS THAT MAY WELL DETERMINE FUTURE DIRECTIONS OF LAW ENFORCEMENT IN OUR SOCIETY.

Chapter 7

POLICE COMMUNITY RELATIONS: PROBLEMS AND PROCESS

ROBERT C. TROJANOWICZ

INTRODUCTION

TYPICALLY, police-community relations programs are established to help the community better understand the role and
problems of the policeman. One of the specific goals is to reduce
tension through communication between the police and minority
groups within the community.

The police-community relations concept, however, can be elusive and ambiguous. Because of this, the functional process of
establishing police-community relations programs does not necessarily follow the good intentions of the designers of the program.

The purpose of this paper will be to discuss and identify some
of the difficulties and faulty assumptions that exist when police-
community relations programs are initiated. The paper will also
describe an action process that will facilitate the effective establishment and perpetuation of such programs.

DEFINING THE ROLE OF THE POLICEMAN

Not only is the police-community relations concept often elusive, role and expectations of policemen in our ever-changing
society is likewise not well defined. The lack of a well defined
role contributes to the public's perception of the policeman as an
authoritarian symbol of government. He then becomes the recip-
ient of much displaced hostility and resentment.

Even traditional police functions and methods are presently
being challenged, further contributing to the policeman's feelings

Reprinted from *Criminology*, Vol. 9, No. 4, February, 1972 by permission of the
publisher, Sage Publications, Inc. and with permission of the author.

of frustration and abandonment by the community. These feelings are often compounded and increased for the policeman assigned to a police-community relations unit.

The police-community relations officer not only feels abandoned by the community, but he is often rejected by his own police peers, many of whom do not acknowledge that a police-community relations unit is a legitimate or necessary function of a police department. Even the uncertainty of the role of the "regular" police officer often provides more security than the role of the police-community relations officer.

To further complicate the situation, the officer assigned to the PCR unit (especially in small and medium-sized departments), many times does not actively seek or desire the position, but is assigned to the unit because of factors other than personal motivation.

Thus, the uncertainty of the policeman's role in general, the compounded uncertainty of the police-community relations officer's role; a lack of legitimacy and well-defined goals and functions for the PCR unit; plus the possible absence of motivation and commitment by the PCR officer can all contribute to a dysfunctional PCR program.

DYSFUNCTIONAL ASPECTS OF SOME PCR PROGRAMS

Defining the role of the "regular" policeman is difficult even though many of his activities, such as patrol, traffic control, and investigation, are routine and specific.

Defining the role of the PCR officer is even more difficult because of the intangible and abstract aspects of his job. He is expected, for example, to "develop positive lines of communication," help "reduce prejudice," and explain "the role and functions of the police" in the contemporary community (explain a role that is at best loosely defined) .

Because of this abstract nature of many of his duties and the lack of well-defined role expectations, the PCR officer naturally attempts to make these functions more concrete, so that his job will be more absolute and predictable. The result is that he tries to make his functions routine and apply simple formulas to such complicated concepts as "prejudice," "role perceptions," and "communication process." Routinization of functions does not solve his problem. It complicates it because the artificiality of routinization is perceived by those persons (both internally and externally) who are supposed to be influenced by the PCR program.

Another result of the PCR officer's attempt to define his duties more absolutely is that he confuses the PCR concept with public relations. The PCR program often assumes characteristics not unlike those of public relations programs in industry or business. A public relations program in industry emphasizes "selling the company" to the public. The PCR officer who utilizes a public relations approach is often perceived by the community as a "sweet talker." He is rejected especially by minority group segments of the community because they feel that his "singing the praises" of the department are overplayed and in some cases unwarranted.

Furthermore, in public relations, there is little room or necessity for feedback and involvement by the public. Conversely, in order for a PCR program to be effective, I feel the process of influence has to be reciprocal. The views, perceptions, and the inputs of the community are mandatory. In addition, the community has to be kept involved in the planning, implementation, and operation of the program if the program is going to be successful and responsive to the needs of the community. An effective PCR program that involves the community should be influential and instrumental in producing change and innovation in the police department so that the department will be more effective in serving the total community. The process for securing perceptions, inputs, and involvement by the community will be stated later.

Finally, the PCR officer does not fare any better in his endeavor to define his role and make his duties more absolute when he seeks to utilize the services and expertise of resources external to his department.

Most often he looks to the university for answers to his problems. He oftentimes finds or perceives the university as alien and hostile as the community to whom he is trying to respond. Because of his unwelcome reception and the "new and radical" concepts that are presented to him, he reacts with suspicion and skepticism, and sometimes retreats back to the secure confines of the "station-house."

He often views the academician with the same disrespect and distrust that the officers within his own department view him. The PCR officer feels that the academician has failed to develop positive lines of communication between the university and the police department, yet the academician is attempting to teach the positive communication process between the police department and the community, two subsystems that have normative orientations much greater in variance than do universities and police departments. The same "phony" inconsistency that the community perceives of the police department's public relations approach is also perceived by the officer when he makes contact with the university. The process for rectifying this dilemma will be discussed later.

THE SELECTION OF THE PCR OFFICER

Not only are PCR units often hastily and vaguely defined, they are many times, as mentioned previously, not considered a legitimate or necessary function of a police department. PCR programs are often introduced reluctantly by police administrators because of community and political pressure. Hence, persons assigned to the PCR unit are often considered "outcasts" or "pseudo policemen."

The "outcast" role can affect the amount of positive influence that the PCR officer can exert in his organization. Furthermore, if he is perceived positively by the community, the positive perceptions will not be generalized to the rest of the department by the community because of his "outcast" or "pseudo policeman" role.

It is an enigma that the very unit of the department that is established to facilitate positive communication between the department and the community is unable, many times, to communicate effectively with the other units within the department.

The selection process for the PCR officer can also contribute to ineffective intra-organization communication. Motivation and commitment are usually prerequisites for effective job performance. As mentioned earlier, the officer assigned to the PCR unit often does not actively seek the PCR unit position but is assigned to the unit for other reasons.

He may be selected because of some personal characteristic (such as being a member of a minority group), or because of factors that are considered unique for a police officer (a college degree), but which may or may not be functional for the effective operation of a PCR unit. (The person may also be selected from outside of the department which may be viewed negatively by the "police fraternity.") If the selection criteria is not considered functional, the program will have difficulty gaining legitimacy and may be perceived as a "phony do-gooder outfit" (intraorganization criticism) or a token "white-wash job" (community criticism).

The officer can also be selected for negative personal characteristics by the skeptical administrator. It has been said that some administrators assign an officer to the PCR unit because the officer was not adequate or successful as a "regular" officer performing the traditional police functions of patrol, traffic control, or investigation. If an officer is selected for the PCR unit because he was dysfunctional in traditional tasks, this not only has ramifications for the effective operation of the PCR program, but also for the transmission of positive intra-organizational communication which can be a factor in producing change and innovation in the department.

When the PCR officer is not respected by his peers because he was dysfunctional as a "regular" officer, then his sphere of influence for positive change within the organization is limited and the legitimacy of the PCR unit within the department will be continually questioned.

Hence, the skeptical administrator can subvert the PCR program by selecting dysfunctional officers for the PCR unit. The influence and operation of the unit is "doomed to failure" when this technique is utilized. If the unit proves dysfunctional, the skeptical administrator can proudly state, "I told you so."

Responding to the Community

In the past the policeman "on the beat" did not many times have a major problem relating to the community. Hence it was not usually necessary to develop specialized units concerned with relations between the police and the community.

The policeman "on the beat" was in constant contact with the public (often living in the same community). He understood their concerns, could empathize with their feelings, and was cognizant of their perceptions.

Because he understood the community and could respond directly to its needs, it was not necessary for him to learn the "communication process." He was communicating effectively in his day to day contacts.

Because of many factors, including urbanization, and the impersonal nature of present communities, the concept of the policeman "on the beat" no longer exists. Programs have had to be developed that teach the communication process and "condition" and train the policemen to respond effectively and appropriately to the citizens of the community. The direct extended "face to face" relationship between policemen and citizens is missing and the conditioning approach becomes artificial and superficial, the communication process sterile. Verbalizations often replace positive action, because the policeman is no longer as concerned or influenced by both formal and informal community sanctions and pressures.

In addition, the situation is much more complicated today. The policeman "on the beat" was many times of the same ethnic background as the residents in the community he was policing. This increased his identification with the community. Today the policeman, especially in the inner city, is not only physically removed from "the beat," he is many times psychologically removed because of a different ethnic or racial background. He has difficulty understanding the culture, life style, and value orientation of the community. Hence, it is much more difficult for him to identify with their needs, concerns, and life style.

Because of this, many officers tend to evaluate as deviant, behavior that is different but still within the parameters of acceptable conduct. Decisions are often made that negatively effect the community because the officer does not understand the community residents or the process of involving them in decision-making that affects their lives and the process of social control.

Hence most PCR programs are initiated, defined, and implemented without the benefit of community input. When there is not reciprocal involvement, the program will usually be a public relations effort with emphasis placed on "expounding the company line." This type of program is self-defeating and will only compound an already serious problem.

A MODEL FOR ACTION: NORMATIVE SPONSORSHIP THEORY

The normative sponsorship theory approach to community problem solving has been utilized to assist communities develop programs such as establish more positive relations between the police and the community. The theory was originated and developed by Dr. Christopher Sower, Professor of Sociology at Michigan State University.

Simply stated, normative sponsorship theory proposes that a community program will only be sponsored if it is normative (within the limits of established standards) to all persons and interest groups involved.

One of the major considerations when attempting to initiate community development programs is to understand how two or more interest groups can have sufficient "convergence of interest" or "consensus" to agree on common goals which will result in program implementation.

Each group involved and interested in program implementation must be able to justify and, hence, legitimize the common group goal within its own patterns of values, norms, and goals. The more congruent the values, beliefs, and goals of all participating groups, the easier it will be for them to agree on common goals. The participating groups, however, don't necessarily have to justify their involvement or acceptance of a group goal for the same reasons. (Sower, Christopher et al., *Community Involvement,* The Free Press, Glencoe, Illinois, 1957.)

Whenever areas of consensus and agreement are being identified between groups with a different normative orientation, it is important not to deny the concept of self-interest. As pointed out above, it cannot be expected that all groups will have common or similar motivations for desiring program development. Self-interest is not dysfunctional unless it contributes to inter-group contest or opposition and diverts energy that should more appropriately be directed at problem solving.

Programs which follow the tenets of normative sponsorship are more likely to succeed than those which do not. Violation of this process usually results in apathy or even concerted subversion and resistance to program development.

Before the normative sponsorship theory process is explained, it will be illuminating to provide an example of a community that has been successful in utilizing this approach.

This method has been most successful in communities where there are several interest groups and a diverse orientation to problem solving and the expression of needs. An account from the Kerner report states that:

> As the riot alternately waxed and waned, one area of the ghetto remained insulated. On the northeast side (of Detroit) the residents of some 150 square blocks inhabited by 21,000 persons had in 1966 banded together in the Positive Neighborhood Action Committee (PNAC). With the professional help from the Institute of Urban Dynamics, they had organized block clubs and made plans for improvement of the neighborhood. In order to meet the need for recreational facilities, which the city was not providing, they had raised $3000 to purchase empty lots for playgrounds (challenge instead of conflict).
>
> When the riot broke out, the residents, through the block clubs, were able to organize quickly. Youngsters agreeing to stay in the neighborhood, participated in detouring traffic. While many persons reportedly sympathized with the idea of rebellion against the "system," only two small fires were set—one in an empty building. (*Report of the National Advisory Commission on Civil Disorders*, Bantam Books, 1968, p. 96.)

The PNAC neighborhood was organized and its positive programs developed using the concepts of normative sponsorship theory. (One of the programs is a viable police-community relations program which includes a scooter patrol, the closest thing to the policeman "on the beat.") The above quotation illustrates that when people are actively involved in the community problem solving process and have some control over their own destiny, they will respond positively and effectively to the implementation of community development programs.

The quote also illustrates two other important concepts of normative sponsorship orientation to community development. First, the role of the Institute of Urban Dynamics was one of providing technical assistance. The technical assistance concept is much different than many contemporary assistance roles. Too often assistance means (either directly or indirectly) "paternalism" or co-option of community problem solving.

Effective technical assistance recognizes the vast amount of human resources within the community and the peoples' willingness to develop positive community programs if their efforts are appreciated and if they are meaningfully involved in the problem solving process.

Technical assistance, according to our definition, does not mean co-option. It means making readily available, assistance to help the community "plug into" available and appropriate resources. Technical assistance is provided only upon community request. After the specific assistance is rendered, the technical assistance unit withdraws until further requests are made. It is interesting to note that as the community becomes aware of available resources and learns the "problem solving process" (which many of us take for granted), their requests for assistance decreases.

It is important to point out that it takes a special type of professional to operate effectively in a technical assistance role. He must be competent and knowledgeable in the areas of resource identification and problem solving, yet he must avoid a "dogooder" or "paternalistic" approach. He is not expected to "save the world" only help make it run more smoothly.

The second important concept that the above quote illustrates is that challenge is a more effective means of program development than is conflict. Normative sponsorship theory postulates that programs that challenge the "skeptics" through involvement, participation, and cooperative action, will be more effective than programs that are conflict-oriented. Not only do the "skeptics" and "cynics" gain support when there is conflict, interest groups (in the case of PCR, the police and the community) polarize their positions—the community makes unreasonable demands, while the police react by over-justifying their position and actions. The longer and more intense the conflict, the less chance there is to develop and identify consensus points from which viable programs can be developed and implemented.

In sum, the technical assistance role is more conducive to community involvement and participation than are contemporary approaches. Many contemporary "experts" who have attempted to provide "expertise" to PCR problem solving have "come under fire" from both the community and the police. The community feels that external "experts" have been high on verbalization and low on action. The "experts" many times expect the community to act as a "human laboratory." The "experts," however, do not have a "stake" in the community, and many times are unconcerned about the frustration and disruption they create because of promises they fail to keep.

The police feel that the "expert" although teaching communication and emphasizing empathy is unwilling himself to empathize with the police and understand that the police are usually merely a reflection of the larger "power structure" of which the "expert" is also a part. The policeman feels that if the "expert" would provide him with alternatives for action rather than merely castigate him, then he would be more receptive to constructive criticism and "new and radical" ideas. A technical assistance unit assumes a neutral position in problem solving, emphasizing cooperative action not disruptive verbalizations. Cooperation can also be an elusive concept if normative sponsorship theory is not utilized as a model.

RELEVANT SYSTEMS

Before programs that necessitate cooperation of more than one group can be implemented it is necessary to identify the relevant interest groups (relevant systems). In the case of police-community relations there are two major relevant systems, the police and the community (especially that segment of the community where positive communication and cooperation needs facilitation). The following is a brief description of the systems relevant to the development of a PCR program.

The Police System

The police department is a governmental agency established to preserve the peace, maintain law and order, service the community and respond to its needs.

The Community System

The community is a group of people living within the geographical boundaries of a governmental unit who are dependent on services provided by that governmental unit. The police department is one of the service organizations.

The technical assistance unit whose services are secured by the relevant systems is not a relevant system itself because it is usually not an integral part of the community. It is a neutral external resource.

The discussion of relevant systems can be somewhat general and abstract. The logical question to be asked is how can these relevant systems be made manageable so that perceptions and areas of consensus can be identified and viable programs initiated? This is the beginning of the normative sponsorship process.

Step Number 1: The Identification of Leadership

To make each relevant system manageable, leadership people interested and concerned with solving the problem of inadequate relations between the police and the community will have to be identified. There are persons within any relevant system who are able to reflect the system's norms, values, and goals, and are knowledgeable about how it functions. They also exert a great deal of influence and their opinions and suggestions are respected and implemented.

They may hold a position in the formal structure of a community orgainzation such as an officer in a block club or they may hold a command rank in the police department. However, they may not have a formal position in either a community organization or the police department but yet exert influence through the informal structure.

Identification of these leaders is accomplished through a process of sampling members of the relevant organizations and asking such questions as:

"Who do you or most of people in the organization go to for advice on problem solving?"
"Who in the organization is respected, has power and influence and has the reputation for getting things done?"

After the sampling process is completed it is possible to construct a list of those individuals whose names have been mentioned most often as leaders. The sampling process is important for leadership identification. It should not be assumed that sampling is not necessary because leaders are already known. Leadership is not static and those persons *assumed* to be leaders because of their formal or informal position are not necessarily the major source of power or influence. The identification of "true leadership" is mandatory if the process of program development and implementation is to be successful.

Step Number 2: Bringing Leaders of Relevant
Systems Together

After leaders have been identified in each relevant system the next step is to bring the leaders together for a meeting. It will be explained to them that they have been identified by their peers as influential leaders interested in the area of police-community relations.

The initial meetings (the meetings are chaired by a technical assistance advisor) will be somewhat unstructured. The major purposes of the initial meetings will be to:

1. Facilitate the expression of feelings about the apparent problems.
2. Encourage the exchange of perceptions between relevant systems about each other.

3. Produce an atmosphere conducive to meaningful dialogue so that misperceptions can be identified and the constellation of factors that contributed to the causation of the problem discussed.

4. Identify self-interest, pointing out from the self-interest standpoint of the police, that cooperative problem solving will make their job easier. There is also self-interest for the community because effective program development will increase police responsiveness to the community's needs.

It is not the purpose of the initial meetings to produce attitude changes or develop a "love relationship" between the relevant systems. Attitudes will change when positive perceptions between the systems increase and when meaningful involvement and positive behavioral action is initiated and carried out.

Whenever there are diverse interest groups assembled together there will be biased opinions, misinformation, and negative perceptions. If there is extensive defensiveness by the relevant systems and if an atmosphere of freedom of expression does not prevail then the initial stages of the process will be hindered which can have implications for future program implementation.

In my experience with groups who are assembled to discuss police-community relations there are initially many accusations made by the community toward the police and vice versa. Police, for example, are accused of brutality and authoritarianism while the community is accused of complacency and lack of cooperation. If there is a too hasty denial of the accusation, if "elements of truth" in the accusations are not handled in an honest manner, if the constellation of factors that contributed to the problem are not identified and if perceptions are not discussed then the communication process will be shallow and the total problem will not be understood.

The technical assistance advisor can play a very important role in these early stages. He can help control the meetings so that they are not monopolized by one interest group or that expression of feelings do not become inappropriate and offensive to the point of disruption and ultimate disbandonment of the group. He can also help clarify the issues and provide insight into the problem and reasons for its existence. This will help support the relevant systems in the expression of feelings and in explaining their perceptions of this complex problem.

The admission of obvious facts such as the police acknowledging that brutality does exist (it is readily admitted and acknowledged within the police fraternity) to varying degrees among some departments and among some policemen will transmit to the community that the police are "reality-oriented" and willing to honestly look at the situation. This will facilitate understanding and cooperation by the community and establish credibility when the police make future positive statements of fact about their organization that will have to be accepted on "good will" or hearsay by the community.

The communication process should be more than merely the denial or the admission of fact. It should also include a discussion of the constellation of factors that can contribute to, for example, police brutality. It could be mentioned that the police are no better or no worse than the community in which they are operating and that they are merely a reflection of the feelings and expectations of the community power structure. If brutality exists, it is usually tacitly approved of by the political "powers that be." Likewise if the police department is utilized as a controlling force to contain minority groups within the inner-city, this again has the tacit approval of the political structure and the larger dominant community. A logical and "in-depth" discussion of the problem will not only facilitate understanding but will eliminate the role of "scapegoat" for policemen, reducing their defensiveness.

Conversely, the community can admit the obvious reality facts in terms of their lack of cooperation with the police. Because it may be a "fact" does not mean the situation cannot be remedied and the reasons for this behavior identified. Inner-city residents, for example, perceive the police department many times as an "occupation force" that controls and contains minority groups within the inner-city. The common perception among many black citizens is that police officers today are no different than the county sheriff of the past who often mobilized and either led or tacitly approved of attacks against blacks. Even though this is an over-generalization, today the perceived possibility of brutal treatment by the police of a peer takes precedence over cooperating with the police to control crime and apprehend offenders. The admission of "reality facts" by the systems when the facts are evident will increase credibility and trust and provide a basis for future understanding and cooperation.

After the first few meetings which are usually typified by the unstructured expression of feelings, the admission of "reality facts," the discussion of the constellation of contributing factors, the facilitation of understanding and the increasing of positive perceptions, the meetings begin to take a more focused and a less emotional orientation. If the initial meetings have achieved the purposes listed above then the stage is set for the next phase of the process, the identification of areas of consensus and dissensus.

Step Number 3: The Identification of Areas of Consensus and Dissensus

In the third stage of the process, the matrix method is utilized for the identification of areas of consensus and dissensus. In dealing with this kind of methodology, Ladd appears to have made a very important contribution. (John Ladd, *The Structure of a Moral Code,* Harvard University Press, 1957.) He obtained the following kinds of information for each of the major positions of the small society which he studied. This same kind of information will be helpful in understanding the relevant systems involved in PCR.

a. What are the prescriptions of expected behavior?
b. Who makes these prescriptions?
c. To what extent is there consensus about the prescriptions?
d. Who enforces them?
e. What are the rewards for compliance?
f. What are the punishments for deviance?

As illustrated in Table 7-I, this kind of information as well as additional information can be assembled into a matrix pattern for the analysis of any system or systems.

TABLE 7-I
DIAGRAM OF THE MATRIX METHOD OF IDENTIFYING AREAS OF
CONSENSUS AND DISSENSUS

Norms and Behavior Perceptions Held By:	*Norms and Behavior Perceptions Held About:*	
	The Police Department	*The Community*
The Police Department	*Self Concept* 1. Perceived Norms and Expected Behavior as it Relates to PCR 2. Description of Actual Behavior 3. Defined as: a. Normative b. Deviant 4. Statement of Alternatives for Problem-Solving	1. Perceived Norms and Expected Behavior as it Relates to PCR 2. Description of Actual Behavior 3. Defined as: a. Normative b. Deviant 4. Perception as to What Alternatives the Other System Will Select for Problem-Solving
The Community	1. Perceived Norms and Expected Behavior as it Relates to PCR 2. Description of Actual Behavior 3. Defined as: a. Normative b. Deviant 4. Perception as to What Alternatives the Other System Will Select for Problem-Solving	*Self Concept* 1. Perceived Norms and Expected Behavior as it Relates to PCR 2. Description of Actual Behavior 3. Defined as: a. Normative b. Deviant 4. Statement of Alternatives for Problem-Solving

This method serves as a vehicle for visually and objectively comparing the perceptions among and between relevant systems. For example, the perception the police have on their role in PCR (self-concept) can be compared with the perception that the community has of the police role and vice versa.

The perceived roles of the systems can also be compared with the actual behavior of both systems and then an evaluation made regarding whether the behavior is deviant or normative, functional or nonfunctional. Finally the statement of alternatives for problem solving of each system can be compared with the perceived expected alternatives. It may be learned, for example, that the alternatives contemplated by each system are not incompatible or as different from each other as originally perceived.

As a result of the intra and intersystem comparisons it then becomes an easy task to compile the information about how each system expects and perceives both its own members and members of the other systems to behave. From this it is not a difficult research task to classify the categories of information as either normative (that is as it should be) or deviant (different than it should be) to the relevant systems.

A special usefulness of the matrix method of arranging the findings is that it provides a means for detecting the chief nexus points of normative consensus and dissensus among and between the systems.

Step Number 4: Program Implementation

After areas of consensus and dissensus have been identified, a program can be developed which will incorporate the areas of consensus so that the program will be normative to all systems. The systems won't necessarily agree or have consensus in all areas but there will usually be enough common areas of agreement so that cooperation and sponsorship will be predictable.

It will be surprising and enlightening to the relevant systems, after using the matrix method, to learn how many areas of consensus are present, which at first glance, after a subjective evaluation, would not be considered to exist. There generally will be consensus on major goals such as the need for positive relations between the police and the community, the need for more positive and effective communication between the two systems, the need for more responsive service by the police, and the need for more cooperation by the community. Areas of consensus may decrease as specific techniques for problem solving are identified and alternatives for program implementation are suggested by each system. This will be a minor problem however because if the normative sponsorship process has been followed then an atmosphere of cooperation will prevail and compromise will be facilitated.

Step Number 5: Quality Control and Continuous Program Development and Updating

As is the case with any viable program there is a constant need for quality control and continuous program development and updating. There needs to be meaningful feedback and reciprocal involvement and program evaluation by the relevant systems as well as individual and system introspection.

CONCLUSION

The normative sponsorship theory method has been used in many situations to assist communities in problem solving. Presently we are using the method to link the university to the community through extension courses. The extension course can serve the same general purpose as community meetings if the courses have a wide variety of participant representation. The same type of problem-solving process, as it relates to PCR, that was described earlier in the paper can be facilitated in the classroom. The classroom is conducive to meaningful communication and the transmission of ideas and feelings. Furthermore, there are not the organizational constraints and pressures which many times inhibit the communication process. The instructor can function in the same technical assistance role that was described earlier for the technical assistance advisor. Community improvement projects can be initiated in the community through a cooperative team effort. The team (which is composed of representatives of all groups) can return to the classroom periodically to provide feedback and receive inputs and an objective evaluation of their project by the instructor and class peers.

In summary, a meaningful police-community relations program (which ultimately facilitates community problem solving) results only through a cooperative "first-hand" experience in the problem-solving process of the relevant systems. A maximum of active involvement and a minimum of shallow verbalization will facilitate cooperation and mutual understanding between the police and the community.

The most effective means of motivating people is to transmit to them that their opinions will be valued, that they will have a voice in decision-making over their own affairs and that they will be kept involved in the decision-making process. Programs will be sponsored and perpetuated if the above criteria are adhered to because the concerned parties will have a personal investment in the process.

There is much skepticism and distrust of the police, especially in the inner-city, because of the past and present behavior of some policemen. These negative perceptions can only be destroyed through action programs which involve both the community and the police in a reciprocal cooperative process. When this is accomplished, the police will demonstrate through actual behavior that they are concerned about responding positively to the needs of the community.

Furthermore the problems of dysfunctional PCR programs discussed earlier in the paper will be eliminated. The PCR officer will have less uncertainty about his role because the PCR program will be defined more concretely as a result of cooperative input by both the community and the police. He will also not "fall into" the public relations "trap" because as a result of joint police-community involvement he will have learned, through a first-hand experience, the reciprocal communication process on which effective PCR programs have to be established. He will also better understand such abstract concepts as prejudice because they will have become more meaningful, understandable, and concrete as a result of his actual involvement with the community.

The success of a PCR program will not only necessitate commitment and involvement by the community and PCR officers, it will also require commitment by police administrators to the PCR concept. They will have to give the program a chance by assigning officers who are functional, adequate, and respected by their peers. As pointed out earlier in the paper, an effective PCR program that involves the community should be influential and instrumental in producing change and innovation in the police department so that the department will be more effective in serving the total community.

Even more important, however, is that after problems have been identified and discussed in depth both the police department and the community can together exert pressure on the political structure and the economic power points in the community to respond to the problems and provide resources for their alleviation. In other words, effective problem solving will necessitate the mobilization of the efforts and resources of the entire community. (The police department cannot do it alone nor can it continue to occupy the role of convenient "scapegoat.") This, coupled with the process previously described, will guarantee meaningful program development and program implementation which will create a new normative relationship between the police and the community that will be mutually beneficial.

"The nature of the group (and group goal) serves to fulfill certain needs of its members, and the satisfaction of these needs is its function. Through the symbolic system of the group, its roles, role-systems, and norms, individual behavior is differentiated and at the same time integrated for the satisfaction of needs, the fulfillment of its functions." (Greer, Scott A., *Social Organizations,* Random House, New York, 1955, p. 24.)

Chapter 8

PROJECT PACE: AN ATTEMPT TO REDUCE POLICE-COMMUNITY CONFLICT

TERRY EISENBERG

THE DISCUSSION in this chapter focuses on a description of Project Pace (Police and Community Enterprise), a two-year police-community relations training and action program which was conducted in the City of San Francisco between 1969 and 1971.[1]

It is to be emphasized that the PACE program was *not* just another study. Although there was a study phase, this component of the program served as an input to, not a product of, the subsequent phases. PACE was designed and operated as a local, social-action program.

The chapter is divided into three sections. Part I contains a description of the model employed, emphasizing its methods and processes. In Part II, the results of the program are discussed. Finally, Part III focuses on the implications of the PACE project to present and future police-community relations programming.[2]

THE PACE MODEL
The Background

"Symptons of loss of faith in the law enforcement establishment are increasingly manifested among this country's citizenry,

---

[1]Project PACE was funded by the Ford Foundation under Grant No. 690-0200. Although persons undertaking projects under Ford Foundation sponsorship are encouraged to express freely their professional judgments, findings and conclusions, points of view or opinions stated in this chapter do not necessarily represent the official position or policy of the Ford Foundation.

[2]Project PACE was conducted while the author was with the American Institutes For Research (A.I.R.). A full and complete final report of the PACE program may be obtained by contacting A.I.R., 8555 16th Street, Silver Spring, Maryland 20910.

especially minority group members. This is evidenced by increases in crime rates and riots; by community indifference; by charges of police prejudice, brutality, and disrespect for citizens; and in complaints of lack of police protection. On the other side, police officers frequently appear to have lost faith in the country's leaders and citizens. They indicate that they function under strong political pressures coupled with undue restraints upon their activities; that they are held accountable for most social ills, but are accorded low status and respect by the community; that they have little opportunity for redress of grievances; and that they must perform a tremendously complex job under conditions which, at best, are frustrating."

These observations are quoted from the original PACE program proposal completed in October of 1968. The proposal was addressed to the topic of policy-community relations and how they might be improved. It was believed that the reclamation of the lost middle ground necessary for the de-escalation of antagonisms and the resolution of differences could be accomplished by mobilizing the good will and good sense of responsible members of the community and of the law enforcement establishment.

Belief in this premise was partially based on seven years of experience the American Institutes of Research had acquired overseas in the context of troop-community relationships. In reviewing these experiences, it was found that many important analogies existed between cross-cultural relations abroad (i.e. Korean-American relations) and subcultural relations here in the United States (i.e. police-community relations). For example, in the overseas experience, one of the critical issues isolated which created hostilities between Americans and Koreans was foreign aid. Americans basically felt that we were giving money away to people who did not want to work and who were lazy. The analogous critical issue in the police-community relations context was welfare. It was believed that there were many other applicable analogies.

It was not just the seven years' experience overseas which provoked consideration of the troop-community relations model to a police-community relations context, but also the successes the previous program had achieved. Through extensive evaluations, it was found that the troop-community relations program in Korea was quite successful measured in terms of both attitude and behavioral change. For example, in terms of attitudes, there was a reduction in the percent of Americans holding the view that local people were to blame for anti-Americanism (e.g. Americans came to realize that they were, at least in part, to blame for anti-Americanism). In terms of behaviors, it was found that the number of offenses committed by host nationals against U.S. personnel during the period of the project was reduced by approximately 50 percent.

By virtue of these and other success indices and the similarities between soldiers interacting with indigenous peoples and policemen with citizens, the troop-community relations model was converted for use in a police-community relations context. Explicit to this conversion was a thorough understanding of police-community relations programs which had previously taken place in this country. This understanding evolved through a review of the literature and consultations with a large number of people who had been intimately involved in the police-community relations field. In this regard, people from the following organizations were consulted: U.S. Department of Justice (Community Relations Service and Law Enforcement Assistance Administration), Ford Foundation, Potomac Institute, Michigan State University, Howard University, Houston Police Department and the International Association of Chiefs of Police.

The Approach

The original PACE proposal was designed to consist of three major components: (1) the conduct of a series of attitude surveys to assess feelings of police toward citizens and citizens toward police; (2) the development and presentation of educational materials based on the analyses of attitudes to *both* police and citizen groups; and (3) the implementation of individual and group action programs designed to improve the police-community relationship. These three conceptual elements were translated into four operational phases with each phase composed of a number of specific tasks.

Phase I, *the planning study,* was designed to focus on the selection of police districts to be involved in the program; the creation of local and national advisory groups; the recruitment, orientation, and training of staff; the search for criteria to evaluate program effectiveness; the development of measurement instruments; an understanding of historical and contemporary police-community relations programming which operated in the selected city; and the development of tactics for dealing with program publicity.

Phase II, *data collection and analysis,* was composed of a number of tasks including attitude measurement, instrument refinement, and criteria data collection and analysis.

Phase III, *training and action programs development,* was to focus on curriculum development and testing; acquisition of educational facilities; the specification of group size, composition and time schedules; visual aids development; publicity tactics for the program; development of an action programs catalogue; and discussion leader recruitment, selection and training.

Finally, Phase IV *training and action programs implementation,* was to be addressed to the presentation of lecture-discussions to participating policemen and residents, program evaluation and revision, implementation of individual and group action programs, and program institutionalization.

Accurate and comprehensive reporting and documentation procedures would be maintained throughout the four phase operational plan.

In summary then, the PACE program was designed to identify the critical police-community relations issues as perceived by police and citizens; to then utilize this attitudinal information and supporting educational materials to shatter various myths and misunderstandings which each group endorses of the other; to identify and implement bright and/or sensible ideas proposed by participating policemen and citizens which are expected to be potentially effective in improving the police-community relationship; and finally, to provide continuity to the initial two-year program through institutionalization.

The Objectives

". . . to progressively and constructively induce and sustain socially desirable behavioral changes among police and citizens . . ." "The behavioral modifications expected include both verbal (i.e., attitude) and performance (i.e., action) dimensions."

These statements taken from the original proposal reflect the broad definition of objectives set for the PACE program. More specifically, the proposal articulated the following objectives: (1) police and citizen attitude changes; (2) behavioral and institutional changes (e.g. a mechanism for policemen to express dissatisfaction with the establishment, recruitment of more minority-groups officers, a youth education program conducted by law enforcement personnel, etc.) ; (3) mass media changes; and (4) program acceptance by police and community.

RESULTS OF THE PACE PROGRAM

The results of the PACE program can perhaps best be organized by reference to the three major conceptual elements or components described earlier.

Attitude Surveys

The conduct of attitude surveys among residents and policemen was primarily for the purpose of identifying the critical police-community relations issues in San Francisco. Without going into great detail concerning various procedural issues, which are discussed at length in the PACE final report, it can be said that in the conduct of the attitude surveys few problems were encountered and the data obtained were considered to be reasonably accurate and valid by the program staff. With the assistance of local police and resident interviewers who were recruited, selected and trained by the PACE staff, critical subpopulations of policemen and residents were identified. Policemen were sampled primarily by duty assignment; residents primarily by geographic location and socioeconomic position.

Both individual interviews and group-administered questionnaires were employed. A total of 459 interviews was conducted;

216 policemen and 243 residents. Of the 216 policemen, 22 were non-white. Of the 243 residents, 68 were white, 122 were Black and 53 were Spanish-speaking. Based on the interview data, a list of 10 critical police-community relations issues was developed.

FIG 8-1

CRITICAL POLICE - COMMUNITY RELATIONS ISSUES

I   *Non-police department city agency factors:*
     effects of other city agencies including the courts, corrections, education, employment, etc. (Citizen).

II   *Police service factors:*
     ghetto protection, response time, community control, citizen complaints, firearms policy, police procedure, rights of policemen, etc. (Citizen).

III *San Francisco police department internal factors:*
     favoritism and preferential treatment, police-community relations personnel and unit functioning, black and white police officers associations, tactical squad and PCR unit, etc. (Citizen and Police).

IV   *Understanding and cooperation factors:*
     restraints on both sides, courtesy vs. weakness, fear of retaliation, press, cooperative crime prevention and control programming, the arrested/accused and the victim, etc. (Citizen and Police).

V   *Brutality, abuse and harassment factors:*
     verbal and physical abuse, respect, overreaction, name-calling, authority, superiority and inferiority, etc. (Citizen and Police).

VI   *Silence and dissent factors:*
     dissent vs. subversion, peer vs. individual reactions, social change processes, silent majority and guts, blue power, etc. (Citizen and Police).

VII *Judgment and physical appearance factors:*
     fear, dress, incident observation and interpretation, apology vs. effigy, the inital contact, assumption of guilt, etc. (Citizen and Police).

VIII *Welfare, poverty, crime and race factors:*
     interrelationships, comparative wealth differentials, motivation, racial intelligence, self-respect, causes of crime, etc. (Police).

IX   *Customs and cultural factors:*
     sanitation, sexual morals including pimps and prostitution, the minority family, language and slang, food preferences, parental control of offspring, live for today phenomenon, etc. (Police).

X   *Employment, education, health care, housing factors:*
     racial differences and causes, relationships to human behavior and crime, survival, etc. (Police).

This list of issues is presented as Figure 8-1. From the interview data, 80 specific questions, (eight in each of the ten categories) were developed and administered to additional samples of policemen and residents. Using statements requiring responses on a five-point Likert scale, 758 questionnaires were completed; 412 policemen and 346 residents. Approximately 16 different units within the police department completed the questionnaire ranging from community relations to tactical squad personnel. Some 17 different resident groups completed the questionnaire ranging from local government organizations to neighborhood self-help clubs.

The questionnaire data were analyzed in such a way as to provide the PACE staff with comparisons in attitudes between policemen and residents on each of the 80 questions. In this way similarities and discrepancies in attitudes could be identified. To provide the reader with a feeling for this data and the manner in which it was analyzed, two of the ten critical police-community relations issues with their corresponding set of eight questions and responses are presented as Figures 8-2 (Police Service Factors) and 8-3 (Brutality, Abuse and Harassment Factors).

From this data, both attitudes held in common and discrepant attitudinal positions were identified. Attitudes held in common in various areas (e.g. the processing of citizen complaints) were used in the subsequent police-resident discussion sessions to serve as a point of similarity and as a basis for entertaining the notion that perhaps the police-community relationship could be improved. Discrepant attitudinal positions identified areas of curricula research needed to "move" both parties closer together (e.g. firearms policy). Although it was recognized that some discrepancies existed in fact and could not be reduced or closed (e.g. police response time in Black neighborhoods), others were a question of myth or misunderstanding (e.g. use of the tactical squad) and did lend themselves to attitudinal convergence.

The attitude survey data along with supporting curricula research and information (i.e. poverty, race, welfare, delinquency, crime, sex, marriage, sanitation, and slavery; patrol procedures, departmental organization and policy, police recruit selection, citizen complaint processing, police commendations and awards, promotion and transfer, and others) constituted much of the substantive content of the subsequent discussion sessions composed of both policemen and residents.

FIG. 8-2

II POLICE SERVICE FACTORS

	Strongly Agree	Moderately Agree	Neutral	Moderately Disagree	Strongly Disagree
Citizen complaints should be processed effectively, fairly and quickly.	BWP				
The majority of the Black community want more police protection in their neighborhoods.	BP	W			
Policemen should become more constructively involved with school-age children and adolescents.	PW	B			
More policemen on the beat would improve the police-community relationship.	B	W	P		
Firearms policy applicable to the police should be revised and stated more clearly.		PW	B		
When utilized properly, the SFPD's Tactical Squad is an important aspect of police department activities.	P		BW		
An all-Black community controlled police department is the best solution to the Police-Black community relations problem.			BW		P
Regardless of the reasons, Police repsonse time is slower in Black neighborhoods than in White neighborhoods.	B		W	P	

P = Policemen,   B = Black residents,   W = White residents

FIG. 8-3

V   Brutality, Abuse and Harassment Factors

	Strongly Agree	Moderately Agree	Neutral	Moderately Disagree	Strongly Disagree
There is too much name-calling on *both* sides.	BP	W			
Name-calling by policemen adversely affects the citizen.	PW	B			
Some policemen have been guilty of either physical or verbal abuse of citizens.	B	PW			
Name-calling by citizens adversely affects the policeman.		PW	B		
If name-calling on both sides was stopped, the police could do their job better.		PW	B		
The current status of Police-Black community relations today in San Francisco is excellent.			W	B	P
Policemen give the impression of feeling superior to Black people.		B	W	P	
Statements of police brutality and harassment are sometimes a consequence of misunderstanding or lack of information about the situation.	P		BW		

P = Policemen,   B = Black residents,   W = White residents

Discussion Sessions

The City of San Francisco is divided into nine police districts. Three of these nine districts were selected for inclusion in the PACE program. The selected districts were all "difficult problem areas" as measured by just about any index of social disorder.

All policemen assigned to each district were required by Departmental order to participate in the discussion sessions. Residents were recruited from within the geographic boundaries of each police district. Although initially an attempt was made to involve residents without any form of financial compensation, it was found that participation could be greatly improved with nominal compensation. Participating policemen received compensatory time for their off-duty involvement in the discussion sessions.

Police and resident discussion leaders were recruited, selected and trained by the PACE staff. The use of lay discussion leaders proved to be effective although during the discussion sessions, the PACE staff monitored and occasionally assumed direction of the session and dialogue. The three police districts were taken one at a time. The scheduling and sequencing of discussion sessions was rather complicated but generally consisted of eight groups (four police and four resident) of approximately 15 members each in each police district. Each of the eight groups were exposed to six three-hour sessions over a period of six weeks. During the first two sessions, all resident and police groups met separately. For the remaining four sessions, the groups were mixed (i.e., composed of both policemen and residents), but each resident group consistently met with one group of policemen. Each participant, whether policeman or resident, was exposed to a total of 18 hours of discussion.

The six-week discussion session format basically consisted of three parts. The first part, consisting of the separate sessions, was designed to establish a constructive climate for the up-coming mixed sessions. The second part, composed of the first two mixed sessions, was designed to promote understanding of divergent points of view and to expand the base of awareness and causes of good and poor police-community relations. Finally, the third part, consisting of the last two mixed sessions, was designed to solicit bright and/or sensible ideas from the participants which were bilaterally endorsed and amenable to implementation efforts by the PACE staff.

During the separate sessions, attempts were made to shatter misconceptions and myths, reduce the pervasive use of exaggerations and set the occasion for future meaningful and constructive dialogue. Another purpose of the separate sessions was to describe the PACE program to the participating policemen and civilians. Since the PACE program was met with substantial skepticism among both residents and policemen, many questions were asked about the purposes and objectives of the program. These questions had to be dealt with as early as possible in order to move on to the critical police-community relations issues.

Because the initial separate sessions were so important in determining the value of future mixed sessions, two detailed 40-minute orientation lectures were developed for use in the first separate meeting with resident and police groups. A number of critical points were made including: the historical consequences of internal turbulence in determining the survival of a country or civilization; the role that each of us plays in improving police-community relations; the importance of the survival value; the impact of a "superiority complex;" and some specific police-community relations issues including police brutality and prejudicial press. For instance, one point we tried to make with policemen was the impact of individual police behavior on the entire police community relationship. A remark made by an ex-San Francisco policeman during the curricula development task was used during the orientation. In making the above point, what he said was, "It bothers me when I see policemen act like a jack-ass, because he may be putting a gun to *my* head." This comment proved to have great impact. One point we tried to make with civilians related to the issue of police brutality and why some policemen may overreact in a particular tense situation. During the interview task, we were discussing this very issue with members of the San Francisco Police Department's Tactical Squad, a special unit trained to deal with civil disorders and serious crimes against persons. One of the remarks made was, "I'd rather apologize than be dead." This comment proved to have substantial impact on residents in providing a greater understanding of police brutality and overreaction.

The separate sessions proved invaluable and most likely prohibited the blowups and walk-outs frequently characterizing straight encounter sessions between residents and policemen which have typified many historical police-community relations programs. Not a single incident of this type occurred during the PACE program. During the last separate session, police and resident groups were given giudelines or tips on how to make the most of the forthcoming mixed discussion sessions.

Curricula materials were brought to bear on the discussion as appropriate. Usually, this would take the form of providing the groups with factual data in the absence of such data or when data was presented by a participant erroneously. For instance, allegations would often be made by residents that the police department doesn't process citizen complaints nor discipline its own men for police malpractice. On these occasions, it was brought to the attention of the residents that in 1969 some 220 citizen complaints were investigated; that of this number approximately 40 were sustained representing 17.5 percent; and finally, that the disciplinary actions taken involved a loss of some $20,000 in police salaries. On the other side, allegations would often be made by policemen that Blacks are poor because they simply do not want to work and are lazy. When these statements were made, the following facts were offered: that Blacks will not occupy 10 percent of the clerical jobs in this country for approximately 20 years at the present rate of change (35 years for skilled jobs and 150 years for sales jobs) ; that black high school and college graduates earn $\frac{3}{4}$ as much as their white counterparts; and that between 1954 and 1964 there was only a change of $\frac{1}{2}$ percent (55.5 to 56%) in the average black family income in comparison to the average white family income. Other data were presented on related topics such as education and welfare.

Numerous visual aids were employed during the discussion sessions. Many of these are presented in the PACE final report, but to provide the reader with some feeling for these aids, a number of attitude data training charts are provided in **Figure 8-4.**

Fig. 8-4

Attitude Data Training Charts

More dialogue is needed between diverse groups such as the Black Panthers and the Tactical Squad.

	BLACKS	POLICE	
YES	V	V	NO
	74%	54%	

The press reports the facts of incidents objectively and fairly.

		BLACKS	POLICE	
YES		V	V	NO
		62%	90%	

Black people would rather be on welfare than work for a living.

		POLICE	BLACKS	
YES		V	V	NO
		70%	83%	

If Blacks and Whites can join together against a common enemy overseas, they can do the same here against crime and poverty.

	BLACKS	POLICE	
YES	V	V	NO
	86%	80%	

At the very beginning of the PACE program, it was decided to recruit those kinds of residents who were not favorably disposed toward police and the law enforcement establishment; residents who were likely to be extremely critical of police and often involved in confrontations with them. This strategy was explicit in the kinds of groups contacted and in discussions with recruiting resource people and staff. "Tea-parties" were to be strictly avoided. Preponderantly, the residents participating in this phase of the PACE program were poor and/or young; in either case, having little power or influence in modifying the establishment, city government and the police.

The recruitment of residents proved to be very difficult and consumed a great deal of staff time. As the reader might expect, there was substantial skepticism and feeling that nothing would really change as a consequence of the discussion sessions. Other programs, which had previously been conducted in the city, were cited as a basis for this feeling. However, successful recruitment of those kinds of residents desired was effected in the first police district. However, because of the difficulties encountered, some groups of residents in the next two districts were financially compensated. This tactic slightly reduced the complexity of resident recruitment efforts. Generally, a *group* of residents composed of 15 to 20 people would receive between $50 and $200 for the entire six sessions. All successful resident recruitment efforts were effected by PACE staff making personal contacts with leaders of various groups and organizations.

Resident participation in the three police districts consisted of the following 11 groups: homophiles (N=15), adult probation officers (N=10), two black teenage youth groups (N=30), juveniles on probation (N=15), drug addicts (N=15), a group composed of people from San Francisco State College, the ACLU and a half-way house for ex-offenders (N=15), staff from a district EOC office (N=10), businessmen (N=10), law school students (N=15), and staff and youth from a neighborhood self-help organization (N=15).

In summary then, a total of 150 residents, organized into 11 groups, *consistently* participated in the discussion sessions along with a comparable number of policemen also composed of 11 groups. It should be realized however, that many more residents and policemen participated in some of the discussion sessions. *Consistent participation* has been defined in terms of attendance at all separate and mixed sessions involving 18 hours per participant. If partial participation were to be included in the numbers cited above, they would almost be doubled for both residents and policemen.

For those policemen and residents who *consistently* participated in the discussion sessions, it was indeed a meaningful experience accompanied by indications that attitudes on *both sides* were modified. Some of these attitude changes and participants' views of the PACE program are briefly discussed below.

The discussion sessions were evaluated by participants in the first two police districts. (The absence of an evaluation in the third and last district is discussed in depth in the PACE final report.) Evaluations were limited to determining the attitudes of policemen and residents on two different forms. One form consisted of 20 questions which were completed by the participants *both before and after* the discussion sessions. The second form consisted of 12 questions which were completed by the participants *only after* the discussion sessions. Highlights of the *before and after* evaluation include:

A change from 71 to 83 percent among the first district policemen and a change from 55 to 81 percent among the second district policemen responding "yes" to the question, "Do you *personally* respect most Black people in the district where you work?"

A change from 47 to 57 percent among the first district policemen and a change from 34 to 56 percent among the second district policemen agreeing with the statement, "Poverty and wealth are primarily determined by geographic location and environmental conditions."

A change from 27 to 57 percent among the second district residents responding "yes" to the question, "Do you *personally* respect most policemen in this neighborhood?"

A change from 69 to 40 percent among the second district residents agreeing with the statement, "The only person who would help a policeman in trouble would be another policeman."

In appraising these encouraging attitude changes, a number of issues must be kept in mind. First of all, some ground was lost on a number of issues and not all changes were positive in nature. Secondly, it is conceivable that the positive changes cited above were, in part, caused by attrition among participants in the police and resident groups. The number of participants who completed the "after" questionnaire was always fewer than the number who completed the "before" questionnaire; there is no reason to believe that the attrition was "random."[3] Finally, the evaluations are limited to verbally expressed attitudes which may have no association with the actual behavior exhibited by residents and policemen on the street. Highlights of the *after only* evaluation include:

The PACE program was evaluated by policemen in the first two districts as being the second most meaningful and valuable *formal* police-community relations activity of seven that were listed. (It is interesting to note that the Police Athletic League was considered to be the most important and the San Francisco Police Department's Community Relations Unit to be the *least* important.)

64 percent of all first district policemen and 51 percent of all second district policemen felt that the PACE program should be continued for an indefinite period of time.

The PACE program was evaluated by residents in the first two districts as being the *most* meaningful and valuable *formal* police-community relations activity of seven that were listed.

51 percent of all first district residents and 40 percent of all second district residents indicated that they changed their minds about certain issues as a consequence of participating in

[3]A fourth police district was used as a "control" to test the validity of attitude changes in the first two districts. No important changes occurred between before and after administrations of this questionnaire on any of the 20 questions.

the PACE program. (Qualitative analysis of this question indicated that approximately 75 percent of the responses were positive in nature.)

Action Programs

The original PACE proposal called for an action programming phase which would be effected subsequent to the completion of the police and resident discussion session phase. This phase would be devoted to the implementation of bright and/or sensible ideas proposed by residents and policemen during the preceeding two phases; ideas or programs which appeared to have the endorsements of both sides. It became apparent shortly after completion of the first phase that it would be best to conduct the second and third phases concurrently; that is, to implement ideas or programs at whatever time they developed as long as they met the basic criteria of potential effectiveness and bilateral endorsement.

At least 30 ideas or action programs were identified. With few exceptions, these ideas came from policemen and residents during the survey and discussion phases. The latter phase provided a forum for the discussion and evaluation of proposed ideas and programs. On a number of occasions, inputs made by residents and policemen resulted in the modification and detailing of ideas which were subsequently submitted to the San Francisco Police Department for consideration in regard to implementation.

Of the some 30 action ideas catalogued during the PACE program, 17 were extensively pursued. Ten were successfully implemented, five were rejected by the Department and two were not completed.

The ten action programs which were successfully implemented either solely through PACE efforts or with the assistance of other local organizations are briefly described and evaluated below:

1. A two-pronged police recruitment strategy involving the utilization of policemen to recruit applicants along with provisions for compensation to those policemen who successfully recruited. This feature was coupled with a tutorial program conducted by police academy personnel for those interested applicants who would be taking the written Civil Service En-

trance Examination. No data were acquired on the success of this strategy, but based on conversations with the Director of Personnel for the San Francisco Police Department it appears to have been effective. As a matter of fact, for the first time in many years, the San Francisco Police Department was at full authorized strength.

2. A suggestion system within the San Francisco Police Department allowing for suggestions by policemen to be submitted to the administration. Adopted suggestions result in financial compensation to the policeman and a number of suggestions have been implemented by the administration. This action program was not implemented solely as a consequence of PACE efforts but with its very early support.

3. A reemphasis of the importance of explaining to residents why they may have been stopped for questioning on the street by policemen after the decision had been made not to effect an arrest. This procedure was discussed during a patrol bureau staff meeting held by the supervising captain with the presumption that the procedure would be communicated to all district station policemen by each of the nine district captains. No data are available on the extent to which this procedure was effectively communicated to the rank and file.

4. A police-conducted tutorial program entitled, Project "PAIRS" (*P*olice *A*cademic *I*nstruction *R*eaching *S*tudents) whereby policemen would tutor on a one-to-one basis elementary school age students having difficulty with reading and mathematics. Inquiries about the program among policemen, students, teachers and parents suggested that the program was moderately successful although on a very small scale.

5. A drug use and abuse conference conducted in cooperation with the Community Relations Unit of the San Francisco Police Department. Guest speakers included the president of the board of supervisors and the chief of police. The one-day conference was composed of experts presenting papers in the morning and workshops in the afternoon. Over two hundred people attended representing a wide range of organizations concerned and involved with the drug problem in San Fran-

cisco. No information is available on the outcome or follow-up to this conference.

6. A jail reform conference conducted in cooperation with "Citizens Alert," a local residents group historically concerned with citizen complaints against policemen. Speakers included the president of the board of supervisors and various experts in jail reform and criminology. The afternoon of the one-day conference was devoted to a number of workshops. Over 300 people attended this conference. No information is available on the outcome or follow-up to this conference.

7. In-service training of experienced patrolmen and sergeants in the areas of human and community relations was conducted by the PACE staff. One-hour training sessions were conducted with 11 groups of policemen totaling approximately 300 men. This training was conducted independently of and in addition to the discussion sessions earlier described. No PACE evaluations were performed, although departmental-initiated appraisals obtained from the participants were very favorable.

8. Recruit training in the areas of human and community relations in conjunction with descriptive information on the PACE program was conducted by the PACE staff. Three different classes of 50 recruits each were involved for periods of from two to four hours. No PACE evaluations were performed, although departmental-initiated appraisals obtained from the participants were very favorable.

9. Discussion sessions between the San Francisco Police Department's Community Relations Unit and patrol force police personnel in the first two district stations. These sessions were especially effective in bridging the long-standing gap in communication and understanding between these two police groups. The PACE staff initiated, planned and moderated these sessions. One tangible outcome was the initiation of a periodic newsletter entitled "Insight" which is designed to improve relationships between community relations unit and patrol force police personnel. Three issues had been published before the PACE program was completed. A critique of these

sessions by the commanding officer of the first district station was very favorable.

10. A meeting among seven of the nine key administration of justice agency heads in San Francisco to discuss ways and means of improving inter-agency relationships. The following agencies were represented; usually by the agency head: public defender's office, district attorney's office, sheriff's department, police department, juvenile probation department, adult probation department and the juvenile court. No representatives appeared from the municipal and superior courts. The only significance which can be attached to this action program was that it was the first time these agency heads sat down together as a group to discuss the inadequacies of the administration of justice system in San Francisco and how they might be resolved. However, it was a start and a move in the right direction.

The five action programs which were *not* adopted by the administration of the San Francisco Police Department are briefly described below:

1. A plan for the reorganization of the community relations *mission* within the San Francisco Police Department which basically called for broader-based programming involving more district station police personnel; civilian conducted police-community relations efforts; the community-relations unit; and the complaints, inspection and welfare unit which processes citizen complaints. This proposed reorganization would pull together a number of presently independent and autonomous activities which are directly related to police-community relations. In addition, it was proposed that the mission be administered by a police officer with substantial rank in the San Francisco Police Department thereby providing greater administrative support for and coordination of the police-community relations mission.

2. A series of 13 one-half hour TV talk shows addressed to various critical police-community relations issues. Discussants would be composed of a wide range of residents and police-

men. A number of TV stations were interested in sponsoring the series and providing the necessary production inputs. This TV series would have provided the vehicle necessary to pervasively display to a large audience of residents and policemen the dynamics and configuration of police-community relations in San Francisco.

3. The utilization of a credible and legitimate member of the homophile community to address police recruits and policemen in the police academy on the topic of homosexuality.

4. With the recent availability of monies from the Department of Justice through the Law Enforcement Assistance Administration, it was suggested that *at least* one policeman be assigned to function *full-time* in a proposal writing and funding capacity.

5. The creation of a special unit within the San Francisco Police Department charged with the responsibility of investigating and studying those circumstances surrounding the assaults and shootings of policemen. The objective of such an effort would be to reduce the frequency with which they might occur in the future through the modification of police policy, procedure, training and management.

Two additional action programs were seriously explored involving substantial PACE staff efforts. A lack of time and resources prohibited their completion and likely implementation. These program ideas are briefly described below:

1. The identification and utilization of genuine alternatives to incarceration which exist in San Francisco with administrative sanctions for their use by policemen. The first part of this action program was completed whereby all genuine alternatives and gaps in alternatives were identified.

2. A pamphlet entitled, "The Police and You" which would be distributed to thousands of residents in San Francisco. Contents of the pamphlet would focus on citizen rights, citizen responsibilities, and the shattering of numerous myths and misconceptions which residents endorse concerning policemen, police policy and police operations. Drafts of the

pamphlet were reviewed by the San Francisco Police Department's legal department and approved for publication. The draft pamphlet came to the attention of the Hayward (California) Police Department, and at the time of completion of the PACE program was being adapted to the city for subsequent publication by the Hayward Police Department.

In addition to attempts to implement action ideas, which were in part, successful, a number of positive incidents and observations are worthy of noting. These are briefly discussed below:

1. The absence of strong and sincere top administrative support for the PACE program can be contrasted with the relatively high level of support from most of the policemen directly involved in the program. Policemen who functioned as interviewers, discussion leaders, curricula developers and participants in the discussion sessions were, with few exceptions, very supportive of the PACE program. The previously mentioned fact that the PACE program was rated second only to the Police Athletic League in terms of formal police-community relations programs which have or were currently being conducted in San Francisco documents this support.

2. While attending a rally addressed to the "War on Dangerous Drugs" conducted by "Youth For Service," a viable youth servicing agency, the author got to talking with a former Black San Francisco policeman who had been a severe and outspoken critic of the PACE program. By virtue of what the program had accomplished at that time he said, "PACE is *really* doing some significant things in police-community relations." Although he spoke specifically of the community relations unit and patrol force discussion sessions which PACE had conducted, he mentioned a number of other things including the critical points we had been trying to make with policemen during recruit, in-service and district station discussion sessions.

3. During the conduct of the PACE program, effective working relationships were established with close to 100 local community organizations.

4. During the discussion sessions in the third and last

district station when police participation began to seriously dissipate,[4] participating residents came to strongly endorse the PACE program requesting that it be continued and that the PACE staff should do whatever they could to bring more policemen into the sessions. In one case, when one combination of police and resident groups had to be aborted halfway through the six weeks, the leaders of the resident group actually felt bad that the sessions would be discontinued. This is especially significant in that this particular resident group had a history of extremely poor relations with the police and represented the most "militant" resident group involved in the PACE program.

5. In attempts to continue the PACE program, a letter of endorsement was received from Mr. Orville Luster, the Executive Director of "Youth For Service." This gentleman has directed an organization in San Francisco for the past twelve years which has provided many needed services to the minority communities in the City. His reputation in San Francisco is pervasive and outstanding having been honored by the Chamber of Commerce and appointed to the Mayor's Committee on Crime. During the last six months of the PACE program, he became a very strong supporter saying that, ". . . has taken a great step to develop new techniques in breaking down the barrier of the police relations in the ghetto . . ."

6. A fight broke out between Black and Samoan students at a local high school in the third PACE district. The first officer on the scene was one of the PACE program police discussion leaders who cooled down the situation and suggested that the two groups of students have a meeting the following day to try and resolve their differences. This officer was requested by the watch lieutenant of the third district to mediate the upcoming meeting *by virtue of the officer's experience with the PACE program.* The meeting was held and mediated by the officer with very encouraging and fruitful results.

---

[4]A full treatment of the experiences encountered in the third district, which were substantially different from those in the first two districts, is discussed in the final report of the PACE program.

7. Upon completion of the discussion sessions in the first PACE district, a police sergeant assigned to that district requested transfer into the Community Relations Unit of the San Francisco Police Department. His transfer, which was subsequently approved, *was based on his experiences with the PACE program* and a desire not only to improve police-community relations but also relationships between community relations police personnel and patrol force personnel. Subsequent to transfer into the Community Relations Unit, this sergeant was instrumental in setting up discussion sessions between community relations and patrol force police personnel to resolve their differences. He also played a vital role in initiating the Community Relations Unit's newsletter, "Insight."

8. The PACE program, while in San Francisco, experienced some 14 significant treatments by the press and numerous radio and television accounts. In addition, as of the present time, interest has been expressed in the program by people from 60 cities in 30 states.

IMPLICATIONS OF THE PACE PROGRAM

Program Impact

A reasonably strong case supporting the PACE program is evidenced from the preceeding discussion. Certainly the reader must agree that some modest but nevertheless real accomplishments were effected by the program. To summarize, these accomplishments were program survival, bilateral attitude change, meaningful bilateral participation, successful action program implementations, interest in the program among non San Francisco residents and policemen, adherence to the original "game plan," positive incidents of bilateral behavioral change and the incorporation of program evaluation procedures.

In the final report of the PACE program, three major improvements (i.e. techniques for increased visibility and impact, improved curricula, and greater support from city and police department officials) and a number of minor improvements were suggested. The assumption implicit in these suggested improvements was that their manifestation would carry the model closer to achieving greater accomplishments. In addition to these suggestions, a number of explanations were offered to account for the fact that at the end of the initial two-year period the PACE program would not be continued nor institutionalized. The explanations offered were essentially based on a lack of necessary support for the program among city and police department officials. The absence of a sufficiently high level of support was not solely attributed to such officials but was also created by virtue of programming errors made by the PACE staff.

Yet it must be concluded that in the presence of greater city and police department support coupled with the incorporation of the major and minor suggestions for improvement, the PACE model and others like it must be seriously questioned as to their viability and ability to significantly reduce conflict between the police and the community. The ultimate fact of the matter is that with all the energy, skill and financial resources which were devoted to the program, it was not continued nor institutionalized; it "reached" a very small percentage of the 700,000 residents and 1800 policemen in San Francisco; and finally, it did not install stable behavioral changes even among a significant proportion of the *participating* policemen and residents.

At best, traditional police-community relations efforts and programs (Are there any others?) *may* help polarized groups better communicate with one another, *may* increase their understanding of one another; and *may* result in additional efforts to work toward more productive working relationships. *At the same time, these things are not synonymous with the reduction of police malpractice, the reduction of unprovoked verbal and physical abuse of policemen by citizens, nor the effective prevention and control of crime.* "Police-Community Relations," as we have known it, is deserving of a quiet and respectful burial.

I offer nothing specific to replace "Police-Community Relations." However, I should like to place the topic in perspective.

Complexity of the PCR Concept

"The Black kids and the white cops—their pride, their fear, their isolation, their need to prove themselves, above all their demand for respect—are strangely alike: victims both, prisoners of an escalating conflict they didn't make and can't control." This quote taken from Colin McGlashan of the London Observer, partially depicts and captures the complexity of the police-community relations concept.

In addition to the attitudes and behaviors exhibited by citizens and policemen toward one another, the following factors all have an impact on the police-community relationship: ineffective courts and corrections systems; the Vietnam War; unenforceable and absurd morals laws; inequities and inefficiencies in city services such as public health, public works, employment, education, housing, transportation and recreation; biased and prejudicial press; the tradition of Southern police department operations; the activities of adjacent police departments; poor and/or nonexistent parental supervision; ineffective police training, supervision and management; the rhetoric of left and right-wing groups; and the activities and special interests of political hacks. Each of these factors, in its own unique way, determines the nature of the police-community relationship at any time, in any city. Among residents, hostilities are directed toward the police largely because of unresponsive and unresponsible city administration and what are preceived to be misguided national priorities. Among policemen, hostilities toward residents occur because of unresponsive city and police department administration and the fact that they are truly a "pawn" of the establishment and society's "whipping boy."

Attempts to improve the relationship which are based on vacuum-like programming focusing solely on the principals (i.e. policemen and residents in conflict) are doomed to failure from the very beginning. Although the problem is primarily one of poor police-*minority* (i.e. not only racial) relations, the solutions lie in broader-based programming involving those who traditionally have not been involved (e.g., the wealthy businessman or industrialist). Efforts cannot be limited to involving the hardheaded militant and the raving liberal but must also include the passive "Uncle Tom," the staunch conservative and all those inbetween.

TWO POLICE ROLE DILEMMAS

I should finally like to discuss two dilemmas which presently confront the police establishment. The first is one which has been with us for some time. It can be referred to as the *mollycoddler/law and order controversy* and represents a debate concerning the question of how to deal effectively with crime and the offender; a debate whose principals are those advocating revenge versus those advocating rehabilitation.

"In sum, America's system of criminal justice is overcrowded and overworked, undermanned, underfinanced, and very often misunderstood. It needs more information and more knowledge. It needs more technical resources. It needs more coordination among its many parts. It needs more public support. It needs the help of community programs and institutions in dealing with offenders and potential offenders. It needs, above all, the willingness to reexamine old ways of doing things, to reform itself, to experiment, to run risks, to dare. It needs vision."[5]

To many people in this country, the contents of the preceding paragraph are rubbish. For them, the answers rest with more and bigger penal institutions, harsher sentences, less leniency in the courts, and more strict enforcement of the laws.

Yet, it appears now that most everyone, regardless of philosophical disposition, has come to recognize that the administration of justice system is simply and clearly not working. The need for change has perhaps finally been recognized.

At the expense of precision, let me briefly and perhaps unfairly, dispense with this first dilemma by suggesting that the "mollycoddling" and "law and order" approaches, as they have been referred to by their respective opponents, *both* contain features which make good sense. That is to say, although neither will prove effective by itself, both possess aspects of substantial merit. What seems to be called for is a compassionate and intelligent melding of their desirable features into one scheme which will work. For instance, it makes no more sense to be lenient with a serious

---

[5]Excerpt taken from *The Challenge of Crime in a Free Society;* A Report by the President's Commission on Law Enforcement and Administration of Justice; February, 1967.

criminal offender because he had a bad childhood (i.e. the strict mollycoddling approach) than it is to be indiscriminately severe with anyone who "breaks the law" (i.e. the strict law and order approach) .

The second dilemma facing the police establishment is more difficult to deal with not only because it is a relatively new controversy but because it touches upon the overall quality of life in our cities today and the manner in which services are delivered to the public. It can be referred to as the *law enforcement/public service (i.e. "helping") controversy*.

What is happening today across the country is that our police institutions are taking on more of the service responsibilities which traditionally have been the province of numerous other city agencies.[6] As a matter of fact, they have been doing this for a long time as reflected in a number of studies describing what policemen do and how they spend their time. Because the police are "open for business 24-hours a day," these activities have been performed by police personnel. What happens under these conditions is that the police get involved in every city agency's business and during their spare moments, attempt to deal with the crime problem. This may be as it should, but let us not expect them to do the latter very well.

The fact that the police currently spend 75 to 90 percent of their time in non-crime fighting, "helping" or public service activities has led to the recent development and enthusiastic endorsement of innovative projects and police training programs which have focused on the pursuit of the public service or "helping" role (e.g. Morton Brad's work in New York and Hans Toch in Oakland) . Many other efforts are presently underway to modify the police role with a concurrent reduction of emphasis in the law enforcement and crime control aspects. Many authorities, police and non-police alike, have concluded that training curricula, for example, should be programmed to fit the data; that if present police training curricula devote 75 to 90 percent on crime fighting

---

[6]The recent civilianization of some traditional police functions, such as traffic for example, is not contrary to this statement because the traffic mission, under such civilianization, has remained administratively within the police agency.

and control, it should be reduced to 10 to 25 percent and the remainder or bulk of the training devoted to curricula which is of a public service nature.

May I suggest, without going into an extended and elegant discussion of crime and social disorder in this country, that the trend discussed above should be carefully appraised. It could be a great blessing or an insidious trap. Serious crime is no myth or fiction; its reality demands preventative and controlling measures. Citizens who are victimized and who subsequently come into contact with the police, regardless of their ethnic or socioeconomic background, want equitable and respectful police treatment. They also want police protection and effectiveness; that is, the solution of crimes which have immediately brought them in touch with the police and the prevention of future similar occurrences.

The responsibility for preventing and controlling crime surely rests with every social institution, city agency and individual; each also plays a role in creating crime and social disorder. However, the police agency represents one social mechanism which has both the mission and potential capability for effectively dealing with the problem. The problem cannot be ignored. Nor can it be avoided by encouraging the police institution to dabble with the responsibilities of many other city service agencies which have failed to perform their missions effectively.

Perhaps the time has come to focus at least some of our attention and constructive criticism on the entire city services delivery system for to concentrate on but one diseased limb will surely allow the others to strangle the body.

Chapter 9

EVALUATION REPORT OF A POLICE-COMMUNITY RELATIONS LEADERSHIP TRAINING PROGRAM

LAWRENCE SOLOMON AND KENNETH VISSER

A PPROXIMATELY FOUR YEARS AGO, the National Advisory Commission on Civil Disorders (Kerner Commission) undertook a survey of 24 disorders which had occurred in 23 cities across the U.S. in 1967. The report of this Commission (1968) states that "although specific grievances varied from city to city, at least 12 deeply held grievances can be identified and ranked into three levels of relative intensity." The first item identified at the first level of intensity was "Police practices." Specifically, with regard to the police and their relationship to the community, the report stated:

"The abrasive relationship between the police and the minority communities has been a major—and explosive—source of grievance, tension and disorder. The blame must be shared by the total society.

"The police are faced with demands for increased protection and service in the ghetto. Yet the aggressive patrol practices thought necessary to meet these demands themselves create tension and hostility. The resulting grievances have been further aggravated by the lack of effective mechanisms for handling complaints against the police. Special programs for bettering police-community relations have been instituted, but these alone are not enough." (p. 17)

The training program assessed in this report may be conceived to represent a continuation of efforts to enhance the effectiveness of police-community relations. Although instigated on a statewide level, the project reported here appears particularly appropriate to the recommendations made by the San Diego Urban

This research was supported by the California Commission on Peace Officer Standards and Training (POST) and was administered by San Diego State College Foundation.

Coalition in April, 1970, in its report, "Urban Coalition Looks at Law Enforcement." In that report, the recommendation was made that:

> "The Steering Committee of the Urban Coalition should request the City Manager to retain the services of a private or otherwise independent agency to evaluate the effectiveness and quality of the human relations training offered at the Police Academy and to in-service personnel following consultation with the Police Chief, and to submit recommendations based upon such evaluation."

The present research effort seeks to evaluate the effectiveness of an experimental training program for police-community relations officers funded by the California Commission on Peace Officer Standards and Training (POST). The California State Legislature, through action in 1968 and 1969, specifically charged the Commission (functioning under the Department of Justice) to develop and implement a statewide community relations program. After examininig several proposals, POST selected three institutions to refine and develop these programs.

Subsequently, three separate projects were initiated at the University of California at Los Angeles, San Jose State College and San Diego State College. Each training program was scheduled to be repeated three times at the locations indicated, with approximately 20 trainees participating in each training session. The three training sessions conducted at San Diego State College are the focus of the present evaluation report.

The specific goals of the San Diego program were to:

1. Teach officers how to analyze communities and identify present and emerging problems of law enforcement.
2. Impart knowledge and develop analytical skills for examining responsibilities of law enforcement agencies during a period of rapid social change.
3. Develop new approaches to community-police relations based on the knowledge, skills and perceptions gained from this program.
4. Develop methods for implementing these approaches and adapting them to the needs of particular police departments.

Following guidelines laid down by POST, the course content was divided into three major components:

1. Instruction covering the study of various cultures in American society. The values and life styles of subgroups within our society were examined from the point of view of their development and intergroup similarities and differences. The behavior associated with these values and life styles which may eventually involve the police were studied.

2. Consideration of various roles of the police. Discussion focused upon the implications of interacting with many different subgroups while performing these roles during a period of rapid social change, and the conditions under which these roles are mutually supportive or conflicting.

3. Study of the forces producing and accommodating to social change. Special emphasis was placed upon the problems created by the process of change itself.

An effort was made to program approximately 134 hours of classroom instruction and 140 hours of field and laboratory experience during the six week training session. The introduction to the first training session included the following statement:

> "The methodology developed to implement the learning objectives is designed toward student experience and involvement whenever possible as an alternative to lecture and discussions. We desire this experience to be student centered, recognizing that the students themselves are, in a real sense, experts and will be responsible, as a group, for acceptance or rejection of program input."

The curriculum, therefore, contained classroom instruction (lecture and discussion and demonstration) on such topics as: understanding America as a political system, as a legal system, as a social system, as a cultural system; the role of law enforcement in today's America; police role conflict; the role of the police community relations office; and community relations skills. Additionally, simulation gaming and small group laboratory learning were employed to enhance the personal meaningfulness of the program. Internship field experiences were provided in such locales as San Diego Police Department Store Fronts, County Welfare Department, County Probation Department, Citizen's Assistance Office, Youth Services Bureau, Neighborhood Youth

Corps, Drug Education for Youth Project, and the Mexican American Advisory Committee Service Center.

METHOD AND PROCEDURE

A pre, post-testing design, with matching central group, was employed as the basic research scheme. A total of 53 police officers comprised the trainee group; the control group consisted of a total of 54 policemen, matched as closely as possible with the trainee group.

The following Table 9-I presents the number of trainees and control subjects tested during each of the three training sessions, as well as other information regarding the testing and training schedules and the characteristics of the two subject groups.

TABLE 9-I
TRAINEE AND CONTROL GROUP CHARACTERISTICS

	Session I (11/9/70- 12/18/70)	Session II (2/8/71- 3/19/71)	Session III (4/26/71- 6/4/71)	Total
Trainee Group				
N	19	16	18	53
Aver. Age	37.5	38.9	34.7	37.0
Rank				
Lt. & above	9	7	7	23
Sgt. & below	10	9	11	30
Community Relations				
assignment	10	2	8	20
Control Group				
N	15	39	0	54
Aver. Age	41.6	34.1	—	37.8
Rank				
Lt. & above	15	5	—	20
Sgt. & below	0	34	—	34
Community Relations				
assignment	0	0	—	0

Subject Population

The trainees were all active duty police officers, assigned to law enforcement agencies in locales throughout the state of California. None were from the San Diego area. Thirty-seven percent of the trainees were actively engaged in police-community relations work at the time of the training program, or had been designated to assume such an assignment upon completion of the training program.

The control group consisted of active duty police officers attending classes to enhance their understanding of law enforcement. One class (N=15) was at San Diego State College in management training; the other (N=39) was a special studies course at the police department in public administration—criminal procedures.

Measuring Instruments

A number of paper-and-pencil questionnaires were employed to assemble the pre-post data. Pretesting was conducted on the first day of a given training session; post-testing was accomplished on the last day of the training session. All three training sessions were six weeks in duration. Control group data were collected concurrently with trainee data, with the exception of data for training session III. Since a sufficient number of control subjects had been tested by the end of the second training session, it was deemed unnecessary to generate further control data during training session III.

The following tests were administered on this pre-post schedule:

The Pre-Lab Post-Lab Inventory

The Pre-Lab form of this inventory consists of 44 items on which the subject is to rate his behavior in relating to other people. The respondent is asked to check those items which he judges to be accurate descriptions of his present interpersonal and group skills in communication, listening, dealing with feelings, sensitivity, etc. An individual's score on the Pre-Lab inventory is *the number of items checked.* The higher the score, the greater number of interpersonal and group skills the individual perceives himself to possess.

The Post-Lab form of this inventory asks the respondent to check those skills in which he feels he has improved. The same list of 44 items is utilized. The individual's score is *the number of items checked.* The higher the score, the wider is the range of improvement as judged by the trainee.

Dimensions of Value Test

This test, devised by Withey (1965), is designed to assess the extent to which an individual places value upon (a) Acceptance of authority, (b) Need-determined expression (as opposed to value-determined restraint), (c) Equalitarianism, and (d) Individualism. The test consists of 12 Likert-type items, to which the respondent indicates his degree of agreement-disagreement on a five-point scale. A high score for each dimension indicates a high value placed by the respondent on that dimension.

Modified Polarity Scale

A modification of the Tomkins Polarity Scale (1964) was employed to assess an individual's position on a value dimension ranging from humanistic to normative. The scale consisted of 16 Likert-type items, similarly constructed to those of the Dimensions of Value Test, above. All items were selected from the original Tomkins scale, with selection limited to those items correlating most highly with the statement "Human beings are good" (or its polar opposite, "Human beings are basically evil").

Eight items were "humanistic"; eight were "normative." The individual's score was the difference between the summated ratings of these two sets of items. Differences were computed in such a manner that a *higher* score always indicated a more *humanistic* orientation.

Group Task

This exercise was utilized as a data generating device, although it is not psychometric measuring instrument in the usual sense. The participants were asked, on a pre-post basis, to form into two groups and do two things: (a) develop a list, by consensus, of ten objectives of a police-community relations department; and (b) rank order the first five of these in terms of importance.

Qualitative differences between the two lists so generated were assessed. This procedure was employed only with the trainee group; there was no control group data with which to make a comparison.

Additionally, the post-only assessments were conducted with the trainee group. These were as follows:

Evaluation Interview

Four trainees were picked at random at the conclusion of each training session and interviewed by a member of the research staff. The interview lasted approximately 15 minutes and was tape recorded. Each interview asked the following questions:

(a) What is your overall evaluation of the training experience? What were its strengths? What were its weaknesses?

(b) What are your short-term goals as a community relations officer? What are your long range goals?

(c) What else would you like to comment on about the last six weeks?

Transcriptions of the tapes were assessed to provide qualitative data regarding the program's perceived effectiveness.

Course Evaluation

All participants were asked to complete a course evaluation form on which they rated each component of the training program. The ratings were on a five-point scale, ranging from 1= excellent to 5= poor. Each program component was judged in terms of (a) topic, (b) presenter and (c) usefulness. The components of the program were identified for the rater by title and individual making the presentation; e.g. Civil Rights Legal Movement—Peter Clarke.

Average ratings for each program component were computed, summing over trainees within each training session. These ratings guided the modification of subsequent sessions, based upon the relative value of each component as judged by the participants.

Results

Pre-Lab Post-Lab Inventory

Table 9-II below presents the mean number of items checked by the trainee and control groups on the two forms of this instrument.

TABLE 9-II
MEAN NUMBER OF RESPONSES TO PRE- AND POST-LAB INVENTORY

	Pre	*Post*
Interpersonal Skills		
Trainee Group	19.43	16.87
Control Group	17.20	11.90
Group Skills		
Trainee Group	9.51	7.40
Control Group	7.64	4.75

On the Pre-Lab form of this inventory, the trainee group indicated that, on the average, they perceived themselves as possessing slightly more skills, both interpersonally and in group situations, than the controls indicated for themselves. For the interpersonal skills, the trainees checked, on the average, about 19 of the 28 items possible; the control group checked approximately 17. On the group skills, the trainees averaged almost 10 of the 16 items possible, while the controls averaged approximately 8. While these differences between trainees and controls are not statistically significant, there is a weak indication that the trainee group may have judged itself to be slightly more skilled in human relations than did the control sample.

The Post-Lab form measures perceived improvement. It is noteworthy that the trainee group evidences a significant increase in interpersonal skills over self-reported improvement by the controls (P < .005). There is a similar trend in favor of the trainees for the group skills; this difference is also statistically significant (P < .005).

The findings on the Pre-Lab Post-Lab Inventory are generally supportive of the training effort in that they indicate a greater degree of self-reported improvement in human relation skills for the trainee group as compared to such change in the control group.

Dimensions of Value Test

Data from this inventory were cast into a three-way analysis of variance format for statistical evaluation. The three factors assessed by this analysis were groups (trainee vs controls), testing (pre vs post) and scales (the four value dimensions indexed by the test.) None of the sources of variance were found to be statistically significant. Table 9-II (following) presents the mean sources on this test.

TABLE 9-III

MEAN SCORES FOR THE TRAINEE AND CONTROL GROUPS, PRE AND POST, ON THE DIMENSIONS OF VALUE TEST

	Pre	*Post*
Acceptance of Authority		
Trainee Group	2.67	2.52
Control Group	2.27	2.18
Need Determined Expression		
Trainee Group	3.53	3.52
Control Group	3.67	3.42
Equalitarianism		
Trainee Group	2.74	2.65
Control Group	3.40	3.21
Individualism		
Trainee Group	3.11	3.03
Control Group	3.09	3.02

The results on this inventory were disappointing in that they did not differentiate between the trainee group and the control group in terms of changes on any of the value dimensions assessed. Apparently, the values assessed by this inventory are unaffected by the training program as experienced by the trainee group.

Polarity Scale

Table 9-IV presents the mean score obtained by the trainee and control groups on the modified polarity scale. A higher score indicates a more humanistic orientation.

TABLE 9-IV

MEAN SCORES FOR THE TRAINEES AND CONTROL GROUPS, PRE AND POST, ON THE MODIFIED POLARITY SCALE

	Pre	*Post*
Trainee Group	1.37	1.48
Control Group	1.17	1.01

The trend in favor of a greater humanistic orientation on the part of the trainee group is clearly evident in these data. Although the trainee group was more humanistic than the control group to begin with, it evidences an increase in that orientation on the post measure. Change in the opposite direction is evidenced by the control group, with their posttest score moving in the direction of a more normative orientation.

Although these trends are not statistically significant (P > .10), they are clearly in the direction postulated.

Group Task

The list of five objectives of a police-community relations department, generated in the group task exercise, are presented in Table 9-V. Qualitative differences between that which was perceived to be important *prior* to training as compared to similar concerns *following* training may be observed in these data.

Review of these data reveals the following trends over the course of the training experience:

(a) A shift of focus inward, toward improving training and functioning within the police department rather than a primary emphasis upon bringing about changes within the community

(b) An increased emphasis upon *two-way* communication between police and community, rather than one-way communication from police to community

(c) A shift away from total action orientation toward one involving personal attitude changes within individuals

(d) An increased recognition of the necessity to build feedback mechanisms (evaluation) into CR programs to help assess, objectively, the effectiveness of these programs

(e) A stronger emphasis upon a participative, joint-effort orientation, with police and community cooperatively expending joint effort toward common goals

Evaluation Interview

No attempt was made to categorize or paraphrase the responses to the evaluation interview. Instead, the verbatim transcrip-

TABLE 9-V

OBJECTIVES OF A POLICE-COMMUNITY RELATIONS DEPARTMENT, AS
DETERMINED ON A PRE-POST BASIS BY THE TRAINEE GROUP

TRAINING SESSION #1 *Pre*	*Post*
Group A 1. Determine community needs 2. Determine effective programs to fit the needs 3. Assist in training officers in community relations field 4. Selection of officers to carry out program 5. Inter-department liaison	1. Provide interaction between police and community 2. Develop internal support for community relations 3. Establish comprehensive training relative to community relations 4. Provide for community input into CR program 5. Establish an evaluation (feedback) system for programs
Group B 1. Reinforce positive attitudes toward us in the community 2. Open avenues of communication with minority, youth and low income 3. Develop techniques of evaluation for CR programs 4. Education community as police role 5. Educate police officers to community problems	1. Determine attitude profile of police department by analytic methods 2. Survey community needs and develop community programs 3. Institute remedial attitude training through ALL levels of police department 4. Establish avenues of communication between police and community 5. Involve all police department personnel in CR programs

TRAINING SESSION #2 *Pre*	*Post*
Group A 1. Define the objectives of the Community-Relations Program 2. Make effective lines of communication with the community 3. Learn to listen to community needs 4. Train all police officers in community relations 5. Change the police attitudes and image	1. Promote intradepartmental understanding, and include all officers in CR effort 2. Establish better avenues of communication with other community agencies 3. Identify problems and disorders in the community 4. Develop programs to alleviate community problems 5. Establish community acceptable methods for handling grievances

TABLE 9-V—(cont.)

Group B	1. Sell CR to every officer 2. Identify particular community needs and tailor program to these needs 3. Find and open lines of communication with every sector of the community 4. Promote programs that utilize these lines 5. Broaden CR on the basis of community feedback	1. Establish and define role of police in society, and determine goals for the department 2. Total police acceptance and understanding of the CR unit and its goals 3. Bring all community resources together to help promote law enforcement and accept responsibility for maintaining social order 4. Establish credibility between police and community 5. Develop programs that involved whole department in goals of CR

TRAINING SESSION #3	*Pre*	*Post*
Group A	1. Establish priority of community needs through research and planning 2. Create communication bridges between police and community 3. Decentralize the CR to its lowest level (patrol) with coordination by CR division 4. Change image of the peace officer and present him as a human being through CR programs 5. Develop liaison between youth and police through youth programs for crime prevention and educate public in these	1. Develop lines of communications, cooperation, and understanding between police and community through research and planning 2. Utilize community resources 3. Orient and educate line officers on community problems and stress total departmental involvement 4. Develop departmental understanding of P-CR objectives and goals through training 5. Relieve tensions and conflicts through programs and develop evaluation processes
Group B	1. Encourage interdepartmental acceptance 2. Establish lines of communication between police and public 3. Encourage community involvement and participation in programs 4. Educate department employees 5. Be a clearing house for department/community problems and information	1. Crime prevention 2. Improve departmental image and acceptance by department 3. Establish lines of communications within and outside the department 4. Obtain community involvement through use of community resources 5. Accurate research and planning for CR programs

tion of replies to the questions asked are presented below, to give a fuller understanding of the quantitative assessment of the training program by the trainees. The Roman numeral at the end of each quotation indicates the training session to which the response refers.

Replies to Interview Questions

Question #1: What is your over-all evaluation of the training experience? What were its strengths? What were its weaknesses?

"It was great. Some things could have been better—the contact with the campus community. Also, there was a lack of cooperation in the internship program. Both of these areas are important.

"I have a better understanding of minority people now. I think my communications skills are also much better." (I)

"It was an excellent program and I got a lot of skills and information. Some weakness that the program had were the lack of college students. There should have been more black students involved. My internship program was a wasted day.

"Strengths included session in S.E. San Diego dealing with minority problems—a lot of good information." (I)

"It was very worthwhile. Some refining is needed. The input of law enforcement people is not necessary. We need people from the outside like the human behavior people. The school did not get behind this program and this was too bad. Facilities were a problem and getting it going the first week was a problem.

"The strengths I got are in awareness and insight in the problems of the minorities. We were exposed and this was really good because we really found out why the people felt as they did. I am much more aware. I am a bigger person." (I)

"It was a good six weeks. I wish we had more on campus time because the time that we did have was very good and we should have had more."

"It gave me a chance to see that we the police do have things that we need to do to change ourselves. Gave me more skills to know what to do, with the problems that I face from day to day—they have given us some expertise." (I)

"It gave me a better understanding of the police role in the community—especially with different cultural groups. I will be able to react more intelligently with greater awareness to the problems in our community."

"Its weaknesses—more sessions with other cultures on a one to one basis rather than always with the group." (II)

"It was extremely profitable—I am a hard core cop and this gave me some real understanding of other people so that I will be able to do the job better. I will also be able to deal with my wife and child better because of the experience that I have had here. I can relate better to the minorities. It put a lot of knowledge that I had had all together so that it makes sense. I can make decisions more wisely because of the added knowledge."

"Weaknesses—some instructors overlapped. The internships can be improved—some were not expecting us and others just did not have much to say to us." (II)

"Great program. It has helped me to understand people and the community. The youth culture was important to me. We need more youth culture stuff."

"Weaknesses—the Black culture was given by a Mexican which I thought was strange. There wasn't enough on the minorities and this includes the youth culture. Some of the instructors were not aware of the police problems." (II)

"It's been quite enlightening. More contact with the minority groups. I can relate better to these groups because of this program and where we conflict." (II)

"It was basically a good program, although there were a number of speakers that talked too long. I'm glad that I came, but it lasted too long. Also, too many of the speakers just talked from their head they didn't have anything that we could apply." (III)

"I think that this program needs to be aimed at the patrolman and not the P-CR man. The patrolman is the one that gets in with the people while the P-CR man just plans priorities and programs. As a patrolman, this program was very helpful because I got some skills that will help me relate to the people that I run into on the street every day." (III)

"The minority representation both by the speakers and the students in the program itself needs to be improved. Surely San Diego has more blacks and Chicanos to choose from. Overall, the program was good, but too often we were lectured to rather than being involved in talking with the various experts." (III)

"I think that this program has been very useful and will assist me in the field. I also have noticed attitude changes toward minorities in several of the officers in the group. They have become more tolerant in their attitudes. This type of program should be made available to every officer and to all police departments." (III)

Question #2: What are your short-term goals as a community relations officer? What are your long-term goals?

"Implementation of programs that better establish communications with the youth in our community. Interaction between school groups. Discussion of the drug problems."

"To get total community involvement in the problems of the community. This helps me in a promotion also." (I)

"Form a better relationship internally with the other departments of the police. We got to get our house in order."

"Long term goals—better rapport with the police and the community. This is preventative work and would help to reduce crime. Get into Junior Highs and High Schools and communicate with them. My own goals really didn't change that much. It strengthened my own goals." (I)

"We have a program going on right now. Get more feedback on what we are doing—are we being effective?"

"Long term—have everyone of our people attend this class. Personally, I feel that there is a need for people in the police department that are in human behavior and in other fields besides criminology." (I)

"Short term—I have to start with the head of administration and get them to change by talking to them about what I have learned. An attitude survey about what the patrolmen now think about R.R. and then see where we have to start changing within the department is a good start."

"Long range—more and more rap sessions getting in with the militants and talking about the problems that they have and really meeting them and getting to the point where neither side sees the other as the enemy." (I)

"Short range goals—instill among my men some of the insights that I have received about the groups around us and communication."

"Long range—to influence the whole state through my office. Successes would be letting other people know that my skills and insights can be learned." (II)

"I can pass on the concepts of dealing with people as people to the men that work under me. I can help the ideas of the P-CR division through my understanding. Pick two people who will come to this next school—improving our own power base."

"Long range—retire the man at the top of our P-CR division. We have to have a division that has a man that has the understanding of this type of program." (II)

"Short range—start speaking to the schools; ride along programs. We need some sort of complaint programs. At the schools I just want to sit down and talk to the kids in small groups and answer anything that they wish to talk about. I need to be more personal. I have broken my stereotypes of the kids and now they have to break theirs of me. From what I have heard from a man in our department, this is the best of the three courses that is being offered." (II)

"Short range—evaluate our practices and policies and see where we have to change. We need to build a base. Look at our structure and see what our CR program is now. I got to sell the boss on this first. I also have to do some selling to city hall. Selling the concept of CR which is community involvement."

"Long range—build programs that include the whole community, county government, welfare, probation and so on. We need to get to the youth. Doing work with kids and guiding them." (II)

"Want to work with getting my men into the High Schools and just rapping with the kids." (III)

Question #3: What else would you like to comment on about the last six weeks?

"The whole program was great." (I)

"I think that this was a good representation of the total California police from patrolmen to captains." (I)

"The program was so good that I really did not want to leave and feel sad that I am leaving now. This is not usual behavior for me." (I)

"The program was a very well structured program—everyone had the chance for their own input." (II)

"The program was very profitable. It was wise that they cut the program back from the first week. The night classes are not good because we were just tired." (II)

"The program was great, and I learned about many aspects of community work that I did not know before such as social work." (II)

"Over all, a very good program. We need more involvement with the minority cultures. Really getting in and being with families and getting down to the nitty-gritty. I need to feel the things that we were lectured on. Some program could go—some of the internships are not worth the time. Model cities could be cut out because it cannot be applied to our town. We need to evaluate after each segment of the program rather than just at the end." (II)

The lack of responses to Questions #2 and #3 from training session III may be partially explained by a note from one of the research staff, following his interviews with that final training group. He wrote, "These men seemed more tired than the other groups—or more bored. I got the feeling that they had very little emotional involvement in the program."

Generally, the replies to these open-ended interview questions appear to reflect a favorable attitude toward the training experience; that it was judged to be helpful and of practical value by the trainees; and that specific weaknesses of the training program could be easily identified for subsequent modification.

Course Evaluation

The specific responses to this questionnaire were utilized each session to assess the relative value of each component of the training curriculum. On the basis of relative ratings, some components were modified, deleted or expanded. The particular ratings of "topic" and "presenter" aided the program directors in their staffing decisions each session. Information most generally derived from this questionnaire relates to the relative "usefulness" of each lesson, as judged by the trainees. The ten lessons rated most useful in each session are presented in Table 9-VI. The number of parentheses in the body of Table 9-VI gives the average rating of the lesson on a five-point scale where 1= excellent, 2= good, 3= average, 4= fair, and 5= poor.

A review of these lessons reveals that:

(a) The participants seem to like lessons in which they can actively participate (e.g. "Star Power").

(b) They are interested in topics that are currently social issues (e.g. Black culture).

(c) The participants are interested in how others see them (e.g. the media's view of police, how blacks see police).

(d) The participants find topics useful that have direct "back home" application (e.g. communication skills, the role of a police community-relations officer).

TABLE 9-VI
THE TEN MOST "USEFUL" LESSONS IN EACH TRAINING SESSION

Training Session #1
  1. Techniques for communicating with community (1.30)
  2. American cultural system (1.35)
  3. The internship (1.53)
  4. Case study "Sunday in the Park" (1.55)
  5. Differential perception — Black culture (1.60)
  6. Community Relations teaching skills (1.60)
  7. "Star Power" Game (1.62)
  8. The role of the P-CR officer (1.63)
  9. The media's view of police (1.65)
  10. How Black see police (1.65)

Training Session #2
1. Introduction to culture (1.06)
2. "Star Power" (1.13)
3. Communications skills (1.13)
4. "Metro Politics" (1.25)
5. Personal development (1.31)
6. Overview of minority culture (1.31)
7. Program orientation (1.38)
8. Program goals and objectives (1.40)
9. Social forces and directions (1.56)
10. Black culture (1.56)

Training Session #3
1. Systems of justice (1.11)
2. Communication skills (1.17)
3. Internal police perception minority panel (1.37)
4. CR management and leadership skills (1.50)
5. Community relations (1.55)
6. Tijuana and border facilities (1.66)
7. Melting pot — urban problems (1.67)
8. News media panel (1.78)
9. Introduction to culture (1.93)
10. The road to professionalism (1.94)

Summary and Conclusion

A total of 53 police officers participated in a six-week community-police relations leadership training program. A number of pre-post and post-only assessment instruments were administered to evaluated attitudinal and perceptual chances related to attendance in the program.

As compared to a control group (N=54) which received no training specifically designed to enhance community relations understanding and skills, the trainees evidenced

(1) a significant improvement in interpersonal and group human relations skills, based upon self-ratings

(2) an increase in a humanistic perspective, as opposed to a normative orientation.

Additionally, the trainees appeared to gain

(3) increased acceptance of the need for intra-departmental training and programs in the area of community relations

(4) enhanced appreciation of the tools and knowledge of the

behavioral and social sciences, and of systematic feedback and evaluation in assessing applied efforts to improve police-community relations

(5) a greater acceptance of the need for cooperative, participative undertakings wherein police and community undertake joint efforts toward common objectives.

By all standards applied to assess this training program, it may be judged a success. The long-term, back home consequences of such a training experience, however, need assessing in order to quantify the degree to which attitudinal and perceptual learnings are translated into behavior by the community relations officer on the job. Such assessment remains yet to be accomplished.

REFERENCES

Report of the National Advisory Commission on Civil Disorders. New York, Bantam Books, 1968.

Tomkins, Silvan S.: *Polarity Scale.* New York, Springer Publishing Co., 1964.

Withey, S.: The U.S. and the U.S.S.R.: A report of the public's perspective on United States—Russian relations in late 1961. In Bobrow, D. (Ed.): *Components of Defense Policy.* Chicago, Rand McNally, 1965, 164-174.

Chapter 10

POLICE-COMMUNITY RELATIONS: THE HOUSTON EXPERIENCE

Melvin P. Sikes

THE *Report of the National Advisory Commission on Civil Disorders*, dismissed by white America and disavowed by white officialdom, identified "white racism" as the basic cause of urban riots. The Commission, which ranked "police practice" as number one among major grievances, listed Negroes in the 23 cities surveyed, found that "almost invariably the incident that ignites disorder arises from police action."[1] What may seem routine or innocuous to the police officer may symbolize a long history of injustice to the Black community.

The Commission on Civil Disorders was appointed by President Lyndon B. Johnson on July 27, 1967, approximately two months after the May 16-17 disorders on the campus of Texas Southern University in Houston, Texas. While other major cities were experiencing violent civil disorders, Houston, Texas, was busy congratulating itself for being the only major city that had experienced no violent disturbance. The incidents of May 16 and 17 shook the city out of its apathy and false security. Dr. Blair Justice, a social psychologist and assistant to the mayor, surveyed the Black community following the Texas Southern incident and found tensions rising at an alarming rate.[2] This sudden turn of events caused great concern among city officials and the business community.

A group of these business leaders met with Mayor Louie Welch and Dr. Blair Justice, his assistant for human relations, to discuss

---

Reprinted from *Professional Psychology*, 1971, 2, 39-46.

[1]U.S. Riot Commission: *Report of the National Advisory Commission on Civil Disorders* (Kerner Commission), New York, Bantam Books, 1968.
[2]Blair Justice, *Violence in the City*, Texas Christian University Press, 1969.

ways of preventing a "Watts" or a "Detroit" in Houston. Immediate intervention was deemed so urgent that these men sought a preventive "crash" program consisting of lectures to the police on how to handle minority group problems. The author, who had worked with Dr. Justice on other occasions, was asked to implement the program by delivering a group of lectures on human relations to members of the Houston Police Department.

The writer was of the opinion that any lecture-discussion approach as a means of relieving tensions and improving police-community relations would be ineffective. It would deal with problems largely at an intellectual level and fail to reach the deeper, emotional level at which the problems really exist. Most importantly, the police officers would be hearing the "measured" responses of *one Black psychologist* who could in no way speak for the Houston Black community—or more appropriately, the Houston "concerned population."

Small group discussion involving a cross section of community representatives and police officers in face-to-face relationships seemed much more appropriate. It seemed that goals of mutual understanding and cooperative endeavor might be achieved more readily and more realistically through this medium of exchange than through a series of lectures. Small group interaction would permit an exchange of attitudes and feelings as well as an opportunity to develop cooperative programs of positive action.

The suggestions of the author were accepted and after much persuasion, he accepted (reluctantly) the responsibility of developing and directing the program that was to be called the Houston Cooperative Crime Prevention Program. Community Effort, Inc. (a group of outstanding business leaders who preferred to remain anonymous) was formed by Houston attorney Gail Whitcomb to underwrite the endeavor.

DESIGN

The design and methodology of the Houston Cooperative Crime Prevention Program followed closely the model provided by the Black-Mouton-Sloma union-management intergroup laboratory for resolving intergroup conflict.[3] It consisted of a series of human relations training laboratories involving police and members of the Houston community.

The need for improved police-community relations is not solely a minority group function. For this reason, community participation in the project was solicited on a broad basis. Persons from all races, age levels, socioeconomic backgrounds, and the like were invited. A special effort was made to recruit these persons so that they could attend the meetings.

Each series of human relations laboratories was designed to accommodate 200 police officers and to last for a period of six weeks. Individual laboratories were designed to meet once each week for a period of three hours and to consist of 40 officers and an equal number of community representatives. This group then was to be divided into three separate, smaller groups that met concurrently. The series was to continue until approximately all of the 1400-man Houston police force had been exposed to 18 hours of human relations training experiences in this laboratory setting.

Doctoral level clinical psychologists and others with training and experience in the behavioral sciences were employed as group leaders. Advanced graduate students in psychology were used as assistant group leaders.

Meetings were held both at the Police Training Academy and at various community centers in predominantly minority areas of the city.

The goals of the program were simple. The Houston Cooperative Crime Prevention Program sought to create an environment and an atmosphere in which police and community representatives could exchange views and attitudes that seemed to be creating a chasm between them. Through the use of group technique it was hoped that antagonizing behaviors of both groups could be explored and examined, with a view of bringing about change. Attitudes do not change quickly, but there is sufficient validation of the fact that if behavior change can be accomplished, attitude change follows much more rapidly.

[3]R. R. Blake, J. S. Mouton, and R. L. Sloma: The union-management intergroup laboratory: Strategy for resolving intergroup conflict. *Journal of Applied Behavioral Science*, 1965, 1, 25-27.

METHODOLOGY

An exchange-of-image model advanced by Blake, Mouton, and Sloma (1965) in their union-management conflict-resolution laboratory program was employed in the initial meetings of the laboratories. This technique required that each group develop a list of self-images and a list of their images of the other group. Upon completion of this task, the two subgroups confronted each other with their lists. This exchange provided the structure and material for discussion.

Group leaders employed a number of techniques to clarify issues, to stimulate participation, and to deal with specific crises. Psychodrama, role reversal, mirroring, and "doubling" proved very effective in situations that required their use.

To achieve the goals of the program, the two subgroups examined these lists of images and stereotypes that very often proved to be not only derogatory but very damaging to the group in question. The causes and effects of these false premises as they related both to the perceiver and the perceived were discussed and means of dispelling such harmful myths were explored. A strong endeavor was made to develop in each laboratory a cooperative problem-solving attitude that might carry over into the day-to-day relationships between the officers and their public.

Lists of stereotypes and images were almost exhaustive, but there were many repetitive themes or images across the entire group of community participants as well as the police officers.

Police Self-Image

Most officers saw themselves as "police first." That is, they were dedicated, honest, well-trained, ethical, and fair. They admitted being a clannish group, both suspicious and distrustful of anyone who was not a law enforcement officer. However, these police officers saw themselves as warm, understanding, and concerned, despite the fact that the community (according to the officers) perceived of them as callous and indifferent. They felt ostracized by the community and the victims of severe scrutiny and criticism. They felt that no one understood or cared about their problems.

Police Image of the Community

Most police stated that they believed the majority of the public to be law-abiding citizens, but very uninformed about the law, as well as the duties of a policeman. Feelings about the affluent and the upper class seemed to be ambivalent. On the one hand, these people were perceived as supportive of the police, but on the other hand they were seen as feeling above the law and as using their influence to avoid penalties to which they or their children might be exposed as a result of breaking the law. The middle class was different. They were civic-minded, law-abiding, and very supportive of the police. They committed few crimes and had minimal police contact. That contact was usually the result of minor traffic violations. The lower class was seen as usually unco-operative, lackadaisical, and often in conflict with the law. They were perceived as having a different sense of values and lived by the law of immediacy. The police agreed generally on two types of Blacks—Negro and "Nigger." Whereas the "Negro" was law-abiding, respectful, not violence-prone, highly moral and industri-ous, the "Nigger" was no good. He was immoral, dishonest, criminally-inclined, lazy, and violent. Militants and Hippies? The worst!

Community Self-Image

The majority of the persons from the community admitted not involving themselves in civic affairs. They feared police and avoided being witnesses in criminal cases. Particularly was this latter self-image true of Blacks, who saw themselves as largely law-abiding, hard-working taxpayers but victims of police brutality. All segments of the community felt alienated from each other and from the police. The community felt a strong lack of knowledge about their rights, obligations, and duties regarding the law. How-ever, they did see themselves as self-respecting persons who were striving to uphold the law and to learn more about its "workings."

Community Image of Police

These images varied by race, age group, residence, and many other factors but there was rather general agreement in many areas. For instance, police were seen as persons who often did abuse their authority. They discriminated against minorities, youth, and the poor. Police were seen as cold, indifferent robots who answered only to themselves and left citizens without recourse in cases of abusive behavior by another officer. The comment was made that police officers see the world "only through their squad car windshields." No distinction was made on the basis of race when referring to a policeman. Whether the officer was Black or Mexican-American, he was viewed first as a police officer. The overall image was extremely negative.

PROBLEMS

Despite all efforts to the contrary, the program did not enjoy the luxury of a smooth, undisturbed course. The "problems" began with the naiveté of the director. As has been indicated, the Black community was angry, and a large segment of the white community had expressed concern about police actions. In view of this, the author (and director of the program) was certain that the recruitment of community persons to participate in the laboratories would be no problem. Blacks were expected to respond in great numbers. This did not happen. Fears of reprisal, harassment, and the like from the police appeared to be combined with apathy and served to reduce, drastically, the number of expected participants in the early stages of the program.

The Houston Council on Human Relations, whose Executive Director (John P. Murray) was the assistant director of the program, assumed responsibility for community recruitment and preparation. The first widely publicized call for "interested citizen involvement" resulted in a total response of approximately twelve whites and two Blacks. Community involvement fluctuated, but recruitment was extremely difficult throughout the program. Getting the desired "mix" was only rarely achieved. That is, getting a cross section of persons from various races, age groups, and the like in each laboratory was virtually impossible. On some occasions the police in certain groups were exposed to an almost totally white population. One group of police was exposed only to a youth group.

Naturally this drew severe criticism from the officers. Most of them wanted to talk only to Blacks. The comment, "We have no problems with these (white) people" was often heard in predominantly Caucasian community participation. This, of course, quickly proved not to be true—much to the surprise and chagrin of the officers. Nonetheless, some balance was achieved in most groups and gradually criticism of this situation subsided.

A more delicate situation arose when an entire session was literally invaded by members of the John Birch Society, distributing literature on "sensitivity training" and on "brain-washing" of police by communists. On another occasion a group of teenage so-called militants went from group to group taunting the police and hurling invectives. At another time, several persons impersonating police joined the group. When they were discovered, they maintained that they had come to "support" the police, who were being subjected to harassment and intimidation by the group leaders and communists. Despite all of this, a balance of input was managed across groups and the extreme activist forces largely were ignored by the officers.

The fourth laboratory was in session when the assassination of Dr. Martin Luther King, Jr. was announced. The effects of this traumatic intervention was reflected in this laboratory. Extremely negative attitudes were shown to persist throughout the six sessions. There was both hardening and deterioration of relationships between the police and the community. Very few positive results were observed or reported by group leaders or participants.

A police "walk-out" during a laboratory in a predominantly black section of town gained widespread publicity on TV. No explanation seemed satisfactory to the news media, and when normal activities resumed without further problems, they warranted no publicity. The final response to this crisis by police and community participants proved to be a validation of the earnest effort on the part of the program and its sponsors to improve relations between police and the Houston community and served to dispel minor rumors that the entire program was a "whitewash by the establishment."

An unfortunate interruption of the laboratories midway

through the program was almost disastrous. Sessions had to be interrupted because funding was becoming a problem and the city had to find legal means by which to compensate officers for their attendance during off-duty hours. Community participation at this time had reached an all-time high and enthusiasm by the officers and the citizens was highly apparent. Rumors about "suspended support by the city," "sabotage of the program," and the like caused extreme disruption. It was very difficult to dispel these rumors and to develop renewed enthusiasm for the program.

The most difficult problem was a lack of commitment to the goals of the program by a substantially vocal and devious body of police officers. These men openly attempted to sabotage the program by excessive overt expressions of hostility, refusal to participate (just sitting silently and glowering), or by endeavors to ridicule other participants. No remonstrations by the leaders or imploring of other officers brought about any change in their behaviors. Fortunately they were unable to gain enough support to destroy our endeavors.

A most unexpected problem involved the group leaders. Leader bias and leader anxiety are not uncommon phenomena in group settings. However, these very human elements usually are controlled to the degree that they are only minimally (if at all) influential. Clinical psychologists and other highly trained behavioral scientists are expected to be least affected by these factors.

This was not the case in Houston. When it was suggested that the triethnic group of leaders should attempt some advance preparation for their responsibilities with police-community sessions, some of the clinical psychologists actually resented the suggestion. They felt certain that the training and experience which qualified them as therapists would be more than adequate for discussion group leadership. Others felt that it would be a waste of time. They did agree, however, to hold weekly meetings to discuss problems, successes, failures, innovative ideas and the like that might emerge from the sessions.

The strain of working with these groups became apparent after the second series of meetings. During our weekly feedback session one leader said, "If my son were to tell me that he wants to be a policeman, I would . . .!" This led into a prolonged discussion of leader attitudes toward the police. They varied from extremely negative, in general, to fairly accepting. Some leaders felt that they reflected only the hostility of many of the officers toward them (the leaders). Others indicated that they had difficulty having positive feelings toward officers who openly expressed bigotry, hate, close-mindedness and the like. On the other hand, some of the leaders talked about the warmth and understanding expressed by some of the policemen in their groups. This particular feedback session was excellent for it set the stage for more fruitful interaction between the leaders and both the police and the community members in their sessions. Real acceptance and objectivity was evident in following feedback meetings.

One of the strong feelings expressed after the first two meetings (and one that persisted at different levels throughout the program) was leader anxiety. Some of the psychologists became so anxious that they asked to be replaced. Others dealt with their anxiety through leader discussions or through talking about their feelings while in the groups. It seemed that dealing with emotions of the mentally disturbed, no matter how violent, was something that the psychologist could handle. He was much less adept at coping with open hostility and recurring violent outbursts from "normal" people. No less unnerving was the fact the police officers refused to take off their guns while in session. In a general sense the weapon seemed to be so much a part of the man that no pressure was applied to have him remove it during the group meetings.

Despite all of this, minority group leaders enjoyed some advantages over their white counterparts. Officers commented often that they preferred the "Negro guys." In all honesty, leading this type of group is emotionally exhausting and the lack of visible reward only increases the strain. The one woman leader survived but even *I* wonder how. The leaders found themselves the target of direct hostility from the police and community participants at some point during *every* laboratory. Often the attacks were quite personal. It took a strong leader to place positive interpretations on these behaviors and to see his personal growth enhanced by virtue of his ability to accept all of this "with personal positive regard."

PROGRAM EVALUATION

The kind of rigorous evaluation and follow-up that should be a part of any program designed to bring about change in human behavior was not possible with the Houston Cooperative Crime Prevention Program. Many police officers mutilated or refused to complete even a simple and direct questionnaire soliciting their general opinion of the program. This attitude may have been a reflection of the officer's suspicious nature and defensive posture.[4] These traits characterized the police generally and in particular cases made two-way communication impossible. These pervasive (and at times directly revealed) attitudes often served as real barriers to optimum group interaction.

Nevertheless it was possible to make some determination regarding the results of the program from approximately 800 police and 600 community responses to one questionnaire. A general positive attitude toward the program can be found in the fact that 85 percent of the police officers rated it either good, very good, or excellent, and 93 percent of the community rated it good, very good, or excellent. Whereas 18 percent of the community rated the program excellent, only 4 percent of the police rated it that high. On the other hand, 15 percent of the police rated the sessions poor, but only 7 percent of the community indicated the program as a poor activity. In terms of attitudes toward each other, 65 percent of the community expressed more positive attitudes toward the community. Only 2 percent of the officers indicated a more negative attitude and 61 percent reflected no change. For the community 31 percent were unchanged and 4 percent more negative.

Indices of results probably are revealed more accurately in other ways. One officer stated, "It (the program) made me understand that although I may have preconceived ideas or biased opinions about people, that I must strive as a policeman to keep

---

[4]Melvin P. Sikes: The police psyche. *The Church and Metropolis,* No. 20, Spring 1969.

these out of my personal dealings with others. I should go further to understand what might motivate this person to feel the way he does." Many officers were shocked to find the degree and extent of hostile feelings toward them expressed by members of the white community. This brought to them in a vivid manner the fact that one cannot judge on the basis of color or race. The difficulty in admitting weakness or misconduct on the part of police was pointed out by the community and grudgingly acceded to by the officers. On the other hand, the community began to see warmth, humanity, and feeling on the part of many of the officers and invited them into their homes and organizations. Community participants became deeply interested in learning more about law and police responsibility and pledged to become more civic-minded as well as active in civic affairs. To many Blacks, this was the first positive contact with law enforcement. Many fears were dispelled and active cooperation promised. One elderly Negro was heard to say, as he left a session, "Thank God! Thank God! Today I'm a man!" If nothing else were accomplished, this would have been an appropriate benediction.

SUMMARY

As with any program designed to deal with human behavior and to bringing about positive change, many questions could be raised. The basic question always is, "Was it a success?" Who knows? One can point only to what several police officers and some city officials cited as a "cool summer of '68" as opposed to the spring and summer of 1967. The same officials indicated the thousands of dollars of savings to the city in monies that had gone into "police overtime" to protect against violent civil disturbance during the preceding summers. No riots followed the assassination either of Dr. Martin Luther King, Jr. or of Senator Robert F. Kennedy. The NAACP and the mayor's office reported a 70 percent drop in complaints against police officers over a seven-month period following the program. An effort, though abortive, was made to organize police-citizen community teams. Interdepartmental relationships between Black and white officers improved. One white officer requested a Black officer as a partner.

Another white officer attempted to have interracial group meetings in his home.

A dramatic incident worthy of publication[5] dealt with a laboratory held in the Texas Southern University area. Upon being assured of his right to open honesty and free speech, one command officer exclaimed, "I hate Niggers! I especially hate Texas Southern young Niggers! Anytime I see a Texas Southern sticker I'm going to give a ticket if I can!" Applause from the predominantly Texas Southern student participants surprised the police officers, who seemed equally shocked by the frank admission of their fellow officer. One male student quickly explained, "We applauded because he was honest. We can trust an honest cop even if he doesn't like us." According to later reports, the young man who responded and the officer who made the statement became fast friends before the laboratory was completed. In addition, the officer was said to have gained the respect and friendship of a large group of students and other members of that community.

Are these positive incidents related to the Houston Cooperative Crime Prevention Program? We would like to think so.

Despite the fact that the program grew out of crisis and was "precipitated" rather than planned over time; despite the too large groups; despite the lack of opportunity to get police involvement in the planning of the program; despite a continuing desperate climate in Houston, so far no riot has occurred. There have been outbreaks of "police violence," according to reports, but these have failed to spark a "Detroit" or a "Watts." People are still trying. This does not mean "it can't happen" or "it won't happen."

Eighteen hours of human relations training cannot completely wipe out years of fear, hate, and distrust. At some time, white officialdom as well as white America must read the Kerner Commission Report and *The History of Violence in America* with understanding and must find ways of implementing their suggestions. Until America attacks its national psychosis, "white racism," at its roots, police-community relations programs largely will remain exercises in futility.

---

[5]Police: Group therapy, *Time Magazine*, April 12, 1968, 57-58.

FUTURE DIRECTIONS

"If it were to occur today, what do you think would be the precipitating cause of an urban riot?" Should this question be posed, the majority of respondents would reply, "Police practices." This is stark and disturbing evidence of the distressing resistance to change on the part of too many policemen. It reveals the degree to which conscientious efforts on the part of many behavioral scientists have been demeaned and the positive effects of potentially good educational and/or training programs nullified by recalcitrant police behavior. In addition it points up the frightening fact that too many chiefs of police and others are of the antiquated and mistaken opinion that any problem can be solved by sheer force.

Proof of this latter accusation can be validated by a review of the manner in which police departments have expended federal funds directly granted to them for "improvement." So much of this money was expended on riot gear and armament (including tanks) that some of the agencies responsible for the approving of funding became alarmed. In many grant requests from police departments, allocations for programs designed to improve police-community relations were almost nonexistent. Where larger amounts were requested for such programs, implementation was to be accomplished largely through innocuous activities. This assured no change in police practices.

Directions for the future demand more rigorous screening of applicants to reduce the number of sadists, bigots, unstable and abusive men, sociopaths, and other misfits who manage to become police officers. This, of course, requires the development of sensitive evaluative techniques to be used in the selection of police candidates. Presently, an alarming number of police are recruited and sworn to duty without *any* type of psychological evaluation or personality test. Some uniformity in recruitment and selection must be achieved nationally and some method for assuring such careful evaluation and adherence to national standards *must* be accomplished.

Directions for the future demand fair and impartial means of handling alleged police misconduct. Departments, and seemingly, grand juries refuse to indict men who are known even within the ranks to be violently abusive. Protection of a fellow officer regardless of his guilt becomes a way of life. The police officer must not suffer, but guilty officers must not go unpunished. Despite popular belief, police cannot themselves be above the law and the general public (but more especially the poor and minority groups) must be assured of this by action—not by empty promise.

The opportunity for educational advancement for interested officers is a hopeful sign. Many men are earning higher degrees and assisting in the development of real professionalism among police. Other men become disenchanted with their supervisors over time and resign to use their educational achievement in fields other than law enforcement. Hopefully this trend will not continue.

Police are a vital and necessary part of any ordered society. The future must provide officers who will have the education, training, and personal stability that will prevent "police action" from being the inciting force in violent social disruption.

REFERENCES

Blair, J.: Detection of potential community violence. Dissemination document—Grant 207 (5.044), Office of Law Enforcement Assistance, U.S. Department of Justice, Washington, D.C., 1968.

Blair, J.: Violence in the city. Fort Worth, Texas, Texas Christian University Press, 1969.

Blake, R. R., Mouton, J. S., and Sloma, R. L.: The unionmanagement intergroup laboratory: Strategy for resolving intergroup conflict. Journal of Applied Behavioral Science, 1965, 1, 25-57.

Graham, H. D. and Gurr, T. R.: The History of Violence in America. New York, Bantam Books, 1969.

Police: Group therapy. Time Magazine, April 12, 1968, pp. 57-58.

Sikes, Melvin P.: The police psyche. Church in Metropolis. 1969, 20 (Spring).

U.S. Riot Commission: Report of the National Advisory Commission on Civil Disorders (Kerner Commission). New York, Bantam Books, 1968.

SECTION III

POLICE ATTITUDES
AND CHARACTERISTICS

INTRODUCTION

THE ATTITUDES OF POLICE TOWARDS THEIR JOBS REPRESENTS A RECENT ATTEMPT TO "GO TO THE SOURCE" REGARDING SUCH VARIABLES AS ROLE SATISFACTION, JOB INVOLVEMENT, AND OTHER RELEVANT VARIABLES. IT MAKES SOME EMPIRICAL SENSE THAT TO CHANGE, MODIFY AND PROFESSION-ALIZE AN INSTITUTION, RESEARCHERS SHOULD SEEK INTERNAL SATISFACTION RATINGS. HOW DO POLICE FEEL ABOUT THEMSELVES AND THEIR JOB? THIS AREA OF EXPLORATION ALSO INCLUDES STUDIES UTILIZING OCCUPATIONAL COMPARISON DATA TO CLARIFY CHARACTERISTICS OF POLICE TO ASSESS THEIR RELATIONSHIP TO OTHER ROLE CATEGORIES IN OUR CULTURE.

THE LEFKOWITZ STUDY IS AN ATTEMPT TO DELINEATE FACTORS RESPONSI-BLE FOR JOB SATISFACTION AND ATTITUDES. DESPITE SOME SAMPLING PROBLEMS, HIS STUDY IS A USEFUL FIRST STEP IN ANALYZING THE ROLE OF POLICEMAN.

OLSONS' RESEARCH IS AN ATTITUDINAL STUDY AND ATTEMPTS TO DETER-MINE HOW POLICE OFFICERS FEEL ABOUT THEIR JOB. IN ADDITION, HE HAS DEVELOPED A POTENTIALLY USEFUL QUESTIONNAIRE THAT COULD BE VALUABLE IN FURTHER RESEARCH.

THE BERMAN ARTICLE, ALTHOUGH IT DOES NOT INCLUDE POLICE OFFICERS WHO WORK ON PATROL, IS A THOUGHTFUL ANALYSIS OF CHARACTERISTICS OF CORRECTIONAL OFFICERS. IT HAS RELEVANCE TO URBAN POLICEMEN SINCE MOST MAJOR DEPARTMENTS DO DEPLOY REGULAR OFFICERS IN A JAIL-TYPE SETTING. HIS CONCLUSIONS PROVIDE MUCH FOOD FOR THOUGHT AND HE HAS DONE SOME INITIAL WORK USING THE MMPI TO ASSESS POLICE CHARACTERISTICS.

THE WALTHER, MCCUNE AND TROJANOWICZ ARTICLE IS BOTH INTEREST-ING AND INFORMATIVE IN ITS PREMISE AND OUTCOME. WITH CONCEPTIONS OF THE ROLE OF POLICE OFFICERS CHANGING OVER TIME, THIS ARTICLE ADDRESSES ITSELF TO A POSSIBLE DIRECTION SUCH CHANGES MIGHT TAKE.

THE STODDARD RESEARCH INCLUDES THE USE OF THE STRONG VOCATIONAL INTEREST BLANK FOR ANALYSIS OF POLICE RELATED JOB CHARACTERISTICS. SUCH DATA HELPS RESEARCHERS PLACE POLICE WORK IN ITS LEGITIMATE PLACE AMONG OTHER OCCUPATIONAL GROUPS.

Chapter 11

ATTITUDES OF POLICE TOWARD THEIR JOB

Joel Lefkowitz

THE SOCIAL and occupational isolation of the policeman is extremely salient in determining his behavior (Clark, 1965. Westley, 1953). The degree to which the impetus for his isolation stems solely from the physical and social demands of his job, in contrast to possibly more basic personality characteristics of the individual policeman, himself, remains in large measure unanswered. In either case, however, it seems clear that such isolation serves several (largely invidious) functions for the public at large.

Chevigny (1969) makes the point that in a dynamic society in which injustices exist, it is extremely difficult to obtain efficiency quick work, and order from our police, as well as due process and equal justice. Failing this, society tends to settle for the appearance of order ("peace and quiet") preserved by the tough actions of the police. He goes on to say,

> The enlightened feel a little guilty about their own impulse to coerce respect by force, and it's easier for them to turn the police into a whipping boy than to admit to such instincts themselves . . . (p. 279).

Ramsey Clark (1971), in a similar vein, adds that society has dumped on the police the task of enforcing unenforceable laws (with respect to alcoholism, gambling, prostitution, homosexuality,

This research was supported by the National Institute of Law Enforcement and Criminal Justice, Law Enforcement Assistance Administration, U.S. Department of Justice, Grant No. NI 70-065-PG-12.

[1]This chapter is based upon research supported in part by Pilot Project Grant #NI70-065-PG-12 of the National Institute of Law Enforcement and Criminal Justice, Law Enforcement Assistance Administration, and reported in *Job Attitudes of Police,* August, 1971.

drug addiction) which, in many cases, we hypocritically don't want enforced anyway. The individual policeman, then, in the exercise of his discretion, tends to behave in accordance with society's implied directive. A recent national survey (Institute for Social Research, 1971) found that,

> While men agreed that the basic causes of violence rest with social problems such as unemployment, discrimination, and lack of education, 30% said the way to prevent violence is through more police force and stricter, more punitive legislation (p. 3).

Since they reflect society's wishes (largely frustration-induced, consciously disavowed aggressive and guilt-laden impulses) ". . . it is hardly reasonable to ask the police to change when society is demanding that they remain the same" (Chevigny, 1969, p. 238). The isolation of the police, therefore, is an individual one (more relevant at the interpersonal level than societal) which permits the police to respond vicariously to the wishes of the larger society.

The unrealistic aspects of such isolation may be reduced by adding the job of policeman to the community of occupations which are studied by social and behavioral scientists. For too long, portrayals of the policeman and his job have had tendentious qualities aimed more at promoting particular points of view than with describing reality. Whether it is "the romantic image of (a grown man) inordinately fond of small animals and children . . ." (McCaghy, 1968, p. 245), or the police officer who "offers to each and every one of us the security and safety which we alone cannot provide . . ." (Nolan, 1950, p. 455), or the poster which pictures "a pot-bellied policeman clubbing a bloody unconscious Negro" (McCaghy, 1968, p. 246), little is added to our understanding of the behavior of men performing their chosen vocation.

The present research was aimed at investigating a variety of job attitudes, the degree and nature of job satisfactions, personal need satisfactions, and aspects of the belief systems of the members of one police department. These attitudes have been investigated rather extensively (primarily by social and industrial psychologists) with respect to a wide variety of occupational groupings and status levels, but infrequently and haphazardly among policemen. Some normative comparisons of the data obtained from this sample of policemen with other occupational samples were enabled because, wherever possible, standardized and/or frequently-employed measuring instruments were used. This investigation is an initial stage of exploratory research in an eventual program of relating such attitudinal variables to overt performance characteristics. In other words, we will eventually wish to answer the question as to whether differences in attitudes "make a difference" with regard to job behaviors, such as quantity or quality of performance, tenure, absences, willingness to assume responsibilities, disciplinary charges, and so forth.[2]

PREVIOUS SOCIAL AND BEHAVIORAL SCIENCE RESEARCH: PERSONALITY CHARACTERISTICS AND ROLE REQUIREMENTS[3]

The first and foremost issue with which one must come to grips concerns the question as to whether there exists a typical "police personality." More precisely, what is the evidence for describing policemen as a relatively homogeneous group (in this context) in comparison with the general population? If indeed, policemen are more like one another than they resemble the general norms, then one should certainly be interested in investigating why that should be so.

At that point we would be forced to recognize the distinction between role demands ("pressures of the job") and more basic personality attributes of the incumbents as alternative (but not necessarily independent) explanations. The two are often confused. Just as the technology of modern industry fosters the erroneous view of the worker as a basically childish, ignorant, and unmotivated employee (because the assembly line production system requires that kind of behavior), it is thought by some that

---

[2]The problem of developing reliable, valid, and meaningful measures of job performance (the "criterion problem") is only recently receiving the attention it deserves.

Whether attitudes determine behavior propensities, or behavior predisposes toward certain attitudes, is an unresolved psychological issue. There is often a correspondence between the two, however, and ascertaining the extent and degree of that association is our ultimate aim.

[3]The original report, upon which this chapter is based, contains an extended literature review in this area.

we may think of policemen as being a certain way, e.g. "authoritarian," merely because of observing them in the performance of their prescribed (authoritative) roles.

Most researchers (whose academic training has tended to be in the social sciences of sociology or political science) have concluded that whatever "typical" characteristics may exist are fostered almost entirely by "the system" (Bayley and Mendelsohn, 1969; Chevigny, 1969; Dodd, 1967; Niederhoffer, 1967). That view is probably similar to the attitude of policemen themselves:

> One often hears . . . that only 'potential cops' seek out a policeman's job . . . That is not true . . . The only real difference between the cop and any other man is their rate of adjustment to the realities of life (Radano, 1968, preface).

Niederhoffer (1967), in discussing violence among police, espouses this view most graphically in stating that the ". . . police officer swings his club in response to the thrust of organizational and occupational imperatives . . ." (p. 93). That point of view is reiterated sympathetically in the press (Astor, 1971; Whelton, 1971).

One must consider with skepticism that portion of the literature which is primarily opinion. They are informed opinions of men experienced in the law enforcement field, perhaps, but subjective, unsystematic, and unverifiable opinions nevertheless.

A frequently-encountered opinion is what one might refer to as the "omnibus qualities" or "hero" theory approach—usually advanced by way of singing the praises of the average policeman. Perhaps the foremost example is offered by August Vollmer, as quoted in a modern textbook of police management (Leonard, 1964), who said that we expect the police officer

> ". . . to have the wisdom of Solomon, the courage of David, the patience of Job, and leadership of Moses, the kindness of the Good Samaritan, the startegy of Alexander, the faith of Daniel, the diplomacy of Lincoln, the tolerance of the Carpenter of Nazareth, and finally, an intimate knowledge of every branch of the natural, biological, and social sciences" (pp. 101-102).

The opposite extreme is represented by views such as that of Radano (1968), a policeman, who simply asserts that the policeman is like "any other man."

Somewhere in the middle-ground of informed opinion are those who feel that there is a constellation of traits and attitudes or a general perspective on the world which particularly characterizes the policeman (Black, 1968; Chevigny, 1969; Dodd, 1967; Wilson, 1968). This constellation is presumably comprised of such interrelated traits as authoritarianism, suspiciousness, physical courage, cynicism, conservatism, loyalty, secretiveness, and self-assertiveness. In addition, these authors uniformly are of the opinion that these traits are fostered primarily by occupational demands and do not especially characterize those who become police candidates before their exposure to the life of a policeman.

Based on a review of the empirical psychological research, it seems clear to this author that the bulk of the evidence favors the notion that the personalities of policemen *do* differ in systematic ways from the rest of the population—that there is, indeed, a "typical police personality" (subject, of course, to the limitations of any such broad generalization). The results, however, are somewhat equivocal because of design inadequacies in the research. As pointed out by Wolfe (1970) ". . . non-random selection of subjects and lack of appropriate comparison groups endanger the validity and restrict the generalizability of results" (p. 1). Moreover, there are contradictions among the research.

Also relevant here is the notable lack of any longitudinal research, which precludes conclusions being drawn regarding the origins of those common traits among policemen. The authors, however, invariably disregard such limitations in their eagerness to ascribe the personality characteristics to "the job," "group pressure," or "the system," vigorously denying the likelihood of systematic preselection influences (either initial self-selection, or organizational selection). In light of this theoretical bias displayed by most of the social scientists, it would seem imperative to design research so as to systematically observe men from the "applicant" through the "veteran" stage.

Much of the resistance to the notion of personality trait communalities seems due to an assumption that comparisons with the general population are necessarily pejorative and are the results of attempts to document a high incidence of psychopathology among policemen. For example, Bayley and Mendelsohn (1969) report that their police sample, in comparison to the general population control group, was less anomic, more sanguine about the future, less authoritarian, more conservative, and had a greater sense of personal efficacy in shaping the future. However, they conclude, inexplicably, "We find no evidence that particular personality types are recruited to police work" (p. 15). They go on to state that, "One does not need a special theory to explain why men go into police work—as many police detractors would suggest" (p. 32). It is difficult to fathom why entertaining the highly tenable notion of occupational "self-selection" necessarily makes one a "police detractor."

In reviewing the available research concerning personality attributes of policemen, one cannot help feeling that the traditional psychometric interpretation of standardized paper-and-pencil tests has been less than fruitful. The clinical evaluation of individual protocols seems to have been more useful in the few occasions where it was tried—as compared with gross descriptive and correlational summaries. It is likely that the use of more "unobtrusive measures" (Webb, 1966) may yield more meaningful data, if one can guard against misinterpretation of the researcher's intent.

RESEARCH DESIGN

Previous psychological research concerning the police have usually been marked by several inadequacies which this study sought to overcome. Significant features of this investigation were (A) Minimal sampling error, data obtained from 80 percent of the entire police department, making the results fairly representative of this department; (B) Utilization of an extensive battery of attitude measures, thus permitting investigation of the relationships among many variables; (C) Utilization, however possible, of standardized and/or frequently-used measuring instruments, many of which had never before been administered to policemen.

The research was designed as an exploratory survey. The primary aim was to obtain a substantial amount of descriptive attitudinal and demographic data. It is decidedly non-hypothesis-testing in nature (except for the hypotheses implied in performing comparisons among various subgroups).

The Research Site and the Sample

Data were collected from members of the police department of the city of Dayton, Ohio, in February, 1970.

The Dayton Police Department (DPD) has been, through most of its recent history, a traditional police organization—characterized by a classical organizational structure with highly centralized, and somewhat rigid, authoritarian command processes, and a typically narrow definition of "law enforcement." The present Director of Police was appointed in 1967 and, at the time of this study, was engaged in attempts at "modernizing" and "professionalizing" the department. This entailed, among other things, innovations in training procedures and content, increased delegation of authority to command, greater restriction on the use of deadly force, increased use of civilian personnel at high levels, and a growing "community service" orientation. The DPD, in early 1970, seemed to be characterized by confusion resulting from the conflict of values between the "old police code symbolized by the 'tough cop' . . . and the new ideology glorifying the 'social scientist police officer'," as described by Niederhoffer (1967) in connection with the New York City Police Department.

The DPD is comprised of approximately 425 sworn, and 115 civilian personnel. This study is concerned only with sworn personnel. Questionnaires were returned by 337 of the approximately 425 policemen and policewomen. Many of those who did not respond were unavailable because of vacation, illness, or absence. Twenty-one respondents were eliminated from the study because they omitted significant portions of the questionnaires. All four female respondents were eliminated in order to make the sample homogeneous in that regard, yielding a final sample of 312 policemen.

Based on the demographic characteristics assessed, the "typical" Dayton policeman is 35 years of age, has been on the force for 11 years, is married, is at least a high school graduate, has used firearms in the line of duty at most once or twice,[4] was raised in a small city in the Midwest, and is the only member of his family to have become a policeman.

Data Collection Procedures

Several meetings were held with the top command of the DPD (chief, majors, captains) wherein the purpose of the survey was explained and the questionnaires were examined and reviewed. The anonymity of all respondents was assured. Each captain distributed sets of questionnaires to his lieutenants, each of whom was responsible for distributing them to his command. No member of the DPD had access to, nor saw any of the completed questionnaires.

The Attitude Measures

The attitudes which were chosen for investigation are those suggested by the literature review (Lefkowitz, 1971) or are those which seem especially significant for understanding the psychological environment of any given occupational group. In every case, the specific instruments chosen as the operational measures of these variables are copyrighted and/or are readily available from published sources to which we have made reference.

1. *Job description index (JDI).* The JDI measures satisfactions with five job areas: the *Type of Work,* itself, the *Pay, Opportunities for Promotion, Supervision,* and the *Co-Workers* on the job.

Several minor changes were made in the standardized JDI in order to make it more relevant for administration to policemen. An item with respect to pay was changed from "Satisfactory profit sharing" to "Satisfactory maintenance allowance for uniform and equipment." The item "insecure" was eliminated from the pay scale. An item on promotions was changed from "Good opportunity for advancement" to "Good opportunities for promotion."

2. *Need satisfaction questionnaire.* This questionnaire has been used previously in a number of studies involving over 5,000

---

[4]Firearms "use" was defined as discharging a weapon in earnest—not firing range use nor merely drawing a revolver as a precaution, or for detention of a prisoner.

managers (Porter and Lawler, 1968). It contains 13 items designed and grouped to measure five levels of personality needs in the Maslow (1954) hierarchy, in relation to one's job: *Security* (one item), *Social* needs (two items), *Esteem* (three items), *Autonomy* (four items), and *Self-Actualization* (three items). The questionnaire has been described in detail by Porter (1962) and Porter & Lawler (1968).

For each item, the respondent is required to give three Likert-type ratings on a scale of one (minimum) to seven (maximum). The ratings are in response to the three questions: (a) "How much (of this characteristic) is there (in your job) now?" (b) "How much should there be?" and (c) "How important is this to me?"

The answers to the first question are a measure of "need fulfillment" or "need gratification" in each area. The differences between the second (the perceived equitable amount) and the first (reality) questions are a measure of "need satisfactions" (or, more precisely, "need (dis) satisfactions," since the second question invariably receives a higher rating than the first). The third question is a measure of the "importance" of the various needs. We introduced another derived measure by multiplying the "need (dis) satisfaction" results by the "importance" rating to yield a "weighted (dis) satisfaction" score.

The word "management" was deleted from our form of the questionnaire, so that questions regarding "my management position" read "my position." Also, every reference to "the company" was changed to "the police department."

3. *Job involvement scale.* This scale consists of 20 items designed to measure one's degree of "job involvement." By "job involvement" is meant such things as the degree to which a person's work performance affects his self esteem (Lodahl and Kejner, 1965). An alternative phrase is "ego-involvement in one's work."

All such definitions describe the job-involved person as one who is affected very much personally by his whole job situation—his work is an integral part of his psychological world. He is not necessarily happy with his job; very angry or dissatisfied workers may be just as involved as very satisfied workers.

Each of 20 statements is responded to on a four-part discrete scale from "strongly agree" to "strongly disagree."

4. *Leadership opinion questionnaire (LOQ).* This questionnaire has received widespread use (Fleishman, 1969; Robinson, et al., 1969; Stogdill and Coons, 1957). It measures two primary dimensions of supervisory leadership behavior which were originally identified in the Ohio State University leadership studies. The dimensions, as defined in the test manual (Fleishman, 1969) are as follows:

> *Consideration* (C). . . . the extent to which . . . job relationships with subordinates (are) characterized by mutual trust, respect for their ideas, consideration of their feelings, and a certain warmth . . . indicative of a climate of good rapport and two-way communication.
>
> *Structure* (S). . . . the extent to which an individual is likely to define and structure his own role and those of his subordinates toward *goal attainment.* A high score on this dimension characterizes individuals who play a very active role in directing group activities through planning, communicating information, scheduling, criticizing, trying out new ideas, and so forth . . . (p. 1) .

The LOQ was administered only to those members of the police department with supervisory responsibilities (above the rank of patrolman) .

5. *Supervisory behavior description questionnaire (SBD).* This questionnaire has also received frequent use and is described in detail elsewhere (Robinson, et al., 1969; Stogdill and Coons, 1957). It measures the same two dimensions of leadership, *consideration* and *structure,* as measured by the LOQ, and the scoring is the same. This form, however, is filled out by subordinates in order to describe their supervisor's behavior.

The "Consideration" scale contains 28 items in its original format. In order to render the SBD more nearly equivalent to the LOQ for comparison, we retained only 20 items—corresponding to the 20 items on the "C" scale of the LOQ. (The "structure" dimension of the SBD contains 20 items as originally developed.) Eighteen of the 40 items were modified slightly in order to eliminate use of the industrial term "foremen."

6. *The dogmatism scale (D-Scale).* This questionnaire, along

with number 7, the anti-Negro scale, was presented as the "Personal Opinion Questionnaire."

The D-Scale is a measure of closed-mindedness with respect to one's system of beliefs. Dogmatism relates to the individual's degree of psychological flexibility—rigidity, and the degree to which his thinking is determined by irrelevant internal drives and/or arbitrary reinforcements from external authority (rather than by objective logical relationships which resist irrelevant motivational or reinforcement pressures).

The advantage of the D-Scale over earlier measures of "authoritarianism" is that it is a more generalized measure and is not related to political ideology—liberalism or conservatism. There are highly dogmatic individuals of both left and right persuasion.

The finally revised (Form E) scale contains 40 items and has been extremely widely used (Vacchiano, et al., 1969) and is described in detail by Robinson and Shaver (1969) and Rokeach (1960).

7. *Anti-Negro scale.* This is a 16-item Likert-type scale developed by Steckler (1957) and reviewed favorably by Shaw and Wright (1967). It is one of the few existing scales of prejudicial attitudes toward Negroes which is not extremely transparent and offensive, nor hopelessly "dated" in its terminology.

It was originally developed for use in assessing the attitudes of Negro samples. One item was modified in order to enable its use with whites. In addition, two references to "colored people" were changed to "Black people."

8. *Cynicism scale.* This scale was presented as the "Policeman C Scale." It consists of 20 open-ended statements concerning significant areas of police work developed by Niederhoffer (1967).

The scale is presented as a measure of cynical attitudes toward police work and in relation to the role of police in society.

RESULTS I: DESCRIPTION OF THE TOTAL SAMPLE ON THE ATTITUDE VARIABLES

The raw scores upon which results are based are presented in Table 11-I.

TABLE 11-I
RAW SCORES FOR THE TOTAL SAMPLE (N = 312)

Variable[a]	M	S
13. JDI—Work	33.71	11.20
14. " Pay	15.15	12.07
15. " Promotion	18.40	14.65
16. " Supervision	40.65	13.68
17. " Co-Workers	41.42	12.74
18. Job Involvement	52.15	10.66
19. Cynicism	56.50	15.13
20. Dogmatism	146.11	35.81
21. Anti-Negro ideology	72.26	24.62
22. n Security—Fulfillment	4.53	2.03
23. " How much should be	5.90	1.77
24. " Importance	6.03	1.84
25. " Deficiency (Dissatisfaction)	1.23	2.68
26. " Weighted Deficiency	6.96	15.59
27. n Social—Fulfillment	10.44	3.16
28. " How much should be	12.12	2.94
29. " Importance	11.53	2.97
30. " Deficiency (Dissatisfaction)	1.84	3.21
31. " Weighted Deficiency	9.76	18.12
32. n Esteem—Fulfillment	11.99	4.67
33. " How much should be	17.90	4.13
34. " Importance	16.89	4.72
35. " Deficiency (Dissatisfaction)	6.00	5.41
36. " Weighted Deficiency	34.42	32.66
37. n Autonomy—Fulfillment	15.96	7.28
38. " How much should be	22.94	5.27
39. " Importance	22.93	7.22
40. " Deficiency (Dissatisfaction)	7.29	6.37
41. " Weighted Deficiency	45.09	38.04
42. n Actualization—Fulfillment	13.46	5.36
43. " How much should be	18.86	3.46
44. " Importance	18.74	3.37
45. " Deficiency (Dissatisfaction)	6.36	6.09
46. " Weighted Deficiency	36.24	33.19
47. SBD—Consideration	50.73	14.31
48. SBD—Initiating Structure	41.90	9.64
49. LOQ—Consideration[b]	56.13	9.18
50. LOQ—Initiating Structure[b]	47.15	8.37

[a]Variable numbers correspond to the original research design. Variables 1 - 12 are demographic items omitted here.

[b]Variables 49 and 50 (the LOQ) are relevant only to the "command" subsample (N = 54).

Job Satisfaction

Normative comparisons on the five scales of the JDI are enabled by data reported by Smith, et al. (1969) for a cross section of approximately 2,000 male industrial workers in 21 plants in 16 different metropolitan communities. The mean scores, for those workers, on the 5 JDI scales are 36.57, 29.90, 22.06, 41.10, and 43.49, respectively.

The outstanding trend revealed by the comparisons with the mean scores presented in Table 11-I is the uniform relative dissatisfaction of the DPD in comparison to the norm group of industrial workers with respect to the *work* itself (t=4.27, p<.01), *promotion* (t=2.15, p<.05), *supervision* (t=2.05, p.<.05), and *co-workers* (t=9.90, p<.01). (The difference for *pay* is assuredly significant, but no significance test was performed because of our having altered the number of items on that scale.)

Nevertheless, however, the pattern of satisfactions (i.e. rank order of degree of satisfaction with respect to each of the five job factors) is highly similar for the police and the industrial group. This is probably indicative of their common origin from the working class population. Both are most satisfied with their *co-workers* and *supervision,* and moderately satisfied with the nature of the *work* itself. *Pay* and *opportunity for promotion,* which rank fourth and fifth for the industrial workers, reverse position in the case of the police because of the extreme dissatisfaction with *pay* (in part attributable merely to the reduction of one item on that scale, and undoubtedly, in part, due to the beginning of contract negotiations at the time of the survey).

Job Involvement

The mean job involvement score of 52.15 compares somewhat unfavorably with the limited normative data available. Samples of nurses, engineers and students scored, on the average, 56.63, 57.38, and 51.94 respectively (Lodahl and Kejner, 1965). The differences for the nurses and engineers are significantly different (t=17.23, and 4.71, p.<.01).

The industrial psychological literature indicates that we should expect acknowledged professional groups (engineers, nurses) to be more "involved" in their work than lower status groups. On the other hand, the particular nature of police work might lead us to have expected a higher mean score from this occupational category. The observed average is just past the midpoint of the measuring scale.

Need Fulfillment

The answers to the question, "How much (of this job characteristic) is there now in your job?" indicate the degree of psychological fulfillment (gratification) received from one's job in each of the five Maslow need categories.

The average responses for 260 industrial managers are presented in the first part of Table 11-II for comparison purposes. The averages were calculated from data presented by Porter and Lawler (1968, p. 133) for a cross section of managers from civil service divisions of state governments, private manufacturing, and privately-owned utility companies. The inappropriateness of the (managerial) norm groups is recognized. Their data is presented only to enable the most tenuous comparisons, and because published data on the need questionnaire deal primarily with managerial groups. Any observed differences may be more a function of the generally working-class backgrounds of the policemen, than of their positions as policemen in particular.

The police receive the greatest degree of need fulfillment in the area of their Social needs. They are most deprived with respect to their needs for Esteem and Autonomy. However, interpretations of these findings are suspect without considering the degree of actual satisfaction—dissatisfaction experienced by the subjects. That is, the absolute amount of "fulfillment" of these needs may be of less significance than the perceived *relative* level of fulfillment in relation to how much "ought to" be fulfilled.

The overall level of fulfillment, or gratification, experienced by the policemen is less than that obtained by the managerial group—especially as regards security and esteem needs. However, the police apparently derive more fulfillment of their social needs than do the managers.

TABLE 11-II
NEED FULFILLMENT, DISSATISFACTION, AND PERCEIVED IMPORTANCE
OF NEEDS FOR THE TOTAL POLICE SAMPLE AND COMPARISON GROUPS
OF INDUSTRIAL MANAGERS

| | Mean Scores | |
Need Category	DPD (N = 312)	Managers
Need Fulfillment (Gratification)		(N = 260)
Security	4.53	5.13
Social	5.22	4.90
Esteem	4.00	4.50
Autonomy	3.99	4.23
Self-Actualization	4.49	4.63
Need Dissatisfaction (Deficiency)		(N = 260)
Security	1.23	.60
Social	.92	.48
Esteem	2.00	.63
Autonomy	1.82	1.13
Self-Actualization	2.12	1.16
Importance of Needs		(N = 386)
Security	6.03	5.14
Social	5.77	5.25
Esteem	5.63	5.21
Autonomy	5.73	5.73
Self-Actualization	6.25	6.31

Note — See text for the source and description of the Managerial comparison groups.

Need Satisfaction

We might more appropriately label this "Need *Dis*satisfaction," since a high score indicates greater perceived *deficiency*.

For comparison, the average responses for the same 260 managers referred to under "need fulfillment" are again presented in Table 11-II. The scores were calculated from data presented by Porter and Lawler (1968, p. 136).

The areas of greatest perceived deficiency, or dissatisfaction, for the police in our sample are the higher-level needs for self-Actualization, Esteem, and Autonomy; they are least dissatisfied with regard to their Social needs. These results are a logical mirror-image of the perceived absolute amount of need fulfillment obtained from the job—as presented in the previous section.

Congruent with the previous findings, we note that members of the DPD uniformly experience greater need deficiency, or dissatisfaction, than do the managers—for all five need areas.

Importance of Needs

The answers to the questions of "How important is (the job characteristic) to me?" enable inferences to be made regarding possible motivations to become a policeman. Those inferences are limited, of course, by the current status of the respondents as experienced policemen, rather than applicants.

Managerial comparisons have been made (see Table 11-II) utilizing data presented by Porter (1963a). In order to obtain the most relevant comparison group available, overall averages were computed by combining only the two lowest levels of management ("lower middle" and "lower" management) reported by Porter, at only the two lowest age categories (20 to 34, and 35 to 44). This yielded a national sample of 386 managers.

The police view as most important, the opportunity to achieve Self-Actualization and Security. They view Esteem and Autonomy as least important to them.

Overall, the police seem to attach greater importance to these psychological needs than do the managers—especially as regards the lower-level Security, Social, and Esteem needs—in that order.

Leadership Style

The self-descriptions of leadership style offered by the 54 command personnel on the Leadership Opinion Questionnaire (LOQ) were compared with the analagous perceptions of leadership style offered by the total sample with regard to each man's immediate superior (as described on the Supervisory Behavior Description questionnaire). We noted only overall mean scores, and have not "matched" specific superior-subordinate relationships. The comparisons are also limited by the unknown degree of scalar similarity between the two measures, thus, no formal tests of significance have been computed between them. However, the content and number of items comprising each factor are the same for each of the two measuring instruments. The data are presented as variables 47 to 50 in Table 11-I.

The police command (all supervisors) score "high-average" on Consideration: raw score equivalent of the 65th percentile for general supervisory norms; they score "low-average" in Initiating Structure:32nd percentile. The relatively low Structure score probably reflects the infrequent direct contact of supervisors with subordinates, the high individual discretionary use of time, and centralized type of command typical of police departments.

Subordinates' descriptions of their immediate superiors tend to be lower, on both scales, than the supervisors' self-descriptions. This may be interpreted as a somewhat negative evaluation based on research which indicates the "best" supervisors to be those high on both characteristics (Fleishman, 1969).

Cynicism

The average Cynicism score of the total sample (56.50) is significantly lower than that of 186 New York City policemen reported by Niederhoffer (1967) (62.24, t=2.74, p<.01). The average score is, in fact, slightly below the midpoint of the cynicism scale, which was defined as indicating a "common sense, middle-of-the-road approach." This may be attributable to the organizational differences between Dayton's police department and one as large as New York City's, or it may be due to an inherently more cynical outlook characteristic of the large city-dweller, or some other unknown reason (s).

Dogmatism

The average Dogmatism score of the policemen (146.11) may be compared with that of some representative norm groups presented by Alter and White (1966), Robinson and Shaver (1969), and Rokeach (1960).

The average score of 158 Ohio State University students was 142.13; that of 36 industrial department heads was 132; and 390 psychiatric patients averaged 168.80. (The midpoint of the scale is 160.)

The results support the limited previous findings that policemen do *not* appear to markedly inflexible, authoritarian, or dogmatic, as measured by paper-and-pencil psychometric measures.

Anti-Negro Attitudes

The mean score of 72.26 on the scale of anti-Negro ideology indicates the police to be characterized by a slight anti-Negro bias (the theoretical "neutral point" is a score of 64).

The degree of prejudice is no greater, however, than that reported for a sample of 449 middle-class Negro college students (Mean = 72.80) (Steckler, 1957).

RESULTS II: RELATIONSHIPS AMONG DEMOGRAPHIC FACTORS AND ATTITUDES[5]
Personal Background Characteristics

1. *Level of education.* As is to be expected, there is a significant inverse relationship between amount of formal schooling attained and the Age, Tenure, and Time in Rank of the policemen. This reflects the increasing educational level among newer appointees.

Those without a high school diploma are significantly less satisfied with the type of Work itself. Those with some college education are significantly more satisfied with their Pay, and are more highly Involved with their jobs.

There is a direct relationship between amount of formal schooling and the degree to which the policeman *seeks* Self-Actualization in his work, and how much *importance* he places in Self-Actualization.

2. *Marital status.* In comparison with the married majority, those few men who are not married are younger, with less job tenure.

They view job Security and achieving Self-Actualization as more important to them. They also seek more Self-Actualization.

3. *Size of place in which raised.* The degree of urbanization

---

[5]Space limitations preclude presentation of raw scores for stratified subsamples. Results are merely summarized here. Refer to original source for raw data and results of significance tests. All relationships noted here are statistically significant at the .05 level of confidence, or better.

in which the policemen were raised has affected their job attitudes. In general, it seems that those brought up on a farm are most dissimilar from their peers in their expressed attitudes.

Those brought up on a farm are uniformly least satisfied with the type of Work, their Pay, and derive less gratification of their Social needs and Autonomy needs. They seek less security in their jobs, and view Security and Self-Actualization as less important to them.

They also feel as if they receive more directive, structuring, and active supervision from their immediate superiors than do other policemen.

4. *Age.* More than one-half the study variables were found to be significantly related to the policemen's age. As expected, older officers tend to be of higher rank, have longer tenure, larger families, less education, and have used firearms in the line of duty somewhat more often than younger officers.

Summarizing the findings for the personal need variables, it seems that older officers seek less gratification of their personal needs from their jobs, feel that such gratification is less important to them, and consequently are *less dis*satisfied with the extent to which their personal needs are gratified via their jobs. This is especially marked in regard to the higher-level needs for Esteem, Autonomy, and Self-Actualization. This confirms the finding that older officers also tend to be less "Job Involved."

Not only do older officers tend to expect less from their jobs and be less involved, but they describe the type of Work they do less favorably, and are less satisfied with Promotional Opportunities.

Contrary to what one might expect, we observe significant inverse correlations for Dogmatism, Anti-Negro ideology, and Cynicism. That is, despite their higher educational attainments, the *younger* men tend to be more cynical, closed-minded and biased against Negroes. This probably reflects their lower rank, greater likelihood of being in the field in direct contact with the public, on tough assignments, in ghetto areas, rather than on "inside" and/or "soft" jobs.

Organizational Varibles

1. *Rank.* Stratification on this variable was achieved by comparing patrolmen (N = 258) with all higher ranks ("Command") combined (N = 54). More than one-half of all variables studied differentiated significantly between these two groups.

As expected, command personnel are older, have longer tenure, and are more satisfied with their Pay than are patrolmen. Command are, however, significantly less satisfied with Promotional Opportunities (probably reflecting the limited number of positions at the top of the organizational heirarchy).

It should be noted that both patrolmen and command personnel are similarly most satisfied with their Co-Workers, Supervision, and type of Work, and least satisfied with Pay, and Opportunities for Promotion.

As is to be expected, in comparison with patrolmen, command personnel are more personally Involved in their jobs, and less Cynical, Dogmatic, and Anti-Negro in their feelings. This may reflect a greater likelihood of having been promoted for those who are characteristically open-minded, flexible, optimistic, and non-prejudiced. That is not likely, however, in light of the traditional orientation, until recent years, of the DPD. It more likely reflects the diminished pressures of command in comparison to the greater pressures of patrol work "on the street" to which patrolmen are more exposed.

There are many significant differences between patrolmen and command personnel with regard to need satisfactions. Patrolmen seek significantly greater amounts of Security, Social gratification, and Esteem from their jobs, and also consider the gratification of Security, Social, and Esteem needs to be of greater importance to them.

However, patrolmen obtain significantly less Esteem and Autonomy from their jobs, and are uniformly more dissatisfied with regard to the gratification of their needs for Security, Socialization, Esteem, Autonomy, and Self-Actualization.

2. *Bureau Assignment.* Stratification on this variable was achieved by comparing those men in Feld Operations (N=155), Investigative Operations (N=28), Special Operations (N=81), Information Services (N=18), and Management Services, In-

spectional Services, plus "other," combined (N=30). The large number of significant results (again, over one-half the total number of variables considered) indicates the necessity of accounting for particular job assignment when considering the job attitudes of DPD personnel.

As expected, the men in Field Operations tend to be younger, with less tenure, than those in other bureaus. They may be characterized as more Cynical regarding police work and the policeman's job, more closed-minded (Dogmatic), more prejudiced against Negroes, least satisfied with their Pay and (to a lesser extent) their Co-Workers.

Those in Special Operations are less "Job Involved" than other personnel.

Summarizing the findings for the personal need variables, it appeared that those in Field Operations (and to a somewhat lesser extent, Special Operations) tend to seek the fulfillment of personal needs to a greater extent, view that fulfillment as more important to them, but are less satisfied with the degree of fulfillment actually obtained.

3. *Frequency of firearms use.* Those who have never used firearms in the line of duty are those who have had less opportunity to do so (younger, with less tenure).

Those who have most used firearms in the line of duty are *more* satisfied with their Pay, and are *less* prejudiced against Negroes. Those frequent-users also obtain a greater sense of personal Esteem and Autonomy from their jobs; they seek less gratification of Social needs.

RESULTS III: FACTOR ANALYSIS

Factor analyses were performed for the total sample, for patrolmen alone, and for command personnel alone. The relatively small size of the command subsample, in relation to the number of variables, renders that analysis somewhat tenuous.[6,7]

The purposes of factor-analyzing the data are to achieve a

---

[6]However, Rummel (1970) states that a number of cases merely in excess of the number of variables is sufficient even for inferences to universal factors.

[7]The number of variables factored for the total group and patrolman subsample are 48. For command personnel, 50 variables (including the two LOQ scales) are factored.

parsimonious description of the inter-relatedness of the 50 variables used in the study, and to explore the domain of job attitudes of policemen with an aim toward, possibly, contributing to efforts at theory-construction in this area.

The common factor analysis model was employed with squared multiple correlation coefficients as communality estimates. The rotations were orthogonal to a criterion of simple structure (Varimax) . Only those factors with *eigenvalues* equal to or greater than one were rotated, and rotated factors were described by only those variables with loadings of at least ± .40.[8]

The *eigenvalue-one* criterion resulted in the rotation of 6 factors for the total sample, 9 for the patrolman subsample, and 12 for the command subsample. These rotated factors account for 55 percent, 55 percent, and 73 percent of the total variation in the three samples, respectively.

These are bipolar group factors and they range in complexity from highly complex (substantial loadings on 17 variables for Factor I, total sample) to several doublet factors (number III, total sample; Factors VI and VIII for the patrolman subsample) .

The factor comparisons summarized in Table 11-III indicate that the primary dimensions of attitudes are similar for both patrolmen and command personnel, confirming the factors noted when the total undifferentiated sample is analyzed. Those reliable factors are *Psychological Growth, Intrinsic Job Satisfaction, Job Tenure, Satisfaction—Security,* and *Satisfaction—Social Relations.* Those factors are not, however, identical for both subgroups. There are subtle differences in the content.

Satisfaction with supervision and with co-workers seems to be an element of *Intrinsic Job Satisfaction* only for command personnel, indicating social interaction to be an inherent aspect of their jobs. Conversely, cynicism and satisfaction with the degree of esteem derived from the job are loaded in *Intrinsic Job Satisfaction* only for patrolmen. This probably reflects the assertion of personal prestige and status as inherent aspects of the job for the policeman in close contact with the public.

---

[8]Only a brief summary of the factor analysis results is presented. All details, including descriptions of the variables which define each factor, are presented in the original source.

TABLE 11-III
FACTOR COMPARISONS: APPROXIMATE RELATIONSHIPS AMONG
THE ROTATED FACTORS

COMMAND	*TOTAL SAMPLE*	*PATROLMEN*
II. Psychological Growth	I. Psychological Growth	II. Psychological Growth and Socialbility
I. Intrinsic Job Satisfaction	II. Intrinsic Job Satisfaction	I. Intrinsic Job Satisfaction
VIII. Job Tenure	III. Job Tenure	III. Job Tenure
III. Satisfaction—Security	IV. Satisfaction—Security	IV. Satisfaction—Security
IV. Satisfaction—Social Relations	} V. Satisfaction—Social Relations	{ V. Satisfaction—Social Relations
V. Satisfaction—Esteem		{ IX. Satisfaction—Esteem
X. Psychological Growth Avoidance		{ VI. Psychological Growth Avoidance
VII. Closed-Mindedness	} VI. Defensiveness	{ VIII. Closed-Minded Racial Prejudice
XI. Status		
VI. Satisfaction—Advancement		
IX. Leadership		
XII. Satisfaction—Supervision		VII. Satisfaction Supervision

Note—Relationships determined by Visual (non-Mathematical) Comparisons.

Sociability (interest in social interaction with others) seems more strongly related to personal *Psychological Growth* for patrolmen, than for command.

An interesting finding is that satisfaction with Pay and with the type of Work itself are elements in the amount of security felt by command people, but the *Satisfaction—Security* factor is more specific for patrolmen.

As a result of performing the subgroup analyses, we learn that two minor factors for the total group, *Satisfaction—Social Relations,* and *Defensiveness,* are apparently complex factors composed of two or more dimensions each. (The definition of "defensiveness" is highly inferential. A policeman scoring high on this factor is one who views job security as very important to him, seeks a great deal of such security, is prejudiced against Negroes, satisfied with his pay, and is of low rank in the department.)

The complex social relations factor is comprised of both *Satisfaction—Esteem* and *Satisfaction—Social Relations*. Moreover, these two factors hold for both subgroups independently.

Factor VI for the total group, tentatively labelled *Defensiveness*, breaks down into *Growth Avoidance* and *Closed-Mindedness* for both patrolmen and command. (*Closed-Mindedness* seems to be a more general complex cognitive factor for command, whereas for patrolmen it seems more specifically related to anti-Negro prejudice.) Moreover, *Defensiveness* is also composed of a third factor, *Status,* for command personnel only.

A minor *Satisfaction—Supervision* factor emerges for both subgroups, whereas it did not appear in the analysis for the total sample.

In addition, there are two factors, *Satisfaction—Advancement* and *Leadership* which play minor roles in accounting for the job attitudes of the command personnel in our sample, but which are not pertinent at all to patrolmen. (For patrolmen, the variable "opportunities for promotion" loads most heavily on *Intrinsic Job Satisfaction*.)

DISCUSSIONS AND IMPLICATIONS

It seems appropriate to emphasize, again, the *caveat* concerning the relationship between attitudes and behavior. Evidence exists which indicate attitudes to affect behavior, as well as *vice versa*. However, there is no necessary nor invariably direct relationship between the two. Attenuating factors which may modify the link between any given attitude and overt behavior include all of the other motivational and environmental determinants of that behavior, constraints on the expression of certain attitudes, the relevance of other attitudes to the behavior, and the nature and intensity of the attitude (Kiesler, 1971).

We have neither assessed any of these attenuating factors nor systematically observed occasions for the overt expression of the attitudes with which we are concerned. Nevertheless, like most field surveys, this study accepts the significance of such job attitudes as influential determinants (and effects) of occupational behavior, as well as accepting their intrinsic relevance to gaining an understanding of police personnel.

From an overall point of view, this study confirms most of the less-systematic available published research in the area of job satisfaction. In comparison with industrial workers, the DPD is relatively more dissatisfied with respect to all five job aspects measured. They are most satisfied with their co-workers, supervision, and the type of work, and very dissatisfied with their pay and opportunities for promotion.

These policemen attach considerable importance to the gratification, through their jobs, of their personal needs for security, social contact, esteem, autonomy, and self-actualization—especially self-actualization and security. The emphasis on personal growth, self-fulfillment, and worthwhile accomplishment offer a relatively new dimension to the study of personal attractions to the police job. It is enhanced by the results of the factor analysis—to be discussed shortly.

In contrast with their view of the *importance* of self-actualization, it is the area in which their needs are most dissatisfied (along with autonomy and esteem). This probably accounts for their lack of any marked "job involvement" despite their interest in self-fulfillment through the job.

The paper-and-pencil measures of particular personality traits indicate these policemen to be not particularly cynical, nor dogmatic in their thinking, and only slightly prejudiced against Negroes. This generally confirms previous findings on paper-and-pencil instruments, and, in part, does not coincide with the more negative evaluations often arrived at by more informal, casual, and/or subtle measurement techniques and observations of overt behavior. We have, in one instance, offered as a tentative explanation for this type of discrepancy, the notion that a crucial factor may not be (for example) the *degree* of authoritarianism or aggression which characterizes the policeman, but the manner in which it is experienced, controlled and expressed by him (Lefkowitz, 1971).

All of the generalizations with respect to job satisfactions, need satisfactions, and personality attributes must be hedged in light of the significant effects of stratifying the sample by various demographic and organizational variables. It was found that, for many attitude variables, the men's responses were influenced significantly by their educational level, marital status, family size, size of community in which raised, age, rank, bureau assignment, frequency of firearms use, and job tenure. It is only with some reservation, then, that we generalize to attitudes of the entire police department.

In the continuing advocacy of increased "professionalism" among police, there is no more-frequently sounded cry than that for increased educational standards for recruits. However, there is usually no empirical justification offered for that advocacy. Moreover, some critics are not convinced that college-educated men would necessarily make better police officers and that, in any event, it is extremely unlikely that well-educated people would find a police career attractive (Cross, 1964; Wilson, 1968). Our findings regarding the stratification by educational level are pertinent.

While we have dealt only with attitudes and have not measured actual job performance, the implications of the positive association between higher educational attainment and increased job satisfaction, job involvement, and a self-actualizing orientation are clear.

Whether other family members have even been policemen, and the region of the United States in which raised, were nonsignificant influences on reported attitudes. While those findings are not crucial, they do support those who advocate more widespread recruiting for police, and the elimination of residency restrictions.

Command personnel described themselves as fairly "considerate" leaders, but relatively low on "initiating structure." Moreover, the pattern was confirmed by their subordinates' descriptions of them. This description of a moderately warm, considerate supervisor, who remains relatively passive in directing his subordinates' activities confirms less formal observations of the DPD command. It reflects traditional police department command processes wherein most authority resides with the chief, with little down-the-line delegation. In such situations, supervisors tend to "sit back" and let the formal rules and regulations guide their sanctions of extreme behavior; little is done as long as subordinates remain "within bounds." The situation is exacerbated by relatively infrequent personal contact between ranks.

The situation, as manifested in the DPD, is described by the Director of Police as "management by abdication." A contradictory finding, however, is that command personnel view the gratification of their autonomy needs as important to them and seek a high level of such gratification ("Autonomy" being defined as having an authoritative job, with opportunities for independent thought and action, for participation in goal-setting, and for participation in the determination of methods and procedures). This would seem to be an important area worthy of further investigation and management development efforts.

An important finding emerging from the factor analysis is that the underlying general constellations of factors which are the most significant determinants of the sample's attitudes are a motivational factor labelled "psychological growth" and a satisfaction factor concerned with "intrinsic" aspects of the job.

These are important in light of the repeated emphasis in the literature on extrinsic job factors (pay, benefits, social relations, security) as exclusive determinants of police behavior. It means that police administrators need pay greater heed to the possibility of alternative job designs insofar as the dull, routine aspects of the job may be reduced in favor of increased challenge, autonomy, and opportunity for personal accomplishment. This is especially pertinent in light of the continually increasing educational level among police personnel and seems consistent with the assumptions underlying the increased responsibility given to policemen in the experimental "Team Policing" programs supported by the Law Enforcement Assistance Administration in several cities.

A highly suggestive finding is the emergence of a factor inferentially labelled "defensiveness" as a determinant of individual responses. It seems to be a complex factor comprised of security-striving (psychological growth avoidance), closed-mindedness, racial prejudice, and status considerations. It would certainly be advisable, in future factor analytic research, to include variables which are presumably related psychologically to this syndrome. Only in that way might we ascertain the extent and reliability of its occurrence. It might, perhaps, be an indication of the suspiciousness, defensiveness, and misperceptions of public attitudes toward them which several investigators have found characteristic of policemen (Bayley & Mendelsohn, 1969; Matarazzo, et al., 1964; Mills, 1969; Niederhoffer, 1967; Preiss and Ehrlich, 1966; Reiss, 1967b; Rhead, et al., 1968; Westley, 1956).

Based on this study, primary suggestions for future research concern the area of performance measurement and evaluation. First, are these job attitudes related significantly to the way in which a police officer actually performs his job, and how well he performs it? Secondly, is it possible to develop relevant, reliable, objective, and fair indices of police performance for use in performance evaluation, and the administration of organizational reward systems? From the standpoint of morale, confidence in the department, and attractiveness of a career in police work, few tasks are as significant as solving this "criterion problem."

REFERENCES

Alter, R.D. and White, B.J.: Some Norms for the Dogmatism Scale. *Psychological Reports,* 1966, *19,* 967-969.

Astor, G.: The New York Cops. Article VI: The Spirit of the Force, *New York Post,* June 19, 1971.

Bayley, D.H. and Mendelsohn, H.: *Minorities and the Police: Confrontation in America.* New York, The Free Press, 1969.

Black, A.D.: *The People and the Police.* New York, McGraw-Hill, 1968.

Chevigny, P.: *Police Power: Police Abuses in New York City.* New York, Vintage Books, 1969.

Clark, J.P.: Isolation of the Police: A Comparison of the British and American Situations. *Journal of Criminal Law, Criminology and Police Science,* 1965, *56* (3) September, 307-319.

Clark, R.: *Crime in America: Observations in Its Nature, Causes, Prevention and Control.* New York, Pocket Books, 1970.

Cross, G.J.: The Negro, Prejudice, and the Police. *Journal of Criminal Law, Criminology and Police Science,* 1964, *55* (3), September, 405-411.

Dodd, D.J.: Police Mentality and Behavior. *Issues in Criminology,* 1967, *3* (1), Summer, 47-67.

Fleishman, E.A.: *Manual for Leadership Opinion Questionnaire.* Chicago, Illinois, Science Research Associates, 1969.

Institute for Social Research: Violence in America—How Men Justify It. *ISR Newsletter,* Spring, 1971.

Kiesler, C.A.: *The Psychology of Commitment: Experiments Linking Behavior to Belief.* New York, Academic Press, 1971.

Lefkowitz, J.: *Job Attitudes of Police.* National Institute of Law Enforcement and Criminal Justice, Law Enforcement Assistance Administration, United States Department of Justice, August, 1971.

Lefkowitz, J.: Evaluation of A Supervisory Training Program for Police Sergeants. *Personnel Psychology,* 1972, in press.

Leonard, V.A.: *Police Organization and Management,* 2nd edition. Brooklyn, New York, Foundation Press, 1964.

Lodahl, J.M. and Kejner, M.: The Definition and Measurement of Job Involvement. *Journal of Applied Psychology,* 1956, *49,* 24-33.

Matarazzo, J.D., Allen, B.V., Saslow, G. and Wiens, A.N.: Characteristics of Successful Policeman and Fireman Applicants. *Journal of Applied Psychology,* 1964, *48* (2), 123-133.

McCaghy, C.H.: Cops Talk Back. *Urban Affairs Quarterly,* 1968, *4* (2), 245-256.

Mills, R.B.: Use of Diagnostic Small Groups in Police Recruit Selection and Training. *Journal of Criminal Law, Criminology and Police Science,* 1969, *60* (2), 238-241.

Niederhoffer, A.: *Behind the Shield: The Police in Urban Society.* New York, Anchor Books, 1967.

Nolan, J. B.: Mental Hygiene in the Day's Work: A Day in the Life of a Police Officer. *Mental Hygiene,* 1950, *34,* 477-455.

Porter, L.: Job Attitudes in Management: I. Perceived Deficiencies in Need Fulfillment as A Function of Job Level. *Journal of Applied Psychology,* 1962, *46,* 375-384.

Porter, L.: Job Attitudes in Management: II. Perceived Importance of Needs as A Function of Job Level. *Journal of Applied Psychology,* 1963, *47,* 141-148 (a).

Porter, L.W. and Lawler, E.E., III: *Managerial Attitudes and Performance.* Homewood, Illinois, Richard D. Irwin and The Dorsey Press, 1968.

Preiss, J.J. and Ehrlich, H.J.: An Examination of Role Theory: *The Case of the State Police.* Lincoln, Nebraska, University of Nebraska Press, 1966.

Radano, G.: *Walking the Beat.* New York, World Publishing Company, 1968.

Reiss, A.J.: Career Orientations, Job Satisfaction, and the Assessment of Law Enforcement Problems by Police Officers. *Studies of Crime and Law Enforcement in Major Metropolitan Areas,* Vol. II, Section II. U.S. Government Printing Office, 1967 (b).

Rhead, C., Abrams, A., Trasman, H., and Margolis, P.: The Psychological Assessment of Police Candidates. *American Journal of Psychiatry*, 1968, *124* (11), 1575-1580.

Robinson, J.P., Athanasiou, R., and Head, K.B.: *Measures of Occupational Attitudes and Occupational Characteristics.* Ann Arbor, Michigan, Institute for Social Research, 1969.

Robinson, J.P. and Shaver, P.R.: *Measures of Social Psychological Attitudes.* Ann Arbor, Michigan, Institute for Social Research, 1969.

Rokeach, M.: *The Open and Closed Mind.* New York, Basic Books, Inc., 1960.

Rummel, R.J.: *Applied Factor Analysis.* Evanston, Illinois, Northwestern University Press, 1970.

Shaw, M.E. and Wright, J.M.: *Scales for the Measurement of Attitudes.* New York, McGraw-Hill, 1967.

Smith, Patricia C., Kendall, L.M., and Hulin, C.L.: *The Measurement of Satisfaction in Work and Retirement.* Chicago, Illinois, Rand McNally, 1969.

Steckler, A.: Authoritarian Ideology in Negro College Students. *Journal of Abnormal and Social Psychology*, 1957, *54*, 396-399.

Stogdill, R.M. and Coons, A.C. (Eds.): *Leader Behavior: Its Description and Measurement.* Columbus, Ohio, Ohio State University Bureau of Business Research, 1957.

Vacchiano, R.B., Strauss, P.S., and Hochman, L.: The Open and Closed Mind: A Review of Dogmatism. *Psychological Bulletin*, 1969, *71* (4), 261-273.

Vollmer, A.: *The Police and Modern Society.* Berkeley, California, University of California Press, 1936, 222.

Webb, E.J.: *Unobtrusive Measures: Nonreactive Research in the Social Sciences.* Chicago, Illinois, Rand McNally, 1966.

Westley, W.A.: Violence and the Police. *American Journal of Sociology*, 1953, *59*, 34-41.

Westley, W.A.: Secrecy and the Police. *Social Forces*, 1956, *34*, 254-257.

Welton, C.: Cooling the Rage of the Cop in the Street, Village Voice, June 24, 1971.

Wilson, J.Q.: *Varieties of Police Behavior: The Management of Law and Order in Eight Communities.* Cambridge, Massachusetts, Harvard University Press, 1968.

Wolfe, J.B.: Some Psychological Characteristics of American Policemen: A Critical Review of the Literature. *Proceedings of the Annual Convention of the American Psychological Association*, 1970, *5* (Pt. 1), 453-454.

Chapter 12

POLICE OPINIONS OF WORK: AN EXPLORATORY STUDY

BRUCE T. OLSON*

IN RECENT YEARS local law enforcement has received more attention than in any period of its history. The proper study of mankind, it seems, is its police.

While a rather large amount of law enforcement data is now accumulating, one extremely crucial area of police work remains relatively uncharted: the job itself. Some research into local law enforcement has been directed at matters peripheral to the work role, for example, whether officers would advise young men to become policemen; how policemen feel about pay, security, their comrades; what can be done to minimize crime, statistical analyses of the time policemen spend on various aspects of their work;[1] styles of police management;[2] improving police selection techniques.[3] Space does not permit an extensive list of the social science literature concerned with police work, but an inspection of this literature indicates that while useful data regarding many dimensions of police work are available, there is little information regarding the policeman's opinion of his work.

This is unfortunate for a number of reasons. For example, the

Reprinted from *Police Chief*, July, 1971, *38*, 28-38.

*The Author wishes to thank the police officers who voluntarily participated in this study. Also Mr. M.N. Hendrickson, Coordinator of the Police Science Program, Solano Community College.

[1]Albert J. Reiss, Jr., "Career Orientations, Job Satisfactions, The Assesssment of Law Enforcement Problems by Police Officers," Working Paper, Ann Arbor, Michigan: The University of Michigan, 1966.

[2]John A. Webster, "Police Work and Time Study," *The Journal of Law Criminology and Police Science*, Vol. 61, March, 1970, pp. 94-100.

[3]Melany E. Baehr, *et al.*, *Psychological Assessment of Patrolmen Qualifications in Relation to Field Performance*, a Report submitted to the Office of Law Enforcement Assistance, Washington, D.C.: U.S. Government Printing Office, 1968.

233

desire for improved salaries and other benefits cannot by itself account for the rising interest in unionization. No doubt other pressures contribute to this interest, among which must be the attitudes police officers have about their work. But what are these attudes? In what way, if any, do they account for specific behavior, such as decisions to leave the police service, or supervisor-subordinate tensions?

Another crucial issue today is the relationship between the community and its police. Can improvements be made in this area if the internal climate in which police work is carried out is not improved? Perhaps policemen are highly satisfied with their work, but if they are not, it is important that we know more about the sources of this dissatisfaction, since these may be related to poor community-police relations.

If social science has neglected this important field, professional police literature has been even more silent. This may be explainable in terms of the orientation of many police administration theorists. In the framework of classical management theory, the attitudes and beliefs of organizational members are subordinate, as objects of concern, to the proper construction and alignment of the organization itself. If, for example, the correct span of control is implemented, idiosyncratic employee behavior can be minimized. In short, the classical management emphasis is on organizational control rather than personal development. This may explain why a number of police administration texts do not list the word "morale" in their index, or, if morale is considered it is seen as something occurring under conditions of "positive discipline."[4] There is, of course, nothing wrong with this assertion, so far as it goes, but given the nature of police work, it is obvious that some of the factors which lead to negative morale are not subject to the mechanisms of direct administrative control while, on the other hand, some factors may be amenable to managerial problem-solving.

In time the actual nature of the policeman's work role, and his attitudes regarding it, will be better understood. If either

---

[4] See Edgar H. Schein, *Organizational Psychology,* Englewood Cliffs, New Jersey: Prentice-Hall, Inc., 1965, Chapter 4, for a discussion of classical versus contemporary management perceptions of subordinates.

unionization or professionalization becomes crucial in the next decade, intense analysis of the police work role must occur. This will be particularly true if the trend is toward professionalization, since one of the characteristics of this process is a heightened interest in gaining autonomy over the nature of the work role, usually for the purpose of purging it of non-professional elements.

The research reported in this article has been termed "police opinions of work" rather than a study of morale. Morale in its broadest sense may include factors which do not directly arise out of one's work, although these factors may, certainly, be involved in feelings about work. An illustration would be a worker employed in a low-status job which he enjoys, but whose family is ashamed of his work. In such a case, he could report himself as being low in morale (in a broad "satisfaction with life" sense) but happy with his work, in a narrow sense.

This is a preliminary report of a project initiated by the writer in 1966 to find answers, if only tentative, to two questions:

1. What do police officers perceive as crucial job-related problems?

2. How are these problems ordered in terms of magnitude?

Before discussing some of the findings which have been developed in the preliminary phases of this project, it will be helpful to discuss the development of the project's research instrument, the "Police Opinion of Work Questionnaire."

DEVELOPMENT OF THE POLICE OPINION OF WORK QUESTIONNAIRE

The study's first research question required that police officers themselves should be enlisted as informants. Alternatively, we might have read professional literature, interviewed city managers or staff members of various professional police associations, police science instructors, etc., but this would have resulted in a census of problems which "outsiders" defined as contemporary police problems. By enlisting working policemen as principal informants, the problems were expected to be more representative of the "police problem universe." This is not to say that other sources were not used: professional police journals were read, various knowledgeable civilian observers of the police field were consulted, and even letters to the editors of various newspapers and popular magazine articles provide insights into contemporary police problems, but police officers provided the main source of job-related problems involved in this study.

The prototype of the present version of the Police Opinion of Work Questionnaire (POWQ) consisted of 200 items developed from hand-written responses to an open-end questionnaire which had been distributed in an early phase of a management survey conducted in a Michigan police department.[5] Four questions comprised the open-end questionnaire:

1. What are the good things about this department?
2. In what way should the department be improved?
3. What do you think the citizens in your town want you, as a policeman, to do?
4. What do you think your job as a policeman is?

Over 90 percent of the officers of all ranks voluntarily responded to these questions; each response was carefully read by the writer and over 400 separate, one-sentence statements were developed. This list was reduced to 200 items after a series of conferences with police officers in other departments (including a state police agency) who helped the writer check each item's readability and general applicability.

Another source of items was an open-end questionnaire, similar to the one described above, which was administered to officers of all ranks in 30 small, medium, and large-sized police departments throughout the United States. These officers voluntarily completed the open-end questionnaire as an exercise in a home-study correspondence course in which they were enrolled. Still another group of police officers was involved in the item generation phase of the project: open-end questionnaires were completed by nearly 100 officers attending police science courses conducted by colleagues of the writer in various western, midwestern, and eastern states.

[5]John K. Longstreth and Bruce T. Olson, *A Study of the Benton Harbor, Michigan Police Department,* East Lansing, Michigan: Michigan State University, Institute for Community Development, 1967.

The POWQ items were not only generated by police officers, as described above, but other officers subsequently read and criticized them as they moved through many pretesting stages before appearing in their present form in the POWQ. These officers were employed by city police departments, county sheriffs' departments, and two state police agencies. This item development and review process accounts for the generally local law enforcement orientation and tone of the 145 items in the present version of the POWQ.

Present Form of the POWQ

The police opinion of work questionnaire consists of two sections. Section 1 is comprised of 145 one line statements; for example: Degree to which citizens support this police organization.

Respondents are asked to rate each statement as to the degree they perceive it to be a problem, ranging from "major problem" to "no problem." Thus, each officer decides the magnitude of each statement as a problem he perceives. The five response options are "major problem," "moderate problem," "no opinion or undecided," "small problem," "no problem."

Section 2 of the questionnaire, "Some Final Questions," consists of seven demographic questions asking for information about rank, years in police work, length of service in the present police organization, age, sex, race, education. Another question asks the respondent about the size of the department employing him. In addition, the respondent is asked to answer four attitude questions: (1) whether he prefers traffic- or crime-related police work; (2) the degree to which POWQ items cover the problems respondents experience in their work; (3) whether he enjoyed completing the questionnaire very much, somewhat, or not at all; (4) how satisfied he is with his job.

The first attitudinal item relates to a particular issue in which the writer is interested and need not be discussed here. The second and third items were designed to yield data regarding the generalizability of POWQ results and the frame of mind of the respondents regarding the instrument. If most respondents indicated it covered few of the problems they experienced, and if the same respondents reported they did not enjoy completing the POWQ, serious doubts regarding the data would have to be entertained.

The fourth attitudinal question is Kunin's faces scale, which is a questionnaire item to obtain data regarding respondents' feelings about their job in general.[6] It consists of six renderings of a man's face ranging from very happy to very unhappy. Respondents are asked to check the face ". . . which expresses how you feel about your *job in general,* including the work, pay, supervision, opportunities for promotion, and the people you work with." The use of faces, rather than words, is thought to minimize distortion, since words are more subject to interpretation than pictures.

The faces scale was included for this reason: if the POWQ were actually tapping sensitive work-related problem areas, officers who reported they were happy with their jobs in general should rate most items differently than those who were not. To put it another way, if the POWQ items were irrelevant as job-related items, there should be little or no difference in scores between officers who reported themselves happy with their jobs and those who reported themselves unhappy. The faces scale, in short, was included as a rough measure of the validity of the POWQ.

QUESTIONNAIRE DISTRIBUTION AND ANALYSIS

While the POWQ evolved through many pretests and critiques, it was still necessary to test it under the conditions for which it was developed, that is, as a self-administering, mailed questionnaire. A distribution strategy was developed whereby the POWQ was voluntarily completed by a large number of officers employed in 16 California and Oklahoma police departments. These departments ranged from 9 to 558 sworn employees. It will be seen that the distribution plan was not based on an overall random sampling procedure with the exception of the highway patrol agency which participated on a random-sampling basis.

[6]Theodore Kunin, "The Construction of A New Type of Attitude Measure," *Personnel Psychology,* Vol. 8, 1955, pp. 65-78. For information about Dr. Kunin's scale, see Patricia Cain Smith, *et al., The Measures of Satisfaction in Work and Retirement,* Chicago, Illinois: Rand, McNally, 1969, p. 176.

Thus, just over one-third of the respondents whose scores are reported in this article were selected randomly, according to rank and geographical assignment. Several police chiefs distributed questionnaires to men assembled at roll calls, and in several cases the writer and Mr. Hendrickson distributed questionnaires within departments with which they were familiar on a roughly random basis. In all cases, it was emphasized that participation was voluntary and anonymous.

By the time the data processing cut-off date arrived, 620 questionnaires were returned to the writer in self-addressed, pre-stamped envelopes which bore the writer's name, academic title, and address. Of this number, 19 were not data processed because of one or more of these reasons: (1) respondent failed to complete more than 10 items in Part I, (2) respondent failed to complete certain crucial demographic items, (3) in several cases, either Section 1 or Section 2 was completely blank. Many questionnaires arrived after the cut-off date and were not included in the present analysis. In all, 601 questionnaires were data processed.

General Nature of Response

Since participation was voluntary, the more highly motivated officers are, no doubt, represented in the POWQ findings reported in this article. Perhaps under distribution conditions which were not quite so permissive the overall frame of mind of respondents would have been less positive than it was in this preliminary study. For example, in only three cases did respondents show aggressive hostility to the POWQ: two officers expressed anger at receiving the questionnaire and one expressed a distaste for participating in anything in which "sociologists" were involved. Some were critical in more specific ways and offered constructive suggestions which they felt would improve the POWQ. Additional information regarding respondent attitudes will be discussed below, but the point is that it appears that the amount of negative feeling which attached to returned POWQs was minimal.

Preparation for Analysis

Each questionnaire was read by the writer and prepared for key punching. In less than 1 percent of the returned questionnaires, a few responses to Parts 1 and 2 were blank and these were indicated by an appropriate key-punch code. In addition to key-punch verification, a validation program was written to double-check coding procedures.

Statistical Procedure

Two statistics were used: mean scores $(\overline{X})$ which are arith-metical averages and the Leik score, which is a measure of agreement.[7] The Leik score is particularly useful since maximum agreement is reported as 1.00 while maximum disagreement would be reported as −1.00.

Response options in Part I were weighed as follows: a major problem was weighted 1, moderate problem 2, no opinion or undecided 3, small problem 4, no problem 5. Thus, the lower the mean score for an item, the greater the problem it was perceived to be. For example, item 86, "The extent to which U.S. Supreme Court decisions have affected law enforcement policies," received an overall $\overline{X}$ score of 2.19, which places the item in the moderate problem range, but close to the major problem category. Item 94, "Willingness of men to help each other in a tight spot," received a $\overline{X}$ score of 4.87, which places the item in the no problem range.

The Leik score shows the degree to which there is consensus about the mean score; for example, item 86, regarding the Supreme Court, received a Leik score of .140, which means there is considerable disagreement regarding the item. But item 94, regarding perceived *esprit de corps,* received a Leik score of .888, which indicates great agreement.

FINDINGS

The potential data yield from the POWQ is large because the demographic items may be cross-tabulated against the 145 problem items in literally dozens of ways. For example, one might inquire how black officers with college degrees, but whose morale is reportedly low, differ in their POWQ item scores from black offi-

---

[7]A complete explanation of this statistic will be found in: Robert K. Leik, "A Measure of Ordinal Consensus." *Pacific Sociological Review,* Vol. 9, Fall, 1966.

cers with college degrees, but whose morale is reportedly high, Space considerations, however, require that only a small portion of the data can be reported in this article. Before reporting the data which answered, if only tentatively, the two research questions discussed above, readers may find a brief discussion of respondent characteristics useful.

Returns by State

The rate of returned usable questionnaires was about the same for each state. Thus, 61 percent of the number of questionnaires (977) distributed in California and Oklahoma departments were data processed.

Respondent Characteristics

Unfortunately, most police departments do not have information regarding the distribution of their sworn employees by rank, years of total police work, length of service in present department, age, sex, race, level of education. Therefore, there is no precise way of analyzing how respondents differed from non-respondents according to these characteristics. The writer's general conclusion is that respondent's probably were not crucially different from non-respondents on these characteristics. Possibly officers with college education are somewhat over-represented, as were somewhat younger officers. Also, it is likely that non-Caucasian officers were somewhat under-represented in the study. On an overall basis, small police departments (i.e. those with thirty or less men) are under-represented; thus, the data are based on perceptions obtained from officers serving fairly large urban governments, except for highway patrol and sheriff department respondents.

By including the faces scale, we were able to acquire some insight into the reported job satisfaction of our respondents: 75 percent selected one of the happy faces to indicate their job satisfaction; 18 percent selected the neutral face, while 7 percent selected an unhappy face. Since the industrial job dissatisfaction average is about 13 percent (where employees have responded to various morale self-reporting instruments), it seems possible that persons experiencing a low degree of job satisfaction tended not to participate in the present study.[8]

Attitudes Toward the Questionnaire

To determine how relevant POWQ items were perceived to be, respondents were asked if the items covered "most, some, or few of the things you feel are problems in your work." Seventy percent of all respondents reported the items covered "most" of the problems; 20 percent said the items covered "some" problems, while 8 percent said the items covered "few" problems. Generally, respondents in each of the two states made about the same assessment of the POWQ's comprehensiveness, although more Oklahoma officers felt the POWQ covered "few" problems than California officers (10 percent and 7 percent, respectively).

To determine whether the POWQ was perceived as a burden, respondents were asked if they enjoyed ". . . completing this questionnaire very much, somewhat, or not at all?" Thirty-four percent in both states reported they enjoyed completing it "very much," 56 percent reported they enjoyed completing it "somewhat," while 7 percent reported they enjoyed completing it "not at all."

The Nature of Job-Related Police Problems

The project's primary research objective was to identify what kinds of job-related problems were experienced by policemen. This objective was met, if only tentatively, when the item generation phase of POWQ development was finished, resulting in 145 single-sentence statements which were judged representative of statements made by most of the policemen who provided us with responses to our earlier open-end questionnaires. After the 145 items had been extensively pretested, they were analyzed to see if any order was implicit within them. This effort resulted in an arrangement of the items into ten major and thirty-two minor categories. These are shown in Table 12-I, "Classification of Police

---

[8]For a discussion of the nature and extent of industrial job dissatisfaction, see Robert F. Blauner, "Extent of Satisfaction: A Review of General Research," in Costello and Zalkind, *Psychology in Administration*, Englewood Cliffs, New Jersey: Prentice-Hall, Inc., 1963, Ch. 6.

Opinion of Work Questionnaire Items by Ten Categories and Thirty-Two Subcategories."

TABLE 12-I

CLASSIFICATION OF POLICE OPINION OF WORK QUESTIONNAIRE ITEMS BY TEN CATEGORIES AND THIRTY-TWO SUBCATEGORIES

CATEGORIES AND SUBCATEGORIES		*NUMBER OF ITEMS*	*PERCENT OF TOTAL*
COMMUNITY-POLICE RELATIONS			
Citizens		10	
Criminal Justice System Officials		4	
News Media		4	
Other Officials		6	
Other Police Departments		2	
	Subtotal	26	17.9%
EQUIPMENT AND FACILITIES			
General		2	
Civil Disturbance Equipment		1	
Uniforms		2	
Vehicles		2	
	Subtotal	7	4.8%
INTERNAL COMMUNICATIONS	Subtotal	4	2.8%
MANAGEMENT	Subtotal	15	10.3%
OPERATIONS			
Patrol Strategies		4	
Prisoners		3	
Resources		3	
Other		4	
	Subtotal	14	9.7%
ORGANIZATIONAL EFFECTIVENESS			
Coordination		3	
Criminal Law Enforcement		6	
Crime Prevention		2	
Traffic		2	
Other		2	
	Subtotal	15	10.3%
RECORDS AND DISPATCHING			
Dispatching		2	
Records		7	
	Subtotal	9	6.2%
SUPERVISION			
Evaluation of Supervisors		12	
Performance Evaluation		2	
Role Ambiguity		2	
	Subtotal	16	11.0%

TABLE 12-I (Cont.)

CATEGORIES AND SUBCATEGORIES		NUMBER OF ITEMS	PERCENT OF TOTAL
TRAINING AND EDUCATION			
Education		1	
In-Service Training		4	
Pre-Service Training		6	
	Subtotal	11	7.6%
WORKING CONDITIONS AND PERSONNEL MANAGEMENT			
Assignment		4	
Compensation, Retirement, Vacations		3	
Discipline		4	
Esprit de Corps		10	
Promotion		4	
Selection		3	
	Subtotal	28	19.3%
	TOTAL	145	100.0%

The largest single category, "Working Conditions and Personnel Management," includes twenty-eight items relating to how officers are assigned, disciplined, selected, and promoted, as well as items regarding fringe benefits and internal cohesion.[9]

The next largest category, "Community-Police Relations," includes items regarding citizens, other participants in the criminal justice system, the news media, other (non-criminal justice) officials, and other police departments. These items relate to perceptions of problems which arise in connection with persons or agencies external to the organization.

The third largest category, "Supervision," contains sixteen items permitting respondents to assess the quality of supervision

---

[9]Readers will notice that no item relating directly to salary was included. In actuality, "Pay" or "Salary" was one of the most frequent responses noted in the open-end phase of the study. Indeed, there seemed so little variance potential in an item relating to this topic that a decision was made not to include it in the final POWQ. In retrospect, this may have been a mistake, especially since it subsequently proved to be possible to administer the instrument in two states. It would have been interesting, for example, to see whether perceptions of the adequacy of salary by state were related to the actual amount of compensation by state.

in their departments. Instructions in the POWQ explicitly define supervisors as "sergeants or other persons who directly supervise the work of troopers or policemen." As in the industrial setting, supervisor-subordinate relationships are crucial in police work, particularly at the sergeant-patrolman level. Two items in this category deal with the way in which the officers' work is evaluated and two items refer to how ambiguous the officers' role is as a result of perceived supervisory problems.

The fourth and fifth place categories are "Management" and "Organizational Effectiveness." They are logically related to each other and each accounts for 10.3 percent of the total items.

The five categories discussed immediately above account for 68 percent of the 145 items in the POWQ. Except for the "Compensation, Retirement, and Vacations" items in "Working Conditions and Personnel Management," all the items in these five categories may be defined as interpersonal in nature. This, of course, is a reflection of the nature of the police work role and represents a problem configuration which is probably similar to other people-oriented crafts, semi-professions and professions.

"Operations" is a category which, as the sixth largest item cluster, refers to the strategies which are used in the execution of police work. It, too, is largely an interpersonal relationship type category. Similarly, "Training and Education" refers to the ways in which officers are trained and re-trained for effective role performance. An item relating to college-level education was included because many officers in the open-end questionnaire item generation phase expressed an opinion that management should encourage officers to pursue a college education.

Following "Training and Education" (the seventh largest category) are two relatively small categories which can be characterized as non-interpersonal in their nature: "Records and Dispatching" and "Equipment and Facilities" which account, respectively, for 6.2 percent and 4.8 percent of the total items. These items, which are somewhat of a "hardware" nature, account for 11 percent of the problem items in the POWQ. The two items comprising "Internal Communications" relate to interpersonal communications problems.

Magnitude of Job-Related Police Problems

The second question which guided the project was concerned with the magnitude of perceived job-related problems. Space does not permit reproducing mean and Leik scores for all 145 POWQ items, instead the five highest and five lowest problems will be discussed. The five highest problems were:

Item	Scores	
	Mean	Leik
Extent to which U.S. Supreme Court decisions have affected law enforcement policies.	2.19	.140
General attitude of national TV networks toward the police.	2.50	.138
Citizens, understanding of what police officers can and cannot do in discharging their responsibilities.	2.71	.065
Degree to which [command officers are] willing to consult with subordinates before new policies are put into effect.	2.81	–.151
The department's effectiveness in dealing with narcotics in the community.	2.85	–.093

All these items received low Leik scores which means that while they were rated as "major" or "moderate" problems by many respondents, many, others rated them "small" or "no probblem,"—in other words, high disagreement exists about these items. The minus values on the last two items indicate that unusually high disagreement exists on these items.

The five lowest problems were:

Item	Scores	
	Mean	Leik
Willingness of organization to cooperate with other police departments.	4.60	.666
Use of excessive force in handling prisoners.	4.61	.678
Relationships between black and white officers.	4.64	.696
Use of force in obtaining confessions.	4.86	.881
Willingness of men to help each other in a tight spot.	4.87	.888

The scores shown above were obtained from all 601 respondents. When scores are examined by departments many striking differences are seen. For example, one of the participating departments was housed in a particularly decrepit building. Item 57 in the POWQ reads, "Adequacy of facilities in which our organization is housed." The overall mean and Leik scores on this item were, respectively, 3.14 and −.436. (Again, the minus figure indicates exceptionally high disagreement as to the degree the concept is seen as a problem.) Mean and Leik scores for the department whose building was notoriously inadequate were 1.48 and .599, respectively. Many other departmental-specific examples could be cited, if space allowed, but the point is that there is evidence of the POWQ's sensitivity to local, department-specific problems.

Effect of the Faces Scale

As a group, respondents who reported themselves unhappy with their jobs differed in mean and Leik scores from those who, as a group, reported themselves happy with their jobs. The general trend was that those who reported themselves unhappy with their jobs rated most of the POWQ items as greater problems than those who reported themselves happy with their jobs. A separate report on this aspect of the POWQ is now being prepared for publication by Mr. M. N. Hendrickson.

DISCUSSION

The POWQ data reported in this study should be regarded as highly tentative. Since it was not politically or logistically feasible to construct an overall scientific sampling procedure for questionnaire distribution, the scores no doubt reflect a certain amount of bias. On the other hand, an inspection of respondents by their demographic characteristics reveals no particularly damaging over- or under-representation. Possibly the most limiting characteristic of our respondents as a group is that low morale officers may be under-represented.

Most respondents believed that the POWQ at least covered some problems and a large number believed it covered most problems. Also, it was not seen as a burden by most respondents. The average completion time for most respondents in the pre-test stages was about one-half hour, which is perhaps slightly longer than it should be. On many occasions, however, officers participating in POWQ pretesting had been asked which items might be omitted, in the interest of shortening the questionnaire, but so far it has been difficult to do this without losing useful data. Certain statistical procedures can be enlisted for this purpose and, in time, the present length of the POWQ may be shortened.

The fact that officers reporting themselves low on the job satisfaction scale also tended to rate most POWQ items higher as problems (compared to officers reporting themselves high in job satisfaction) suggests that the POWQ is, to some extent, sensitive to job satisfaction feelings, which does not seem undesirable since it is of considerable interest to determine which work-related problems are relatively independent of overall job satisfaction.

Whether this project has identified something which could be termed the structure of perceived job-related police problems is difficult to say. Only a microscopic section of the nation's local police was involved in this exploratory study, but those who were, generally attested to the ability of the POWQ to represent the universe of their job-related problems.

Some Future Uses of the POWQ

The POWQ was created to learn more about the nature of job-related police problems. The ten categories and thirty-two subcategories may be regarded as a kind of inventory of these problems (or, at least, many of them) which can be used as a preliminary organizational reconnaissance technique for persons involved, for example, in management analysis, designing in-service training curricula, or who wish to compare police departments in a given area according to their internal climates. It would be useful to employ the POWQ as part of a before-after test to see if problems which existed before a new police executive attained office were affected by several years of his incumbency. Also, the POWQ might be useful to determine whether black officers differ from white officers in their assessment of job-related problems.

Research Applications of the POWQ

As previously mentioned, considerable dissensus existed on many POWQ items. It would be useful to know how age, education, length of service, etc., account for these differences, e.g. are college-educated officers significantly different from non-college-educated officers in the type and magnitude of the problems they perceive? In what specific ways do low job satisfaction officers differ from high job satisfaction officers in their percpetions of the magnitude of the problems? Perhaps factor analysis would yield a cluster of POWQ items which were specific to high or low job satisfaction, a finding that would be of value to persons who are interested in attacking the problem of police officer motivation. Similarly, it would be useful to know which demographic characteristics distinguish the groups of respondents whose divergent assessments result in high amounts of disagreement—what accounts for most of this variance, age, rank, education, or length of service?

CONCLUSION

Few empirically derived data exist in the literature regarding police opinions of work, a concept which is closely tied to needed changes in contemporary law enforcement. To ignore how policemen feel about their work is to ignore a powerful force which may hinder or enhance police progress. Police executives who are concerned with the relationship of police officer motivation to organizational effectiveness may find the POWQ—or some similar instrument—useful as a diagnostic device for identifying issues which may be subject to managerial solutions in contrast to those which lie outside the zone of administrative influence. In either case, police problems appear to differ among organizations and, therefore, no all-purpose solutions can be proposed for them. Survey research techniques (such as the one described here) can add useful data to the police administrator's battery of problem-identification strategies he employs in attempting to increase his organization's effectiveness, realizing that the quality of service is closely related to his officers' opinions of their work.

Chapter 13

MMPI CHARACTERISTICS
OF CORRECTIONAL OFFICERS

ALLAN BERMAN

PASSAGE OF A RECENT STATE LAW made it mandatory that all people wishing to be employed as officers in adult or juvenile correctional institutions be psychologically evaluated to determine their suitability for this type of work. Communication with a number of sources around the country resulted in the finding that there has been no significant published research in this area. Neither are there any established criteria for determining which psychological characteristics are desirable or undesirable in correctional officers. The present study was designed to (a) provide psychological screening of applicants, (b) generate data concerning personality characteristics of correctional officers, since this has been an issue of increasing public concern and since this is a group for which little data currently exists, and (c) provide initial information which could be used later in follow-up research to help determine which characteristics relate to satisfactory performance on the job.

SUBJECTS

Subjects were the first one hundred men to complete other application procedures and who were ready to be employed as officers at one of the state correctional institutions. A certain amount of screening, therefore, has already taken place. During the period when data were obtained, individuals without at least a high school education were excluded, as were those with criminal records (although this latter restriction is no longer systematically used). In addition there are no records kept on the number of men who begin application, go through the other screenings, then withdraw when they are told about the nature of the psychological screenings. Discussion with personnel clerks suggests that this group may range up to 20 percent of the original applicants.

PROCEDURE

All men included in the sample had completed other screening and were declared eligible for employment pending results of the psychological evaluation. It should be stressed that the men, at the time they take the MMPI, have not already been declared eligible. The test is administered by personnel clerks on the same day that they fill out other application forms, but the profile wasn't included in the sample unless they were otherwise eligible. Strict procedures were followed to guarantee confidentiality of results. Completed answer sheets were scored and interpreted by the author. MMPI's were also obtained from a random group of fifty inmates, as part of a battery given during orientation to all men sentenced to over three months.

RESULTS

Results were analyzed in several ways to help provide the most complete picture of the characteristics of this population. Comparisons were made with data from other populations obtained from the literature, and with the group of inmates.

A mean profile for officer candidates was determined, and z-score analysis indicated significant differences from the normal population on 2 of the 3 validity scales and 7 of the 10 clinical scales. The greatest differences were shown on scales 4, 9, 5, and 3. This resulted in a composite high-point code of 4953.

Comparison of the mean profile of officer candidates along with the mean profile of the inmate group, and the typical 4-9 profile of Marks and Seaman (1963) reveals that the curvature of the three profiles is almost identical, but there are differences in elevation.

Data were also studied for differences in the number of individual officer profiles hitting scores above 70, compared to the expected distribution of a sample representative of the normal population. It was found that the officer group scored above 70 significantly more often (p less than .001) than expected.

TABLE 13-I

Scale	Empl. Mean	z (rel. to normals)	p	Inmate Mean	z (rel. to employees)	p
L	4.91	+3.73	.01	4.87	+1.45	N.S.
F	3.78	+1.76	N.S.	2.66	+1.12	N.S.
K	15.66	+3.78	.01	12.45	+2.21	.05
1	49.85	— .18	N.S.	50.54	+ .09	N.S.
2	54.85	+5.45	.001	55.12	+ .68	N.S.
3	55.15	+6.55	.001	48.37	—5.77	.001
4	60.05	+1.49	.001	63.19	+3.75	.05
5	55.55	+5.91	.001	56.72	+1.11	N.S.
6	52.95	+2.05	.05	54.73	+4.48	.05
7	51.40	+1.53	N.S.	49.97	— .05	N.S.
8	52.35	+1.95	.05	55.70	+ .52	.05
9	55.85	+5.96	.001	59.08	+6.38	.01
0	45.55	—6.07	.001	48.79	—2.87	.05

Characteristics of employee applicants, their relationship to the normal population and to a group of prison inmates.

Finally, a comparison was made of first high-point code frequencies of the officer group with our random inmate group (NI), and with Normal Adults (NA), College Students (CS), Psychiatric Patients (PP), Psychiatric Outpatients (PO), Medical Outpatients (MO), and a Prison Inmate group (PI) from the literature (Dahlstrom and Welsh, 1960). Most pertinent is that the officer group scored scale 4 as first high point with a frequency not statistically different from the Prison Inmate population or our Random Inmate group; and scored scale 9 as first high point significantly more often than Prison Inmates (p less than .01), Random Inmates (p less than .01) and Psychiatric Patients (p less than .001). In addition, the officers scored scale 3 as high-point significantly more often than Prison Inmates (p less than .001) and Random Inmates (p less than .01).

DISCUSSION

The similarity between the profiles of correctional candidates and the Prison Inmate population occurs most vividly on Scales 4 (Psychopathic Deviate) and 9 (Hypomanic). This would indicate that correctional officer candidates, like Inmates, show emotional shallowness, alienation from social customs, and relative inability

TABLE 13-II

Employee Group is	1 X²	2 X²	FIRST HIGH POINT SCALE						
			3 X²	4 X²	5 X²	6 X²	7 X²	8 X²	9 X²
HIGHER Frequency Than	none	none	PI***	NA* CS** PP* PO*** MO***	PI***	none	none	none	PP*** PO* MO** PI**
LOWER Frequency Than	PP*** PO** MO*** PI**	PP* PO*** MO***	NA* MO**	none	NA*	none	CS* PP* PO**	PP* PI***	none
Not sign. diff. from	NA CS	NA CS PI	CS PP PO	PI	CS	NA CS PP PO MO PI	NA MO PI	NA CS PO MO	NA CS

*p. .05   # Data unavailable for scale 5 for 3 groups
**p .01
***p .001

Comparison of high point code frequencies of employee applicants with Normal Adult group (NA), College Students (CS), Psychiatric Patients (PP), Psychiatric Outpatients (PO), Medical Outpatients (MO), and Prison Inmates (PI).

to profit from social sanctions. All the while, however, they profess poise and confidence and deny social estrangement. In addition, a 49 profile may indicate tendencies toward uncontrolled temper outbursts, unproductive overactivity, and general unreliability of goal-directed behavior (Dahlstrom and Meehl, 1960). Other descriptions of 49 profile include: lack of control of impulses, frequent acting-out, incapability of close personal relationships, excitability, irritability, and self-centeredness (Marks and Seeman, 1963).

The additional element in the officer profiles of significant elevation on Scale 3 (Hysteria) is provocative. Megargee and Mendelsohn (1962) have found that elevations of Scale 3 in the presence of a high score on Scale 4 indicate individuals who are "generally inhibited" but who "occasionally lash out and express their chronic hostile feelings directly and intensely."

Other findings in the Megargee and Mendelsohn study become important here. Mainly, they found that on two structured measures of aggressiveness, assaultive criminals indicated better control and less hostility than either nonviolent criminals or normals. This is intriguing since the usual assumption is that the assaultive criminal, by the very nature of his crime, demonstrates lack of control. However, they suggest an alternative explanation. The assaultive person is often a taciturn, long-suffering type of individual who buries all of his aggressive and angry feelings behind rigid but tenuous controls. In certain instances he may lash out and release all of his aggression in one calamitous act, then afterward return to his usual overcontrolled defenses. This is a very different way of functioning from the more "normal" type of person's way of handling anger. Typically, the hostile, angry noncriminal has found ways of releasing his feelings more gradually, thus forestalling the point where he might have to engage in a more flagrant aggressive act. But drawbacks to this method of handling anger are that this bit-by-bit release leaves the person in a more constant state of high resentment and aggressiveness; and secondly, this person must constantly be searching for ways of discharging his feelings that will allow this gradual release without having to engage in overt assault. So that, from Megargee and Mendelsohn's research we get some basis for feeling that the criminal may, during his assaultive crime, be temporarily dangerous and without adequate controls, but that most of the time he is actually in better control and feeling less of an urge to act out than the chronically aggressive, resentful person who never fully vents his feelings and may always be just under the threshold for more overt assaultive behavior.

Thus, the detection of aggression becomes a highly difficult thing, because we must distinguish the overly controlled but explosively dangerous kind of person from the aggressive person who has poor controls. Nevertheless, thinking about this explanation may be useful in looking at the present results. Both the officer candidates and the inmates seem to be about equal in their feelings of aggressiveness, hostility, resentment, suspicion and desire to act out assaultively. Yet one group obviously has acted out and the other hasn't—at least not overtly. It is tempting to try to find explanations for this in the subtle differences that exist in the current mean profiles. The differences on Scale 3 are interesting. They imply that the officer group actually has the potential for even more unexplained lashing out than does the inmate group. This would be in keeping with the explanation offered earlier, and would suggest that the officers may be the "gradual releaser" type of angry person, whose aggressiveness is chronically dormant under the surface.

Another interesting profile difference occurs on Scale 8, where the inmates score significantly and consistently higher than the officer candidates. Moderate differences on Scale 8 are often used to indicate appropriateness and rationality of thought processes. This, combined with the difference on Scale 0, could imply that a problem that the inmates have is an inability (or unwillingness) to apply social standards of conformity to their aggressive thinking—that, once the threshold has been passed they are unconcerned with appropriateness and think only of immediate acting out. Nevertheless, even though the inmates score higher than the officers on Scales 8 and 0, it is rarely that even an inmate's score on either of these two scales is deviant enough to be considered abnormal.

Another important difference is in the F-K ratios. In both cases, for officer candidates and inmates, profiles show consistently high negative ratios, indicating strong attempts to "look good" and answer in socially desirable ways. The degree of this desire to look good seems strongest in the officer candidates. This is understandable since they obviously would have more to lose by looking "disturbed" than an inmate would. The important thing is to consider where their defensiveness might have had its greatest effect. It is often felt that this occurs mostly on the questions which have the most manifest face validity to the layman. Among the first scales to be affected, then, would be Scale 8, which is loaded with items which have the most obvious meaning to the nonprofessional. It is likely that a highly defensive person without much psychological sophistication would produce very low Scale 8 scores. This is exactly what happens in our sample of officer candidates. The higher the negative F-K ratio, the lower the score on Scale 8. This would seem, then, apparently to wipe out the significance of the differences in Scale 8 scores for the two groups.

There is still the problem of differentiating between the two groups; and considering the current discussion, the "reverse control" hypothesis of Megargee and Mendelsohn seems more attractive. In their study they also found that, even using two separate indicators of hostility and aggressiveness, there were not predictable differences occurring among their groups of violent criminals, nonviolent criminals and normals. They went on to demonstrate that the MMPI by itself could not differentiate between the assaultive likelihood of different aggressive people. It seems that we have run into the same type of roadblock. While it is apparent from the present results that officer candidates and inmates have similar aggressive tendencies, similar hostility and resentment, and similar inner desires to be rebellious, it cannot be determined from the MMPI profiles what the probability is that a person will act out more or less blatantly on these impulses.

This leaves the question of whether the failure of the MMPI to discriminate assaultive tendencies between the two groups is due to a deficiency of the MMPI. This would assume that there actually is such a difference between the two groups, but that the MMPI (and the other eleven measures used by Megargee) was unable to measure the difference. The obvious alternative to this is the possibility that the two groups indeed do not vary on this dimension—that the officer candidates are as likely as the inmates to engage in assaultive behavior. This would carry along the correlative implication that the reasons why one group is behind bars and the other group is guarding them may be due to incidental factors such as intelligence, pure chance, or simply the bad luck involved in getting caught. Certainly, after some of the studies by Meninger (1969) and others, the possibility of such close similarity between the two groups is not impossible to conceive.

Another issue that becomes significant here is the role of society in setting up the officer role to attract men with this type of personality. Despite many intellectualized rationalizations to the contrary, most prisons are set up for punishment. It is as though the public is seeking to punish or take vengeance rather than to reform or correct. It is not surprising, then, that the prisons attract "punishers"—people whose tendency to be punitive will carry out the public will.

These considerations are based partially upon the assumption that correctional work is a chosen field—that men select this occupation to meet their needs. My discussions with officers and administrators do not support this assumption. One gets the feeling that the men who end up as adult or juvenile correctional officers have simply been unable to find other employment. This seems especially true with regard to the juvenile officers. "The situation is so bad that we always have many vacancies and have to hire nearly anyone who applies, even if we have reason to feel that he doesn't have the personal attitudes we want." This was told to me by a personnel officer involved in hiring, as we discussed possible usefulness of screening batteries for applicants.

A look into the backgrounds of the officers—particularly those in the juvenile facility—substantiates these impressions. Men apply who have had many other jobs, who have no particular training for any skilled work, and who essentially consider the officer position as strictly a custodial or punitive one. The turnover rate is quite high as men quickly leave once they find other employment. Nevertheless there are many who do stay and settle into the positions permanently.

It is apparent that differences between adult and juvenile corrections officers also appear in our data. Examination of the MMPIs indicates that, while the shape of the profiles is similar, those of the juvenile officers are considerably more elevated than the results of the correctional officers at the adult institution. Thus, it appears that the juvenile officers are the most hostile, alienated and bitter of the whole group, as well as the least likely to be suitable for other employment.

We must be concerned about the effects of these officers' characteristics on the inmates. Criminals and Delinquents have been characterized as individuals whose acting-out is an attempt to break away from frustrating and hopeless lives, where they have existed too long in a state of tenuous over-control. The violent act may be the desperate attempt to preserve some dignity by asserting power and identity. Yet the result is imprisonment under hostile, angry officers who themselves help perpetuate the very feelings of frustration and helplessness which form the basis of the vicious cycle of continued associality. It is not difficult to see how this cycle of despair and resentment may be erupting in the waves of prison out-breaks occurring currently.

The research seems to support, therefore, a rethinking of personnel practices. Certainly the job of corrections officers must be made more attractive. It seems that the basic ingredient for such a change is a fundamental switch in administration and political attitudes concerning the treatment of prisoners. As long as criminals are to be punished, prisons will attract men whose temperments make them punishers. As long as working conditions for officers are overtiring, unsafe, and beset with petty rules and regulations, these conditions will aggravate the bitterness, anger and fear the officers already feel.

Finally, many prisons include in their programs activities which allow prisoners to "let off steam" to ventilate some of their anger before it gets to the point of impulsive release. The current data suggests that it may be realistic to include such energy-releasing activities for the guards also. Administrators should not forget that the officers, like the inmates, are "locked up" all day, occupied in sedentary, monotonous, sometimes frustrating chores. Activities or other kinds of group experiences may help relieve some of the pent-up feelings. And because of the similarity of some of the officer and inmate feelings, joint activities involving both officers and inmates might not only help vent and release, but also create desirable rapport.

There were many problems encountered in carrying out this research, particularly the resistance of most applicants toward taking the MMPI, raising questions about the reliability of the data obtained. Further study seems critical, especially: (1) adequate follow-up information on the current applicant group to relate specific profiles to success or failure on the job; (2) the necessity for a control group of subjects of similar socioeconomic and intellectual backgrounds as the applicants but who are not employed in correctional settings; (3) a breakdown of results separating the applicants for adult correctional institutions from those for the juvenile institutions; and (4) separation of inmate groups according to whether their offenses were assaultive or nonassaultive.

REFERENCES

Dahlstrom, W.G. and Welsh, G.S.: *An MMPI Handbook*. Minneapolis: University of Minnesota Press, 1960.

Marks, P.A. and Seeman, W.: *The Actuarial Description of Abnormal Personality*. Baltimore: Williams and Wilkins, 1963.

Megargee, E.I. and Mendelsohn, G.A.: A Crossvalidation of Twelve MMPI Indices of Hostility and Control, *Journal of Abnormal and Social Psychology*, 1962, 65, 431-438.

Meninger, K.: *The Crime of Punishment*. New York: Viking, 1968.

Chapter 14

THE CONTRASTING OCCUPATIONAL
CULTURES OF POLICEMEN
AND SOCIAL WORKERS

Regis H. Walther, Shirley D. McCune and Robert C. Trojanowicz

THIS IS a report of a study of occupational personality in the fields of police and social work that tests hypotheses developed from an earlier study of personnel in the juvenile court system (Walther and McCune, 1965). The report is presented in five sections: general background, review of relevant research relating to the police and social work professions, the design of the study, the results, and a discussion of implications.

BACKGROUND

There is abundant research evidence that different occupations produce different occupational personalities. Occupational personalities tend to be most sharply differentiated in the professions; and students of the subject are in general agreement that, over a period of time, every profession develops a common set of beliefs, values, attitudes, and working styles which tend to characterize members of that profession. The specific mechanisms which establish the professional subculture include the attraction of particular types of personalities to a profession, the informal and formal selection process for entry into a profession, the formal professional training, and the reinforcement of desired characteristics and behavior within the profession. These mechanisms serve to shape the personality which characterizes the members of a profession and can be expected to result in a common set of values, attitudes, and beliefs. This process is often referred to as the "socialization

Reprinted from *Experimental Publications System,* December, 1970, *9* Ms. No. 314-256 and with the permission of the authors.

of the professional" and is based on shared assumptions within the profession regarding the ideal philosophy, the ideal set of behavior, and the ideal person for the profession. The resultant personality structure consists of those interests, attitudes, values, modes of relating to others and other characteristics that make the individual maximally receptive to the cultural ways and idealogies of his profession and that enable him to achieve adequate gratification and security within the profession.

In a dynamic society, professions tend to differentiate into fields of specialization making it necessary to include in studies of professions both the common cultural characteristics as well as the sub-speciality configurations. Grouping psychiatrists and surgeons together even though both are medical doctors would result in an imprecise description of both groups as would grouping trial attorneys who enjoy legal combat with research lawyers who are uncomfortable in the courtroom. The pragmatic test for sub-specialities is the degree to which the members of a profession are interchangeable with a reasonable amount of training. Lack of interchangeability points to the existence of sub-specialities.

Kelly and Goldberg (1959), Terman (1954), Strong (1955), and Rosenberg (1957) have provided evidence of the existence of occupational personality patterns and their results suggest that cognitions, wants, interpersonal response traits, values, interests, and attitudes of individual members help define these patterns. The research reported in this paper continues the exploration of occupational personality patterns through a study of policemen and social workers.

The research instrument used in the research, The Job Analysis and Interest Measurement (JAIM),[2] has evolved over a ten-year period through a series of studies of mature workers in over 40 occupations and professions, including business executives, juvenile court judges, ambassadors, physicists, social workers, policemen, army officers, engineers, lawyers, and secretaries. The be-

---

[2]Distributed for research purposes by the Educational Testing Service, Princeton, N.J. Studies using the JAIM are reported in Walther (1964, 1965), Walther and McCune (1965), and Peterson and Lippitt (1968).

ginning point for the development of the JAIM was the discovery that certain self-description items answered by the U.S. State Department personnel when they entered on duty were useful in discriminating among employees assigned to different jobs, and in predicting both staying power and performance ratings within these jobs. These results led to the conclusion that the achievement of a satisfactory level of job satisfaction and performance requires an adequate psychological match between job and the individual and that self-reported beliefs, typical behaviors, preferences, and values provide useful information for judging the adequacy of the match.

The notion that the study of the internal frame of reference of the individual is a useful approach for understanding behavior is consistent with the views of many personality theorists (Rogers, 1961; Combs and Snygg, 1959; Kelly, 1955; Rokeach, 1960). Kelly, for example, in proposing his psychology of personal constructs states that man creates his own ways of seeing the world in which he lives; the world does not create them for him. Thus, if we examine a person's philosophy closely, we find ourselves examining the individual himself. To understand how a person behaves, we need to know the manner in which he represents his circumstances to himself.

The research leading to the development of the JAIM found persuasive support for Kelly's point of view regarding the importance of personal constructs and for the predictive power of self-descriptive statements. It also led to the conclusion that a useful way to subdivide personality variables for role or occupational analysis purposes is into behavioral styles, activity preferences, and values. In general, behavioral styles are the consistent ways in which individuals organize and direct their mental, physical, and energy resources to accomplish goals. Activity preferences reflect the anticipation of intrinsic satisfaction from the performance of certain types of tasks. Values are the criteria against which the individual judges the "goodness" or "badness" of the work. These variables influence the degree of occupational match as follows:

— Different roles or jobs have different behavioral requirements and provide varying opportunity for personal satisfaction and feeling of value;

— Individuals bring to their roles or jobs behavioral styles, activity preferences and values; and

— It is the degree of match between the role or job and the individual in these dimensions which significantly influences how well the individual will perform in or be satisfied with the role or job.

THE POLICE PROFESSION

Law enforcement functions have not always been delegated to men working in a formalized structure like a police department. The professional policeman is a product of the 19th Century. Prior to the 19th Century law enforcement was usually a private matter and amounted to a self-protection of property and rights. With the establishment of police forces, the public, in effect, delegated its law enforcement power to a relative handful of professional guardians. For the most part these guardians were given a low status in the view of the general public. A study of North and Hatt in 1947 (Form and Nasow, 1962) sought to determine the prestige of 90 occupations. The results showed that policemen ranked 55th. A replication of this study by Hodge, Siegal and Rossi (1964) showed that the police still ranked only 47th.

Other studies have attempted to describe the policeman's personal characteristics and his working milieu. From a survey of backgrounds of more than 1,200 recruits who graduated from the New York Police Academy from 1952 to 1967 it was found that most of the candidates were from the upper-lower class. Only a few were above that class. About 95 percent had no college training. The typical characteristics of recruits are a cautious personality, a working class background, a high school education or less and average intelligence (Niederhoffer, 1967).

Sheldon (1942) has extensively studied body types and tried to correlate temperament factors to various body classifications. Niederhoffer (1967) feels that the policeman's physique fits Sheldon's mesomorphy category perfectly. Temperament characteristics associated with the mesomorph category are the need to dominate, assertiveness, competitive aggressiveness, ruthlessness and other traits associated with authoritarianism.

The supposed authoritarian orientation of policemen was not supported in a study using the well-known F-scale (Adarno et al., 1950). The mean score on the F-scale was 4.15 as compared with a score of 4.19 for the working class. Niederhoffer (1967) concludes that police candidates are generally no higher in authoritarianism than the rest of the working class and also suggests that there is no self-selection among authoritarian personalities prior to appointment.

Niederhoffer (1967) believes that the police system is the major factor in transforming a man into a special type of authoritarian personality required by the police role. As a result of the socialization process in the police system the officer feels justified and many times righteous in using power and toughness to perform his duties. When he is criticized for brutality he feels like a martyr and abandoned by society. Niederhoffer also believes that policemen vary in the amount of authoritarianism which they exhibit. This he feels may be due to the differential impact that experience, training and role models have on the individual policeman. The patrolman on the beat, because of his close proximity to the public, is involved in most of the situations that require a display of authority. Hence he is the most authoritarian. As the officer's career progresses he is promoted and removed from "on the line" contacts with the public or else, if not promoted, he is rewarded with a quiet job in the station house which also removes him from daily contacts with citizens. As an "old pro" he transmits his reverence for toughness to each new generation of recruits.

In terms of the specific role and working milieu of the policeman Skolnick (1966) believes that the two principle variables involved in police work, danger and authority, operate in an atmosphere of a constant pressure to appear efficient. Danger in his work requires that the policeman be especially attentive to situations that have a potential for violence and law breaking. Thus danger, as an integral part of police work, generally contributes to the policeman being a "suspicious" person. Furthermore, danger as a common element in the policeman's working milieu, discourages friendship. Not only does the element of danger isolate the policeman socially from that segment of the citizenry which he regards as symbolically dangerous but it also isolates him from the conventional citizenry with whom he identifies. Thus there is generally a great social distance between the policeman and all segments of the citizenry.

The above, of course, is only a brief description of the policeman's personal characteristics and his working milieu. These same general characteristics will be discussed in relation to the social work profession. First, however, two previous studies that utilized the JAIM with police samples will be discussed. The purpose being to give a brief description of those behavioral styles that were most evident in policemen. The first, a study of new recruits in Washington D.C., showed the policemen compared to a sample of Episcopal ministers, nurses, physicists, secretaries, and Foreign Service officers, were high on scales measuring obedience to authority (Accepts Routines and Accepts Commands) and moderately high on a tendency to fight back when confronted with aggressive behavior (Move Against). On other scales, measuring a tendency to try to please authority, please other people, and to be socially isolated, the average scores of the policemen were neither high nor low compared to the other occupational groups (Walther, 1964).

The second study compared a sample of policemen from several metropolitan systems with lawyers, juvenile court judges, social workers and probation officers. Police patrolmen and youth officers were studied separately (Walther and McCune 1965). The scales which differentiated the police patrolmen from the other occupational groups were Prefers Routines, Directive Leadership, External Controls, Role Conformity, and Mechanical Activities. The first four scales measure attitudes toward authority and society. The Prefers Routines scale measures the degree to which the individual likes to have definite procedures available in his work which he can follow. Directive Leadership measures the degree of the belief that the best results are obtained by supervisors who make decisions themselves rather than delegating them to subordinates. External Controls measures the strength of the belief that behavior can best be regulated by external controls and punishment. Role Conformity measures the degree to which the individual values himself according to how successfully he has conformed to the role requirements of society. Individuals scoring high say that they prefer to be considered reliable, dependable, trustworthy, and industrious.

In addition to the above scales, the police patrolmen were moderately high on Move Against the Aggressor and low on Self-Confidence, Persuasive Leadership, Problem Analysis and Intellectual Achievement.

The picture of the policeman which emerges from JAIM analysis is one of an individual who has identified with the standards and values of society, wants to work in structured situations and is oriented more toward things than toward either data or people. His tendency toward self-assertiveness is, perhaps, limited by his relatively low self-confidence.

THE SOCIAL WORK PROFESSION

Barber (1963) describes social work as an "emerging or marginal" profession. The profession is presently facing many problems because of the changing and complex environment within which it is practiced (French, 1964).

According to Wilensky and LeBeaux (1958) social work began to have a distinct realm of its own when the Charity Organization movement provided a system wherein a visitor came frequently and systematically in contact with "cases"—the heads of poverty stricken families primarily—with special attention given to what were seen as individual or family causes of difficulty and as individual resources to meet the problem. Thus, as Wilensky and LeBeaux point out, a setting and a vehicle were provided for the observation of human behavior and for the practice of skills in helping people out of trouble.

Although there has been comparatively little research relating to the social workers' occupational milieu, there have been several reports relating to the personal characteristics of those persons who choose a social work career. Kadushin (1958) for example comments that there is a pattern that applies to social work, and that certain types of persons are likely to be attracted to it. A profile of such a person, as reflected from Kadushin's research, would be a female of above average intelligence, of professional middle class parents, living in a Northern city, whose occupational interests and values revolve around a desire to work with people in an effort to help them through the use of verbal skills. Pins (1963) does not agree with Kadushin's findings. He says that social work is attractive to people in their early twenties coming from lower-middle class homes in large Eastern cities, with college majors in social science achieving average academic records, had previous experience in social work and enjoy people. Gockel (1966) adds to the picture by stating that social workers place high value on jobs or careers which give them an opportunity to be of service; they are relatively uninterested in jobs which contain an intellectual component; and they are relatively uninterested in monetary rewards and the opportunity to operate independently on the job. In summary, he says that rates of recruitment in social work are relatively low among students who indorse the following values: freedom from supervision, a chance to exercise leadership, opportunities to be original and creative, living and working in the "world of ideas" and making a lot of money.

Kidneigh and Lundberg (1958) in the comparison of social work students with six other professional schools found that social work students were more liberal in their thinking than students attending other professional schools.

In a later study McCormack and Kidneigh utilized the Strong Vocational Interest Blank in studying a sample of members of the American Association of Social Workers. After computing the results there was an indication, as would be expected, that social workers liked those activities which involved working with people. They also enjoyed verbal activities and indicated a dislike for "conservative" people. In reference to differentiation of attitudes depending on the sex of the social worker it was found that male social workers disliked physical sciences and athletic men while women disliked athletic women as well as scientific, selling, and clerical activities (McCormack and Kidneigh, 1959) .

As was mentioned above in the discussion of the police profession, a sample of social workers associated with the juvenile court system was included in the JAIM study of policemen, lawyers, juvenile court judges, and probation officers (Walther and McCune, 1965). As might be expected, social workers differed most from the members of other occupational groups on the Social Service scale. They were also high on optimism and tended either to keep away from or to conciliate rather than fight persons acting aggressively toward them (Move Toward or Move Away rather than Move Against the Aggressor). They tended to be participative or delegative rather than directive in their leadership styles and emphasized knowledge of results rather than external controls as motivational strategies. They tended to be low on perseverance and orderliness and value group participation and approval from others.

STUDY DESIGN

The Job Analysis and Interest Measurement (JAIM) has been described above. This self-report inventory was used in a study of Juvenile Court personnel and produced results indicating significant differences in the occupational personalities of social workers and policemen. On the basis of these results, it was possible to predict which JAIM scales would differentiate between samples from these two professions.

In the present study the JAIM was administered to the following samples of social workers and policemen:

A. First-year social work students at five graduate schools of social work (Tulane, Portland, Denver, Maryland, and Howard) were requested to complete the JAIM.[3] Sixty-three percent were females and thirty-seven percent males. The age range was from 21 to 58 years with a median of 27 years. Usable responses were obtained from 436 subjects, a completion rate of about 85 percent.

B. The JAIM was distributed to 100 social workers in the Lansing, Michigan area. All of the social workers had masters degrees in social work. There was a completion rate of 91 percent. Two answer sheets had to be eliminated because of coding problems. In the sample, 24 worked in a Mental Health unit, 44 in Social Service, 18 in private

---

[3]The data were collected by Shirley D. McCune in connection with her doctoral dissertation (McCune, 1966).

agencies, and 12 were school social workers. Nineteen were consultants, 28 were supervisors, and 51 were case workers. Fifty-one were males and 47 were females, and 30 were 20-29 years of age, 36 were 30-39, 23 were 40-49, and 9 were 50-59.[4]

C. The JAIM was distributed to 100 members of the Michigan State Police. There was a 100 percent completion rate, although one answer sheet had to be eliminated because of coding problems. In the police sample 8 were from the juvenile division, 9 from the training division, 11 from the crime lab division, and 71 from the patrol division. Twenty-nine policemen were command officers and 70 were troopers. All the policemen were male, 41 were 20-29 years of age, 35 were 30-39, and 23 were 40-49.

D. The JAIM was administered to 52 students at two schools of social work at the time of entering school and again at the end of their professional training two years later.

It was predicted that JAIM results would generally confirm the Juvenile Court study results; and that, specifically, comparisons of JAIM scale scores would show significant differences in predicted directions.

RESULTS

Predictions were made that significant differences in a predetermined direction at the .05 level of confidence would be found between the mean scores of the samples of policemen and social workers on 28 scales. Twenty-two of these predictions were confirmed for both samples and for an additional scale the prediction was confirmed for one sample and came close to being confirmed for the other. The predictions for four scales were not confirmed by either sample, and for one scale the results were significant in the opposite direction for one sample but not for the other (See Table 14-I).

Further support for the predictions was provided by the high

---

[4]These data were collected by R. C. Trojanowicz in connection with his doctoral dissertation (Trojanowicz, 1969).

TABLE 14-I
COMPARISON OF PREDICTED AND ACTUAL DIFFERENCES IN THE
JAIM SCORES OF SAMPLES OF POLICEMEN AND SOCIAL WORKERS

	Predicted^a	Policemen Compared with	
		Social Work Students	Social Work Practitioners
Optimism	—	—*	—
Self-Confidence	—	—**	—***
Perseverance	+	+***	+***
Orderliness	0	—***	—**
Plan Ahead	+	+**	+***
Moral Absolutes	+	+***	+***
Slow Change^b		+***	+***
Persuasive Leadership	0	+**	+
Self-Assertiveness	+	+***	+***
Move Toward Aggressor	—	—***	—***
Move Away From Aggressor	—	—	+
Move Against Aggressor	+	+	—
Prefers Routine	+	+*	+***
Identifies With Authority	0	—*	—
Prefers Independence	—	—*	—***
Directive Leadership	+	+***	+***
Participative Leadership	—	—**	—**
Delegative Leadership	—	—***	—***
Knowledge of Results	—	—**	—*
External Controls	+	+***	+***
Systematic-Methodical	+	+*	+***
Problem Analysis	—	+**	+
Social Interaction	—	—***	—***
Mechanical Activities	+	+***	+***
Supervisory Activities	0	+***	+**
Activity-Frequent Change	—	+	+
Group Participation	—	0	—
Status Attainment	0	+**	+
Social Service	—	—***	—***
Approval From Others	—	—***	—***
Intellectual Achievement	—	—	—***
Maintain Societal Standards	—	—**	—**
Role Conformity	+	+***	+***
Academic Achievement	—	—***	—***

^aA plus [+] indicates that mean scores of policemen were higher and a minus [—] that social workers were higher. The asterisks indicate level of confidence as follows: * = .05; ** = .01, and *** = .001. The predictions are all made at the .05 level.
^bNot included in Form 663.
^cNinety-nine policemen compared with 497 social work students.
^dNinety-nine policemen compared with 98 social work practitioners.

confidence level achieved in most of the comparisons. Out of 56 predictions, 45 or 80 percent were confirmed. Fifty-five percent of the predictions were confirmed at a confidence level of .001 or better, 16 percent at .01 and 9 percent at .05. (See Table 14-II).

TABLE 14-II
NUMBER AND LEVEL OF CONFIDENCE OF SUPPORTED PREDICTIONS

Level of Confidence	N	Percent
Supported at .001 level	31	55%
Supported at .01 level	9	16%
Supported at .05 level	5	9%
No difference found	10	18%
Significant in opposite direction	1	2%
TOTAL	56	100%

In addition to comparing a sample of policemen with two samples of social workers, comparisons were made with the norms of the JAIM based on scores of subjects from 11 occupational groups. (See Table 14-III). On the basis of both the between group comparisons and the comparison with the norms of the instrument, a profile for each profession emerged.

PROFILE OF A POLICEMAN

According to his self report, the policeman is characterized most distinctly by his orientation toward the values and standards of society. He places a high value on being considered reliable, dependable, trustworthy, industrious, and following a way of life based on duty. To a much greater degree than the average, he believes that external controls, discipline, and punishment are necessary to control the behavior of other people. Thus he tends to endorse the statements "Spare the rod and spoil the child" and "Obedience and respect for authority are among the most important virtues children should learn," and to believe that parents get the best results from children if they maintain strict discipline.

The conservative outlook of the policeman is reflected in his endorsement of the statements that laws and social conventions are seldom or never useless and hamper an individual's personal freedom; that it is usually best to do things in a conventional way;

TABLE 14-III
STANDARD SCORES[a] OF POLICEMEN, SOCIAL WORKERS
AND SOCIAL WORK STUDENTS

	Policemen N = 99	Social Workers N = 98	Social Work Students N = 497
Optimism	—18	3	10
Self-Confidence	—57	19	—21
Perseverance	45	—21	—25
Orderliness	42	—53	—10
Plan Ahead	—59	—9	—12
Moral Absolutes	69	—29	—26
Slow Change	50	—5	0
Persuasive Leadership	14	—7	—29
Self-Assertiveness	71	—31	—46
Move Toward Aggressor	—32	17	37
Move Away From Aggressor	—11	—26	—7
Move Against Aggressor	2	26	—11
Prefers Routines	46	—32	15
Identifies With Authority	—23	—17	14
Prefers Independence	—42	32	—7
Directive Leadership	44	—56	—42
Participative Leadership	—26	13	14
Delegative Leadership	—9	45	37
Knowledge of Results	—34	3	12
External Controls	70	—46	—39
Systematic — Methodical	8	—64	—23
Problem Analysis	0	—18	—46
Social Interaction	—36	37	38
Mechanical Activities	93	—25	—32
Supervisory Activities	24	—14	—30
Activity-Frequent Change	0	—16	—8
Group Participation	31	43	31
Status Attainment	—21	—48	—68
Social Service	—22	87	119
Approval From Others	—55	2	33
Intellectual Achievement	—56	—11	—40
Maintain Societal Standards	8	47	45
Role Conformity	101	—12	—10
Academic Achievement	—81	—10	—13

[a]The standard scores are ased on a norm group selected from eleven occupations with the mean of the norm group set at 0 and the standard deviation at 100.

that when things are going smoothly it is best not to make changes which will disrupt things; and that moral principles come from an outside power higher than man.

The policeman prefers to boss and be bossed and to work within structured situations. He likes to know exactly what is expected of him rather than to decide for himself what to do and how to do it, and favors a directive rather than a participative or delegative style of leadership.

While he reported himself as self-assertive in pursuing his own goals, the policeman scored slightly lower than the social worker on the Move Against the Aggressors scale, indicating that he was no more likely than the average individual in the norm group to counter-attack when someone acted toward him in a belligerent or aggressive manner. Perhaps this result reflects the selection practices of the Michigan State Police Department from which the sample was drawn, and might not be characteristic of samples from other police departments.

Other significant characteristics of the policeman are that he tends to have mechanical and outdoor interests; he does not value himself particularly through intellectual attainments, nor does he think it of prime importance to be well-liked or to be considered gracious, attractive, or pleasant. He is also somewhat lacking in self-confidence and does not do well in academic situations. His social distance from other people is reflected in the more frequent than average endorsement of the statements, "Familiarity breeds contempt" and "If you give someone an inch he will take a mile," and his below average participation in parties and social events. These results provide support for Skolnick's thesis that the role and milieu of the policeman discourages friendship outside his profession.

In summary, the policeman is oriented toward the standards and values of authority and toward things rather than toward people or data. He likes to work within structured situations, has a conservative point of view, and believes that the behavior of people should be controlled through discipline. He is self-assertive rather than accommodating in his relations with other people but does not respond to the aggression of others with above average forcefulness. He is also below average in self-confidence and academic achievement.

PROFILE OF A SOCIAL WORKER

The social worker is oriented primarily toward social service, social interaction, and professional standards. He says that he values himself most through being sympathetic, understanding, unselfish, and helpful to others. He likes work which permits him to work as a member of a group, to interact with other people, and to apply professional standards. His people orientation is reflected in the belief that he gets along best when he respects the feelings of others rather than to respect their rights or to do what has to be done even if it doesn't please everyone.

The social worker does not place a high value on the status symbols established by his culture, nor on intellectual achievements. He does not consider himself self-assertive or competitive; does not like to work with tools, and does not believe that he is particularly orderly or systematic and methodical in processing information and reaching decisions.

A strong anti-authoritarian point of view is reflected in his perference for a delegative or participative rather than a directive leadership style and his emphasis on internal rather than external controls. Thus a social worker is more likely to say that parents get the best results when they praise and encourage their children or give them the freedom and opportunity to learn from their own experiences rather than to praise them sometimes but also maintain strict discipline.

In summary, the social worker's profile is almost the exact opposite of the policeman's. While he shares with policemen a low interest in data, he is oriented more toward people rather than toward things, or authority. He does not like structural situations and is more accommodating than self-assertive in his relation to other people. In addition to social service, he places great value on applying professional standards. He emphasizes internal control and personal growth rather than discipline and punishment as primary strategies for social control, and believes in a delegative or participative rather than a directive style of leadership.

EFFECT OF SEX COMPOSITION OF SAMPLES

Since the samples were not matched with respect to sex, policemen were compared separately with male and female subsamples of social workers (See Table 14-IV). While there were significant

TABLE 14-IV
JAIM STANDARD SCORES OF MALE AND FEMALE SOCIAL WORKERS
AND POLICEMEN

	Female Social Workers	Male Social Workers	Policemen
Optimism	21	—16	—18
Self-Confidence	15	24	—57
Perseverance	—21	—21	45
Orderliness	—59	—46	42
Plan Ahead	—20	2	59
Moral Absolutes	—41	—5	69
Slow Change	— 8	— 2	50
Persuasive Leadership	—12	— 1	14
Self-Assertiveness	—75	16	71
Move Toward Aggressor	—38	— 5	—32
Move Away From Aggressor	—12	—41	—11
Move Against Aggressor	9	45	2
Prefers Routines	—31	—33	46
Identifies With Authority	—12	—22	—23
Prefers Independence	34	30	—42
Directive Leadership	—78	—32	44
Participative Leadership	25	0	—26
Delegative Leadership	51	39	— 9
Knowledge of Results	31	—26	—34
External Controls	—56	—36	70
Systematic — Methodical	—54	—75	8
Problem Analysis	—42	7	0
Social Interaction	49	25	—36
Mechanical Activities	—51	2	93
Supervisory Activities	—30	3	24
Activity-Frequent Change	—46	15	0
Group Participation	75	10	31
Status Attainment	—75	—20	—21
Social Service	78	96	—22
Approval From Others	25	—22	—55
Intellectual Achievement	— 7	—15	56
Maintain Societal Standards	37	57	8
Role Conformity	—16	— 8	101
Academic Achievement	28	—49	—81

differences in the average scores of men and women social workers, the pattern of differences with policemen remains substantially the same. On 21 of the 24 scales, the differences between policemen and the two subsamples of social workers is significant and in the same direction indicating that a substantial proportion of the differences between policemen and social workers is independent of the sex of the subjects (See Table 14-V).

THE PROCESS OF ACCULTURATION

The above results have identified some distinctive characteristics of policemen and social workers. An important issue is the cause and effect relation. To what extent does the policeman and social worker develop these characteristics because of the demands of his job, and to what extent was he that way to begin with? While only comprehensive longitudinal studies can answer these kinds of questions, some information bearing on this issue was developed in this research and will be discussed next.

The JAIM was administered to entering and graduating students at two schools of social work. The results for the social work students were consistent between the two schools and indicate that graduates were more independent, less likely to accept routines or emphasize orderly procedures, and less directive and more delegative than they were when they started the social work curriculum (See Table 14-VI). With the exception of the Academic Achievement scale, the changes were all in the direction of making the social work student more like the social work practitioner (See Table 14-III).

The increase in mean scores on the Academic Achievement scale suggests that most social work students earn better grades in graduate school than in their undergraduate programs. The other changes may reflect the liberal, antiauthoritarian orientation of the profession as a result of which the educational programs develop independence and reduce dependence on structure and routines.

It should be noted that these findings are contrary to Glockel's conclusion that social workers are relatively uninterested in the opportunity to operate independently in the job. Perhaps

TABLE 14-V

POLICEMEN COMPARED WITH MALE AND FEMALE SOCIAL WORKERS[a]

	Policemen [N = 99] Compared With	
	Male Social Workers	Female Social Workers
	[N = 51]	[N = 47]
Optimism	—	—*
Self-Confidence	—***	—***
Perseverance	+***	+***
Orderliness	+***	+***
Plan Ahead	—***	—***
Moral Absolutes	+***	+***
Slow Change	+***	+***
Persuasive Leadership	+	+
Self-Assertiveness	+**	+***
Move Toward Aggressor	—	—***
Move Away From Aggressor	+	0
Move Against Aggressor	—**	—
Prefers Routines	+***	+***
Identifies With Authority	0	—
Prefers Independence	—***	—***
Directive Leadership	+***	+***
Participative Leadership	+	+**
Delegative Leadership	+**	+***
Knowledge of Results	—	—***
External Controls	+***	+***
Systematic-Methodical	+***	+***
Problem Analysis	—	+*
Social Interaction	—***	—***
Mechanical Activities	+***	+***
Supervisory Activities	+	+**
Activity-Frequent Change	—	+**
Group Participation	—	—*
Status Attainment	0	+**
Social Service	—***	—***
Approval From Others	—*	—***
Intellectual Achievement	—**	—**
Maintain Societal Standards	—**	—
Role Conformity	+***	+***
Academic Achievement	—	—***

[a]A plus [+] indicates that mean scores of policemen were higher and a minus [—] that social workers were higher.

Glockel's comparisons are with college students while the JAIM comparisons are with established occupational groups.

TABLE 14-VI
CHANGE IN JAIM SCORES OF SOCIAL WORK STUDENTS ASSOCIATED
WITH SOCIAL WORK TRAINING

	School 1 N = 25	School 2 N = 27	Total N = 52
Orderliness	—2.78***a	—5.61***	—5.46***
Prefers Routines	—3.58**	—3.20**	—4.78***
Prefers Independence	3.92***	2.77*	4.58***
Directive Leadership	—2.90**	— .10	—1.99
Delegative Leadership	1.55	1.25	2.00
Academic Achievement	1.55	2.29*	2.69*

aRefers to t-test values for the differences between means on before and after measures for the same individual. A plus (+) value indicates that the mean score at end of training was higher than the beginning score. A minus (—) value indicates the opposite.

An important issue which this research does not examine is the relationship between JAIM scores and performance in social work or policeman roles. It would be hazardous to assume that the closer an individual conforms to the typical policeman or social worker profile, the better his performance. Survival in a profession is not necessarily a measure of competence. The markedly different profiles of these two occupational groups, however, suggest reasons why the members of these professions might have great difficulty communicating with each other, and why as Wilensky and Le-Beaux have pointed out, schools of social work have exhibited only minor interest in working with criminal offenders. Successful work with many delinquents and criminals may require greater use of external controls than social workers believe desirable. A different research design than the one used in this study would be necessary to shed light on these issues.

In summary, the JAIM studies of policemen and social workers have demonstrated distinctive characteristics of these two occupational groups which for the most part are consistent with earlier research. In almost every dimension measured by the JAIM, the policeman and the social worker differed significantly. The most pronounced characteristics of the policeman are his valuing of the standards of authority, his orientation toward mechanical or outdoor activities, his competitiveness and self-assertiveness, and his conservatism. Whether he should also be considered as authoritarian depends on how this term is used. Niederhoffer (1967) has stated that when the authoritarian concept is discussed the collection of traits and combination of these traits becomes astronomical with many variations depending on the theorist. In terms of JAIM concepts, the policeman might be considered authoritarian in that he prefers a directive leadership style and external controls. There is no evidence provided by this study, however, indicating that he goes out of his way to seek conflict.

The identification that policemen feel toward authority is toward the standards and not the person of authority. Thus it will be noted that the policeman scored somewhat lower than most groups on the Authority Identification scale which measures the degree to which the individual identifies with his superior and tries to please him.

The most pronounced characteristics of the social worker are his valuing of social service, his orientation toward people, and his rejection of routines, structure, and authoritarian attitudes.

REFERENCES

Adorno, T.W., Frenkel-Brunswick, E., Levinson, D.S., and Sanford, R.N.: *The Authoritarian Personality*. New York: Harper, 1950.

Barber, B.: Some problems in the sociology of professions. *Daedalus,* Fall, 1963. pp. 669-689.

Combs, A.W., and Snygg, D.: *Individual Behavior*. New York: Harper, 1959.

French, G.F.: *Needed Research on Social Work Manpower*. A report to the Task Force on Social Work Education and Manpower. Washington: Welfare Administration, Department of Health, Education, and Welfare, 1964. p. 1-7.

Gockel, G.: *Silk Stockings and Blue Collar: Social Work as a Career Choice of America's 1961 College Graduates*. National Opinion Research Center, Univ. of Chicago, (April, 1966).

Hatt, P.K. and North, C.C.: Prestige ratings of occupations. In S. Nasow and W. Form (Eds.): *Man, Work and Society*. New York: Basic Books, 1962, pp. 277-283.

Hodge, R.W., Siegel, P.M. and Rossi, P.H.: Occupational prestige in the United States, 1925-1963. *American Journal of Sociology,* 1964, 70. pp. 287-294.

Kadushin, A.: Determinants of career choice and their implication for social work. *Social Work Education*. April, 1958. pp. 37-43.

Kelly, E.L. and Goldberg, L.R.: Correlates of later performance and specializations in psychology. *Psychological Monographs.* 1959, Vol. *73,* No. 12. pp. 22-23.

Kelly, G.A.: *The Psychology of Personal Constructs.* New York: Norton, 1955.

Kidneigh, J. and Lundberg, H.W.: Are social work students different? *Social Work.* (May, 1958). No. 3, pp. 57-61.

McCormack, R. and Kidneigh, J.: The vocational interest patterns of social workers. *Social Work Journal.* Vol. *35,* No. 4 (October, 1959). pp. 161-163.

McCune, S.D.: *An exploratory study of the measured behavioral styles of students in five schools of social work.* (Doctoral Dissertation, Catholic University) Washington, D. C., 1966.

Niederhoffer, A.: *Behind the Shield.* New York: Doubleday and Co., Inc., 1967.

Petersen, P.B. and Lippitt, G.L.: Comparison of behavioral styles between entering and graduating students in officer candidate school. *Journal of Applied Psychology.* 1968, *52.* pp. 66-70.

Pins, A.M.: *Who Chooses Social Work, When and Why? An Exploratory Study of Factors Influencing Career Choices in Social Work.* New York: Council on Social Work Education, 1963.

Rogers, C.R.: *Becoming a Person.* Boston: Houghton-Mifflin, 1961.

Rokeach, M.: *The Open and Closed Mind.* New York: Basic Books, 1960.

Rosenberg, M.: *Occupations and Values.* Glencoe, Illinois: Free Press, 1957.

Sheldon, W.H.: *The Varieties of Temperament: A Psychology of Constitutional Differences.* New York: Harper, 1942.

Skolnick, J.H.: *Justice Without Trial.* New York: John Wiley, 1966.

Strong, E.K.: *Vocational Interests 18 Years After College.* Minneapolis: University of Minnesota Press, 1955.

Terman, L.M.: Scientists and non-scientists in a group of 800 gifted men. *Psychology Monograph.* 1954, *68.*

Trojanowicz, R.C.: *A comparison of the behavioral styles of policemen and social workers.* (Doctoral Dissertation, Michigan State University) East Lansing, Michigan, 1969.

Walther, R.H. *The Job Analysis and Interest Measurement.* Princeton, N.J.: Educational Testing Service, 1964.

———: *Orientations and Behavioral Styles of Foreign Service Officers.* New York: Carnegie Endowment for International Peace, 1965.

———: and McCune, S.D.: *Socialization Principles and Work Styles of the Juvenile Court.* Washington D.C. The George Washington University Center for Behavioral Sciences, 1965.

———: Juvenile Court Judges in the United States. Part II: Working styles and characteristics. *Crime and Delinquency.* 1965. *11* (4), pp. 348-393.

Wilensky, H. and LeBeaux, C.: *Industrial Society and Social Welfare.* New York: Russell Sage Foundation, 1958.

Chapter 15

CHARACTERISTICS OF POLICEMEN OF A COUNTY SHERIFF'S OFFICE

Kathleen B. Stoddard

To achieve the highest quality of police service it is essential that the best candidate be selected for appointment and promotion. It seems reasonable to assume that applicants should be evaluated on such factors as mental ability, academic achievement, interests and personal characteristics as well as knowledge of police procedures and supervisory aptitude when considered for advance level positions (Wilson, 1952).

A review of the literature (Terman, 1917; DuBois and Watson, 1950; Mullineaux, 1955; Frost, 1955; Colarelli and Siegel, 1964; and Matarazzo et al., 1964) related to the selection and promotion of police officers during the 1900's suggests that the successful police applicant of the 1960's comes from a better educated and more intelligent sector of society than did his counterpart of fifty years ago. Johnson (1965) has noted that educationally the successful applicant in Terman's 1916 study had attained an educational level slightly below the national average while a comparable applicant in a study by Matarazzo et al. (1964) was close to the national average in number of years of formal schooling. The most prominent difference between the two studies was in intellectual ability. The average applicant in 1916 possessed an IQ in the dull-normal range (e.g. 80-89) while the typical successful applicant in 1959-1962 measured within the bright-normal range (e.g. 110-119).

Typically, qualifications for a police applicant suggest that he should be a high school graduate or have passed a written examination considered to be equivalent to a high school diploma, be a United States citizen between the ages of twenty and thirty, of good moral character, possess minimum intelligence above that of the general population and be mentally, emotionally and physically fit (Smith, 1925; Vollmer, 1936; Gourley, 1950; Leonard, 1950; Wilson, 1950, 1952; and Frost, 1955). The inclusion of interest measurement (Matarazzo et al., 1964; and Golarelli and Siegel, 1964) in the evaluation of police applicants demonstrates a recent further effort to obtain the best qualified recruit.

In addition to the desired qualifications for selection of an applicant into police service, other factors must be taken into account when a candidate is considered for promotion. According to Wilson (1952), promotions should be based primarily on qualities of leadership and supervision. One of the few studies reported in this area done by Caughley and Taylor (1957) evaluating leadership qualities of promoting constables to sergeants in New Zealand.

As indicated earlier, areas that previous research (Terman, 1917; DuBois and Watson, 1950; Mullineaux, 1955; Colarelli and Siegel, 1964; and Matarazzo et al., 1964) has shown to be useful in selection were mental ability, academic achievement, and interests. In addition, knowledge of police procedures (Wilson, 1952) and leadership qualities (Caughley and Taylor, 1957) have been considered valuable in evaluating a candidate for advancement. The purpose of this study was to develop data on these areas that would differentiate among the ranks of a county sheriff's office. The characteristic of personality assessment, typically thought to be important (Kates, 1950; Sterne, 1960; Zaice; 1962; Colarelli and Siegel, 1964; and Matarazzo et al., 1964), was not examined because of the negative attitude of the sheriff's office to such assessment.

METHOD

Subjects

The *Ss* were officers of a county sheriff's office in the western United States. The law enforcement agency served a county with a population of 466,624 including a city of 176,793. The 165 officers employed by the force consisted of 6 captains, 12 lieutenants, 30 sergeants and 117 deputies. Of these men, 112 had served a minimum of three years in-rank and were thus eligible for promotion. Eligibility was further determined through a test of police knowledge and an investigation of physical and moral qualifications.

The 112 *Ss* consisted of 7 lieutenants, 30 sergeants and 75 deputies. The mean age of the lieutenants was 44.6; sergeants, 39.1; and deputies, 34.0. The lieutenants had an average of 13.0 years education; sergeants, 12.5; and deputies, 12.5. At least 28 percent of the men had attended college while only 13 percent had not completed the twelfth grade. The lieutenants had spent an average of 17.4 years in law enforcement service; sergeants, 10.5; and deputies, 6.0. The lieutenants had been employed by the county sheriff's office an average of 15.7 years; sergeants, 9.3 years; and deputies, 4.8 years.

Instruments

The *Ss* were administered the Strong Vocational Interest Blank (SVIB) : (1) because it had a policeman scale (2) for comparison purposes as it had been used in a number of studies measuring the interests of policemen (Kates, 1950; DuBois and Watson, 1950; Zaice, 1962; and Matarazzo et al., 1964). The Differential Aptitude Tests (DAT) of Verbal Reasoning (VR) and Numerical Ability (NA), form A, were chosen (1) to obtain measures of verbal and quantitative ability (2) because the authors have stated that the combination of scores on these two tests would serve "the same purpose as would so-called intelligence tests and make the administration of the latter unnecessary" (Bennett et al., 1948, p. 4), and (3) to reduce the perceived threat of academic tests by choosing instruments designed for a high school population. How Supervise? was included to measure knowledge of general principles of supervision as the presented norms for general foremen, production area supervisors and regular office supervisors seemed appropriate for this group. The purpose of the test of police knowledge was to evaluate achievement in the area of law enforcement information and procedures.

Strong Vocational Interest Blank (SVIB)

The SVIB for Men, a commonly used instrument, was originally developed by E. K. Strong, Jr. in 1927 and has been most recently revised by David P. Campbell (1966). The inventory was designed to measure interests in comparison with the known responses of persons who were considered successful in particular occupations. Results are reported in terms of standard scores with a corresponding letter system for ease in interpretation. An A rating suggests interest similar to people successful in an occupation while C indicates dissimilar interests with B—, B and B+ representing the middle range.

The 1966 revised consists of 55 scales which comprise 11 occupational groupings. Four non-occupational scales, academic achievement (AACH), masculinity-feminity (MFII), occupational level (OL), and specialization level (SL) were also reported on the profile.

The criterion group for the policeman scale consisted of 254 policemen from the cities of Berkeley, Los Angeles, and Palo Alto, California; Cincinnati, Ohio; Duluth, Minnesota; and Wichita, Kansas. Their mean age was 35; mean educational level, 10.4 years. The men were tested in 1933.

The test-retest reliability on the policeman scale ranged from .90 for 139 University of Minnesota sophomores tested over a two-week period to .56 over an eight-year period for 171 high school seniors to .58 for 191 Stanford University seniors over a period of twenty-two years. Darley and Hagenah (1955) concluded that behavior measured on the occupational scales seemed to remain fairly stable over time.

Differential Aptitude Tests (DAT)

The DAT was developed in 1947 by George K. Bennett, Harold G. Seashore and Alexander G. Wesman. The tests were designed to measure the abilities of boys and girls in grades eight through twelve. A further use was a screen employment applicants.

Correlations between the combination of the VR and NA tests are presented in the manual (Bennett et al., 1948). On a sample of 175 males, the correlations of the higher level of the Otis Self-Administering Test of Mental Ability with VR and NA were .81 and .69 respectively; for 68 men the Henmon-Nelson IQ correlated .73 with VR and .70 with NA. The Ohio State Psychological Examination (N=137 males) and the Terman-McNemar IQ (N=279 males) correlated .79 and .77 respectively with VR and .47 and .35 with NA.

How Supervise?

Form M of How Supervise? was developed by Quentin W. File and H. H. Remmers in 1948. The test, based on situations commonly found in industry, was composed of three sections: supervisory practices, company policies and supervisor opinions. The first two concern activities which would seem desirable for a supervisor or organization to initiate. The third deals with interpersonal relations between supervisor and workers. The corrected split-half reliability coefficient on Form M was .87 (File and Remmers, 1971).

Police Knowledge Test

The test of police knowledge was constructed by one of the county commissioners for this administration. It consisted of 100 objective and short-response questions based on information from the police handbooks.

Procedure

The 112 candidates eligible for promotional consideration were tested at a nearby state university. The assessment took 3 to 4 hours per candidate and consisted of the DAT-VR, DAT-NA, How Supervise?, the SVIB, a locally developed test of police knowledge, and collection of autobiographical information pertaining to age, education, and law enforcement experience.

Scoring was according to manual specifications with the exception that the correction factor was not used in scoring NA. The intended purpose of the instrument was to obtain a measure of computational ability without regard to the nationally established norms which were inappropriate for this group. The results of VR and NA were then combined to yield a single quantitative measure of intellectual ability.

In preparation of the data for computer analysis, negative

standard scores on the SVIB were recorded as zero. One *S* was dropped in the SVIB analysis because of insufficient data. With regard to age, formal education, number of years spent in law enforcement and in the employment of the sheriff's office, the recorded figures were rounded to the nearest whole number.

Analysis of Data

Means and standard deviations were computed for each variable. Coefficients of correlation (Garrett, 1962) were calculated among all the variables and intercorrelation matrices established for the lieutenants, sergeants and deputies. Further analysis consisted of computing t-tests of differences between the means for the differentially ranked groups (Guilford, 1965). The level of significance was established at .05.

FINDINGS

Occupational Interests

For the total group, the mean standard score on the policeman scale of the SVIB was 38.7 or a letter grade range of B. The mean scores and corresponding letter grades by rank were: lieutenants 43.2, B+; sergeants 38.9, B; and deputies 38.3, B. This scale did not statistically differentiate between the groups.

In looking at the overall occupational patterns of the three ranks, scales where the mean letter grades were A or B+ were of particular interest. From Figure 15-1a & 15-1b it is apparent that the lieutenants had interests in common with man engaged in the three technical supervision occupations: production manager, army officer and air force officer. In comparing these occupations across the ranks, production manager did not differentiate between the lieutenants and either of the other two groups; however, a significant difference (t = 2.66; p<.01) was found between the mean scores for sergeants and deputies on this scale. Significant differences were discovered between the lieutenants and sergeants on both the army (t = 1.98; p<.05) and air force officer (t = 2.65; p<.01) scales and between lieutenants and deputies (t = 2.01; p<.05) on the latter scale.

On the public administrator scale, the lieutenants obtained a

SVIB MEAN STANDARD SCORES AND STANDARD DEVIATIONS FOR LIEUTENANTS, SERGEANTS AND DEPUTIES

GROUP	SCALE	MEANS Lt	MEANS Sg	MEANS Dp	S.D. Lt	S.D. Sg	S.D. Dp
I	Dentist	23	25	27	8	9	10
	Osteopath	32	26	29	6	8	8
	Veterinarian	27	35	34	4	10	8
	Physician	27	24	28	9	10	9
	Psychiatrist	30	18	19	6	14	9
	Psychologist	23	15	17	8	9	8
	Biologist	26	17	22	12	10	10
II	Architect	17	20	23	11	9	12
	Mathematician	12	10	13	7	9	10
	Physicist	16	11	14	10	10	11
	Chemist	26	19	21	15	11	13
	Engineer	27	24	25	14	11	12
III	Production Manager	42	40	35	8	6	10
	Army Officer	45	38	36	12	8	12
	Air Force Officer	46	37	37	6	8	11
IV	Carpenter	29	29	30	14	13	14
	Forest Service Man	38	32	35	4	9	10
	Farmer	28	37	36	7	10	10
	Math-Science Teacher	37	26	31	8	7	11
	Printer	30	33	35	8	9	10
	Policeman	43	39	38	7	7	9
V	Personnel Director	37	29	28	14	12	12
	Public Administrator	50	43	39	15	12	12
	Rehabilitation Counselor	39	31	31	13	12	11
	YMCA Secretary	36	38	33	18	11	13
	Social Worker	34	27	27	16	12	12
	Social Science Teacher	28	33	32	15	12	10
	School Superintendent	21	19	15	12	10	11
	Minister	16	9	11	17	9	11
VI	Librarian	20	16	20	8	5	8
	Artist	16	22	24	8	7	10
	Musician Performer	25	26	30	8	7	8
	Music Teacher	17	21	22	9	10	9
VII	C. P. A. Owner	17	20	20	8	10	9

Chart legend:
- △—△ Lieutenants (N = 6)
- o----o Sergeants (N = 30)
- ●—● Deputies (N = 75)

15-1A

GROUP	SCALE	MEANS			S.D.		
		Lt	Sg	Dp	Lt	Sg	Dp
VIII	Senior C. P. A.	28	25	26	11	10	10
	Accountant	29	28	26	10	10	9
	Office Worker	34	32	31	10	9	8
	Purchasing Agent	31	40	36	6	7	8
	Banker	23	30	27	8	9	8
	Pharmacist	27	35	32	8	8	8
	Mortician	28	39	34	11	9	7
IX	Sales Manager	22	34	28	9	8	8
	Real Estate Salesman	28	40	37	9	7	7
	Life Insurance Salesman	18	31	28	13	8	9
X	Advertising Man	17	28	27	6	8	10
	Lawyer	24	30	29	6	6	10
	Author-Journalist	20	28	28	4	6	10
XI	Pres., Mfg. Concern	19	27	22	7	5	8
Suppl. Occup. Scales	Credit Manager	42	37	33	8	10	12
	Chamber of Commerce Exec.	37	39	35	12	9	10
	Physical Therapist	50	41	42	15	9	12
	Computer Programmer	38	26	29	15	13	11
	Business Education Teacher	35	34	31	13	10	11
	Community Recr. Admin.	41	33	36	18	11	13
Non-occupational Scales	Specialization Level	42	34	35	9	9	9
	Occupational Level	52	54	52	5	6	8
	Masculinity-Femininity	56	53	52	8	6	8
	Academic Achievement	44	33	37	7	11	10

Fig. 15-1B

mean A rating and the sergeants a B+ rating. This scale significantly differentiated between the lieutenants and deputies (t = 2.29; p<.05) suggesting that the interests of lieutenants and to a lesser degree, sergeants, lie more in the areas of supervision than do those interests associated with the patrolman. The lieutenants also received B+ ratings on the credit manager and community recreation administrator scales, but these occupations did not statistically differentiate between the groups.

Physical therapist was the only scale on which the lieutenants, sergeants and deputies all obtained A or B+ ratings. It significantly differentiated between lieutenants and sergeants (t = 2.33; p<.05). Further, it was the only scale where the deputies obtained a mean letter grade of A or B+. Possibly the variance within each occupation for the deputies tended to pull the group letter grades toward the mean explaining the lack of more A or B+ scores. In other words, the deputies as a group possessed the least crystalized pattern of interests.

For the three sales occupations: sales manager, real estate salesman and life insurance salesman, the sergeants obtained scores that were significantly higher than those of the lieutenants and with the exception of life insurance salesman were also significantly higher than the deputies. In addition, the deputies' scores on real estate salesman and life insurance salesman were significantly higher than those of the lieutenants. All of the t-values were greater than that required for .05 significance. These findings suggest that the sergeants have more interests in common with persons engaged in sales occupations than do the lieutenants or deputies, and deputies possess stronger interests than lieutenants in the sales area. A similar result occurred for president, manufacturing concern where the sergeants' mean score was significantly higher than the lieutenants (t = 3.48; p<.001) and deputies (t = 3.26; p<.01).

The mean scores for the sergeants on the verbal-linguistic occupations; advertising man, lawyer and author-journalist were also significantly higher than those of the lieutenants. All of the t-values were greater than the 2.04 required for .05 significance. In addition, the advertising man scale differentiated deputies from lieutenants (t = 2.39; p<.05).

The sergeants' mean scores on three of the business-related occupations: purchasing agent, pharmacist and mortician were significantly higher than the lieutenants and with the exception of pharmacist were also significantly higher than the deputies. Again, all the t-values were greater than that required for .05 significance.

Three of the life science occupations: psychiatrist, psychologist and biologist differentiated between lieutenants and sergeants. The t-values were greater than the 2.04 required for .05 significance. The lieutenants also obtained higher scores than deputies (t = 2.63; p<.01) on the psychiatrist scale while deputies had more interests in common with biologists than did sergeants (t = 2.41; p<.05).

The deputies obtained significantly higher scores than sergeants on the SVIB scales of librarian (t = 2.41; p<.05) and musician performer (t = 2.43; p<.05).

One further occupational scale which produced significant differences was math-science teacher. Both lieutenants (t = 3.17; p<.01) and deputies (t = 2.18; p<.05) had more interests in common with this field than did sergeants.

The only non-occupational scale which significantly differentiated was academic achievement between lieutenants and sergeants (t = 2.18; p<.05) suggesting lieutenants have interests more similar to persons who persist in academic endeavors.

In summary, the lieutenants appeared to have more interests similar to men engaged in the areas of technical supervision, administration and the life sciences while the interests of sergeants seemed to be more related to the sales, verbal-linguistic and several business occupational areas. As a group, the deputies possessed the least crystalized pattern of interests.

Intelligence

The combination of VR and NA of the DAT yielded a mean of 47.6 for the total group. Lieutenants obtained an average of 48.1; sergeants, 43.0; and deputies, 49.3. As shown in Table 15-I the results significantly differentiated between the deputies and sergeants (t = 2.27; p<.05).

TABLE 15-I

CHARACTERISTICS OF LIEUTENANTS, SERGEANTS, AND DEPUTIES

	Lieutenants N=7			Sergeants N=30			Deputies N=75		
	Mean	Standard Deviation	t-value Lt./Sgt.	Mean	Standard Deviation	t-value Sgt./Dep.	Mean	Standard Deviation	t-value Lt./Dep.
Police Knowledge	71.9	13.3	.63	69.4	8.5	.07	69.5	8.2	.69
DAT: VR+NA	48.1	16.5	.82	43.0	14.5	2.27*	49.3	12.2	.24
How Supervise?	70.4	12.5	2.32*	55.7	15.7	2.53*	63.6	13.9	1.26
Formal Education (Years)	13.0	2.5	.63	12.5	1.6	.08	12.5	1.6	.75
Law Enforcement Service (Years)	17.4	4.0	3.52**	10.5	4.9	4.15**	6.0	5.0	5.84**
Sheriff's Office (Years)	15.7	5.7	4.14**	9.3	3.1	5.58**	4.8	4.0	6.66**
Age	44.8	6.8	1.63	39.1	8.1	2.96**	34.0	8.0	3.38**

*Significant at the .05 level
**Significant at the .01 level

Supervisory Knowledge

The mean score for lieutenants on How Supervise? was 70.4; sergeants, 55.7; deputies, 63.6; with 61.9 as the average for the total group. Comparing the three ranks with the national norms for Level II—office and middle-level production supervisors, the lieutenants placed at the 62nd percentile; the sergeants at the 30th percentile; deputies, 48th percentile; and total group, 43rd percentile. How Supervise? significantly differentiated between lieutenants and sergeants ($t = 2.32$; $p<.05$) and between deputies and sergeants ($t = 2.53$; $p<.01$). However, it did not distinguish between lieutenants and deputies; thus of the three groups, the sergeants displayed the least knowledge of supervisory practices.

Police Knowledge

On this locally developed test, the lieutenants obtained an average score of 71.9; sergeants, 69.4; deputies, 69.5; with 69.6 for the total group. A statistical test on the results did not differentiate among the three ranks.

Relationships of the Variables

Correlation matrices were established to explore the relationships of the measurement variables. All of the following coefficients of correlation were reported to be significant at or greater than the .05 level.

For the lieutenants, age was related to education (–.83), knowledge of supervisory practices (–.78), years of experience in law enforcement service (.84) and in the employment of the sheriff's office (.81). Service in law enforcement and the sheriff's office corresponded with police knowledge (–.75, –.85) and education (–.87).

For the sergeants, intelligence was related to police knowledge (.60), education (.53) and knowledge of supervisory practices (.45). The SVIB policeman scale was related to police knowledge (–.59), intelligence (–.64) and knowledge of supervisory practices (–.44). Age corresponded with law enforcement service (.63) and police knowledge (–.42).

For the deputies, intelligence correlated with education (.48), police knowledge (.60), supervisory practices (.43), age (–.34), years of law enforcement service (–.27) and employment by the sheriff's office (–.32). Knowledge of supervisory practices was associated with formal education (.29) and number of years spent in the sheriff's office (–.29). In addition, deputies with more education demonstrated less interest in the SVIB occupation of policeman (–.34). Knowledge of police procedures was related to knowledge of supervisory practices (.48), education (.41), age (–.55), employment by the sheriff's office (–.51) and law enforcement experience (–.39).

In summary for the total group regardless of rank:

1. The men performed better on the intelligence measure evidenced low interest in the SVIB occupation of policeman, possessed greater knowledge of supervisory practices and police procedures, had more formal education, were younger and had less experience in law enforcement service and in the employment of the sheriff's office.

2. The men who scored higher on the measure of supervisory practices had more schooling, greater knowledge of police procedures, had spent fewer years in the sheriff's office and indicated less interest in the occupation of policeman.

3. Knowledge of police procedures was associated with formal education and inversely realted to age, employment by the sheriff's office, and experience in law enforcement.

4. Education was inversely related to police interest as measured by the SVIB.

5. Age, employment by the sheriff's office and experience in law enforcement were interrelated.

DISCUSSION

Comparison of SVIB results for this study with the mean profiles for new recruits (Matarazzo et al., 1964) and experienced policemen (Zaice, 1962) suggests that the profiles generally followed similar patterns. The interests seemed to be most like those of men employed in the technical and skilled trade areas as well as social service and the business related occupations.

Results of the SVIB policeman scale suggest that the officers of the county sheriff's office have fewer interests in common with Strong's criterion group than do the applicants and experienced officers in Portland. The differences might be accounted for by the fact that the criterion group for the policeman scale was composed of a limited number of city policemen from metropolitan areas in the midwest and on the West Coast; therefore, it would be expected that a group of men similarly employed would obtain higher ratings (DuBois and Watson, 1950; Kates, 1950).

The policeman scale was the highest ranking occupation in the technical and skilled area which was consistent with both Portland studies. This comparison was limited to the occupations common to the 1938 and 1966 forms of the SVIB.

Similar to Zaice's command personnel, the lieutenants of the sheriff's office obtained a mean A rating on the SVIB public administrator scale, and it too was higher than the rating on the policeman scale. Lieutenants and command personnel no longer performed the duties of the deputies or patrolmen but were generally more involved with administrative activities.

Physical therapist was the only SVIB scale on which the lieutenants, sergeants and deputies obtained ratings of B+ or better. They appeared to have interests more similar to this occupational group than to the policeman scale. Sheriff's officers and physical therapists seem to be interested in areas related to technical skills, social service, and physical, recreational and military activities.

Although the deputies obtained scores that were significantly higher than the lieutenants on the SVIB sales group and significantly higher than sergeants on two of the aesthetic-cultural occupations, physical therapist was the only scale where they rated as high as B+. One conclusion might be that the deputies possessed a wide range of interests which could be an asset in law enforcement. Another possibility is that the deputy position is a trial period. If a man were promoted to sergeant, he most likely remained with the force; if he were not advanced, he might have sought other means of employment. Hence, interest patterns seemed more crystalized for sergeants than deputies.

It further appeared to this author that while deputies seemed to eventually get promoted or leave the force, sergeants may or may not have been advanced but in most instances probably remained with the force. This conclusion was based primarily upon the significant age difference found between sergeants and deputies but not between sergeants and lieutenants. Also the deputies performed significantly better than the sergeants on both the intelligence and supervisory knowledge measures. Thus, the deputy ranks are continually being revitalized with new recruits; the more qualified sergeants get promoted, but what happens to the older sergeant who keeps getting bypassed?

RECOMMENDATIONS

As a result of the findings of the present study, it is recommended that further research evaluating desirable qualifications of the differential ranks of policemen would be valuable. Then data collected at the time of recruitment could be used to discriminate potential supervisory personnel from those who might be best qualified for intermediate ranks. Mandel (1970), one of the few reported studies in this area, attempted to predict on-the-job performance of policemen from information obtained during the initial selection procedure.

Further research is suggested to explore what happens to the men who do not get promoted. Are deputies more often than sergeants or perhaps lieutenants apt to seek other fields of employment if they are not advanced? This question raises another issue, that of the legitimacy of a man remaining within a particular rank because he is most appropriately qualified at that level.

It is suggested that the criterion group for the policeman scale of the SVIB be more specifically defined as to the ranks and duties of the "policemen" to permit a more accurate interpretation of results. It is further recommended that the criterion group be based on a more geographically representative sample of "policemen" throughout the country. In addition, from the findings of this study, it would seem desirable to develop local norms.

REFERENCES

Bennett, G. K., Seashore, H. G., and Wesman, A. G.: *A manual for the Differential Aptitude Tests.* New York: Psychological Corporation, 1948.

Caughley, J. G. and Taylor, A. J. W.: New methods in the promotion of constables to sergeants in the New Zealand police force. *Journal of Criminal Law, Criminology and Police Science,* 1957, *48,* 207-212.

Colarelli, N. J. and Siegel, S. M.: A method of police personnel selection. *Journal of Criminal Law, Criminology and Police Science,* 1964, *55,* 287-289.

Darley, J. G. and Hagenah, Theda.: *Vocational interest measurement.* Minneapolis: University of Minnesota Press, 1955.

DuBois, P. H. and Watson, R. I.: The selection of patrolmen. *Journal of Applied Psychology,* 1950, *34,* 90-95.

File, Q. W. and Remmers, H. H.: *How Supervise?* New York: Psychological Corporation, 1971.

Frost, T. M.: Selection methods for police recruits. *Journal of Criminal Law, Criminology and Police Science.* 1955, *46,* 135-145.

Garrett, H. E.: *Elementary Statistics.* New York: David McKay Company, 1962.

Gourley, G. D.: Police discipline. *Journal of Criminal Law and Criminology,* 1950, *41,* 85-100.

Guilford, J. P.: *Fundamental statistics in psychology and education.* San Francisco: McGraw-Hill, 1965.

Johnson, R. W.: Successsful policemen and firemen applicants: then and now. *Journal of Applied Psychology,* 1965, *49,* 299-301.

Kates, S. L.: Rorschach responses, Strong Blank scales, and job satisfaction among policemen. *Journal of Applied Psychology,* 1950, *34,* 249-254.

Leonard, V. A.: *Police organization and management.* Brooklyn: The Foundation Press, 1951.

Mandel, K.: The predictive validity of on-the-job performance of policemen from recruitment selection information, unpublished doctoral dissertation University of Utah, 1970.

Matarazzo, J. D., Allen, Bernadene V., Saslow, G., and Wiens, A. N.: Characteristics of successful policemen and firemen applicants. *Journal of Applied Psychology,* 1964, *48,* 123-133.

Mullineaux, J. E.: An evaluation of predictors used to select patrolmen. *Public Personnel Review,* 1955, *16,* 84-86.

Smith, B.: *The state police.* New York: Macmillan Company, 1925.

Sterne, D. M.: Use of Kuder Preference Record, Personal, with police officers. *Journal of Applied Psychology,* 1960, *44,* 323-324.

Strong, E. K., Jr.: *Strong Vocational Interest Blanks Manual.* (Revised by David P. Campbell). Stanford, California: Stanford University Press, 1966.

Terman, L. M.: A trial of mental and pedagogical tests in a civil service examination for policemen and firemen. *Journal of Applied Psychology,* 1917, *1,* 17-29.

Vollmer, A.: *The police and modern society.* Berkeley, California: University of California Press, 1936.

Wilson, O. W.: *Police administration.* New York: McGraw Hill, 1950.

Wilson, O. W.: *Police planning.* Springfield, Illinois: Charles C Thomas 1952.

Zaice, J. E.: Measured interests, personality and intelligence of professional policemen. Unpublished master's thesis, Washington State University, 1962.

SECTION **IV**

POLICE AND MINORITY GROUPS

INTRODUCTION

THE LONG-STANDING DEBATE BETWEEN POLICE OFFICERS AND MEMBERS OF VARIOUS MINORITY COMMUNITIES HAS CAUSED INCREASING TENSION, VIOLENCE AND FEAR. SUCH TENSION IS UNFORTUNATELY CONTAGIOUS ON THE ONE HAND, AND A MICROCOSM OF HOW "PEOPLE" IN GENERAL FEEL, ON THE OTHER. NO AREA OF POLICE WORK AND COMMUNITY RELATIONS IS IN MORE NEED OF CLARIFICATION, RELIABLE DATA AND SOLUTION.

THE POWERS AND MCENTIRE BOOKLET A GUIDE TO RACE RELATIONS FOR POLICE OFFICERS WAS PUBLISHED IN 1946 BUT HAS MUCH RELEVANCE FOR THE PROBLEMS AND CONCERNS OF TODAY. IN THE FOREWORD TO THIS 38-PAGE PAMPHLET, ROBERT W. KENNY, THEN ATTORNEY GENERAL OF CALIFORNIA STATED.

> DURING RECENT YEARS, WE IN THE PROFESSION OF LAW ENFORCEMENT HAVE REALIZED MORE AND MORE THE IMPORTANCE OF TRAINING IN HUMAN RELATIONS AS WELL AS IN THE DETECTION OF CRIME. IN AUGUST, 1943, THE GOVENORS' PEACE OFFICERS COMMITTEE IN CIVIL DISTURBANCE, RECOGNIZING THAT "THE POLICE PLAYED A VITALLY IMPORTANT ROLE IN RACE RELATIONS," STRONGLY URGED THE NECESSITY OF SPECIAL TRAINING TO EQUIP OFFICERS TO MEET THEIR RESPONSIBILITIES IN THIS REGARD.

THE BOOKLET WAS AN OUTGROWTH OF A CONFERENCE HELD IN RICHMOND, CALIFORNIA PROMPTED BY THE SEVERE RACE RIOTS OF 1943. THE CONFERENCE WAS PLANNED AND CARRIED OUT AS FIVE DISCUSSION SESSIONS FOR TWELVE SELECTED OFFICERS. AS THE READER LOOKS OVER THIS ARTICLE, HE WILL NO DOUBT BE STRUCK BY THE FAMILIAR SOUND OF ISSUES AND ANSWERS DISCUSSED IN THIS PAMPHLET. IN MANY WAYS LITTLE HAS CHANGED DURING THE LAST THREE DECADES. THE ENTIRE PAMPHLET WAS REPRODUCED SO THE READER MIGHT ALSO SEE SOME DATED ASPECTS OF THE PRESENTATION.

THE MORALES ARTICLE REPRESENTS A CONTROVERSIAL HYPOTHESIS OFTEN PUT FORWARD BY VARIOUS MINORITY GROUPS. THE DIFFERENTIAL APPLICATION OF POLICE DEPLOYMENT HAS LONG BEEN AN ISSUE AND WILL PROBABLY BE SUBJECTED TO SUBSTANTIAL STUDY OVER THE NEXT FEW YEARS.

THE RESEARCH BY KELLY AND WEST DOCUMENTS THE PROBLEMS AND PROCESS OF AN URBAN POLICE DEPARTMENTS' ATTEMPT TO BRING ABOUT

RACIAL BALANCE. ALTHOUGH VERY PRELIMINARY, THE AUTHORS OFFER USEFUL INSIGHTS INTO THE PAINFUL TRANSITION THAT IS NOW TAKING PLACE THROUGHOUT THE UNITED STATES.

THE WALLACH AND CARTER ARTICLE REPRESENTS THE CONCLUSIONS REACHED AFTER AN EXTENSIVE ATTITUDE STUDY. IT IS INDICATIVE OF RECENT TRENDS TO SEEK DATA FROM CONSUMERS TO ASSESS INSTITUTIONAL PERFORMANCE. HOPEFULLY, SUCH STUDIES WILL MAKE THE POLICE MORE AWARE OF THE NEEDS OF A COMMUNITY.

Chapter 16

A GUIDE TO RACE RELATIONS FOR POLICE OFFICERS

Davis McEntire and Robert B. Powers

I

POLICE PROBLEMS OF MINORITY GROUP RELATIONS

1. Tension among racial groups is a constant threat to the peace and public order.

A. Violent incidents demand the immediate attention of police officers. Fights, assaults, and disturbances of the peace are examples.

Sometimes, in disregard of law, members of one group try to terrorize members of another group to "keep them in their place" (Whites versus Negroes) or to force them out of certain localities (Chinese, Japanese, Negroes who are moving into white residential areas). Members of terrorized groups sometimes retaliate with violence, in equal disregard of law.

When incidents occur between individuals of antagonistic groups, there is always a danger of inflaming the groups. A fight between a Negro and a White may be just a fight between two persons, but if others interpret it as a race fight, the stage may be set for a clash of groups. When a White person is attacked by a Negro, Whites are inclined to feel they have a grievance against the entire Negro population.

B. Police are always in the "middle" of any racial dispute. They are often charged with racial discrimination. If they

Reprinted from a Police Training Bulletin 66294, Department of Justice, State of California, 1946, with the permission of the Department of Justice, State of California.

302

try to be fair, prejudiced people may call them "Nigger-lovers" or "Jap-lovers."

C. Minority groups often fear the police and distrust their fairness. As a result, police have difficulty in working with these groups.

D. The race riot. This is the extreme disruption of public peace, disorder on a large scale. It is extremely destructive of life and property. The Detroit riot of June, 1943, cost 34 fatalities, over a thousand persons injured, and $2,000,-000 in property damage. Over a million man-hours of work were lost in war plants. The Harlem, New York City riot of August, 1943, killed five, injured 307, including 53 policemen, and destroyed $5,000,000 worth of property.

Riots are only the explosion of long-accumulated tensions. The impending danger to law and order is apparent long before tensions blow up in open conflict. Race riots never happen suddenly or unexpectedly except to those who can not see the symptoms and signs of danger.

2. Race tensions at present are high and liable to increase unless relieved. Basic factors in the present situation are:

A. Population shifts—huge migrations, bringing thousands of white and colored workers together in a new environment.

B. Return of previously evacuated Japanese-Americans. A number of attacks were made on Japanese-Americans when they first began returning to California early in 1945. The action of State law enforcement agencies and local public officials effectively discouraged this terrorism and the attacks stopped. This problem appears now to be settled from a law enforcement standpoint, but may recur in some communities.

C. Post-war dislocations. Reconversion and demobilization are causing new population shifts.

If jobs become scarce, there may be efforts to exclude minority groups from various kinds of employment. If unemployment becomes concentrated among minority groups, they will feel discriminated against and White workers will feel that the unemployed minority groups are a threat to their jobs. This may cause serious racial trouble, especially if employer attempts should be made to use minority group workers to keep wages down or to break strikes.

Some white people think, now that the war is over, that it is time "to get the Negroes in line" or make them stay "in their place." Negroes are also tense—afraid they are going to be discriminated against in postwar jobs and housing. They will do everything they can to hold on to their wartime gains.

D. Community tensions. In troubled times, people suffer from many tensions and frustrations. The housing shortage, economic fears and insecurities, overcrowded transportation, and inadequate recreational facilities, all contribute to the general unrest and discontent. Nearly everyone seems to have a grievance of some sort.

Community tensions have a tendency to focus on minority groups. People look for someone to blame for their troubles. They may blame "the Administration," "the Communists," "the unions," "grasping capitalists," "corrupt police," etc. Often minority groups get the blame. People will say "the Jews are ruining the country," or "the Negroes have spoiled this community."

3. The present situation on the West Coast is similar to that in northern cities after World War I.

A. There was heavy migration of Whites and Negroes from the South to northern industrial centers during that war.

B. Racial tensions and community tensions were built up during the war. Practically nothing was done to relieve the tensions.

C. Postwar dislocations aggravated the problem; still nothing was done to solve it.

D. Outbreak of race riots occurred in 26 cities during the year 1919.

4. Cities and counties, under California law, are responsible for property damage caused by riots, and this responsibility is heavy on the shoulders of peace officers.

Political Code Section 1452, makes every county and municipal corporation responsible for "injury to real or personal property situated within its corporate limits, done or caused by mobs or riots."

II

OFFICIAL ATTITUDE OF POLICE TOWARD RACE RELATIONS

1. What should be the objectives of a police department and of individual policemen in dealing with racial problems? What is the selfish interest of police officers in the matter?
   A. "Essentially, the policeman wants to be in a strong position when he is on his beat or when working on an investigation. He wants to be in such position that he can deal with any condition arising with the greatest of freedom from restrictions and the greatest of latitude insofar as positive action is concerned."—*Attorney General's representative, Richmond.*
   B. A police department wants the same thing—to be in a strong position; to have the support and confidence of the public in its policies; to have the necessary freedom for a good job of law enforcement; and to have the capacity for dealing effectually with any situation which may arise.
   C. Charges of racial discrimination, unfairness, or brutality hamper a police department—even if untrue, they still hurt.
   D. Lack of public confidence in the police, on the part of any considerable section of the people, hurts and hinders the effectiveness of law enforcement officers.
2. What can police officers do to attain these desired objectives?
   A. Being prepared to suppress a riot, if one should develop, is necessary but *it is not enough.*
   B. They must exert every effort to prevent major disturbances because police are the real losers in a race riot. When a race riot once starts, loss of life and extensive property destruction are practically inevitable.

Unless a riot is handled with exceptional skill, police will be the target of serious criticism from one source or another.

The barrage of criticism growing out of a race riot destroys public confidence in the police and tends to hamper them in subsequent enforcement of the law in interracial and other situations. No race riot settles anything. Except for directing attention to its fundamental causes, conditions after the riot are usually worse than they were before.

C. The best hope of the police lies in *prevention*. This requires knowledge of the causes of racial unrest and ways of reducing tensions. Special techniques are required.

"Race problems have not received the special study their importance merits. In attempting to cope with such problems, the police have sometimes used routine methods which, for a variety of reasons, have not proved successful. Race riots involve special social problems which must be understood before they can be met successfully."—*Report of the Peace Officers Committee on Civil Disturbances*.

D. Police should not underestimate the importance of what they can do in race relations; nor should they be deterred from action by an attitude that the problem is insoluble. Experience proves that they can do a great deal to improve race relations, to the benefit of the police and the whole community.

"The police play a vitally important role in race relations. No agency of government can be more effective in furthering good race relations and in preventing race riots than the police. *Police can prevent race riots*. Not only can they prevent such riots from occurring, but should they occur, intelligent police methods can minimize their consequences."—*Report of the Peace Officers Committee, etc.*

"At the same time, lax police policies contribute to race riots and antiquated methods of coping with riots can greatly aggravate their consequences."—*Ibid.*

3. The first essential in a preventive program is a *professional approach to the problem.*

   A. This is in keeping with the trend toward professional status of police work.

   "During the past 20 years we have seen police work develop from the category of unskilled labor to a semiprofession. * * * We may some day take our place among the truly professional vocations such as medicine, law, and education. * * * Many aspects of police work indicate that we are already approaching professional status."—*E. W. Lester, Member, Adult Authority, formerly Deputy Chief of Police, Los Angeles.*

   B. A professional attitude is essential to success in the problems of human relations. Neutral, impartial, unbiased, inquiring—these are attributes of the professional.

   Fundamental principle of law enforcement: All citizens are equal before the law. Race, color, politics, or religion make no difference.

   The policeman is an arm of the law—therefore, all citizens must be *equal* in his official eyes. This is the starting point of professional policemanship.

   "I believe that if the policeman were not to show any partiality one way or another, if he should judge each case as if there were all Whites or all Negroes involved, he would be doing his job as he should. He shouldn't lean over backwards to protect the Negro, nor should he discriminate against the Negro. He should enforce the law as it is."—*Captain George W. Bengley, Richmond Police Department.*

   "Adopt a professional attitude, basing decisions and action on observation, evidence, and probability, rather than on prejudice, rumor and possibility. The physician's diagnosis and treatment of physical ills is based on symptoms, and on the differences in individuals, not on prejudices, races, and religion. The police officer's decision and action must likewise be determined not on a basis of group mem-

bership but on individuality."—*Attorney General's representative, Richmond.*

"Expression of bias invariably leads to charges of discrimination, prejudice, and intolerance. We must never
forget that we are representatives of government—a Democracy, and as such we must be impersonal and unbiased
in every act. * * * We must rigorously enforce the law
against all transgressors * * * without regard to the race,
religion, or political views of the violator."—*F. W. Lester.*

Almost all police officers firmly believe that they do
treat citizens alike, regardless of race or color. Nevertheless, policemen are human beings and like everyone else
they have opinions and prejudices. "Police officers often
fail to realize that their prejudices make impartiality impossible. Believing, as many do, that 'Negroes have criminal tendencies' leads to unconscious discrimination."—
Attorney General's representative, Richmond.

A high ranking peace officer in California once stated
in an official report that Mexicans had a "biological disregard for the value of life," that they had an "inborn desire
to kill or at least let blood." Negroes, also, he said, had
this same hereditary blood lust, while Filipinos were biologically disposed to crimes of violence, especially over
women. These interpretations are scientifically as wrong as
anything could be. As one anthropologist remarked, "it
would be just as logical to charge Americans with being
hereditary killers because they kill so many people with
automobiles." This example of a tendency to regard an
entire group as inherently criminal, blinds the officer to
facts and destroys his standard as a professional. And if
minority group members learn that such ideas are held by
enforcement officers, they may rightfully feel that they are
convicted without hearing and have no chance of fair
treatment.

Just as a new police officer has to *learn* the techniques
of making an arrest, detecting a crime, or preserving evidence, so he has to *learn* to be aware of his human preju-

dices and to curb their expression. An *impartial, professional* attitude does not come naturally; it has to be acquired and cultivated.

C. Use of expressions which may antagonize members of racial, religious, or other groups, such as "nigger," "kike," "wop," "cholo," "chink," "chili-picker," "Jap," etc., is unprofessional conduct.

"When we stoop to call names * * * we are simply injuring ourselves and making our job more difficult. Such conduct * * * nullifies the possibility of cooperation from those so addressed. * * * When we offend the sensitiveness of those with whom we deal, even our most just act becomes discriminatory from the standpoint of its interpretation. *We lose the professional standing of an impartial agent of government and are vulnerable to almost any charge of intolerance."*—E. W. Lester.

To same effect are New York City Police Department. Instructions: "Remember that actions and language if improper, will be the subject of much criticism. Be careful not to do or say anything improper. At all times remain calm, cool, and collected. Act firmly but courteously. * * * Make no comment or give opinions concerning the disorder or disturbance."

Note.—The New York Police Department received high praise from both Negro and White leaders for its handling of the Harlem riot in 1943.

D. Professional knowledge and training are also essential to success in the field of human relations. Is modern police work any less exacting or responsible than school teaching or social work? Should not professional standards for police be at least as high as for social workers and school teachers?

A distinguished foreign observer who notes the trend toward professional status of police work, advocates that it be strengthened. He urges that training for police work "should not be directed only on the technicalities of crime detection. Even more important is an understanding of the wider aims of crime prevention. Ideally, the policeman should be something of an educator and a social worker at the same time that he is the arm of the law. Even * * * where standards of professional policemanship are highest, too little interest has been given to social and educational viewpoints. One result of this is that the policeman in America is not commonly liked and trusted as he rightly ought to be."—*Gunnar Myrdal, Swedish economist, author of "An American Dilemma," authoritative study of the Negro problem in America.*

For professional approach to law enforcement problems in race relations, a police officer should have a practical working knowledge of:

(1) The psychology of race prejudice—its nature, causes, and manifestations.

(2) The essential facts of racial and cultural differences among people. What characteristics are inborn and which result from environment? Why is there more crime among some groups than others?

(3) The psychology of minority group behavior and attitudes. Why are members of minority groups frequently sensitive and defensive?
Why are they often aggressive and overbearing in behavior?
Why do Negroes and Mexicans, for example, so often fear and distrust the police?
What effects do segregation and discrimination have on the behavior of people?

(4) Basic facts of social and economic conditions under which minority groups live in the community.

(5) How to recognize the symptoms of rising tension among groups, creating potential riot conditions.

(6) Practical police methods, based on experience, of reducing tensions and preventing routine police incidents from assuming riotous proportions.

III

PREJUDICE

1. The successful policeman has to be a practical psychologist—he has to know something of how people's minds work.
2. Prejudice, which takes some form in all persons, is a common way of thinking which creates problems for law enforcement officers.
   A. Prejudice is literally a "prejudgment"—an opinion formed before knowing the facts.
   B. Everyone has prejudices. It's only human to substitute prejudice for thinking. It's easier to *believe* than to *think*.
3. There are many kinds of prejudice.
   A. Prejudice exists against certain foods (horsemeat), certain colors, kinds of clothing, makes of automobiles, and certain animals. Such prejudices are harmless.
   B. But prejudices against groups of people can be harmful and dangerous, from the standpoint of public safety.
   C. For example: There is the prejudice which many people have against police officers—the idea that "cops" as a group are stupid, brutal and crooked. This is certainly harmful. It undermines public confidence in the police and makes it hard for them to do a good job of law enforcement.
   D. Race prejudice causes bad feelings between racial groups, sometimes breaking out in violence.
4. Prejudice of one group against another always complicates the police problem.
   A. Ordinary offenses are magnified. Incidents between individuals of antagonistic groups may lead to conflict of groups.
   Example: White rioters said in Detroit, "The black bastards had it coming to them." A whole racial group was condemned for the sins, real or imagined, of individuals.
   B. Police are hampered by prejudiced criticism.
   "I think a lot of white officers are a bit reticent about speaking up for the Negro because there is always some

guy standing around the corner who will say, 'He's a nigger-lover.' I think there would be a lot more of us who would do more if it were not for this."—*Richmond officer.*

While prejudiced Whites will criticize the police officer for being fair, prejudiced Negroes will condemn him for fancied discrimination. This hampers the police officer in any case involving members of different racial groups because of the danger that an ordinary arrest, if regarded as discriminatory, may precipitate a racial incident.

5. Group prejudices are based on stereotypes—i.e. fixed ideas which people hold about groups other than their own.

A. Many people have definite ideas regarding the characteristics of all Italians, Mexicans, Jews, Negroes, and others. This is one of the most common ways of thinking about groups of people.

Examples: Beliefs that Negroes are lazy, dirty, and immoral; Jews, shrewd and wily; Italians, emotional and criminal; Irish, ignorant and superstitious; that Japanese are tricky.

B. The same sort of fixed notions are also held about occupational groups such as policemen, professors, or social workers.

Many people hold the belief that policemen are fat, stupid, and flat-footed; professors, absent-minded and impractical; social workers, sentimental and idealistic.

"We don't have to look at a racial minority group to make that point. We can just think about ourselves. I run into far too many people who think of a policeman as an ignorant, flat-footed, stupid fellow that any private detective or layman can outwit. This stereotype of us has been developed in detective stories, in the movies, in cartoons, and on the stage. We know there are as many different kinds of people in police work as there are patterns of fingerprints. Yet some of us have the stereotyped idea that a Negro is lazy, indolent, lustful, and carries a razor. And that thinking doesn't work for us as policemen. Until we realize that there are just as many different kinds of

Negroes as there are different kinds of policemen, we shan't be able to make intelligent and creditable decisions."—*Attorney General's representative, Richmond.*

6. To recognize prejudice in themselves and combat it in others, policemen must understand its causes.

A. Psychologists agree that prejudice is 100 percent learned. No one inherits his prejudices. Small children are not prejudiced. A child may be told by his mother that if he doesn't behave, she will send for a policeman who will put him in jail. Repeated often enough, the child acquires a fear of, and consequent prejudice against, all policemen.

In the same way, children hear their parents and older associates talk about Negroes, Jews, Catholics, etc., and they acquire prejudiced ideas about these and other groups.

B. Tolerant attitudes can be taught as easily as prejudices. But there is very little teaching of tolerance and much inculcation of prejudice. Hence, most people grow up with all sorts of fears and dislikes of various groups. When circumstances require a person to act without prejudice (such as in discharging the duties of a police officer in a professional manner), strenuous efforts usually have to be made to overcome prejudices taught since childhood.

C. Prejudice is the bastard child of fear and ignorance. In general, the more intelligent, experienced, and educated a person is, the fewer prejudices he will have. The intelligent person thinks in terms of individuals; the ignorant thinks of groups.

D. Prejudice is largely based on insecurity and fear. In genereral, the more sure of himself a person is, the less prejudice he will have. Thus, the most spiteful and bitter feelings toward minority groups are found among the most ignorant and poverty-stricken classes, notoriously among the Southern poor-whites, and insecure Whites in other parts of the country.

E. Everyone has a natural desire to feel superior. Those who can satisfy this desire by being a better-than-average officer, a successful executive, a distinguished teacher, or other desirable achievement have little need to fall back upon the mistaken belief that their group is superior to minority groups. In general, it is the people whose achievements are the least or whose social position is the lowest who insist most strongly on the inferiority of the Negro and other non-white groups. For such people, the Negro is practically the only group toward which they can feel superior.

F. "The prejudice of the policeman is also based on the fact that even with experience he has little or no contact with the better type of Negro—the stable citizen. Because his duty involves the curbing of antisocial behavior, he comes to know only the rowdy, the hoodlum, and the criminal. The law-abiding citizen is ignored by the patrolman on a busy beat; attention is focused on the law violator. Consequently, in careless thinking, the policeman comes to stereotype all Negroes as being like those with whom he makes contact.

"In his desire to find a simple answer on which he can base action, the police recruit becomes one of the worst offenders insofar as he regards people as behaving according to group patterns. On the other hand, the experienced officer has learned that the characters and personalities of Negroes, Whites, Jews, or Mexicans vary as much as do the patterns of fingerprints—no two being alike. Prejudice is retained only where knowledge is limited and the opinions of others are accepted without question."—*Attorney General's representative, Richmond.*

7. The tyrant, prejudice, is an enemy of democracy. Its consequences, like those of fascism and criminality, are of serious concern:

A. *For the objects of prejudice:* They are set apart from the general society and regarded as different, inferior, dangerous, or all three.

Individual members of such groups are deprived of a fundamental freedom: the right to be judged according to individual merits or faults. Instead they are judged according to ideas about the groups to which they belong. (A Negro is judged in a certain way, so is a Jew, so is a policeman, not because they individually deserve these judgments but because they are members of a group.) Such judgments are always wrong, of course.

Individuals are discriminated against because of the group to which they belong. They are deprived of rights and privileges which others enjoy. (Right to compete for jobs in accordance with ability; right to live in any neighborhood of their choice in accordance with their ability to pay; right to be served in public facilities—hotels, restaurants, etc.)

People react to prejudice by becoming sensitive and defensive. (See section on "Minority Group Behavior," below.)

B. *For the holders of prejudice.* Prejudice limits and distorts an individual's point of view, closes the mind to facts, makes unbiased judgment impossible. Some people become possessed by their prejudices. They can't think. They can only fear and hate. Such people are *bigots.* They are usually insecure, frustrated, and ignorant individuals and they blame whole groups of people for whatever is wrong in the community, nation, or world. This is *scapegoating.*

Jews, Negroes, Japanese-Americans, Catholics have all been scapegoats. Police, too, have had many experiences of being made "the goat."

Bigots are the support of race-hatred campaigns. They circulate the vicious rumors, agitate, and engage in race riots.

Most extreme case of bigotry and racial scapegoating in modern times was the persecution of the Jews in Nazi Germany. The same tendencies are evident in postwar United States.

C. *For law enforcement.*

(1) People who suffer from prejudice and discrimination acquire thereby attitudes of sensitiveness, defensiveness, and suspicion which interfere with cooperation

with the police. This is aggravated in the case of many Negroes from the South who have had bad experiences with police in their former communities.

(2) Bigotry is a serious problem for police, leading to racial persecution and violence.

(3) Insofar as police officers themselves are prejudiced against certain groups, it is impossible for them to be impartial; their judgment is clouded; their professional attitude is nullified.

"Prejudice—that is, the combination of ignorance and fear—precludes expertness in the field of human relations. Since a policeman must be a human relations expert, he must constantly extend his acquaintance with individuals, including those who are members of minority groups."—*Attorney General's representative, Richmond.*

IV

BASIC FACTS ABOUT MINORITY GROUPS

1. A minority group is *any* distinct group toward which others have prejudices; i.e. preconceived ideas about what the group as a whole is like.

2. Minority groups are set apart from the general population by differences in race, color, religion, language, other cultural characteristics, or occupation.

   A. Policemen are a good example of a minority group based on occupation. Their occupation makes them distinct, and the general public has definite ideas about what policemen are like as a group. Therefore, they are a minority group.

   B. Jews, Mormons, and Catholics are set apart by their religion; Negroes, by race and color; Chinese and Japanese by race and culture; Mexicans by color and culture; Russians, Poles, French, Italians, etc., by culture only.

3. Group differences in race, color, religion, culture, or occupation are significant because they are pegs upon which prejudices can be hung. (Difference plus prejudice equals probelm.)

4. From a *problem* standpoint, the most important differences are those of race or color.

Because these surface differences are permanent and inescapable, every member of a distinct racial or colored group can usually be instantly identified.

Contrast: Policemen can not be recognized as policemen except when in uniform; Mormons and Catholics can not be identified as such on sight; Italians, Russians, etc., cease to be set apart when they become "Americanized." But a Negro is a Negro 24 hours a day all his life.

What would police officers think of a condition which (a) required all policemen to be in uniform at all times, and (b) prohibited policemen from ever leaving the profession?

5. Race differences.

A. "Race" is biological—it refers to *inherited, physical* characteristics.

B. Scientists do not agree on how many races there are. Some say—only one race—the "human race." Others describe hundreds of races.

C. All agree—human beings the world over are much more alike than they are different.

In body structure, organs, skeleton, physical functioning-human beings are all alike.

Race differences are in the outermost layer only—skin color, head shape, nose shape, lip shape, eye shape, amount and texture of hair, other details.

Compare race differences among human beings with differences among breeds of animals. Human differences are much smaller. No variations in mankind are comparable, for example, to the difference between a Pekinese and a Great Dane.

D. Races cannot be ranked in an evolutionary scale. No race is more primitive or more advanced biologically than any other.

Compare with apes: Negroids are most like apes in regard to skin color, nose shape, and jaw shape; but apes have very thin lips. Mongoloids are most ape-like in this respect while Negroid lips are most human. In regard to amount and texture of hair, Caucasoids are the most ape-like; Negroids the least. Apes have long arms, short legs; Negroes are most like apes in length of arms, least ape-like in length of legs.

E. Race mixture has been going on since time immemorial. There are no pure races; all races are intermingled.

Of the Negroes in America, probably not more than 20 percent are of pure Negro ancestry.

The White Race includes a wide variety of physical types from tall, blue-eyed blondes to the short, very dark types of Southern and Eastern Europe. Many "Whites" are actually darker than many Negroes.

Race crossing produces neither superior nor inferior types.

6. Mental differences among races.

A. There is a popular belief that since races differ physically, they also differ mentally. Race prejudice among Whites is based on the belief that non-white races are inferior.

B. A vast amount of scientific research has been made on the subject of racial differences in mentality. Intelligence tests have been given to millions of people of all races. All this research has revealed no evidence of any differences in mentality due to race. All racial groups have the same capacity for mental development.

C. It has been proved that environment has a great influence on the mental development of people.

Slum dwellers test lower on the average than the middle-class; people in the North and West test higher than people in the South, on the average; city dwellers average higher than rural people. These differences cut across racial lines; that is, middle-class Negroes average higher in intelligence than poverty-stricken Whites.

Intelligence tests given to Army recruits in World War I showed the average intelligence of Negroes from several Northern States to be above the average for Whites in some Southern States.

In World War II, rejections for military service because of failure to meet minimum intelligence standards were higher among southern Whites than among northern Negroes.

These differences reflect differences in environment; that is, in opportunity for mental development.

D. Because Negroes on the whole are poorer and have fewer opportunities than Whites, it would be expected that their average mental development would be lower than the average for whites, and that is the fact.

But the Negro population, the same as the white, includes the whole gamut from inbecile to genius.

Negro and white groups on the same social-economic level are equally intelligent.

Intelligence tests in Los Angeles city schools showed Negro children slightly above the average of white children.

E. *Conclusion:* All the evidence shows there is no such thing as racial superiority or inferiority. The color of a person's skin does not determine the kind of intellect he possesses.

V

MINORITY GROUP BEHAVIOR

1. Police officers will notice certain distinctive behavior traits of Negroes as a group, and of other minority groups. It is of the utmost importance that the reasons for such behavior be correctly understood.

A. Behavior is not racial. Physical appearance excepted, there are no known differences among racial groups that are the result of race or heredity. Any differences in group behavior are due to differences in the environment.

B. Prejudice and discrimination are important parts of the environment of minority groups and affect their behavior in significant ways.

2. Members of minority groups are more than usually sensitive and defensive.

A. This results from prejudice and discrimination against them. (When people are made to feel, from childhood, that they are "different" from other people, they are bound to be affected in some way.)

B. Because minority individuals feel that others are prejudiced against them, they become apprehensive and continually fearful of insult or discrimination. Therefore, they often develop strong self-protective reactions.

"I know that a lot of members of minority groups are supersensitive. They have been discriminated against so much that they are on the anxious seat all the time. You can't put yourself in the position of a minority group person. In Richmond *you* can walk into any hotel or restaurant. But if I go in I would be very alert to anything that might appear to be an insult. I would have a certain amount of apprehension in going into any public restaurant or any hotel. I know the different forms in which insults occur. There might be delays—it might be normal delay but I would feel that it was unusual delay—maybe delay telling me to get out, that they are not serving me."— *Walter A. Gordon.*

C. When a person is treated as an inferior, he will begin to feel inferior. He may develop aggressiveness or shyness to cover up his inferiority feelings. This is not peculiar to minority groups. It is a universal human reaction. Anyone who feels insecure or inferior is bound to develop some defense mechanisms. (Psychologists know that arrogance is more often than not a cover-up for an inferiority complex.)

D. Discrimination means that members of minority groups are subject to many deprivations and their ambitions and desires are constantly being frustrated. Many rights and privileges which people generally take for granted are denied to minority groups, such as the privileges of hotels, restaurants, and bars; free choice of residence and free competition for jobs. People react to frustration either by aggression or by withdrawing and trying to avoid further frustration.

Negroes and Mexican-American youth, as groups, seem more inclined to react aggressively to discrimination. This shows up in the crimes for which members of these groups are most frequently arrested—crimes of violence. The Chinese, on the other hand, have generally withdrawn from contacts with Whites which would expose them to discrimination. Japanese and Jews have responded by aggression but of a competitive character—they compete vigorously and try hard to be better than anyone else.

E. Police officers should readily be able to understand what the minority groups are up against and why they react defensively as they do, because, as Chief Lester observed, "In many respects we are a minority group."

"An exaggerated illustration that we often bring out in training new officers is, 'You may have been beating your wife before you joined the force, but you were just a guy up the street who beats his wife; now, you are that policeman who beats his wife. Or, you were that harum-scarum who drives like wild up the street; now, you are that policeman who drives like wild. The public generalizes about policemen just as it does about Negroes. That is the basis of the squawks about those portrayals (of policemen) in the motion pictures and the press. The cartoons always depict him as a fellow with a little head, big stomach, big feet, reaching back and getting an apple or banana off the fruit stand. Law enforcement officers are striving to professionalize the service and develop a code of ethics which will demand recognition as a profession—this constant stereotyping just crucifies them."—*E. W. Lester.*

3. Fear and distrust of police.

A. One aspect of the sensitiveness and defensiveness of minority groups which is of special concern to the police is the fear and distrust of police which these groups generally have.

"The average Negro, * * * believes that if he gets arrested he will immediately get his head beaten in with a club. * * * Far too many Negroes believe that they will get the worst of it everytime they get arrested. * * * We don't realize as policemen how deep that fear goes in them."—*Attorney General's representative, Richmond.*

"There is a resentment on the part of minority groups toward the police in general—not always justified. But in many instances there is justification. * * * It is based on the fact that a lot of them feel they are treated unfairly. Maybe they are over-sensitive. It's a normal reaction for them to be over-sensitive in view of their general treatment in America."—*Walter A. Gordon.*

B. Negroes coming to California bring with them a deep suspicion and a deadly fear of all police officers, based on their whole experience.

Far too often the police make no pretense of impartiality where Negroes are concerned. Many police officers consider it their job not only to enforce the law but also to enforce "White Supremacy" and keep the Negroes "in their place."

"It is part of the (southern) policeman's philosophy that Negro criminals or suspects, or any Negro who shows signs of insubordination, should be punished bodily."—(*Myrdal.*)

A Richmond officer states, "In parts of the South for example, Negroes aren't allowed on the street after dark. A Texas officer told me, 'We don't have any trouble in niggertown. If a nigger kills a nigger it's a routine investigation. If a nigger kills a white man, we kill the nigger and that's all there is to it.' "

The result is that the southern Negro frequently regards the police officer as his mortal enemy. When he migrates to California, he naturally brings these attitudes with him.

A Richmond officer: "We have gained the confidence of the Negroes to the extent that they will call us if they need us. But to try to get a Negro witness to an incident to talk is like getting blood out of a turnip."

Other officers, however, reported favorable experiences

in gaining the cooperation of Negro witnesses. It was generally agreed that the Negroes who had lived in Richmond for a period of years were reasonably cooperative with the police.

C. Mexican-American youth are inclined to show attitudes similar to those of Negroes.

"They start in the gangs as a self-defense mechanism. They realize they are members of a minority group and feel a certain amount of frustration and animosity from society. They are particularly fearful of police. This fear comes out in aggressiveness and in an attempt to show that they are not afraid. In Los Angeles they often feel that they are being picked on and singled out for police attention because of nationality or dress (zoot suits). That's the thing the police have to watch very carefully—not to identify police activity with a given minority group, giving them the impression that they are being singled out for special attention. Anything that looks like special treatment to them is discrimination—whether the action is good or bad."—*E. W. Lester.*

D. This attitude of fear and distrust for the police, regardless of whether justified or not, presents a serious problem in public relations for the police.

Police officers must have the confidence and support of the public in order to do a good job of law enforcement.

In the field of race relations, police can't accomplish much unless they have the confidence of both sides—majority group and minority groups.

There is always a strong tendency for prejudice to be paid back by prejudice. If Whites dislike the Negroes, the latter will respond by disliking the Whites. If minorities are antagonistic and uncooperative toward the police, it is only human for police officers to respond in kind, especially if they have had bad experiences with members of minority groups.

When a condition of mutual antagonism develops between police and minority groups, it is almost impossible for police to do a fair and effective job of law enforcement. A situation is created which is very dangerous to the public peace. This was the situation in Chicago before the 1919 riot and also in Detroit in 1943.

4. Adjustment of the in-migrant southern Negro to life in California.

A. Negroes recently arrived from the South at times are likely to behave in strange and seemingly obnoxious ways because of their unfamiliarity with the new environment. A world of difference exists between the life of the Negro in the South and the life in Pacific Coast cities. The in-migrant Negro has to learn a whole new way of living, ranging all the way from urban standards of sanitation and garbage disposal to new ideals and aims of life. Great personal uncertainty and insecurity are involved in this shift. To some degree, this, of course, is true of any in-migrant, underprivileged group, black or white.

B. The Southern Negro is compelled to be subservient to the white man in all ways. In trying to cast off this life-long habit of subservience, he is often likely to be rude and arrogant, or at least ill-mannered.

C. The immigrant comes to California expecting to be a free man and as good as anyone else. He does find more freedom than in the South, but he is still segregated and discriminated against in various ways. He doesn't know the limits of the new freedom; in trying to discover the limits, he is likely to go too far. He encounters many disappointments and frustrations, to which he may have an aggressive reaction.

D. *Police officers will see an analogy between the in-migrant Negro testing his new freedom and a new policeman vested with authority for the first time in his life. The recruit policeman is also insecure in his new authority, he doesn't know how far he can go in any situation, and he is liable to commit his share of "boners" before he becomes an experienced officer.*

5. The majority of Negroes and Mexican-American youth live under conditions conducive to crime.
   A. It is well known that slum conditions and a vicious environment breed crime. Practically always, in any city, the highest crime rates occur in the poorest districts.
   B. The economic status of most Negroes and Mexicans is very low. Due partly to poverty and partly to segregation, these groups live mainly in the slums. Their housing is poor and overcrowded. Recreational facilities are generally inadequate. The slum neighborhoods in which they live are also frequently the centers of organized prostitution, gambling, and other vicious activities.

      "The police will allow gambling dives, houses of prostitution, and other forms of vice to exist in a Negro neighborhood because the officers think it solves their immediate problems to some extent and keeps the people off the street. But what are you doing to the Negroes when you do that?"—*Walter A. Gordon.*
   C. These conditions mean that members of minority groups are more exposed to vicious associations and other conditions conducive to crime than are members of the general public. This is part of the explanation for the relatively high delinquency and crime rates in these groups.
6. Restrictions on normal activities of minority groups often cause exaggerated behavior in other directions.
   A. Minority groups suffer from restrictions on many types of activity which other people take for granted (enjoyment of hotel, restaurant, and tavern facilities, bowling alleys, swimming pools, for example). Discrimination has the effect of narrowing a person's field of opportunities and activities. It is only normal that people so restricted, should intensify their activities in fields where they are not interfered with. Sexual activity is an example. It has been aptly described as "the poor man's recreation." Religion is another. This is part of the reason why church activities play such an important part in Negro life.
   B. An example significant for law enforcement: In the Berke-

ley-Albany public housing project, white residents complained that the Negroes were drinking and partying excessively in their apartments. Investigation revealed that the numerous bars and taverns along San Pablo Avenue adjoining the project refused Negro trade and had signs posted to that effect. While white people could do their drinking at the bars, if they cared to do so, the only way a Negro could get a drink was to buy a bottle and take it home with him.

VI

PRACTICAL POLICE METHODS IN RACE RELATIONS

The *Interim Report of the Peace Officers Committee on Civil Disturbances* (revised edition, 1945) contains a list of 39 suggestions for meeting the problem of racial tensions. These deserve careful study. The police conferences at Richmond and the study materials used therein, including the Peace Officers Committee Report, emphasized the following as preventive measures:

1. A professional attitude and professional knowledge on the part of police officers. This is fundamental. Racial problems are after all only a rather severe test of a police department's efficiency. A good department staffed with officers who are professionals in their field will handle racial tensions in stride and will not allow conditions to develop which would cause a race riot. On the other hand, a poor department, which is unable to handle the ordinary problems of law enforcement effectively, will never be able to cope with racial tensions.

2. Absolute impartiality. Essential to a professional approach but is not easy to achieve. The following points should be emphasized:

   A. Enforcement of the law against ALL violators without regard to the race, color, or religion of the violator.
   Example of good practice: "We had an experience in Los Angeles. * * * There was a white fellow who had for two or three years visited a Negro woman on week-end

trips to Los Angeles. She was married. Her husband was a railroad man and was usually out of town. On this particular occasion, this man came into Los Angeles and went to see the girl, and she told him she couldn't see him that week-end. He was pretty rude and hard-boiled—had had a couple of drinks. He went out and proceeded to get really drunk. He came back about sundown. He broke the door down and went in and got this woman. * * * A crowd of people gathered. The police were called, and the man was taken down to the station. The captain of detectives said, 'Well, go ahead, book the man for rape or attempt to rape.' Someone spoke up, 'You can't do that. Why, this man is a white man, and the woman is a Negro. We couldn't book a man like that. Every white person in the division will be disturbed about it.' The captain said, 'Well, did he attempt it or didn't he? That's the question.' There was further objection, 'We think you'd better book him for drunkenness and disturbance of the peace.' But the captain of detectives insisted on the correct booking. He asked, 'Well, what if it were the other way around?' And the reply was, 'We'd certainly book him for rape.' 'Then,' ordered the captain, 'that's exactly what we're going to do in this case.' * * * The men respected this captain for his cool and calm judgment, for his attempt to secure equal justice as far as the racial groups were concerned. It made it a lot easier for the policemen to work with the Negroes who were a majority of the population of the district. It meant that the Negroes were going to be treated fairly."
—*E. W. Lester.*

B. A "human" approach, regarding every individual as different from every other, and treating every person as an individual. The contrary is the "stereotype" approach which views the members of any group as all alike and regards the various groups as superior or inferior to each other.

C. Avoid use of insulting terms and names. Some expressions, used casually without thought of offending, are nevertheless offensive to members of minority groups. Such as:

"He looks like an Okie to me."

"Black as a Negro."

"Who do you mean, that nigger?"

Terms such as "kike," "nigger," "chili-picker," "wop," "cholo," invariably antagonize the person and the group to whom they are addressed. If an officer thinks he has to use an insulting name, it is better to use one which insults only the individual and not his group. The consultant from the National Association for the Advancement of Colored People observed that a Negro would rather be called a "black sonofabitch" than a "nigger." The term "Negress," while technically accurate is found to be offensive to Negro women.

Police feel the same way about derogatory names applied to their group. "We don't mind calling each other 'cops' or 'flatfeet,' but we don't want other people to do it." —*E. W. Lester.*

Because of the sensitiveness and defensiveness of minority groups and their ingrained fear of police, "every act of an officer, even to the tone of his voice, is examined for prejudice. It behooves us to treat members of such groups with the same professional courtesy that we use in our contacts with the general public."—*E. W. Lester.*

"The wise officer in the discharge of his duties will so conduct himself that his work is made easier by creating the desire to cooperate on the part of those with whom he works."—*F. W. Lester.*

D. The same kind of law enforcement in a minority group district as anywhere else in the city.

A paternalistic attitude toward minority groups is one of the most difficult kinds of discrimination to get away from—the attitude that one can't expect too much of a given group because they are Negro, Mexican, or whatnot. There is the related attitude that crimes of minority group members don't matter very much so long as they only affect other members of the same group. Too often, police will allow conditions to exist in a Negro neighborhood that they would never tolerate in a white district.

"Those Negroes who are thinking about the future of the race feel that every Negro should be made to toe the mark just the same as every other individual. Until police departments accept that as a basic philosophy, you are going to find that the Negro will deteriorate morally, physically, and otherwise. I know of police departments right here in California that will permit dens of vice, gambling, prostitution, etc., to exist in Negro neighborhoods because it will keep the Negroes off the streets, and as long as they are just Negroes, it doesn't make any difference. Now that is a paternalistic attitude which we don't appreciate because it affects our whole racial uplift."—*Walter A. Gordon.*

3. Employment of qualified members of minority groups on the police force.

A. The problems of overcoming prejudice against the employment of minority group members will vary with community attitudes. Likewise, the problems incident to Department and public acceptance of a minority group officer assigned to general police duty will vary.

B. No person should be appointed to a police force *because* he is a member of a minority group, and no one should be appointed to *represent* a minority group. While superior qualifications are desirable in a minority group member initially appointed to a force, in order to overcome prejudice, minority group members should be required to meet the same standards of qualification and performance as anyone else.

C. For maximum benefit in preventing crime, protecting life and property, and improving race relations, officers who happen to be minority group members should be treated like anyone else on the force without discrimination insofar as assignments and duties are concerned.

D. Harm, rather than good, is the frequent result of (1) appointing poorly qualified members of minority groups and (2) restricting their activities and opportunities only to patrol in minority group areas.

E. Great good may come from assigning a member of a

minority group to majority group areas where, in addition to his general qualifications, he has a genial and engaging personality.

(1) His presence is a constant education to the majority community who thus will become accustomed to seeing minority group members in official positions.

(2) His presence will tend to break down the stereotype that minority group persons are and should be in inferior positions.

(3) His tactful handling of job situations will build good will toward the group of which he is a member.

(4) He, in turn, through integration as a "member of the force" rather than a "representative of a minority group," will be an agent of goodwill in the minority community when he is acting off duty and as a private citizen.

(5) His presence on the police department will stimulate a better attitude in all other officers toward the minority group. Their tendency toward group classification will be deterred because of their acquaintance with a group member who differs from the stereotype.

4. Recognize and stay within the proper field of law enforcement.
  A. One reason why relations between Negroes and police in the South are so bad is that the police in many cities consider it part of their duty to enforce "White Supremacy" and keep the Negro "in his place." The result is that the police officer becomes a living symbol to the Negroes of all the discriminations that they have to face.

    Policemen must be careful to refrain from intervening in the lawful social relations of people and the association of individuals, on the theory that people of different races should be kept apart.

    "Police officers many times try to tell a white person that he can't go to this dance or into that neighborhood, etc. Police departments often refuse to issue permits or licenses for dance halls without inquiring who is going to to be at the dance, and sometimes they request that the permit state the hall shall be closed to Negroes or to Whites. You have them refusing to recommend to the city council to give cabaret permits unless they agree that no Negroes or Whites shall be on the dance floor at the same time either as mixed couples or as White couples and Negro couples."—*Walter A. Gordon.*

B. The intent of police in taking action such as the foregoing is usually not to subordinate any group, but to preserve the peace. There is serious question, however, whether such actions really serve the purpose intended. They do expose the police to criticism on the grounds (1) of exceeding their lawful authority, and (2) of making color rather than conduct the test of a permissible activity.

The only sound and impartial rule is: *The proper object of police surveillance is conduct, not color.*

5. Contact with minority group leaders and organizations.

A. Such activity is helpful in gaining confidence and cooperation of minority groups and overcoming their unfavorable attitudes toward police.

B. On a friendly basis, police can make suggestions to minority group leaders for the education and guidance of their respective groups, and can receive suggestions for the improvement of law enforcement work among the minority groups.

C. Liaison with these groups will be extremely valuable in dealing with any troublesome situations.

In the expertly handled 1943 riot in Harlem, for example, "The mayor himself toured the Negro sections in company with well-known Negro leaders, exhorting the people by loud speaker to get off the streets and assuring them of protection. * * * All during the night Negroes *known to the people* of Harlem broadcast from sound trucks exploding the false rumor that a Negro had been killed and urging the people to return to their homes and stop vandalism and other violent acts. Coupled with this was the magnificent restraint and efficiency of the police." *(New Republic, August 16, 1945.)* Quoted in Report of the Peace Officers Committee on Civil Disturbances.

D. Irresponsible and inflammatory movements among minority groups frequently create problems for police. Cooperation with responsible leaders and organizations will help in handling such problems.

"Seek out the responsible leadership in the community, talk frankly to them about your problems * * * present your facts and make it plain that you will not jump on a man because he is a Negro, and you will get your response."—*Walter A. Gordon.*

"Perhaps the most important of all things to be kept in mind by law enforcement officials in communities newly confronted with the possibility of riots is that there are responsible, law-abiding elements in every racial group whose cooperation can be secured by friendly and intelligent efforts. These responsible elements can do more to prevent the spread of riot infection than any number of police officers who might be added to the force." *(Report of the Peace Officers Committee.)*

E. Contact with individuals of minority groups on a non-official "person-to-person" basis will be very helpful.

6. Liaison with school authorities and other youth-serving agencies to work out programs for reducing racial tensions among the youth.

A. Recent events in Gary, Indiana; Chicago; Los Angeles; and Richmond have indicated a serious condition of racial tension among the children in many junior high and high schools.

Investigations indicate such tensions have arisen where school conditions generally are bad (overcrowded classes, shift sessions, poorly prepared teachers, inadequate equipment, lack of recreational programs, community dissatisfaction with the schools, etc.) .

Tensions among the youth involve the parents and hence the whole community.

B. The schools can do much to reduce tensions by (1) eliminating the conditions which cause friction, (2) preparing the teachers to do a better job of promoting interracial understanding, and (3) educating the parents to cooperate and produce interracial goodwill through their parent teachers' associations.

7. Consult with the press to work out a constructive policy of handling news of racial matters and ensure cooperation with the police department.

   A. Newspapers have been often criticized for handling racial news in an inflammatory manner. Minority groups frequently charge the press with playing up unfavorable news about their members while giving little attention to their praiseworthy activities. (Some papers seem to love headlines such as "Sheriff Arrested" or "Negro Rapist at Large.")

   B. In self-defense, many newspapers have adopted a policy of printing as little news as possible about racial matters. This policy, while better than a sensational one, ignores the important contribution which the press can make toward a constructive handling of racial problems. Some newspapers are sincerely trying to do a job in this field.

   C. A constructive press policy cooperating with the police department would include:

      (1) Unbiased, accurate reporting of all newsworthy events in the interracial field.

      (2) Elimination of racial identifications in crime stories except where publication of the race of a suspect would be helpful in his apprehension.

      (3) Adequate publicity to constructive programs in race relations, such as programs in the schools, activities of interracial committees, etc.

      (4) Publication of facts to counteract rumors.

      (5) Close cooperation between newspapers and police to ensure that the press always promptly receive the full and correct facts of any racial incident.

8. Contacts with minority press.

   A. Relations between minority group newspapers and police are bad in most cities. The press is constantly playing up stories of police discrimination and brutality; the police consider the newspapers inflammatory.

B. Straightforward and frank discussions would help in some instances to produce a better understanding here on both sides. Police would find it worth while to gain the cooperation of the minority press in a preventive program. This might be done through frequent press conferences involving the entire local minority press.

9. Investigation and control of rumors.
A. Rumors are both a symptom and a cause of trouble. They have played an extremely important part in every major race riot that has occurred in this country.

Rumor is such a characteristic sign of tension that the degree and seriousness of tension at any time can be judged from the number and character of rumors prevalent.

B. As tensions rise, rumors increase and take on a more menacing character.

In periods of high tension, people will circulate and believe the most extraordinary and outlandish stories. During the Detroit riot of June, 1943, the Negro community was full of stories of Negro babies being thrown off a bridge and Negro girls being attacked, while white people were excited over similar stories with white babies and white girls as victims.

The New York Harlem riot of August, 1943, began with the utterly false rumor that a Negro soldier had been shot and killed by a white policeman.

In Richmond in October, 1945, when a white boy received a knife wound in the leg during a fight with a Negro boy, stories circulated all over the East Bay that the white boy's leg had been amputated and later that he had died.

C. A rumor that circulated all over the country in 1943 and 1944 said that Negroes were organized in "Bumper Clubs" for the purpose of "bumping" white people on the streets, in streetcars, etc. Concerning this rumor, Chief Lester said,

"This information would come from all types of sources and be told in detail without thought of its being anything but the truth. Time after time these rumors were investigated (by the Los Angeles Police) with the definite purpose of finding out the true origin, and in every case that we investigated—and the FBI was working on these cases too—it just blew up in thin air. There was absolutely no foundation. Yet after this rumor got spread around, people by the hundreds were convinced that groups of people were going out on certain days each week to make as big a nuisance of themselves as possible. Investigations were made in Boston, Chicago, and Philadelphia, and no one could trace the rumors down there either. It was most revealing. Some of the most intelligent people in Los Angeles were passing on that rumor with the utmost confidence that it was the truth. Even after they were told about the investigation, their faith still wasn't entirely shaken in those rumors. * * * I have heard high police officials state the rumor as a fact."—*E. W. Lester.*

D. Even though they are false, vicious rumors do great damage. They heighten the tension and aggravate people's fears and hatreds. When people begin to suspect that others are plotting and arming against them, the result may be as disastrous as if it were true. Even groundless atrocity stories can lead to retaliations and "what is in the beginning fictitious eventually becomes real."

E. Police experience indicates that efforts to track down the source of inflammatory rumors are seldom productive. Officers can, however, and should be on the lookout for rumors and get the facts to counteract them.

F. *Never repeat a rumor, even to deny it.* The rumor is usually so much more sensational than the fact that the latter will be overshadowed. The only antidote for poisonous rumor is fact.

Get the facts promptly, and publish them as widely as

possible. Cooperative relations with the press will be helpful here, but use should also be made of radio, civic ogran-
izations, minority group organizations, and other channels
of information.

10. Persuade proprietors of restaurants, bars, etc., to remove signs
such as "Colored Trade Not Solicited," or "No Japs."

Open flaunting of discrimination by means of posted signs
is insulting to the groups affected and a cause of antagonism.

*The California Civil Code prohibits restaurants, hotels,
and other places of public accommodation or amusement from
discriminating against any customer because of race or color.
The remedy is only civil.* Police, however, by virtue of their
responsibilities, should concern themselves with conditions
threatening the public peace.

The Berkeley Police Department, on several occasions, has
been successful in securing the removal of discriminatory
signs.

11. Investigate inflammatory publications or agitating groups
which promote prejudice against Negroes, Jews, Japanese-
Americans, or other minority groups.

A. While it is *conditions* rather than any specific persons or
groups which cause racial tensions, nevertheless, groups
frequently appear which seek to advance their selfish interests by playing upon the fears and prejudices of the people.

"In most of the riots that have been investigated, the
existence of a pattern of action has been indicated by the
evidence. In most cases there has been instigation, provoca-
tion, or manipulation."—*Peace Officers Committee Report.*

B. The following is quoted from the Richmond Police Department Conference on September 14th:

"Mr. Powers: It is my thought that race riots are
seldom if ever caused by one organized group attempting
to cause a riot. They are an outgrowth of misunderstanding and bad social conditions, generally. We can't say,

"This or that group caused this riot." It has to do with housing, with unintelligent handling by the police, etc. * * *

"QUESTION: Are there organizations though that make a business of stirring up bad feeling among racial groups?

"MR. POWERS: Certainly, there are. In the Japanese-American situation we have organizations which work to stir up bad feeling. We have many groups based on a race hatred of Negroes. I can't think of any organization which attempted specifically to start race riots, but there are organizations which have contributed greatly to setting them off.

"QUESTION: What about Los Angeles, Mr. Lester? Have you had any organized antagonism there?

"MR. LESTER: We have had deliberate attempts from individuals. Some are unscrupulous fellows going around using this as a means of livelihood. Some of them preach discrimination to the point of making the listener feel a hatred and do not give him a proper outlet of seeing any other solution than one of violence. They create hatred. * * *"

C. One type of organization whose activities often lead into anti-racial campaigns is the property owners' association or improvement club which seeks to keep minority groups out of a certain neighborhood. Their avowed purpose is economic; they claim to be interested only in property values; but in trying to exclude minority groups, they often slide over into preaching race hatred and stir up much bad feeling.

"A lot of your community clubs in any given city are consciously or unconsciously fomenting racial tensions. * * * They say it is economic and that they are protecting their property values. But they will go to the extent of trying to make the Negro person lose his or her job. They will go to the banks and bring pressure on them to not loan money. They will spread the rumor that people should stop depositing at the bank. They will go to the realtor who sold the property and see that he loses his job. They will sometimes, as a last resort, by innuendo suggest force. * * * In Oakland one man tried to get a group of white people aroused and couldn't. He said, 'What's the matter with you people? You ought to be mad enough to put somebody at the end of a rope. * * *' That is doing something not only to their thinking, but it is doing something to the Negro in the community."—*Walter A. Gordon.*

D. *Police action:* Report any agitational or propaganda activities which appear to be subversive to the FBI. For the others (most operate within the law), point out to them what they are doing; warn them of the dangers involved; keep them under surveillance.

12. Observe and report symptoms of trouble.
   A. Race riots never happen suddenly or without warning. They are the product of tensions which accumulate over a fairly long period, sometimes for years. These tensions can be recognized and measured closely enough to permit preventive action. In other words, the growth of a dangerous racial situation can be diagnosed in the way that a doctor diagnoses a disease.
   B. The thing to watch is *change* in the existing situation: the *growth* or *decline* of tensions.
      The following are generally accepted as reliable indicators of rising tension:
      (1) An *increasing* number of rumors, together with an *increase* in their sensational character.
      (2) An *increasing* number of incidents of violence or threats of violence.
      (3) *Increasing* activity of race-agitating organizations, including groups seeking to exclude minorities from certain districts.
      (4) *Growing* distrust of police by minority groups. An *increase* in the number of charges and complaints of "police brutality" would be one evidence of this.

(5) An *increase* in labor unrest (strikes and threats of strikes, etc.)

(6) An *increase* in altercations on street cars and buses.

(7) Minority reaction to the increasing tension, as reflected in the minority press.

13. A definite public relations policy. Cooperation with the press and contacts with minority group organizations, already mentioned, are important parts of a sound public relations program.

In addition, talks of police officers before service clubs, church groups, youth groups, on the radio, etc., are desirable to build public confidence in the police department, and also to guide public opinion on racial matters.

14. Establish a Human Relations Detail in the Police Department. To centralize responsibility for the Department's action in the field of race relations.

Human Relations Detail should be primarily responsible for carrying out Points 5 to 13, above listed.

15. Dealing with Riot Situations. Emphasis in this bulletin is laid on *preventive* measures rather than riot tactics.

The importance of sound police tactics in an emergency is not underestimated. However, a department which is capable of developing a sound preventive program will be in the best possible position to handle a riot, should its preventive efforts fail.

Most of the preventive principles discussed above will be valuable in bringing a riot under control with minimum loss of life and property damage.

Unless the situation is extremely aggravated by conditions beyond the police department's control, there is no reason why a thoroughgoing preventive program should fail.

In a tense situation, the police have to deal almost every day with the makings of a riot, that is, rumor, violent incidents, crowds. The way of handling these minor situations will determine whether tensions go up or down.

Recent incidents in the Richmond schools, for example,

have had riot potentialities. There was tension to begin with, followed by a violent incident, rumors, crowds, and widespread fear. The situation was competently handled and the danger abated. If the good work done by the police in that immediate situation is followed up by longer-range preventive measures, the danger in the schools may well be removed entirely.

Chapter 17

POLICE DEPLOYMENT THEORIES AND THE MEXICAN-AMERICAN COMMUNITY

ARMANDO MORALES

August 1970

THE HEART OF THE POLICE law enforcement effort is patrol, that is, the movement around an assigned area on foot, vehicle, or helicopter by police personnel. Patrol is the largest of police divisions, and it was once referred to by Orlando W. Wilson as the "backbone of police service."[1] Although police experts agree that patrol is an essential activity, the issue of how many policemen under what orders and using what techniques to patrol what activity is a highly complex question. A review of the literature regarding theories of police patrol deployment with some emphasis on ethnic minority communities therefore is in order, as a beginning. Thereafter, a specific community case will be analyzed in light of the theories presented, followed by a discussion, recommendations, and the raising of questions for future research.

All police departments have the problem of patrol force deployment, how many men to assign to each shift and to each precinct. Most departments assign men equally to all shifts, which reduces scheduling problems but is an inefficient use of manpower.[2] Some police departments use a formula such as the propor-

---

Reprinted from *El Grito, 4*, No. 1, 1970, 52-64 and with permission of the author who has copyrighted this entire article.

[1]Orlando W. Wilson. *Police Administration* (New York: McGraw-Hill Book Compan, 1963), p. 231.

[2]The Challenge of Crime in a Free Society. A Report by the President's Commission on Law Enforcement and the Administration of Justice, U. S. Government Printing Office, 1967, p. 257.

tional need theory[3] that weights the previous year's reported crimes, radio calls, population, etc., for each patrol area or precinct and then assign the patrol force proportionately to the precinct's weighted score.[4] A question arises, however, regarding what specific weights to assign to what specific crimes. The literature regarding police patrol deployment theory is rather modest—one possible explanation being that a small fraction of 1 percent of the criminal justice system's total budget in the United States is spent on research.[5]

A law enforcement professional in recent years who began discussing factors underlying police patrol deployment was the late William H. Parker, Chief of the Los Angeles Police Department (1950 to 1966). In his 1957 book he said:

> "Every department worth its salt deploys field forces on the basis of crime experience. Deployment is often heaviest in so-called minority sections of the city. The reason is statistical—it is a fact that certain racial groups, at the present time, commit a disproportionate share of the total crime. Let me make one point clear in that regard—a competent police administrator is fully aware of the multiple conditions which create this problem. There is no inherent physical or mental weakness in any racial stock which tends it toward crime. But, and this is a 'but' which must be borne constantly in mind—police field deployment is not social agency activity. In deploying to suppress crime, we are not interested in why a certain group tends toward crime, we are interested in maintaining order."[6]

According to Parker, therefore, police deployment is heaviest in minority sections of the city because, based on statistical reasons,

---

[3]Proportional distribution was conceived as early as 1909 when Chief August Vollmer assigned the Berkeley, California, patrol force (which then was bicycle-mounted to two twelve hour shifts in accordance with the number of calls anticipated in each part of the city. The Proportional Need Theory is defined by Robert Benedict Gaunt as a system which studied police problems in the immediate past in order to project what might be anticipated in the near future and thus deploy police manpower to areas and at times when these problems were anticipated. For further information, see Robert Benedict Gaunt, Field Deployment of Police Patrol Forces and the Use of Electronic Data Processing Equipment, unpublished Master's Thesis, School of Public Administration, University of Southern California, June, 1965, p. 34.

[4]*Ibid.*

[5]*Ibid.*, p.x.

[6]William H. Parker. *Parker on Police*, ed. by O. W. Wilson (Springfield, Illinois: Charles C Thomas, Publisher, 1957), p. 161.

he *believes* it to be a *fact* that racial minority groups commit more crime. Parker made these statements in an address delivery at the National Conference of Christians and Jews Institute on Police-Community Relations, Michigan State University, in May, 1955.[7]

However, in comparing the 1955 crime statistics in the low-socioeconomic, predominantly Mexican-American community (LAPD Hollenbeck Division) with the middle class predominantly Anglo-Saxon community (LAPD Hollywood Division), there does not appear to be a statistically significant difference in the crime rates[8] per ratio of population in these two communities. In the Mexican-American police division there was a crime rate of 3,682.9 per 100,000 population compared to the Anglo-Saxon area which revealed a rate of 3,681.1 per 100,000 population.[9] This means that there were 1.8 more crimes per 100,000 population in the Mexican-American community. *Would this minute statistical difference warrant heavier police deployment in the ethnic minority community?* Parker further stated,

"At the present time, race, color, and creed are useful-statistical and tactical devices. So are age groupings, sex and employment. If persons of one occupation, for some reason commit more theft than the average, then increased police attention is given to persons of that occupation. Discrimination is not a factor there. If persons of Mexican, Negro, or Anglo-Saxon ancestry, for some reason, contribute heavily to other forms of crime, police deployment must take that into account. From an ethnological point of view, Negro, Mexican and Anglo-Saxon are unscientific breakdowns; they are fiction. From a police point of view, they are a useful fiction and should be used as long as they remain useful. The demand that the police cease to consider race, color, and creed is an unrealistic demand. Identification is a police tool, not a police attitude."[10]

Parker does not elaborate as to how ethnicity and creed may be a "useful fiction" from a police point of view, or how the po-

[7]*Ibid.,* p. 133.

[8]The Los Angeles Police Department reported these crime rates on the basis of Part I Offenses (Homicide, Rape, Robbery, Aggravated Assault, Burglary, Larceny and Auto Theft).

[9]Los Angeles Police Department 1955 Annual Report, City of Los Angeles, p. 28.

[10]Parker, p. 162.

lice administrator determines when this ceases to be a useful criteria in police deployment. He feels that race, color and creed for identification purposes are a police tool and not the result of a police attitude. Might not these criteria be based on *attitudinal perceptions* that may or may not be based on fact? How is *fact* determined? Would it not be possible to heavily deploy police in an ethnic minority community as a response to a *perceived* fact or assumption which in turn has the result of making it appear as if indeed it is a fact? As Gilbert Geis has said:

> "A belief, based on real or imagined information that a particular minority group commits more crimes than other groups will often lead to a greater saturation of this group's neighborhoods by police patrol. Such saturation will likely turn up more crime and produce a larger number of arrests of persons belonging to the group, though it will often inhibit some kind of criminal activity as well because of the increased likelihood of apprehension. But it is the police activity and not the behavior of the group itself which is conditioning the crime rates for the group as these eventually appear in the printed statistics."[11]

The phenomenon described by Geis leads to what Robert K. Merton called a "self fulfilled prophecy." Within this conceptual framework, it would be possible for law enforcement to unknowingly generate its own need for more services thereby utilizing more critical manpower that could have been used for some other activity.

Orlando O. Wilson advocates the use of "police hazards" as a theoretical basis for the deployment of police patrols in communities. He states:

> "The need for patrol service derives from police hazards. The total hazard in a community resulting in need for police service is the sum of a multitude of varied and complex conditions and situations, many of them intangible and difficult to isolate for purposes of analysis and measurement. However, hazards result in crimes, offenses, accidents, complaints, and arrests whose frequency may be taken as a measure of the hazards. The measure is made, not in terms of the hours and minutes spent in handling cases or in neutralizing or minimizing the hazards, but in terms of the proportional distribution of the incidents

---

[11]Gilbert Geis. Statistics Concerning Race and Crime," unpublished paper submitted to the U. S. Commission on Civil Rights, September 13, 1962, p. 6.

that result from these hazards among the various patrol areas and time periods."[12]

The purpose of patrol, according to Wilson, is to achieve police objectives through the action of officers moving about within prescribed areas. Their tasks are divided into three classes, *viz.,* services called for (incidents requiring police action reported by a victim or witness, or they may be discovered by a patrolman), inspectional services (routine examination of business premises, etc.), and routine preventive patrol (directed primarily at diminishing less tangible hazards that are not readily isolated and identified).[13]

While a formula has not yet been developed to determine the needed strength of a police department, states Wilson, the minimum number of men needed for the special divisions can be estimated on the basis of essential duties that must be performed; and the number needed for patrol may be estimated by ascertaining the number required to provide an amount of patrol service in terms of called-for service and routine patrol. The relative need for routine preventive patrol and called-for services, according to Wilson, may be measured in terms of the relative frequency of occurrence of Part I offenses (seven major crimes), Part II offenses (all other crimes), accidents, reports, and arrests, because these are the incidents that routine patrol is intended to prevent, and their frequency establishes the extent of called-for services.[14] Wilson suggests that the procedure for working out the patrol deployment is simplified if those factors which determine the relative need for called-for services and routine patrol are consolidated into a single factor, or index.[15] The factors then are assigned weights. In describing this procedure, he states:

> "A weight of one should be assigned to all incidents in each of the categories of arrest, accidents, and miscellaneous reports, since it is assumed that they are of approximately equal importance and that approximately equal time is required to deal with them. A weight of two

[12]Wilson, p. 257.
[13]Wilson, p. 238.
[14]Wilson, p. 251-252.
[15]Wilson, p. 263.

should be assigned to Part II offenses, and a weight of four to Part I crimes. In applying the weights, Part I crimes should be multiplied by four and Part II incidents by two, since it is assumed that they are, respectively, four and two times more serious than incidents in the other three categories and that a similar increase in time is required to deal with them."[16]

Thereafter, the weighted number of incidents in each type are added, and the proportion of the total on each shift to the total for the 24 hours of the day are computed. This percentage is then used to apportion the man-hours to be devoted to called-for services and preventive patrol among the shifts.[17] This approach would meet the requirements of the "proportional need theory."

Within recent years, the Los Angeles Police Department Patrol Bureau has instituted its own theoretical rationale for the distribution of personnel within a geographic patrol division.[18] The policy states that "by evaluating past experiences, the police administrator can anticipate the distribution of the need for his patrol force on the basis of the past distribution of the problem."[19] This policy is also consistent with the proportional need theory. There is, however, no way of measuring the validity of the original theoretical base upon which later personnel deployment policies may evolve. The LAPD distributes its manpower on the basis of criminal activity and called-for services. The manpower distribution is made on the basis of four factors: selected crimes, called-for services, felony arrests, and misdemeanor arrests. The following crimes are selected, tallied and combined for machine tabulation: "Burglary," "Robbery," "Theft from Person," "Auto Theft," "Burglary and Theft from Auto," "Bicycle Theft," "Murder, Rape and Felonious Assault," and "Other Thefts." The policy states that:

"These crimes were chosen as they are more susceptible to prevention by the presence of uniformed patrol officers, or because they are indicators of the need for police services, or both. Bicycle thefts were in-

---

[16]Wilson, p. 264.
[17]Wilson, p. 264.
[18]"Distribution of Personnel Within a Geographic Patrol Division," Patrol Bureau, H/8, 8:43.2, Los Angeles Police Department, February 11, 1965, p. 1.
[19]*Ibid.*, p. 2.

cluded because of their correlation to those "less serious" juvenile crimes not covered by the other selected crimes. A question arises as to the inclusion of murder and rape with felonious assaults. Murder and rape are crimes of passion and are not responsive to the mere knowledge that the police are in the area. However, simply because a crime falls into a group of crimes which we think cannot be prevented does not preclude its value as an indicator of a police problem area. Aggravated or felonious assault are to a certain extent susceptible to prevention, especially when those assaults might occur in a public place. Additionally, the general geographic location of such assaults is usually predictable when considered in volume of number and time. Murders, rapes, and felonious assaults tend to indicate the need for the presence of uniformed officers in those areas which, because of socio-economic or ethnic conditions, seem to present a much higher proportion of crimes of violence."[20]

Again, as was the case with the late Chief Parker, the deployment policy is based upon a *belief* that socioeconomic and ethnic conditions lead to a much higher proportion of crimes of violence. There is no further clarification or elaboration of these ethnic, socioeconomic variables to demonstrate how this is true (or not true). The local police administrator in effect has to accept this premise as a "given" and thereafter, plan accordingly. A weight factor is assigned to called-for services, felony arrests, and mis-demeanor arrests. These three factors are combined and form *work units* and are used as a *single factor*. The percentage of work units, and the percentages of crimes are then averaged to determine the workload by reporting district. The workload then is determined separately for each watch.[21]

The operationalization of the LAPD patrol deployment policy *should* reveal that more police are assigned to those areas that reflect the most need based on LAPD criteria. To accomplish this, two police divisions were selected for contrasting purposes because one area was a low, socioeconomic, predominantly ethnic minority community, and the other a middle-class, predominantly Anglo-Saxon community. The LAPD Hollenbeck Division is comprised of 73.4 percent Spanish-Surname persons with a me-

---

[20]*Ibid.*
[21]*Ibid.*

dian family income of $4820.[22] The LAPD Wilshire Division is comprised of 68.6 percent White, non Spanish-Surname persons with a median family income of $6517.[23] The basic crime profiles and the number of police in the two communities are compared as follows:

TABLE 17-I

LAPD SELECTED CRIMES USED FOR DISTRIBUTION OF PERSONNEL
WITHIN A GEOGRAPHIC PATROL DIVISION

Division	Population	Burglary	Robbery	Larceny and Theft From Person	Auto Theft	Bike Theft, Burglary and Theft From Auto, and Other Theft	Murder, Rape and Felonious Assault	Total
Hollenbeck								
1965	110246	1517	245	2206	1150	303*	576	5997
1966	109749	1574	279	1998	1030	392	606	5822
Wilshire								
1965	259178	5335	936	7752	1903	659	851	17436
1966	214750	4487	707	6584	1520	325	778	14701

*The 1965 and 1966 LAPD Statistical Digests do not reveal a specific crime category for Bicycle Theft, Burglary and Theft From Auto, and Other Thefts. However, the digests reveal a category both in juvenile and adult arrests labeled "Other," and it is these figures that were used for this column.

TABLE 17-II

AREA CRIMES RATES AND POLICE PER POPULATION

Division	Total Selected Crimes	Crime Rate Per Population	No. of Police Per Population (in thousands)
Hollenbeck			
1965	5997	5.4%	1/1070
1966	5822	5.3%	1/1086
1969	7932	7.3%	1/1016
Wilshire			
1965	17436	6.7%	1/1200
1966	14701	6.7%	1/1256
1969	18453	8.2%	1/1118

[22]Mental Health Catchment Areas of Los Angeles County. Population and Health Care Resources, UCLA School of Public Health, Division of Behavioral Sciences, April 1968, p. 123.

[23]*Ibid.*, p. 5.

Contrary to common belief, Table 17-I and Table 17-II reveal that *even though there is a higher incidence of crime in the middle-class Anglo-Saxon community, there is a greater amount of police deployment in the poorer, Mexican-American community.* One possible explanation might be that police administrators, by placing a greater emphasis on a historical policy *belief*—that lower socio-economic ethnic minorities commit a much higher proportion of crime, accordingly assign more police to those areas even though statistical analysis do not warrant this deployment. Does this therefore suggest that there is an element of *subjectivity* in police patrol deployment? N. F. Iannone in his 1970 book expresses this viewpoint when he states:

> "The determination of proportionate need for the distribution of the patrol force depends upon the selection and use of factors which indicate the extent of the police problem in a given city. Herein lies the element of subjectivity since the selection of factors which reflect the nature of the police problem is, in large part, a matter of opinion. Each administrator should select those factors which he believes most accurately reflect the police problem in his community.[24]

The police administrator is very much alone in making those subjective decisions and perhaps even more important, when functioning under the proportional need theory, the greatest shortcoming of this theory is that there is no provision for feedback and control. In other words, not only is there no direct relationship between the deployment scheme and the activities of the officers in the field, there is also no method by which the activities of the officers in the field can be related to the achievement of the objectives of the deployment scheme.[25] How does one measure the police deployment *outcome?* Is crime actually prevented?

The President's Commission on Law Enforcement and the Administration of Justice found that policemen spend half of their time on "preventive patrol," but that no police chief can obtain even a rough estimate of how much crime is thereby "pre-

---

[24]N. F. Iannone. *Supervision of Police Personnel* (Englewood Cliffs, New Jersey: Prentice-Hall, Inc., 1970), p. 29.

[25]Robert Benedict Gaunt, Field Deployment of Police Patrol Forces and the Use of Electronic Data Processing Equipment, unpublished Master's Thesis, School of Public Administration, University of Southern California, June 1965, p. 34.

vented."[26] The Commission also discovered that the ratios of policemen per 1000 residents in cities of over 500,000 ranging from 1.07 to 4.04, showed no differences in the incidence of reported crime in those cities.[27] Although it might be difficult to measure the crime preventive outcomes of police patrol, it would be possible to measure what James Q. Wilson calls "Police-Invoked Order Maintenance." The most common *police initiated intervention* (Police-Invoked Order Maintenance) occurs in situations dealing with drinking related offenses.[28]

Drunkenness arrests vary from place to place—some police departments strictly enforce drunkenness statutes, while other departments are known to be more tolerant. The President's Commission concluded that the number of arrests in a city may be related less to the amount of drunkenness than to *police policy*. To prove its point, the Commission compared drunkenness arrests in three cities and found that the Washington, D.C. (51.8 percent drunk arrests) and Atlanta, Georgia (52.5 percent drunk arrests), police departments were guided by stricter enforcement policies to arrests than was the more tolerant St. Louis, Missouri police department (5.5 percent drunk arrests).[29] Undoubtedly there are many complex variables to consider when different cities in different states are compared as to drinking arrests. It would be possible, however, to consider these arrest patterns as they affect a specific Mexican-American ethnic minority community in East Los Angeles as data are available for careful analysis. Drunk and drunk driving arrests account for a little over 50 percent of all offenses in East Los Angeles—a significantly higher ratio than other communities. Table 17-III compares the East Los Angeles and West Valley populations with regards to numbers of police and frequency of drunk and drunk driving arrests,

Table 17-III reflects dramatic differences in arrests related to drinking. From its information, one must conclude that more

---

[26]The President's Commission, p. 247.

[27]The President's Commission, p. 96.

[28]James Q. Wilson. *Varieties of Police Behavior* (Cambridge, Massachusetts: Harvard University Press, 1968), p. 118.

[29]The President's Commission, p. 234.

TABLE 17-III
DRUNK AND DRUNK DRIVING ARRESTS PER AREA AND POPULATION

1968	LAPD Hollenbeck Area & ELA Sheriff's Station*	LAPD West Valley Area†
Total Population	259,275	260,832
Square Miles	26.44	54.81
Ethnicity	50-60% White, Spanish-Surname	95% White, Non-Spanish Surname
Median Family Income	$5680	$8440
Number of Alcoholics per 100,000 population	8143	8143
Drunk and Drunk Driving Arrests	Per Month: 800 Per Year: 9676 Per Sq. Mi.: 3.72	125 1552 28.5
Police Agencies	CHP, LAPD, Sheriff	LAPD‡
Total No. of Officers	375	151
Number of Officers per Square Mile	13.5	3.5
Major Crime per Ratio of Population	4.9%	4.8%

*"Total Population" and "Square Miles" includes Bell Gardens, 29,491 people, 2.40 square miles; and City of Commerce, 10,763 people, 6.56 square miles. Bell Gardens and Commerce accounted for 1,168 of the drunk and drunk driving arrests.

†As defined by LAPD.

‡CHP statistics in the West Valley area were not available but even when CHP arrests are subtracted from the East Los Angeles Area (approximately 3000 arrests), there still is a significantly higher ratio of arrests for those offenses in the ELA area as compared to the West Valley area. The LAPD made 2954 ELA arrests and the Sheriff's office produced 3722 ELA arrests.

LAPD — Los Angeles Police Department (city)
CHP — California Highway Patrol (state)
Sheriff — Los Angeles County Sheriff's Office (county)
The ethnicity and income factors appear in Mental Health Catchment Areas of Los Angeles County, Population and Health Care Resources, UCLA School of Public Health, Division of Behavioral Sciences, April, 1968.

police are present to observe drinking infractions of the law in the East Los Angles area, and that drunk and drunk driving arrests increase as the number of police per population and square mile increase. *It is not that Mexican-Americans are drinking more than their affluent neighbors. The Division of Alcoholic Rehabilitation of the California Department of Public Health re-*

port an identical ratio of alcoholism per population.[30] *The situation described in Table 17-III may not be unusual as the affluent users of alcohol seem to be very much underrepresented in criminal statistics.* Jack W. Bishop, Director of the USC Research Project on the Drinking Driver and Traffic Safety, found that most convicted drunk drivers are between 31 and 40 years of age, and that most of those convicted are laborers or unskilled workers. He remarked:

> "If we say that drunken drivers are only from lower economic groups or minorities, we are fooling ourselves. Drunk drivers come from every social stratum and occupation."[31]

The head administrator of the Los Angeles County Jail, Chief Kramer, informed the writer on August 2, 1968, that they did not keep racial or ethnic statistical data on prisoners. There are 12,000 prisoners in the county jail. During 1967, 153,221 persons were booked into the county jail, with a third of these being arrested for offenses related to drinking.[32] Since Mexican-Americans comprise 20 percent of state adult inmates and parolees, and 25 percent of California Youth Authority wards, there would be reason to believe that Mexican-Americans represent 20 percent (2,400) to 25 percent (3,000) of the county jail inmates in Los Angeles. This is not difficult to conclude when one considers the large numbers of people in East Los Angeles being arrested for drunk and drunk driving offenses. Better statistics regarding ethnic arrest patterns are needed in this area for exact documentation.

How should the police administrator deal with the "police invoked order maintenance" phenomenon such as was presented in Table 17-III? Patrol deployment policies and theories do not seem to take this kind of self-generated outcome into consideration in patrol deployment planning. Might there not be too much emphasis placed on "police hazards" and the "police problem"

---

[30]California State Plan for Community Mental Health Centers, State of California, Department of Public Health, Bureau of Health Facilities Planning and Construction, June 1968, p. 301.

[31]*Los Angeles Times,* Section C, p. 1, June 1, 1969.

[32]Los Angeles County Sheriff's *Biennial Report,* 1965-1967.

which may lead to many intangibles, assumptions and variables that, in the end result, require arbitrary, subjective decisions? In 1965, one of every three arrests in America were for the offense of drunkenness (two million arrests).[33] The great volume of these arrests places an extremely heavy load on the operations of the entire ciminal justice system. Not only does it burden police, but it clogs lower criminal courts and crowds penal institutions throughout the country.

Perhaps police administrators should deliberate beyond the *traditional* criminal justice system (courts, police and corrections) in comprehensive planning. Other systems that should be part of the criminal justice system—particularly as it pertains to drinking related offenses, are mental health and public health agencies. While over 50 percent of all arrests for law enforcement agencies in East Los Angeles are for offenses related to drinking, only 2 percent of all the patients seen at the County East Los Angeles Mental Health Regional service were for drinking problems.[34] With the exception of three or four Alcoholic Anonymous groups in East Los Angeles, and a very modest, recently established outpatient public health satellite service, there are no detoxification or professional services available to Mexican-Americans with drinking problems. In other words, it is not just a police problem, it is a bio-psychosocial problem—it is a community problem. Involving the criminal justice system with these agencies and the community system in comprehensive planning, could result in a more totally efficient system for processing drinking behavior—thereby reducing law enforcement's most time consuming burden. Law enforcement cannot afford not to be concerned with the outcome of the patrol deployment scheme it it wishes to keep pace with the growing crime problem in America.

---

[33]The President's Commission, p. 233.
[34]Patient and Service Statistics," Los Angeles County Department of Mental Health, Evaluation and Research Division, January 1969, p. 52.

Chapter 18

THE RACIAL TRANSITION OF A POLICE FORCE: A PROFILE OF WHITE AND BLACK POLICEMEN IN WASHINGTON D.C.

Rita M. Kelly and Gormon West Jr.

THE RACIAL composition of police departments has become an important political issue in most of America's large inner cities. Supporters of more community control of police argue that the police must be a part of the people they are employed to serve; the police must represent them physically in appearance and physically in spirit. If the policemen are racially, ethnically, and culturally like the community they are supposed to protect, then, it is argued, they will more naturally know when and how to use their discretionary arrest powers as well as be more likely to improve, by their ordinary behavior, police-community relations. In addition, if more Blacks and other minority group individuals are hired as policemen, more employment for minority groups is obtained.[1] Opposed to these populist views are numerous

Reprinted with permission of the American Institutes for Research, Incorporated and the Authors.

The reported evaluation was performed pursuant to a contract with the Office of Economic Opportunity, Washington, D.C.

[1]For different versions of this position, see

Andres Taylor, Report on "Law and Order Seminar" at Federal City College, Washington, D.C., January 30, 1971, as cited by Garmon West, Jr. in Memorandum for the Record, dated January 30, 1971.

George C. Edwards, *The Police on the Urban Frontier* (New York: Institute of Human Relations Press, 1968), p. 27.

George C. Edwards, "Order and Civil Liberties: A Complex Role for the Police," *Michigan Law Review*, No. 64 (1965), pp. 17-56.

Bruce J. Terris, "The Role of the Police," *The Annals of the American Academy of Political and Social Science*, CCCLXXIV (Nov. 1967), pp. 58-59.

Allen D. Grimshaw, "Police Agencies and the Prevention of Racial Violence," *The Journal of Criminal Law, Criminology and Police Science*, LIV, No. 1 (March, 1963), pp. 110-113.

law enforcement experts who assert that increased professionalization is the main way to resolve existing police-community relations problems. The argument here is that a good policeman is a
good policeman regardless of race, color, or creed. With proper
training and socialization Whites can be effective policemen in
predominantly Black areas and vice versa.[2]

The riots of the late 1960's, as Scott points out, led to the
recognition that "personnel recruitment practices of police organizations reveal much of the same kind of racial discrimination that
undergirds the more general problem of intergroup violence."[3]
Because of this discrimination in recruitment very little information has been readily available to determine whether or not racial
group membership actually does or does not have a significant impact upon the quality of policing, upon personnel recruitment
and selection activities, or indeed, upon police departments as a
whole as they enter upon a racial transition comparable to that
of the cities to whom they belong.[4]

---

[2]For discussions of this position and its implications, see

Louis A. Radelet, "Implications of the Professional Concept in Law En-
forcement for Police-Community Relations," in *Police Community Relations,*
(Ed.): Norman E. Pomrenke (The University of North Carolina at Chapel Hill,
Institute of Government, 1966).

Nelson A. Watson and James W. Sterling, *Police and Their Opinions,*
(Washington, D.C.: IACP, 1969) *passim.*

Paul H. Ashenhurst, "Trends in Police Training," *Sociology of Crime* (Ed.):
Joseph Rourek, (New York: Philosophical Library, 1961), 353 pp. Donald H.
Bouma, *Kids and Cops* (Grand Rapids, Michigan: Wm. B. Erdmans Publishing
Co., 1969), p. 25ff. James Wilson, *Varieties of Police Behavior: The Management
of Law and Order in Eight Communities* (Cambridge, Mass.: Harvard Univer-
sity Press, 1968) *passim,* and Ray Jeffrey, "The Sociology of the Police," in *The
Sociology of Crime (Ed.):* Joseph Rourek, (New York: Philosophical Library,
1961).

[3]James F. Scott, "Racial Group Membership, Role Orientation and Police Conduct
Among Urban Policemen," In *Phylon: The Atlanta University Review of Race
and Culture,* XXXI, No. 1 (Spring, 1970), p. 5.

[4]International Association of Chiefs of Police, *Washington, D.C. Police Personnel Selection Survey* 1968. unpaged. The qualifications required of policemen
throughout the U. S. are compiled in this pamphlet. They are listed by state,
although the requirements for some major cities in each state are also included.

Robert Mast, "Police-Ghetto Relations: Some Findings and a Proposal for
Structural Change" (London: Institute of Race Relations, 1970), *Race,* XI, No.
4, pp. 447-462.

PURPOSE

One police department that has begun this racial transition is the Metropolitan Police Department of Washington, D.C., a city whose current population is 72 percent Black. In 1966 only 17 percent of its 3100 policemen were Black;[5] by the fall of 1970, after extensive recruiting efforts the proportion of Blacks had been increased to 38 percent of 5100 men.[6] Although this proportion of Black policemen falls far short of the proportion of Black people living in the nation's capital, it easily surpasses the national average. To illustrate, the popular Black magazine *Ebony* reported in May of 1971 that only 7 percent (30,000) of the approximately 420,000 policemen in the United States are Black.[7]

The purpose here is to present a summary profile of a sample of 509 Washington, D.C. policemen, comparing Whites and Blacks, in terms of (1) their current socioeconomic status and position on the force; (2) their reasons for becoming policemen; (3) their background prior to becoming policemen; (4) the impact of race on the type of news media they read and listen to; and (5) the reasons they give for why they would leave police work. By means of such data it is hoped that some partial insights into the results of the racial transition of police forces will be obtained.

THE SAMPLE AND PROCEDURES USED

In December of 1970 as a part of an evaluation of an OEO funded experiment in police-community relations, 509 Washington, D.C. policemen, chosen by means of a stratified, disproportionate random sampling procedure, were administered a questionnaire which, among other things, sought data on each of the above five topics. The police sample was stratified first by rank and second by extent of contact with community residents.[8] Since our

---

[5]Alex Poinsett, "The Dilemna of the Black Policemen," in *Ebony*, XXVI, No. 7 (May, 1971), p. 130.

[6]Personnel Department Report, District of Columbia Metropolitan Police Department, Fall 1970.

[7]Poinsett, in "The Dilemna of the Black Policemen.

[8]For more details on Rita Kelly, *et al.*, the sampling procedure and the larger study, see *The Pilot Police Project in Washington, D.C.: A Description and Assessment of a Police-Community Relations Experiment* (Washington, D.C.: The American Institutes for Research), 1972.

purposes here are to indicate general similarities and differences among Black and White policemen on the total force, to get a snapshot, if you will, of the racial transition occurring, only summary data for the total samples are discussed. Of the 509 policemen in the sample, 316 or 62 percent are White and 193 or 38 percent are Black. As was indicated earlier, this is the precise percentage of Blacks on the total Washington, D. C. police force.

Current Socioeconomic Status and Position on the Force

It is self-evident that the socioeconomic status of a policeman is highly correlated with his rank and assignment. Previous studies have found that Black policemen tend to have low ranks and to be assigned to patrol and detective work with a relatively small proportion of them being assigned as administrators.[9] Our data confirm these findings.

TABLE 18-I
POLICEMAN'S RACE AND DIVISIONAL ASSIGNMENT
(In Percentages)

	Patrol Division (N = 389)	Administrative Technical, Inspection and Special Services Division (N = 120)	Total (N = 509)
Black	43	22	38
White	57	78	62

$\chi^2 = 7.62$; d.f. = 1 ; p <.001

As Table 18-I shows, the racial distribution of the policemen within the various divisions is not based upon chance alone. A much larger proportion of Black policemen are assigned to the Patrol Division than to all the other department divisions combined. While 43 percent of the 389 policemen in the Patrol Division sample are Black, only 22 percent in the remaining divisions are. Table 18-II shows an even sharper difference in racial distribution within the hierarchy of the police department. Only 12 percent of the 155 police respondents with ranks higher than that

---

[9]Nelson, A. Watson and James W. Sterling. *Police and Their Opinions* (Washington, D.C.: IACP, 1969) p. 6.

TABLE 18-II
POLICEMAN'S RACE AND RANK
(in percentages)

	Lowest Rank (Officer) (N = 354)	Higher Ranks (N = 155)	Total (N — 509)
Black	43	12	38
White	57	88	62

$\chi^2 = 45.48$; d.f. = 1 ; p <.001

of officer are Black. Looking at the same data slightly differently
Table 18-III shows that 91 percent of the 193 Black policemen
sampled from the Washington, D.C. police force have the lowest
rank of officer, while 57 percent of the 316 White policemen have
this rank.

TABLE 18-III
POLICEMAN'S RANK VERSUS RACE
(in percentages)

	RACE		
	BLACK (N = 193)	WHITE (N = 316)	TOTAL (N = 509)
Lowest Rank	91	57	70
Higher Rank	9	43	30

$\chi^2 = 66.78$; d.f. = 1 ; p <.001

Given the fact that the proportion of Blacks on the force has
only recently doubled it is quite conceivable that the racial differences found in the assignment of officers and their current rank
stem from a more youthful composition of the Black policemen
sample and fewer years of experience on the police force. The data
in Table 18-IV reveal that of the 509 policemen in our sample 281
or 55 percent are under 30. Only 87 men or 17 percent are 40
years of age or older. This high proportion of young policemen is
not surprising given the rapid expansion the District of Columbia
Metropolitan Police Department has undergone in the past two
years. Approximately 2,000 new officers, almost all new recruits,
have been added to the force in an effort to attain full authorized
strength.

A comparison of the age and race of the policemen reflects the

The Racial Transition of a Police Force 359

TABLE 18-IV
POLICEMAN'S AGE AND RACE
(in percentages)

AGE	RACE BLACK (N=193)	WHITE (N=316)	TOTAL (N=509)
20-29 years old	75	43	55
30-39 years old	21	32	28
40 or over	5	24	17

$\chi^2 = 52.12$; d.f. = 2 ; p <.001

intensive effort of the DCMPD under Chief Wilson to recruit young Blacks to the force in the past few years. Of the 193 Black policemen, 75 percent are 29 years of age or younger; only 5 percent are 40-years-old or older. In contrast the age distribution of the White sample is more even. Only 43 percent of the White policemen are 29-years-old or less, while 24 percent are 40 or older.

The sharp difference in the age distribution of the White and Black policemen indicates not only that Blacks have been recently recruited, but also that in the future a more evenly balanced racial distribution is likely to occur in the hierarchical rank structure, assuming, of course, that racial discrimination in promotion of officers is a thing of the past for the District of Columbia Metropolitan Police Department.

If comparable levels of general educational attainment are critical factors in promotions, the Black policemen in Washington, D.C. should not as a group be handicapped. Table 18-V reveals

TABLE 18-V
POLICEMAN'S EDUCATION AND RACE
(in percentages)

EDUCATION	RACE BLACK (N=193)	WHITE (N=316)	TOTAL (N=509)
No answer	1	1	1
No High School Diploma	3	16	11
High School Diploma	61	54	57
Some Higher Education	36	29	31

*$\chi^2 = 20.43$; d.f. = 2 ; p <.001

*All chi-squares for this report are computed excluding the no answer/don't no category.

that a higher proportion of Blacks than Whites have high school diplomas and some higher education. Conversely, a smaller percentage of Black than White policemen had no high school diploma. The proportionately lower rank and greater youthfulness of the Black police sample suggest that the Black respondents will also tend to have a lower socioeconomic status relative to the White respondents. The data in Table 18-VI support this assumption. As of July 25, 1970, 78 percent of the 193 Black policemen earned less than $10,000 a year as policemen, but only 45 percent of the White police respondents did.

TABLE 18-VI
POLICEMAN'S 1970 SALARY AND RACE
(in percentages)

| | RACE | | |
SALARY	BLACK (N = 193)	WHITE (N = 316)	TOTAL (N = 509)
No Answer	1	0	0
$5000-$9999	78	45	58
$10000 or above	21	55	42

$\chi^2 = 55.02$; d.f. = 1 ; p < .001

A comparison of White and Black policemen was also made in terms of home ownership and amount spent on rent if a house was not being purchased. The data in Table 18-VII reveal a larger percentage (52 percent) of the White policemen than of the Black policemen (22 percent) own their own homes. Sixty-nine percent of the Black respondents rent homes while a smaller 42 percent of the White respondents rent. Table 18-VIII indicates that of those who stated they rent a home, a substantially higher proportion of the Black policemen pay less than $150.00 a month than the White policemen. The difference in distribution of the responses on both of the variables is statistically significant at the .05 level or below.

Although some might be inclined to read racial prejudice in these differences, a portion of the variation in home ownership and monthly rent paid stems, it seems, not principally from a lower socioeconomic status of Blacks, but rather from differences in family status and place of residence. For example, Table 18-IX

TABLE 18-VII
HOME OWNERSHIP STATUS AND RACE

HOME	*RACE*		*TOTAL (N = 509)*
OWNERSHIP	*BLACK (N = 193)*	*WHITE (N = 316)*	
No Answer	2	2	2
Rent	69	42	52
Own	22	52	40
Other	7	4	5

$\chi^2 = 43.10$; d.f. = 2 ; p <.001

TABLE 18-VIII
MONTHLY RENT AND RACE
(in percentages)

MONTHLY	*RACE*		
RENT	*BLACK (N = 193)*	*WHITE (N = 316)*	*TOTAL (N = 509)*
No Answer	25	52	42
Less than $150	47	24	33
$150 or more	28	24	26

$\chi^2 = 5.24$; d.f. = 1 ; p <.05

TABLE 18-IX
MARITAL STATUS AND RACE
(in percentages)

MARITAL	*RACE*		
STATUS	*BLACK (N = 193)*	*WHITE (N = 316)*	*TOTAL (N = 509)*
No answer	2	0	1
Single	29	17	21
Married	63	80	73
Other	6	3	4

$\chi^2 = 15.46$; d.f. = 2 ; p <.001

shows that the proportion of single Black policemen is almost twice as high as the proportion of single White policemen (29 percent and 17 percent respectively). Table 18-X reveals considerable differences between the races in terms of the number of children per policeman as well. The Black policemen have fewer children than the White policemen. Forty-three percent of the Black policemen have no children as compared to 32 percent of the White policemen; 47 percent of the Blacks have one or two children, while 36 percent of the Whites do. In addition, only 10 percent of the Black respondents have three or more children,

TABLE 18-X
NUMBER OF CHILDREN AND RACE
(in percentages)

NUMBER OF CHILDREN	RACE		
	BLACK (N = 193)	WHITE (N = 316)	TOTAL (N = 509)
None	43	32	37
1 or 2	47	36	40
3 or more	10	32	24

$\chi^2 = 30.13$; d.f. = 2   ; p <.001

whereas 32 percent of the White respondents have three or more children. It seems, thus, that as a group the Black policemen have less of a need to buy a home or to rent a large apartment than the White policemen.

Another factor affecting whether or not one might rent or buy a home is the place of residence of the policemen. Since all Washington, D.C. policemen are required by law to live within a 10-mile radius of the city, to live outside of the city almost invariably means living in a Virginia or Maryland suburb of the nation's capitol. Most of the housing units in these suburbs are private houses.

As Table 18-XI shows, 36 percent of the 509 policemen surveyed lived in the District of Columbia, the city they police. Forty-nine percent resided in Maryland, 15 percent in Virginia. The comparison by race indicates that while 70 percent of the 193 Blacks sampled live in the District of Columbia, only 16 percent of the 316 Whites do. Conversely, 61 and 23 percent of the Whites reside in Maryland and Virginia, respectively, while only 28 and 3 percent of the Blacks do, respectively. It is evident that by in-

TABLE 18-XI
RESIDENCE AND RACE
(in percentages)

RESIDENCE	RACE		
	BLACK (N = 193)	WHITE (N = 316)	TOTAL (N = 509)
District of Columbia	69	16	36
Maryland	27	61	48
Virginia	3	23	16

$\chi^2 = 152.08$; d.f. = 2   ; p <.001

creasing the proportion of Blacks on the police force, the proportion of policemen residing among the residents served in Washington, D.C. by this police force will also increase.

Reasons for Becoming Policemen

So far as we know there are only two empirically-based studies that focus in a major way upon the reasons why Blacks become policemen. The first study is Nicholas Alex's *Black in Blue*, 1969.[10] On the basis of intensive interviews with self-selected Negro policemen in New York City during December 1964 and October 1965, Alex identified two basic types of Blacks who chose this career. The first type consisted of those who became policemen because they really wanted to be policemen. These men are policemen first, Blacks second. These were in a minority in Alex's study (about 29 percent). He describes them as follows:

> They joined the police department because they wanted to become policemen, because it offered more prestige than other jobs they had, and because it offered the potential of satisfying their personal interests in youth, community work, and law. Because they feel police work has brought them status and mobility, they identify with the job and the functional value of police service.[11]

The second type, the majority, was the civil service-oriented policemen. According to Alex, for these Blacks ". . . their goal was not police work as such but the benefits of a civil service job.

> Civil service represents to these persons the attainment of a relatively high, secure income, with no lay-off periods, the opportunity for advancement based on civil service examinations up to the rank of captain, and the opportunity of getting an education or continuing one's education either in police science or in some field outside police administration. The strong regulations in civil service requiring non-discriminatory job practices were also considered a crucial factor. . . . Thus police work had no meaning in and of itself, but for the external economic meaning of being a member of a class of jobs. Police work was actually considered an occupational area to avoid because it was thought of as a routine job, menial and onerous, limited in scope for the individual with talent and imagination, and the 'butt of everybody's problems.'[12]

---

[10]Nicholas Alex, *Black in Blue: A Study of Negro Policemen* (New York: Appleton-Century Crofts), pp. 34-55.

[11]*Ibid*, p. 46.

[12]*Ibid*, pp. 34-35.

On the basis of the identification of these above two types of reasons why Blacks become policemen a number of assumptions are evident. Those that are examined in this paper are as follows: (1) those Blacks who choose a police career do so for quite different reasons than Whites who choose a police career; (2) a relatively small proportion of Blacks are really interested in a police career and service to the community; (3) if they left the police force after joining, the majority of the Blacks will do so for economic, pecuniary reasons; and (4) Whites will leave the police force for reasons different from those given by the Blacks. In sum, the Alex study indirectly suggests that an increase in the proportion of Blacks on a police force will lead to an ideological transition of the force as well as to a racial transition.

A second study focusing on why (and how) Black's become policemen was conducted by Isaac C. Hunt, Jr. and Bernard Cohen.[13] This study was sponsored in part by the City of New York, in part by the Law Enforcement Assistance Administration of the U.S. Department of Justice and in part by the New York City Rand Institute during the period from October 1968 through July 1969. On the basis of extensive interviews with Black, White, and Puerto Rican youths, Hunt and Cohen found that "Black and Puerto Rican youths, unlike their White counterparts, find the service aspects of police work more attractive than the pay, fringe benefits, or job security."[14] This finding was not expected by them. "Because of the comparatively high payscale of the NYCPD and the still limited, albeit expanding, job opportunities available to minority youths, this study anticipated that the economic benefits resulting from joining the NYCPD would be more important to minority youths than to White applicants."[15]

In order to determine if major differences exist in stated reasons why Blacks and Whites chose a police career in the city of Washington, D.C., the questionnaire included an item asking the respondents to "think back to the time when you became a policeman. . . ." Having set the time frame for them, the respond-

---

[13]Isaac C. Hunt, Jr. and Bernard Cohen, *Minority Recruiting in the New York City Police Department* (New York: The Rand Corporation), pp. xiii-xv.

[14]*Ibid*, p. xiii.

[15]*Ibid*, pp. xiii.

ents were then asked to indicate what the most important reasons were for their becoming policemen. The responses they could check were derived from an open-ended question included in the pretest given to 30 Black and White policemen prior to the larger survey of the 509 policemen. The responses, organized here into the two categories of police orientation and civil service orientation for the purpose of examining Alex's conclusions, are as follows:

Police Orientation Responses	*Civil Service Orientation Responses*
Opportunity to enforce the law	Possibility of a secure career
Value of policeman to society, its prestige and esteem	Possibility of good pay
Desire to be involved in community affairs	Good fringe benefit
Chance to work directly with people	Best opportunity available
It seemed exciting and was a challenge	
My general admiration for the police	

An additional response available for checking was "The possibility of achieving personal satisfaction." It has been excluded in the examination of the orientation of the police respondents, since this response could legitimately fall into either of the two categories.

As the data in Table 18-XII show, a higher proportion of the Black policemen's responses are in the police orientation category (48 percent) than White policemen responses are (39 percent). The difference in the distribution of responses is statistically significant at the .10 level, which, while not a particularly sharp difference, does indicate that a difference between Blacks and Whites does tend to exist in the reasons given for selecting a police career as Alex indicates. These same data reveal, however, that in contrast to the implication of Alex, Blacks tend to be more police-oriented than the Whites; conversely, Whites were the most civil service-oriented of the two racial groupings. Moreover, within the Black group itself a higher proportion (48 percent) are police-oriented than civil service-oriented (37 percent). Hence, it is not true, in Washington, D.C. at least, that only a small proportion of Black policemen are really interested in a police career and service to the community.

TABLE 18-XII

MOST IMPORTANT REASON WHY BECAME A POLICEMAN BY RACE
(in percentages)

REASONS	RACE		
	BLACK (N = 193)	WHITE (N = 316)	TOTAL (N = 509)
No answer	12	8	9
Police Orientation	48	39	42
Civil Service Orientation	37	43	41
Personal Satisfaction	4	10	8

$\chi^2 = 3.49$; d.f. = 1 ; p <.10
Chi-square excludes the no answer and personal satisfaction responses.

Socioeconomic Background Prior to Becoming a Policeman

The argument that Blacks will be less police and service oriented than Whites is based upon the fact that as a group Blacks tend to have fewer opportunities to enter into middle class and well-paying occupations. Further, it seems to be assumed that Blacks who enter into the police profession will tend to come from lower socioeconomic status positions than Whites who become policemen.[16]

The debate over the social class origins of policemen is not new. Watson, for example, notes that "many of the actions of the police which have been called undesirable, improper, and inhuman are said to be a consequence of the lower middle-class values of the police."[17] Watson, however, challenges the assumption that most policemen are from the lower class. He feels that in order to deal with the question of the relationship between

[16]*Ibid*, p. xiii.
[17]Nelson A. Watson and James W. Sterling, *Police and Their Opinions* (Washington, D.C.: IACP), p. 126.

social class and behavior it is essential to distinguish between the social class into which one is born and reared and the one which the individual has attained as an adult. According to Watson, the occupation of one's father is the key to discovering a policemen's status prior to becoming a policeman. He states that occupations in the crafts, foremen, clerical and sales, proprietors and managers, and professional or semi-professionals are middle-class and above occupations while the remaining are lower-middle, working-class or below. Through research using the Bureau of the Census classifications, he concludes that the common belief that most policemen are products of the lower middle-class environment should be viewed with some doubt. His classification of his sample indicates an over-representation in relation to the general population of the police respondents' father's jobs at the level of craftsmen and foremen and at the service level. So, if one applies the rule that occupations above the level of craftsmen and foremen are middle class or better, the statement that most policemen are products of the lower middle class is not supported as 56 percent reported that their fathers held jobs at or above craftsmen or foreman.[18]

Sterling, in his study, "Changes in Role Concepts of Police Officers During Recruit Training," indicates that 42 percent of the subjects held jobs at middle-class level or better.[19] McNamara, in his article "Uncertainties In Police Work: Recruit's Background and Training," analyzed the previous employment of 574 recruits in New York City. Using the highest skilled job held as his variable, he found that the majority worked in clerical and sales jobs. One must remember that he did not use the last job held, but, the highest job skill attained.[20]

In our survey of Washington, D.C. policemen several questions related to the socioeconomic status of the respondents' fathers were asked. The first to be discussed here is the highest educational level attained by the father. As Table 18-XIII shows, over 50

---

[18]*Ibid,* p. 113.

[19]*Ibid,* p. 113.

[20]John H. McNamara, "Uncertainties in Police Work: The Relevance of Police Recruits. Background and Training," in *The Police: Six Sociological Essays* (New York: John Wiley & Sons, Inc.), 1967, pp. 163-252.

percent of the fathers of both the White and Black police respondents has less than a high school education. Although there is almost no difference between the racial groupings on this category,

TABLE 18-XIII
FATHER'S EDUCATIONAL ATTAINMENT AND RACE
(in percentages)

FATHER'S EDUCATIONAL ATTAINMENT	RACE		
	BLACK (N = 193)	WHITE (N = 316)	TOTAL (N = 509)
No answer	7	5	6
Less than high school	52	51	54
High school graduate	20	24	23
Some higher education	21	15	17

$\chi^2 = 3.85$; d.f. = 2 ; p <NS

some difference appears in the other two categories. While 24 percent of the White policemen's fathers stopped their education with a high school diploma, 20 percent of the Black policemen's fathers did. A higher proportion of the Black respondents' fathers (21 percent) had some higher education as well as a high school degree than the White police respondents (15 percent). Comparatively speaking, thus, it seems that the fathers of Black policemen are not, as a group, very different in their educational backgrounds from the fathers of White policemen.

The 509 police respondents were also asked to indicate (1) what their fathers' occupation at their birth was and (2) what their fathers' main occupation throughout most of his life was. In coding the responses the occupation categories, divisions, and groups developed by the Bureau of the Census was used. To get some idea of the relative social class standing of the fathers of the two racial groups, those responses falling in the professional and clerical/sales categories are considered middle-class/white-collar status, while those falling in the farming, fishing, forestry, processing, machine trades, bench, structural and miscellaneous work are considered working-class/blue-collar status; military service is classified as working-class/blue-collar and those falling in the service and unemployed categories are designated here as lower-class/general "have-not" status.

As Table 18-XIV reveals, there is no statistically significant difference between the Black and White police respondents with regard to the proportion having fathers with either middle-class/white-collar type of occupations at their birth or with lower-class/"have-not" status. While 17 percent of the Black policemen's

TABLE 18-XIV
FATHER'S OCCUPATION AT RESPONDENT'S BIRTH AND RACE
(in percentages)

| | RACE | | |
	BLACK (N = 193)	WHITE (N = 316)	TOTAL (N = 509)
Middle class/ No answer	16	9	12
white collar	17	17	17
Working class/ blue collar	54	61	59
Lower class/ "Have Not" status	13	12	13

$\chi^2 = .38$; d.f. = 2 ; p <NS

fathers had white-collar occupations, 17 percent of the White policemen's fathers also did. Thirteen percent of the 193 Black policemen said their fathers had lower class/"have-not" status at their birth while 12 percent of the 316 white policemen did.

Table 18-XV further shows that, using these classifications,

TABLE 18-XV
FATHER'S MAIN OCCUPATION AND RACE
(in percentages)

| | RACE | | |
	BLACK (N = 193)	WHITE (N = 316)	TOTAL (N = 509)
No answer	13	7	9
Middle class/ white collar	22	22	22
Working class/ blue collar	52	60	57
Lower class/ "Have-Not" status	13	10	11

$\chi^2 = 2.36$; d.f. = 2 ; p <NS

there is no substantial difference between the main occupation held by the respondents' fathers and the race of the respondents. Twenty-two percent of both racial groups had fathers with middle-class/white-collar occupations, with around 10 percent of each group having fathers with lower-class/"have-not" status.

To get some self-assessment of the socioeconomic status from which they came the police respondents were asked to rate the neighborhood they grew up in as poor, average, or well-to-do. Three percent of the White officers and 6 percent of the Black officers said they grew up in well-to-do neighborhoods (see Table 18-XVI). A higher percentage of the White policemen (66 percent) said they came from average neighborhoods as opposed to a lesser percentage of Black policemen (57 percent). Similarly, 31 percent of the Whites and 36 percent of the Blacks indicated they came from poor neighborhoods. The difference in the distribution of responses to this item is statistically significant at the .10 level of confidence.

TABLE 18-XVI
SELF-ASSESSMENT OF SOCIO-ECONOMIC BACKGROUND AND RACE
(in percentages)

NEIGHBOR-	RACE		
HOOD RATING	BLACK (N = 193)	WHITE (N = 316)	TOTAL (N = 509)
No answer	1	0	0
Poor	36	31	33
Average	56	66	62
Well-to-do	6	3	4

$\chi^2 = 5.04$; d.f. $= 2$; p $< .10$

On the basis of the above data on the occupations of the respondents' fathers at birth, the respondent's fathers' main occupation, and the respondents' self-assessment of the financial well-being of the neighborhood he grew up in, one has to conclude that, in Washington, D.C., at least, the racial transition of the police force from almost no Blacks to a relatively high proportion has not in any significant manner changed the general socioeconomic class background of the total force.

To get some idea of the occupational history of the respondents themselves a series of questions about their own job history were also examined. As indicated earlier, one would expect that a higher proportion of the Black respondents would have held lower-class/"have-not" status jobs and a lower proportion of middle-class/white-collar jobs than the White respondents. Table 18-XVII shows that this assumption is indeed correct when the respondents' first full-time occupation is compared to the race of the policeman. The difference in the distribution of the responses is statistically significant at the .001 level. While 16 percent of the Black police respondents said they held a middle-class/white-collar type of job first, 25 percent of the White police respondents did. Conversely, 24 percent of the Blacks held lower-class/"have-not" status type of positions as their first full-time job, but only 12 percent of the Whites did. The percentage points of the responses falling within the working-class/blue-collar category is almost the same for both racial groups.

TABLE 18-XVII
RESPONDENT'S FIRST FULL-TIME OCCUPATION AND RACE
(in percentages)

| | RACE | | |
	BLACK (N = 193)	WHITE (N = 316)	TOTAL (N = 509)
No answer	4	4	4
Middle class/ white collar	16	25	22
Working class/ blue collar	56	59	58
Lower class/ "Have-Not" status	24	12	17

$\chi^2 = 16.39$; d.f. = 2 ; p <.001

When the question is changed from the first full-time job held to what was your immediate occupation immediately prior to joining the Washington, D.C., police department, a considerable change in responses occurs. There no longer is a statistically significant difference between the two racial groups in terms of the socioeconomic class standing of occupations held (see Table 18-XVIII). About 30 percent in both groups identify jobs of a middle-class/white-collar nature, while close to 50 percent specify a working class/blue-collar type of job and 17 to 18 percent identify lower-class/"have-not" status jobs.

TABLE 18-XVIII
OCCUPATION IMMEDIATELY PRIOR TO JOINING POLICE FORCE
AND RACE
(in percentages)

| | RACE | | |
	BLACK (N=193)	WHITE (N=316)	TOTAL (N=509)
No answer	5	5	5
Middle class/ white collar/	30	29	29
Working class/ blue collar	47	49	48
Lower class/ "Have-Not" status	18	17	17

$\chi^2 = .35$; d.f. $= 2$; p $<$NS

Comparing the responses given to the question about the first full-time job and the occupation held immediately prior to joining the District of Columbia police force (Tables 18-XVII and 18-XVIII), one sees that the proportion of Blacks indicating they held a middle-class/white-collar type of job almost doubled between the first full-time job and the last job held. One reason for this doubling is that a relatively larger proportion of the Black respondents than the White respondents went back to school after their first full-time job and were college students immediately prior to becoming policemen, (the coding procedure used placed students in the middle class/white collar category). An additional reason for the change in percentage level for Blacks but not Whites is the age differences between the two groups. The Black sample is considerably younger than the White sample as a whole. Young people often try out many different jobs before settling upon a career or occupation for life, one would expect greater variability among this group. Further, during the time period the younger people in our samples would be seeking jobs the job market opened up considerably to Blacks, providing them with greater opportunities to occupy white-collar types of occupations than previously.

Given the great stress placed upon recruiting policemen from the military service, special attention was paid to whether or not differences exist in the veteran status of the two racial groupings of policemen. Close to three-fourths of the Washington, D.C. police force are veterans. Conversely, slightly more than one-fourth (26 percent) of the D.C. police force sampled are not veterans. Thus, the vast bulk have some military experience. Statistically significant racial differences do appear on this variable. While 22 percent of the 316 White policemen sampled are not veterans, 33 percent of 193 Black policemen are not.

TABLE 18-XIX
VETERAN STATUS AND RACE
(in percentages)

| | RACE | | |
	BLACK (N = 193)	WHITE (N = 316)	TOTAL (N = 509)
No answer	2	1	1
Veteran	65	77	73
Non-veteran	33	22	26

$\chi^2 = 7.96$; d.f. = 1; p < .01

Only 23 percent of the Washington, D.C., police force sampled were born in the city they now serve. Twice as many Black policemen were born here as were White policemen. While 33 percent of the 193 Blacks were born in the District of Columbia, only 17 percent of the 316 Whites were (see Table 18-XX).

Regionally, most of the 509 D.C. policemen come from the South (36 percent). If one adds the 23 percent who were born in Washington, D.C., which is also considered Southern in U.S.

TABLE 18-XX
PLACE OF BIRTH AND RACE
(in percentages)

| | RACE | | |
	BLACK (N = 193)	WHITE (N = 316)	TOTAL (N = 509)
Northeast region	8	43	30
South	51	27	36
D.C.	33	17	23
Other	9	13	11

$\chi^2 = 83.67$; d.f. = 3 ; p < .001

census terms, then a total of 59 percent of the policemen are of Southern origin. Only 2 percent come from the West, 8 percent from the North Central region (both in the "other" category), while 30 percent come from the Northeast. A very small 1 percent were born in a foreign country.

An examination of place of birth by race reveals some interesting phenomena. The proportion of the 193 Black policemen born in the South is almost twice as high as the proportion of the 316 Whites born in the South (51 percent compared to 27 percent), or the District of Columbia (33 percent) the bulk of the Whites tend to come from outside the South (43 percent come from the Northeast and 9 percent from the North Central region). Only 27 percent of the Whites come from the South and an even smaller 17 percent come from the District of Columbia.

Impact of Race on Type of News Media
Policemen Read and Listen To

Although the racial orientation of the news media read and listened to is not necessarily related to socioeconomic status, it is related to race, to strategies for recruiting minority groups to police forces, and to arguments that Black policemen will be more likely to know and understand problems currently facing the Black populations in America's inner cities. Hence, our findings about the racial type of newspapers and magazines read by policemen and radio stations listened to are included here, even though more detailed and extensive analyses of the impact of any differences found because of this type of racial exposure received from the news media will need to await another study.

As Table 18-XXI shows, a higher proportion of Black police-

TABLE 18-XXI
NUMBER OF NEWSPAPERS READ REGULARLY
(in percentages)

	(1) B N = 193	(2) W N = 316	Total N = 509
No answer	4	4	4
One	38	51	46
Two or more	58	45	50

$\chi^2 = 8.81$; d.f. = 1; p <.01

men state that they read two or more newspapers than the proportion of White policemen who indicate this. While 58 percent of the Black respondents say they read two or more newspapers, 45 percent of the White respondents say they read as many papers regularly. The difference in the distribution of responses between the two racial groups is statistically significant at the .01 level.

One possible reason why the Black respondents tend to read more newspapers than the Whites is revealed in Table 18-XXII. A much higher proportion of the Black policemen sampled read both White and Black-oriented newspapers than the White policemen did, 3 and 25 percent respectively. In other words, the Black police respondents more often report they read *the Washington Post* (classified as White-oriented) and the *Afro-American* or the *Panther Party Paper* than White respondents do.

TABLE 18-XXII
RACIAL TYPE OF NEWSPAPER READ AND RACE
(in percentages)

	RACE		
	BLACK (N = 193)	*WHITE (N = 316)*	*TOTAL (N = 509)*
No answer	4	4	4
Black only	1	1	1
White only	70	93	84
Black and White combination	25	3	11

$\chi^2 = 60.89$; d.f. = 2 ; p <.001

In the case of the magazines read, a comparable situation exists. Table 18-XXIII shows that 81 percent of the Black police respondents read two or more magazines regularly, but only 54

TABLE 18-XXIII
NUMBER OF MAGAZINES READ AND RACE
(in percentages)

	RACE		
	BLACK (N = 193)	*WHITE (N = 316)*	*TOTAL (N = 509)*
No answer	7	20	15
One	12	27	21
Two or more	81	54	64

$\chi^2 = 23.08$; d.f. = 1 ; p <.001

percent of the White police respondents do. It seems that the more youthful and generally better educated Black sample of policemen is more news media oriented. Table 18-XXIV reveals that an even higher proportion of the Black policemen read both Black- and White-oriented magazines than the proportion of Blacks who said they read both Black- and White-oriented newspapers. Sixty-seven percent of the Black sample said they read both racial types of magazines, 14 percent said they read only White-oriented types,

TABLE 18-XXIV

RACIAL TYPE OF MAGAZINES READ AND RACE

(in percentages)

| | RACE | | |
	BLACK (N = 193)	*WHITE (N = 316)*	*TOTAL (N = 509)*
No answer	7	20	15
Black only	11	0	5
White only	14	79	54
Black and White combination	67	1	26

$\chi^2 = 316.48$; d.f. = 2 ; p <.001

and another 11 percent said they read Black oriented magazines only. In contrast to this distribution of responses, the 316 White policemen almost entirely identified predominantly White-oriented magazines as their regular reading fare. Seventy-nine percent of their responses fell here, with none being in the Black magazine category, and only one percent identifying both Black- and White-oriented magazines. The magazines considered Black are, for example, *Ebony, Jet,* and *Black Dollar.* The ones classified as White are the more general ones, such as *Life, Time, Look,* the *National Observer, National Geographic,* and the like.

The findings analyzing the type of radio stations listened to are comparable to the findings described above for the newspapers and magazines. When a list of the radio stations was presented to the police respondents, most of the White respondents (82 percent) listen to White radio stations and most of the Black respondents listen to both White- and Black-oriented radio stations or to Black radio stations, 52 and 32 percent, respectively (see Table 18-XXV). The difference in the distribution of responses is, again, statistically significant.

TABLE 18-XXV
RACIAL TYPE OF RADIO STATIONS LISTENED TO AND RACE
(in percentages)

RADIO STATION TYPE	RACE BLACK (N = 193)	WHITE (N = 316)	TOTAL (N = 509)
No answer	2	8	6
Black only	32	1	13
White only	14	82	56
Black and White combination	52	12	26

$\chi^2 = 268.72$; d.f. = 2 ; p < .001

On the basis of the data on the number and types of magazines and newspapers read and radios listened to, it appears that it is indeed true that Black policemen are more inclined to be intellectually aware of the concerns and interests of the general Black population than the White policemen are. The fact that almost no White policemen questioned indicate they read regularly a Black-oriented magazine or newspaper or ever listen to Black-oriented radio stations might suggest one area where greater understanding and knowledge of the inner city resident could easily and relatively painlessly be gained.

The fact that the vast majority of the Black police respondents tend to read or listen to general (or White-oriented) news media suggests that general advertisements recruiting men to the police force should be effective for Blacks as well as Whites. However, again further research specifically on this question is greatly needed to verify the accuracy of this speculation.

Why Policemen Would Leave Police Work

The sharp racial differences between the police samples on most of the questions discussed so far, as well as the implications of the Alex study suggest that statistically significant differences between Black and White policemen will probably occur in response to the query about why they would leave the police profession. As in the case of the question about why they became policemen in the first place, the responses included in the final survey were derived from a comparable item included in the pretest of the police questionnaire. To determine if the Black police-men would be more inclined to leave for pecuniary reasons than the White policemen as Alex's study suggests, the responses for this analysis were grouped into two general categories. The first of these is "Negative View of Police Career" and the second is "Pecuniary Economic—Security Reasons."

Negative View of Police Career

Lack of opportunity to enforce the law.

Lack of value of police to society.

Difficulty of achieving personal satisfaction in present career.

Desire to get away from unsolvable social problems.

Possibility of a more exciting and challenging career.

Chance to work directly with people.

Pecuniary Economic-Security Reasons

Possibility of a more secure career.

Possibility of better pay and fringe benefits.

Possibility of achieving greater prestige and esteem.

Using the responses regarding the first most important reason why they became policemen, Table 18-XXVI shows that a statistically significant difference between the Black and White policemen does indeed exist. While 59 percent of the Whites considered negative features of a police career as the most critical reasons for leaving rather than economic, only 50 percent of the Blacks did.

TABLE 18-XXVI
MOST IMPORTANT REASONS WHY RESPONDENT WOULD CHANGE
CAREER AND RACE
(in percentages)

REASON	RACE		
	BLACK (N=193)	WHITE (N=316)	TOTAL (N=509)
No answer	6	6	6
Negative view of police work	50	59	55
Pecuniary reasons	45	35	39

$\chi^2 = 4.24$; d.f. = 1 ; p <.05

The data on why the police would leave do not, however, support the implication of Alex's study that the large majority of Blacks would leave for economic, pecuniary reasons. While 45 percent would leave for such reasons, 50 percent would leave because of a negative view of police work. Nonetheless, the data do show that a greater proportion of Blacks (45 percent) would leave principally for economic reasons than Whites (35 percent) would.

SUMMARY AND CONCLUSIONS

Racially, the Washington, D.C. Metropolitan Police Department has undergone considerable change within the past four years. In 1966 only 17 percent of its 3100 policemen were Black; by the fall of 1970, after extensive recruiting efforts the proportion of Blacks has been increased to 38 percent of 5100 men. To obtain insights into the results of this racial transition of the D. C. police department, 316 White D. C. policemen are compared with the 193 Black D. C. policemen selected from a sample of the entire Washington, D. C., police force. Some of the resulting summary profiles that were statistically significant are reiterated here.

The analysis of the D. C. police force sample indicated that Black policemen tend to have low ranks and to be assigned to patrol and detective work with a relatively small proportion of them being assigned as administrators. The data indicated, however, that the racial differences found in the assignment of officers and their current rank might well stem from the more youthful composition of the Black policemen sample and the fewer years of experience they as a group had on the police force. This youthful composition of the Black police sample suggested that the Black respondents would have a lower socioeconomic status relative to the White respondents. The data analyzed supported this assumption. As of July 25, 1970, 78 percent of the 193 Black policemen earned less than $10,000 a year as policemen; but only 45 percent of the White police respondents did. Educationally, a higher proportion of Blacks than Whites had high school diplomas and some higher education. Conversely a smaller percentage of Blacks than Whites had no high school diploma.

There is currently much discussion on the national and local level, especially in Washington, D.C. as to whether policemen should be required to live in the communities they serve. Thirty-six percent of the 509 Washington, D.C. policemen surveyed lived in the District of Columbia. Forty-nine percent resided in Maryland, 15 percent in Virginia. The comparison by race indicates that while 70 percent of the 193 Blacks sampled live in the District of Columbia, only 16 percent of the 316 Whites do. It is evident that by increasing the proportion of Blacks on the force, the proportion of policemen residing among the residents served in Washington, D.C. by this police force will increase.

In an analysis of the reasons Blacks and Whites give for becoming policemen and the reasons they give for leaving if they were considering a change in their police careers, it was hypothesized that (1) those Blacks who choose a police career do so for quite different reasons than Whites who choose a police career; (2) a relatively small proportion of Blacks are really interested in a police career and service to the community; (3) if they left the police force after joining, the majority of Blacks will do so for economic, pecuniary reasons; and (4) Whites will leave the police force for reasons different from those given by the Blacks.

With regard to why they became policemen, Blacks tended to be more police service oriented than the Whites; conversely, Whites were the most civil service oriented of the two racial groupings. Moreover, within the Black group itself a higher proportion were police service oriented than civil service oriented. Hence, it is not true, in Washington, D.C. at least, that only a small proportion of Black policemen are really interested in police careers and service to the community.

The data on why the police would leave a police career indicates that the majority of Blacks would leave for economic, pecuniary reasons, while the Whites considered negative features of a police career as the most critical reasons for leaving.

From the comparison of the socioeconomic background of the White and Black respondents the following conclusions can be made:

1. The fathers of Black policemen are not, as a group, very different in their educational backgrounds from the fathers of White policemen.

2. There is no substantial difference between the two racial groups of policemen in terms of the main occupation their fathers held at their birth and the father's chief occupation as an adult.
3. On the basis of the data on the occupations of the respondents fathers at birth, the respondents' fathers' main occupation, and the respondents' self-assessment of the financial well-being of the neighborhood he grew up in, the racial transition of the police force from almost no Blacks to a relatively high proportion has not in any significant manner changed the general socioeconomic class background as defined in this paper of the total Washington, D.C. Police force.
4. The proportion of Black policemen having military service is significantly less than the proportion of Whites having military service.
5. The highest proportion of southern-born Washington, D.C. Policemen are from the Black sample, not from the White sample. The White Washington D.C. Policemen tend to come from the Northeastern region of the United States, while the Black Washington, D.C. Policemen come either from the South or Washington, D.C. area itself.

The data on the impact race had on the reading and listening habits of policemen revealed that *almost no* White policemen questioned indicated they read regularly a Black-oriented magazine or newspaper or listened to Black-oriented radio stations. Hence, an obvious, readily available way of increasing their understanding and knowledge of the Black inner-city residents is not being utilized. Black policemen tended to read and listen to both Black and White news media.

As expressed in the beginning of this report, it is hoped that the data analysis has given new insights into some of the general results that might be connected with the racial transition of a police force. It is obviously necessary with the racial transition of a police force. It is obviously necessary for further study in the area of recruitment of Blacks to police careers and for further study to assess the results of the racial transition of police forces.

Chapter 19

PERCEPTION OF THE POLICE
IN A BLACK COMMUNITY

Irving A. Wallach and Colette C. Jackson

THIS REPORT presents a description and analysis of how a cross section of residents in an urban Negro community perceive the police, and their activities and behavior. The point of view of these residents is contrasted with that of the local police who function in the same community. The community studied is the Western Police District of the City of Baltimore. Data were gathered in late 1969 and early 1970 by conducting fifty in-depth interviews with local residents. Data indicating the police perspective—with which resident data are compared—were collected between October 1968 and September 1969 by participant observation, interviews, and the use of expert informants.[1]

Two problem areas are addressed in this study. The first is the police function and its implementation in an urban Negro community, as viewed by community residents. The second area deals with the nature and significance of differing resident and police perceptions of the police role, functions, and behavior in the community.

The study represents an attempt to systematically describe and compare the points of view of both police and residents *in the same community.* A basic limitation of the study is that the sampling procedure does not permit statistical generalization to the larger population. Because of the exploratory nature of the study, the capability of generalization was sacrificed in favor of a qualita-

This project was funded by the Office of Economic Opportunity Grant No. B99-5018 and is reprinted with permission of Research Analysis Corp., Los Angeles.

[1]This police study, performed under other auspices, was published in August 1970. See, Irving A. Wallach, *The Police Function in a Negro Community,* Research Analysis Corporation, McLean, Virginia, 1970 (2 volumes).

tive, in-depth exploration of the complexities of community-police relationships.[2]

THE COMMUNITY

The Western Police District is one of nine districts (precincts) established within the City of Baltimore by the police department for operational and administrative purposes. This precinct in West Baltimore can be described in overall terms as a small, heterogeneous, densely populated, primarily residential, high crime, all Negro area.

Among the salient characteristics of the District are its small size (2.61 square miles), its large population (105,201 people), its racial composition (98 percent Negro), and its variation in terms of the kinds of people who reside there. The population exhibits great variation in age, household composition and family structure, education and economic characteristics. The majority of the population is under 25 years of age, but a substantial portion is over 50 (20 percent). Most families are headed by a male, but over one-third are female-headed households. Two-thirds of the heads of households have less than a 12th grade education, but 6 percent have taken college courses and 2 percent are college graduates. Similarly, wide variation was also found for income, home ownership, occupation, and welfare assistance.

The major difference between a factual description of the Western District and the perceptions of our respondents is their view of the size of their community. Almost all respondents perceive their community as a much smaller area than the Western District. For most it is an area not larger than five square blocks in size. All respondents see problems in their environment but the intensity of these problems varies by neighborhood of residence. For most the area is a relatively satisfactory place to live.

The data on the community social environment indicate that residents form patterns of interaction with neighbors to deal with personal and community problems. Informal interaction with neighbors is indicated by approximately three-fourths of our

---

[2]See Volume II, Appendix A for a detailed description of the study methodology and its rationale.

sample, although the nature, content, and intensity of these contacts varies considerably. For most of this group, such contacts are related to emergencies which individuals cannot handle alone. On the other hand, one-fourth of the respondents indicate varying degrees of isolation from their neighbors. For this group, isolation, i.e. non-involvement in the affairs of others and "minding one's own business," is a way of coping with an unfriendly, unconcerned, or dangerous environment. Approximately 25 percent of the sample indicate that the formal interaction required for community projects occurs either on a sustained basis or for a specific event. However, the rest see the community as inactive for a variety of reasons.

There appears to be little or no difference between the conception of the community held by respondents and the way the community is perceived by the police. Great similarity exists in the views of both groups regarding the nature of the community, its problems, and its demographic characteristics. Exceptions to this statement are that some police officers see racial factors as a cause of many community problems, and the tendency of the police to characterize much of the District population in terms of the behavioral characteristics of lower-class elements with whom they are in frequent negative contact. The police perception of informal and formal interaction patterns in the Western District, based upon their experience, results in a low expectation of sustained community effort to resolve local problems, without outside assistance.

PERCEPTIONS OF CRIME IN THE COMMUNITY

The perception of the Western District derived from police department statistics is that of a high crime area in both an absolute and relative sense. Major and minor crimes occur in the community with great regularity. During 1969, a total 9,074 index crimes were reported and the crime rate was substantially higher in the district than it was city-wide. Interpersonal violence is a major community problem. This is indicated by the number of homicides, forcible rapes, robberies, and assaults which occurred during this one-year period. Crimes against property are also a serious problem in the community.

The subjective perception of crime in the community provided by the interview data is in agreement with the description based upon police sources. Most respondents see their community as having a high level of crime and are greatly concerned about it, whether it exists in their immediate vicinity or in surrounding neighborhoods. Crimes involving physical violence are viewed by the majority of respondents as the most serious and threatening, and narcotics is viewed as a community problem. The experience of the residents in our sample provides ample justification for their concern about crime in the community. Only two of the respondents indicate that they have had no experience with crime. Of the remaining 48, one-half have been victims of crime within the past three years, while the other half have either witnessed crimes or have knowledge of others in their neighborhood who have been victimized. The most frequent form of victimization reported is burglary.

The data indicate that district residents are affected by the fear of crime in varying degrees. Forty-one of fifty respondents feel safe in their homes, but only twenty feel safe on the streets, especially at night. Most respondents do not take precautions in terms of weapons, but take prudent steps to avoid crime, such as locking car doors, avoiding groups of teenagers, installing extra door locks and limiting activities after dark. Some, although aware of the crime problem, do not appear to feel greatly threatened by it. Most respondents indicate that they attempt to deal with the threat of crime without drastically disrupting their lives. The fear of crime is heightened by the reluctance of many residents to intervene when others are being victimized. Most respondents attribute this reluctance to a fear of injury.

The residents who comprise the sample believe that young males from lower-class neighborhoods commit most of the crimes in the Western District. Thus, 47 of 50 respondents indicate that the crimes which occur most frequently are perpetrated by teenagers, e.g. burglary, yoking, assault and robbery. Other crimes, such as car theft, vandalism, and purse snatching are attributed to youngsters between the ages of 9 and 15. Armed holdups and drug pushing are generally believed to involve a higher percentage of adult males.

The local residents interviewed express definite views concerning the causes of crime in their community. Most respondents attribute criminal activity to the family. Eleven responses indicate poor home environment as a cause, e.g. illegitimacy, working mothers, and other factors that affect training and discipline; and ten responses cite a lack of parental control. A large group of responses (15) presents economic factors, particularly poverty resulting from unemployment and underemployment, as a cause of crime. Eight responses note a lack of recreation and jobs as a constructive alternative to crime. There was surprisingly little black militant rhetoric in the data. Few respondents feel that crime is the result of oppression of Blacks by the larger society.

Almost two-thirds of our sample also have ideas about what should be done to alleviate the crime problem in the community. These fall into the broad categories of preventive and control measures. Of the 20 responses in the preventive category, 11 indicate that if parents raised their children properly, they would not engage in delinquent and criminal behavior, and 9 responses see a requirement for community and recreational programs as preventive measures. The 15 responses in the control category are directed at the immediate threat. They aim at controlling crime by family action, employment and rehabilitation programs, and recreation facilities. Respondents also advocate control measures involving the police. The major emphasis of the responses is on reducing crime by proper family training, making more jobs available, and providing community activities for youth.

Respondent and police perceptions concerning crime in the community are in broad agreement in a number of basic areas. These include the incidence and types of crime in the community; the kinds of people who are engaged in criminal activity; concern regarding citizen victimization and citizen safety; the lack of parental control and a poor home environment as a major cause of crime; and the importance of the family as a mechanism for crime prevention. There is somewhat less agreement in other areas. A direct causal relationship between crime and poverty, lack of recreation facilities, and general societal conditions was postulated by some of our respondents. Negro officers, in general, tend to agree with this formulation. White officers, while recognizing a relationship, frequently do not see it as basic because they often ascribe both crime and the related factors to racial and cultural causes. The police, based upon their experience, are less optimistic than the respondents regarding the value and effectiveness of employment, rehabilitation, and recreation programs as crime control measures.

THE POLICE AND CRIME

Most of the respondents perceive the police to be unsuccessful in their efforts to control crime in the Western District. Many specifically point to the narcotics problem, but most feel that the police are not effective in controlling any crimes. A majority of the sample attributes the lack of success in crime control to factors external to the police. This is particularly true of female respondents, the males being more critical of police efforts.

Most often mentioned as a reason for police ineffectiveness is the lack of community cooperation with the police. Next, in terms of frequency is the police inability to relate to and work with the community. In general, however, the largest proportion of respondents feel that community cooperation is the factor most related to the police force's inability to control crime. At a much lower frequency, respondents indicate the following as causes of ineffective crime control: lack of proper police training; limited police authority, police corruption and miscellaneous factors (e.g. police salaries, manpower, and the amount of crime in the community).

The majority of respondents feel that the police can become more effective in controlling crime. Most frequently mentioned as measures to improve crime control were cooperation between the community and the police, a concerted drive on narcotics, and a change in police operational procedures and resources. The latter measures to include increased patrolling, more police, and foot patrols. A much smaller group of respondents feels that the problem of crime goes beyond the police and that there is little that the police can do about it.

In general, the police are viewed by most respondents as providing some level of protection to community residents. Female respondents generally see the police as providing protection in their neighborhood, while males see this function as limited or nonexistent. The vast majority of respondents, both male and female, feel a need for increased protection, while a majority of these want more police in their neighborhood. Contrary to militant rhetoric, almost all respondents perceive the police function to be that of protecting the community, rather than serving as the protectors of special interests.

Most residents sampled are not completely satisfied with the level of protection provided. However, even those who view police protection as highly limited derive some sense of security from present police activity in their community. Respondent dependence upon the police is clearly indicated by their view, with a few exceptions, that crime would increase greatly if the police were withdrawn from the community. Most respondents feel that they could no longer reside in the Western District if there were no police functioning there. Thus, in a community that has been increasingly characterized as hostile to the police, the data show a high level of reliance on and faith in the police to protect community residents.

The data indicate that respondents make a distinction between crime control and protection. Most respondents recognize the difficulty of controlling crime in their community, particularly with the low level of cooperation currently existing between the police and the community. Protection, while related to crime control, is linked by respondents to the visible presence of the police in the community.

Present police patrol techniques in the district are viewed as satisfactory by most respondents. However, over three-fourths of the residents in our sample express a desire for foot patrolmen in their community. In their view this will provide them with increased protection. The use of dogs to patrol the community was not acceptable to a majority of the respondents. However, a large minority (21 of 48) indicate that they are not totally opposed, and some feel that dogs are useful in controlling crime.

The use of special police is becoming relatively common in business establishments and public facilities in the Western District. Most respondents see them as necessary but do not see them as part of the crime control picture in the district.

Police and respondent data reveal a high level of general agreement on a number of topics related to crime control. Among these are the lack of success of present crime control efforts; the reasons for police inability to control crime, particularly the lack of citizen cooperation; the need for more police protection for residents; and the reliance of residents on the police. Areas in which there is less agreement are who is responsible for the lack of citizen cooperation with the police, the need for more police authority and more stringent punishment of criminals, the level of resident hostility toward the police, and the use of police dogs in the community. Police data do not agree with respondent data on the effectiveness of foot patrol as a deterrent to crime.

POLICE-CITIZEN INTERACTION

On the ideal level our respondents view the police role in the community in a law and order frame of reference and most see their main functions to be the crime control, and the protection of residents and the community. However, the operational definition of the police role held by a majority of respondents includes functions not related to crime, and their utilization of the police for a variety of supportive services determines the actual police role in the community.

Police-resident contacts in the Western District are a common occurrence. During the past three years 47 of 50 respondents have had direct and formal contact with the police. A minimum of 90 such contacts took place. The personal characteristics of respondents do not appear to influence whether or not a contact occurs but do affect the type of contact. For example, contacts of a threatening or potentially threatening nature were almost exclusively with lower-class males. Only 18 respondents reported informal contacts with the police during the same time period.

Respondent perception of direct contacts depends upon a variety of factors such as the extent to which their expectations are fulfilled, what occurs during the contact, and their prior experience with the police. Most respondents indicate dissatisfaction with the police response to their requests for service. Of 53 respondent-initiated requests, 31 were termed unsatisfactory. Reasons cited are, in order of frequency, slow police response, the way police handled the case, and the demeanor of the police officer. Dissatisfied respondents are more often young, better-educated residents of middle and upper-middle class areas. Perception of indirect police-citizen contacts, because the respondents are not primary participants, is often based upon incomplete and inaccurate information. Missing elements are generally derived from previous experience and knowledge, and mythology concerning the police.

A sizeable majority of residents sampled indicate that they want more rather than less interaction with the police, and they express a desire for a more personal relationship with the police officers who patrol their neighborhood. The shift from foot patrol to motorized patrol has depersonalized the interaction between residents and the police. Our respondents would like to restore the former relationship and would feel more secure and more comfortable with the presence of foot patrolmen in the community. Apparently residents find it more difficult to anticipate and accommodate to the behavior of the motorized patrolman because their interaction with him is less regular and personal. The depersonalization of police-resident interaction generates anxieties and a less comfortable relationship with the police than existed in the past.

Respondent and police data are in agreement concerning the police role in the community and major police functions. However, these data indicate important differences in the perception of police-resident interaction in general. Among the factors which operate here are differing perceptions of police response time, including what the response time is and whether it is possible to respond more quickly; resident expectations of police action, and what actually occurs during contacts because of legal and operational constraints; and police expectations of resident hostility. Respondent perceptions of the need for more personalized interaction between residents and the police are paralleled in the police data but with less intensity.

POLICE-COMMUNITY RELATIONS

Police-community relations in the Western District are directly influenced by resident perceptions of police behavior and attitudes and by resident interactions with the police. Whether these perceptions are positive or negative is often directly related to the type of experience the resident has had with the police. However, positive experience with the police does not always result in a favorable perception, nor is experience with the police a necessary prerequisite for judging police behavior. Most respondents who see police behavior and attitudes as generally bad have had unsatisfactory contact with the police or witnessed unacceptable police behavior. The opposite was true for almost all respondents who had a positive view of police behavior and attitudes. Further, some respondents with positive police contacts nevertheless had a negative perception.

Most respondents have a generalized perception of the police that is less than favorable. They share an expectation that police will not always behave courteously or impartially in contact with community residents. Almost one-half of our sample (23) view police behavior in the community as unacceptable. These respondents, primarily men, see the police as generally discourteous, prejudiced, not performing their duties properly, or brutal. However, a slightly larger group of respondents (24) do not take such a negative view. Most of this group (13) state that only some police do not behave properly in their interactions with residents while the rest (11) see police behavior as good. Respondents holding an unfavorable perception of police behavior are often ambivalent because of the realization that resident behavior plays a part in "improper" police behavior, and that only some police behave unacceptably. Respondent perceptions of police attitudes parallel those of police behavior.

A majority of respondents (32 of 43 responding) perceive that police behavior has changed during recent years and that these changes have affected police-community relations. Of this group, over half (18) think police behavior has changed for the worse, 10 see it as changed for the better, and four see it as more forceful now, but necessarily so. Those who perceive negative changes ascribe them to diminished interaction between police and residents, primarily as a result of the substitution of motorized patrol for foot patrol (13) and to increased use of force and other means of harassment and intimidation (5). Those who perceive positive changes cite less police prejudice and brutality and better-educated policemen as the reasons. The four other respondents who see more force being used by the police see it resulting from worse resident behavior, hence appropriate. The type of change perceived appears to be related to the age, sex, and education of the respondent.

The relatively high frequency of incidents in which residents resist arrest and assault police officers in the Western District is viewed by many respondents as directly related to the existing perception of relations between the police and community residents. In this view, police behavior in their past and current interactions with community residents very often determines whether a resident resists arrest or submits peacefully. The 20 responses which fall into this category indicate the following as causal factors: the police approach to the resident; police behavior and attitudes; the expectation of police brutality, resentment of police authority, and a lack of respect for the police. On the other hand, 18 respondents view residents rather than the police as usually responsible for resisting arrest. Among the reasons cited are drunkenness, dislike of jail, belief that arrest is unjustified and resentment at being caught. Male respondents more often see the police as responsible in resisting arrest situations, while female respondents more often place the responsibility on the resident. The responses as to why policemen are assaulted were similar to those cited for resisting arrest, both in content and distribution.

The level of physical danger which the police perceive to be associated with the performance of their duties in the community can, and often does, influence their interactions with residents.

Forty of forty-five respondents providing information on this topic believe that it is dangerous to be a police officer in the Western District, and nine of these feel that foot patrolmen should be provided with dogs for their protection. All 40 respondents see the danger as coming from within the community, but only 11 perceive the danger as related to past or present police behavior towards residents. These data vary greatly from those presented on resisting arrest and assaults on police officers, in which a majority of respondents attribute most of these situations to police behavior. Apparently, consideration of the danger associated with policing results in a greater identification with the police role than occurs in considering resisting arrest and assaults on police.

Resident perception of community support for the police is a reflection of the perceived state of police-community relations. Sixty percent of the respondents believe that there is either general or limited support for the police in their neighborhoods, while 40 percent feel that their neighbors will not support the police in any way. Those who indicate general support (17) are not referring to total support but to such specific acts as reporting a crime, assisting an officer in trouble, or both. The respondents who speak of limited support (13) indicate that some of their neighbors will perform the specific acts noted above. Responses indicating no community support for the police (20) indicate a lack of trust and confidence of the police (13), and apathy and fear (7) as the primary reasons.

Race plays a part in the perception that our sample of local residents has of police-community relations and policing in the Western District but not always in the way that is generally believed. Most of our respondents believe that race affects some aspects of policing. Surprisingly, however, very few respondents judge either the entire police force or police operations and procedures in terms of race relations. Most view expressions of race prejudice in police behavior as an individual occurrence rather than a characteristic of the police department in general. The data show that black residents do not necessarily prefer black to white police. Thirty-six of fifty respondents state that they have no racial preference in police officers so long as they perform their duties adequately. Only 14 respondents say that they prefer black officers. When asked about the preferences of other community residents a majority of the respondents (27) still believed that residents had no preference regarding the race of police officers working in their community. Concerning perceived differences between black and white officers in terms of their behavior, the majority of respondents (28) perceive no difference in the behavior of black and white officers towards residents. This group of responses views officers of both races as equally good or equally bad. A minority of respondents (20) see differences in the behavior of officers by race. Twelve respondents believe that black officers have a better understanding of the community and its residents, while eight see black officers as rougher, tougher, or more brutal than white officers. No respondents reported that white police were more brutal than black police.

A comparison of police and resident data on topics related to police-community relations reveals many similarities and some differences. Both police and residents agree that modifications in behavior are required to improve relations between police and residents. Although both groups recognize that internal changes are necessary, the police view changes in resident behavior as most important, while most respondents stress changes in police behavior. Both police and respondents agree that changes in police behavior have occurred during the past several years and that these changes have had both positive and negative effects on police-community relations. Most interesting here is agreement that motorization of patrol has had a negative effect. However, over 25 percent of those responding do not perceive any changes in police behavior, and 21 percent see a greater use of force than in the past. These views are contrary to those expressed by the police. Respondent data support the police perception that they have only limited resident support, that policing in the Western District is a dangerous job, and that prejudiced behavior by police is an individual rather than an institutional phenomenon. Police and respondents are in general agreement concerning the causes of citizen violence against the police, with the exception that many respondents attribute it to the perceived state of relations between the police and residents, while many police do not. Respondent data support the general police point of view that residents perceive police as police, i.e. "blue," rather than in racial terms. Most respondents express no racial preference and see no difference in the behavior of black and white officers. Beyond this point there is less agreement. Black officers believe that they better understand the community and its residents. One in four respondents also express this view. Many white officers believe that residents prefer white officers because they are not as rough and brutal. Eight respondents support this belief with reference to behavior, but not necessarily with regard to resident preferences.

PERCEPTIONS OF FORCE AND BRUTALITY

The vast majority of our sample of local residents (84 percent) believe that force is a necessary ingredient of police work in the Western District.[3] However, a majority of respondents (60 percent) also believe that the police use force unnecessarily on occasion. Despite this majority perception over half of the respondents report that they have never witnessed aggressive police behavior that was inappropriate to the situation. When the definition of force is shifted from aggressive behavior to the use of physical force (i.e. guns, clubs, or fists) only a minority of respondents (46 percent) perceive that the police occasionally use excessive force. Less than 20 percent of those interviewed (predominatly males) said they had personally experienced or directly observed police brutality; but a larger group (46 percent) believes that such behavior occurs.

The willingness of those who have not had relevant, direct experience to believe that the police are currently overly aggressive or brutal can be ascribed to factors which operate to structure their perceptions in this area. These include historical factors (e.g. past police behavior) ; the mass media, which highlight examples of forceful police behavior; black militant propaganda; and oral communication which incorporates the factors cited

---

[3]The definition of force used by these respondents equates force with aggressive behavior. Thus, for them, force is that broad range of aggressive behavior from verbal abuse and a forceful presence to rough handling and the use of weapons.

above and the direct experience of other community residents with the police.

A substantial proportion of our respondents (and by extension of the Western District population) believe that the police use unnecessary force of various types. This belief has a direct effect upon resident expectations of police behavior and an adverse effect upon police-citizen interaction.

Police data agree with respondent views concerning the need to use force in police work, and the occasional use of unnecessary force of various types in the Western District. The police data disagree, however, concerning the frequency with which force is used inappropriately. This difference in perspective is due, among other things, to the use of different criteria to evaluate the appropriate use of force; differing definitions of force; the different roles of the respective groups; and, the amount of direct relevant experience with the application of force which exists within each of the groups.

POLICE-COMMUNITY RELATIONS PROBLEMS

Our data indicate perceived areas of conflict and hostility between community residents and police in the Western District. However, they also show a fair amount of open goodwill towards the police, and a great deal of ambivalence about how bad the police actually are. A majority of respondents indicate that some aspects of policing arouse complaints from community residents. At the same time most respondents indicate that such complaints are often generalizations and not necessarily the fault of the police, and also that the police are sometimes falsely accused. The most frequent complaint cited is that the police are not present when needed. Only ten respondents feel that complaints alleging police brutality have some justification. Few respondents have ever made a formal complaint against a police officer or know anyone who has. Most are not aware of how and to whom one makes a formal complaint. While most respondents feel that there are some justified reasons for complaining about the police, very few express any real concern.

A majority of those responding believe that the present complaint review procedure will not result in a fair hearing of complaints against police officers, and that no action will be taken on complaints. Men generally distrust the procedure and often express the view that it should be partially or totally handled by non-police personnel. Women, on the other hand, more often express confidence in the procedure and a willingness to have it remain within the police department.

Our data do not support the view that community control of police, or black officers in the black community, are necessary preconditions for resolution of existing problems between police and residents. Only four respondents suggest community control as a way to improve police-community relations, and only one suggests black officers as a solution. The vast majority of respondents see improved police-community relations coming about through increased two-way interaction and cooperation between residents and the police.

Several important differences are apparent between police and respondent data. The residents sampled perceive that complaints against police officers are relatively unimportant and ineffective in modifying police behavior, while the police data indicate that the opposite is true. Further, respondent data do not support the points presented in police data concerning widespread resident knowledge of the complaint review procedure and the inhibiting effects of police counteraction on the filing of citizen complaints against police officers.

APPROPRIATE POLICE BEHAVIOR

A large majority of the residents sampled are able to specify the characteristics of a good policeman. The major criteria used in characterizing appropriate police behavior are related to police-citizen interaction. These include courtesy and respectful behavior towards community residents, the ability to relate to residents and to interact skillfully with them, and knowledge and understanding of the community and events occurring within it. Many respondents believe that better police training can improve police performance in areas that residents consider important, e.g. self-discipline and restraint, understanding of residents, and fair and objective treatment of citizens.

A majority of responses indicate the belief that most police do not now behave appropriately in the Western District, but a sizable minority (45 percent) express the opposite view. As on other topics, males are more critical of police behavior than females. Our respondents see more courteous and respectful behavior, and better police training as the way to make police behavior more acceptable to the community.

There is broad general agreement between police and respondent data concerning the characteristics of a good policeman. However, there is also a considerable difference in emphasis in such areas as courtesy, training, and the need for qualities related to the physical aspects of policing. Both sets of data indicate an awareness of the divergence between ideal police behavior and the reality situation, and both attribute it, at least in part, to resident and police behavior.

ILLEGAL AND UNDESIRABLE POLICE BEHAVIOR

Our data indicate that most respondents suspect some police involvement in the illegal activities which exist in the Western District. However, these suspicions do not necessarily detract from either the perceived effectiveness of the police or the image of the police force, because it is believed that only a limited number of individual officers are involved in illegal behavior. Few respondents see it as a major problem for the community.

Most respondents believe that a small number of police officers are involved in illegal activities, e.g. gambling, numbers, and narcotics. By far the largest number of these respondents see police involvement as limited to accepting payoffs; only a few accuse the police of more extensive involvement, e.g. participation in and/or backing of criminal activities. This belief concerning police corruption is based primarily on indirect evidence or no evidence at all. Only a small number of respondents claim direct knowledge of police involvement. A large majority, however, base their belief upon hearsay or suspicion. Those respondents who claim neither direct knowledge nor hearsay evidence base their suspicions of police corruption on mass media accounts of corrupt officers, the continuing high crime rate in the face of presumed police knowledge, and a belief in the basic weakness of human nature. All respondents who believe the police are involved in corruption view it as detrimental, but few see corruption as a major reason for police inability to control crime.

A majority of respondents also believe that a limited number of police officers engage in various forms of misconduct. Fewer respondents see the police involved in such behavior than in corruption. Respondent beliefs concerning corruption are based primarily on hearsay and suspicion, while those related to misconduct are based upon specific incidents witnessed by the respondent. Thirty-one respondents reported 36 incidents which they perceive as police misconduct, neglect of duty, or dishonesty. These incidents range from wasting time, lying in court, and drinking on duty to accepting money for not issuing traffic tickets and demanding payoffs from hackers. Respondents view these incidents as inappropriate or dishonest behavior rather than police corruption. Most view them as minor offenses and some do not view them as offenses at all.

CONCLUSIONS

1. Residents are aware of and greatly concerned about the high level of crime which exists in their community. Many fear for their personal safety on the streets, particularly at night, and they identify the criminal element primarily as indigenous lower-class youth.

2. Few respondents see crime as the result of oppression by the larger society. A large proportion view both the causes and solutions to the crime problem to lie within the community. They emphasize poor home environment and a lack of parental control as key causal factors and advocate related measures as solutions. Poverty resulting from unemployment and underemployment, and a lack of constructive alternatives for youth, are also perceived as directly related to the crime problem and its solution.

3. Despite ambivalence and disapproval of some police behavior, most residents in our sample have a basically positive

orientation toward the police. The widespread hostility against the police which is generally believed to exist in the black community is not supported by the data. Almost all respondents perceive the function of the police to be protection of the community and its residents, rather than the protection of special interests. Most respondents want more police in their community, rather than less, and they derive a sense of security and well being from the police presence. Even the use of police dogs, which is generally believed to be totally unacceptable to the black community, was opposed by only a bare majority of respondents.

4. The level of hostility towards the police generally believed to exist in the black community is most closely approximated among the younger male residents who are a minority of our sample. Male respondents under 40 are as a group consistently more hostile to the police and more critical of their activities and behavior than are female respondents or older respondents of either sex. This was true on virtually every topic examined during the study.

5. The majority of residents in our sample want more rather than less interaction with the police officers who patrol their neighborhoods, and they want this interaction to be more personalized and reciprocal than it is at present. The evidence for this conclusion is quite strong. The overwhelming respondent desire for the return of foot patrol is based, to a great extent, on their wish to reestablish the kind of relationship which existed before the motorization of patrol resulted in the depersonalization of police-citizen interaction. In their discussion of the characteristics of a good policeman, respondents stress the ability to relate to residents and interact with them, and knowledge and understanding of the community and its residents. Further, the majority of respondents see improved police-community relations coming about through increased interaction between residents and the police.

6. The need to increase resident cooperation with the police is perceived as a key problem area by the majority of residents sampled. Most respondents perceive police efforts to control crime in the community to be ineffective. However, they ascribe police

ineffectiveness to a lack of citizen cooperation. Greater police involvement in the community is viewed by many as necessary to secure greater citizen cooperation with the police.

7. Most respondents have a generalized perception of police behavior towards residents that is less than favorable. They share an expectation that the police may not always behave acceptably in contacts with residents. This perception, which appears to be based partly on experience and partly on beliefs concerning police behavior and attitudes, affects the nature of resident-police interaction and citizen cooperation with the police. However, a substantial minority of respondents view negative interaction between police and residents to be the result of resident behavior, rather than of police behavior.

More acceptable police behavior can only partially modify the majority's negative perception of police behavior towards residents because the beliefs underlying the perception are not necessarily based upon experience, and their existence to some extent determines whether police-resident contacts will be positive or not.

8. Few respondents evaluate the police and their operations and behavior primarily in terms of race or race relations. Thus, the data do not support the widely prevalent conceptions of the importance of race in police-community relations in the black community. Our conclusions in this content area are:

a. Most respondents view racially-prejudiced police behavior as the behavior of individual officers and do not generalize it to all white police officers or to the police department as a whole.

b. Black residents do not necessarily prefer black police officers. Most respondents express no racial preference, but stress satisfactory job performance in the black community.

c. A majority of respondents perceive little difference in the behavior of white and black officers towards community residents. The minority does see differences, but not all of these are unfavorable to white officers.

9. Changes in police behavior in the Western District during the past five years are perceived as changes for the worse by a

majority of respondents. This is true despite technological changes in police operations to provide more timely and efficient service to community residents, and modification of police behavior to make it more acceptable to the community. The major cause of this negative perception is the motorization of patrol with attendant changes in police-citizen interaction patterns. If not for this cause, a majority would view changes in police behavior positively because many note less discourtesy, less prejudice, and less force and brutality now than in the past.

10. A substantial proportion of our respondents believe that the police use unnecessary force on occasion despite the fact that they have neither experienced nor witnessed the inappropriate use of force by the police. This negative perception which derives from historical factors, the mass media, hearsay, and ideological orientations, has a negative effect on police-citizen interactions. It establishes expectations of inappropriate police behavior and affects resident behavior in these interactions.

11. The majority of respondents do not consider the existing police department complaint review procedure to be an important problem area, despite their belief that it will not result in a fair hearing or appropriate action on citizen complaints against police officers. However, a majority of our sample appears satisfied to have the process remain under the exclusive control of the police department.

12. A majority of the residents sampled believe that some police officers are involved in the illegal activities which exist in the community and in other forms of misconduct. Because such behavior is believed to involve only a small number of officers, it is not perceived as a major problem affecting overall police effectiveness or the police image in the community.

13. There is a broad base of common perception and opinion among a majority of residents sampled and the police, which can serve as a foundation for action programs directed toward improving police-community relations and police effectiveness in the black community. Police and respondent data show a surprising level of agreement on most of the content areas studied, at least insofar as a majority of residents are concerned. The data indicate

almost identical views on a large number of topics, and a difference in emphasis on many others. There are, of course, some content areas on which there is marked disagreement between the police and residents. These, which are far fewer than the areas of agreement, are also most important for action programs because they will constitute the more difficult program areas from the point of view of planning and implementation. However, it is quite possible that successful handling of areas of agreement will establish a climate of opinion which makes problem resolution in the areas of disagreement less difficult.

14. The data indicate the existence of a sizable minority within the Western District population whose perceptions of the police and police activities and behavior differ markedly from those of the majority. This minority, which seems to be comprised mainly of males under 40 years of age, generally has a strong negative perception of the police and their behavior in the community. It is among this group, which is quite large in absolute terms, that one finds the greatest concentration of negative contacts with the police.

Here one finds a wide divergence of opinion between police and respondent data, and very little in common upon which to build action programs to improve police-community relations. Quite obviously, the previously discussed majority and the minority discussed here represent discrete target groups for police-community relations action programs. Each group will require programs which are significantly different in approach and program content, and quite different results must be anticipated.

SECTION V

SPECIALIZED INNOVATION
IN TRAINING

INTRODUCTION

The methods of clinical psychology and psychiatry have only recently found their way into police training programs. Crisis intervention, counseling techniques, group training methods, and conflict resolution models have all become standard words and methods in many urban police departments. There is little doubt that these methods will contribute significantly to the re-evaluation of the role of police officers and hopefully their effectiveness in violence prevention.

Bard's article represents the philosophical justification of newer roles for policemen. The possibility that police might have a role in dealing with crisis in a meaningful way will probably continue to be an issue for debate for several years to come.

Liebman and Schwartz offer a review of programs designed to train officers in appropriate methods of crisis intervention. The data seem to indicate that such specialized training of police officers yields significant reductions in violence against and by police.

Han Tochs' report on the Oakland project is now a classic in the field of police science. It represents the first systematic attempt to alter patterns of behavior that for years had been seen essential in police work.

The Danish and Ferguson project reports a study in personal awareness of police officers and the effects of such awareness on interpersonal relationships of the officers.

Bieliauskas and Hellkamp present data on long experience in working with police. They also discuss how to deal with departments and overcome common problems.

Chapter 20

THE ROLE OF LAW ENFORCEMENT IN THE HELPING SYSTEM

Morton Bard

IT IS ONE OF THE IRONIES of social existence that the greatest progress often occurs at times of greatest social unrest. Indeed, it is the threat of violence that is frequently the most powerful force to promote change in the institutions of society. History attests to the fact that the most dramatic technological advances in science and industry have occurred during periods when our nation was imperiled by war. There is little question that when "under the gun" we are able to marshal our resources, we can reappraise our priorities, and we can alter our institutions to enhance survival as a social order.

Today, threats of violence are legion—not so much from without but from within our society. And the crucial question is, "Are we prepared to undertake critical appraisal of our institutions and alter them to insure survival?" If the past is prologue, we will. The signs are already evident that the necessary changes are taking place, even if haltingly.

Two institutions are currently in the forefront of social reappraisal: law enforcement and academe. It is hardly accidental that these two should be paired at this time in history. Both play critical roles with respect to the internal harmony of society: one primarily by thought, the other primarily by action; the one given to change; the other committed to the *status quo*. Unfortunately, both have failed to adapt to rapidly changing conditions. The simplistic notion of the police as a repressive force in the defense of property is no more viable today than is the naive notion that the university is a medieval cloister given to abstract thought far

Reprinted from *Community Mental Health Journal*, June, 1971 and with permission of the author.

removed from the realities of everyday life. As a consequence of adhering to outmoded functional concepts, both institutions find themselves increasingly remote from those they serve and decreasingly effective in fulfilling their primary missions.

Perhaps the key issue for both of these institutions lies in their failure to acknowledge present-day realities. Much of the university's prime function is regarded as irrelevant today. There seems to be less and less tolerance for abstract research exercises which do not contribute to the world of real people. A similar charge of irrelevance is directed at law enforcement. There is increasingly less tolerance for police behavior patterned after the Hollywood-reinforced stereotype of the tight-lipped, gun-slinging frontier marshal.

There was a time when the myth of academic intellectual purity excluded practical application of knowledge in much the same way that law enforcement tended to reject all functions but those based upon force. But each institution has had to confront its own myths. The university did so initially by incorporating elements of the practical in science and technology, creating schools of engineering and agriculture; later, medical colleges, schools of social work and schools of education were added to the array of interests which could be said to serve the community without compromising the university's mission to extend the horizons of knowledge. The university accepted its responsibility in the preparation of society's professional helpers. Interestingly, save for rare exceptions, the university ignored the education of one of the most direct helpers in society. . .the police. It is the thesis of this presentation that our present national crisis makes it imperative that law enforcement be acknowledged as a participating profession in the helping system. To do so will mark our maturation toward progress and responsibility. There is no better barometer of the state of any society than the state of its law enforcement.

Recent changes in the helping system have created a particularly favorable climate for embracing the police as appropriate participants. Increasing population density, growing economic inequities and ever greater complexity and alienation have caused helping institutions to examine some of *their* myths. Selectivity in the delivery of services, organizational inadequacies and other givens of the "helping game" have suddenly become irrelevant (that word again). Agencies with long traditions of helping in particular ways have found their hallowed methods under attack. The pressure for change has grown increasingly insistent . . . the call for revolution, more strident. It is a never ceasing source of wonder that this kind of social unrest succeeds in bringing about the adaptive changes which, in the end, make for a better society.

The goals of the university, law enforcement, and the helping system can be said to converge at the issue of relevance. When one examines the point of convergence, one is struck by how naturally congenial they are. One is prompted to exclaim, "Why, of course—how simple! Why wasn't it seen before?" It is suggested here that, like certain distant planets, their communallity could not be seen until all conditions were in harmony. Ironically enough, it is at this time of social disharmony that conditions seem best for the incorporation of the police as full participating professional members of the helping system.

At this point, it must be emphasized strongly that there is no intention here to minimize the primary peace-keeping function of the police. The police officer's first responsibilities are to enforce the law and to maintain order. This is a "given" in every known society. But there is ample evidence[2,3,6,7,12] that in the United States between 80 and 90 percent of a policeman's daily activity in rural, suburban, and urban areas involves maintenance of order as distinct from law enforcement. Wilson pointed out that:

> The vast majority of police actions taken in response to citizen calls involve either providing a service (getting a cat out of a tree or taking a person to the hospital) or managing real or alleged conditions of disorder (quarreling families, public drunks, bothersome teen-agers, noisy cars, tavern fights). Only a small fraction of these calls involve law enforcement such as checking on a prowler, catching a burglar in the act or preventing a street robbery.[13]

Wilson's distinction between order maintenance and law enforcement is a crucial one.

> The difference between order maintenance and law enforcement is not simply the difference between "little stuff" and "real crime." The

distinction is fundamental to the police role, for the two functions involve quite dissimilar police actions and judgments. Order maintenance arises out of a dispute among citizens who accuse each other of being at fault; law enforcement arises out of the victimization of an innocent party by a person whose guilt must be proved. . . .Because an arrest cannot be made in most disorderly cases, the officer is expected to handle the situation by other means and on the spot, but the law gives him no guidance on how he is to do this; indeed, the law often denies him the right to do anything at all other than make an arrest . . . .Alone, unsupervised, with no policies to guide him and little sympathy from onlookers to support him, the officer must "administer justice" at the curbstone.[13]

The helping system has virtually ignored the implications of that aspect of the policeman's function which Wilson calls maintenance of order. This is made particularly striking by the fact that the police in every community have been functioning as social and mental health agencies by virtue of their order maintenance function. Instantly available 24 hours of each day (unlike other helpers, who operate between the hours of nine and five and not on weekends), they come when called (eliminating the frustrating delays of waiting lists and return visits) and they do something (unlike the typical verbal abstractions of the usual "planned intervention").

The "something" policemen "do," however, is the centrally crucial issue. The police establishment is not geared to recognizing the validity of order maintenance as "real" police work. Like the rest of society, the institution recognizes and rewards the quick draw on main street as the prototype of police excellence. It is loathe to acknowledge service functions, one suspects, because compassion and helping might in some way tarnish the masculine mystique of law enforcement. However, this institutional insensitivity to the "order maintenance"function of police work has been costly indeed. Recently, the FBI reported that 22 percent of policemen killed in the line of duty nationally were slain while intervening in disturbances such as family disputes (4). Estimates of time lost because of injuries sustained in the line of duty indicate that about 40 percent occur in the same way.

It is therefore more than curious that there has been so little interest by society in the policeman's helping role. Indeed, this is particularly striking when one compares society's investment in the helper most like him. . .the physician. There are no other two professionals in the helping system whose identities and responsibilities approximate each other so much. The physician is an authority with the power of life and death in situations which involve physical disorder. The policeman, on the other hand, is an authority with the power of life and death in situations of social disorder. And yet, the average physician receives a minimum of 11,000 hours of training to prepare him for his role; the average policeman receives less than 200 hours of training to prepare him for his.[5]

There are undoubtedly many factors which contribute to the disparity in training. But in view of the escalation of social disorder, it is highly questionable that society can continue to ignore the extensive ramifications of the range of functions subsumed under the rubric of law enforcement. Perhaps the time has come for the kind of creative collaboration between law enforcement and the academic-professional communities which would maximize the potentials of the police as acknowledged members of the helping professions.

For almost two years now an experimental program has been in operation which may serve as a model for demonstrating the potentials inherent in police-helping system collaboration. The program has shown the mutual distrust of both institutions can be minimized while they cooperate to serve the community more effectively. What is more, the collaboration permitted each agency to remain faithful to its own primary mission. For the police. . . enhancement of its law enforcement and order maintenance mission; for the university. . .the education of helping professionals (in this instance, clinical psychologists), research, and community service. Impetus for the program was derived from a number of sources: increasing crime rates, increasing violence and aggression, worsening police-community relations, and increasing social and professional pressure for innovation in preventive mental health.

The President's Commission on Law Enforcement and Administration of Justice commented on a phenomenon well known to every policeman:

A great majority of the situations in which policemen intervene are not, or are not interpreted by the police to be, criminal situations in that they call for an arrest. . . .A common kind of situation. . . is the matrimonial dispute, which police experts estimate consumes as much time as any other kind of situation.[13]

The program to be described was designed to deal with this social reality. Crime statistics indicate that between 35 and 50 percent of all homicide victims in the United States are related to their killers and that in fewer than 20 percent of the cases are homicide victims and perpetrator complete strangers. It is apparent from these startling figures that family crisis intervention offered unlimited experimental and preventive prospects.

The psychological helping professions have become increasingly disenchanted with traditional methods of diagnosis and treatment. Not only are their methods found wanting in themselves, but they seem to have lessening social impact as the demand for psychological services quickly outdistances manpower resources. Prevention appears to offer the greatest promise of relief. The project in police family crisis intervention embodies principles of at least three distinct tracks of mental health theory and research: (1) the training of the frontline mental health workers; (2) the role of the family in determining disordered behavior; and (3) preventive crisis intervention.

As Reiff and Riessman[8] and Rioch[10] have demonstrated, indigenous mental health aides can effectively extend the social impact of the highly-trained professional. There appears little question that intelligent laymen can be trained to render effective mental health services under supervision. In such an approach, the highly-trained supervisor does little direct service but instead influences the functioning of those he supervises, thus extending the effects of his education and experience. We proposed the selection and training of a group of policemen to serve in the capacity of indigenous mental health personnel *in the course of their regular police duties.* This was based on the supported contention that policemen were already engaged in quasi-mental health roles and that specific training would simply enhance their effectiveness in doing what they were already doing.

And so, a program was conceived which embodied crime prevention and preventive mental health principles—but, more important perhaps, afforded a research framework within the psychological and social matrix of a living community. . .an opportunity to explore a variety of hypotheses regarding the natural history of aggression. Most important, perhaps, was the design of a model for the utilization of policemen as primary crisis intervention agents.[1]*

Briefly, 18 police officers were selected from among 45 volunteers. Because the community surrounding the campus (west Harlem) is largely Black, the design called for the selection of nine White and nine Black patrolmen who were to be paired interracially. No effort was made to induce participation except for the offer of three college credits. Selection was based upon evidence of motivation and aptitude for family crisis intervention and a minimum of three years' experience as patrolmen to insure sufficient skill in police work.

For the entire month following selection, the men were released from all duties to engage in an intensive training program which included lectures, workshops, field trips and a unique opportunity to "learn by doing." Three Family Crisis Laboratory Demonstrations involved the enactment of specially written plays by professional actors in which the patrolmen intervened in pairs. The value of the experience was to enable the men to see how different interventions could produce different outcomes. All the practice interventions were subjected to extensive critique and reviewed by all members of the unit. The intensive training also included human relations workshops which helped sensitize the men to their own values and attitudes about disrupted families.

After the month of intensive training, the Family Crisis Intervention Unit began its current operational phase. For a two-year period, one radio car is designated for use by the Unit and is dispatched on all complaints which can be predetermined as involving "family disturbance." A special duty chart permits 24-hour-a-day coverage by men of the Unit in a circumscribed experimental area of about 85,000 people.

*This project was supported in part by the Office of Law Enforcement Assistance, U.S. Department of Justice, Grant #157; the New York City Police Department and The City College, The City University of New York.

The men have continued their training by appearing on campus in groups of six for discussions with a professional group leader each week. In addition, each man has an individual consultation with an advanced graduate student in clinical psychology who uses the experience to enhance his own training as a mental health consultant.

Finally, the project will undergo evaluation to determine if, indeed, the method reduces the number of homicides, suicides and assaults in the demonstration area. Comparable data are being collected in a neighboring precinct which does not have the services of a specially-trained unit.

Since being operational, the Family Crisis Unit has engaged in more than 1,400 interventions with more than 900 different families. In addition, the men of the Unit have performed all routine police duties on a par with the men of their command. However, despite the high hazard work involved in family crisis intervention, *there has been only a single minor injury* sustained by one member of the Unit. During the same period, three patrolmen not trained in family crisis intervention have sustained injury in domestic disturbances.

While conclusions based upon the method described will have to await final evaluation, preliminary findings are beginning to serve as a basis for speculation. For example, the remarkable absence of injury to a group of officers exposed in the extreme to dangerous and highly volatile aggressive situations strongly suggests the importance of the role played by the victim in the exacerbation of violence. Recently Sarbin characterized danger as connoting *a relationship,* pointing out that assaultive or violent behavior which leads to the designation *dangerous* can be understood as the predictable outcome of certain antecedent and concurrent conditions. . .among these conditions are degredation procedures which transform a man's social identity.[11]

Sarbin develops the notion that social identity is formed out of role-relationships and that individuals who do not meet minimal social expectations may be classified as "brutes" or as "nonpersons," or, to put it another way, are deprived of their social identity. By the nature of his work, a policeman is always ready to classify conduct as potentially dangerous. The officer's negative valuation of the other person in the power relationship may entail degrading behavior toward those he classifies as "non-persons." Indeed, the officer may even engage in premature power display, thus further provoking the untrusted "non-person" to behave as the expected "wild beast." In this connection, the conclusion may be drawn that the dangerous person may, in large measure, then be the outcome of the very institutions we have created to control him. In a Mertonian sense, the self-fulfilled prophecy.

It may be that the officers engaged in our project, through their sensitivity training, have avoided premature power displays and have eschewed classifying people as "non-persons" and hence have avoided potentiating danger and violence directed at *them*. Perhaps an illustration will clarify the concept as it occurred in our "laboratory" for the study of aggression. After repeated family difficulty, yet always reluctant to summon the police, in desperation a Black family requested assistance. Two members of our unit responded, took appropriate action, and started to leave the apartment. The White patrolman went out the door and his Black partner was about to follow when the lady of the house asked him to stay a moment. She described previous difficulties and spoke of her reluctance to summon aid before—because of her fear of the kind of treatment she might receive. "Finally," she said, "we called for help and the first one through the door was your partner. I looked at that White man and said to myself, 'Now we've had it!' " "But," she said, looking squarely at the officer, "I want you to know how much it meant to us that he and you treated us as a family and treated my husband *like a man.*" This illustrates how the men of the unit may avoid making negative valuations which transform individuals to the status of non-persons and so do not also engage in premature power displays which provoke danger and violence. Indeed, the Family Crisis Intervention Unit's performance in this regard has been acknowledged in the recent Report of the National Advisory Commission on Civil Disorders. Taking note of domestic disputes as precursors to violence, the report included the project as a recommendation.[9]

This project has many implications; space permits touching upon only a few. If there is a single most significant element in our approach, it is that we have managed to avoid role identity confusion in our officers. Throughout the project, every effort was made to avoid giving the men the notion that they were functioning in any way other than as police officers. Their professional identities were respected and preserved and, indeed, constantly reinforced. The members of the unit never lost sight of their primary objective: restoring and maintaining the peace. Our view, and theirs, was that their insight and training served to enhance their performance as policemen.

This aspect of the experience has been paramount, perhaps because it highlighted one of the greatest pitfalls in mental health community consultation. Most community consultants succeed in confusing the role identity of their consultees. Undoutedly, many of you have witnessed the consequences of this. . .most notably in the field of education. Well-meaning consultation programs in the schools almost universally succeed in confusing the classroom teacher. Before very long, the teacher is not quite sure about whether she is a teacher or whether she is a psychotherapist. It may be that pride and conscience endow many consultants with a subtle form of proselytizing enthusiasm which only serves to confuse the consultee. Awareness of the problems of role identity confusion must be regarded as a keystone in the mental health consultation process.

The validity of the concept of utilizing as mental health resources those individuals already in the psychological front-lines needs no further emphasis here. What should be underscored, however, is the importance of identifying those in society who are in this front-line role. Mental health personnel typically move *in safe social sub-systems*. The most popular is the educational sub-system; working through that institution is usually justified by the claim that the child is father to the man and as such represents the best of all preventive possibilities. While this may be true in part, it may not be the real reason for investing so much effort in the schools. A more subtle reason may be that the educational sub-system is more familiar, more comfortable, and hence *safer* for the mental health professional. The school establishment is well-travelled ground and requires little re-orientation. Not so in other subsystems. The police establishment, for example, is a subsystem as remote from the world of mental health professionals as it is possible to be. And, as such, it is regarded as uncomfortable and, in a way, unsafe. There are many subsystems which offer unusual and creative opportunities for extending preventive mental health principles. They exist, however, outside of the safety of the schools and of the hospitals and the like; they exist in abundance elsewhere in the community. They represent the real challenge in preventive mental health, but it remains for us to search them out and use them effectively.

Aside from service potentials and fulfilling the objectives of prevention, such approaches open a wide range of research possibilities. The world of people as seen through the eyes of those in unfamiliar subsystems can only enlarge and add dimension to our knowledge of human behavior. For example, in our police family crisis intervention program, we expect to learn a great deal about the social psychology of aggression—not in the context of the scientifically pure experimental laboratory, but in the pulsating, real-life laboratory that every community represents. We already have some preliminary data with interesting implications in tracing the epidemiology of the family fight. We should be able to trace hourly, daily and even seasonal trends in the frequency of family fights requiring police intervention. We already have some basis for questioning the commonly held conviction that Friday night (pay day) is the time of greatest incidence. Our preliminary data indicate that there is indeed a peaking on Friday night but that it maintains the same level on Saturday night, and, even more surprisingly, all day Sunday and into Sunday night. Also, interestingly, there is a precipitous drop in incidence on Monday and Tuesday, with a slight building from then to the first peak on Friday. This all may be more suggestive of increasing tension as the dreaded weekend of togetherness approaches, while the dramatic drop on Monday perhaps is related to the opportunity for "getting away" from one's "loved ones."

Typical of the kinds of clinical hypotheses to be tested is a study now being prepared which will involve a representative sample of children from among the families served by the unit.

For a long time there has been endless debate regarding, and laboratory experimentation on, stimulus threshold in aggression. We now have the opportunity to identify and study young children actually raised in an atmosphere of violence and aggression in order to understand the effects of such early experiences on subsequent development and the quality of aggression.

We also have an opportunity to discover whether there is a homicidel signal emitted by the person who ultimately kills, just as the suicide repeatedly cries for help. Do frequent and repeated requests for police intervention in family fights presage a fatal outcome? Do individuals know that they will kill and ask, in this way, to be stopped? From the statistics on homicide and intimacy, there is a suggestion that such may be the case.

Or what role does alcohol play in murderous and assaultive behavior within the family? Are there certain styles of family interaction which are characteristic? Can we develop an assault or homicide index? These are only a few of the questions to which we hope to find answers.

The family crisis project with the New York City Police Department is The Psychological Center's first venture into serving the mental health needs of the community by collaborating with existing community institutions. Others are in the planning or funding stages. For example, we are currently awaiting funding for a project proposal prepared jointly by The Center and the New York City Fire Department. This two-stage project will attempt to understand and modify a very recent and particularly destructive kind of urban behavior—harassment of fire fighters and the increasing rate of false alarms of fire.

If The Psychological Center does its job properly, however, it should terminate its collaboration, leaving the cooperating institution with capacities and insights it did not have before. An exciting spinoff of the police family project is the promise it holds for a new structuring of police organizations. Typically, police departments follow the specialist model. Individual police officers are assigned to highly specialized tasks, e.g. traffic control, emergency services, community relations, youth detail, etc. The officer so assigned performs his specialized function to the exclusion of generalized law enforcement. But, unfortunately, that approach has had results with which specialists in other fields are only too familiar—psychiatrists, for example. The specialist officer is quickly regarded by his fellows as no longer a "real cop" and, following a fundamental biological principle, he is rejected as a foreign body. What is more, the public also views the behavior of the police specialist as not being typical of the police in general.

Our project suggests the viability of the generalist-specialist model of police patrol. It would entail utilizing the special talents and interests of each patrolman, while at the same time having each perform over-all patrol duties. The unit operating as family crisis intervention specialists patrol as do all other members of their command but are available within their precinct area whenever a family disturbance occurs. The same approach might be taken in relation to youth disorders, alcoholics, attempted suicides, or psychotics. It is too much to expect that every policeman should have specialized capacities in relation to the enormous range of human problems. It does make sense, however, to assume that a patrolman with special proclivities in managing a psychotic may not be so well suited to managing a group of unruly adolescents. . .or vice versa. What is more, the public is exposed to police whose behavior is consistent with special capacity and special training, thus vastly improving their impressions of the police. If the public attitude toward police is to improve, it won't be because of highly-touted community relations gimmickery, but because policemen are handling their order-maintenance functions with skill, understanding and compassion. If professionalism is to occur in law enforcement, it will be necessary to modify outmoded organizational structures which are no longer relevant in today's complex society.

These remarks have seemed to focus on the issue of relevance. It is perhaps one of the most fortunate characteristics of the current scene that so many of our institutions are questioning organizational structural forms which have clearly become irrelevant. In the last analysis, relevancy is probably the benchmark of adaptation. If we are to change and continue to grow, we must constantly question the relevancy of what we do. In these comments, the measure has been taken of the helping system, of the academic-professional community, and of law enforcement.

These three social institutions share more in common at this time in history than could ever have been thought possible even a short time ago. Perhaps we can take solace in these troublesome times in the thought that our national crisis may produce the kind of synthesis from among the three that is bound to make for a better society.

REFERENCES

1. Bard, M. and Berkowitz, B.: Training police as specialists in family crisis intervention: a community psychology action program. *Community Mental Health Journal, 3,* 1967, 315-317.
2. Cumming, Elaine, Cumming, Ian, and Edel, Laura: Policeman as philosopher, guide and friend. *Social Problems, 17,* 1965, 276-286.
3. Epstein, Charlotte: *Intergroup Relations for Police Officers.* Baltimore, Williams and Wilkins Company, 1962.
4. *FBI Law Enforcement Bulletin,* January 1963, p. 27.
5. Lipset, S.M.: Why cops hate liberals and vice versa. *Atlantic Monthly,* March, 1969, 76-83.
6. McCann, R., director, Chicago Police Department Training Division. Personal communication .
7. McCloskey, C.C. Jr., Executive Director, Division of Police Administration Services, Office for Local Government, State of New York. Personal communication.
8. Reiff, and Riessman, F.: *The Indigenous Non-Professional: A Strategy of Change in Community Action and Community Mental Health Programs.* U.S. Dept. of Health, Education and Welfare, Report No. 3, November, 1964.
9. *Report of the National Advisory Commission on Civil Disorders.* Bantam Books, 1968.
10. Rioch, M. et al.: National Institute of Mental Health pilot study in training mental health counselors. *American Journal of Orthopsychiatry, 33,* 1963, 678-689.
11. Sarbin, T.: The dangerous individual: an outcome of social identity transformations. *British Journal of Criminology,* July 1967, 285-295.
12. Wilson, J. Q.: *Variety of Police Behavior.* Cambridge, Harvard University Press, 1968.
13. Wilson, J.Q.: What makes a better policeman. *Atlantic Monthly,* March, 1969, 129-135.

Chapter 21

POLICE PROGRAMS IN DOMESTIC CRISIS INTERVENTION: A REVIEW

Donald A. Liebman and Jeffrey A. Schwartz

THE PAST FIVE years have witnessed the development and implementation of a rapidly increasing number of police programs in the area of domestic crisis intervention. As of 1966, no law enforcement agency in the nation had a training program in this area despite the fact that between 5 to 10 percent of an urban policeman's assignments might involve domestic disputes; as of 1971, at least fourteen law enforcement agencies have conducted training in crisis intervention and dozens more are making plans for training in the near future.

What is domestic crisis intervention and why has it become a major police function? Broadly defined, it is the assistance of an independent agent to parties having some problem or dispute that demands immediate attention. In the case when the police officer is the intervening agent, the range of problems that are encountered are diverse. The police may be called to settle violent husband-wife fights, disputes between parents and teenagers, arguments caused by alcohol or drugs, struggles over child custody or any of the myriad problems that arise among people in domestic situations. While urban police are called more and more frequently to provide this service, there are a number of reasons why handling domestic disputes remains one of the least desirable jobs that an officer must perform. First, most officers maintain that handling family disputes is not "real" police work. Rather than getting involved in citizens personal problems, officers feel that police should be pursuing criminals and performing patrol functions. Coping with family fights is often viewed as "social work." In addition, there is little or no job recognition or reward within the police system for doing a good job handling domestic disputes (while, for example, there is considerable reward for making a good felony arrest). Secondly, few officers feel they are equipped to solve other peoples "problems."

Traditionally, training in handling domestic disturbances has consisted of one recruit academy lecture and some on-the-job training (observing other officers, handling disturbances by trial and error, and listening to fellow officers tell stories of particularly strange or dangerous family fights). Thus, the police have not been adequately prepared to cope with the complexities or demands of the domestic crisis situation. Domestic disputes have the added dimension of being extremely dangerous and unpredictable, partly as a function of the often violent emotions that the citizens are experiencing, and partly as a result of the lack of officer training. Not surprisingly, family fights have come to be viewed as undesirable assignments, and worse. Faced with a situation which had so many negative aspects, police officers have traditionally used either expedient or legalistic methods of handling domestic disputes (21). The most common solution to these situations has been inducing one party, (usually the man), to leave the premises for a period of time since it permitted the officer to keep the peace and to get out quickly (28). It is axiomatic among experienced policemen that arrest (even when a battery has been committed) is generally a poor choice because few of the citizens actually follow through the press charges. Consequently, most officers distaste for responding to family fights is magnified by the generally unsatisfactory outcome of those interventions. In fact, officers frequently find themselves returning to the same house a few weeks later to settle the problem again. It is also apparent that the police make few friends as a result of their work in this area since one party usually feels that he has been sided against.

It is acknowledged by both police and a goodly number of citizens that police service is neither the best nor the most desirable possible intervention in a domestic dispute. Why, then, is it that the police are continually drawn upon to handle these fights? The reasons are numerous and somewhat complex. An extensive discussion of these factors is beyond the scope of this chapter, but a brief summary of these issues provides the framework within which family crisis training has been developed. Pragmatic rather than theoretical issues are the primary reasons for the widespread urban dependence in police to cope with family fights. The police (until recently) have been the only meaningful 24-hour service agency in most cities. Since most family disputes occur in the evening hours there are few, if any, other resources to turn to. Just as important is the speed with which police respond. What other service agency will appear at a citizen's house within 15 minutes of a request for aid with a fight? Police appear when a crisis is happening. Moreover, they are visible, available, and very well known.

The sad reality is that there is no one to call for a wide range of community needs and that the police are used for lack of a more appropriate service. In the last several years, some community mental health centers have attempted to fill part of the vacuum by organizing home visiting services and 24-hour crisis clinics. However, few communities have educated their citizens to call those 24-hour clinics. Perhaps more importantly, many citizens who call the police are as distrustful (or more so) of the mental health disciplines as they are of the police. Presently, mental health crisis services in most cities are not equipped to handle the volume of crisis work that befalls the police.

Another pragmatic issue is that the police are the only agency equipped (both physically and legally) to deal with the violence which is a frequent concommitant of domestic disputes. Even if sufficient manpower from the social service agencies were available, they would not now have the expertise necessary, nor the desire, to deal with the physical aspects of a violent family fight. It has been apparent for some time that the number of trained professionals in the mental health disciplines severely limits the direct services that can be provided to most communities. Most public and private social service agencies have too short hours of operation and too few personnel to meet the great demands for third party crisis intervention in America's cities. One potential solution is the cooperation of the police and the local mental health facilities to provide joint services with each group maintaining priority in their area of expertise. Historically, few attempts of this kind have been made and much of the explanation may be mutual distrust. Finally, as was alluded to above, many of the poor and uneducated citizens who call upon the police are unaware of other agencies that might be of assistance. For those citizens the police are the "court of only resort." While some poor citizens may be aware of other resources, they are also aware that the police do not charge for their services while almost all other agencies do.

Although it is possible to postulate a number of sociological hypotheses regarding the breakdown of the extended family and the need for external agents regulating family quarrels, it is likely that the pragmatic issues outlined above have had the most significant influence in the continuing use of police services in this area. A combination of circumstances led police command personnel and social scientists to recognize the potential for cooperation in family crisis training. Specifically, these factors were statistical evidence pointing towards the dangers to both police[15] and citizen[10,12,33] alike in family fights; increasing awareness by police executives of the degree to which police behavior is service oriented[19]; recognition by trained professionals in the social sciences of the need to train para-professionals[17] to do tasks once thought of as solely the province of professionals; and the increasing involvement in social-action-type programs on the part of the social scientists. As a result of these factors, family crisis intervention has become one of the few areas of police training in which social scientists have directly affected police operations. But in spite of the increasing number of social scientists involved in family crisis intervention programs, there has been a wholesale failure to carefully examine (and improve upon where necessary) the efforts of other professionals working in the area. There has been almost no attempt at an integration of the results of the various programs and it is clear from the research summarized here that few departments know of the existence of other projects besides the original New York program. In only one city (New York) was there knowledge of the existence of more than three other programs.

Thus, family crisis intervention programs become important

to review for a number of reasons: First, training programs like these are prototypes of what may be the "new wave" in police training. Second, it permits a brief look at the increasing involvement of social scientists in police departments. Third, these programs provide training in an area of police functioning where the quality of service has drastic consequences on the situation's outcome. Fourth, it permits some initial attempts at drawing together the results of the various projects. Finally, and perhaps most importantly, as innovations in major police departments become more and more synonomous with "federally-funded projects," it is instructive to look at one innovation across a number of quite different police agencies (most of which did obtain federal funds for family crisis intervention projects). In fact, this chapter can profitably be viewed as a case study of a single concept as it visited different law enforcement agencies. The chapter is divided into three sections—the preceding introduction; Project Summaries; Specific FCIU Recommendations and Implications.

While each of the following programs had its unique aspects, there were also certain similarities in terms of philosophy and method. Rather than summarizing these issues within the body of each program description, a few parallels that exist across programs will be briefly discussed below:

1. *Generalist-specialist philosophy:* Not a single department has opted for a large-scale, pure-specialist approach. This appears to be a part of an overwhelming tide against patrol specialization. In each agency, all of the officers who were specially trained in domestic crisis intervention continue to perform regular patrol duties when not intervening in family fights. This went a long way towards reducing negative reactions from other officers about special units. It was also a reflection of the feeling among most police command officers that few departments can afford the extra manpower to have specialists.

2. *Outside consultants:* No department has relied totally on "in-house" talent for their training. Consultants, usually psychologists, have been hired to develop and conduct the training and to work with patrol supervisors in agreeing upon an operational plan. The use of an outside consultant can be a double-edged sword. He may

have the skill to teach family crisis intervention, and he may have fresh perspectives to offer the department but, at the same time, he may be unfamiliar with local regulations and procedures and/ or with police work in general. Thus, a department may have to educate the consultant to their specific needs before he may usefully train in his area of expertise.

3. *Small group training:* One of the most fundamental consistencies of the program has been the attempt to maintain a small group format in training. Strong arguments have been made for the impossibility of imparting the special skills needed in family fights to large classes. It is also felt that the need for discussion among the officers regarding the new procedures and philosophy requires a small enough group for everyone to air his thoughts. Some programs in which group meetings were similar to sensitivity groups would have been unable to conduct their kind of training had large groups been demanded by the police agency.

4. *Training methods:* There has been an effort to use innovative teaching techniques. Role playing, usually with video tape as an additional training aid, has been included to some degree in almost all of the training programs. Typically, actors have been hired and a series of scripted plays are dramatized until the officers intervene. Then the participants and observers discuss what happened and replay video tapes to stimulate additional critique.

5. *Referral systems:* One of the most encouraging aspects of the domestic crisis programs has been the arrangements that have been made with local community resource agencies. In some instances, these working arrangements have produced a substantial rapprochement between the police and mental health system. The referral system commonly involves a broad network of social agencies that agree to provide whatever services they offer to any citizen referred by the police. Since many of the agencies involved are public, this may not be looked upon as an important step. However, knowing of the commitment and concern of the service agencies has often exerted a positive influence on the police officers' attitudes. Unfortunately, most of these referral systems fail to provide adequate feedback to the police about the appropriateness and effectiveness of their referrals. Such

feedback would greatly enhance the usefulness of the referral system.

PROJECT SUMMARIES

This section will be devoted to a summary and review of 14 training programs in family crisis intervention. The programs are broadly grouped into three categories (the New York approach, the Richmond, California approach, and the Oakland approach) on the basis of the three different conceptual models used in training. There are considerable differences within each category in terms of variables like the number of officers trained, the methods of operation, the kind of law enforcement agency (e.g. housing authority police, sheriffs, city police) and how the program fits into the department as a whole. These factors, however, may not be as crucial to the effectiveness of the program in the long run as are the differences in conceptual models.

It would not be feasible to describe each of the family crisis intervention programs in detail.[1] An attempt will be made to briefly state the basic elements of the program and to highlight any aspects of special significance. In each of the three general categories, a more intensive critical summary will be attempted with at least one of the programs. Three extended critiques (one for each model) will be presented first, followed by brief summaries of the programs that have developed from those models. Nine family crisis intervention projects were variations on the New York approach, one project derived from the Richmond approach and one program was developed from a combination of the New York and Richmond methods. At this point, Oakland's F.C.I.U. model has not been attempted by any other city.

Model One: New York Police Department

The New York Police Department, in cooperation with Dr.

---

[1]For additional details on any of these programs, contact either the specific department or the authors. Many of the programs that will be described have never published reports; consequently, the authors have relied on many personal communications and relatively few formal program summaries. This increases the possibility of slight inaccuracies or some personal bias in the program reviews presented here.

Morton Bard and the Psychological Center of City University of New York (C.U.N.Y.), undertook the creation and training of the first Family Crisis Intervention Unit (FCIU). The demonstration project was funded by an Office of Law Enforcement Assistance grant of approximately $95,000. Being the first and most ambitious of the experiments in family crisis intervention training, it is considered the theoretical and methodological foundation for almost all the other family crisis intervention units. It is also the only program to have a sufficiently rigorous evaluation to permit careful critique. Because of the special historical significance of this program (as representative of a particular training model) and as the most influential program yet implemented, detailed discussion of the strengths and weaknesses of the program is presented.[2,3,4,5,32]

Selection:

During the pre-operational prepatory phase, 18 experienced officers (nine White and nine Black) were selected on the basis of interviews with the project leaders from among 42 volunteers. An attempt was made to select officers on the basis of motivation, commitment, sensitivity and personal stability.

Training:

The eighteen officers began an intensive training program during which they spent a full month (160 hours) at the Psychological Center of City College. The training consisted of lectures on relevant topics, films, field trips to community resource agencies, role-playing demonstrations, and group discussions similar to sensitivity groups.[4] It was felt that the success of the training would "be dependent upon significant alteration of the interpersonal perceptual set of each participating officer."[32] Therefore, the trainers contended that the training required two levels of approach: (1) Intellectual: learning selected and highly specific behavioral science content relevant to functions to be performed and (2) attitudinal: gradual modification of personal values and attitudes and a generalized increase in self understanding.[32] The first level (intellectual) was addressed primarily through lectures by a variety of speakers, most of whom had little familiarity with police operation but had expertise in specific areas of mental health. The second level of the training model involved primarily group discussions oriented towards personal growth.

Operations:

The 18 officers (divided into nine biracial teams) were assigned to a multiracial precinct and divided into three groups, thereby insuring 24-hour coverage. One specific car was designed as the "family car" and it was dispatched to all the complaints in the precinct which could be predetermined to be family disturbances. When not responding to family fights, the car was to patrol a regularly assigned sector. If men in another sector responded to a family crisis, they were under instruction to summon the special team. The employment of the officers as generalist-specialists was, of course, vital to the functioning of the program, since it allowed the officers to maintain their identity as police officers doing patrol work. While still having patrol responsibilities, the officers were able to spend whatever time they deemed necessary to adequately deal with the crisis situations, without the pressure that a regular patrolman might experience to "get back on the street." Weekly consultation from students in the City College clinical psychology graduate program continued throughout the two-year period in which the officers were locked into the family crisis intervention unit.

One of the most noteworthy operational aspects of the family crisis intervention unit operations was the use of social agencies as resources. This program's attempt to develop a referral system set a precedent that was to be followed by most of the other projects. While the operations of the system encountered difficulties, it nonetheless pointed the way to a new and important collaboration between the police and the mental health system.

Evaluation:

This program must be given considerable credit for its attempts at an extensive and rigorous evaluation. The evaluation was primarily directed at the effectiveness of the program in relation to crime control and police personal safety. Furthermore, the project directors were able to obtain permission to use a second nearby district for comparison with the operations of the experimental district. Comparisons were made between this control district and the demonstration district on indices like total number of family disturbances, recurrence of complaints, total number of homicides and assaults, changes in number of homicides and assaults among families and injuries to officers. In addition, the evaluation attempted to gather normative and descriptive data on what constituted a domestic disturbance. This was the first evaluation of a family crisis intervention unit project and it remains today the only major quantified assessment of the effectiveness of such programs. Therefore, its results must be reviewed quite carefully. The project found it beyond its scope to make a large-scale assessment of its effect upon the community, which is regrettable.

New York Police Department: Family Crisis Intervention Unit Critique

Selection:

Since the officers were carefully selected on the basis of criteria which seemed to reflect a likelihood of proficiency in family fights prior to training, it is not possible to determine whether the training, in fact, made any difference. It is possible that if the selected officers were compared to unselected officers and neither group had any special training that there would still be a difference in the performance of these two groups.

Training:

As noted in the program description above, the training was attempted through two levels. The intellectual or cognitive level consisted primarily of lectures. It would appear that this segment of the course was not dissimilar to most recruit academy training. That is, experts were brought in to cover a variety of topics, but no attempt was made to integrate their presentations into a consistent model which could direct actions in real family fight interventions. These lectures did not generate any specific curriculum material for the department to adopt. Consistency of the training program seems an impossibility when speakers are given a "carte blanche" in a content area. Finally, no quality control of the material presented is possible when the responsibility for information is subcontracted out of the hands of the project directors.

The second or attitudinal level was addressed through sensitivity-type group meetings designed to foster personal growth. The allegiance to a personal growth approach undermines the replicability of the project. A basic tenet of a demonstration project is that if it works well, others must be able to adapt and use the same program. The New York Family Crisis Intervention Unit is not replicable in a scientific sense, primarily because the model for training is one of personal growth (which is neither precise nor specific). It is not surprising to also find that the model is not operationalized consistently. Rather, as must follow from such a model, one finds different methods depending on the approach of the particular group leader, the investment of the group participants and the nature of the group experience.[32] As one of the group leaders put it, ". . . a good meeting is similar to an excellent bull session."[32] If that is so, it is hardly the basis for a replicable training program. Moreover, even in parts of training which address "skills" in crisis intervention, it appears that besides labeling the stages (e.g. mediation, referral, information gathering) of an intervention, little specific instruction on how to achieve the ends of a particular stage was given. It is highly unlikely that an officer can mediate a dispute with the vague instruction to "assist them in communicating with each other."[18] Specific methods of facilitating communication need to be imparted, and it is clear that no single technique (or group of techniques) were generated which might accomplish the behavioral goals of an intervention.

Operations:

One of the primary aims of any intervention program is to help families in crisis. Often, however, crisis intervention is not sufficient service, and additional referral (perhaps to an agency providing social services) is necessary. From the statistics available in the New York project it appears that the Family Crisis Intervention Unit did not make effective discriminations in choosing *who* they would refer. Only one quarter of all interventions were made without referral to some social agency. Therefore, 75 percent of all calls were referred—an unrealistic percentage to anyone who has experience in handling family fights. This probably reflects poor training of the officers in what type of family would most benefit from a referral. Thus, it is likely that a great number of referrals were either ineffective or the individuals just did not appear at the agency (because of an inappropriate or unnecessary referral). Not only does it appear that the training was insufficient in who to refer, but also in *where* to refer. Nearly half of the total referrals were made to one agency. Though that agency did provide a number of different services, it is probably true that specialized agencies were available but generally unused. The excessive referral to one agency probably taxed the resources of that agency to the point where effective processing and disposition of the families was seriously affected.

While the Family Crisis Intervention Unit did indicate an interest in getting feedback from the social agencies receiving referrals, they were unable despite a number of troubleshooting efforts to get an effective feedback system into operation. Thus, one of the prime reinforcements for the officers, knowledge that they had taken effective action by getting a family to "the right place," was removed. In addition, the self-correcting aspects of feedback were not available to the officers.

One of the most regrettable parts of the program design was the failure to take any steps in following up interventions. While this was apparently an issue of departmental policy rather than a bias of the project itself, it would appear that having a follow-up system of some sort would help to clarify some of the muddy issues relating to the referral system and offer a valuable service to the community. The potential benefits of follow-up in terms of the image of the "concerned cop," and better community relations might have been substantial.

Evaluation:

Although it is clear that the crux of the program is police training, one of the best indirect ways to measure the training's effectiveness is by asking the citizens served about police performance. Rather than using any objective or quantifiable means to evaluate the community's thoughts about, the program, the project unfortunately was forced to rely exclusively on anecdotal evidence. Anecdotal reporting, while extremely entertaining and readable, should be used as supplemental and clarifying information for quantified results. Any program with the scope and duration of the Family Crisis Intervention Unit project clearly should have invested substantial efforts in surveying community response. Two years after the project's completion, the final data is still unavailable. This is unusual since the majority of the data summarization was to be done by computer. It appears that their planning of the data collection process was inadequate for a large-scale project. Perhaps more important, it is doubtful whether the data collected (Appendix G of Project Report) will provide useful information to answer crucial questions regarding family fights. It is certainly apparent that few officers will gather the amount of information necessary to complete the data form in a 30 minute intervention.

Results and Conclusions:

This is probably the most important and widely quoted aspect of the program. Everyone who has attempted a program in family crisis intervention is familiar with the positive results and conclusions of the New York project. Yet, a careful examination of these sections of the project report is puzzling and disturbing. *Many of the conclusions are unsubstantiated by the data; some are actually contra-indicated.* None of the criteria measured showed success but some did show failure. Some examples of the results are as follows:

(a) The experimental precinct had a significantly higher percentage of repeat calls than did the comparison district.[32] The report's attempt to interpret this finding as positive stretches experimental reasoning. One clear goal of the project was to reduce the number of chronic fighting families who were dependent on the police system, and the project failed with regard to this goal.

(b)   The experimental precinct had more homicides and more family homicides than did the control precinct. Further, the 30th precinct (experimental) showed a sharp increase while the 24th precinct (comparison) showed a decline in these indices during the period of the project. This would seem to indicate another negative finding.

(c)   The experimental precinct showed an increase in assaults while the comparison precinct showed a decrease in assaults. This reflects either an inconclusive finding or a negative finding, depending on the outcome of an appropriate statistical significance test, which the project report fails to provide.

(d)   Family assaults appear to follow the same pattern as general assaults (see "c" above). The project report points out that arrests in family disturbances were 2.5 percent less for the experimental precinct and suggests that a lessening of the burden on the courts may have resulted. Since the experimental precinct showed a sharp increase in family fight calls, the overall result must have been an increase in total arrests in the 30th precinct. The arrest data is almost surely nonsignificant statistically and should be shown and discussed as such. In addition, the percentage of family assaults (in relation to total assaults) was approximately the same in both precincts—another inconclusive finding.

(e)   The injury data shows fewer injuries to Family Crisis Intervention Unit members than to members of patrol in the 24th precinct. No single result of this study has been as widely publicized. This finding is based on *no injuries to officers in the experimental district and one injury in the control district.* The projection from three injuries (one in the 24th, and two non-family crisis intervention unit injuries in the 30th) to 135 city-wide injuries is methodologically unjustified and misleading.

There is considerable disparity between the results and the conclusions; it is not worthwhile to again cover the results point by point, but it should be noted that the conclusions bear no resemblance to the actual data and that most of the conclusions are based on impressions rather than results. One example should suffice: the *results* show clearly that family assaults and family homicides *increased* in the family crisis intervention unit district relative to the comparison district; the first *conclusion* of the report is "sensitive and skillful police intervention in family disturbances may serve to *reduce* the occurrence of family assaults and family homicide."[32] Finally, it must be noted that there are no negative conclusions in the report.

Effects on the System:

The New York Family Crisis Intervention Unit program received tremendous publicity. On one hand, the New York Family Crisis Intervention Unit has been more influential in other police departments adopting family crisis intervention unit programs than any other single factor. The project directors engaged in a major public relations effort and were extremely effective in widely disseminating the "positive" results of the project. Yet, it is this same dissemination issue which has led to other problems.

Was it in the best interest of the New York Police Department or the Office of Law Enforcement Assistance to promote the project as if it accomplished things which it did not? Is it in anyone's best interest to present only the positive aspects of a program and ignore the problems and failures within the program? In this case a great number of people within mental health and within police administration have been convinced that New York's Family Crisis Intervention Unit was a great success and held high promise for other police departments. A detailed examination of the project shows that this is not wholly true. In fact, other police departments have begun experimenting with family crisis intervention units based in part on the illusion of New York's success. Had the New York project been presented with a realistic discussion of strengths and weaknesses, then other agencies could have benefited from their experience, rather than being misled.

The program was not institutionalized in the same format as the family crisis intervention unit training. Eight hours on family crisis intervention have been added to the recruit academy, but the classes are large and the FCIU methods of training have been forsaken.

The project "intended to demonstrate innovative methods of crime prevention and preventive mental health."[32] Thinking strictly in those terms, it is difficult to assess if the project can be considered a success. First, the data on the crime prevention aspects of the project must be considered negative or, at best, inconclusive. Second, it is impossible to ascertain if the project had any effect in a "preventative mental health" sense. The data that was collected did not permit a clearcut statement in this area. The data that was gathered regarding referrals does not warrant conclusions about any actual sensitive detection or identification of potential mental health problems.

Model Two: Richmond, California Police Department

The Richmond Police Department was the first agency to make domestic crisis intervention a part of its regular in-service training and the first police department in the nation to train its entire patrol force.[24] It is additionally distinctive because it is the only program of this type which did not have external federal or state funding. Rather, the training was developed and implemented by the authors (who were already consulting to the Richmond Police Department on a regular basis) in conjunction with the department leadership. Moreover, the training program constituted the first major effort that did not use the crisis intervention training model developed by Bard.[32] Instead a skill-related "how to" model was successfully developed and used.[30] The development of a serious alternative to the Bard model suggests the possibility of a future study which compares the relative costs and effectiveness of the differing models.

Selection:

In considering training for intervention in family fights in Richmond, it was decided not to train specialists, but rather to provide training for the entire patrol division. The major factors in the decision to train all the men were (1) desire to avoid "elitism," (2) an awareness that all officers will occasionally handle family fights even if specialists have been trained, (3) an unwillingness to "lock in" specialists who might then be kept out of the usual promotional and training opportunities, and (4) a recognition that the tone of police community relations are often shaped by the crucial role that police play when intervening in family fights, thereby indicating a need for all uniformed officers to be skilled in this area.

Since the Richmond Police Department has been using the team policing concept[22,23] for several years, the Uniform Division was already subdivided into eight teams of ten to twelve men, which were appropriately sized groups for training. Thus, approximately 80 officers completed the training course. No officer was denied the opportunity to participate in the training.

Training:

The emphasis in the training program was on teaching concrete, learnable skills which can be employed in real life situations. Particularly important was the recognition of and attention to the time constraints under which the police operate. The intervention model is designed so that an intervention can be successfully completed in less than 20 minutes. For each of the stages of an intervention (e.g. safety precautions, defusing, information gathering, mediation, referral) specific procedures were taught to help achieve specific behavioral goals. Additionally, emphasis was placed on knowing why and when to choose one alternative over another, as well as how to employ the methods. Each team was individually given approximately 14 hours of inclass training along with a comparable time requirement for outside reading. Assignments involving practice with the new skills supplemented the reading.

Since many police have had training experiences with social scientists in which the consultant has come in poorly prepared and tried to lead a "bull session," the materials received a great deal of planning and organization. Class outlines were prepared in detail and distributed so that officers did not have to try to participate and take notes at the same time; rather than assigning long readings, the consultants summarized the best available literature and then reproduced these highly condensed and edited summaries for the men to read. Class time was employed pri-

marily to demonstrate and practice the new skills. Extremely helpful in this regard was the use of simulated crisis interventions
based on actual cases that the officers reported. No direct attempt
was made to change officer attitudes toward family fights or toward
people in general. It was believed that giving the officers new behaviors rather than changing his attitude would be successful in
producing effective crisis intervention. A basic concept in this approach was that attitude change most easily follows behavior
change, and that a direct attack upon undesirable attitudes often
does nothing except solidify those negative attitudes. Finally, there
was another innovation which, while auxilliary, played an important role in the program. Prior to beginning training, all men in
patrol were surveyed about their training needs in the area of
domestic fights; information was also collected on problems
specific to family crises, as well as present procedures. This information proved invaluable in designing the training to meet the
needs of the men on the street, and prevented the program from
becoming theoretical or academic. Many officers were aware that
their own responses on the questionnaires were instrumental in
shaping the training. They also knew that the authors had done
extensive observational riding in patrol cars in Richmond and
were not strangers to the realities of family fights. These two facts
were central to the acceptance given the authors in their role as
trainers.

Operations:

The Richmond Police Department uses one-man patrol cars
which frequently necessitated an officer waiting for his cover car
before entering a domestic dispute. Since all officers were trained
in the new procedures there was very little trouble in coordinating
the intervention strategy even though there were often different
cover cars coming to aid an officer. There were no special patrol
cars that were designated as family crisis cars nor was there any
special group designated to handle family crises. Thus, 24-hour,
city-wide service was continually available.

The average time spent on family crisis calls after the training
was still comparable to the amount of time spent on those calls
prior to the program; thus, there was little conflict between super-

visors and patrolmen. Such conflict was also prevented by the nature of the team system, in which supervising sergeants were in training classes with their men. The supervisors knowledge of crisis intervention procedures allowed for close supervision of patrolmen and generated opportunities to review and discuss effective crisis intervention methods.

A referral system employing a wide range of city service agencies was developed and implemented. Agencies participating in the program met all the following criteria: they agreed to (1) accept police referrals, (2) provide immediate service, and (3) handle indigent families. The 33 participating agencies offered services in such areas as alcoholic and drug abuse, medical and dental care, psychiatric counseling, juvenile problems, financial assistance, legal problems, suicide prevention, etc. The necessary information for effective referral to these agencies (hours, address, fees, etc.) was condensed into a 3×5 inch loose leaf notebook designed to fit comfortably into the uniform shirt pocket. Each man trained was given a copy of the "Community Resource Manual" and the Department made carrying them a requirement for all patrol officers.

Evaluation Plan:

Since there were no grant funds to support a large evaluation of the long range effect of the program on the various systems and individuals involved, an evaluation of the training classes themselves was conducted. Informal interviews with supervisory personnel as well as patrolman were planned to assess officers' response to the course. Additionally, on-going evaluative data were secured from each officer trained at the end of each class. These data were reviewed after every class session in order to modify training procedures. However, no attempt was made to assess the entire body of data from these evaluations.

Richmond Police Deaprtment: Domestic Crisis Intervention Unit Critique

Selection:

The reactions of the uniformed officers to this program was generally very favorable. One disadvantage of training generalists rather than a small group of volunteers is that most of the men were initially skeptical, or openly hostile, to efforts in this area by psychologists. Over the course of the training sessions, however, most of the men became involved, receptive and enthusiastic, although a small number (perhaps 15 percent) remained negative and unwilling to give the new techniques a chance. There was little indication of role or identity confusion on the part of the officers despite the fact that no selection process was involved. This is probably attributable to the emphasis placed on using procedures that were consistent with normal patrol operations.

Training:

The single strongest area of this program was the training. Nothing received more attention than the preparation of training materials. The training model is internally consistent and easily grasped. Moreover, it is highly replicable because of the specific procedures taught. The training model was itself dependent on the effectiveness of the consultation model which emphasized the consultant's familiarity with the police system, the use of the officers' experiences as major sources of expertise and the commitment to develop skills that were consistent with the needs of the job. The consultation model appears to be a major factor in the successful development and implementation of the training.

The team training process was a particularly useful crucible for learning. The opportunity of each officer to view himself in a variety of stress situations was unusually instructive. This was especially true of the role playing aspects of the training. The video tape playbacks of an officer's performance gave him new perspectives on both his strengths and weaknesses. It also increased the frequency with which the patrolman discussed his actual crisis interventions with other team members as well as with his supervisors.

An unanticipated problem with training an entire patrol force was the degree to which some men would not do reading assignments. Frequently, half the officers would come well prepared (having carefully read and studied the assignment) while the other half of the men were not. This was apparently a reflection of the varying amount of motivation that was brought to the course, although some officers were obviously involved and interested in class but would not do four to eight page reading assignments. This was a significant problem since the procedures are similar to building blocks where new information must be added to knowledge previously mastered. Valuable class time was spent helping unprepared officers catch up with the rest of the class. Training time was lost and the amount of training time was insufficient to begin with. Doubling the number of hours devoted to the course would have allowed time to practice each of the new techniques until the officers were highly skilled in their application.

Operations:

Since the whole patrol force was trained, there were always skilled officers handling family fight calls. A frequent problem in other programs where only a few officers were trained was that the majority of domestic disturbance calls would be handled by untrained officers. One of the great advantages of the Richmond approach is that there is city-wide coverage on a 24-hour basis.

A significant result of training all patrolmen was the active participation of the officers in modifying and improving departmental dispatch procedures regarding disturbance calls, and in updating relevant rules and procedures. The changes proposed by the officers received support from Chief Robert Murphy (now Chief, San Jose Police Department) and his successor Chief Lourn Phelps. Administrative support for the training and its operational application was a strong point of the program.

The program failed to build in an effective feedback system from the referral agencies to the police department. This has been a problem for almost every family crisis intervention program. It requires a major organizational effort and constant vigilance to assure the necessary participation of the service agencies. It also demands that the "confidentiality of records" issue be attended to by both police and referral agencies. There was also no follow-up procedure developed to contact a family (that was referred) to see if they had made use of the referral. Citizen satisfaction was also not assessed, and this might have been done with follow-up. The community resource manual was an important and well received part of the program. It met both the practical and informational needs of the officers. Of all the programs reviewed, Richmond has developed the best method of aiding officers in making appropriate referrals.

Evaluation:

The failure to rigorously evaluate the effects of such a unique program is a serious loss to the law enforcement community at large. A well-designed and useful evaluation would, however, have involved considerable expense and there were no funds available. The failure to adequately evaluate was due to a lack of funding rather than a lack of inclination. Impressionistic data based on the interviews with team sergeants suggested that arrests resulting from family fights had decreased as a result of the training program, but the validity of such data is highly questionable.

Officers evaluations of the course presentations, course materials and the relevance of the techniques to job needs were overwhelmingly positive. Particularly strong were the responses to the role playing demonstrations and to the value of video tape.

Effects on the System:

Though the Richmond Police Department was interested in incorporating the training program into recruit training, it was not possible. The department is not large enough to conduct its own academy, and recruits are sent to a regional academy. Thus, the effects of the initial training will be lost as each class of recruits enters the department unless additional in-service training is conducted. The department has encouraged new officers to take the course at a local junior college where it is now offered as part of the police science curriculum.

The success of a training program in an area which is service oriented has strongly influenced the command personnel to support the development of other service related training programs. For example, plans are now being made to develop a comparable training program in handling juveniles.

Model Three: Oakland Police Department

The Oakland Police Department has implemented a six-month experimental family crisis intervention program which is, perhaps, the most unusual of all the programs in operation.[20] While partially funded by a National Institute of Mental Health grant in the broad area of violence prevention, the funds for the program came primarily from the department budget. The program was initiated at the recommendation of a committee of patrolmen (called the Experimental Project Committee) who were part of the Violence Prevention Unit. This committee presented the idea to Chief Charles R. Gain, who then pressed for the implementation of such a program. Chief Gain has continued to foster the growth of this program with his active support.

Selection:

Four experienced officers were chosen from among 17 volunteers to man the "family crisis" cars. The officers were chosen on the basis of group interviews plus the recommendations of other experienced patrolmen. Each of the selected officers met the following criteria: (1) the member must have volunteered to work with the program, (2) the member must have demonstrated a capability of calming disturbances and maintaining control throughout the call with minimal friction between himself and those involved, (3) the member must have demonstrated a willingness to utilize the service and problem-solving approach to the family disturbance, and (4) the member must have had recent street experience.[20]

Training:

This is one aspect of the family crisis intervention unit program which distinguishes it from all others. Rather than conducting formal training classes run by consultants as had all other programs, the Oakland Police Department felt that this was unnecessary. They had no formal training program; instead, Oakland "is relying upon the good judgment and experience of officers."[20] The central element of their informal training was peer group critiques of tape recordings made in actual family fights. The four family crisis intervention unit officers would meet and listen to each others tapes of recent interventions with an eye to determining what factors affected the outcome. One day was spent in a seminar with representatives of participating social agencies in an attempt to familiarize the officers with the functions of those agencies.

Operations:

Oakland Police Department researched the frequency, location, and hours of family disturbance calls and found that the majority of calls for service were between the hours of 7 P.M.-3 A.M., Wednesday through Sunday. They were also able to determine that the calls occurred predominatly in two low-income areas of the city. They proceeded to organize their family crisis intervention unit to work those hours and days of the week. The unit consisted to two, two-man teams in unmarked vehicles whose primary responsibility was family disturbance calls. When not engaged in handling family disturbances, the teams were to function as cover cars and do preventive patrol. Operational difficulties eventually led to a change in the functioning of the unit so that they were reassigned to engage in normal patrol duties when not responding to family fights. Each unit was assigned to one of the areas that had the highest incidence of family disturbance calls. The plan was to have street supervision provided by the regular district patrol supervisors. Close liaisons were established with local social service agencies. It was the responsibility of the family crisis intervention unit staff to maintain frequent contact with these agencies. This was unlike most of the other family crisis intervention unit projects which have had the training consultants establish and maintain referral contacts.

Oakland also built a follow-up procedure into the program. Officers had the option of returning to a family to inquire whether that family took advantage of a referral and if so, whether the referral agency was successful in providing assistance.

Evaluation:

Oakland has one of the best evaluation components among the family crisis intervention programs. They were aware of the limits of the New York project evaluation, as well as their inconclusive results. Oakland's evaluation had five major components:

1. Descriptive data on families calling the police.
2. Outcome data on family crisis intervention unit effectiveness.
3. Comparative data on family crisis intervention unit patrol activities.
4. A survey of officer reaction to the family crisis intervention unit.
5. A survey of citizens served by the family crisis intervention unit.

While the Oakland project is small in size, the results of this evaluation will provide extremely valuable information on the operation and the effectiveness of its family crisis intervention unit.

Oakland Police Department: Family Crisis Intervention Unit Critique

Selection:

The selection process employed by Oakland is a departure from the procedures of other programs. The use of a selection committee manned by patrolmen is an exciting concept. While the family crisis intervention unit did have a high officer turnover rate during initial periods of operation, it is not clear whether this is in any way attributable to the selection decisions.

Training:

The practice of tape recording all crisis interventions to permit later study and evaluation is an excellent one. It should be profitably adopted by every family crisis intervention program with a minimum of difficulty. The consequence of such a method would probably be the reinforcement of an officer's role as an effective intervention agent and his continual growth in the job. Recording all interventions enhances the possibility of establishing a library of edited training tapes which might be used in conjunction with the training of new officers. While the Oakland program is no longer recording their interventions (due to lack of time and failure of equipment), they hope to do so again in the near future.

Oakland's decision to avoid any formal training procedure can be viewed as a reaction to the expense and the non-specific nature of the training programs that were known at the time of the programs inception. It is to Oakland's credit that they were willing to take a chance on their untested training approach rather than accept a training model which did not meet their needs. It is clear, however, that a skill-related training program would usefully supplement their peer group critique methods.

Operations:

Oakland has been troubled by operational difficulties since the program's beginning. Yet, the program has not floundered due to the strong support from the chief and the troubleshooting efforts of the project coordinators. The project appears to be reasonably flexible in altering its procedures to reduce or minimize operational problems.

After the project was underway, disagreements arose over the deployment of the family crisis intervention unit officers when they were not intervening in family fights. After considering a number of procedures, it was finally agreed that the initial design would be modified so that the family crisis inervention unit's did normal patrol work rather than just special assignments or preventive patrol. Supervision problems developed because of the special hours that the unit worked. The family crisis intervention unit was placed under the supervision of the regular district sergeant, but the unit found that it received split supervision since their special hours overlapped two different patrol shifts. This situation proved unworkable. The family crisis intervention unit did not have a daily information line-up, nor did they receive any of the frequent line-up in-service training. The line-up is designed to insure that the officer has knowledge of current developments which are vital to effective patrol work. The family crisis intervention unit's failure to participate in line-ups led to complaints from supervisory personnel. On the whole, the coordination with patrol division was poor. The most effective step to meet these difficulties has been the change of family crisis intervention unit patrol hours to coincide with the 8 P.M.–12 A.M. shift.

The referral system and the liaison system with the participating service agencies has been one of the best among all programs reviewed. There has been almost no problem in getting cooperation from these agencies. Feedback on referrals has been excellent and extremely reinforcing for the officers. It would be valuable to study in detail the way in which Oakland was able to keep the system functioning effectively.

The follow-up procedure where an officer returns to a family to see how they have used referral information has been a working part of the operational procedures. This is done in about 10 percent of the cases. The citizens response to this procedure has been very positive and the officers have not been adverse to doing the follow-up.

Regrettably, the manpower devoted to the program is small. The family crisis intervention unit handles only 10 percent of the total number of family crisis calls in the City of Oakland. Additional officers would be very useful in determining if the systems that have worked so well on a small basis could respond to the demands of city-wide program.

Evaluation:

While the evaluation design has been one of the most comprehensive of all family crisis programs, much of the data is not available in its final form. Preliminary indications of the effectiveness of the Oakland program are positive and encouraging.

The survey of partol officers working in the same district as the experimental unit has produced nearly unanimous praise. The random survey of the 10 percent of the families served by the unit also showed overwhelming satisfaction with the quality of service. The preliminary data on the outcome of family crisis intervention unit's interventions has been most encouraging. Few arrests have resulted (in less than 5 percent of the calls), only one minor injury to an officer, no cases of resisting arrest and few assaults on an officer. The average time spent on family crisis calls has been 33 minutes. Better than one-third of the families referred actually made appointments at the agency and 80 percent of those families actually appeared. Work surveys indicated that the family crisis intervention unit patrolmen actually performed more patrol work than regular patrol officers. An attempt was made (by extensively reviewing all police service calls to single families) to determine whether the family crisis intervention unit had any effect on chronic disputants. The preliminary evidence suggests that two visits by the family crisis intervention unit stops all further calls. This is seen as an extremely positive result.

The total evaluation, when completed, should be extremely informative and may have a major impact on police personnel's view of special family crisis intervention units.

Effects on the System:

The experimental program has produced a number of positive effects on the system. First, the unit has begun to train other local social service agencies in the techniques they have employed. This has led to increasingly closer cooperation between these agencies and the police. This is a major step since some of the agencies (e.g. probation) have not in the past had good relationships with the police. Second, the apparent effectiveness of the program has led National Institue of Mental Health to give additional funds for ten more patrolmen and one supervisor to be assigned to the unit. Third, the department has formulated plans to put crisis intervention into the recruit academy. This academy training will, in large part, consist of role playing demonstrations. The long range planning goal is to have training for all the men via in-service training for experienced personnel and academy training for recruits.

San Francisco, California, Police Department

This program is a direct descendant of the Richmond program. It is as significant for what was not accomplished as for those things that were accomplished.

Former Chief Alfred T. Nelder, of the San Francisco Police

Department, personally decided in early 1971 to seek specialized training in family crisis intervention, partially as a response to the unusually high incidence of off-street assaults during 1970. An agreement was reached between Chief Nelder, and the psychological consultants who had designed and recently completed the Richmond program (these consultants were the authors of this chapter plus John Silk, a third psychologist). Plans were evolved by this group for an ambitious and very extensive FCI project. The major goals of the project proposal were to provide the San Francisco Police Department with city-wide training in family crisis intervention techniques, to install similar training within the police recruit academy, and to train police personnel to function in the role of trainers so that the project would at the duration of the grant period, be independent of external funding and expertise. In addition, the project would concurrently test several methods of training in family crisis intervention and determine the most effective of these methods. The teaching methodology and curriculum of this project were all to be designed in such a way as to maximize the feasibility of other law enforcement agencies utilizing them.

Chief Nelder decided to seek funding for this project (approximately $285,000 over a two-year period) and to concurrently begin training in one of San Francisco's nine police districts (Northern) as both a pilot and a demonstration. Most of the preparations for this program were based on the assumption that the city-wide project would be funded. Thus, several months of intensive planning, coordination, meetings and the like were engaged in to provide a firm foundation for the larger project and, incidentally, for the imminent training in the Northern district. This phase of the project went unusually smoothly; the police officer associations cooperated in planning, as did J. M. Stubblebein, the director of mental health services for the City and County of San Francisco (now the Director of the Department of Mental Hygiene of the State of California) and a host of other agencies.

While planning was proceeding very well, funding efforts were proceeding poorly. A private foundation had been approached, as had LEAA. Each of these possibilities appeared quite promising for a while, and then each, in turn, proved futile. Several other sources were contacted in an effort to secure funds, but each effort ended in failure. Just as training in Northern district was about to begin, it became clear that there was little chance of getting any funds for this program. It was decided to proceed with the training in the pilot district without money, primarily to honor commitments at many levels, from patrolmen to mental health center staffs. This meant that the training was done without funds for equipment, evaluation, salaries, space and support services.

A meeting was held with all supervisory personnel at Northern Station to explain the training program and introduce the training staff prior to beginning any actual training. This meeting was quite successful at avoiding the development of covert hostility towards the project on the part of mid-management personnel, although active support was not really achieved until the end of the training classes. Also, in preparation for the training program, the two community mental health centers nearest the Northern Police District were contacted, and their cooperation was solicited and received. Some 60 other community agencies were contacted in order to establish avenues for police referrals. Training in Northern District was begun in September of 1971 and completed in November, 1971. Seventeen men were trained, including fourteen volunteers from the patrol force (including two supervising sergeants) in Northern District, two officers from Police Community Relations Bureau, and one officer who has functioned as liaison officer between the Police Department and the City's mental health centers.

The skill-related intervention model developed in Richmond was employed. The training materials were basically the Richmond curriculum, although presented in expanded and considerably more sophisticated form (e.g. entire sections on legal issues and cultural issues were developed, and some reading assignments were presented in programmed text format). Each group of eight to ten officers was given 24 hours of in-class training and asked to do a comparable amount of work outside of class on written and reading assignments. At each class, as in Richmond, a detailed outline of that class session was distributed along with a reading assignment for the next class session, a written assignment, and a feedback form on which the officers registered their evaluation of the class session and made suggestions for changes.

The training was extremely successful and resulted in positive feelings not only on the part of the men being trained, but also on the part of men in Northern District who were not involved in the training program but who had heard about it informally. Much of the success of the training can be attributed to the extensive and careful preparation that preceded training. The consultants who were in charge of the training efforts all had prior experience consulting to police systems, and, as in Richmond, each of them made many observational rides in patrol cars in the Northern District across all three shifts. It was decided to try to obtain at least an informal evaluation of that training from an independent agency. Langely Porter Neuro-Psychiatric Institute's Community Mental Health Training Program agreed to do such an evaluation. All of the men who were trained, as well as most of the police executives involved in this program, and a sample of men at Northern District who are not involved in the training program, were individually interviewed. This evaluation, while limited because of its dependence on interview data, suggested that officers saw the new skills as reducing the risk of violence in family fights. The officers interviewed were also impressed with the degree to which the skills were applicable in a broad range of police tasks unrelated to family fights.

Operationally, the trained officers were assigned across all shifts, thereby providing 24-hour service to the Northern District. One major problem was that trained officers were sometimes paired with untrained officers, and found it difficult to use their new skills when there was no coordination with an untrained partner.

The departmental commitment to and support for this project remains excellent, even though there has been a change of chiefs. The new Chief, Donald M. Scott, has made several departmental commitments to this project, including a guarantee of a minimum 12 hours in the Recruit Academy Program in which to install this training so that it will be given to all recruits. These commitments, like much of the preparation and planning, will be futile if funding is not secured.

This program remains an enigma. While most of the projects reviewed here had easy access to money, most had problems with planning deficiencies, lack of experience in police training and a disinclination to do good evaluation research. The S.F. program started with a well-developed and field-tested training program, departmental and community support, months of preparation, familiarity with the other FCIU projects in the country, and a rigorous evaluation design—and was then the only major program to fail to find funding. One positive note is that other cities may be able to benefit from San Francisco's training curricula, evaluation plan, etc., even though the City of San Francisco probably will not.

Capsule Comment:

Long on training sophistication and short on accomplishments. By far the best training of any program reviewed, and the best planning and evaluation design. In the end, ironically, a lack of rigorous evaluation and a token training effort.

Variations on the New York Approach:

The following nine programs are all derivatives of the original New York Police Department project. Some of these programs remain quite similar to the original New York project, while others have varied considerably.

NEW YORK HOUSING AUTHORITY POLICE. When Morton Bard was unable to come to an agreement with the New York Police Department over the second phase of the original Family Crisis Intervention Unit project, he approached the New York Housing Authority Police. The Housing Authority Police (with a complement of 1400 officers) are responsible for 600,000 high-rise, public housing project residents, and were receptive to an experimental program in family crisis intervention. With support from a Law Enforcement Assistance Administration (L.E.A.A.) grant, a two-stage training program was devised. The first phase of training involved one-half day a week for 12 weeks for 54 recruits who were also attending the police academy. This class of 54 recruits were randomly divided into two groups. Twenty-four of the recruits (plus six senior patrolmen) were placed in the "conflict resolution group," and the remaining 30 recruits were assigned to the "behavioral and social science group" (BASS). The major difference between the groups was the kind of training the group was to receive. The conflict resolution group received 42 hours of affective-experiential training designed to imporve their conflict resolution skills.[25] The BASS group received 42 hours of conventional academic training covering a broad range of the behavioral and social sciences. Following the classroom training, the conflict resolution group took part in weekly discussion groups and individual consultation for a period of three months (ending in May 1970). At the conclusion of training, randomly-selected officers from the conflict resolution group were assigned to patrol two preselected housing projects. A group of recruits from the BASS group were also randomly selected and assigned to another housing project. A fourth housing project, with no changes in its staff, was to serve as a control.

It was hoped that such a training design would test the project assumption that affectively oriented training methods were superior to cognitive training methods. While this is an interesting question, it is probably not the most important one to test. Nonspecific curricula, more appropriate to a liberal arts education than to reality-based police needs, are not likely to be an effective means of training an individual to handle family disturbances. In this sense, a weak "straw man" has been set up to compete against. Even the traditionally poor police academy training is likely to be more helpful in teaching how to handle such disturbance situations than vague and general BASS training. An important comparison that should be made would be between the affective-experimental training and specific skill-related training based on a clearly specifiable intervention model. Such a comparison would provide answers regarding the relative effectiveness of truly viable models of training.

Bard recognized the need to build careful evaluation into the project design and attempted to correct some of the oversights in the evaluation of the original New York family crisis intervention unit program. Of particular note in the evalution plan is the carefully designed community attitude survey and an attempt to collect family dispute data similar to that collected in the original project. However, the data collected on police performance will be of greatest import. If the results are as inconclusive as those obtained in the original family crisis intervention unit project, serious consideration will have to be given to less expensive, more productive methods of training. At present, none of the results on these dimensions (or any of the other measurements) are available.

Capsule Comment: An ambitious project for housing police with an experimental approach that is addressed to the wrong question; the extensive evaluation section (when completed) will be very useful.

LOUISVILLE, KENTUCKY POLICE DEPARTMENT. The Louisville, Kentucky, Police Department, impressed with the New York project, submitted a $25,000 grant (in addition to $75,000 in state and local money) to Law Enforcement Assistance Administration (L.E.A.A.) to conduct an eight-month experiment in family crisis intervention.[26] The police department approached the University of Louisville Psychology Department and was able to make arrangements for consultation and training. A strong statement by the command officers of the police department on the value of such a program yielded forty police volunteers who were screened and interviewed. Twelve officers were selected to participate in a four-week, 100-hour, full-time, training program. The orientation of the training was behavioral as opposed to the sensitivity training approach of New York. This was the first program to use video-tape as a teaching technique.

The operational plan was to have at least one pair of trained officers on duty for each of the three work shifts. They were to handle all of the family fights in a given sector of the city (covering 115,000 of the 800,000 citizens) and if another car were to come upon a family fight in that sector, the specialists were to be called in. Arrangements were made with local agencies to accept police referrals. This referral plan seemed to work out quite well and is in operation today despite the recent conclusion of the rest of the program. Students from a local university were hired to contact citizens who have been served by the specially trained officers to get their reactions to the police service. Responses were consistently positive. While the data gathered here was not extensive, it was a step in the right direction.

One major problem in the program was acquiring and maintaining support from supervisory personnel. Supervising sergeants, in particular, were upset over the excessive amounts of time that the trained patrolmen would spend in family fights. Despite some attempts at mollifying the supervisors objections, the supervisor-patrolman problem was not adequately resolved. While the program's formal evaluation is not as ambitious as New York's the results that were obtained were very encouraging. The department felt positively about the program and requested refunding.

The project has resulted in changes in two major areas. First, thirty hours of training in the general area of crisis intervention has been instituted within the academy. Second, the city mental health agencies have begun a 24-hour crises intervention service which coordinates with the police. Finally, at the conclusion of the grant period, the specially trained officers were reassigned around the city and the project as a formal entity was disbanded.

Capsule Comment: A promising program which has formally ended. Department and consultants have learned a considerable amount about what makes a program effective and would be ready for an effort on a larger scale. Major problems with mid-management.

CHARLOTTE, NORTH CAROLINA, POLICE DEPARTMENT. The Charlotte, North Carolina, Police Department, knowing of the attempts the Louisville police department was making in the area of crisis intervention and, secondly, responding to the results of an informal survey of field officers in which they expressed interest in training in the area, received a $45,000 grant from Law Enforcement Assistance Administration (L.E.A.A.) to organize a family crisis intervention unit.[21] The department recognized that finding volunteers for such a program might be somewhat of a problem and arranged to have the officers who had been trained in Louisville visit Charlotte to speak to officers at the different roll calls. Forty-seven officers volunteered and twenty-four men were chosen from that group by a captain who had personal knowledge of the officers.

The training course was contracted to a local mental health agency that arranged for 55 different speakers to contribute to the 100-hour program. The mental health agency also took care of providing referral information to the officers and arranging for the police referrals to be handled promptly by other local agencies. The representative of the mental health agency responsible for the training felt that the early and intimate involvement of the various community agencies (as distinguished from less direct contact in New York and Louisville) contributed greatly to the effectiveness of the program.

Operationally, Charlotte employs one-man patrol cars and, as a result, a trained officer would frequently get an untrained officer as his cover car. Attempts were made to familiarize the supervisory personnel (only one sergeant had been included in the training program) with the program methods in an effort to avoid patrolman-supervisor conflicts. This seemed to work out satisfactorily and patrolmen were able to spend up to an hour handling a family fight without fear of supervisor complaints.

There has been little systematic evaluation in this program except to count referrals. No comparison group of untrained officers was used to evaluate the relative effectiveness of the trained officers. The local agency in charge of the training was responsible for the evaluation, and it did not have the resources for an extensive effort. They do note, however, that informal figures suggest that as many as 66 percent of the citizens who are referred by the police are appearing at the specific local agency, which is extraordinary.

The department reports it is pleased with the functioning of the program and plans to train additional men as of January 1972. They hope to use only volunteers and to get a more representative cross section of the force in order to avoid some of the selection they had in their first effort.

Capsule Comment: A program which lacks a coherent training model but which has nonetheless been well received and commands considerable departmental support.

REDONDO BEACH, CALIFORNIA, POLICE DEPARTMENT. The Redondo Beach Police Department in Redondo Beach, California, attempted to adopt the New York City program to a small, primarily middle-class, white community.[1] Operating under a $6,000 Law Enforcement Assistance Administration (L.E.A.A.) grant, the Acorn Project, as it was called, consisted of 44 hours of training. Ten officers were chosen (eight from patrol division, one from detective division, and one policewoman from juvenile division) with a deliberate eye toward selecting officers who represented disparate points of view on the value of such "service" programs.

Operationally, the program involved only the eight officers in patrol division who continued to respond to family disturbance calls in the course of their normal patrol duties. Attempts were made to keep at least one trained officer on each shift, but shortly after the training concluded the officers were scattered throughout patrol and other assignments and the program was, in effect, disbanded. The officer-in-charge within the department felt that a more careful follow-up of the training program for the officers who had participated might have helped the program greatly.

A lack of coordination existed between the police department and other community resource agencies and this became apparent during the program. Some troubleshooting efforts to improve inter-agency cooperation was attempted with ambiguous results.

The training and evaluation was made the responsibility of a local psychology research institute. The training encountered resistance from the men, particularly those who were negatively inclined to begin with. The evaluation of the program was, in the words of the evaluators, "sketchy"[1] and did not reflect sufficient planning. There was little evidence from the statistical evaluation that the program was effective in achieving its aims.

The project report of this program is noteworthy in that it is one of the few documents in print on a family crisis intervention training program and (perhaps even more startling) it discusses successes, failures and future recommendations for such projects with real candor.

Capsule Comment: An unsuccessful project due to insufficient planning and resources as well as poor departmental support on an operational level.

DAYTON, OHIO, POLICE DEPARTMENT. The Dayton, Ohio, Police Department's program in family crisis intervention must be considered unique because it is embedded with a general crisis intervention program.[7,8,31] In fact, it was only a small section within a larger extended training program concentrating on team policing and conflict management (which included other areas such as investigative training, exposure to the community and its resource agencies and handling community conflict).

Forty-three patrolmen, four sergeants, and one lieutenant were selected from a group of volunteers. While the actual time spent studying family crisis intervention was limited to two days, many of the techniques that were dealt with in other areas of study might be considered relevant; in particular the role playing involving youth conflicts and community conflicts. Part of the training involved the trainers returning on a regular basis (over a period of months) to consult with the officers on recurring problems.

The training for the family crisis segment was contracted to a New York psychology consulting firm. As a result, many officers felt that the consultants were unfamiliar with both local conditions and police operations. The attempt on the part of the trainers to gather research information led to a suspiciousness and resentment on the part of the officers which further compounded problems. Despite these problems, officers' ratings of the course were mildly positive.

The program did not have a rigorous evaluation component, a seemingly recurrent problem for this area. The department leaders are extremely proud of the total program and view it as an innovative model for future programs. However, they are less certain about the role of family crisis training within the team policing concept.

Capsule Comment: The Family Crisis Intervention Unit component of the total program was not well received, due in great part to the lack of rapport between the officers and the consultants.

St. Louis Housing Authority Police. St. Louis Housing Authority, under a joint grant from HUD and the Department of Labor developed an in-service training program for all members of the housing authority police. The program was run by the Housing Authority's Director of Training who is a criminologist.[13] Rather than asking for volunteers, a decision was made to train all 120 police (including four women), in groups of twelve, with each group receiving approximately 44 hours of training. The training was conducted from March to July 1971. Besides the Richmond Police Department project, this is the only major program that has attempted to train all police personnel. The Director of Training reports that 20 percent of the officers continued to respond negatively to the program while 80 percent seemed to enjoy the course and tried to use the methods.

Twenty hours of the training consisted of representatives from various community agencies speaking to the police about the services their agency offered. While it was one of the stated goals of the project to increase the number of referrals, the trainers were unsuccessful in modifying the negative attitude of the officers about making referrals and as a consequence there was almost no use of the community's resource agencies. At least four, and sometimes as many as twelve officers were on duty on a 24-hour basis to serve the housing projects, which had about 8,000 residents, primarily poor and Black. (All the officers were required to be residents of the project).

The program did not have a large or rigorous evaluation component. A number of informal evaluations were conducted and a report is presently being prepared. One of the most surprisingly impressions in that report is that the female officers seemed to be especially good (more so than men) at handling family disturbance calls. Whether this is a skill which is attributable to women as a group or to just that particular sample of female officers is unknown, but plans are being considered to train 50 female officers as a demonstration project. The Housing Authority is very pleased with the program and is planning to make it a regular part of its recruit training now that all in-service personnel have been trained.

Capsule Comment: A significant program which has avoided the token efforts of other agencies by attempting to train all its personnel (including women). The program would have benefited from a solid evaluation, a more coherent training model and an improved approach to referrals.

MULTNOMAH COUNTY, OREGON, SHERIFF'S OFFICE. The Multnomah County, Oregon, Sheriff's Office, using a $60,000, three-county grant from Law Enforcement Assistance Administration (L.E.A.A.) had made family crisis intervention a part of their in-service training.[25] To date, 60 line officers, about half of whom volunteered to take the training, have completed the 40-hour, one-week course given at a local mental health clinic. This was the only program among those reviewed that had a psychiatrist as the director of training. The training included sufficient supervisory personnel to insure operational support of the program. While the program began with the idea of teams of specialists it quickly switched to a generalist philosophy when administrative and operational roadblocks were encountered. The Sheriff's Office made no effort to assign equal numbers of men to each watch. They did find that because they had trained a rather large group of officers, 24-hour service was provided as a function of the natural distribution of the officers across shifts.

The program did not involve many community resource agencies, and as a result, there has been very little referring by the officers. Further attempts will be made to enhance the possibility of referrals.

An evaluation is being planned but, as is frequently the case, it will not be large enough or comprehensive enough to answer major questions about the general effectiveness of work in this area.

One interesting aspect of this program is the employment of Portland State graduate students to assist the officers in their crisis interventions. The students ride with the officers and are supposed to act as partners in handling the crisis (though more often than not, the students have wisely sat back and let the officers handle the dangerous cases).

Because there was a generally positive response from the officers, the program is now being made a part of the recruit academy. The plan is to extend the length of the academy by one week and use that week for full-time training in crisis intervention. A first group of recruits has been trained and were enthusiastic about this innovation.

Capsule Comment: An improving program that has overcome a shaky start. It should continue to develop as consultants become more familiar with police systems, but better referral training is needed, as is evaluation.

BRIDGEPORT, CONNECTICUT, POLICE DEPARTMENT. The Bridgeport, Connecticut, Police Department, using some of the personnel who had participated in the original family crisis intervention unit experiment in New York, also received a Law Enforcement Assistance Administration (LEAA) grant to establish a family crisis intervention program.[11] The original goals of the project involved some training for all officers in the Bridgeport Police Department in addition to the planned training for the specialists. However, practical consideration led to the temporary abandonment of the original objectives and the adoption of a 30-hour training course which included 40-officers from the Bridgeport Police Department plus 20 officers from the housing police. Each of the five sector Bridgeport police commanders selected eight men from his sector to participate (two from each shift, in order to have trained officers available on a 24-hour basis). The department recognized that involvement of supervisory personnel was vital to the reception of the program on the streets and made great efforts to involve patrol commanders with the hope of minimizing any potential conflicts in the operation of the program. Bridgeport appears to be the only department which had the person in charge of the field utilization of the program attend all the training sessions. This attendance served the dual purpose of monitoring the presentations and making a command-level officer intimately familiar with the program content and procedures, and is an excellent practice. While the department hoped to arrange for consultation and research on the project by local mental health centers, they have not been able to realize that goal. Similarly, careful evaluation of the programs effectiveness is not being carried out. At the end of the training, information on resource agencies was still unavailable, but efforts are now being made to compile the information necessary for effective referral.

Capsule Comment: A program which has failed to realize its initial objectives and lacks an effective training program. Strong operational support partially overcomes other problems.

LOWELL, MASSACHUSETTS POLICE DEPARTMENT. The Lowell, Massachusetts Police department, working with a regional planner, applied for and was awarded a $25,000 six-month grant for family crisis intervention from the state planning agency.[14] The consultants, the same group who had worked in the Dayton program, selected nine officers from approximately thirty that were interviewed. The nine officers received eight consecutive days of classroom training and then participated in bi-weekly follow-up meetings over a period of months with the trainers.

While the training was generally well received, the implementation of the program experienced certain problems. The grant included funds for a patrol car designated for a given sector of the city. The officers in the crisis car were expected to do regular patrol duties when not intervening in family fights. However, unclear communications had led to one shift staying in the specified sector while another shift would respond all over the city. In terms of relative workload, the family crisis intervention unit actually handles only a small percentage of the city's total number of family fights.

The department's project coordinator was responsible for making arrangements with local community agencies. The patrol officers indicated which agencies they wanted additional information on, and then speakers from each of those agencies came to a training session devoted to community resources. However, the officers have made relatively infrequent use of those agencies as a referral resource. The hard crime-related data that the project coordinator planned to gather was not collected because of a variety of administrative and planning problems. The remaining portion of the evaluation, like almost all the others in this area, will be more of a token appeasement to the granting agency than a serious attempt to critically evaluate the program's effectiveness.

It is likely that the real test of this program's importance in the department will be determined when the follow-up consultation with the specially-trained policemen ends in January 1972. The original command officers who were enthusiastic about the program are no longer in the department and the present command is not equally receptive to the program.

Capsule Comment: Token manpower commitment. Future is in doubt due to turnover in command personnel.

TACOMA, WASHINGTON POLICE DEPARTMENT. The Tacoma, Washington Police Department and the local Sheriff's Office combined resources for a program as a result of a local community and mental health cooperation. A grant for state block funds was prepared.[9] Two-year funding ($37,000 first year; $50,000 second year) was obtained for a dual program in family crisis intervention and suicide prevention. Thirteen officers were selected, seven from the police department and six from the sheriff's office. The officers attended ten training sessions with each session lasting three hours. An attempt was made to combine aspects of both the New York project and the Richmond project, with some degree of success. The trainers felt that approximately half the officers responded positively to the training while the other half were mildly negative.

On an operational level, there were a number of problems. First, both departments were unwilling to lock officers into watch assignments, so trained officers were not on duty on a 24-hour basis. Second, while the city of Tacoma had a number of agencies to handle referrals, there were practically no agencies available within county jurisdiction to handle citizen needs. Third, the officers viewed family crisis intervention as a low priority area which created a certain amount of apathy regarding the training. Fourth, the department failed to provide a ranking liaison officer for the program who could troubleshoot for the consultants when necessary. Fifth, no supervisors were trained and, as a result, supervisory concerns about the program were frequent.

An evaluation comparing the effectiveness of the trained versus the untrained officers is presently being attempted, but no statistics are as yet available. Again, there is no major evaluation built into the program. Plans are also being made for an extensive follow-up team that will be responsible for home visits and post intervention phone calls, but that has not yet been operationalized.

Capsule Comment: The department's low priority for this program minimizes its importance. Some excellent planning attempts.

SPECIFIC FCIU RECOMMENDATIONS

In the preceding section, 14 FCI programs were reviewed while delineating issues basic to the success or failure of the programs. At first glance, the lessons derived from the experiences of the various FCIU programs appear to be good criteria for departments thinking of instituting family crisis training. Further examination reveals that these are recommendations that might profitably be considered in developing any innovative programs in law enforcement.

Secure and Maintain Administrative Support

For any program to succeed, there must be demonstrable support and commitment from the top of the police heirarchy. This condition is not a problem when a project idea emanates from the chief. However, if the impetus for the project is external to the department, involvement of the top command personnel early in the project planning stage should be considered mandatory. The best indication of the problems encountered when the command is not committed to a program can be found in those FCIU programs where there was a change of chiefs during the life of the project. The new chief did not view the project as "his" and therefore gave it lower priority and less support when faced by requests from project personnel. The lesson learned in programs like New York was that continuing support from the command is as vital to the success as is initial approval and enthusiasm. If a program is isolated from the chief (whether by intent or poor planning) the consequences will frequently be diminishing support and minimized chances of success. Early in the planning stages, command officers should have a genuine understanding of the goals, methods and needs of the project.

Set Goals That Are Realistic and Measurable

Frequently, programs which have modest and reasonable goals to begin with are discussed or publicized as projects that will revolutionize judicial systems. Such discussions only raise unrealistic expectations about a project's accomplishments. The police and the consultants should maintain a reasonable picture of what a project has been designed to do, and these realistic expectations are the proper basis for information disseminated to the public.

Goals should be specified and unambiguous conclusions should be drawn about the success of the project in meeting those goals. Many projects fail to develop measureable criteria which directly indicate the project's effectiveness in achieving its stated objectives. Often the problem is that the goals are so vague or so global that they cannot be directly measured. In other cases, the project designers fail to measure the appropriate areas. Either error is costly and useful conclusions concerning the success of the program turn out to be impossible. It is crucial that appropriate goals be developed and relevant criteria be measured if a program is to be helpful to future projects that might be attempted.

Also, well-designed evaluation should provide an agency with information regarding some aspects of the project (those that can effectively be measured in an ongoing fashion—this is *not* possible with many criteria) while the project is in operation. This kind of information can pinpoint areas of weakness or failure, and permit ameliorative changes to be made.

Avoid Token Programs

Training some small number of men or training for a small area of an agency's jurisdiction does not appear to be worthwhile. Such programs may receive much favorable publicity, but in the long run they are merely a facade of innovation behind which an organization can more easily resist true change. There is no evidence that small demonstration projects are stepping stones for department-wide training; rather, these programs remain outside the mainstream of departmental activity and disintegrate rather rapidly, leaving few traces of their youthful promise.

The only two agencies that currently have general capability in FCI are the Richmond, California Police and the St. Louis Housing Authority Police, and both of these programs began with deep commitments to department-wide generalist training. If one looks at the other FCIU programs and the total number of family fight calls in those cities since the inception of their FCIU programs, one finds that the vast majority of these calls have been, and are, handled by rank-and-file patrolmen without special training. Until there is evidence that a small number of men working as specialists can effectively cover the bulk of some city's family fight calls, the training of small numbers of specialists should be considered an operational dead end.

Plan for the Project's Institutionalization

A good FCIU program should include provisions for training recruits, so that the program is self-perpetuating. Otherwise, considering the high turnover in patrol in most agencies, the skills of the specially-trained men will be quickly diluted by untrained recruits. It is not easy to institutionalize FCI training within an academy. Small departments may have to influence their regional academies (since they do not operate their own) and this can prove to be very difficult. For large departments, generalist training is easier to institutionalize than specialist training, because the former usually totals 15 to 30 hours while the latter may be as much as 160 hours. Commitments for time for such training in the academy should be sought from police executives early in the planning of any FCIU project.

Avoid Negative Consequences for Participants in the Program

Project planning must show sensitivity to the needs of the men who will be trained. Men who participate in the training must not be "locked-in" (denied usual promotional and transfer opportunities), or they will have been done a disservice and may well become bitter towards the project and its goals. On the other end of the continuum, the specially-trained officers must not develop into an elite "clique," or the rest of the agency personnel may become resentful, and this resentment will probably generalize to the FCIU project. The easiest way out of both binds is to train department-wide, but even if specialist training is desired, these problems can be avoided by careful planning. In the case of specialists, it is important that the program be thoroughly explained to those men who will *not* participate in it. This is best accomplished by patrolmen, as opposed to consultants or command officers.

It is the responsibility of the consultants and of the police administrators to do some planning for failure. This review has shown that FCIU programs may ultimately fail for a wide variety of reasons, many having nothing to do with operational issues. The men participating in a project must not be allowed to be stigmatized with the failure of that project if they have acted in good faith.

Include Supervisory Personnel in Planning and Training

No single issue has been more of a problem for the programs reviewed here than lack of mid-management support. It is unrealistic to ignore supervisors in planning and in training and then to expect them to cooperate with the specially-trained men in the field. Sergeants and lieutenants should be informed early about the project, their advice should be solicited during planning, and some of them should be included in the actual training—even if only as observers. It must be remembered that it is easier to teach rookies new methods than it is to teach supervisors who have used the same techniques for 10 or 20 years. Nevertheless, mid-management is a strong source of support for FCI training provided they are informed and involved, rather than "railroaded" by command officers.

Make Long-Term Plans for Program

Obtaining a grant for FCIU training for two or three years and working on the implementation of the grant program is not sufficient to ensure long-range success. It is important to involve departmental executives in long-term plans for the program *prior* to considering operational issues. In some cases, the long-term project needs will dictate the short-range operational decisions.

Specific plans should be formulated for methods of retaining the program beyond the duration of the grant period. This may include provisions for academy training for recruits, preparation of police personnel as trainers, in-service training at regular intervals and the inclusion of some aspects of the program into the operating budget of the agency. The plans of the San Francisco program seem optimal in that the police department would have had no need for external funding or consultation at the end of the grant period. (These plans were never tried, so that their practicality remains conjecture.)

Plan FCIU Operations to be Compatible with Normal Patrol Operations

Most of the programs reviewed have planned to have their FCIU personnel operate very differently from other uniformed personnel. Further, they have asked the FCIU officers to handle the actual family crises in ways that radically conflict with other job demands. The clearest example is the time issue, which has been discussed in detail previously. In short, FCI training has been far better received when it did not demand that an officer spend an hour or more on a single intervention. The same kind of issues arise with regard to the referral process, training for handling legal issues during family fights, the design of an evaluation and more. Any of these areas can be the focus of major problems if the FCI training and operations do not take account of other patrol functions and procedures.

Arrange Coordination with Referral Agencies

Most programs reviewed have made some efforts toward establishing working referral systems, but have not been successful

(Oakland is a notable exception). This aspect of FCI demands careful attention throughout the program. Initial efforts to establish relationships may be positive, but they will not guarantee long-term working relationships. Such relationships are predicated upon regular (if infrequent) contacts, careful planning, mutual knowledge and an arrangement that meets the needs of the police and the referral agency.

It will be far more difficult to achieve a feedback system so that each officer gets some information on the appropriateness of his referrals, but this is an excellent goal to work toward. The issue of confidentiality of records must be acknowledged and dealt with by all agencies concerned.

The use of a single agency for most referrals is contraindicated. Sending citizens to an agency that is itself a referring, screening, or clearing house is also a mistake. If an officer is able to effectively refer a family, and they arrive at an agency door, then in many cases a minor miracle has occurred. To ask that the family be seen without treatment in order to give them another referral is to guarantee that they will not reach help.

Training Consultants Should be Experienced with Police Systems

The choice of consultants is one of the crucial early decisions facing a police chief who wants to start FCI training. Usually, the consultants will help design the training, the operation and evaluation of the program as well as take charge of the training phase. If the consultants are inept, or receive no acceptance by the rank-and-file of the department, or design things poorly because of lack of familiarity with the police system, then the FCI project will have an uphill struggle for success.

Police agencies should not give "carte blanche" to professional consultants. Rather, some police personnel (a working project director, if possible) should work with the consultants on *all* phases of the project. The training itself should be carefully monitored by the department to insure the quality and relevance of the program. The department must determine that the intervention model being taught is consistent with the philosophy and practice of the agency.

Insist on a Meaningful Evaluation

This point is a recurrent failure theme in the review of various programs. No FCIU project to date has been adequately evaluated. Even a modest evaluation must be based on empirical techniques and provide answers to relevant questions (e.g. will FCI training reduce repeat calls?). Citizen reaction cannot be ignored in an evaluation in this area, nor can it be the sole avenue of research. Crime reduction, injury reduction, referral information, officer acceptance and more must be included if the evaluation is to be comprehensive, and behavioral research skills are a prerequisite if the evaluation is to be rigorous and reliable.

Develop Early Plans for Disseminating Information About the Project

The time has come for police journals and police symposia to stop presenting every new program as if it were the panacea for all police problems. All social and judicial programs have operational difficulties as well as benefits, hidden costs as well as savings, and most have major problems. It is simply too inefficient for one agency to repeat another's mistakes unnecessarily just because the head of the first agency wanted to look good. A candid discussion of a program's strengths and weaknesses is far more professional than the mindless but self-serving paeon's of praise which currently fill the police literature.

The importance of communicating the results of an innovative project should not be underestimated. Police executives should carefully consider the best way (or ways) to share information with other agencies. In many cases, a short journal publication will receive far more attention than a project report. In other instances, several journals may be used in order to reach different audiences. The manner of dissemination of project information should be consistent with the degree of impact the information is expected to have and with its potential usefulness to others.

REFERENCES

1. *A Program to Train Police Officers to Intervene in Family Disturbances* Final Report United States Department of Justice No. NI-056.

2. Bard, M.: *Family Intervention Police Teams as a Community Mental Health Resource. Journal of Criminal Law, Criminology and Police Science, 60,* (2) 1969, 247-250.

3. Bard, M.: Alternatives to Traditional Law Enforcement (Ed.) : Korten, F.F., Cook, S. W., and Lacey, J. I. *Psychology and the Problems of Society,* p.p. 128-132.

4. Bard, M. and Berkowitz, B.: Training Police as Specialists in Family Crisis Intervention. *Community Mental Health Journal, 3* (4), 1967, p.p. 315-317.

5. Bard, M. and Berkowitz, B.: Family disturbance as a police function. *Law Enforcement Science and Technology II* (Ed.): S. I. Cohn, Chicago, Illinois, IIT Research Institute, 1968 p.p. 505-508.

6. Bard, M. and Zacker, J.: Design for conflict resolution, paper, *Third National Symposium on Law Enforcement Science and Technology.* Chicago, Illinois, 1970 p.p. 1-10.

7. Barocas, H.: A Community Mental Health Program in Police Crisis Intervention. *Experimental Publication System,* April, 1971, *11,* Ms. No. 429-56.

8. Barocas, H. and Katz, M.L.: Dayton's Pilot Training Program: Crisis Intervention. *Police Chief,* July, 1971.

9. Barry, Kinney: Consulting Psychologist, Tacoma Police Department, personal communication.

10. Bensing, R. C. and Schroeder, O.: *Homicide in an Urban Community.* Springfield, Illinois, Charles C Thomas, 1960.

11. *Bridgeport Police Department Family Crisis Training Program.* Final Report, United States Department of Justice, A70-15-45.

12. Bullock, H.A.: Urban Homicide in Theory and Fact. *Journal of Criminal Law, Criminology and Police Science, 46,* 1955.

13. Director of Training, St. Louis Housing Authority Police, personal communication.

14. Family Crisis Project Coordinator, Lowell Police Department, personal communication.

15. *F.B.I. Law Enforcement Bulletin,* Jan, 1963, p. 27.

16. *F.B.I. Uniform Crime Reports,* 1967, United States Government Printing Offce, Washington, D.C.

17. Joint Commission on Mental Health and Illness: *Action for Mental Health.* New York: Basic Books, 1961.

18. New York City Police Department: *Police Response to Family Disputes: A Training Manual for Family Crisis Intervention.* 1969.

19. Niederhoffer, A. and Blumberg, A.: *The Ambivalent Force: Perspectives on the Police,* Ginn and Co., Waltham, Massachusetts, 1970.

20. Oakland Police Department: *Information Bulletin,* Family Crisis Intervention Program, January, 1971.

21. Parnas, R. I.: The Police Response to the Domestic Disturbance, 1967, *Wisconsin Law Review,* 914-960.

22. Phelps, L.: Richmond Police Department Revises Patrol System. *Journal of California Law Enforcement,* April, 1969, p. 185.
23. Phelps, L. and Murphy, R.: The Team Patrol System in Richmond, California. *Police Chief,* June, 1969.
24. Phelps, L., Schwartz, J. A., and Liebman, D. A.: Training an Entire Patrol Division in Domestic Crisis Intervention, *Police Chief,* 1971.
25. *Police Management of Conflicts Among People,* United States Department of Justice, NI-028, 1970.
26. *Police Training in Family Crisis Intervention.* Final Report, Kentucky Crime Commission, 1971.
27. Project Supervisor, Charlotte Police Department, personal communication.
28. Project Co-ordinator, Multnomah County (Oregon) Sheriff's Office, Personal communication.
29. Schwartz, J. A. and Liebman, D. A.: A Police Survey of Family Crisis Intervention, unpublished.
30. Schwartz, J. A. and Liebman, D. A.: *Domestic Crisis Interventon: A Programmed Text for Law Enforcement Officers,* Charles C Thomas, in press Springfield, Illinois.
31. *Training Police in Crisis Intervention.* Final Report, Director of Police, Dayton, Ohio, 1971.
32. *Training Police as Specialists in Family Crisis Intervention.* United States Department of Justice No. PR 70-1 1970.
33. Wolfgang, M. E.: *Patterns in Criminal Homicide.* Philadelphia: University of Pennsylvania Press, 1958.

Chapter 22

CHANGE THROUGH PARTICIPATION (AND VICE VERSA)

Hans Toch*

L ATE ON A WEDNESDAY EVENING a fleet of motorcycles turned into a parking lot in Oakland, California. Several Hell's Angels dismounted and crossed the street, heading for the lobby of the Oakland Police Building. Five minutes later the men entered a meeting room, shook hands with seven police officers, and helped themselves to coffee. The group then settled down to serious business.

The cyclists were serving as consultants to an unusual team of policemen who work as change agents, groping for ways to solve a complex social and practical problem. Their problem areas, of concern to both society and professional police, are those of conflict between police and citizens. Their mission involves imaginative ways of eliminating avoidable confrontations, and creating an atmosphere that reduces risks of violence.

FROM CHANGE CLIENTS TO CHANGE AGENTS

The unique feature of the project lies in its choice of personnel. Other things being constant, we seek to employ officers who have themselves participated in more conflict than their peers. We assume that these men can become not only personally effective, but especially powerful agents of police professionalization.

Our premise is that an individual's liabilities can be not only

Reprinted with permission of the National Council on Crime and Delinquency, New York, New York and the Author.

The project described in this paper was supported by the National Institute of Mental Health. The project was entitled "Training Police Officers for Violence Prevention." Raymond Galvin, Co-Director; J. Douglas Grant, Consultant.

*The Author wishes to thank the Oakland Police Department, and its Chief, Charles Gain.

neutralized, but turned into assets. At first blush, this prescription sounds overly optimistic. But history furnishes us several examples of its viability. Consider, for example, the roster of saints who started their careers as sinners. I would argue not only that sainthood is rehabilitative, but that sinning provides helpful background for a successful spiritual militant. For one, I suspect that when sinner-saints discuss humanity, they must know whereof they speak. They have accumulated variegated first hand experiences that put flesh on the bones of their theological concerns. They can address themselves to the spiritual struggles of their fellows with empathy and credibility. Moreover, they have reason to care. Having (as they see it) faced the abyss of their own destruction, they are motivated to save others from a comparable fate.

The same logic applies to more mundane transitions. The police officer who over-eagerly responds to the hostility of citizens invites physical confrontations. If we can induce such an officer to adopt a more sophisticated perspective, he can draw upon a wealth of data about violence not possessed by less aggressive officers. Moreover, he is uniquely able to see the point of the violence prevention effort. He can think back to his own narrow escapes—the near-riots, injuries, courtroom inquisitions and reprimands from superiors. He can recall the necessary deceptions and their risk.

Of course the question is whether—and how—we can convince a problem person to abandon habits of a lifetime and to modify his premises and goals. Why should he cooperate? He may not only feel comfortable with his pattern of conduct, but may derive dynamically suspect satisfaction from it. He may see no "problem," and he may view himself in favorable terms.

What counts is the fact that a demonstrable problem *does* exist. We need only help the person to discover the (for him) undesirable consequences of his acts. We need also offer attractive rewards on our side of the fence. What is involved is not material incentive, but more intimate psychological gain such as an important role in life or increased grounds for self-respect.

In all of this, I think the fundamental rule to remember is

Lewin's adage that you cannot induce change through frontal assault. A person moves if and when he wants to, and he must arrive at this juncture himself. The best any of us can do it to provide an atmosphere that facilitates innovative thinking.

THE POLICE PROJECT

What we have done in the Oakland Police Department is to create an environment in which violence-experienced officers can become experts on violence. In this environment, the officers can evolve ways of reducing conflict for themselves as well as for others.

We have started modestly. We have brought together seven patrolmen and assigned them (half-time) the task of educating themselves and of training others. Our first group is exceptional (for us), because it is not one of problem policemen, although several members have backgrounds of violence involvements. The men were chosen on the basis of group interviews, so as to insure that they could handle themselves constructively in a group setting.

The procedure worked. As it stands, we have a team that represents a solid variety of resources. The senior member is Bob Prentice (41), who joined the police department in 1951. Bob is physically imposing, direct and resourceful, with qualities that bring him to the fore in any situation. He is a natural politician and leader. Bob's personal experience extends into the "rough and ready" days of law enforcement, but at present, Bob is far from "rough and ready." His perspective is flexible, and he argues forcefully for the sophisticated exercise of police discretion.

Next to Bob in seniority is Mike Weldon (32) who has spent seven years on the job. Mike is a policeman's policeman, thoughtful, firm, consistent and immensely patient. Mike personifies stability, and his interventions in our group are measured, pointed and relevant. Mike—like Bob—commands respect among the rank and file of the Oakland Police.

Carl Hewitt (28) has five years of police work to his credit. He has a sparkling, inventive mind, and an awesome command of language. Carl is a consumate actor, with a spontaneous capacity for mimicry and role playing. He is intuitively skilled in human relations and flexible in the management of interpersonal encounters.

Two of the group who have four years on the force are Roy Garrison (29) and John Dixon (28). Roy has accumulated numerous college credits. His academic work includes several subjects of relevance to the project, including group dynamics and management. John Dixon has no college training, but an omnivorous reader, and successfully self-educated. John is quiet, perceptive and thoughtful.

Larry Murphy (31) has spent two years in police work. He is a mature person, having been discharged by the Navy as a chief. Larry is invariably able to focus group attention on priorities and on the means necessary to reach them. Larry provides a reservoir of technical skills (communications and electronics) and much leadership experience.

The comparatively young member of the group is Mike Nordin (26) who joined the department over two years ago. Mike packs power into a quiet, even, soft-spoken approach to others. He is insightful in his dealings with fellow officers and civilians, and is able to skillfully reduce tensions and prevent conflicts.

The Oakland Police Department Violence Prevention Unit (as we called ourselves) started functioning July 2, 1969. Ten of us—seven police officers and three staff—met for two eight-hour days each week. The officers in the group led double lives. Half their working time was spent in uniform, answering calls and responding to routine police business; the rest of the time, in casual attire, they engaged in discussion and research, similar to that of graduate students and professors.

What did the group do? To provide some flavor of their activities, I shall try to describe one or two of the Unit's projects.

The Violence Tape Library

During our first meeting, an officer (Prentice) brought up the idea that we could record live incidents of potential violence. He suggested that tapes of real confrontations could provide research data, and could permit informed review by others. The group noted the suggestion (among others), but let it drop.

In the fifth session, the tape recording idea was brought forward again. This time, the group worried over ethical and practical implications. What of police who might arrive on the scene? What about the Unit's image, if the men were known to carry concealed recorders? How could one run such a project to avoid repercussions? The group decided the idea might be worth the risk, perhaps on a one-shot trial basis.

At the sixth session, we examined a miniature recorder, purchased by the Police Department for other uses. We decided to give the machine a field test. A week later, the recorder reappeared with a successfully captured incident. This incident, discussed in detail, seemed potentially useful as training material. The group decided to add recorded comments to the tape, and to listen to it. This package—in modified form—led to the creation of a Violence Tape Library.

The tapes we produce are spontaneous documentaries. In each of them, an officer confronts citizens in an explosive situation. We hear screaming and cursing, furniture crashing into walls, and people rushing about. We hear recriminations, challenges, and demands for help. We hear the police placed in the vortex of sometimes irreconcilable pressures. And we hear the officer trying to appease, to pacify—to somehow prevent an extreme act. The officer may use various strategies (there are no rule books here) and he may succeed or fail. Whatever happens, there is a lesson, both for him and other police officers faced with like problems.

In the tapes, each officer takes a look at his own experience. In the relative calm of an impromptu studio (Murphy's workshop), the man edits his tape, provides background information, and adds a running commentary as needed. His talk is added "on sound," so that the action evolves as the man talks.

The tapes include an analysis section, in which our officer second-guesses or criticizes himself; this is followed by comments from other group members. The "package" is a lesson—drawn from life—of applied human relations. It can be used as is, ready-made, as raw material for comments, or as a model for others if they are equipped with a tape recorder on the street.

The prospective market could include officers who permit street situations to degenerate because of poor self-control or bad judgment. Such strategies (or non-strategies) could yield to systematic review of failures. Memory is no help here because (even with honesty) errors blur. The tape recorder preserves (in sequence), and it details (inescapably) their sometimes tragic consequences.

Positive alternatives—featuring constructive approaches—can also be dramatized. To illustrate such options, as seen by our group, it might help to review excerpts from a tape. These feature one of our officers (Hewitt) responding to a family disturbance call.

The Problem Situation

Few people realize that the police do not typically deal with crime in process. Only infrequently do officers confront a burglar in the act of burglary, or a fleeing mugger or car thief. More routinely, the police deal with emotionally aroused citizens—with persons who are angry, fearful, excited, resentful or upset. Officers sometimes arrest such persons, but they have other choices of action, and they must carefully assess individuals and circumstances before deciding what to do. A technical violation of the law is a factor they must consider, but there are more human considerations—and they must be weighed.

Hewitt's encounter is instructive in this regard, because it shows the options of the officer and resolves these without the use of sanctions. As Hewitt recalls—"I received a call about 10:30 in the morning Saturday, of a family fight that had just occurred on —— Avenue, involving a husband and wife. It had occurred in the street and he (the husband) had allegedly beaten her and torn her clothing off. I responded to the call being covered by wagon officers."

The opening conversation on the tape is with the wife, who makes it clear—and repeatedly clear—that she wants her husband arrested:

WOMAN: I want to take care of him for tearing off my sweater! That's what he done two weeks ago, and then he threw a knife at me again last night. I'm tired of this!

CARL: Didn't you have him arrested?
WOMAN: Yeah, but I had to go to the District Attorney. But now I mean it!
CARL: You mean it this time?
WOMAN: I do. I want him picked up!

While this sort of dialogue is going on, the husband appears (at first, unnoticed) on the scene; the situation at this point becomes potentially explosive:

"The lady lunged past me, grabbed for the baby, in an attempt to get it from her husband's arms. My main concern now was keeping them apart from physical contact."
CARL: Why don't you go inside? All right, go inside!

Hewitt takes the opportunity to question the husband in detail, in an effort to get his side of the story. The man represents himself as a rescuer of infants from irresponsible intoxicated women, and describes the ripping of the sweater as an accidental consequence of an unstable hold:

CARL: Now, how did you happen to tear her sweater off like that without hurting the baby?
MAN: Well, I asked her to stay there. You know, she started out of the car. Then I reached for her and she just ripped. You know, jumped out. She was standing by the car, and she jumped out of the car. And I had my hand on her sweater like this and it ripped when she jumped.

At this junction, the tables turn. While the officer talks to the husband, the wife enters the scene, and new conflict threatens. This time, the officer engages the wife:

She attempts again to get near the husband. And our main concern is keeping them apart. The wagon officer has come over and attracted the woman's attention in asking her her name, her address and so forth, in an attempt to keep her from her husband. Now he's getting the lady inside the house so that I can talk to her about the incident and try to establish whether or not an arrest should be effected.
WOMANS I mean it; I'm tired of this! Look what he done to me. . .
CARL: Do you think it might be a good idea to go inside rather than let everybody in the neighborhood know your problem? Huh?

While the other officer distracts the husband, Hewitt takes the wife into the house. He reports that this strategy pays off in some respect (peace is temporarily restored), but brings him new problems. Mainly, the lady welcomes the opportunity for what she regards as a gripe session. Hewitt listens, but tries to turn the conversation back to the marital difficulty:

> Now, I find that the wife is running rather rampant about a great many problems. She's beginning to tell me things that happened a week ago, two weeks ago—things that have happened the night before, things that are completely irrelevant to the problem at hand. Which leads me to believe at this point that she may in fact just need somebody to talk to.
> WOMAN: We had a bottle in here... (some incoherent sentences)
> CARL: The baby can upset you a great deal, huh? Sometimes?
> WOMAN: Sometimes he does. I'm getting too old to take care of little babies. And Jim don't help me. If he'd help me, I wouldn't care.
> CARL: How old are you now?
> WOMAN: I'm 45.
> CARL: 45. How long have you and Jim been married?
> WOMAN: Six years.

As the conversation progresses, Hewitt comes to feel that the wife wishes "to use me, the officer, as a threat to her husband." He says: "At this point I feel she doesn't want an arrest. She merely expects me to scare the man, or to bring to his attention that she in fact does have the power to have him arrested." Having sensed the lady's reluctance to prosecute (despite her vigorous demands for her husband's arrest), Hewitt explores the consequences, and works out a solution that seems satisfactory to the lady:

> CARL: ...It's kind of tough for a young man like myself to come in here and have to tell people you and Jim's age—you know, how to get along with each other. We don't want to arrest people unless we absolutely have to. You say it's going to mess up his check. Now I'm going to leave it up to you.
> WOMAN: Well, we get $124 and I ain't got no money.
> CARL: You think it's going to worsen the situation to have to put up bail?
> WOMAN: It will, cause when he gets out it will be worse.
> CARL: Well, financially, anyway. Besides that, he's going to have to pay bail, which is going to cost money.
> WOMAN: Right.
> CARL: So maybe arrest isn't the answer, do you think?

WOMAN: I know, but when you guys leave, that's when I'm really going to get it!

CARL: Do you really believe that? Do you really believe the guy will work you over if I tell him that if I have to come back here today or anytime, he's going to go to jail, and I'm not going to even talk about it? That he's just going! You don't think that'll do any good?

WOMAN: It might, if you talk to him real stern.

CARL: Do you want me to try it?

WOMAN: Yeah.

CARL: All right, fine! And if you have any more trouble, just give us a call, O.K.?

WOMAN: O.K.

The husband is notified of the disposition of his case, and seems grateful:

CARL: I kind of want to put it on you this way: I talked to her and kind of convinced her that arresting you wouldn't be a good thing, and believe me, she has grounds to lock you up, pal! If you're going to beef with your wife, do it in your house. And do it without ripping her clothes off! If I were you, I'd stay the hell away from her for awhile. Let her cool off. Because she's really upset. Well, I'm going to leave that up to you, but I'll tell you right now, if I get another call . . .

JIM: If you come back you take me to jail.

CARL: You're going—there's no doubt about it, if I come back! O.K.?

JIM: Fine. Thank you.

This concludes the incident, as well as Hewitt's running analysis of it. The remainder of the tape consists of additional inquiry into the officer's strategy, and the reasons for it. The following excerpt illustrates this process:

GROUP MEMBER: Prior to the husband's arriving at the scene where you were with the woman, Carl, the woman insisted about six or seven times that she wanted the man arrested, and you seemed to be deliberately avoiding this question, or any response to this question. Why?

CARL: Well, at this point, I hadn't yet confronted the other party involved in this altercation, and I hadn't really established enough facts to know whether or not an arrest was going to have to be effected. Until I could establish this fact, I did try to avoid it, in an attempt to bring out more details of what happened.

GROUP MEMBER: Right at the end, when you were talking to the husband, you told him five different times in five different ways that you didn't want to come back—that he wasn't to hit his wife anymore. Why did you go into this so often?

CARL: I was trying very hard to get the point across to the man that I was very serious in what I was saying. Many times an officer will use this on calls, and I have also, as an out—as a parting statement. But I really was serious at this point, and I wanted to impress this fact upon the individual to the point that he felt the import of what I was trying to say. Although it was rather redundant, at that time I felt it was necessary to get the point across to him.

This tape—and others like it—are a violence-reduction tool because they permit sequential review of situations. If the problem is solved without violence, the strategy can be teased out in steps for possible application elsewhere. If the incident degenerates, the analysis of taped material can reveal how and where it did. The group can then propose alternative courses of action, and trace out their consequences. The result is an inventory of police-civilian games and of how these are won or lost.

VIOLENCE AS AN OPTION

The objectives of the police civilian "game" cannot be understood when separated from the rules that govern it. Thus, a topic which proved of constant interest to our group was the relationship between violence and "good" police work. How much conflict results from a real need to move into explosive situations? How much of it results from ill-conceived interference in situations calling for no action? In other words, what would constitute commendably aggressive—as against unprofessionally over-aggressive—police work?

The group tackled this question with research. They constructed a critical incident questionnaire based on situations actually experienced by themselves. They pretested this instrument, reconstructed it through item analysis, and re-administered it to a sample of officers including recruits, command personnel, and the chief himself.

One set of their findings was that different groups gave different responses to different items. To cite an example, there were items which produced arrests only among recruits. The following is one of these:

A telephone complaint received of a family disturbance; the complainant refuses to identify himself. The officer responds, and encounters a black man, approximately thirty-years-old. The report states:

> "Officer approaches scene and hears sound of argument. Officer knocks. Argument stops. Door opened by subject wearing T-shirt. Officer asks if police needed. Subject says, 'No, pig!' and slams door in officer's face."

What happens next? For the older officers, nothing much. Some would leave at once, and others would seek information first. But a largish number of recruits (8 out of 22) felt that they would seek to arrest. What accounts for this difference? The crux of the problem is the perception of critical information, such as the availability (or nonavailability) of complaintants. Regardless of the merits of the issue, here is a topic which recruit training has seemingly missed.

On a different level, the questionnaire yielded diagnostic information. In reviewing patterns of responses, we found that some officers demonstrated chronic indecisiveness, which left them pensively lingering in the wrong places. Other officers showed an affinity for mobilizing help, and thus produced organizational "over-kill." Others manifested a "bull in the china shop" syndrome, and charged indelicately into every crisis. A fourth group showed a propensity to retaliate verbally, thus escalating conflict.

A third approach to the questionnaire focussed on communications within the police department. Several of our incidents resulted in arrests, although command personnel indicated they would not take action. In at least one instance, the issue was an interpretation of law, easily subject to clarification.

These sorts of findings illustrate how action research conducted by subject-matter experts can increase the sophistication of staff, open new areas of investigation, and suggest reforms.

ORGANIZATIONAL CHANGE FROM WITHIN

Several of our group projects were directed at organizational change. We conducted surveys of departmental activities—communication and training—that could affect the chances of violence. We made recommendations, and members of the group were delegated to work out the details of new programs.

One example of such activity was a survey of the selection of training officers—men who "break in" recruits when they reach the street. The importance of this area rests on the premise—as valid among police as in universities—that peer training can neutralize the impact of academic work. The novice is susceptible to the views of "experienced" tutors, because initiation experiences tend to be overwhelming in their complexity. A misassigned trainer can thus leave his charge with career-long habits that spell problems to himself and others.

In considering the problem, our group became concerned about the pairing of trainers and trainees, and about monitoring of the process. They made recommendations suggesting a new position (training officer coordinator) and streamlined procedures.

FROM PROFESSIONAL POLICE TO POLICE PROFESSIONALS

I have illustrated the range of our group's activities. As noted, we have collected data; we have brought about review and reform. Our efforts have evoked interest around the country, where they have been described—by the officers themselves—at state and regional meetings.

But I would suggest that these impressive pay-offs are far less important than that of converting our group members into professionals who can help mold their profession. These seven men can now better affect their own work, and they can become more helpful to their fellows. They can conduct training, and thus improve the quality of police contacts. More important, future generations (the men training by the men who are trained by our men) can play similar roles. This trend—once initiated, is designed to be self-perpetuating. It creates a vehicle whereby the police institution—and other institutions—can renew themselves and improve themselves from within.

THE PSYCHOLOGY OF PARTICIPATION, REVISITED

Three decades ago, Gordon Allport enjoined social scientists to consider "the psychology of participation." Allport cited laboratory findings and summarized pioneer work in industry. He pointed out that effective group membership (large and small) presupposes the sharing of goals; that it presumes that each member plays a meaningful role in the achievement of democracy.

On the current scene, participation is an endemic and obsessive theme. It preoccupies adolescents, and concerns black militants, welfare clients, women, and institutional inmates; it permeates the ideology of radicals and conservatives; it is a publicized tenet of government.

What of social science? The issue (as a slogan) has us hotly divided. Yet, Allport's injunction remains unheeded. We have no systematic inquiry into "the psychology of participation," and no body of thought or knowledge. No one has defined "participation," nor classified it, sorted its components, or traced its implications. We have not studied the impact of participatory membership on individuals and institutions. We assume participation "works," but we can furnish no blueprints or instructions.

Because the gap exists, the practitioner must fill it. Change-oriented projects must show results—and failures—in detail. They must trace the landmarks of progress and plot its pitfalls. They must self-consciously inventory the anatomy of change.

Chapter 23

TRAINING POLICE TO INTERVENE IN HUMAN CONFLICT

STEVEN J. DANISH AND NANCY FERGUSON

CHANGE IN OUR SOCIETY is necessarily reflected in the institutions which we create to serve us. As society has undergone massive change in the past decade, its institutions, which tend to change more slowly than the society itself, have been under considerable pressure to reexamine its directions and purposes. One institution which has been particularly subject to pressure by the community at large is the police. The police as an agency are not separated from the community but part of the community itself. Consequently, the way in which the community behaves necessarily influences the behavior of the police, and sooner or later a community molds its police force in its own image (Lopez-Rey, 1968). For example, as a result of the social changes taking place many traditional social values and customs are rapidly being altered and new social and political groups are evolving to challenge the authority and practices of establised interests. These changes requiring the discarding of old values and the accepting of new standards cause much unrest among the police. The unrest occurs because society has failed to inform the police of the new code of conduct and, therefore, the police are not yet prepared to handle the resulting confusion.

The pressure placed on the police is perhaps greater than on other institutions because it is one of the first to face the consequence of social change. The sense of urgency and insistence which accompanies the demand for change often results in tension, distrust, rumors and sometimes even physical violence within the community.

486

INTRODUCTION

Change in our society is necessarily reflected in the institutions which we create to serve us. As society has undergone massive change in the past decade, its institutions, which tend to change more slowly than the society itself, have been under considerable pressure to reexamine its directions and purposes. One institution which has been particularly subject to pressure by the community at large is the police. The police as an agency are not separate from the community but part of the community itself. Consequently, the way in which the community behaves necessarily influences the behavior of the police and sooner or later a community molds its police force in its own image (Lopez-Rey, 1968). For example, as a result of the social changes taking place many traditional social values and customs are rapidly being altered and new social and political groups are evolving to challenge the authority and practices of established interests. These changes requiring the discarding of old values and the accepting of new standards cause much unrest among the police. The unrest occurs because society has failed to inform the police of the new codes of conduct and, therefore, the police are not yet prepared to handle the resulting confusion.

The pressure placed on the police is perhaps greater than on other institutions because it is one of the first to face the consequence of social change. The sense of urgency and instistence which accompanies the demand for change often results in tension, distrust, rumors and sometimes even physical violence within the community. When these stressful events occur it is most often the police who are asked to serve as the primary mediator and reduce the conflict (Sikes and Cleveland, 1968). However, because both the citizens and the police are under stress during the mediation process, the potential for negative feelings and confrontation between the two groups is high.

THE STATUS OF POLICE TRAINING

How have the police handled the pressures resulting from the social changes? Both police administrators and large segments of the public have called for more and better training for police so they can effectively handle the results of social change. However, the call for training has been more a recognition that training is necessary rather than a consideration of what kind of training will be most helpful. Much of the interest in training has centered around words such as "human-relations training," "community-relations training" and "communication training."

The broad discussion given these terms indicates general agreement on what the problem areas are. However, when one attempts to identify specific skills to incorporate into training programs, he is confronted with gross generalities. For example, some of the goals reported from a police-community relations conference held at Michigan State University were:

1. To foster and improve communication, and, hopefully, mutual understanding in the relationship of the police and total community.
2. To assist police and community leaders in an understanding of the nature and works of complex problems in people-to-people relations; therefore, to encourage intelligent and prudent handling of the problems (Radelet, 1964).

Further, Newman and Steinberg (1970) posit that the success of a modern police force is dependent on the human-relations skills of its officers. As noted above, it would appear that general agreement exists about the importance of communicating and relating effectively with others, but *what does that really mean and how does one do it*. We wonder whether the vagueness with which these goals have been defined has not contributed to the suspicion that exists among some police officers about this new orientation in police training.

Realistic Goals for Police Training

The status of police training appears confused. There has been little progress made toward the identification of either reasonable goals for training or of definitive procedures by which training should take place.

What are realistic goals of police training and how can we determine what they are? It first seems necessary to identify what police do; what their major functions are. There seems to be two appropriate means of determining these functions: (1) ask the police themselves to identify their major roles and functions and (2) assess by role or function analysis how police spend their time.

A recent study by Sterling and Watson (1971) under the auspices of the International Association of Chiefs of Police (IACP) sought to identify the policeman's perception of his role. One of the conclusions drawn from the study is that the policeman sees his role as having little to do with "policing." Eighty percent of police work is seen as "social work;" i.e. giving directions, interceding in domestic relations, counseling, etc.

How does the policeman's perception of his role compare to analyses done on what the police really do? Cumming, et al. (1965) studied the hypothesis that the police role was explicitly concerned with control (keeping the law from being broken and apprehending those who break it) and only implicitly involved in supportive, service functions. The requests for help received by an urban ghetto police department and police responses to these calls were investigated. Over 82 selected hours during a two-month period, data was collected on 801 calls that were received. The 652 calls used for analysis (149 were excluded since they were callbacks or otherwise not useable) were dichotomized into requests for service in connection with things or possessions, and calls for support or assistance with regard to health, safety or interpersonal relationships. The latter category was subdivided into persistent problems (those occurring during the week) and periodic problems (occurring mainly on weekends). Results indicate that "support" type calls were received at the desk 50 percent of the time. The most dominant activities in persistent problems dealt with health (ambulance escorts, investigation of accidents, suicides) or child problems (complaints regarding trespassing or destructive behavior). For periodic problems, the most frequent service involved intervention in disputes and quarrels of all kinds, both in families and among unrelated people.

More recently, Bard (1969) noted that an average of 63 calls per month fitted the designation of family crisis and that an average of 30 minutes per call was spent by family intervention police teams handling the crisis. The President's Commission on Law

Enforcement and Administration of Justice in 1967 noted that 90 percent of police time is spent in solving non-criminal type problems relating to personal crisis. Fifty percent of police calls nation-wide are requests to intervene in family disputes. Misner (1969) on reviewing data about the nature of police work concluded:

> "Enough data has been collected from a variety of cities to show clearly that the uniform policeman in large urban areas typically spends less than 30 percent of their working time dealing with crime or other enforcement duties . . . (they are) engaged for the most part in work which should properly be classified as 'public service.' This is often true even in 'high crime neighborhoods.' It seems that neighborhoods that have high instances of crime also have high instances of calls for other police services."

Therefore, one can conclude that the 20th Century policeman's job involves something more than being adept at the "cops and robbers" function. The policeman has become a helping agent. However, before we start replacing policemen with social workers as some law enforcement administrators fear and some social scientists wish to do, let us examine more closely what the helping role of the police entails.

THE PUBLIC SERVICE ROLE OF THE POLICE

It seems evident from the analysis of the police role that the major police function is that of helping and public service. Some of this helping and public service work is performed in clearly demarcated circumstances; for example, community relations work having to do with drug education. However, the majority of service occurs in situations where either the citizen or the police or both are under stress, and when someone's physical or mental health or perhaps one's life is in jeopardy. Such situations include: helping accident victims and their families, intervening in family disputes, intervening in racial or generational conflicts, helping victims in various environmental crises and situations which involve citizen (offender) -police confrontations. It is clear that few police have any training which facilitates them in handling these human conflict situations. This work is often talked about disparagingly as "social work."

Police often react negatively to functions and training in which they see themselves being required to perform "social work" duties. We have similar reactions to the demand that the police become "social workers." Let us examine what this demand really means. The role and function of the social worker is, in part, to help the citizen learn to understand himself and his place in society and if the citizen is uncomfortable with his present existence to help him change it. The social worker, then, is concerned with helping the individual in his quest to better himself psychologically socially and physically. This concern requires a strong commitment of time and energy to the individual (s) the social worker helps.

The police, on the other hand, have a mandate to keep society healthy rather than the individual by helping and serving its citizens. Their focus is not on any one individual's concerns but on society's welfare. While his duties do involve service to individuals it is as part of his mandate to society and when the crisis is over it is his duty to transfer his work with the individual to someone who can commit himself wholly to that individual's welfare. It might be nice for the police to follow through on all their commitments to individuals and we are sure many social and behavioral scientists would want this, but we contend that someone must concern themselves with society's welfare and the policeman seems in the best position to do this. The social workers and other mental health personnel should assume the role of agent to the individual.

A second reason why police may not be the best choice to establish intense helping relationships with the public is the personal qualities of the police. Mills (1969) developed a small diagnostic group game for police selection which tapped the following attributes: cooperation, leadership, persuasiveness, group participation and ability to function under pressure. The diagnostic game yielded a composite picture of a person who has difficulty recognizing and admitting to aggressive emotions and typically projects his own aggression to others as a self justification; has low levels of interpersonal trust and a high degree of suspicion toward others; and has an intolerance for ambiguity. Also, Zacker (1970) infers from an examination of a number of studies that empathy and interpersonal sensitivity, two qualities many behavioral scientists consider essential in helping relationships, are not prominent attributes of the "typical" policeman. In sum, it appears that police do not have the qualities commonly attributed to effective helpers.

While the police may not have the qualities to be considered the primary community mental health agent, there are pressing reasons why the police should learn effective helping skills. The most important reason is to facilitate their service to society. As Bittner (1967) notes, activities which involve peace-keeping contain elements of control and support in a unique combination that requires high level skills. For example, Toch (1969), in his recent study of violent incidents involving policemen, concluded that violence is frequently triggered by persons in authority because they allow themselves to fit into a preconceived stereotype which contributes to acting our behaviors. Conversely, the occupational experiences of the police lead the officer to think of citizens in legal categories or stereotypes. Unfortunately, such a tendency severely obscures essential helping skills, which may be appropriate to the situation. This stereotypic thinking provides a base for a "self-fulfilling prophecy" in situations where the labels and their imputed characteristics are communicated to people who may respond with violence.

Bard has coined the term "iatrogenic violence" to label the phenomenon of police intervention which results in increased conflict for the disputants as well as causing possibly death or injury to the policeman. For family crisis intervention, the problem of iatrogenic violence is particularly critical. In research on 588 homicides in Philadelphia over a five year period, approximately 25 percent were relatives, 28 percent were close friends and 20 percent were husband-wife homicides. Bard (1969) notes that about one-third of homicides and even more assaults take place in the family. He also indicates that nationally 22 percent of the police killed and 40 percent of the injuries occurred while police were intervening in family disturbances. Said another way, police attempts at helping resolve family disturbances as well as civil disorders, can be for the better or for the worse, but rarely leave the situation the same (Gormally, 1971). The physical safety of police and citizens, not to mention mental health of the community, demand that police receive adequate preparation to intervene successfully in behavioral problems.

If the police are not to be the community's primary mental health agent, what is their role to be, and what skills are essential for them to effectively perform the functions associated with this role? As noted earlier there are two basic kinds of helping situations police confront. The first is an information and community relations function. As part of this function the officer provides information about the law and customs of the community such as acquainting the public about the drug abuse problem. Also, the officer acts as a public relations agent for the department emphasizing the importance of the police role and of obeying the law. In general, he is serving as a visible representative of the police profession. To effectively perform this function police often take public speaking courses and programs designed to create favorable impressions upon people ("how to make friends and influence people").

The second police function is that of providing assistance in human conflict situations. We contend that the skills involved in this function have been either overlooked or inadequately taught; in part, because they have not been accurately identified. Some of the essential skills would seem to be (1) an ability to ferret out the needs of the citizens in conflict and therefore an understanding of the communication of another including observing what he does, hearing what he says and how he says it, and sensing what he has not said or done but wishes to. In order to understand these aspects of the communication of another the police must acquaint themselves with various verbal and non-verbal (body language) behaviors; (2) an understanding of what effect police have on various segments of community and the likely reactions to them; (3) the skill of relating to others in a manner which communicates their desire and ability to be an effective helper. This skill requires their using effective non-verbal attending behavior and verbal response behavior; (4) an understanding of their needs for being public service agents and (5) to learn an effective use of one's own emotion in conflict situations. This fifth skill would entail the police being able to identify their emotional reaction to various crisis situations and the consequences of acting according to these emotional responses, and if alternative behavioral responses would prove more effective to identify these responses and use them.

The above skills are more specific than the global human relations skills or communication training mentioned earlier. The advantage of the specificity is that the skills can be behaviorally defined and therefore more readily teachable (Danish, 1972). For example, effective non-verbal attending behavior is defined as:

> "Eye contact—*good* eye contact includes looking at another individual when he is talking to you or when you are talking to him. The eye contact should be spontaneous glances expressing an interest and desire to communicate. *Poor* eye contact includes never looking at another—constantly and blankly staring at another; immediately looking away from another as soon as he looks at you.
>
> Postural position (including gestural and facial expressions) —*good* postural position includes sitting with one's body facing another; hands either on lap or desk loosley clasped or *occasionally* being used to gesturally indicate what is being communicated verbally; being responsive facially, i.e. sopntaneous smiling or nodding of head in agreement or understanding and frowning when not understanding; body should be erect but not rigid with occasional leaning toward the other to emphasize a verbal point being made or to indicate a "withness" to the other. *Poor* postural position includes sitting with body and head not facing another person; slouching; sitting in a very fixed, rigid position without moving; being restless or frigid, being preoccupied with hands, papers on lap or desk; cleaning fingernails; making no gestures at all with hands; constant moving and thrashing of hands and arms; no facial expressions (stonefaced); too much inappropriate smiling, frowning or nodding of head" (Danish, 1972).

The behavioral definitions are a part of a paraprofessional training program designed to teach the basic helping skills involved in interpersonal situations. While I am not suggesting that the police are paraprofessionals, I do believe that they are in need of some of the same skills paraprofessionals should possess.

THE PROCESS OF LEARNING EFFECTIVE CRISIS INTERVENTION SKILLS

All too often, behavioral and social scientists have failed to distinguish the goals of training from the processes of learning the goals. Consequently, the process of learning is sometimes amphorous and vague. Again, the vagueness might well contribute to the suspicion police have about these training progrms. The material presented above has focused on identifying the goals of training; the focus of this section will be to identify various processes which have been used to reach past training goals.

One procedure to teach the essential skills outlined above which has been receiving increased attention and support is the use of the university curriculum. Proponents of a mandatory two-year college education for police have suggested that courses in psychology, sociology and other liberal arts subjects will help the police better understand the citizens and environment in which they work.

It is noteworthy that this increased interest in the college experience for police occurs at a time when higher education is under attack by both students and the public at large as being irrelevant. It is questionable whether a general studies education in itself will enable the police to become better prepared to face the psychological confrontations and public service demands of their job. Certainly the authors' experiences with introductory psychology courses were of little value in understanding people. This is not to disparage the value of a college education or many of the law enforcement academic programs. However, many law enforcement programs do not address themselves to teaching police how to handle human conflict. Higher education by itself is no panacea; one must examine the specific police education programs to determine just what goals are being achieved. While higher education may be a valuable experience for a policeman, or for that matter, anyone, there are no indications that it produces better policemen.

A variation of the college experience is the use of increased academy training to teach the police "human-relations or community-relations skills." Many recruit training programs now have large blocks of time devoted to the subject. McNamara (1967) notes, after reviewing one police department's human relations training, that:

> "The training was covered primarily by lectures given by the academic instructors in formal class meetings . . . For the most part, any principles regarding interpersonal skills were presented either in the form of rather general prescriptions, for example, 'be firm but courteous,' or in the form of rules of thumb which individual instructors had evolved from their own experience in patrol work."

During their academy training these recruits had little opportunity to test their human relations skills or to develop and integrate them with the other knowledge and skills they had acquired. The academy personnel, who were for the most part better educated than most of the recruits, viewed interpersonal skills as a matter "of having common sense or not having it," and that it was "an ability that cannot be developed or taught" (Gormally, 1971). Again, it is less the setting where the training occurs than is being trained and how.

Human-relations training (sensitivity training, T-groups) is a second process which has been used to train police. Among some police there seems to be concern, bordering on fear, about this process, in part, because of the negative stories about such experiences. The increased popularity of these groups with the public at large has resulted in some T-groups being led by inexperienced leaders who tend to want to do their "thing" *to* people instead of *with* people. This misuse of groups combined with the generally conservative reactions of police administrators toward these kinds of experiences, has placed the status of human-relation training for police in jeopardy.

If we attempt to look at the value of this mode of training objectively, what can we identify? Often it seems as if the goals of this method of training are vague and undefined (Danish & Zelenski, 1972). Among the stated goals of such training are increased insight and awareness about oneself (Argyis, 1964) and an increased sensitivity to the behavior of others (Bradford, et al., 1964). More recently, the focus has been on community relations training via the group process; i.e. increased understanding between citizens and police. While some of the goals may, in some non specific way, relate to the goals we have defined as important, the process used to achieve these goals is amphorous. For example, it is expected that by having the police call a black citizen "Nigger" and the Black yell back "Honky Pig," understanding will ensue. It assumes that if people "communicate," understanding will follow.

Unfortunately, this thesis finds no conformation in experience. Individuals are not motivated by pure reason. Both the police and the black citizens have prejudices and stereotypes as well as memorial of actual unpleasant experiences which do not disappear through contact. Furthermore, the notion that "communication" is the key fails to take into consideration that both groups have fundamental differences and perceptions about the state of the world what will not easily erode. It is naive to assume that no problems would exist "if only they could talk to each other."

The results of a recent community relations workshop run with white policemen and black inner-city youth (Kroeker, *et al.,* 1971) illustrates this false assumption. A research evaluation indicated that following the workshop the black youth were more fearful of police and both police and the youth were *less willing* to communicate with each other as a result of the workshop than was a control group. In addition, both Blacks and police seemed to lack any ability to understand the feelings, behavior or motivations of the other (Kroeker, et al., 1971). In short, the group experience not only did not succeed, but was actually detrimental.

We are aware that other police-community relations workshops have reported positive outcomes (Sikes & Cleveland, 1968). However, these "positive outcomes" have never been related to the behavior of either citizen or police. The outcomes primarily relate to self-report attitudes following the workshop. It seems to us that what really counts is, do the groups behave any differently toward each other following the workshop, and if so, are these differences related to the workshop? The data presented by Kroeker, et al. (1971) provides little encouragement. It is our feeling that this mode of training be used with extreme caution until there are indications that what is learned in a group situation changes behavior for the better outside the group environment back on "the street."

A third training procedure has involved the use of audio-visual simulation material. Two programs which illustrate this procedure are Rubin (1970) and Danish and Brodsky (1970). Although there is a tendency to view the two programs as interchangeable, there are considerable differences between them.

Rubin (1970) has developed three stress training films. Each film depicts a separate situation which police face: a family dispute, a noisy party of "college militants" and a diabetic drunk with a suspected coronary. The viewer watches the police handle each situation. The films attempt to evoke emotional response in the viewer. Rubin identifies a four-stage training process: (1) to get the trainees to express their own feelings as elicited by the film; (2) to help the trainees to separate their feelings from their actions; (3) to have each trainee talk about a situation which has evoked a feeling similar to those portrayed by the police on the film and (4) a discussion of general feelings unrelated to the film. A leader's manual is provided to assist the leader in structuring the training. In addition to the four stages detailed above, homework assignments are given to help the trainee explore his feeling about a number of situations related to the film.

Danish and Brodsky (1970) showed a series of filmed vignettes to police recruits to sensitize them to their aggressive feelings and self-control problems. The films, known as the Stimulus Films (Kagan, et al., 1967), were developed to help psychotherapy clients understand their feelings and reactions to rejection (Danish and Kagan, 1967), and had nothing to do with police training. However, the film was general enough that it could be applied to the recruits. The authors reported considerable involvement on the part of recruits and a subsequent discussion following the films was directed toward how to handle strong personal feelings in stressful situations.

The major difference between the two film procedures is that the viewer of the Rubin films watches police on the film react to several situations while the films used by Danish and Brodsky require the viewer to participate in the situation since the actor directs his action toward the viewer. It is our opinion that this latter approach provides maximum involvement for the viewer; he becomes a part of the situation.

While the simulation procedures described represent a promising approach, there are several disadvantages to the two reviewed. Both simulation procedures were limited to a very few situations, thereby limiting the number of opportunities for stress training. Secondly, both procedures seem to have been conceived without an overall systematic model of training. No attempt was made to detail what changes were expected nor how these changes would be made. Also, both procedures focus primarily on examining feelings and reactions rather than behavior. Finally, no formal evaluation was done with either procedure to assess its effectiveness.

A final training procedure to be mentioned is the family crises intervention training, developed by Bard (1969). This procedure is to be detailed elsewhere. However, it is important to note that among the training programs we have reviewed, it seems among the best designed. Bard has developed a complete model of training family crises intervention teams. Furthermore, it is one of the few programs which included programmatic research on behavioral differences. In other words, the training that Bard conducted *actually made a difference in police behavior.* Within the scope of family crises intervention training the program is outstanding.

A Model of Training

It is our plan to develop a model of training which will identify specific goals to be learned and a specific training procedure to teach these goals. The specific skills to be taught were identified previously. However, in general, they are: (1) to teach police officers the basic skills of being helpful to another; (2) to enable police officers to deal more effectively with human conflict situations by understanding their emotional reactions to conflict and (3) to help police officers to develop behavioral alternatives which will reduce conflict.

In order to achieve the first goals, that of being helpful to another, an adapted form of the *Basic Helping Skills Program* (Danish, 1972) will be used. The *Basic Helping Skills Program* is a training procedure designed to teach essential helping skills in a structured manner. The essential skills are derived from three components: (1) an understanding of yourself; (2) some knowledge of helping strategies; and (3) practice in applying these strategies. While the total program includes ten stages, the program adapted for police training will utilize five stages:

1. Using effective non-verbal behavior
2. Using effective verbal behavior
3. Understanding your needs to help others
4. Understanding others' communications
5. Establishing effective relationships

An example of the definition of one of these skills, effective non-verbal behavior, was detailed earlier.

As part of the development of the *Basic Helping Skills Program,* several training (instructional) techniques were considered. It was decided to make use of instructional and teaching principles identified by Gage (1963) and Gagne (1965). These principles seemed to provide the most effective and efficient procedure of teaching the various skills. Some of these principles are: (1) identifying explicit behavioral objectives, (2) practice or application of skills to be learned, 3) self-learning by group discussion, (rationale for learning (understanding the importance of certain skills), (5) sequential presentation (learning concept A before concept B), (6) active trainee participation, (7) use of modeling and (8) the use of immediate feedback concerning the appropriateness of trainees responses (Danish, 1971). In order to integrate these principles into a workable training procedure, the following format was used for the teaching of each skill:

1. Identify and define the skill or ability to be learned.
2. Discuss the need for the skill.
3. Give examples of the skill.

4. Specify the level of attainment necessary to demonstrate that the skill or ability is understood.

5. Practice the skill or ability to the point that the participant can demonstrate that the skill has been learned.[1]

To teach the essential helping skills to the police, the *B.H.S.P.* will be adapted for use in police training because much of the program emphasizes a commitment to help people in solving their problems as the motivation to learn the skills being taught. It is our feeling that this emphasis is at best a secondary motivation for policemen to learn these skills. A more effective way of insuring greater participation and commitment on the part of the police would seem to be for the program to appeal to the survival needs of the officers. In other words, the program be sold on its ability to help the police have more control over potentially volatile interactions and reduce "iatrogenic violence."

The first part of the training model, then, is the teaching of several sections of the *Basic Helping Skills Program* to police officers. Without this initial training in essential helping skills we believe it would be a difficult task to train individual police officers to handle volatile conflict in an effective manner since conflict situations involve the use of these skills under considerable pressure. It is almost as if one would be expecting the officer to run before he could walk.

Following the teaching of the sections of the Basic Helping Skills Program, the officer should then be prepared for the film simulation training. The simulation training seems to be a logical extension of the *B.H.S.P.,* since it is expected that the simulation experiences should provide an opportunity for the trainees to practice the skills previously learned.

The film simulation procedure to be employed is similar to that used by Danish and Brodsky (1970). The viewer becomes the individual toward whom the action is directed and therefore becomes a participant in the crises. This differs from much of the

---

[1]The *Basic Helping Skills Program* has been successfully used with nurses, hospital personnel, undergraduate residence hall personnel, Model Cities personnel, OEO "new Careers" personnel, and graduate student counselors in training. In short, it has been used with a wide variety of present and/or future helping personnel at various levels of education and past training.

simulation training where the viewer is a third person watching the interaction between the police and citizen.

The second major difference between the present films and past film simulation is the diversity and specificity of the present films.[2] In order to develop the simulated situations, various police agencies and training institutions were asked to identify specific situations which their officers might have difficulty handling. Over 50 situations were identified; 30 situations are being filmed. The scenes deal with a wide variety of conflict situations which can be categorized into the following areas:

1. The police physically being prevented or restricted from carrying out their duties or functions (demonstrators blocking the entrance to a building where AWOL man is, "We're not doing anything wrong.")

2. The pressures and attitudinal influences engendering conflict about the performance of duties (offers of bribes, interference from other law enforcement agencies, or pleas for leniency from offender, "I'm a traveling salesman and if I get this ticket I'll lose my livelihood. My family will starve.").

3. Attacks on the police as representatives of society and the values and institutions they represent (rational arguments about the danger of marijuana versus alcohol or remarks about illegal or unethical police activities).

4. Attacks on the man who is the policeman (spitting, yelling obscenities).

5. Having to control citizens who can't control themselves (drunk, suicide).

6. Citizens ignoring the police trying to do their job.

The film simulation procedure will be done in small groups (8-12) initially with two leaders, a member of the project staff and a police officer.[3] Prior to the showing of the first filmed vig-

---

[2]The exact situations and procedures used to identify the situations will be contained in the Final Report for the ILEC project entitled: *Human Relations Films for Police Training.*

[3]The long-range goal is for the staff to train law enforcement personnel to do the training themselves since it is the staff's feeling that more effective training can be done when the distrust and fear of outsiders is not present. The training of trainers will be accomplished through workshops and the development of a leader's manual to guide the trainer in using the films.

nette the group will be instructed to react spontaneously to the actor as if they were on-duty policemen confronted with this situation. In other words, it is as if the actor were talking directly to the group member and that he were alone in the situation with the actor. These instructions, then, set up a situation where the individual group members become involved as participants in the simulated action.

Following the showing of each vignette the group will be asked two questions: (1) as an officer, what would you say or do to the actor-citizen, and (2) how do you feel about what the actor-citizen has said to you. A group member is asked to respond to the actor-citizen with the exact response to the actor-citizen with the exact response he would make (rather than something like, "I would say . . . or I would try to explain . . ."). Another group member is then asked to assume the role of the actor and interact with the respondent as if it were a real situation. Therefore, the respondent and the individual assuming the actor's role carry out the crisis interaction until completion. In this way the respondent and the group begin to understand the consequences of his response. If his behavioral response does not reduce the potential conflict, another group member is asked to respond in his way to the film and a second interaction follows. By this procedure the group is able to see examples of behavioral responses which reduce conflict. Interjected in both interactions is an attempt by the trainer(s) to have the respondents examine their feelings toward what the actor-citizen has said to them so that he might better understand his reactions to emotionally provoking situations.[4]

The specific goals of this section of the training are for the trainees: (1) to learn how they (the trainees) feel about what is being said to them; (2) to have a behavior rehearsal experience; to practice and experience their own responses to potentially volatile situations; (3) to understand and experience the consequences of their responses to these situations; and (4) to provide them with a basic repetoire of responses, some of which may reduce the potential conflict more effectively than others. This

[4]Past experience with this type of simulation film indicates that counselors-in-training (Danish, 1971a), police recruits (Danish & Brodsky, 1970) and psychotherapy clients (Danish & Kagan, 1969) all are able to respond to the films. They seem to be able to view this situation as real and learn from responding to them.

procedure with the films is repeated with each of the some 30 vignettes.

The training, then, is primarily focused toward changing the behavior of the trainees rather than changing the trainee's attitudes. There has been considerable controversy among behavioral scientists about which procedure, behavior change or attitude change, is most effective, efficient and permanent. It is our feeling that changes in behavior may or may not accompany changes in behavior may or may not accompany changes in attitudes especially under crisis conditions. It is also doubtful whether change can be effected in a short time and even if it were possible, how could such changes be measured. Therefore, we decided to focus on behavior change. If behavior change can be effected, whether attitudes change or not, becomes less important. For example, we are less concerned how a police officer feels toward, let us say, a minority group member than how he behaves toward him. One does not have to like an individual to assist him. However, he must treat him fairly. Furthermore, there are indications that when one's behavior toward another changes, his attitudes or feelings about him will change as well. In other words, one does not change strong affective attitudes because he is told to change them. Changes in strong affective attitudes can only take place when an individual feels that these changes are justified. The source of such a justification is a positive experience with the object of the negative attitude. After several positive experiences one would be unable to continue to hold negative affective attitudes.

It is expected that the opportunity to experience emotional reactions and test out various behavioral responses to conflict through simulation prior to any actual real-life confrontation will provide the trainee with some valuable learning. Following the simulation training, the trainee may then be able to alter his behavior due to an increased understanding of his emotions and of the consequences of his initial responses. The training places the trainee in an advantageous position somewhat analagous to that of a student who has seen some of the examination questions prior to the examination and is prepared to respond appropriately (Danish, 1971a).

SUMMARY

The purpose of this chapter has been to begin to delineate some specific goals of training police. An attempt was made to define the goals on the basis of an analysis of what police do or feel they do and on the understanding that the more specific the goal is, the better it can be defined behaviorally and therefore, the more likely it can be achieved. In addition, the process of goal identification was separated from the methods employed to achieve these goals. Following the consideration of several methods of training presently being used, a new model based on a form of microteaching and film simulation was proposed.[5] The model focuses on teaching police officers skills which will enable them to more effectively handle the crises which they confront. It is expected that a formal assessment of this procedure will be conducted in order to determine the effect of the training on the behavior of police in the field.

REFERENCES

Argyris, C.: T-groups for organizational effectiveness. *Harvard Business Review, 42(2),* 1964, 60-74.

Bard, M.: Family intervention police teams as a community mental health resource. *Journal of Criminal Law, Criminology and Police Science, 60,* 1969, 247-250.

Bard, M. and Berkowitz, B.: Training police as specialists in family crisis intervention. *Community Mental Health Journal, 3(4),* 1967, 315.

Bittner, E.: Police discretion in emergency apprehension of mentally ill persons. *Social Problems, 14,* 1967, 278-292.

Bradford, L. P., Gibb, J. R., and Benne, K. D.: *T-group theory and laboratory method.* New York: Wiley, 1964.

Cumming, E., Cumming, I., and Edell, L.: Policeman as philosopher, guide and friend. *Social Problems, 12,* 1965, 276-286.

Danish, S. J.: Film simulated counselor training. *Counselor Education and Supervision,* 1971a, 11, 29-35.

Danish, S. J.: The basic helping skills program: a proposed model for training paraprofessionals. Paper presented at the American Psychological Association, September, 1971b.

Danish, S. J.: *The basic helping skills program.* Unpublished, Southern Illinois University, 1972.

---

[5]Additional information about the model (*The Basic Helping Skills Program* and the *Police Training Films*) as well as the results of the project may be obtained from the authors.

Danish, S. J. and Brodsky, S. L.: Training of policemen in emotional control and awareness. *American Psychologist, 25,* 1970, 368-369.

Danish, S. J. and Kagan, N.: Emotional simulation in counseling and psychotherapy. *Psychotherapy: Theory, Research and Practice, 6,* 1969, 261-263.

Danish, S. J. and Zelenski, J.: Structured group interaction. *Journal of College Student Personnel, 13,* 1972, 53-56.

Gage, N. L. (Ed.) : *Handbook of research on teaching.* Chicago: Rand McNally, 1963.

Gagne, R.: *The conditions of learning.* New York: Holt, Rinehart, & Winston, 1965.

Kagan, N., Krathwohl, D. R., Goldberg, A. D., Campbell, R. J., Schauble, P. G., Greenberg, B. S. Danish, S. J., Resnikoff, A., Bowes, J., and Bondy, S. B.: *Studies in Human Interaction: Interpersonal Process Recall Stimulated by Videotape.* Educational Publication Services, Michigan State University, December, 1967 .

·Gormally, J.: The development of police service potential: a behavioral science view of the police role and innovative training models. Unpublished, Southern Illinois University, 1971.

Kroeker, L. L., Forsyth, D. R. and Haase, R. F.: Evaluation of a police-youth encounter group workshop in the city of Rochester. New York State Crime Control Commission, Albany, New York, 1970.

Lopez-Rey, M.: Defining police-community relations. In Brandstatter and Radelet (Eds.) : *Police and Community Relations.* Glencoe Press, 1968, 188.

McNamara, J. H.: Uncertainties in police work: the relevance of police recruits' backgrounds and training. In D. J. Bordua (Ed.) : *The Police: Six Sociological Essays,* New York: Wiley, 1967.

Mills, R. E.: Use of small groups in police selection. *Journal of Criminal Law, Criminology, and Police Science, 60,* 1969, 238-241.

Newman, L. E., and Steinberg, J. L.: Consultation with police on human relations training. *American Journal of Psychiatry, 126,* 1970, 1421-1429.

Radelet, L. A.: Police and community relations. *Police Chief, 31,* 1964, 41.

Rubin, R.: *Stress training films.* Washington, D. C.: International Association of Chiefs of Police, 1970.

Sterling, J., and Watson, N. A.: *Changes in Role Concepts of Police Officers.* Mental Health Program Reports #4, January 1970, 261-280.

Sikes, M. P. and Cleveland, S.: Human relations training for police and community. *American Psychologist, 23,* 1968, 766.

Toch, H.: *Violent men.* Chicago: Aldine Publishing Company, 1969.

Zacker, J. W.: The effects of experiential training upon empathy, interpersonal sensitivity, cynicism and alienation in police recruits. Unpublished, 1970.

Chapter 24

FOUR YEARS OF TRAINING POLICE IN INTERPERSONAL RELATIONS

Vytautas J. Bieliauskas and David T. Hellkamp

O UR CONTINUOUSLY changing and restless society requires changes and adaptations not only from individuals but also from various social institutions. While the individuals as individuals may show considerable flexibility in responding with adaptive behavior to the changes, the institutions or the individuals as members of these institutions usually show less flexibility and greater anxiety in relating to social changes. In most instances the institutions have a tendency to obviate changes and to react to them only instead of meeting them with decisive positive action.

Police departments throughout the country represent institutions of long standing, deeply rooted in traditions and depending upon circumscribed rules of behavior. Not only are they institutions, but they represent the bulwark which guarantees the survival and effectiveness of other social institutions. Therefore, it is quite understandable that police departments and other social institutions perceive present day social changes as threatening and their first reaction is to hold fast on what they have rather than to change.

However, institutions must change and adapt themselves to the social needs lest they will work themselves out of existence. This principle applies to the police departments and most of them realize that they must change. However, they are, many times, at a loss in being too deeply engrossed in themselves and thus being unable to develop new ideas regarding the changes. Seeing this weakness of self-entanglement, many progressive police department since 1965 have been looking for outside help to cope with their dilemmas. They have been and still are looking toward behavioral scientists, and many times they found responses on the part of the educators, sociologists, social workers, ministers, etc. Only more recently some psychologists began to realize that they too can contribute to the development of changes in the police departments and thus police departments are becoming open to psychological consultation. Our experience with such a consultation may be typical of many similar experiences, but then it may also be unique and transferable with modifications into other areas.

THE PROBLEM

In 1966 two command officers of the Cincinnati Police Department came to the senior author asking for aid in developing a program for training all their officers in community awareness. They studied many programs and realized that something should be done in their department, but they did not feel comfortable in trying to solve this problem themselves. They decided to try a psychology department. The idea of working with the police was at that time as foreign to us as to most psychologists today. However, the enthusiasm and openness on the part of these two police officers made us agree to look into their request.

We started looking, reading and studying, and we found out how little we knew about the police work. Some of us were able to recall our army experiences as a basis of departure; some didn't even have this to start with. However, we thought that we must step out of our academic ivory tower and try to determine to what extent we could contribute to a solution of a practical social problem.

One of the first steps was to study police work first hand as an observer. That entailed such things as riding with the police in their cars on weekends and evenings. The riding experience proved to be informative and more risky than was anticipated as riots in the black ghetto area of Cincinnati occurred at that time, the summer of 1967. Needless to say, the riots only accentuated the need for training in police-community relations.

Apart from the first-hand experiences such as riding with police officers, one of the writers (Bieliauskas) was also given the opportunity to travel to various other police departments throughout the country to study their community-relation efforts. Trips to police departments in St. Louis, San Francisco, Los Angeles, Miami Beach, Miami, Chicago and Detroit provided important information regarding police community relations, problems and programs, many of which have been summarized and reported elsewhere (Bieliauskas, 1969).

A final step in the preparation was quantitative in nature. In order to know more specifically existing attitudes of both police and citizens and to determine those attitudes requiring change, we conducted a survey of the citizens of our area regarding their attitude toward the police. This survey consisted of citizens rating police on a seven-point scale on 15 bi-polar characteristics (e.g. understands people in this area . . . does not understand people in this area). The sample consisted of 300 interviews in 30 census tracts in the Cincinnati area, assuring within reasonable limits proportional representation of race, sex, age, socioeconomic status, and head of household. At the same time we also conducted a survey among the police officers concerning their attitudes towards several aspects of their work, especially toward the job, instructions, supervisors, youth, Blacks, and Southern Appalachian Migrants (SAM's).

Slowly, then, on the basis of our reading, surveys and observations of police in Cincinnati and elsewhere, we developed a certain understanding of the police work, and we felt that we were ready to combine our new knowledge with our old expertise to produce a program which could train police officers in community relations and be effective.

TRAINING[1]

The main purpose of our training was to provide a basis for changes of attitudes among the police officers toward community relations. An original approach to rely primarily upon the T-group method was modified so much that we decided to call it

---

[1] A detailed description of the early training was published and is available in very limited number from the Department of Psychology, Xavier University (Ohio). We are currently in the process of writing a detailed Manual for Training of Police in Interpersonal Relations.

"training in interpersonal relations" in order not to confuse it with the sensitivity training. We became convinced also that the best training for the police officer in community relations is for him to be trained in interpersonal relations as a whole rather than making it a typical black-white experience.

Unlike other similar programs, we decided to ask the supervisors to participate in our program first and only then we invited the line officers. The philosophy behind this was based upon our experience with the police. Police departments, as a semi-military organization, depend greatly upon the attitude of the command officers. Therefore, we thought, in order for the program to be acceptable, the supervisors must know it first. The results of our four years' training program supported this approach.

Our first grant was therefore designed to train the police supervisors of the Cincinnati Police Division—who represented the complete supervisory echelon from the rank of sergeant through assistant chiefs and the chief of police. We then trained detectives and specialists followed by the training of patrolmen. Although the original target for training was the Cincinnati Police Department, most of our training time after the first year has also included the training of virtually all police officers in four southwestern Ohio counties—representing over 1500 men from about 30 independent law enforcement agencies.

The training was given on a three-day basis for groups of 25 to 40 officers at a time. The participants were invited to live on campus and to take part in all aspects of the program. They were provided lodging and food on campus. The housing was arranged in a student dormitory and the meals were taken in the university cafeteria. Each three-day training session, called a workshop, was planned to promote maximum involvement on the part of each participant, with minimum time for lectures and maximum time for discussion and small group activities. An intensive schedule was designed to help the participants learn about their own feelings and reactions, to improve communication and understanding, and then to involve them in problem-solving sessions dealing with interpersonal relations, community relations and their attitudes toward community problems, such as race relations, poverty, family-crises intervention, campus unrest, etc. In workshops involving supervisory personnel (sergeants through chiefs), the police officers were also asked to develop a set of recommendations for improvement of police community relations programs in their communities and these recommendations were then summarized and presented to the appropriate chiefs of police along with the recommendations of the training staff. The line officers (patrolmen and specialists) were not asked for recommendations, but were given further training in the roles of the professional policeman.

In addition to the three-day workshop, our training program also included bringing each officer back to the campus for a half-day follow-up or "reinforcement" seminar. The half-day seminar consisted of groups averaging about 35 men at a time and was conducted anywhere from six months to a year following completion of the three-day workshop for each participant. Again, supervisory personnel were generally scheduled at different times than patrolmen in the seminars as we found more openness in the discussions in the segregated rank conditions. Apart from the benefits of reinforcing the community-relations issues, the seminar period was also used for problem-solving tasks and all officers were asked to provide evaluations and recommendations for various community-relations programs. The recommendations were collated along with the recommendations of the staff and sent to appropriate city and county officials for consideration and possible implementation.

Our training program had these three educational aims: (1) to help the individual participants become more effective in interpersonal relations in general—at home, in peer relations, or in community relations, (2) to develop a better understanding of the policeman's role in contemporary society and getting acquainted with behavioral science techniques used in communication and leadership, and (3) to become personally involved in police community-relations problems through the experience of problem solving and the preparation of recommendations.

Results[1]

We have used various questionnaires and have accumulated a considerable amount of statistical data over the past four years. Generally speaking, our results indicate that we have been making an impact upon our trainees. For instance, at the completion of each workshop, we had each police officer answer a questionnaire regarding his pre- and post-workshop attitudes towards police-community relations. Table 24-I lists the eight items of the questionnaire along with the mean increase of each item in the ratings prior to and following the workshop experience for all participants in 16 of the first 18 workshops we conducted. Through an oversight the survey was not conducted during the fifth and sixth workshops. Each item on the questionnaire was rated from 0 (low) to 7 (high) to indicate the participant's feelings on the item prior to the workshop. Each question was then rated a second time to reflect his post-workshop experiences. As

TABLE 24-I

MEAN CHANGES IN PRE- AND POST-WORKSHOP RATINGS OF POLICE
FEELINGS TOWARD POLICE-COMMUNITY RELATIONS

Item	Mean Pre-Pose Workshop Change
1. Degree of understanding why I do what I do	+1.52**
2. Awareness of the feelings of others	+1.68**
3. Willingness to discuss my own feelings about important issues in police-community relations	+1.59**
4. Ability to understand hostility and aggression in myself and others	+1.89**
5. Reaction to opinions on police-community relations which are opposed to mine	+1.50**
6. Ability to use language clearly expressing the difficulties in many areas of law enforcement	+1.32
7. Ability to influence others toward improvement of police-community relations	+1.51**
8. Willingness to see closer personal relationships with members of other cultural groups than my own	+1.56**

**significant at the .01 level
+ Indicates an increase in post workshop ratings for item

[1]Special acknowledgement is given to Dr. Gerald L. Quatman for his analyses of the quantitative results.

can be seen from Table 24-I, a highly significant increase in positive attitudes occurred on each of the eight items across all workshops. The greatest amount of increase was in ability to understand hostility and aggression in themselves and others (item 4), in awareness of the feelings of others (item 2) and in under-standing why they do what they do (item 1). The least amount of increase was in ability to use language clearly expressing the difficulties in many areas of law enforcement (item 6). The results of the questionnaire thus provided quantitative evidence that we were seemingly heading in the right direction in terms of our stated goals for training. That is, the survey was indicating that attitudes had changed in a favorable direction for at least the time of the workshop.

Some additional quantitative evidence supporting the success of our training program came from another survey which we conducted and alluded to in our comments above regarding the preparation stages of our training program. Specifically, some months prior to presenting our first workshops for the Cincinnati police supervisors, 690 Cincinnati police officers answered a 25-item questionnaire concerning their attitudes towards several aspects of their work, including attitudes towards their job, instruction, supervision, youth, Blacks and SAM's. Three months following completion of the workshops in training the super-visors, we were able to again resurvey the majority of Cincinnati police officers with the same questionnaire. When the data from these questionnaires was analyzed from the standpoint of police rank, we found some significant changes occurring for police supervisors who had been through our training. Police super-visors' attitudes towards minority groups, especially Blacks, had changed significantly for the better ($p < .05$). Whereas, attitudes towards Blacks were generally low for most policemen on each survey, the attitudes significantly increased favorably on the second survey for the officers who had been through our program. Moreover, many supervisors' attitudes towards their own super-visors changed significantly for the better ($p < .01$) on the second survey, indicating perhaps better interpersonal relations at work. On the other hand, the attitudes of the line officers showed, but for one exception, no significant changes between the two surveys. The one exception was a significant increase (p<.01) in attitudes of police specialists towards their supervisors. Keeping in mind the fact that the line officers had not been through our training program as yet while the supervisors had, the data appeared consistent with our expressed goals. Such statistical evidence, however, can be challenged concerning its meaning. Some critics may say that our results indicate nothing more than the fact that police supervisors who went through our program learned how to provide better answers to the questions, and that their attitudes really did not change. Granted that such could be a possibility, it still could be argued for the success of our program. If people who participated in the program developed a better facility to answer questions in the surveys, they must have developed more sensitivity to the problems of community relations. If the program accomplished just this much, it would be a sufficient indication of success, because it resulted in an increased sensitivity to the problems and the realization of their importance which was one of the objectives.

In an effort to observe changes in attitudes of citizens in our area towards the policemen, we also conducted a second survey of citizens in the Cincinnati area in 1969 which was one year following the original survey that was referred to earlier in this paper. The second survey consisted of 320 interviews in 30 census tracts of the Cincinnati area, taking into consideration, like the first survey, such variables as race, sex, socioeconomic status, and head of household. The citizens rated police on 16 items on a seven-point scale. In the interval of time between the two surveys, we had completed the workshops with police supervisors of Cincinnati.

Generally speaking, the 1969 survey yielded results similar to the survey conducted in 1968. The results of both surveys for each overall sample are presented in Table 24-II. For the most part, citizens rated their police department in a much more positive than negative light on both surveys. The vast majority of citizens therefore showed highly favorable attitudes toward the police. In comparing the two surveys, one finds small, but sig-

TABLE 24-II

CITIZEN ATTITUDES TOWARD THE CINCINNATI POLICE DEPARTMENT
ON SIXTEEN SEVEN-POINT ITEMS — OVERALL SAMPLES

Item	1968 (N = 300)		1969 (N = 320)		Difference and significance
1. Efficient	5.33	(3)	5.07	(8)	—.26*
2. Kind	5.15	(6)	5.16	(6)	+.01
3. Helpful	5.46	(2)	5.46	(2)	——
5. Confident	5.15	(6)	5.18	(5)	+.03
6. Polite	5.14	(8)	5.20	(4)	+.06
7. Reasonable	5.07	(9)	5.10	(7)	+.03
8. Understands people in this area	5:00	(10)	4.71	(11)	—.29**
9. Quickly responds to calls	4.84	(12)	4.97	(10)	+.13
10. Positive attitude toward people in this area	4.79	(13)	4.79	(12)	——
11. Fair and impartial	4.89	(11)	4.60	(13)	—.29**
12. Obeys laws	4.71	(14)	4.58	(14)	—.13
13. Calms others in emergency situation	5.15	(6)	5.04	(9)	—.11
14. Know policeman personally	3.31	(15)	3.48	(15)	+.17*
15. Deserves respect	5.96	(1)	5.95	(1)	—.01
16. Desire to solve problems	5.30	(4)	5.27	(4)	—.03
17. Interest in me	——		4.80		
Average . . . all 15 items	5.02		4.97		—.05
all 16 items	——		4.96		

*significant at the .05 level
**significant at the .01 level

nificant changes on four of the fifteen items. On the positive side, respondents felt on the second survey that they knew the policemen more personally than on the first survey, while on the negative side, significant decreased attitudes towards the police from 1968 to 1969 were found with regards to the police being considered as less efficient, not understanding people as well in their area, and not being fair and impartial.

When the data of each survey was analyzed from the standpoint of respondent's race, the attitudes of Blacks towards the police were significantly lower (p<.01) than those of Whites, but still generally more positive than negative as the average rating on the seven-point scale across all items for Blacks was 4.20 and 4.17 in 1968 and 1969 respectively. The attitudes of Blacks toward the police that increased significantly in 1969 over 1968 were that the police were rated as being more polite, responding more quickly to calls, and had less negative attitudes towards the people in their area. Significant decreased attitudes of Blacks towards the police from 1968 to 1969 included ratings of being less efficient, not understanding people as well in their area, not obeying laws in the performance of their duties, and showing more preferences rather than being fair and impartial.

As we discovered, it became well-nigh impossible to relate one way or another any changes in the two surveys of citizens to the effect of our training program with the police supervisors as many events were also occurring simultaneously in the community. For instance, the Greater Cincinnati area, like many other American cities, was undergoing sobering riots during the years of our surveys. It was perhaps more surprising that a greater polarization trend in attitudes towards police was not manifesting itself by citizens in the 1969 survey as compared to the 1968 survey.

The various surveys of the police and citizens thus provided us with some quantitative feedback as to the relative success of our training. In addition to such a feedback mechanism, the information gathered from analyzing the surveys from many different points of view was also helpful in aiding us in modifying our continuing workshops in terms of topics to be stressed, etc. For example, our surveys plainly indicated that the police as a group have significantly more negative attitudes towards Blacks than towards Whites. At the same time, however, our survey of the citizens of Cincinnati indicated very plainly that black citizens as compared to white citizens as a group have significantly more negative attitudes towards police. To us, this indicated that to hopefully improve Black-police relations, *both* groups must make efforts, not just one group or the other. By being able to establish racial prejudice as a more *total* community problem rather than just one of the police, we found the police officer to be more understanding and less defensive in discussions on how the police might contribute to improving racial relations. Similar approaches with prejudices towards other minority groups were also many times followed.

More than statistical results, however, are important to us. We were also very interested in the reactions of the officer personnel. As previously mentioned, we have by now trained well over 1500 police officers, and the enthusiasm is still high among most of the participants. They tend to come to us highly skeptical and suspicious as is perhaps illustrated by a remark overheard from one officer on the first morning of one three-day workshop: "What the hell do these kook psychologists think they are going to teach us anyway!" Yet, most men leave us asking when they might be able to come back for more training. We, too, are enthusiastic after four years of hard work, a factor which perhaps takes on extra meaning when considering the fact that we are currently ready to begin training anywhere from 200 to 600 more officers.

Due to the fact that we have been training police officers from over thirty independent police agencies from around the area, we have been able over the past three years to mix officers from different departments (e.g. Cincinnati Police Division officers with Ohio State Highway Patrol officers, etc.) in the workshops and seminars. We have found this to be a very favorable feature in that it permitted greater communications between departments while lending itself for a better understanding and more global problem-solving attack on various community-relations issues at large.

Numerous recommendations for improving police-community relations have been provided by the police officers and training personnel in the over 60 workshops and seminars that we have conducted up to the present time. On the basis of some of these formal recommendations submitted to the chief of police, implementations were initiated where possible. They have included, for example, suggestions as to how to structure and operate the Community Relations Bureau for the specific purpose of effectively reaching the pressure points of the total population at any given time. In addition to the formal recommendations, informal suggestions by training staff also have been made to various command personnel during the past four years. One example deserves special mentioning. Just for our own curiosity and cooperation with the Director of Cincinnati Police Academy we administered the same attitude survey which we gave to the regular police officers and police recruits. We received 100 percent response from the total police recruit class consisting of 43. We compared their answers to those of the rest of the police department. The results indicated very clearly that police recruits had a statistically significant more positive attitude toward minority groups than policemen who have been on duty for two to five years. However, we discovered that the young recruits receive on-the-job-training after they complete their studies at the Police Academy and that their supervisors of this training—called patrolmen coaches—are men who have been on the police force from two to five years. Considering the fact that these "trainers" have the present attitude toward community relations it was thought that something should be done in changing the training procedures. These ideas were brought to the attention of the chief of police and he ordered an immediate change in training procedures. Therefore, since September, 1968, young Cincinnati patrolmen are supposedly not being trained by policemen who have been on the force for less than six years. This is a small change, but very likely it will have extensive results. We observed similar "small" changes in other areas, such as policies governing materials on police bulletin boards, reactions toward student unrest and attempted dialogues with black citizens. There are many things, most of which are intangibles, which compose the attitudes. Our observations suggest that this training program has reached at least a few of these intangibles.

It should perhaps be pointed out that by no means was all our work in the workshops and seminars *content*-oriented. Since the nature of the policeman's role today is filled with frustrations in that the police officer is frequently the man who is caught in the middle (damned if you—damned if you don't phenomenon) many times the groups turned into gripe sessions which provided ample opportunity for constructive ventilations. We have had no emotional breakdowns.

Along similar lines, we also have had no campus riots. As a matter of fact, by having the police living on campus in the same dormitories as students for the three days, we have found the police to interact socially with the students. We have had no police-student disturbances and have had many favorable comments regarding greater understanding from both students and policemen.

Conclusions

There has been extensive give and take on the part of both the police officers and our team members. We believe we have developed much more understanding and empathy for police work, but we still know that we are not policemen. We are impressed with the generally high caliber of personnel in the police departments. Most of them are ethical, intelligent, and very sympathetic to human problems. In this day and age, we are convinced that almost every officer will think twice before using force or firearms. They know that the word is more important than guns, and that dialogue supersedes any polarization. We learned that police officers are human beings and they have human emotions, such as fears, anxieties, hatred, prejudices, etc.; usually they are well trained in controlling their emotions. We also found that they can be trained in changing their attitudes and in substituting positive for the negative feelings. We also found that the police organization, as any other organization, has some weaknesses. One of the weaknesses is in the police semi-military structure which uses the pyramidal basis for authority. The police departments are too heavily dependent upon one man's rule, which in rather large units have severe drawbacks, because no man can provide all answers to all questions. The team approach will very likely be used in the future more and more widely in police administration.

Another weakness in each police department is a small minority of the officers who really don't belong in the police force. We believe that this minority represents three to five percent of most police departments. These men do more harm to police prestige and reputation than 95 percent of the others can sometimes repair. This is an unfortunate truth, and the police supervisors know this. However, the usual civil service regulations provide protection to those who don't belong as well as those who belong to the police departments.

At the present time the police officers need and deserve support from all citizens. We believe that as psychologists we can learn about new dimensions of human behavior while working with the police, and as psychologists we certainly can and should contribute our know-how to make the police an effective and humane organization.

REFERENCE

Bieliauskas, V. J.: *Community Relations Training Program for Police Supervisors.* Cincinnati, Ohio: Xavier University, Department of Psychology, 1969.

SECTION VI

POLICE AND
THE MENTALLY ILL

INTRODUCTION

LITTLE RESEARCH HAS BEEN DONE IN THIS SPECIFIC AREA. HOWEVER, POLICE IN MANY METROPOLITAN AREAS ARE CALLED UPON TO HANDLE THE MENTALLY ILL IN THE COMMUNITY. HOW THEY DISCHARGE THIS DUTY AND THEIR FEELINGS ABOUT IT IS EXPLORED IN THIS CHAPTER.

THE SNIBBE ARTICLE IS AN OVERVIEW OF THE SUBJECT WITH PARTICULAR REFERENCE TO A SINGLE GEOGRAPHIC AREA. THE IMPLICATION FOR OTHER AREAS IS CLEAR AND THE NEED FOR AWARENESS OF THE PROBLEM ESSENTIAL.

THE JACOBSON, CRAVEN AND KUSHNER RESEARCH REPORT PRESENTS EVIDENCE ON HOW "MENTAL" PROBLEMS ARE DEALT WITH. NEW LAWS REGARDING THE RIGHTS OF THE MENTALLY ILL IN MOST STATES, MAKES SUCH RESEARCH A MUST.

Chapter 25

THE POLICE AND THE MENTALLY ILL: PRACTICES, PROBLEMS, AND SOME SOLUTIONS

JOHN R. SNIBBE, PH.D.*

I N ALL LARGE metropolitan areas police are called upon to per- form duties that involve a wide range of activities for which there is often little precedent in the individual officer's life or the department's training manuals. Such activities become even more difficult in view of often inadequate training for dealing with ambiguous situations requiring a high degree of personal and interpersonal skill.

This is particularly true when one considers police handling of the mentally ill, suicidal, or the pathologically-violent in- dividual in the community. Such people often present, at their best, a complex set of stimuli that may set off a myriad of feelings in the police officer who is called upon to deal with them. Even for the highly trained and experienced professional, confrontation with a bizarre, violent, or acutely mentally-ill individual causes some anxiety and confusion regarding the most appropriate course of action.

The basic problem of management and control of the mentally ill in the field is often confounded by inadequate communication between police and professionals, complex legal and bureaucratic difficulties, and local inadequacies or gaps in mental health care that the police are often called upon to fill.

This article will discuss current practices, explore the above mentioned problems, and suggest some tentative solutions. Par-

*The author wishes to express special tanks to Sgt. David Pharr and the men of the Los Angeles Police Department for their invaluable assistance in the pre- paration of this paper.

ticular reference will be made to the current conditions in Los Angeles County.

The author obtained the information for this article by extensive interviews with Los Angeles Police Department officers and participation in the activities of police officers who handle the mentally ill.

CURRENT POLICE POLICY IN LOS ANGELES COUNTY

The Los Angeles Police Department (LAPD) is called upon by professionals, "hot line" operators, hotel managers, relatives, and others to cope with the individuals in the community that may be mentally ill. However, the police feel that their role is to intervene only when police action is deemed necessary. This is usually defined as a situation in which someone is in danger or breaking the law in some way. The police do not feel, and rightfully so, that it is their role to provide psychotherapy, counseling, or aid and comfort for the lonely and confused. Very often, as with much police work, a decision is made to take or not to take a call based on the individual officers invloved and how they feel about the mentally ill. The disposition question also involves discretionary judgment, but this will be discussed later.

It is LAPD policy that when a "mental" call is received, the officers who reach the scene are asked to call the Hospital Detail at Central Receiving (CR). At that time the detectives stationed there will provide referral information, disposition advice, telephone evaluation, or they may request that the patient be brought into Central Receiving for further evaluation. Others who wish police intervention in a case simply call CR, explain the problem, and the officer on duty makes a decision whether or not police action is necessary.

The use of a central clearing house for information and referral of police "mental" cases is not new. It is only currently that this operation is working fully in Los Angeles County. The receiving office is staffed 24-hours-a-day and handles some 2500 to 2600 patients per year. Of these, about 1800 are confined to the hospital involuntarily for 72 hours. This is commonly known as a "72."

In Los Angeles only peace officers, physicians, and psychiatric emergency team staff have legal authority to write a "72." Thus if the patient is evaluated in the field or at Central Receiving and found to be a danger to himself, gravely disabled (i.e. unable to provide for basic needs of food and shelter), or a danger to others, he is taken to the appropriate hospital that services the area in which the patient lives. Generally it is preferred that LAPD officers take the patient to Central Receiving and that the duty officers write up the "72" forms since they have experience in just how to do this. Such a procedure often helps officers avoid serious legal, bureaucratic, and administrative problems.

However, LAPD covers only part of the Los Angeles basin. Officers from small local police departments as well as Sheriff's Deputies cover other areas and do not have the benefit of central offices from which dispositions are made. Thus, individual officers write their own "72's" and make independent judgments.

MANAGEMENT

Face to face confrontations with mentally-ill persons represent a complex problem for police officers. One of these is that police officers are not adequately trained to deal with this population. The LAPD Training Academy currently provides eight hours of instruction on the various aspects of dealing with the mentally ill in the field. This includes some films and lectures on suicide prevention, legal aspects, and some role-playing situation. This training amounts to eight hours out of a total 840 devoted to police recruits. It seems obvious that this is not adequate since management of the mentally ill can have strong implications for control of individuals seen in other aspects of police work.

In three training bulletins issued by the LAPD in June and July of 1971, only two paragraphs deal with attitudes and techniques needed to deal with the mentally ill. Most of the bulletins deal with legal authority to restrain individuals, situations not covered by legal codes regarding the mentally ill (alcoholics and drug abusers), and procedures for investigation.

In the final analysis, dealing with the violent individual, mentally ill or not, requires specific learned skills and attitudes

(Toch, 1970). When the problem of violence is compounded by explosive pathology, delusions, and hallucinations, even more refined skills are necessary.

The need for course work in the recognition and management of mental illness is obvious. There are specific techniques available (Danish, 1970) that help the untrained individual cope with these highly anxiety-provoking situations. Such course work should be instituted with the hope that the growth of these skills will lead to more appropriate management of all people with whom police come in contact.

POLICE-PROFESSIONAL COMMUNICATION PROBLEMS

The police and professional community are often at odds as to the correct procedure for dealing with the mentally ill. Often professionals complain of inappropriate arrests of the mentally ill, poor diagnostic and judgment capabilities on the part of the police, and improper management of the mentally ill in the field. Police officers, on the other hand, complain of being "talked down to," being forced into non-law enforcement rules, and inappropriate referrals by professionals of nonpolice cases (Kushner and Craven, 1970).

This conflict can be best illustrated by a case brought in to a Los Angeles hospital emergency psychiatric clinic. A patient known to the clinic called a psychologist on a ward where she had previously been a patient. She reported that she had been hurt (a head injury) and was very agitated and suicidal. The psychologist called the local psychiatric emergency team and they in turn called the police. They picked the patient up at a phone booth in downtown Los Angeles. After taking the patient to Central Receiving Hospital for routine medical care, they brought the patient into the psychiatric hospital. When they arrived certain legal documents had not been completed (as they should have been at Central Receiving) and there was serious confusion as to who should do what for this patient. While this discussion was taking place, the patient became agitated and bolted. The officers gave chase but were restrained by an orderly who required that they check their side arms in a locked receptacle before entering the hospital proper. By this time the chief of service was involved and a heated discussion began about who had responsibility for this "escaped" patient.

The patient, had, in fact, gone up to see the psychologist on the ward. In a short while she was relaxed and calm. The patient then returned to the admitting area and when the haggard officers spotted her they took custody using handcuffs. The patient then became very agitated and further words were spoken between staff and police officers before the situation was resolved (the police were asked to leave the clinic).

This illustrates how a chain of events based on miscommunication and confusion over legal responsibility can cause serious consequences and lack of trust between professionals and police. The fact is, that police officers often look upon psychiatric treatment as a totally inadequate solution to the problem of the mentally ill. They are constantly faced with people who have received extensive "treatment" who are again and again psychotic, dangerous, or a problem in the community. They wonder what goes on in clinics and psychiatric hospitals. The sad thing about this is, that some professionals often wonder the same thing.

Such conflicts can be simply resolved by coordinated meetings between responsible representatives from both sides. These meetings could be used as mutual training siminars as well as opportunities for information exchange. Such meetings now take place in Los Angeles but are usually not on a formal basis.

Suspicion, mistrust and even open hostility exist between the police and other groups today. In an area as workable as mental health care, it behooves both sides to plan together for adequate training and control.

LEGAL AND BUREAUCRATIC PROBLEMS

In the case of the mentally-ill patient (if he is seen as such by officers in the field) it is not unusual for him to be committing a high-grade misdemeanor, or even a felony while in an acute state. Running nude, disturbing the peace, threatening behavior and assaults are not uncommon scenes when police officers are called to a location on a "mental" (mentally ill individual). The question again arises of how the officers are going to make a judgment on several critical fronts.

1. Can the officer legally intervene in the first place? Does he feel like intervening?
2. Is this individual mentally ill?
3. If he has committed a crime, should he be booked?
4. Does he meet the legal criteria for 72-hour commitment?
5. Does the police officer understand the legal criteria for commitment?
6. Does the police officer know where to bring the patient; his catchment area?

It is obvious from the above that the same latitude in judgment is involved here as it is in all police work (Goldstein, 1960, and Lafane, 1965). Also a good deal of legal expertise is required as well as excellent judgement.

Other legal problems confronted by the police are current trends to avoid violating civil rights of individuals involved with the police. This includes the mentally ill. Such trends often lead to police complaints about the handling of the mentally ill by our courts and hospitals. They often wonder why current laws permit the release of "dangerous mentally-ill individuals," or why chronic community problems are not kept in hospitals for longer periods of time.

In general, the police find it is frustrating to deal with the legal and bureaucratic system. Often this is the consequence of unrealistic perceptions of what police work is or what it should be (Olson, 1970). "Non-police" functions are requiring more and more of a police officer's time. Activities such as coping with the mentally ill, family disputes, juvenile behavior problems, and so on, have become common for most urban officers. It is unfortunate that perceptions of police work are not changing as fast as the task demands. The skills required to be a modern policeman are intellectual and personal in nature. He must have legal knowledge and a high degree of personal skill. For the vast majority of officers, judo, skill with weapons, and military training are not often useful; while driver's training, psychology, law, community resources and development, violence prevention, and social psychology are.

In an attempt to avoid legal problems and help officers cope with the "bureaucratic shuffle," the LAPD has stationed two detectives at Central Receiving Hospital. All individuals suspected of having a mental problem are channeled through this office. All dispositions of "mental cases" are screened by this office either by phone or in person. This process relieves the officer in the field of much of the discretionary powers he once had. It also increases the probability of appropriate decisions since the officers stationed at Central Receiving are experienced in the legal aspects of mental illness as well as community resources.

The development of such special details is a strong step forward in dealing with the mentally ill. However, ideally such a detail should be staffed by mental health professionals. It is unfortunate that other police departments in the Los Angeles area do not have such a resource since the police of any such metropolitan area do process a large number of mentally-ill individuals.

LOCAL MENTAL HEALTH CARE

Many communities suffer from inadequate resources in the area of mental health care. The expensive and complex task of developing mental health centers and other resources has often caused more problems than they were implemented to solve.

In Los Angeles, Psychiatric Emergency Teams (PET) were created to cope with the problems of the non-ambulatory mentally ill in the community. It was hoped that these teams would provide appropriate care and disposition for acute cases formally handled by the police. Working through local mental health clinics, these teams are authorized to go out on emergency calls and provide professional care in the field. They were to be staffed by professionals and be highly mobile.

While the concept is excellent, problems have developed in the formation and functioning of these teams in the community.

Without going into precise detail on administrative, economic and practical problems encountered by these teams, it is fair to say that the program suffered from some serious shortcomings

(Johnson, 1971). Lack of adequate staffing, equipment problems, fear for team members' safety, and inadequate and confused criteria for visits are some current problems.

For the police, this means continuation of their current unofficial role as "Psychiatric Emergency Officers." This role also includes non-statutory activities such as transport. Almost one-half (50 percent) of the "mental" cases the LAPD handles involves transporting the patient to his local mental health agency. This requires a good deal of time and may cause a car to be out of service for as much as half a day.

Another interesting aspect of the relations between the police and PET teams is that the detectives at Central Receiving may transport a highly disturbed individual, whom the PET teams have refused to see, back to the very agency who declined to respond to the call. This is often the way police displeasure at PET team inefficiency is expressed.

Further, the police are the ones that deal with the mental health system "rejects." Such people are the "bad patients" that are often sent from clinic to clinic because they are poor treatment cases with little perceived chance of recovery. These are often people with multiple state hospital admissions and court appearances. This problem is compounded by the fact that much of the professional treatment and hospitalization of the mentally ill does not achieve the desired effect. Professionals just do not know enough about treatment to solve many of the chronic emotional problems that plague some individuals in the community.

The solution to the above mentioned problems calls for increased effectiveness of the PET teams. "Mental Health Patrols" are needed that cooperate with police and answer most of the "mental" calls the police receive. This is the only way to provide professional on-the-spot treatment and disposition in the community. Such a program would free police to perform their real function which is law enforcement, the control of crime, resolving interpersonal conflict, and somehow dealing with a vast spectrum of human behavior.

CONCLUSION

It is currently the vogue in professional circles and the literature to look towards the community for solutions to the mental health problems of some citizens. Long custodial hospitalizations and lengthy treatments have given way to community programs, early release, and the heavy use of medications.

How the community feels about this responsibility is unclear. However, it is clear that as a consequence of this and other factors the police have been given the responsibility to diagnose and treat the mentally ill in the field. Police see this responsibility as it is: they are asked to shoulder duties that no one else wants or can manage.

This situation highlights the chronic gap between theoretical approaches and practical applications. The achievements in mental health care developed in laboratories and universities have little relevance to the real world of day-to-day calls received by police about disruptive individuals in the community. Such a state of affairs also indicates the professional communities' reluctance to help bridge this gap. While positions on PET Teams go begging, untrained police officers perform a needed service for the community which they can neither enjoy nor manage.

As with much public policy each arm of that policy is going its own way. It would seem to be time to develop better lines of communication to solve current problems and provide better planning before policy goes into effect.

REFERENCES

Goldstein, Joseph: "Police Discretion Not to Invoke the Criminal Process: Low Visibility Decisions in the Administration of Justice." *Yale Law Journal*, March, 1960, 60, pp. 543-588.

Johnson, Bernard and Braden, M.: "A Method For Evaluating Psychiatric Emergency Teams." *Program Development Bureau* publication, Los Angeles County Department of Mental Health, January, 1971.

Kushner, S. and Craven, W.: "A Study of Police Referral of Allegedly Mentally Ill Persons to Los Angeles County—University of Southern California Medical Center, Psychiatric Unit III," thesis. University of California, Los Angeles, 1970.

Lafane, Wayne R.: Arrest: *The Decision To Take A Suspect Into Custody*. Boston: Little, Brown, 1965, pp. 102-124.

Olson, Bruce: "An Exploratory Study of Task Preference." *Personnel Journal,*
    December, 1970, 49, pp. 1,015-1,020.
Toch, Hans: "Change Through Participation (and Visa Versa)." *Journal of
    Research in Crime and Delinquency,* 1970, 41, pp. 198-206.

Chapter 26

A STUDY OF POLICE REFERRAL
OF ALLEGEDLY MENTALLY-ILL PERSONS
TO A PSYCHIATRIC UNIT

Doris Jacobson, William Craven and Susan Kushner

THE RECENT PASSAGE in California of the Lanterman-Petris-Short Act has directed attention to police involvement with the mentally ill. The Act, which primarily deals with the involuntary treatment of the mentally disordered, the alcoholic and the gravely disabled, provides for the peace officer to take a person who appears to be dangerous to himself or to others to a facility which will provide evaluation and treatment of his condition (Rock, 1968). When the peace officer, acting in response to a situation arising in the course of his duties, such as investigating a disturbance on the street, decides that the problem is one of mental illness rather than crime, he directs his actions toward hospitalization rather than incarceration. His decision-making power may have far-reaching consequences for those mentally-ill persons he encounters.

In Los Angeles County, police involvement with mentally-ill persons also occurs when a court-ordered petition for psychiatric evaluation is served by a mental health counselor and is not responded to by the mentally-ill person. The peach officer may be ordered to apprehend him and take him to the facility designated for evaluation.

The police have dealt with the mentally ill and have played a major role in initiating hospitalization procedures. In fact, they are in some way involved in about one-fourth of all public hospitalizations of mental patients in the United States.

This research was done in connection with the University of California at Los Angeles, School of Social Welfare.

The police run almost the only 24-hour-day, 7-day-a-week community emergency service and therefore become involved in work with the mentally ill with great frequency. Families decide to call the police because other, more accessible resources are not available or will not offer services to the involuntary patient. When dealings with the mentally ill become unmanageable for professionals, for the clergy or for the family, the police are called on to take over. Initial calls are often directed to more appropriate psychiatric resources who, in turn, refer the problems to the police. Many referrals are directed to the police because of the patrolman's unique mobility and legally sanctioned right and duty to identify and apprehend mentally-ill persons.

The purpose of this study is to add to the limited knowledge available on police involvement with mentally-ill persons. This study will examine police involvement with mentally-ill persons in a specific area; it will include some consideration of the role of the police in working with the mentally ill, and the role of the police in the mental health system. The major study questions are:

I. What forms of behavior prompt police intervention with allegedly mentally-ill persons?
    A. What are some of the characteristics of persons apprehended by the police?
II. What do the police do when called on for help with allegedly mentally-ill persons?
    A. What alternatives do the police attempt prior to making a hospital referral?
    B. What do the police do with the apprehended person when the referral for hospitalization is refused?
III. What are some issues and problems encountered by the police in their work with allegedly mentally ill persons?

Further information concerning the work of the police with the mentally ill is of value in appreciating the importance of police work in this area, the identification of strengths and limitations of the police in working with the mentally ill, considering in what areas police work is effective and desirable and in what areas resources other than police resources need to be strengthened and developed.

LITERATURE REVIEW

Growing interest and conecrn about the activity of police with the mentally-disabled population has led to some studies which reveal information relevant to the above issues. The extent of police involvement has been documented. Bittner (1967) reported that one-fifth of those referred to public hospital psychiatric services in San Francisco had been referred by the police. Liberman (1957) reported that nearly one-half of those admitted to public hospital psychiatric services in Baltimore had come from police stations where they had been detained. Hollingshead and Redlich (1958) found that over one-half the referrals to mental hospitals of those in the lowest socioeconomic class were made by the police and the courts.

> Police of all community officials are most likely to perceive that a psychotic individual is disturbed or in need of psychiatric care. This may occur when an officer is called to the home to take charge of a violent individual or when a disturbed individual is being disorderly in a public place.

Liberman (1957) reports that families often call the police as a mental health resource for help and transportation in emergency situations, a number of which involve the patient's refusal of voluntary treatment possibilities. He states that the "typical police patient" is not an uncontrollable, violent "madman"; he is likely to be a paranoid schizophrenic, personality disorder, or other person who is currently seriously upset and who denies that he has problems which require professional help at this time. Few community resources are available to the family in such emergency situations.

Bittner (1967) points out that the mental health services of the police go beyond duties which are purely official. They often perceive and appraise abnormal behavior and make judgment that the behavior is disturbed, delinquent, or idiosyncratic. This judgment can determine whether a person is taken to a mental hospital or to jail. Bittner (1967) further states that while the police acknowledge that dealing with mentally-ill persons is a large part of their work, they maintain that it is not an appropriate task for them. They do not see a situation as pertinent to police contact unless there is a serious police problem in addition to a psychiatric problem. They say they lack training pertaining to psychopathology and do not feel competent in this area. They see the task of taking someone to the hospital as cumbersome and tedious. They are not eager for this aspect of their job, which the community has allocated to them.

The U. S. Riot Commission (1968) has referred to an aspect of police work termed "non-police work." They point out that the police face increasing manpower and money shortages. Police therefore resist becoming involved in matters in the mental health area, in part because they are not rewarded for their work. They are not rewarded professionally; there is little public recognition. The Commission believes that it is advisable for the police to be involved in "community services," that it is of benefit to them and the public.

METHODOLOGY

This is a descriptive study aimed at formulating problems for more precise investigation and developing hypotheses for further research.

The major sources of data were interviews with police officers who brought in for referral allegedly mentally-ill persons (AMIP) to the Los Angeles County University of Southern California Medical Center (LAC-USC-MC), hospital forms, and observation by researchers.

The sample aimed at interviews with all police officers who brought in allegedly mentally-ill persons (AMIP) to the LAC-USC-MC, Psychiatric Unit III, between 3:00 P.M. and 11:30 P.M. from March 4 to April 3, 1970. The final sample covered 93 percent of all police cases which were brought in during that period. It covered 40 percent of all police cases referred any time of the day or night during that 30-day period. Peace officers work in teams of two. Forty-four interviews with 88 peace officers were held. Interviews were joint interviews. Peace officers came from many departments and divisions of the city. AMIP all lived within or were apprehended within the LAC-USC-MC catchment area; this is in the heart of the city. Interview with peace officers were carried out at Unit III while the AMIP was being evaluated by the hospital psychiatrist. Interviews varied in length from 30 to 60 minutes. A semi-structured schedule was used.

Hospital forms included "Application for 72-Hour Detention," which was filled out by the apprehending peace officer before the person was seen in evaluation by the psychiatrist. This form included factual information concerning the circumstances under which the AMIP was called to the attention of the police and the behavior which precipitated the call. The Hospital Information Form provided data on the characteristics of the patient.

Direct observation of the AMIP and the referring officers was possible for the researchers as they were present when the AMIP was brought in. This provided some material which allowed for a check on data gathered on the forms.

Complete data was not available in all situations. The characteristics of the AMIP were self-reported at the time when they were brought in; many were unable to provide information regarding education, previous treatment, etc. In some situations neither officer on a team could or would answer questions addressed to him. The maximum available answers are reported in each instance, rather than reporting findings of only those areas in which total responses are available. This accounts for numbers which are less than the total number in the study.

RESULTS

What forms of behavior prompt police intervention? Behavior reported prompting police intervention with allegedly mentally-ill persons varied greatly in detail. It generally fell into seven categories:

Aggressive Behavior (three degrees of severity) :

Assault with injury.
Assault without injury.
Verbal assault only.

Confused behavior.
Shouting obscenities and/or paranoid thoughts.
Attempted suicide.
Nude exposure.
Public nuisance.
Drug-Induced behavior.

Some degree of aggressive behavior was the primary behavior prompting police intervention in 33 percent (16) of the 48 cases studied. In four other cases some degree of aggressive behavior occurred secondarily. The total of aggressive behavior was 42 percent (20). Twenty-three percent (11) of the overall sample showed confused behavior as a primary reason for police intervention. It was a secondary behavior problem in four additional cases, making a total of 31 percent (15). Shouting obscenities and/or paranoid thought occurred as the primary behavior in 17 percent (8) of the sample. In one case this shouting was a secondary behavior difficulty, making the total 19 percent (9). Nine percent (4) of the group prompted police intervention as a result of a suicide attempt. There was one instance of attempted suicide after police involvement. Six percent (3) of the sample prompted police involvement as a result of nude exposure. Ten percent (5) involved some nude exposure. Public nuisance behavior accounted for 6 percent (3) of the major reasons for police involvement. Only one situation of secondary nuisance behavior was found. All drug-induced behavior was primary. This was 6 percent (3) of the sample.

Most of the primary aggressive behavior in the sample occurred in the home, 81 percent (13). It is not surprising therefore that in 63 percent (10) of the aggressive cases, a family member was the person who contacted the police. Confused behavior was most commonly found in the street, 40 percent (4); it occurred only once in the home. No person with confused behavior was referred to the police by a family member; 40 percent (4) were contacted by police as a result of a citizen call, while 30 percent (3) were self-referred. Shouting behavior is similar to confusion in that it occurred only once in the home, and in no case was a shouting incident referred to police by a family member. As with confusion, shouting behavior tended to be public and occurred in a drug store (1), market (1), on the street (1), in a police car (1), and hotel (3). Managers initiated contact with police in 50 percent (4) of the shouting cases. No trends can be located in the small numbers of the other categories, except to note that none of the attempted suicide cases were referred to the police by family members.

Two methods of apprehension are employed by the peace officers in their dealings with a mentally-ill person. If verbal persuasion is not successful then force is used by physically overcoming and restraining the individual. Handcuffs are always applied in such cases. Sometimes officers use a "choke hold" which causes momentary loss of consciousness. Substantially less than half of the aggressive cases required the use of force in apprehension by a peace officer, 38 percent (6). Although the samples are small, it is worth noting that two of the public nuisance cases required force in apprehension; two of the attempted suicide cases also required force. All of the nude exposure cases were brought to the hospital through verbal persuasion. The shouting behavior cases were apprehended by force two times; and confused behavior required force two times.

All primary nude exposure, public nuisance, and drug-induced behavior cases were hospitalized, while only 63 percent (5) of the confused behavior cases and 50 percent (2) of the attempted suicide cases were hospitalized. A hospital disposition was made in 86 percent (6) of the shouting cases and 79 percent (11) of the aggressive cases. Fifty percent (2) of the attempted suicide cases were released, and 38 percent (3) of the confused behavior cases were returned to the peace officer.

Data was available on history of treatment and hospitalization for mental illness for two-thirds of the sample. Seventy-five percent (24) of all these cases had a history of prior hospitalization, while only 25 percent (8) were currently receiving any form of psychiatric treatment. Ninety-two percent (12) of the aggressive cases had a prior hospitalization history, and attempted suicide cases had a 100 percent (3) history of prior hospitalization. Confused and shouting behavior cases each had a 40 percent (2) history of hospitalization. The other samples were too small to indicate trends. All of the public nuisance cases had unknown history of treatment for mental illness.

The following tables show sex and age distribution of the sample.

TABLE 26-I.

Sex of Apprehended Person

Sex	%	N
Male	51	(22)
Female	49	(21)
Total	100	(43)

TABLE 26-II.

Age of Apprehended Person

Years	%	N
15-19	7	(3)
20-29	46	(20)
30-44	19	(8)
45-64	12	(5)
65 & Over	16	(7)
Total	100	(43)

Distribution of the referred AMIPs by age group is shown in Table 26-II.

The greatest age representation of individual brought in by the police was between 20 and 29 years, 46 percent (20). Over half of the referred AMIPs in the study were under 30 years of age. Slightly less than one-third—31 percent (13)—were in the "middle years," ages 30-64. Age and sex of the AMIP were not related to the behavior prompting peace officer intervention. Over four-fifths of the sample included persons who were currently without a spouse. Only one-fifth of the persons referred had dependents. Most of the sample was identified by race, and 36 percent (16) were members of minority groups. Blacks accounted for 27 percent (12) of the sample. Information on education and religion was available in about one-half the situations. Thirty-three percent (8) were Protestant; 30 percent (7) were Catholic; 21 percent (5) were Jewish; 8 percent (2) were none; and 8 percent (2) were other. Of those reporting educational background, 64 percent (16) had completed high school; this included 20 percent (5) who had some college education. None of those from whom information was available had less than seven years of education.

Only three categories of behavior leading to apprehension (aggressive, shouting, and confused) had large enough numbers to examine in relation to demographic characteristics. No relationships between age, sex, race, marital status, religion, education and behavior prompting police intervention were found. All categories of behavior showed the same over-representation of young unattached persons, with history of prior hospitalization for mental illness.

What do peace officers do when called on for help? When called on for help with the allegedly mentally-ill person, the police officers may view the problem as a civil matter or a criminal matter. In the researcher's observation, he is presented with several courses of action and may respond to the situation in one of the following ways:

> As a criminal matter, by arresting the individual if a violation of the law has occurred;
> As a civil matter, by referring the individual for 72 hours of psychiatric observation;
> In a number of informal ways, for example by counseling and releasing, or turning the individual over to a responsible relative or friend.

In response to the general interview question regarding the decision to hospitalize or arrest, approximately half, 51 percent (22), of the peace officers responding (43) said that if a crime (law violation) had been committed they will *sometimes* arrest an allegedly mentally-ill person. Twenty-one percent (9) said that they *never* arrest an allegedly mentally-ill person, even if a crime has been committed. Fourteen percent (6) reported *always* arresting a mentally-ill person if there has been *any* violation of the law. Fourteen percent (6) denied having any decision-making responsibility.

The actions of the peace officers in the specific cases in this study indicated much less inclination to arrest than was suggested by their responses to the general question about decision-making. In 46 percent (22) of the studied cases (48) the peace officers were aware that a law violation had occurred. In all but one instance, the referring officers denied having any plans to arrest or to file criminal charges. The one case in which a criminal charge (resisting arrest) was to be filed, a California Highway Patrolman had stopped a 78-year-old man for crossing against a red light. The man became belligerent and swung at the officer, who wrestled him to the ground. It was the officer's first encounter with an allegedly mentally-ill person, and he appeared to the researchers to be quite shaken by the experience.

The reasons given by the police officers for choosing a civil (hospitalization) rather than a criminal disposition in the cases studied where some violation of the law occurred are as follows: 52 percent (11) said that the person was obviously not responsible for his acts; 24 percent (5) said that hospitalization was more helpful than jail; 24 percent (5) said there was no complaint. (Someone must sign a complaint in order for an arrest to be made for disturbing the peace. As one officer put it, "Disturbing the police is not disturbing the peace.")

Alternatives attempted by peace officers prior to the hospitalization were documented in 23 cases. In 56 percent (13) of these cases, some counseling or extensive listening was attempted before deciding to refer for hospitalization. In 35 percent (8) of the cases a hospital referral was the only course of action considered. In 9 percent (2) of the cases an attempt was made to contact a responsible person. As indicated earlier, 42 percent (21) of the total sample were at home when the police intervened. This may account for the small number of attempts to contact responsible persons.

Alternatives to hospitalization were further examined by asking the peace officers what kinds of things they did when hospitalization did not appear to be the proper course of action. Their responses included: 35 percent (15) attempted to contact responsible person; 35 percent (15) counsel mentally-ill person or family; 12 percent (5) arrest, or check outstanding warrants; 4 percent (2) take to medical facility; 14 percent (6) take no significant action. Those persons taken routinely to a medical facility are those who have attempted suicide, taken an overdose of drugs, or are suffering from D.T.s. "Taking no significant action" includes "ignoring" the AMIP or making a brief report of the encounter and returning the individual to the street.

Three-fourths of the officers described alternatives which were intended to have ameliorative effects on the AMIP. The remaining one-fourth either arrested the individual or took no further action because it was not considered a criminal matter.

What are some of the issues and problems encountered? Some of the issues and problems encountered by the police in their work with the allegedly mentally ill were pointed out by them when they were asked to rate their work in relation to the most satisfying and least satisfying aspects of their total job. Over 50 percent of the 67 officers clearly considered work with the mentally ill as an undesirable part of their police duties. Reasons included: it takes time away from "real" police duties; lack of control of the situation; sympathy for the mentally-ill person and family; feels efforts are futile. About one-third of the officers were noncommittal in rating their work with mentally-ill persons. Reasons given included: depends on the situation; it's all part of the job; I don't work with the mentally ill.

Fifteen percent (10) of the sample clearly gave work with the mentally ill a high rating. Their reasons were not specific; nine said they felt that they were helpful in their work with the mentally ill, and one said that such work was "interesting."

Examination of reasons given for low rating of work with the mentally ill suggests several issues and problems:

1. Establishing and maintaining control using traditional police techniques is difficult for the peace officer when dealing with someone who is not defined as a criminal.
2. The peace officer questions the appropriateness of his involvement in civil matters at the expense of what he views as his actual police role.
3. For the peace officer it appears more difficult to separate personal from professional feelings when dealing with the non-criminal.

The issue of appropriateness of police work with the mentally ill was raised by the researchers in the interview with the peace officers. They were asked if they felt it was an appropriate duty for them, and why. A total of 59 officers responded to this question, 73 percent (43) of whom felt that their work with the mentally ill was appropriate. Their reasons given for considering it a proper task are described below. Fifty-four percent (23) said that it was the police officer's duty to protect persons and property and to serve the public; 30 percent (13) said that "no one else would do it"; 5 percent (2) said that the police had special expertise; 11 percent (5) gave no reason.

When asked who would be more appropriate to handle allegedly mentally-ill persons, very few officers responded (11). Those that did suggested crisis teams, a special "professional" detail connected with each division (authorized to carry weapons), and a pool of "mental health professionals" available for them to call on when needed.

Over one-third of the peace officers who considered work with the allegedly mentally ill an inappropriate police task gave inadequate training as a reason.

We were concerned with the issue of training and experience and the peace officers were asked what kind of preparation they had had for working with mentally-ill persons and what would they recommend for further training? Fifty-nine percent (38) had had up to six hours of police academy training in this area; 8 percent (5) had had 16 or more hours of in-service training from the Department of Mental Health staff; 3 percent (2) had had a tour of a mental hospital; 11 percent (7) had had some college psychology; and 19 percent (12) reported no preparation. About one-half of those responding felt that further training was needed. Recommendations for training which they gave included 36 percent (11) recommended field training (i.e. experience obtained while on the job) ; 29 percent (9) recommended classes in human behavior; 16 percent (5) recommended observation of treatment and counseling; 10 percent recommended visit to mental hospital; 6 percent (2) recommended small group training and 3 percent (1) recommended more academy training.

Those who recommended field experience felt that there was no adequate way to be prepared in advance for the diverse situations they would encounter in working with the AMIP. In view of this it is of interest to note that over one-third of the officers interviewed had less than two years of field experience, and for nearly one-fourth this was the first hospital referral.

SUMMARY OF MAJOR FINDINGS

It was found that one-third of all police interventions were prompted by aggressive behavior, usually occurring in the home and called to the attention of the police by a family member. Two other forms of behavior most often leading to police involvement were confusion and shouting of obscenities and/or paranoid thoughts, usually occurring in a public place. To a lesser extent the following behavior prompted police action: attempted suicide, nude exposure, public nuisance, and drug-induced behavior.

Persons referred to the hospital by police were evenly divided between the sexes, but were over-represented by the unmarried young adult population. Of those whose prior history of mental illness was known, three-fourths had been previously hospitalized while one-third of those were currently receiving treatment.

When encountering an individual exhibiting obviously disturbed behavior the peace officer frequently must choose between hospitalization and incarceration. In cases where some criminal act had occurred, an overwhelming disinclination among the officers to arrest or file charges was found.

In considering alternatives to hospitalization, three-fourths of the peace officers described carrying out actions which were intended to have an ameliorative effect on the individual, such as counseling or contacting a responsible person. The remaining one-fourth would either arrest the individual, or not considering it a police matter, would take no further action.

Most peace officers who had had a hospital referral refused had released the individual either to a responsible relative or on his own recognizance. Approximately one-third of the officers had ever arrested such a person.

Over half of the officers questioned clearly consider work with the mentally ill as an undesirable part of their police duties.

Their reasons given for a low rating raise several issues and problems:

1. Maintaining control with traditional police techniques when dealing with someone not defined as a criminal is difficult for the peace officer.
2. The peace officer questions the appropriateness of his involvement in civil matters at the expense of what he considers his actual police role.
3. For the peace officer it appears more difficult to separate personal from professional feelings when dealing with the non-criminal.

Three-fourths of the peace officers questioned felt that their work with the mentally ill was appropriate, however, a significant portion of those consider it so only because "no one else will do the job."

Nearly three-fourths of the peace officers responding had acknowledged no training at all or had less than four hours of police academy training in work with the mentally ill. Less than a third thought there was a need for further formal training. Most officers consider field experience to be the only means of preparation for encounters with the mentally ill.

INTERPRETATIONS OF FINDINGS

The findings in this study suggest that the policeman becomes involved with the mentally ill with greatest frequency when the situation contains elements of both "real police business," and "obvious psychiatric problems." This is demonstrated by the preponderance of persons alleged to be mentally ill and referred to the hospital who had exhibited some form of aggressive behavior.

Most of the aggressive behavior had occurred in the home, which may suggest that those mentally-ill individuals behaving aggressively on the street or in another public place are arrested and incarcerated. Aggressive behavior by a mentally-ill individual constitutes "real police business" because of the possibility that personal or property damage will proliferate. However, in those cases where aggressive behavior prompted police intervention, the use of force was not usually required to induce the mentally-ill person to accompany the peace officer.

None of the cases in this study involving aggressive behavior resulted in serious physical harm, which leads the researchers to speculate that mentally-ill persons who have actually inflicted major injury on another person are handled as criminals.

The findings imply that disturbed behavior in public, such as confusion and shouting obscenities, frequently precipitates police involvement. While such behavior is not necessarily perceived by the police or the public as criminal, it is offensive and results in pressure from the "offended" public to remove the individual. The citizen often will not sign a disturbing the peace complaint, diminishing the "real police business" element of the intervention.

The characteristics of the study sample support Gerald Caplan's (1964) concept of populations at high risk including disproportionate numbers of young adults, unattached persons, minority group members, and former mental patients. Three-fourths of the sample population had a history of prior hospitalization, while only a third of those were currently receiving treatment. This is even more characteristic of the aggressive cases, nearly all of which had a history of prior hospitalization. This points up the clear need for preventive mental health resources.

This study gives strong evidence of a wide divergence of responses by peace officers to basically similar situations. Their responses consistently ranged from arrest for a law violation to hospitalization or "psychiatric first aid." The range of responses indicates broad latitude in decision making.

The individual peace officer tends to deny his decision-making power with such statements as, "If any violation of the law has occurred we must arrest," or "We report to Central Receiving Hospital, which makes the decision." However, a large number of cases referred to LAC USC MC, Unit III, by the police had violated a law, which refutes the first denial. The second denial is mitigated by some peace officers acknowledging that the way in which they choose to describe the allegedly mentally ill person's behavior to the sergeant at Central Receiving (or to not report it at all) determines the outcome of the case.

"Psychiatric first aid" was represented in the study by the peace officers' frequent attempts at counseling and contacting a responsible person. The content of their counseling indicates that the peace officers' conception of mental illness closely approximates that of the general lay public. Counseling is rudimentary and primarily oriented toward management, not toward treatment.

The group of officers studied are from that population of peace officers who have in their repertoire of decision making the consideration of a hospital referral. It is likely that there is another population of peace officers outside the sample who never decide in favor of a hospital disposition when dealing with a mentally-ill individual. The officer's decision making has far-reaching consequences for those mentally-ill persons whom he encounters.

Most of the peace officers in this study freely acknowledge that work with the mentally ill is an undesirable part of their task. Yet, they continue to view it as an appropriate part of their mandate "to protect and to serve." It would appear that most would not easily relinquish their current responsibility for intervention with allegedly mentally-ill persons. This is further shown by the paucity of their suggestions for other resources to handle or assist with this aspect of their job.

An analysis of the reason given for a low rating of work with the mentally ill suggests that the police officer has difficulty establishing and maintaining control using traditional police techniques when dealing with someone who is not defined as a criminal. The allegedly mentally-ill person is commonly irrational and often unpredictable but cannot be simply defined as a "bad guy" to be overwhelmed by superior force. While the peace officers express the need for special training in better understanding of the behavior of the mentally ill, study findings would lead the researchers to speculate that this is not a desire to better "treat" the person. Rather, it is a desire to more efficiently predict behavior in order to protect oneself, prevent proliferation of trouble, and to expediently end the crisis.

Elaine Cumming (1965) argues that where the policeman's

role contains "both overtly supportive and overtly controlling elements," his position is untenable. Her recommendation is that their supportive and mental health function should remain latent and informal. By the peace officer's preference for field training (or for no further training) over more formal academic mental health instruction, he demonstrates his emphasis on the controlling elements of his work. The researchers were impressed with the peace officer's tendency to minimize his supportive role, suggesting that greater psychological knowledge might cause him to experience greater role conflict.

IMPLICATIONS AND RECOMMENDATIONS

The police do not identify themselves as a mental health resource, but are with great frequency called on by the public and by identified mental health resources to become involved with the mentally ill. No other existing mental health agency can match the police in their *availability* (24-hour/day, 7-day/week, in all areas), *authority* (power to arrest, or defend self or others with deadly force; power to call on "reinforcements"), and *mobility* (fleets of radio patrol cars dispersible throughout the community).

The question then becomes, is all this necessary for emergency work with mentally-ill persons, or have the police become the "catch-all" of the mental health system? Have mental health professionals abdicated too much responsibility for decision making in emergency apprehension of mentally-ill persons? Given their superior availability, authority, and mobility, what special handicaps or limitations characterize peace officer intervention? Answers to these questions must be considered in the light of the complexity of the problem and the variety of needs of mentally ill persons.

Some of those individuals referred by the peace officer to the hospital were merely lost and confused; unable to provide pertinent information about themselves. Clearly they only needed shelter until a responsible party could be located. It was learned from the hospital staff that some of these individuals purposely withheld their names and addresses from police in order to avoid the embarrassment of returning home in a police car. It is evident that this type of situation could be appropriately handled by a non-police resource if one were available.

Most of the referrals involved no law violation and in those cases that did, the offense was a misdemeanor and directly related to their being mentally ill. Further, force was used to apprehend in only a small proportion of the cases.

The power to arrest and the application of force in apprehension seems not to be required in the majority of cases. In fact, it could be speculated that in cases where force was employed, more subtle means of apprehension might have been possible. It is difficult to determine the policeman's authority (uniform, etc.) is an irritant or a tranquilizer. This would be a valuable area for further research.

The conflict inherent in adopting both overtly controlling and overtly supportive roles is not a conflict restricted only to the police. It is reasonable to assume that the mental health professional, when confronted by a volatile disturbed person in a public place would have to deal with the potential expansion of trouble and therefore necessarily be concerned with maintaining control. It would be ironic but possible for a civilian crisis team to slowly take on the trappings of authority typical of the police. Citizens responding to the publicly offensive behavior of a mentally-ill person are concerned primarily with the removal of the offending individual and are therefore likely to call on the police even when more treatment-oriented resources are available.

There were a considerable number of calls initiated by family members, many of which were referred to the police after calling Unit III. These cases require police involvement in part because means are not currently available in the community for advising families at home and for transporting mentally-ill persons to the hospital. There are provisions in the Lanterman-Petris-Short Act for emergency crisis units to operate out of the psychiatric admitting and evaluating area of Unit III. A good beginning might be a mobile crisis service staffed only by mental health professionals responding directly to the calls coming in to Unit III from family members of mentally-ill persons in crisis.

The already useful LAPD Hospital Detail at Central Receiving could be enhanced by the addition of mental health professionals acting as full-time consultants on disposition and treatment of mentally-ill persons. In addition, peace officers who demonstrate unusual aptitude for work with the mentally ill might be considered for a special mobilized detail composed of both police and non-police mental health professionals, operating in each LAPD Division.

The study findings have provided some answers to the research questions, and a body of information that is useful in further studies.

REFERENCES

Bittner, E.: "Police Discretion in Emergency Apprehension of Mentally Ill Persons." *Social Problems, 14,* 1967, 278-292,

Caplan, Gerald: *Principles of Preventive Psychiatry.* New York: Basic Books, 1964.

Cumming, Elaine, Edell, L., and Cumming, I.: "Policeman as Philosopher, Guide and Friend." *Social Problems, 12,* 1965, 276-286.

Hollingshead, A. and Redlich, F.C.: *Social Class and Mental Illness.* New York: John Wiley, 1958.

Liberman, Robert: "Police as a Community Mental Health Resource." *Community Mental Health Journal,* Vol. 5 (2), 1969, 111-120.

Rock, Ronald: *Hospitalization and Discharge of the Mentally Ill.* Chicago: University of Chicago Press, 1968.

U.S. Riot Commission Report: *Report of the National Advisory Commission on Civil Disorders.* New York: New York Times Co., 1968.

SECTION VII

CONSULTATION WITH POLICE

INTRODUCTION

INCREASINGLY, OVER THE PAST FEW YEARS, BEHAVIORAL SCIENTISTS HAVE BEEN INVITED TO CONSULT WITH POLICE DEPARTMENTS. CONSULTATION INVOLVES A WIDE RANGE OF PROBLEMS AND SERVICES FROM PSYCHO-THERAPY TO EVALUATION OF RESEARCH PROJECTS. THE ARTICLES IN THIS CHAPTER RELATE PROBLEMS AND PRACTICES OF POLICE CONSULTATION.

THE SCHWARTZ AND LIEBMAN CHAPTER DISCUSSES ROLES AND PROBLEMS OF MENTAL HEALTH PROFESSIONALS IN A POLICE DEPARTMENT. BODIN RELATES THREE WAYS IN WHICH A PROFESSIONAL MIGHT ORIENT HIMSELF TO POLICE DEPARTMENTS. FINALLY, SOKOL DISCUSSES THE ROLE OF COM-MUNITY PSYCHIATRIST IN A POLICE SETTING.

Chapter 27

MENTAL HEALTH CONSULTATION IN LAW ENFORCEMENT

Jeffrey A. Schwartz and Donald A. Liebman

U NTIL RECENTLY, police agencies rarely used any type of consultation from mental health professionals. In the last several years, there has been a burgeoning interest in this area which is attributable to several factors. First, the move by police toward professionalization has had a direct effect on their degree of reliance on civilian consultants of all stripes. Many law enforcement agencies have turned to psychologists and psychiatrists in an effort to improve recruit quality by using psychological screening. Police professionalism has also meant that social scientists have been increasingly used in police training and education. Second, community pressures in some cities have forced psychological testing and/or counseling upon unwilling police executives. Third, the movement within social work, psychology and psychiatry toward active involvement with social problems has meant that some professionals from these fields are approaching the judicial system hoping to define consultation roles. Fourth, the Law Enforcement Assistance Administration (LEAA) has spurred developments in this field in a manner designed to get fast results: by providing money. The LEAA 1970 discretionary grant program set aside money to fund "psychiatric aides"—psychiatrists or psychologists —to work, on a regular basis with a number of medium-sized and large police departments. Finally, the tremendous increase in emphasis upon community relations has seen many departments look beyond their in-house personnel for expertise in areas such as human relations, juvenile counseling, race relations, sensitivity training and the like.

All of the factors reviewed above have converged to produce a quite active interchange between law enforcement and mental health systems, where there was essentially none ten years ago. Of greater significance is that this interchange will almost certainly increase rapidly, probably exponentially, in the next ten years, because all of the factors identified should themselves operate more and more strongly.

As with most new ventures, this rather sudden-and fledgling-rapprochement between police and mental health professionals is not without problems, pitfalls and hidden costs. Primary among these is the fact that mental health professionals and police personnel are blessed by a state of mutual ignorance which often insures that attempts at collaboration are doomed to failure. Most police executives know so little about the mental health disciplines that they are unaware of what services they can expect to obtain, and what cannot be done. Further, given a very specific need, police executives frequently lack the sophistication with the mental health system which would allow them to find the desired service. Thus, a social worker may be asked to provide psychological testing of police recruits, or a sociologist may be asked to provide marital counseling. The other side of this coin is just as problematic in its effects upon mutual efforts: most mental health professionals know essentially nothing about the day-to-day operations of a police department or about the salient aspects of police systems. Thus, a psychotherapist may attempt to teach police about family crisis intervention without any notion of the differences between a therapy office and a hot family fight in a ghetto.

In spite of these and similar problems, the infusion of mental health expertise, concepts, personnel and services into law enforcement is one of the most exciting and potentially useful innovations in police work. This chapter is an attempt to provide some clarity to both police and social scientists about useful—and useless—consultation roles. This chapter is not an attempt to delineate all possible consultation roles in law enforcement. The roles discussed here were chosen because they are common roles, or particularly promising roles, or both. Mental health professionals have been employed by police agencies in capacities which are not considered here (e.g. juvenile work, or resolution of labor conflicts) . Also, important new consultation roles can be expected to evolve during the next ten years and it is likely that many of these new roles are not even anticipated in this discussion.

For the purpose of this chapter, the term "mental health professional" will be used to signify psychologists, psychiatric social workers and psychiatrists. "Law enforcement agencies" is meant to include municipal, county and state police agencies.

TESTING AND SELECTION

This role is the single most common way in which mental health professionals consult to police agencies. A great number of police departments, large and small, now use some form of psychological testing or psychiatric interviews in their recruit selection process. Departments which do use psychological tests or psychiatric interviews almost always have professional consultants in charge of such activities. It has already been noted that there are two avenues by which police arrive at psychological testing: either self-initiated, out of concern for professionalism and improved recruit quality or under duress from community pressures. In either case, a major goal of police in installing psychological testing procedures is the identification of candidates who are potentially brutal, unstable, or racist. Less frequently, police agencies express a desire to improve the probability that a man will remain in police work.

The role issues inherent in such a charge are indeed formidable. Most obvious is the possibility of a mental health professional agreeing to provide services that cannot be rendered. Whether the specific service is psychological testing (almost always done by psychologists) or psychiatric interviews (which might involve social workers, psychiatrists or psychologists), the critical question is, "How effective is psychological screening?" It is not within the scope of this chapter to examine this question in depth, but some general statements are in order. It is clearly *not* possible at this time to identify from a group of recruit candidates those men who will be brutal or racist as police officers. The social scientist who accepts such a charge has entered into an impossible contract and the responsibility for the inevitable failure of the program rests squarely on his shoulders and not on those of the police administrator. There have been many confusing and contradictory statements in the mass media about the effectiveness (or lack of same) of psychological testing, and it is not surprising that lay persons think that much can be done which cannot.

There is no easy answer to the real issue, which is "to what extent will psychological screening *improve* existing recruit selection procedures?" One of the common justifications of psychological testing is that it *at least* identifies the blatant psychotics and keeps them from being policemen, but in fact, the background investigation and oral exam used in most agencies will also identify blatant psychotics; thus, psychological tests may not constitute an improvement in this specific function. Since the effectiveness of testing and selection methods has been one of the most extensive and bitter arguments within academic psychology for the last 15 years, it should not be incumbent on a police chief to be aware of all of the manifestations of this issue. It does seem that the burden of proof should fall on those who extoll the merits of psychological testing. In the area of police selection, such proof is presently non-existent.

It is noteworthy that most law enforcement agencies that utilize psychological testing have hired individual consultants on a retainer or a "per client" basis rather than make arrangements with local mental health centers (even though such arrangements would often be without charge). The explanation is that most police departments are suspicious about "civilian" personnel. Also, in many cities, the relations between the police department and the personnel of the mental health facility are quite bad. Thus, police are likely to try to find a consultant they can have faith in and give him free access to personnel, records, etc.

If the consultation role in police screening is extended to either promotional exams or to diagnostic work with sworn officers, then there is tremendous potential for role conflicts. (This is also true of the counseling and therapy role which is discussed later.) If a consultant is involved with diagnostic work, promotional screening, counseling or therapy with sworn officers, *then he should not be fulfilling any other roles within that agency.* These roles do not, however, conflict with each other.

The rationale for these role constraints is rather simple; even if the consultant feels comfortable working with men in a training capacity and then interpreting test protocols of those same men that may affect their chances of promotion, those men may be ill at ease with the situation but unable to alter it for fear of negative consequences. The professional has allowed his role to be changed from consultant to supervisor. The implications of these role constraints are serious. The mental health professional who wants to consult to law enforcement agencies in ways that go beyond the provision of direct intervention services is prohibited from testing and therapy, which may well be his most comfortable roles and the areas of his greatest expertise. For the police executive, this may also be a bitter pill to swallow. Having overcome his personal pessimism and secured a mental health consultant, and then having found the consultant to be a useful addition to the agency in counseling and/or testing, the administrator is here told *not* to go to that same consultant when a need arises in training or research or the like. It is, nevertheless, a sound and necessary premise.

Because of the restrictions inherent in the clinical consultation roles of testing and counseling, they are the only mental health roles within police agencies that do not demand that the consultant become familiar with the police system. It is possible (but not desirable) to agree upon carefully circumscribed clinical services which can be performed without knowledge of police work (e.g. marital therapy). It is preferable that even in these roles the consultant begin by orienting himself to the agency and familiarizing himself with actual police procedures and working conditions. (A pragmatic aside is that police executives should expect to pay for this period of familiarization, but that the increase in the quality of the services to the department and the increased acceptance of the consultant by the rank and file will more than justify this added expense.)

COUNSELING AND PSYCHOTHERAPY

This role includes the provision of counseling or therapy services for sworn personnel (and may extend to the families of officers) . Where therapy programs are established, marital counseling can be expected to be a major element of such programs. At present, it is quite rare for even the larger police departments to have programs of this type. This is one of the areas in which mental health consultation with law enforcement should show great growth in the next ten years. The primary stimulus for such growth will come not from police administrators, community groups or from professional therapists, but rather from police officer associations (P.O.A.'s) . As P.O.A.'s grow more militant and union-like in their pursuit of improved working conditions and greater fringe benefits, they will increasingly demand individual and marital counseling as a job-related health need.

There is a great deal of justification for the view that psychotherapy for an officer experiencing emotional problems is the responsibility of the police department just as medical care must be provided for officers injured in the line of duty. The job pressures on a policeman in today's urban departments are truly enormous. Young officers in most departments see themselves as facing hostility and danger from the community they serve, while receiving little or no support from police administrators (who are usually viewed as being overly concerned with ameliorating social and political pressures) . In addition, the young officer who hopes to advance in police work must continue his education in his off-duty time, make court appearances and the like. For such an officer, the job is closer to 65 hours a week than 40. The officer's wife probably had no understanding of her husband's job demands when she married him. She also did not bargain for the insecurity, the danger to her husband, or the anti-police feeling she herself may encounter in some social settings. It is not surprising that indices of social alienation are high within police ranks; divorce and alcoholism often reach serious proportions.

The picture of personal stress outlined above underscores the need for readily available counseling services. Unfortunately, some people in police work still regard psychotherapy as a sign of weakness or craziness, and are resistant to efforts to secure such services.

Problems of role definition and potential role conflict are

more critical for the therapy role than for any other type of mental health consultation in law enforcement. As with the testing role, police departments will usually retain individual consultants rather than work with local mental health facilities. In addition to the reasons discussed earlier, there are two additional factors here and a consultant must be sensitive to both. First, if an officer were known to be in therapy, it might adversely affect his promotional chances. Some of his supervisors may have the negative attitudes about therapy alluded to above. Second, many policemen would worry about the possible effect that therapy might have upon their court cases. Thus, counseling or therapy should be established in a manner that preserves an officer's anonymity. This entails the therapist maintaining an office that is *not* within the agency, an answering service, and a therapy schedule that is flexible enough to allow officers to use off-duty time even if they work day shift. Reports to the Department from the therapist should specify the number of clients seen, but not their names. Unless the consultation arrangement accommodates these needs of the officers, then men who may want counseling will choose not to avail themselves of it.

A consultant who provides a department with counseling should fulfill no other role within the agency with the exception of recruit selection. The problems engendered in such role conflicts are subtle, and the consultant may not realize that anything is amiss; officers may choose not to try counseling for fear of being compromised by the consultant's multiple roles.

Another pitfall which must be avoided is allowing the department in any way to select those men who are to be seen in therapy. A police chief may, with the best of intentions, ask a consultant to individually work with men selected by their supervisors. This procedure will be anathema to any valid therapy program. It will identify the consultant as an agent of the department's administrators and prevent the rank-and-file patrolmen from developing any trust in the consultant. Police executives and mental health professionals alike would be wise to avoid this almost punitive use of therapy.

As with psychological testing, it is useful but not necessary for the consultant therapist to become familiar with the police agency with which he will work. In addition, to the direct services that the consultant provides, he will almost inevitably serve the useful secondary function of desensitizing police personnel to mental health services. The consultant can enhance this effect by systematically educating the membership of the agency as to what services he does and does not provide, what types of therapy and diagnostic services other local professionals offer and some notion of what to expect when going to therapists of various types.

For most police agencies, hiring a consultant to do counseling will be an important step forward. However, an even more exciting possibility is that some enlightened police executives may find equally enlightened mental health consultants and establish innovative programs which are preventative in nature. The concept of preventative mental health should have wide applicability within the field of law enforcement. What remains is for viable programs to evolve, and for those programs to rigorously demonstrate their effectiveness.

COMMUNITY RELATIONS

If there is such a thing as a traditional role for social scientists within police agencies, it is working with the police community relations (PCR) bureau. Social scientists of all persuasions have been used as consultants in community relations, and the specific consultation services offered have been equally varied. The consultant may only teach a course in community relations, or he may be deeply involved with the entire community relations effort.

PCR is by far the easiest point of entry into the police system for the mental health professional. Within community relations, the consultant often finds men who are sympathetic to social science perspectives and who represent the "soft" approach to law enforcement. Thus, the consultant may develop close working relationships and personal rapport with one or more of the men assigned to PCR. All is not well, however. The problem is that within many large police agencies, the PCR personnel are isolated from the rest of the department—and often distrusted. Thus, the consultant may feel elated that he is so well received, and he may be optimistic about his impact on the agency when in fact he is cut off from the actual operations of the department and working only with those men whose views are closest to his own and who are least representative of the rank-and-file. PCR can be an excellent way to introduce a department to mental health consultation, but for greatest impact on the department, it is best used as a bridge to areas that are more central to the agency.

Within PCR there are a wide range of activities that may attract the attention of the mental health consultant. One very useful focus for the talents of the consultant is working between the police department and other agencies. Most law enforcement agencies do not enjoy close or effective relationships with other public agencies. While this lack of accord may be only at the administrative level or only at the level of the rank-and-file, it often runs throughout both organizations. Thus, antipathy between police and probation, for example, is the rule, not the exception. It has been pointed out earlier in this chapter that police-mental health center relations usually range from strained cooperation to open warfare. Individual officers often find it difficult to maintain perspective in such situations and are ineffective at taking steps to alleviate such hostilities. The mental health professional is usually in an excellent position to do just that.

The PCR consultant role is not as difficult in terms of role integrity as the roles in therapy and testing, nor is it restrictive. As with the rest of the roles to be described, it is *imperative* that the consultant become familiar with police work.

TRAINING AND EDUCATION

Many police agencies have used mental health professionals in training and education. Like the therapy role, this function may be expected to show a tremendous increase in the next ten years. It is instructive to examine the forces that will produce new emphasis in the training field.

First, current police training is very poor. This fact is acknowledged readily by most police officials, and is now coming to the attention of many concerned citizens at local and national levels. Recruit academies and in-service training classes alike show little awareness of the most rudimentary teaching techniques. Curricula are often patched together hurriedly and are the responsibility of a training officer with few skills in teaching methodology. Departments seldom monitor training classes and do not often ask for evaluative feedback from the trainees, so there is seldom any basis for modifying or improving the courses. An eight-hour day of training for an officer will probably entail eight hours of dry lecture punctuated only by responsive readings from the penal code. In addition, the training seldom approximates the demands of the job. Most police training concentrates on the officers' arrest function; much attention is given to defensive tactics, weapons, training, jailing procedure and the like. While these skills are indispensable, there is another whole side of police work—the service function—in which very little training is available. This is so in spite of recent estimates, that suggest that 70 to 80 percent of a police agency's business is service-related rather than arrest-related.

For police, the formal educational sphere is equally grim. Police training is often the least demanding program on the campus. It is certainly one of the least interesting and useful. The prototype of many police science courses is a class for three semester units in traffic control in which all 20 class members are already proficient at traffic control (being experienced sworn officers) . It is taught by another police officer who knows no more about traffic control than most of the class, and little about teaching. Fortunately, in a few locations in the U.S. there is an awakening interest in developing quality educational programs for police. These new programs tend to de-emphasize traditional police training courses in favor of liberal arts and the social sciences. In many of the educational centers where such developments are occurring, mental health professionals are deeply involved with program design and development. (While teaching at a university would not usually be considered as a consultant role, many police departments arrange for certain types of training and education to be offered through local colleges. In these instances, the instructor is primarily providing service to the police agency, at least in spirit if not by formal definition.)

Police executives must begin to resolve a serious problem that is a byproduct of a well-educated force; how can a man's educational skill be used to advantage while retaining flexibility with regard to his transfer or promotion. As young officers are encouraged by their departments to get useful college degrees, these young officers are going to more and more expect that their skills be put to good use. Currently, police departments are in danger of acquiring the Army's reputation: "if a man is a trained radio operator give him a job as a cook."

The mental health professional is in a particularly good position to consult to law enforcement on training issues because he has expertise in content areas and also in teaching methodology; both are sorely needed. In the content realm, there are several social problem areas which consume much of a policeman's time and energy, but for which he receives little or no training. These areas include family fights, alcoholics, drug addicts, suicides and juvenile problems. The emerging interest among law enforcement officials in family crisis intervention training is an excellent example of a natural congruence of interests of mental health and law enforcement in one of these areas. In the methodology realm, mental health consultants are familiar with the use of video tape feedback, programmed learning texts and other recent developments in teaching. These techniques can be used to excellent advantage in many training situations. For example, most law enforcement agencies currently own videotape equipment, but they typically use that equipment only to make or to show training films. Video tape is seldom used to show an officer how he looks while interviewing a citizen, or to replay an officer's movements during a simulated car stop so that he can see where he failed to take proper safety precautions.

The training role carries the responsibility for insuring the relevance of the training for the people being trained. A good rule of thumb is that training will be effective in direct proportion to the familiarity of the trainer with the job demands of the police officers.

It is not feasible for the policemen to learn enough about the disciplines of psychology and psychiatry to be able to abstract the important elements from a presentation and then to translate them into implications for law enforcement. On the other hand, it is quite reasonable for a consultant, *before* he develops training on handling alcoholics, to find out the conditions under which the police are called on to deal with alcoholics, what the officer's legal options and legal constraints are, and what constitutes normal police procedures in such cases. If possible, the consultant should arrange for observational rides in patrol cars so that he has first-hand knowledge of the situations for which he will provide training.

The consultant satisfying a training function with a police agency must be sensitive to the context in which his training occurs. If he implicitly or explicitly approaches this task as if training occurs in a vacuum, then he will be ineffective. In fact, police training occurs within a system that imposes myriad influences upon the men being trained, their reactions to the training and their subsequent behavior on the streets. An awareness of the most salient of these influences will allow the consultant to maximize his impact. For example, mid-management personnel should be sufficiently involved in the training so that they understand the procedures the patrolmen are being taught, and so that they encourage the use of these procedures. All too frequently police agencies find that attempts at innovation end in failure because of the passive resistance of line supervisors. Similarly, the consultant who trains recruits must be aware of the resocialization process which the rookie will face from older officers, and particularly from his training officer. Thus, an excellent set of ideas given to recruits may be "trained out" of those recruits when they reach the street, simply because the ideas conflict with the standard procedures of the experienced officers. A case in point is family crisis intervention training. In most programs, the specially trained officers take from 30 minutes to an hour and a half to handle a family fight. This alienates line supervisors and fellow officers, whose experience dictates that patrolmen should be able to get out of a family fight and back into service in 15 to 25 minutes. Whether the extra time is well spent or not is unlikely to receive serious consideration; spending 1 hour and 15 minutes in a family fight is a *prima facia* case against the specially-trained patrolman. (Aware of this conflict, the family-crisis programs in Richmond,

California and San Francisco used methods designed to be feasible in less than 20 minutes, and managed to avoid the problems described above.)

There is no simple solution for the police administrator or for the consultant that will guarantee quality training or enthusiastic reception of that training. The police executive must be as demanding about the quality, thoroughness, relevance and preparation of training for his men as he is about the conduct of his officers. This has generally not been true. It does not make good sense for law enforcement officials to set high standards for their men and to carefully scrutinize the behavior of those men in difficult situations, but to provide mediocre training for those same situations. As for the consultant, it is his professional responsibility to determine that his training is, in fact, worth presenting, and that he has tried to maximize its utility for the police officer.

It is not unrealistic to ask that major departments in the next decade advance to the point that they offer excellent training in all of the major functions of the police officer. If this is to happen, mental health professionals will have to effectively collaborate with police agencies.

RESEARCH AND PROGRAM EVALUATION

This is another unusual but highly promising function for the mental health consultant.[1] For the purpose of this discussion, the term "research" includes both basic and applied research; program evaluation is meant to denote the analysis of the effects of any ongoing project, program or procedure.

It is useful to differentiate between basic and applied research within police departments. In general, the climate for basic research is poor. The police system and police as individuals tend to be highly pragmatic. This is not surprising, considering the environmental demands imposed by the job. For the basic re-

---

[1]It should be noted that it is not unusual for law enforcement agencies to employ psychologists and sociologists as project evaluators, but this arrangement is usually contract research—at least in spirit if not in fact—and there is seldom any intent on the part of the department or the researcher that the impact of the evaluator's activity should go beyond the project being evaluated. This type of arrangement is not within the purview of this chapter.

searcher, however, this police pragmatism is an additional problem. Worthwhile studies may find no support among police officials because the probability of short-term practical consequences is small. Projects seen as basic research may be dropped or supported half-heartedly because of a general desire on the agency's part to attend to "important" things and to start action projects. A research proposal often draws a suggestion that "there's been plenty of research, we need to do something about the problem." An extended discussion of the problem almost always discloses that how to deal with the problem is *not* apparent and that good research is *not* available on the subject.

Many researchers in areas such as sociology, criminology and psychology view law enforcement agencies as being particularly uncooperative with regard to research efforts. This is often true. There are, however, easily understood reasons for this police mistrust of researchers. Many police departments have been exploited by researchers, and subsequently have decided to deny access to the agency to other investigators. This exploitation (and negligence) has ranged from relatively mild forms such as failing to provide feedback on the outcome of the research to much more serious cases of breach of faith such as obtaining cooperation from a police agency for a very technical study and then publishing an "exposé" of the department in the mass media. The prospective researcher also falls heir to the police distaste for the academic world in general.

The preceding paragraphs indicate why the research picture in law enforcement has seemed bleak. In fact, the picture is not bleak at all. The researcher who practices a few basic principles should find excellent cooperation, and, in many instances, real enthusiasm concerning his efforts. First, the research proposal should be explained in some detail to the agency administrators. The practical consequences of the agency's participation should be emphasized, even if some of these are negative or restrictive. If administrative permission is secured, the researcher should then insure that the project is explained to all personnel who will be directly or indirectly affected by the study. (This should be done even when police executives do not request it; the consultant should regard this process as a necessity to insure administrative and operational support.) Second, the agency must understand, prior to the research undertaking, the major purposes of the study, what kinds of publications may result and how the agency's role will be presented. Third, prompt feedback should be presented to the department executives *and* to all personnel involved in the project.

There are potentially strong sources of support for research which lie dormant in most law enforcement agencies. For example, the formal values of the policeman are heavily empirical. When the technical complexities and the jargon is stripped from most research efforts, what remains is the systematic application of empiricism in an attempt to answer some question; police personnel tend to appreciate this approach. The consultant who is effective at carrying out a few studies within a police agency will likely find that he stimulates interest in a wide range of research efforts and project evaluations that have no relation to his own studies.

There is an immediate need for research talent within police agencies. The Safe Streets Act of 1968 started a massive infusion of federal funds into local elements of the judicial system, with police departments getting the bulk of these monies. Most federally-funded projects must include an evaluation component, and in many cases this has forced police to hire consultants or firms or contract researchers in order to comply with the requirements of the funding agency.

Unfortunately, even the largest police departments typically do not have anyone with behavioral research skills. This is a far more serious deficit than may be apparent. It means that agencies are, figuratively, at the mercy of the consultant firms they engage for research and evaluation. The research knowledge gap between the project evaluator and the police personnel in charge of the project is usually so great that the evaluation is not designed with consideration of police needs. At the end of the project, the police administrators may discover that the evaluation is of little or no use in guiding future decisions about the project. Even in cases where the evaluation is well done and to the point, it may be presented with so much technical jargon that the law enforcement personnel are unable to decode the final report. Part and parcel of this problem is that police personnel are usually unable to discriminate the competent from the incompetent among research consultants—and there has been no dearth of incompetent consultants.

An interesting sidelight for the research consultant is that this area is an excellent starting point for the behavioral scientist who wants to address social issues but has no clinical training. Thus, the experimental psychologist who is interested in consultation or the physiologist who is interested in the criminal justice system will find research consultation an appropriate beginning that should lead to broader role definitions.

It is a necessity that major police agencies acquire in-house expertise at behavioral research. This is a difficult charge. It can be fulfilled by either of two avenues: trained civilian personnel may be hired, or capable sworn personnel may be sent for university training in this area. The requisite skills are not available at the undergraduate level. It is possible, although difficult, to find Masters-level programs in the behavioral sciences which are good enough and sufficiently research oriented to impart the skill necessary to design and conduct program evaluation research.

The research consultant can influence a police agency far beyond the scope of this designated consultation role. He can sensitize police executives to the potential benefits in good program evaluation. He can develop within the Research bureau of the agency an appreciation of good research and some ability to recognize and evaluate bad research. He can remove much of the stigma attached to the word "research" and cultivate the already data and fact-oriented views of policemen, showing them that many of their concerns and questions are empirical and will yield to applied research. Finally, the consultant may be able to stimulate an interest in program evaluation that carries well beyond specially-funded projects, so that the agency begins to use program evaluation techniques to evaluate everyday procedures. Thus, questions such as the optimal deployment of patrol, the influence of the 10-4 plan upon use of sick leave or the relative effectiveness of individual investigators vs. two man teams in working burglaries are all eminently researchable—and answerable—questions. However, none of those questions can be definitively answered with anecdotal evidence or impressionistic studies; rather, each demands competence with behavioral research design and methodology and a fair knowledge of descriptive and inferential statistics. Again, most police already lean toward mutually defined, mutually observable evidence and away from subjective reports, so that the behavioral research consultant will sow his knowledge on fertile fields.

ADMINISTRATION CONSULTATION

Administrative consultation includes any arrangement in which a mental health professional works with a command-level police administrator on a broad range of issues and in an ongoing manner. In addition, there are a wide variety of other situations which may or may not be considered to be "administrative consultation," depending on one's definition of this term. The primary focus of this discussion is restricted to the type of case described above; that is, consultations at the executive level of the police agency that extend, temporally, and substantively, beyond any one specific task.

There may be many instances in which a police chief will contact a consultant in the mental health disciplines with regard to some limited task. A police chief might want a diagnostic test battery administered to an officer or to a suspect in a criminal case; a police executive might want help with a racial problem in some district of his city or a mental health professional might be called in by management to try to avert a labor dispute.

Any of these examples could be argued to be "administrative consultation." Such arguments are basically semantic disagreements and do little or nothing to improve the quality of consultation available to the components of the judicial system. In this chapter, those consultations which center about single topics are discussed in relation to those topics (e.g. testing and selection) and this section is devoted to working agreements that are not problem-limited.

It is extraordinary today to find an ongoing administrative consultation between a police executive and a mental health professional. This will probably continue to be the case in the near future. It would be most surprising to see any profusion of such roles within law enforcement agencies. Currently, very few people in law enforcement or in psychiatry have a clear conception of the nature of such a consultation. Thus, there is no pressure to initiate such relationships, and little awareness of their potential utility. There is one method by which administrative consultations are occasionally established by police executives: they grow out of specific consultations. That is, a consultant may be retained for some specific task or service and, in the course of his contact with the police chief, the chief finds the consultant adding a new and useful dimension to his outlook. If the specific consultation is successful, and if the chief and the consultant establish some personal respect and rapport, then the chief may initiate a long-term and less-structured consultation. Obviously, this does not happen often. If administrative consultation to police chiefs is to have any real future, support and direction must come from outside police agencies. The two most likely sources for such support and direction are city managers (who would do well to carefully examine the potential benefits of ongoing consultation for their police chiefs) and local mental health agencies (which could offer such services free if they could convince police to try them; and if they have staff personnel capable of filling this unusual role).

Administrative consultation is probably worthy of consideration by the police executive. ("Probably" is used because this kind of consultation has been tried so infrequently that a clear evaluation is impossible.) The urban police chief is one of today's beleaguered men, part of a select and uncomfortable group that includes university presidents, high school principals and mayors. The police executive faces pressures from his own men, the city government, minority groups and more. The interests of these groups are often irreconcilable. In most police agencies it is the chief alone who must bear the brunt of the social and political pressures. This is all the more difficult because the chief probably had scant experience in the political arena prior to assuming the chief's position. Similarly, prior to becoming chief he may have had little knowledge of other municipal agencies and their interaction with the police at an administrative level. A psychologist, psychiatrist or social worker serving as an administrative consultant will surely not be able to rid the chief of these pressures, nor will he be able to alleviate them in most cases. He may, however, be able to furnish the chief with a fresh perspective and thus increase his range of alternative responses. He may also help the chief react to and deal with pressure. Occasionally, he may be able to help the police administrator deal with personal issues which are interfering with his ability to cope with job demands.

The administrative consultant's role is active, not passive. The consultant will spend some of his time as a non-participant observer and may occasionally adopt a passively therapeutic stance, but he will more frequently be suggesting, helping to plan, and actively working with the administrator. Because of this, the consultant who excels within this role will bring to it a great deal of specific knowledge that does not reside in the police department. Thus, knowledge of other local agencies (certainly mental health, perhaps the schools, probation, welfare, etc.), of the community, of potential grant sources and of innovative social programs may turn out to be invaluable in this role, although none of these areas of expertise may seem relevant at the beginning of the consulation arrangement. (The reader who is interested in theoretical issues in mental health consultation will have noted early on that Caplanian definitions of consultation[1] were given short shrift in this chapter. Such definitions are restrictive and unrealistic and, in the growing interchange between police and mental health, play no important part).

Optimally, administrative consultation should be structured so that the consultant spends a healthy amount of time with the police executive. This is particularly crucial early in the consultation. If the consultant can spend one or two half-days per week with the police official, for a period of a few months, then the consultant will have an understanding of how the police official handles a great variety of situations and people. Such an under-

---

[1]Caplan, Gerald, *Principles of Preventive Psychiatry;* Basic Books; NY; 1960.

standing cannot be achieved in years of a one-hour per week consultation. It is important that the consultant have time alone with the police official, and that he also observe the police executive doing everyday tasks unrelated to the consultant. After several months of this procedure, the consultation can easily be changed to shorter sessions which are primarily between the consultant and the police executive.

It is important to maintain some lack of specificity if the consultation is to remain administrative rather than problem centered. The consultant may begin with no individual area of concentration. He may, after some period of familiarization, work closely with the police executive on, say, community relations. He must return to a more general perspective after a time, however, or his role will become restricted to community relations consultant.

It is not possible to enumerate the actual services that the administrative consultant may provide. He may, at various times and in various areas, make suggestions, criticize, listen sympathetically, counsel, socratically question, or provide support. (A major reason why administrative consultation is unlikely to become common is that police chiefs are not given to hiring people to perform services that cannot be specified with regard to problems that cannot be defined.) It should be apparent that one of the prerequisites for a successful administrative consultation is the establishment of personal rapport between the police administrator and the consultant.

Role issues can easily become muddled for the administrative consultant. He will probably be viewed as "the chief's man" and should avoid situations in which members of the agency feel coerced to cooperate with him because of this image. There are no compelling reasons why the administrative consultant should not perform other functions for the department. He must, however, exercise caution so that he is not used as a "pipeline" of information in either direction. The administrative consultant is also in an unusually good position to involve other professionals in consulting capacities with the police agency.

LEADING GROUPS

Within the last five years, this consultation role has become common in law enforcement. Most large police agencies have had some experience with sensitivity training, encounter groups, rap sessions, group therapy or some other group experiences. Typically, such groups are led by consultants and the consultants are usually mental health professionals. Interest in groups among law enforcement officials has followed a more general societal interest in groups, and policemen are not very different from school teachers, nurses or college students in this regard. Police do seem unusual in their expectations about groups, their reactions to groups and their professional needs with regard to groups and group leaders. This discussion is primarily concerned with these differences between police and other populations, and with the role of the group leader; this discussion is not intended as a general statement about group experience.

The range of activities subsumed under the label "groups" is indeed wide. Everything from 3 people discussing politics to lengthy live-in retreats for hundreds of people have been called groups. Before anything meaningful can be said about police groups and police group leaders, it is necessary to make certain simplifying assumptions because there appears to be no conceivable activity which is not championed by some group leader as an appropriate or useful group method. In short, when one says, "we are starting a group for police officers," even experienced group leaders have no idea of what is actually being done. Because of this general lack of clarity, it is important to separate those methods which have a high probability of success from other methods which are higher risks or less appropriate for police groups. The comments that follow should be interpreted in this spirit.

Groups are, in general, a high-risk, high-gain procedure for law enforcement agencies. In many instances, police administrators can direct their energies toward low-risk, high-gain procedures, (e.g. training) which are certainly preferable if they meet the needs of the agency. There are occasions, however, when all of the options facing the administrator involve high risk, and a group may well be the best available alternative. The situations in which police groups are most appropriate include internal problems (racial, communications, patrolman-supervisor), minorities, juveniles (mixed police juvenile groups, police-parent groups) convicts and municipal agency personnel (police-parole groups, police-probation groups).

Sensitivity training is a "trigger word" for most police. This is a bad pun but a good generalization. For many police, the words "sensitivity training" conjure up visions of orgies, vicious personal attacks, public humiliation, homosexuality, and the like. (In some of the urban centers on the East and West Coast, this is no longer true, but it is still applicable for most of the country). Encounter groups and rap sessions are often seen as situations in which a group of angry citizens are encouraged to verbally attack one or two policemen. There is no need to belabor this point; the prospective group leader must be aware of the enormous resistance and hostility that most police feel for groups. Some of this resentment and hostility is based on misconceptions, rumors and lack of knowledge of groups—but some is based on accurate information.

The consultant can be easily misled by a police executive who has a rosey and often unrealistic view of what group experience may do for his men, and of their reactions to a group experience. The executive may be impressively open and risk taking in establishing a group for his men; he himself, will seldom participate. After arranging a group with an optimistic police chief of this type, the consultant is often unprepared for the Armageddon which awaits him. Fortunately, there are a number of ways in which the consultant can avoid having a police group turn into a pitched battle.

There is a tremendous difference between a police officer participating in a group as a citizen (off-duty and without departmental sanction) and an officer participating in a group as a part of his job. The former case is not problematic and is not considered here. The latter case has many problems, and the consultant group leader who is a stranger to police systems will find many of the problems are unique to police. The confidentiality issue is almost always difficult. The group leader will find that the police "grapevine" is fast and effective (though not always accurate) and that incidents within the group will usually become common knowledge throughout the agency. Worse, the group leader *cannot* and *must not* suggest to the group members that they may say anything they wish to, with impunity. In fact, if a police officer insults a superior within a group, the supervisor may punish the officer, subtly hurt the officer's promotional chances, or impose negative consequences in a wide variety of other ways. The group leader has no way to know if this will happen, nor can he prevent it or rectify it; it is not his career which is endangered, it is the group members' careers. Thus, even though the consultant group leader may have boundless faith in the goodwill of the men in the group, he should not attempt to influence the men to be "candid" or "honest" by suggesting that remarks made within the group are privileged communication. They are not.

First, a group should be established only after the potential members of the group have been thoroughly informed of the group's purposes, composition and rules. The police officers must be given an opportunity to question the group leader or a knowledgeable police administrator about the nature of the group. If this approach is not used, the establishment of the most innocuous group can precipitate a grave internal crisis within a police agency. When possible, participation in groups should be voluntary. In some cases, however, agency-wide participation may be desired, or the group may be initiated because of a condition involving a number of officers who must all participate if the group is to come to grips with that condition. Even if participation is voluntary, the personnel of the agency should be well-informed about the group. This will help attract volunteers and also reduce the tendency of the men who do not volunteer to cast aspersions on those men who do participate. The consultant will do well to also remember that "volunteering" in some police departments is not unlike "volunteering" in the Army.

Second, police groups are best led by two people. A single leader becomes a target for much of the resentment that the men feel for the group. While some group leaders will accept this and try to use it constructively, it is a long and difficult process which can be avoided by the inclusion of a second leader. This will sharply reduce the number of personal attacks upon the consultant. Also, police will tend to be more active and involved than other populations (although if the group is going badly enough, the officers may sit in hostile silence). It is very difficult for one group leader to keep track of most of what is going on, and a co-leader is invaluable in keeping track of the entire group. Control can also be difficult to maintain in a police group, and a co-leader is good insurance against loss of control.

Third, police groups should be problem-centered rather than unstructured or process-centered. Police officers tend to be outspoken and emotionally expressive, and the need in police groups is more for techniques to "cool" people than for techniques to "open up" people. In most situations, a police discussion group talking about a mundane work issue will quickly develop all of the emotional expressions, openness and honest feedback that most group leaders could wish for. A group which is established to discuss non-emotional work issues is an excellent entree into communication, feelings, relationships and the like. On the other hand, a group formally established to deal with, say, interpersonal feelings runs a high risk of "turning off" the policemen involved and generating passive resistance.

Fourth, groups involving both police and other citizens should be carefully designed to promote an active interchange, rather than unidirectional attacks. In a police-juvenile discussion group, for example, the numbers of police and teenagers should be roughly comparable. Also, the group leader ought to have some familiarity with both groups (unless he knows nothing about either group, which is workable). Situations in which one or two police officers are on "the hot seat" and grilled by eight or ten hostile adolescents, or where the group leader has worked closely with the non-police members of the group but knows little about the police members, are structured for failure. In such groups, both police and other members are likely to have negative experiences and to strengthen previously held biases, stereotypes, etc. It is also a mistake to have a group that is unbalanced in the opposite direction;

a group of police encountering a single student revolutionary or a black militant is not a group likely to result in anyone's personal growth.

There are no unusual role constraints inherent in leading police groups. However, the consultant will find he has a difficult, challenging and pressured role. He should not be surprised if group members perceive him as having gained confidential information about them and are, thus, uneasy about his performing other functions within the agency. The consultant should assume responsibility for assessing some of the reactions to the group by participants and by non-participants and this assessment should be shared with the police administrator and its implications discussed.

CONCLUSION

In conclusion, there are three issues that transcend specific job functions and are common to most or all of the consultation roles described. The first of these is the entry problem for the consultant who is approaching a police system for the first time. The consultant is a non-policeman, and worse, a "shrink." In order to successfully start a consultation, the mental health professional must carefully consider how to approach the rank-and-file of the agency, what kind of contract to establish with the executive, how much command level support is needed and from whom, how to become familiar with the areas of police work with which he will interact, and where he fits into the organizational structure of the agency. While these problems have been touched upon several times in this chapter, space does not allow a detailed exploration of this issue. The entry problem is an issue of primary importance for all potential police consultants and should be carefully considered.

Secondly, many mental health professionals possess several skills which are extremely useful in most of the consultation roles described. These include technical writing (including the preparation of articles for publication and the preparation of grant proposals), social program development and long-term planning. These abilities are especially helpful because they are areas in which police agencies are traditionally weak.

Finally, for both the consultant and the police executive, mental health consultation can be a rewarding personal experience. It may reduce the degree of isolation of the police from the community while significantly increasing the involvement of trained mental health personnel in the social problems of those same communities. To try to establish the kinds of programs described in this chapter is, in most cases, to venture into uncharted waters. It is, however, a venture filled with high promise for law enforcement and for the mental health disciplines.

Chapter 28

CONNECTING WITH
THE THIN BLUE LINE[1]

ARTHUR M. BODIN

I SHALL FOCUS on how one makes entree into a police department, on some of the pitfalls I fell into, and on some of the
things I have learned in the process. I shall discuss some bridging
devices to make contact with police, and finally, I shall cover some
features within the scope of the course and program that I was
working with, which, though outside the course content, were
central and essential. I think you could say that there are three
R's in orienting yourself to the police: reading, riding, and
rapping.

READING

I have found only a few useful readings for getting oriented to
the police. I think I learned the most from a single book called
The Varieties of Police Behavior by James Q. Wilson, a Harvard
urbanologist. His book conceptualizes three major styles of police
work and illustrates them with comparisons of eight departments.
Also, there is a new book called *The Ambivalent Force: Perspectives on the Police*. This collection of readings on police-community relations (PCR) is outstanding for the scope, depth, selection
and orientation of its contributed chapters. Moreover, it has
much that is timely and much that is timeless. There is a relatively new book by a policeman about policemen. It is *The New Centurians*, by Wambaugh. I gather it is factual enough that the
author was reprimanded by his department: he said that the book
was fiction and that he did not have to clear fiction with the department, but the department apparently held that it was not en-

[1]Adopted from a presentation at Western Psychological Association meeting, San
Francisco, April 24, 1971.

tirely fiction. This book illuminates the edges of police work, but do not expect a best seller to focus on the less dramatic but more central themes of ordinary police at their usual work.

Rivers of Blood, Years of Darkness by Conot, a journalist's account of the Watts riots, is an excellent source. Its coverage of police work has a limited scope, but the police in the classes I have taught—in three different society and law enforcement courses—thought it was one of the best books they had read. When they handed back 3 x 5 cards on their reactions to books assigned, they indicated an overwhelming liking of Conot's book. Although I had assigned only Part I, one policeman reported he had read the entire book three times. It is a very interesting and penetrating psychological study of citizens as well as of police as they interact. I might add that the police in my course did not have such a favorable reaction to all of the books assigned.

I think it is a mistake to overload police with readings if you are going to be teaching them, but I have found three others particularly useful. First, there is the Kerner Commission Report. Since it is dry and statistical, I recommend assigning its 30-page summary rather than the full report for course reading by the police. It summarizes succinctly the social currents which impose problems and constraints on today's policeman. One reading they responded to very well is a special issue of the *Public Administration Review: "Police in a Democratic Society."* It has four articles, including an excellent review of modern police systems in Europe, detailing various practices which we do not have here. To my astonishment, the police were favorably impressed by much that was described. For example, the provision for lateral entry of lawyers at the lieutenant level intrigued them because it opens the door to lateral movement between police departments and hence to greater departmental attention to offering competitive salaries. It also affords greater personal freedom as a consequence of increased interdepartmental mobility. Moreover, the men expressed satisfaction with the idea of finally having within the police department itself lawyers equipped to deal with the flood of complications arising from the lightning pace of change in the procedural requirements of law in these tense times. Finally, there is a pamphlet called *Professional Police in a Free Society* by Skolnick, a sociologist at the University of California, Berkeley, School of Criminology. It offers a brief yet broad perspective of the evolutionary processes underlying today's police practices and problems.

RIDING

Although reading provides fundamental conceptual frameworks for comprehending police work, riding provides direct experience more concrete and vivid than any words on a page. You see a lot when you are riding. You get a "first-hand feel" for what is happening and how. Seventy-five rides in seven police departments sharpened my awareness of the complexities of police-citizen interaction and strengthened my grasp of attitudes, traditions, and relationships affecting the structure and function of police departments. I also began to understand the impact of these factors when civilians from the outside come to work with police departments.

I once had a young man in therapy who was smuggling hash into the country. At one session, he complained lengthily and colorfully about the "pigs," so I asked him whether he would take a ride in a police car as a form of homework between sessions. He and a buddy did just that. They rode in separate cars and then came back and taped a discussion of their experiences in my office. Although they both spoke of important positive changes in their feelings about police based on their eye-opening experience, they also mentioned having felt put off at first by the initial reluctance of police to welcome their participation. Their experience is not necessarily typical, but such resistance is one of the features occasionally encountered in getting a look at police.

Police have strong traditions which are fundamental to an understanding of their roles and functions. Such understanding is vital in working with police. Most civilians have not taken the time to orient themselves adequately, so they harbor numerous unsubstantiated stereotypes and unexamined myths. The police are understandably sensitive to the insensitivity of outsiders who, however well-meaning, have a superficial grasp of police work.

Another source of the coolness occasionally encountered by out-siders is the fact that some police departments have been "burn-ed" by a psychologist or other social scientist who failed to give feedback on research results or published reports which seemed derogatory, particularly after failing to obtain departmental clear-ance for publications stemming from work with police. It does not delight police to have academic freedom invoked as an excuse for circumventing the customary procedures of the department commanding their allegiance—particularly after making the social scientist privy to significant "inside" information. Such faux pas have created real difficulies for many later researchers.

Another block on which some consultants have stumbled is their slavish adherence to a pet-training method or approach with cavalier disregard for the necessity of analyzing the problems and priorities of a particular department. Moreover, some consultants have indulged in vehement ideological arguments with the people whom they were teaching or have gratified who-knows-what per-sonal motives by bringing police into an outnumbered confronta-tion situation in which one or two policemen were pitted against a dozen or more militants. Understandably, such practices re-sult in some defensiveness which can facilitate fiascoes. In view of the fact that some police departments have had unfortunate ex-periences, it is important in making entree to convince them that you share a genuine concern for the function and improvement of the law enforcement system. This requires taking the time neces-sary to become knowledgeable about police work in general and about special features of their department in particular.

RAPPING

Another vital step in starting to work with police is rapping. It usually takes time to build enough rapport for individual police-men to open up and give you a more penetrating and candid pic-ture of his department than the PR face it presents to the public. Such rapport must be nourished; it cannot be forced to flower in a few weeks. Only after you have demonstrated an ongoing con-cern with learning enough to help the police—rather than a more self-centered desire to simply acquire information for a research paper—will you have begun to earn the acceptance of the police so necessary for the success of your consultation.

There are a number of bridges useful in reaching the police. A keystone is the fact that about 90 percent of police work is service rather than catching felons. Some police like this fact, others decry or deny it, and perhaps the majority are ambivalent about it. Yet a similar situation prevails in psychology, and it is useful to point this out in establishing what ground you have in common with police. You can point out that both you and the police are rendering a helping service on a nonroutine basis, by which I mean a service not like the weekly garbage collection. Police, like psychologists, are often called upon to deal with non-routine matters. People are not usually happy about needing the service they request. They are probably suffering. Both police and psychologists are often required to take decisive action without having time to check back with someone else. Of course, there are also some differences in job roles, and these should be acknowledged. The element of danger is considerably greater for the police. They must be prepared for physical action. Police are thrust into a more controlling and even coercive role with the citizens than are psychologists with their clients or patients. There are few decisions psychologists make for patients, except perhaps for unusual situations requiring hospitalization.

I have found that it is helpful to make these bridging points and to demonstrate, perhaps by the language system you use, some familiarity with police lingo. Police use many special code terms and code numbers. For instance, a "turtle shell" is a riot helmet; a "fifty-fifty" is somebody who is only half there; a "PIN-check" is a check through the Police Information Network; "DOB" is date of birth; the "RP" is the reporting party; "ETA" is expected time of arrival, as in the question "What's your ETA?" meaning "How long until your unit arrives on the scene?"; "Black and white" or "unit" is a police car; "POST" is Peace Officer Standards and Training (official body for approving courses). Many other phrases like these will become familiar after a while.

To speed the bridging process, it is very useful to ask a lot of questions, to avoid pretending you know it all, and to be just curious as possible. It is important that in the telling of any "war stories" you be judicious and sparing. If you know some negative stories, beware of using them inappropriately. But if some would be useful in teaching, it would be well to have ridden in more than one police department and to say so, so that your police students *know that they do not know* which of several departments and particular story depicts.

It is also important to understand something about the constraints policemen have on their hours due to rotating shifts, and on their image due to the uniform. This next point may sound trivial or even funny to some, but it can make a definite difference. Shine your shoes if you are working with the police, or at least have a pair of Corfams®; I think you *do* have to be a little spiffier on those days when you are with police. A policeman told me "It helps to look more like a cop when you are riding with one. People you might talk to or hear talking to the officer seem to feel more comfortable." The police may be more comfortable with you, too.

On the other hand, it could be argued that comfort is not your primary goal, and that if you are really good at the entree skills outlined in this chapter, you may achieve more by not looking like a policeman. The combination of your understanding police work while perhaps having a beard and dressing informally may help in teaching about and breaking through some stereotypes.

SYSTEM CONSIDERATIONS

One system consideration derives from the widely-held proposition that police-community relations is the business of every policeman and will fail if perceived by public or police as segregated into a specialized division of a department. This function is further undermined by such separation if the community relations personnel are singled out as an elite group. The well-intended policy of permitting members of police-community relations division to wear civilian clothing can backfire by stimulating resentment on the part of regular beat officers, since an elitist image attaches to the men in the special division. Even more significantly, uniformed beat policemen feel that any goodwill created by such a group will not rub off on them since the civilian clothing of the PCR men marks them in the public eye as hand-picked special troops, and therefore different from the ordinary beat policemen. Another unfortunate effect of such separation is that it cuts off the beat patrolman from the feedback he needs from citizens to feel fully responsible and function accordingly in the area of police-community relations.

A related consideration concerns the question, "How can a department continue to further the development and maintenance of good community relations practices by all its officers once they have completed their classroom training?" *The socialization process,* by which police are inducted into their roles, *the post-probationary de-selection option* and *the periodic evaluation* offer extra-supervisory leverage in this regard.

The enormous importance of the socialization process was brought home to me with painful impact one summer night when I was riding in a two-man car. The driver was a veteran officer and his partner was still in his probationary period. The car pulled up behind a stolen vehicle, already abandoned by its joyriders. A tow-truck was summoned and we were simply parked, awaiting its arrival. We were in a predominantly black neighborhood. Children and youths clustered around the car, a few of the bolder ones leaning their elbows on the open windows. One boy about eleven-years-old stuck his head through the window and said, "Hey man. That your radio? Let me hear your radio. My Daddy's tax money pay for that radio." The younger officer was starting to return the jive, when he was silenced by his older partner, who muttered loud enough to be heard not only by me, but also by the black children, "Don't give them the time of day!" These two white officers went through a similar sequence later that same shift. The driver interrupted his younger partner's friendly conversation with a member of the Soul Brothers, a peaceful black motorcycle club, several of whose members the car had been following. I reflected with new appreciation on the wisdom of some departments in giving careful consideration to the selection and matching of seasoned mentors for the young officers during their probationary period. I was even more impressed than I had been initially by the policy of one local department which attempts to give each new officer some experience with as many as seven different partners, realizing that exposure to many role models allows the young officer a rich choice in selecting good features with which he is personally comfortable.

In one of my courses on society and law enforcement, I asked the policemen what thoughts they had for improving community relations through personnel policies. The resounding recommendation was for a far more liberal use of the deselection option at the end of the probationary period, during which a man's true colors begin to show.

My overall point of view on advancing good police-community relations has changed from one in which I thought that some readings and some good teaching, including guests who are experts on certain topics, would help a lot. I no longer think that. No matter how much knowledge and skill a teacher can inculcate during a police-community relations course, including skill in communication, I do not think a policeman is necessarily going to rush out and start applying what he has "learned" unless there is something in it for him to do so. Does *he* think that his supervisor is paying attention to those particular aspects of his work when it comes time for promotion or pay increase or better duty assignments? That is what I mean by "something in it for him." In one course, I brought in the city personnel director as a guest; we all examined the evaluation blank and found that nowhere on the blank was there anything specifically about police-community relations, and there was precious little about human relations. I felt that it would be useful to have not just one, but a whole cluster of items in this area. Not that anybody has any marvelous way of evaluating it—certainly not the lieutenant who is not often out in the field with the men—but the sergeant can get the feel of it after awhile. If, when each man sees his yearly evaluation, he sees that a concern for human relations is reflected on the evaluation blank, I think he will receive the message that PCR is important, just as the omission of a human relations evaluation will convey the opposite impression.

PITFALLS

There are certain topics to avoid with police, or at least to avoid bringing up belligerently. For example, if you use the phrase "police riot," they want to know "were you there?" and "Just how did you manage to assign the responsibility for the riot to one side rather than to the other?" The topic of civilian review boards is also a very touchy one. If you just think about how much we in psychology have enjoyed non-psychologists evaluating our professional perfomance, I think you will understand parallel police concerns. We have not rushed out to invite the public to evaluate the performance of professional psychologists. "Encounter group" is not a favorite term, having been the topic of some warnings in a police journal. Try "realistic simulation" instead.

INCENTIVES

There are numerous techniques you can employ to help a course gain acceptance in the department once you have obtained some knowledge and some familiarity with the men. One is to offer college credit. Another is to see whether POST (Peace Officers Standards and Training) points can be awarded at the regular rate of one point for each twenty course hours. Another incentive, if you are running a series of such courses, is to start off with a very high prestige group, not necessarily in terms of rank, but in terms of peer respect on the part of rank and file officers. Also, seek to fill the first class with volunteers. To neglect providing some incentives is to invite unnecessary difficulties. It is rough if people are thrown into a course on their own time without college credit, without extra pay, and with a feeling that the course offers low prestige to boot. Finally, whatever the content of your course, foster fun and involvement through much participation. All such measures in your work with police will, at least, avoid saddling it with a hindstart, and, at best, allow you to concentrate on the quality of your police consultation.

HIGHLY RECOMMENDED READINGS

Conot, R.: *Rivers of Blood, Years of Darkness.* New York: Bantam Books, Inc., 1967.

National Advisory Commission on Civil Disorders: *Summary Report.* Reprinted from the Bantam Books Edition of the Report of the National Advisory Commission on Civil Disorders.

Niederhoffer, A. and Blumberg, A.S.: *The Ambivalent Force: Perspectives on the Police.* Waltham, Mass.: Ginn and Company, 1970.

The police in a democratic society: A symposium. *Public Administration Review,* Vol. 28, No. 5, September/October, 1968.

Skolnick, J. H.: *Professional police in a free society.* New York: National Conference of Christians and Jews, 1969.

Wambaugh, J.: *The New Centurians.* Boston: Little, Brown and Company, 1971. Paperback, Dell Publishing Company, 1972.

Wilson, J.Q.: *Varieties of police behavior.* Cambridge: Harvard University Press, 1968. Paperback, Atheneum 156, College Edition, 1970.

ADDITIONAL READINGS

Brandstatter, A.F. and Radelet, L.A.: *Police and Community Relations: A Sourcebook.* Beverly Hills: The Glencoe Press, 1968.

Black, A.D.: *The People and the Police.* New York: McGraw-Hill Book Co., 1968.

Chevigny, P.: *Police Power: Police Abuses in New York City.* New York: Vintage Books, 1969.

Earle, H.H.: *Police-Community Relations: Crisis in Our Time.* Springfield, Illinois: Charles C Thomas Publisher, 1967.

Earle, H.H.: *Student-Instructor Guide on Police-Community Relations.* Springfield, Illinois: Charles C Thomas Publisher, 1970.

Edwards, G.: *The Police on the Urban Frontier: A Guide to Community Understanding.* Pamphlet Series Number 9. New York: Institute of Human Relations Press, 1968.

Hahn, H. (Ed.) : *Police in Urban Soicety.* Beverly Hills: Sage Publications, 1970.

Hewitt, W.H. and Newman, C.L.: *Police-Community Relations: An Anthology and Bibliography.* Mineola, New York: The Foundation Press, 1970.

Miller, M.G.: *A Bibliography on Police and Community Relations.* Mimeographed, May 1, 1966.

Miller, M.G.: *A Bibliography on Police and Community Relations.* Supplements I, II, III. Mimeographed, 1967-69.

Momboisse, R.M.: *Community Relations and Riot Prevention.* Springfield, Illinois: Charles C Thomas Publisher, 1967.

Morris, N. and Hawkins, G.: *The Honest Politician's Guide to Crime Control.* Chicago: The University of Chicago Press, 1969.

Sowle, C.R. (Ed.) : *Police Power and Individual Freedom: The Quest for Balance.* Chicago: Aldine Publishing Co., 1962.

Toch, H.H.: *Violent Men: An Inquiry Into the Psychology of Violence.* Chicago: Aldine Publishing Co., 1969.

Wambaugh, J.: *The Blue Knight.* Boston: Little, Brown and Company, 1972.

Wolfgang, M.E.: *Crime and Race: Conceptions and Misconceptions.* Pamphlet Series Number 6. New York: Institute of Human Relations Press, 1970.

Chapter 29

CONSULTATION WITH POLICE: SOME PROBLEMS AND CONCEPTUALIZATIONS

Robert J. Sokol

WITH THE RAPIDLY CHANGING SOCIAL SCENE, the desirability of working with police has become an absolute need. The nature of the police role is changing. Rather than the typical "cops and robbers" problems, more and more police time and energy are involved in problems with major social and mental health overtones. For example, last year the Los Angeles Police Department (LAPD) spent more than 410,000 man-hours in relation to drug investigation and arrests, this with a force of 7,000 officers. Alcoholism, abortion, drugs, civil disturbances, minority problems, and adolescent "dropout," to mention only a few, represent major concerns for police. Along with this, there is an increasing emphasis on prevention of crime and the reduction of recidivism. All of these reflect an increasing need for an understanding of and techniques of dealing with, the emotional forces involved.

We, in community psychiatry, need to understand the community from the police vantage point and the nature of the police situation. We have to learn much from and teach one another. Certainly the needs for cooperative relationships and mutual understanding are obvious and could be elaborated considerably. The same comments are applicable to other social systems—schools, welfare, etc. Within the criminal justice system, special emphasis should be given not only to police, but to the law, the judicial process and the "correctional" system. There are mental health professionals active in all of these areas, but not enough.

Here my objective will be limited to reviewing actual and potential consultative relationships with police.

Mental health consultation with police presents some unique challenges and problems. Some of these are indigenous to all consultation with large cohesive agencies, but some are very unique to work with police. For the past five years I have been consulting with various police departments. During this time I have had the opportunity to learn from personal experience and also to compare notes with others doing this work. Here I would like to pass on some experiences, observations, and conceptualizations that have arisen from this experience.

When first initiating consultation with our division of a large metropolitan force, I spent four months observing and talking with a group of officers. This was in the juvenile section. The initial suspicion and resistance was easily overcome and at the end of this period I was recognized as their own "private shrink." The hallmark of acceptance came one day when a sergeant in front of the other officers asked for a personal consultation. The problem then arose—where do we go from here. What type of consultation, what format etc. Moreover, although the individual officers accepted me and expressed interest, when it came to formalizing a program, the absence of administrative sanction became obvious. This need for active administrative involvement is paramount and will be discussed at length later in this chapter.

After this experience the opportunity for consultation with another division arose. Here I chose another format and the initial approach was made to the division commander. Somewhat to my surprise I found that my active relations with him did not hinder my relation with the line officers—rather they were enhanced. This observation led me to examine the psychological structure of the department as a whole. This is another area I will comment on at length somewhat later—particularly in relation to its effect on the officers and on the consultative process.

One of the major questions asked by senior police officials was just what can a mental health consultant do? In their frame of reference we were categorized. A psychiatrist treated people with emotional problems. A psychologist did testing. The first task was to spell out in plain language the various ways we could function. This was no easy task. I should like to share with you my own categorization and provide some references as to examples from the literature in each category. Following this I will review some of the problems encountered in consultation. The final section will deal with some recommendations as to the organization of and the development of consultation programs.

I. The various types of mental health consultation with police can be categorized in many ways. The following breakdown has been useful and comprehensible to police. There is obvious overlapping between various groups. Many of the programs referred to could fit into several categories. I have attempted to classify them by their expressed intent and mode of approach rather than by potential effect. In reviewing the literature I have chosen articles and programs as examples in each category. No attempt has been made to compile a comprehensive bibliography.

A. Direct training and Education: The client-oriented case conference would be one example of this category. Others might include didactic lectures, discussion groups, films, seminars etc.

Examples:

1. Training police in family crisis intervention (N.Y.); an extensive two-year program was developed and reported by Bard and his associates.[2,3] The program involved developing special units who were trained with lectures, seminars, roleplaying techniques, and then critiques of field experience.

2. Training police in community relations and urban problems, a program for police trainees developed by John and Susan Talbot (N.Y.).[4] This program primarily involved reading, lecture, seminar and discussion groups.

3. Training police in handling suicidal crisis. There are several active but unreported programs in this area developed by Dr. Michael L. Peck.

B. Programs whose primary object is to modify and enhance work attitudes: Here the major objective would be increased awareness of self and others. This category might include "encounter" and "T" groups. Another type would be the consultee-oriented case conference.

Examples:

1. An intradepartmental encounter group in Sausalito has been reported by Shev.[5] As reported, this type of program has been quite effective in assisting officers in dealing with their own feelings and has significantly improved their functioning, particularly in encounters with minority groups. Similar groups in other departments in this area have corroborated these findings. The departments utilizing this approach are primarily small, 20 to 50 man forces.

2. Training police sergeants in early warning signs of emotional upset and brief counseling techniques. This program, developed and reported by Sokol and Reiser and LAPD, has just completed its pilot phase.[6,7] The program involved lecture and discussion groups with follow-up consultation around actual field problems. The primary objective was to deal with the "up-tight" line officer in the most rapid and effective fashion. The initial results are favorable, and expansion of the pilot program is anticipated.

C. Programs designed primarily to improve communications between police and outside groups.
   Examples:

1. Encounter groups between police and blacks have been reported from Houston by Sikes.[8] The problems of the group leaders in these encounters is reported by O'Connell and Hanson.[9] Newspaper articles have reported other similar projects. The success reported with this type of program has varied considerably, apparently related to the sophistication of the planning and the experience and comfort of the group leader.

2. Seminar and discussion groups with police around a minority problem (Puerto Ricans) was reported from New York by Elkins and Papanck.[10] Here the

necessity of psychodynamic expertise in dealing with group resistances is well documented.

D. Programs to assist in personnel selection and research evaluation:
  1. Several reports are available in this area. Those by Levy,[11] Due,[12] Berman,[13] Blum,[14] and Raubenheimer et al.[15] provide some background. Most departments have some type of psychological screening, from testing to extensive interviewing, in the selection process. As yet, these approaches are not formalized.

E. Programs to assist in intradepartmental planning and development: Here the consultant would participate in providing specialized input into the planning and development of new programs where psychological factors were involved.
  Examples:
  1. Newman and Steinberg[16] have consulted with police in the development and augmentation of a training program in human relations. They helped develop the curriculum and train the police "trainers."
  2. As a police department psychologist, Reiser has reported on his functions in the planning and development process[17] as well as in research.[18]

F. Direct treatment programs:
  1. It is the general consensus that the consultative and therapist role must be separated. In certain circumstances, this dual role may be possible. Dr. Reiser[19] functions as a departmental consultant and also does some direct treatment. The large size of the department and the time limited "crisis" orientation of the treatment approach make this possible. Although not reported, it certainly would be within the consultative function to help plan and develop direct treatment services.

In this brief review, I have attempted to select papers which illustrated various types of consultative programs. As one reads these papers, certain questions arise which are often unanswered.

What happened when the original program was finished? Are there any measures of the impact of these programs on the police —on the community? Is there any on-going consultative continuity? These questions must be answered if a long-term impact is to be hoped for with this type of consultation. It is obvious that the opportunity for creative consultative programs in this area are manifold.

II. THE NATURE AND PROBLEMS OF CONSULTATION WITH POLICE

I should like to divide this section into four divisions. These are arbitrary and overlapping, but I hope it will serve to emphasize what I consider to be certain major considerations.

A. Comments on the Nature and Organization of Police Departments

It is all too easy to consider all police departments as being similar without paying sufficient heed to the differences in size, area served and individual organizational considerations. This is particularly necessary when attempting to develop consultative programs. For example, when the work of Bard and his associates in training New York City's Police in family crisis intervention techniques was first reported, there was considerable pressure for a similar program to be developed with Los Angeles Police. Although an initial survey of police daily logs revealed an apparently much smaller incidence of involvement in such disputes by Los Angeles Police, there were other factors which demanded consideration. The New York program involved a significant amount of training time for a selected group of officers—time away from their normal functions. The New York Department has close to 35,000 uniformed officers to serve a population of 8 million in a relatively compact area. Los Angeles Police Department serves a population of over 3 million (spread over a much larger area) with approximately 7,000 sworn personnel. When this number is divided into three shifts, along with timeoff, vacation and special assignments, the number of police officers on duty at any one time to cover this area and population is approximately 2,000, and only a portion of these are on the uniformed patrol.

I am describing these differences not to indicate that a similar training program is impossible in this area, but rather that these factors must be considered so that the program can be specifically redesigned for this area. Another example along these lines would be attempts to translate the intradepartment encounter group developed by Shev with the Sausalito Police Department to the needs of a large metropolitan force with its many divisions and specialized areas. Sausalito has a 30-man department, and great personal familiarity is possible. It is true that such encounter groups might well have their place in a large metropolitan force, particularly for specific subgroups at a divisional level (e.g. new trainees, vice squads, etc.). However, careful organizational consideration and training of personnel would be necessary to implement this concept. (More will be said about this in Section III.)

I do not mean to belabor this point, but Los Angeles Police Department has almost daily experience with professional groups from the mental health field who propose training or consultative programs with no prior consideration of these factors. When these proposals are not well received, these groups often ascribe it to police "resistance."

B. The Police "Family" and the Need
for Administrative Sanction

Police face stresses of a highly unique nature, both physical and psychological. One way in which they cope with these stresses is by the development of an intense esprit de corps and "family" psychological structure within the department. There is great importance of this "family" dynamic in supporting the discipline to tolerate the physical and psychological danger to which the officer is exposed. However, along with its useful functions, it does present certain problems and considerations for the consultant coming in from the "outside." Among these is the absolute necessity for *active administrative sanction* for any program to be developed.

I would like to distinguish between active and passive administrative sanction. By the former I mean that the administration is actively involved in on-going participation in any program, this compared to providing sanction and passively observing the program from a distance. The active involvement provides the opportunity for the development of personal contact between the consultant and senior administrative personnel (the importance of which cannot be overemphasized). It also provides the opportunity for continuous feedback and modification of any programs and may prevent a potentially useful program from foundering on misunderstandings. Some further ramifications of this need will be discussed in the next section, but at this point let me just reiterate what I believe is its crucial importance in the success of any program. I have personally seen a number of potentially useful programs discontinued due to the lack of such involvement.

C. Resistances to Consultation, Their Nature and Some Dynamic Formulations

In this section, as in others, the nature of the subject is such that a considerable treatise could be written. I have attempted to isolate certain major features which have impressed me in my experience and will only touch on the highlights of these. In utilizing the term "resistances," I am including both conscious overt attitudes as well as unconscious covert factors which may impede the consultative relationship on the part of both the police and the mental health professional. By focusing on these resistances, I do not in any way mean to convey a connotation of hopelessness. Rather, if the resistances are anticipated and their nature understood, they can often be "worked through" expeditiously.

There are some reality bases to certain attitudes of police to mental health professionals. They have had some experience with mental health personnel who took no time to learn the police situation or pains with police sensibilities. One gross example was that of a young psychologist who lectured at the police academy complete with T-shirt, beard and peace medallion. Needless to say, he was seen but not heard. Another example was an intradepartmental "sensitivity" group involving senior officers of different rank. The group leader attempted to deal with the group as equals, his usual approach. In a military organization, a lieutenant does not tell a deputy chief to "shut up." Sensitivity training does not have the most desirable connotation to that police department, to put it mildly.

Another element leading to some confusion is this. Mental health professionals tend to speak and act as individuals. Particularly to police who are used to speaking as a group (in a professional sense), the sometimes controversial pronouncements of individual psychiatrists or psychologists are accepted as reflecting the general attitudes of mental health professionals as a group. Even after a consultant is accepted and respected, he is often seen as one of the few with his "feet on the ground." Unfortunately, the police view of the mental health professional is shared by a significant proportion of the population, including many physicians.

Again relating to the social scene, there often is a polarization along role lines with certain analogies to a family dispute. Here the police role can be analogized to the paternal one where disturbed or recalcitrant behavior is dealt with by superego-reinforcing techniques—the disciplinary approach to behavioral problems. On the other hand, the mental health professional's approach can be analogized to the maternal one where aberrant behavior will be "cured" with love and understanding. I realize the oversimplification involved, but how often do frustrated parents who have different approaches turn on one another when unsuccessful with the child? In a similar fashion, the police are often viewed by the mental health professional as "harsh and punitive" whereas they in their turn view the mental health field as being "soft and mollycoddling" in relation to the offender "child."

The tendency to use and be comfortable with superego-reinforcing techniques on the part of many police accounts in some part for their mutual reaction to outsiders. Just as they are often the recipients of projected superego attitudes, so do they tend to project their own approaches onto the consultant and anticipate judgement and criticism to which they react defensively. The tendency to projection may be aggravated by tendencies to silence and passivity on the part of the consultant. I feel that particularly in consulting with police, it is important for the consultant to make sure that his own personality comes across clearly and distinctly. Police, who are trained in critical observation and, indeed, suspiciousness, are quick to perceive any falseness or role playing, a perception which may easily be misinterpreted.

Let me return once again to the concept of the police "family" and its connotation to the consultant. As mentioned, the police job carries with it many inherent psychological pressures. Some of the obvious ones are the temptations for aggressive acting out, satisfaction of primitive urges of greed and lust, etc. The more subtle stimulants to unconscious forces by exposure to all sorts of sexual behavior (e.g. in vice squad activities) and by the knowledge and exposure to all manner of corruption weigh heavily in the battle between impulse and conscience. It is no happenstance that the policeman's superego structure may oftentimes be harsh and rigidly puritanical to balance the exposure to primitive temptations. Still another subtle but powerful psychological stress is engendered by the transference role in which particularly the young policeman finds himself. Consider the stresses on a young man in his twenties being called upon to adjudicate a dispute between people of his parents age.

These and many other psychological stresses could be documented. One of the ways in which these forces are contained is by the development of the intense "family" psychological structure previously mentioned. However, some of the offshoots of this structure tend to have inhibitory effects on contacts with "outsiders." Within the police family, citicisms and harsh judgements are strict and freely given. Many of us who have witnessed their internal review boards have been amazed at the strictness with which the rules are enforced and the immediacy of penalties for their transgressions. However, as in many close-knit families, the same criticisms from outsiders are viewed as an attack on the family *as a whole* and are a signal for closing ranks and defense.

There are two other observations which I believe have significant psychological import in this area. The first is that police are trained to be suspicious as part of their job. This training is often reinforced by the young officer's dissolusionment as he is exposed to the facts of life in his limited role.

The second observation relates to the tendency to projective identification, or more simply, to the assumption that others think and react as we do. Thus, the police officer who is trained in helping through the use of superego-reinforcing techniques tends to anticipate the same approach from the consultant and will often react defensively and suspiciously. I believe these factors largely determine what is often called the police "paranoia" and that this term is a poor one in relation to its actual technical meaning. In a technical sense, the paranoid mechanism refers to a conflict between internal id and superego forces in which the conflict is "resolved" by projecting the forbidden id impulse onto an object or objects in the outer world. In the instances described, what is projected is not the forbidden impulse but rather the superego attitudes.

In the preceding paragraphs, I have touched on the highlights of certain psychological features common to police and police organizations. I feel the family analogy is particularly important to emphasize the need for active administrative sanction that was previously discussed. I recall well one effort to establish a consultative relationship with one police division in which personal rapport was well established between the consultant and the officers, but no programs were forthcoming as the administrators had not been involved. In a major program in another area, the consultant was asked to review and reorganize the program and did not insist on active police administrative involvement in this task. When the new program was presented, it was viewed as the consultant's program rather than a police program and rejected. Undoubtedly this resulted from the fact that the new program contained features with which the police were unfamiliar and therefore uneasy, but this could have been worked through with active administrative involvement as opposed to passive consent.

D. Consultant Problems

This section on the problems and resistances encountered in consultation would not be complete without some comments on the problems of and the resistances encountered within the consultant. Some of my comments here will be taken for granted by those experienced in consultation. These problems do exist and, I feel, must be acknowledged.

The first problem of consultants is not a frequent one but does occur. That is that the consultant's own social and political philosophy affect his consultative approach. It is true that most police tend to be conservatives in a philosophical or political sense. In contradistinction, most mental health professionals are liberally-oriented. This is no bar to a consultative relationship and indeed may serve as stimulants to interaction if they are kept separate from the task at hand, namely, rendering consultative assistance to police in the area *they* request. Unfortunately, on occasion, consultants will approach police with only thinly disguised attitudes that they will show them the right path or philosophy. If the consultant actively disagrees with a police position, it is best that this be overtly expressed so that it can be in the open rather than allowing for all sorts of transference distortions and misconceptions if it remans covert.

Another stress on the consultant is that to his usual role and reception. Our usual mode of consultation centers around the case study approach, be it client or consultee oriented. Although there are some applications of this approach within the police framework, they are limited. Also the consultant is usually dealing with agencies or groups which are "psychologically-oriented" or at least hungry for this knowledge. Unless he has been specifically invited around a certain problem, the consultant will at first find himself at sea with the police. Here it is necessary for the consultant to assume what may be the unfamiliar role of student until he has had an opportunity to familiarize himself with police procedures, organization and situation. This student role has a dual advantage. Not only does the consultant have time to learn without having to produce, but it also gives the police time to familiarize themselves with the consultant as well as to assure them of his real interest in learning and participating as at least an auxiliary to the family. If he allows himself the opportunity of this student role, the consultant will often be able to appraise the situation and then help propose and develop unique and well-thought-out programs with a much higher likelihood of success and continuity.

An example of a consultative program that failed in its objective can be illustrated here. A new police chief had problems with his senior administration. They were accustomed to the former chief's more conservative approach. When the consultant entered the scene, he was assigned to work with the senior administrator. He was quickly caught up in the developing polarization between the new chief and his staff. Had the consultant insisted on the "student period" against all the pressures to "do something," he might well have recognized the impending polarization and insisted on a second consultant to work with the chief. As it was, the polarization continued until the chief had to leave and the consultant was viewed by him as siding with the staff.

Another problem which may arise from the consultant's uneasiness in this strange environ is the common human tendency to retreat to the familiar. Here the consultant may focus upon such concern as, "What are the unconscious dynamics that lead to becoming a policeman?, an area of familiar interest. I don't mean to imply that this is not a valid area of interest, but that it may also be used defensively to avoid the uneasiness of new areas requiring creative conceptualization.

At this point I would like to mention a brief theoretical formulation which I have found useful. This is not original with me, but I have not seen it written in these terms. That is, when people are faced with a situation for which they do not have a conceptual frame of reference, an uneasiness, tension or anxiety may develop. Often, to cope with this anxiety they will retreat to simplistic or rigid conceptual models. In everyday terms to "hard line" (be they left or right) attitudes. Another manner of dealing with this tension may be psychological withdrawal—manifested as apathy. Still a third coping mechanism may be via action, which is often random and poorly organized—such as directionless militant activism. (I hope that this is not misconstrued as a blanket condemnation of either firmly held views or all activism.)

I am presenting this theoretical construct because I feel it is useful in understanding the value of various types of consultation. Let me give a practical example. At one police division we decided to have a series of "bull sessions" with the members of the vice squad. These took the form of their discussing their work and me discussing the psychodynamics of similar problems as seen in my private office. After an initial period of suspicion (that I was going to tell them how to do their job) the officers became quite involved in the discussion. Comments such as, "I always wondered why prostitutes had pimps" were followed by definitely observable attitude changes. Several officers subsequently reported that although they made the same arrests they were much gentler and compassionate in the way they handled the arrestees. In essence, their broadened conceptual frame of reference served to replace their former "hard line" attitudes with those less likely to interfere with their doing their job professionally.

III. COORDINATED CONSULTATIVE PROGRAMS

To this point, my major emphasis has been on some of the dynamics of consultation with police. In this section, I will emphasize some practical aspects and needs in developing consultative programs with large organizations. In observing numerous consultative programs with such organizations, I have been struck by several observations. Often the consultants, each working in his own individual manner, provide considerable benefit to the individual consultees. However, there is often little effect on the overall approach of the consultee agency to the problems involved. This may often be due to the lack of administrative involvement or the lack of overall planning.

> Example: A probation officer developed a very successful group within her caseload with the consultant's support and supervision. Shortly after consultation was discontinued, the group disbanded and the officer developed negative feelings toward group work which influenced her office. No provisions had been made (or the need recognized) for on-going consultative support for the group leader.

Another problem that frequently arises is that the consultant's approach is not particularly useful to the consultee, but the transference problems prevent the consultant from getting the necessary feedback. The consultation is tolerated and accepted passively rather than being actively utilized and useful.

> Example: In a recent review of a large-scale consultative program, ratings of the consultants by the consultees were largely negative, much to the shock and disappointment of the consulting agency and the consultants. This was the first time in a long period that such a review had been attempted.

Still another problem in consultative programs involving a number of consultants is that the variety of approaches and languages used may vary significantly from one consultant to another. Particularly when consultees are transfered from one office to another, this may lead to confusion and factionalism within the consultee organization.

Example: At one office, a consultant utilizing a "Gestalt" approach was very well liked and received. When workers from this office were transferred to a consultant with a case consultation approach, they were confused and dissatisfied, and their feelings spread to other workers who had previously accepted this approach.

Obviously there are many other problems and examples that could be given relating to the consultative process, but many of these could be circumvented by the development of a coordinated consultative program.

What I would like to propose would be an organization of the consultants in the following fashion. One or more of the consultants would work with the senior administration to identify problems and develop programs. These programs would then be initiated and carried through by other consultant members of this group at the local agency level. The consultants would all go through an orientation period which would serve to acquaint them with the organization and the particular approaches, format and consultative objectives decided upon.

Once the actual operational consultation was initiated, the consultants at all levels—administrative and local, planning and operational—would meet regularly to provide continuing feedback. Simultaneously, there would be regular meetings of the senior consultant with the agency administration. The combination of these would provide not only the feedback necessary for continual supervision and reevaluation of the program but also the opportunity to develop and implement new programs at all levels of the agency.

In order to illustrate the operation of this concept, I will use the program reported by Dr. Reiser and myself as an example. In this case, the problem presented by the police was, "What can we do for emotional problems in our own men?" There were many facets to the request, among which was that police, being unfamiliar with the varying roles of mental health consultants, were requesting the one service they were familiar with. However, given the particular stresses of the policeman and the fact that emotional problems might significantly influence their work, the request had a primary validity. Using the constructs of crisis intervention theory, it was decided to provide the first line supervisors (sergeants) with training in the early detection of such problems, along with brief counseling and referral techniques. We felt that such a training program would only be fruitful if consultants were available to provide follow-up support when the sergeants attempted to utilize the training. Otherwise, an initial failure might lead to more generalized disillusionment with the project. During the program, monthly meetings of the consultants, a senior police official and the division commanders were held. This involvement turned out to be crucial for the success of the program from a number of vantage points:

A. The knowledge of the active administrative involvements (the division commanders also attended parts of the training program) helped overcome the sergeants' initial scepticism and engage them in the program.

B. The feedback provided in these meetings (and those between the consultant-trainers) helped circumvent certain problems at their inception.

> Example: In the training portion, we had decided to use the language of the transactional model to describe the psychic apparatus, i.e. "Adult, Parent, Child." Confusion arose among the sergeants to whom the term "Parent" was a good construct and not the harsh superego model intended in the original theory. When we became aware of this, we were able to substitute the concept of "Put-down Parent" which rapidly clarified the confusion. It should be noted that the initial feedback on this came from the division commanders. Returning to the family dynamic postulated earlier, it is often much easier for the senior officials to constructively criticize "outsiders" than it is for the more junior members.

C. The police were enabled to feel that they had active control of the program. I cannot overemphasize this point. This proof to police that they had active on-going control of the program played a crucial part in their acceptance of and wishes to expand the pilot project.

> Example: Problems of communication developed between one consultant and the division commander. When initial efforts to alleviate this were unsuccessful, the consultant was replaced. The program in that division which had been in jeopardy was rejuvenated.

D. The fact that the consultants all had an orientation program to police (including riding in police cars, attending divisional meetings, etc.) helped insure their acceptance and their understanding of the police situation.

There is one final comment about such a consultative organization. It can be seen that this type of organization would provide the machinery into which many programs could be "cranked." Let me give just several brief examples of some problems and their possible solutions:

> 1. *Problem:* "Our young officers, when they first emerge from the Police Academy, are enthusiastic and anxious to get into the community. When they return for their one-year refresher course, a large number of them are cynical with 'hard line' attitudes."
>
> *Dynamics:* Along with the natural disillusionments, the young officer goes from an environment of intensive "togetherness" with his fellow recruits (at the Academy) to one of "aloneness." There is also constant involvement and observation by older experienced officers. "Hard line" and cynical attitudes are often an attempt at handling anxiety as well as exaggerated attempts at identification with attitudes of older (and apparently more secure) officers. This is quite analagous to the exaggerated "sureness" of the adolescent trying to emulate the adult.
>
> *Possible Solution:* Develop a type of encounter group for the young patrolmen at the divisional level. This group could be led by the division consultant, one who the police administration trusted and was familiar. Here the experience of Shev with a small department could be easily translated to the needs of a larger force .
>
> 2. *Problem:* There is intense antagonism between police and a minority group.
>
> *Dynamics:* Mutual problems of communication and ignorance of each others' situation.

Possible Solution: Here the division consultant could develop and run (or at least oversee) the types of encounter groups between police and minorities that were reported from Houston. Another approach would be to develop the type of intradepartmental seminars and training reported by Elkins and Papanek.

Whether such a consultative organization were developed by the department or in coordination with a private group or another agency (e.g. County Department of Mental Health) would be relative to the funding and consultative talent available. Certainly more administrative and planning time would be necessary, but the additional effort would be more than justified by the potential rewards for all concerned.

One final point of considerable importance: this type of organizational set-up would lend itself to two crucial factors. First, it would ensure a continuity of programs. Second, a continual research and evaluation process could be easily built in. These research and evaluation procedures have been solely lacking in all but a few of the programs reported. Not only is such research necessary from an informational standpoint, but from a purely pragmatic one as well. Only in this manner can such programs be justified to police and to the legislative and funding bodies.

IV. CONCLUSION

I have attempted to review some of the needs and approaches to mental health consultation with police agencies. In summarizing some of my own observations of the dynamics involved and some concepts arising from them, only a brief overview of five years of experience has been possible. I hope I have been able to convey both my respect for police and for the problems involved, as well as my firm conviction that consultation with police can be useful and meaningful to not only the police and the consultant but to the community as a whole.

REFERENCES

1. Kaplan, G.: *An Approach to Community Mental Health.* New York: Grune and Stratton, 1961, p. 236.
2. Bard, M. and Berkowitz, B.: "Training Police as Specialists in Family Crisis Intervention," *Comm Ment Health J, 3:*315-317, 1967.

3. Bard, M.: "Training Police as Specialists in Family Crisis Intervention." U.S. Govt. Printing Office, P.R. 70-1, Washington, D. C., May, 1970.

4. Talbott, J. and Talbott, S.: "Training Police in Community Relations and Urban Problems." *Am J Psychiat, 127*:894-900, 1971.

5. Shev, E.E.: "Psychiatric Techniques in Selection and Training of a Police Officer." *The Police Chief,* April 1968.

6. Sokol, R. and Reiser, M.: "Training Police Sergeants in Early Warning Signs of Emotional Upset." *Mental Hygiene, 55*:303-307, 1971.

7. Reiser, M., Sokol, R., and Saxe, S.: "An Early Warning Mental Health Program for Police Sergeants." (in press).

8. Sikes, M.P. and Cleveland, S.E.: "Human Relations Training for Police and Community." *Am Psychologist, 13*:10-14, 1968.

9. O'Connell, W.E. and Hanson, P.G.: "Anxieties of Group Leaders in Police-Community Confrontations." Paper read at American Psychological Convention, San Francisco, August 1968.

10. Elkins, A.N. and Papanek, G.O.: "Consultation with Police: An Example of Community Psychiatry Practice." *Am J Psychiatr, 123*:531-535, 1966.

11. Levy, R.: "Predicting Police Failures." *J Criminal Law, Criminology Police Sci, 58*:256-276, 1967.

12. Due, F.: "Psychiatric and Psychological Screening of Police Applicants to an Urban Police Department: Computer Analysis of 113 Cases." Paper read at American Psychiatric Convention, May 1970.

13. Baehr, M.: "Psychological Assessment of Patrolmen Qualifications in Relation to Field Performance." L.E.A.A., Washington, D. C., 1968.

14. Blum, R.H. (Ed.): *Police Selection.* Springfield, Charles C Thomas, 1964.

15. Raubenheimer, I. and Tiffin, V.: "Personnel Selection and Prediction of Error." *J Applied Psychol, 55*:229-233, 1971.

16. Newman, L.E. and Steinberg, J.L.: "Consultation with Police on Human Relations Training." *Amer. J. Psychiat., 126*:1421-1429, 1970.

17. Reiser, M.: "The Police Psychologist as Consultant." *Police,* January 1971.

18. Reiser, M.: "Psychological Research in an Urban Police Department." Paper presented at American Psychological Association meeting, Miami Beach, Florida, September 1970.

19. Reiser, M.: *The Police Psychologist.* Springfield, Charles C Thomas (to be published).